Teaching Students with Mild and Moderate Disabilities

RESEARCH-BASED PRACTICES

LIBBY COHEN
ALLTech / The Spurwink Institute

LORAINE J. SPENCINER
University of Maine at Farmington

PEARSON

Merrill
Prentice Hall

Upper Saddle River, New Jersey
Columbus, Ohio

Library of Congress Cataloging-in-Publication Data

Cohen, Libby G.
 Teaching students with mild and moderate disabilities : research-based practices / Libby Cohen, Loraine J. Spenciner.
  p. cm.
 Includes bibliographical references and index.
 ISBN 0-13-088108-2
 1. Children with disabilities--Education--United States.   I. Spenciner, Loraine J.   II. Title.
 LC4031.C64 2005
 371.92′6--dc22

2004015431

Vice President and Executive Publisher: Jeffery W. Johnston
Acquisitions Editor: Allyson P. Sharp
Editorial Assistant: Kathleen S. Burk
Production Editor: Linda Hillis Bayma
Production Coordination: Susan Free, *The GTS Companies*/York, PA Campus
Design Coordinator: Diane C. Lorenzo
Photo Coordinator: Sandy Schaefer
Cover Designer: Linda Sorrels-Smith

Cover image: The cover art was done by Betty Pinette, who is a self-taught artist. She lives in Brunswick, Maine, and is part of Spindleworks, an artists' cooperative where her talent and dedication are encouraged and supported.
Production Manager: Laura Messerly
Director of Marketing: Ann Castel Davis
Marketing Manager: Autumn Purdy
Marketing Coordinator: Tyra Poole

This book was set in Galliard BT by *The GTS Companies*/York, PA Campus. It was printed and bound by R.R. Donnelley & Sons Company. The cover was printed by Coral Graphic Services, Inc.

Photo Credits: Tim Cairns/Merrill, p. 398; Scott Cunningham/Merrill, pp. 7, 68, 80, 97, 159, 190, 201, 246, 336, 394, 431, 492; Laima Druskis/PH College, p. 522; Ken Karp/PH College, pp. 1, 297, 485; Kathy Kirtland/Merrill, p. 476; David Mager/Pearson Learning, pp. 38, 486; Anthony Magnacca/Merrill, pp. 13, 34, 89, 110, 140, 220, 234, 255, 276, 316, 319, 331, 349, 409, 411, 446, 448, 452, 455, 502, 540; David Napravnik/Merrill, p. 117; Pearson Learning, p. 353; Courtesy of Prentke Romich www.Prentrom.com, p. 20; Barbara Schwartz/Merrill, pp. 127, 143, 232, 267, 350, 426; Valerie Schultz/Merrill, p. 506; Rhoda Sidney/PH College, pp. 223, 545; Silver Burdett Ginn, p. 98; Anne Vega/Merrill, pp. 2, 45, 207, 244, 309, 384; Tom Watson/Merrill, pp. 199, 285, 467; Todd Yarrington/Merrill, pp. 72, 173; Shirley Zeiberg/PH College, p. 525

Pearson Education Ltd.
Pearson Education Singapore Pte. Ltd.
Pearson Education Canada, Ltd.
Pearson Education—Japan

Pearson Education Australia Pty. Limited
Pearson Education North Asia Ltd.
Pearson Educación de Mexico, S.A. de C.V.
Pearson Education Malaysia Pte. Ltd.

10 9 8 7 6 5 4 3 2 1
ISBN: 0-13-088108-2

We dedicate this book to the first teachers in our lives, our parents,
Ruth and Joseph Gordon and Ruth Moody Jones,
whom we lovingly remember.

Interactive in format and personal in manner, this book provides research-based practices and strategies for teaching children and youth with mild to moderate disabilities, including those students with learning and behavior problems, in kindergarten through grade 12. This lively text conveys enthusiasm about the practice of teaching and learning. The book emphasizes consistent assessing, planning, organizing, implementing, and evaluating instruction based on knowledge of the learner, the intended student outcomes, and the curriculum. Designed for future teachers and experienced educators or other professionals, this text may be used in undergraduate and graduate courses in methods and curriculum for teaching students with mild to moderate disabilities and students with learning and behavior problems.

FEATURES

This book features comprehensive coverage of traditional and contemporary approaches. The text:

- Encourages high expectations for students with disabilities
- Emphasizes the research base for teaching methods and strategies
- Links assessment with instruction directly
- Integrates diversity as a theme throughout the book
- Addresses the integration of technology and assistive technology into curricula and instruction
- Includes a wealth of teaching strategies and skills
- Highlights important topics—social skills, positive behaviors, reading, written communication, mathematics, science, social studies, study and learning skills, and transition skills

FOCUS

This text conveys research-based teaching methods, strategies, and assessment approaches that facilitate the learning and behavior of students with mild to moderate disabilities. It describes how to consider students' prior knowledge and experiences, needs, capabilities, interests, and intended outcomes when planning, implementing, and evaluating instruction. Separate chapters focusing on teaching reading, written communication, mathematics, science and social studies, and transition emphasize this philosophy.

Several strands appear in each chapter. The first strand focuses on linking research to practice. The research base for instructional strategies is described and connected to teaching practices. The second strand emphasizes diversity. Understanding diversity perspectives is fundamental to teaching. The text describes how educators can ensure equity and fairness in the instruction and assessment of learners. The third strand, using technology, stresses integrating technology into teaching and learning. The text addresses a range of low-tech to high-tech materials, assistive technology devices, and software that can be used when teaching students with disabilities. This strand addresses the concept of *universal design,* which makes teaching and learning accessible to all students. Finally, there is a strand on linking instruction with assessment. This strand is unique because assessment strategies that can be used to assess both state and national learning standards are described.

The book begins with Part I, "Foundations for Teaching," which provides foundational concepts in designing instruction. Separate chapters in this part discuss preparing to teach children and youth and characteristics of students. Part II, "How Teachers Teach," focuses on generic teaching considerations and on developing and enhancing social skills and promoting positive behaviors. Separate chapters in this part discuss linking instruction with assessment, planning and organizing instruction, methods of teaching, selecting instructional strategies, social skills, positive behaviors, and developing partnerships with educators, families, and paraprofessionals. Part III, "Curriculum Areas," provides separate chapters for teaching in content areas and includes suggestions for curriculum integration. Part IV, "Promoting Independence," is designed to provide students with information regarding the teaching of learning and study skills and the transition from school to work and the community.

SUPPLEMENTARY MATERIALS

Supplementary materials include:

- *Instructor's manual:* The instructor's manual contains a sample syllabus, resources, and an extensive test bank.

- *Companion Website:* This website provides a rich resource of supplemental materials related to the book.

ACKNOWLEDGMENTS

Our sincere appreciation is given to the many people who helped and supported us in the development of the book. A very special thank-you goes to Jamie Beam, Kathy Fries, Deb Pluck, Barbara Williams, Nancy Lightbody, Dale Blanchard, Andrea Norwood, and Donna Benjamin, as well as those who reviewed the manuscript: Joyce W. Bergin, Armstrong Atlantic State University; Kathleen Briseno, College of

DuPage/Naperville School District #203; Jim Burns, The College of Saint Rose; Christine Cheney, University of Nevada, Reno; Margaret E. Dixon, Southern Utah University; Maryann Dudzinski, Valparaiso University; Dennis K. Kelleher, California State University, Sacramento; Victoria Morin, Troy State University, Dothan; Maureen R. Norris, Bellarmine College; Regina Helen Sapona, University of Cincinnati; and Phyllis M. Tappe, San Francisco State University.

We extend grateful appreciation to our families, including Les, Seth, Jay, Amy, Dave, and Dina, for their continued support.

Libby Cohen
Loraine J. Spenciner

Discover the Companion Website Accompanying This Book

THE PRENTICE HALL COMPANION WEBSITE: A VIRTUAL LEARNING ENVIRONMENT

Technology is a constantly growing and changing aspect of our field that is creating a need for content and resources. To address this emerging need, Prentice Hall has developed an online learning environment for students and professors alike—Companion Websites—to support our textbooks.

In creating a Companion Website, our goal is to build on and enhance what the textbook already offers. For this reason, the content for each user-friendly website is organized by chapter and provides the professor and student with a variety of meaningful resources.

FOR THE PROFESSOR—

Every Companion Website integrates **Syllabus Manager**™, an online syllabus creation and management utility.

- **Syllabus Manager**™ provides you, the instructor, with an easy, step-by-step process to create and revise syllabi, with direct links into Companion Website and other online content without having to learn HTML.

- Students may logon to your syllabus during any study session. All they need to know is the web address for the Companion Website and the password you've assigned to your syllabus.

- After you have created a syllabus using **Syllabus Manager**™, students may enter the syllabus for their course section from any point in the Companion Website.

- Clicking on a date, the student is shown the list of activities for the assignment. The activities for each assignment are linked directly to actual content, saving time for students.

- Adding assignments consists of clicking on the desired due date, then filling in the details of the assignment—name of the assignment, instructions, and whether it is a one-time or repeating assignment.

- In addition, links to other activities can be created easily. If the activity is online, a URL can be entered in the space provided, and it will be linked automatically in the final syllabus.

- Your completed syllabus is hosted on our servers, allowing convenient updates from any computer on the Internet. Changes you make to your syllabus are immediately available to your students at their next logon.

Common Companion Website features for students include:

FOR THE STUDENT—

- *Chapter Objectives*—Outline key concepts from the text.
- *Interactive Self-Quizzes*—Complete with hints and automatic grading that provide immediate feedback for students.

  After students submit their answers for the interactive self-quizzes, the Companion Website **Results Reporter** computes a percentage grade, provides a graphic representation of how many questions were answered correctly and incorrectly, and gives a question-by-question analysis of the quiz. Students are given the option to send their quiz to up to four e-mail addresses (professor, teaching assistant, study partner, etc).
- *Web Destinations*—Links to www sites that relate to chapter content.
- *Message Board*—Virtual bulletin board to post or respond to questions or comments from a national audience.

To take advantage of the many available resources, please visit the *Teaching Students with Mild and Moderate Disabilities: Research-Based Practices* Companion Website at

www.prenhall.com/cohen

EDUCATOR LEARNING CENTER: AN INVALUABLE ONLINE RESOURCE

Merrill Education and the Association for Supervision and Curriculum Development (ASCD) invite you to take advantage of a new online resource, one that provides access to the top research and proven strategies associated with ASCD and Merrill—the Educator Learning Center. At **www.EducatorLearningCenter.com** you will find resources that will enhance your students' understanding of course topics and of current educational issues, in addition to being invaluable for further research.

How the Educator Learning Center Will Help Your Students Become Better Teachers

With the combined resources of Merrill Education and ASCD, you and your students will find a wealth of tools and materials to better prepare them for the classroom.

Research

- More than 600 articles from the ASCD journal *Educational Leadership* discuss everyday issues faced by practicing teachers.
- A direct link on the site to Research Navigator™ gives students access to many of the leading education journals, as well as extensive content detailing the research process.
- Excerpts from Merrill Education texts give your students insights on important topics of instructional methods, diverse populations, assessment, classroom management, technology, and refining classroom practice.

Classroom Practice

- Hundreds of lesson plans and teaching strategies are categorized by content area and age range.
- Case studies and classroom video footage provide virtual field experience for student reflection.
- Computer simulations and other electronic tools keep your students abreast of today's classrooms and current technologies.

Look into the Value of Educator Learning Center Yourself

A four-month subscription to Educator Learning Center is $25 but is **FREE** when ordered in conjunction with this text. To obtain free passcodes for your students, simply contact your local Merrill/Prentice Hall sales representative, who will give you a special ISBN to give your bookstore when ordering your textbooks. To preview the value of this website to you and your students, please go to **www.EducatorLearningCenter.com** and click on "Demo."

Brief Contents

Contents

PART II
HOW TEACHERS TEACH

PART IV
PROMOTING INDEPENDENCE

Note. Every effort has been made to provide accurate and current information in this book. However, the Internet and information posted on it are constantly changing; it is inevitable that some of the Internet addresses listed in this textbook will change.

Special Features

RESEARCH TO PRACTICE

USING TECHNOLOGY

CONSIDERING DIVERSITY

Foundations for Teaching

1

Chapter

Preparing to Teach Students with Mild and Moderate Disabilities

CHAPTER OBJECTIVES

After completing this chapter, you should be able to:

❖ Discuss what beginning teachers should know about the principles of the Individuals with Disabilities Education Act (IDEA).

❖ Describe how individualized education program (IEP) team members plan specially designed instruction and consider the use of assistive technology devices and services for students with disabilities.

❖ Discuss other federal legislation related to working with students with disabilities including the Rehabilitation Act Amendments of 1998, the Americans with Disabilities Act of 1990, the Carl D. Perkins Vocational and Applied Technology Education Act Amendments of 1998, and the No Child Left Behind Act of 2001.

❖ Describe the continuum of settings in which special educators work.

❖ Identify and discuss federal legislation regarding students with disabilities from diverse cultural, ethnic, racial, economic, and linguistic backgrounds.

❖ Use technology-based resources in locating information regarding changes and updates to federal and state legislation.

❖ *Meet Kalynda* ❖

"Hi! My name is Kalynda—but my friends call me Kay. I love to Rollerblade with my friends. My favorite subject in school is art. I have a learning disability, but I think I'm doing well in school because I have learned to be very organized, to keep up with my work, and to ask for help if I need it.

"My special education teacher has taught me some really neat things, like how to check my writing before I pass it in. She helped me make a cue sheet that I use to check my paper myself to make sure that it has all the necessary requirements. Writing is really important in our school, and everybody has a portfolio of their work. Like I am really, really proud of mine. Last week I added a report to my portfolio that demonstrates how I am working toward one of my school standards in literacy, showing how we understand a story from the point of view of one of the characters.

"My special education teacher has taught me how to be independent and to become an advocate. She invited some leaders from the business community to come speak to our class. One person was an artist who uses discarded items in her sculptures. This artist is so cool, and she also has a learning disability. It was so great to meet her and to hear her story, and sometimes I think I'll be an artist, too. She also talked about individual rights and laws for people with disabilities. It's hard for me to remember all the things that she said. Maybe I'll have a chance to learn them again some day."

. . . AND HER MOTHER

"Bringing up Kalynda has been quite an experience for me as a single mother. I remember her first years of school were pretty difficult. She didn't like to sit still long enough to listen to a story and then, in the early grades, she had a great deal of difficulty in learning how to read—and I didn't know why. It was a relief when the IEP team determined that she had specific learning disabilities in reading and writing.

"I'm pleased with her progress now. Her teacher keeps in close contact with me, letting me know her successes. She is taking an interest in writing short stories and poetry. In fact, her teacher is encouraging her to submit some of her work to the school newspaper!

"When Kalynda experiences difficulties, her teacher lets me know too. This way we can address concerns before Kalynda becomes discouraged with her schoolwork. Like last week, her teacher called to let me know that Kalynda was having some difficulty in math class and wasn't turning in her homework. Now that I know that Kalynda has homework assignments, I can follow up with her at home. Usually I just need to remind her, but sometimes I need to limit her cell [phone] use and instant messaging."

PREPARING TO TEACH

Preparing to teach students like Kalynda begins with learning about federal legislation and how these mandates guide a special educator's work with students, families, other educators, and professionals. As you continue reading this textbook, you will learn more about students with mild and moderate disabilities and the characteristics of the most common disabilities including learning disabilities, attention deficit hyperactivity disorder, other health impairments, emotional disturbance, mental retardation, and autism spectrum disorder. And you'll study effective research-based methods and instructional strategies for teaching students with mild and moderate disabilities. The work of a special educator is both demanding and rewarding. This book starts your journey!

As you read this first chapter, think about the students and the teachers you may have already met. How do the federal laws described in this chapter influence the education and related services that students receive—or perhaps do not receive? Can you describe some of the job responsibilities of a special education teacher that you know? How are these responsibilities tied to federal and state legislation?

FEDERAL LEGISLATION AND THE EDUCATION OF STUDENTS WITH DISABILITIES

Over the past three decades, the passage of federal legislation has greatly shaped the provision of special education and related services along with the settings where students with disabilities receive their education. Beginning in the mid-1970s, a series of federal laws were passed that had a major impact on children and youth with disabilities. These laws came about because parents and others who deeply cared about the civil rights of individuals with disabilities had a vision of what the future should hold.

Political movements, characterized by concerns for the civil rights of others, have occurred throughout the history of our country. In the mid-20th century, Americans began to develop an interest in the problems of people who lived in poverty and others who did not have access to the same privileges and rights that the majority enjoyed. During the 1960s, political leaders and civil rights activists called for action. The notion that people of color should be segregated was challenged in schools, in the community, and in the workplace. Equal access became a driving force as concerned citizens reexamined state and federal laws and school-based policies, including those concerning the education of students with disabilities.

Before the 1970s, few students with disabilities attended public schools in the communities in which they lived. Students with multiple or severe and profound disabilities frequently stayed home or were placed in residential facilities that provided only custodial care; students with mild and moderate disabilities usually attended special-purpose private schools or residential schools designed especially for students with disabilities. Some students had to travel a long distance to attend schools in other communities, and others lived away from home because they attended residential schools. Families often paid for their child's education themselves. Some students with mild disabilities did not receive services at all and were passed through the grades in their local school with little understanding of their special needs.

In 1975, as a result of parent advocacy, court decisions, and many other efforts, Congress passed federal legislation that provided free, appropriate public education for students with disabilities at no cost to their parents. Furthermore, the legislation stipulated that students with disabilities should receive their education in the **least restrictive environment,** requiring schools to offer a variety of settings that provide the most appropriate placement options and from which students with disabilities can benefit. IDEA defines least restrictive environment as follows:

1. that to the maximum extent appropriate, children with disabilities, including children in public or private institutions or other care facilities, are educated with children who are nondisabled; and
2. that special classes, separate schooling or other removal of children with disabilities from the regular education environment occurs only if the nature or severity of the disability is such that education in regular classes with the use of supplementary aids and services cannot be achieved satisfactorily. [20 U.S.C. 1412(a)(5)]

For many students this meant that they could enroll in their local community schools. Since 1975 there have been numerous amendments to this law, today known as the Individuals with Disabilities Education Act.

In 2002, the President's Commission on Excellence in Special Education was convened to study the current state of special education and to make recommendations to improve the special education system. Their recommendations present a challenge to future educators working to meet students' learning needs. The Commission reported the need to establish high expectations for students with disabilities, to increase parental empowerment, and to link school and nonschool transition services for secondary students with disabilities. In later chapters of this book, you will study research-based teaching methods and strategies to help students with disabilities meet high academic expectations across the curriculum, learn about working with parents, and study transition services. First, though, we will provide background information that future educators need to know. The following federal legislation has important implications for you and your work with students with disabilities.

THE INDIVIDUALS WITH DISABILITIES EDUCATION ACT

The Individuals with Disabilities Education Act (IDEA) Amendments of 1990 (Public Law 101-476) changed earlier legislation that focused on ensuring that children and youth with disabilities receive a free, appropriate public education and, at the same time, have their individual educational needs determined and addressed. IDEA requires that students with disabilities have access to the general education curriculum (the same curriculum that students without disabilities have) to the maximum extent possible [Sec. 300.26(b)(3)(ii)]. IDEA expands the scope of education to include preparing students for employment and independent living (Sec. 300.29). Further, IDEA strengthens the role of parents and ensures that they have meaningful opportunities to participate in the education of their child (Sec. 300.345).

IDEA focuses on excellence, high standards, and high expectations, in addition to the earlier issue of providing a free, appropriate public education in the least restrictive environment. Teaching and learning are the primary focus of this legislation; IDEA considers the individualized education program (IEP) as the primary tool for accountability and for enhancing the child's involvement and progress in the general curriculum (Kupper, 2000). This comprehensive mandate for children and youth includes both special education and related services.

What Is Special Education?

IDEA defines *special education* as specially designed instruction, at no cost to parents, to meet the unique needs of a student with a disability. The instruction may be conducted in the classroom, in the home, in hospitals and institutions, and in other settings. **Specially designed instruction** means:

1. adapting content, methodology, or delivery of instruction to meet the unique needs of a child with a disability, and
2. ensuring that the child has access to the general curriculum so that the child can meet the educational standards that apply to all children.
   [Sec. 300.26(b)(3)(ii)]

IDEA requires that students with disabilities have access to the general education curriculum.

Specially designed instruction also includes education and training in one or more of the following areas [Sec. 300.26(a)(2)]:

- PHYSICAL EDUCATION. Physical education includes special physical education, adapted physical education, movement education, and motor development. Teachers help students work toward physical and motor fitness or fundamental motor skills and skills in aquatics, dance, and individual and group games and sports.
- TRAVEL TRAINING. Travel training is a type of specially designed instruction to help a child in developing an awareness of the environment and to move effectively and safely from place to place in school or home, at work, or in the community.
- VOCATIONAL EDUCATION. This specially designed instruction consists of organized education programs that are directly related to the preparation of individuals for paid or unpaid employment, or for career preparation that does not require a baccalaureate or advanced degree.

Who Is Eligible for Special Education Services?

To be eligible for special education services, (a) a student must have a disability and (b) that disability must adversely affect the student's education performance (Sec. 300.7). IDEA describes 14 categories of disability (Table 1.1). Some states follow these federal categories, whereas others use slightly different terms and definitions for describing disabilities.

Table 1.1	**Disability Areas Described by the Individuals with Disabilities Education Act**

Disability	Definition
Autism	A developmental disability significantly affecting verbal and nonverbal communication and social interaction, generally evident before age 3, that adversely affects a child's educational performance.
Deaf–blindness	Accompanying hearing and visual impairments that, combined, produce severe communication and other developmental and educational needs that cannot be accommodated in special education programs solely for children with deafness or blindness.
Deafness	A hearing impairment that is so severe that linguistic information cannot be processed through hearing, with or without amplification, adversely affecting the child's educational performance.
Developmental delay	A delay in one or more of the following areas: physical development, including fine and gross motor, cognitive, communication, social or emotional, or adaptive development. Some states have adopted this term for children from ages 3 to 9 so that these children can receive special education services.
Emotional disturbance	A condition exhibiting one or more of the following characteristics over a long period of time and to a marked degree, adversely affecting a child's educational performance: 1. an inability to learn that cannot be explained by intellectual, sensory, or health factors 2. an inability to build or maintain satisfactory interpersonal relationships with peers and teachers 3. inappropriate behaviors or feelings under normal circumstances 4. a general pervasive mood of unhappiness or depression 5. a tendency to develop physical symptoms or fears associated with personal or school problems The term includes schizophrenia. Emotional disturbance does not apply to children who are socially maladjusted unless it is determined that they have an emotional disturbance.
Hearing impairment	An impairment in hearing, whether permanent or fluctuating, that adversely affects a child's educational performance.
Mental retardation	A condition in which there is significant subaverage general intellectual functioning, existing concurrently with deficits in adaptive behavior and manifested during the developmental period, that adversely affects a child's educational performance.
Multiple disabilities	Concomitant impairments (such as mental retardation–blindness, mental retardation–orthopedic impairment, etc.) the combination of which causes such severe educational needs that they cannot be accommodated in special education programs solely for one of the impairments.

Disability Areas Described by the Individuals with Disabilities Education Act *continued*

Disability	Definition
Orthopedic impairment	A severe orthopedic impairment that adversely affects a child's educational performance. The term includes impairments caused by a congenital anomaly, impairments caused by disease, and impairments from other causes such as amputations and fractures or burns that cause contractures.
Other health impairment	Limited strength, vitality, or alertness, including heightened alertness to environmental stimuli, that results in limited alertness with respect to the education environment. These impairments are due to chronic or acute health problems such as asthma, attention deficit disorder or attention deficit hyperactivity disorder, diabetes, epilepsy, a heart condition, hemophilia, lead poisoning, leukemia, nephritis, rheumatic fever, and sickle cell anemia and adversely affect a child's educational performance.
Specific learning disability	A disorder in one or more of the basic psychological processes involved in understanding or using language, either spoken or written, that may be manifested in an impaired ability to listen, think, speak, read, write, spell, or do mathematical calculations. The term includes such conditions as perceptual disabilities, brain injury, minimal brain dysfunction, dyslexia, and developmental aphasia. It does not apply to children who have learning problems that are primarily the result of visual, hearing, or motor disabilities, mental retardation, emotional disturbance, or environmental, cultural, or economic disadvantages.
Speech or language impairment	A communication disorder such as stuttering, impaired articulation, a language impairment, or a voice impairment that adversely affects the child's educational performance.
Traumatic brain injury	An acquired injury to the brain caused by an external physical force resulting in total or partial functional disability or psychosocial impairment, or both, that adversely affects a child's educational performance. The term applies to open or closed head injuries resulting in impairments in one or more areas, such as cognition, language, memory, attention, reasoning, abstract thinking, judgment, problem solving, sensory, perceptual, and motor abilities, psychosocial behavior, physical functions, information processing, and speech. The term does not apply to brain injuries that are congenital or degenerative or to brain injuries induced by birth trauma.
Visual impairment, including blindness	An impairment in vision that, even with correction, adversely affects the child's educational performance. The term includes both partial sight and blindness.

Source: Adapted from IDEA 34 C.F.R., Sec. 300.7(c).

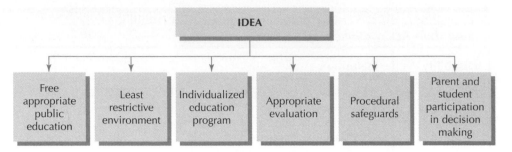

Figure 1.1   **Six principles of IDEA provide the framework for special education and related services**
Source: Adapted from *Six Principles of IDEA,* NICHCY, 2002.

When a student with a disability is eligible for special education, members of the student's IEP team develop a written document that describes the goals that the student will meet during the year. The IEP is a legal document and an accountability tool for educators and parents. Six main principles establish the framework for providing special education and related services described in the IEP (National Information Center for Children and Youth with Disabilities [NICHCY], 2002; see Figure 1.1).

Principle 1. Free Appropriate Public Education

Free appropriate public education (**FAPE**) ensures that no child or youth (3 to 21 years of age) will be excluded from an appropriate public education because of a disability, including students with profound disabilities, students with disruptive be-haviors, and students with contagious diseases. Educators sometimes use the term *zero reject* to describe this mandate of enrolling all students. To help pay the extra cost of providing the special education and related services associated with FAPE, IDEA gives money to state agencies and local schools. Children and youth with disabilities receive FAPE in the least restrictive environment.

Principle 2. Appropriate Evaluation

Educators must determine whether a student has a disability and, if so, whether the stu-dent needs special education and related services. Special education teachers and other professionals conducting assessments must ensure that the approaches used are appro-priate. Assessment approaches should be free from bias and discrimination and should be used for the purposes for which they were intended. Educators and other profes-sionals involved in the assessment process are required to follow assessment stipulations outlined in IDEA (Figure 1.2). If the student is eligible for special education services, teachers conduct additional assessments to determine the student's educational needs. The student's IEP team uses the results of these assessments in planning the IEP.

Principle 3. The Individualized Education Program

Each student with a disability must have an IEP that describes what the student can do, the student's strengths, and the student's needs. The IEP also includes much

Figure 1.2   General requirements of appropriate evaluation according to IDEA

IDEA requires that assessment procedures be fair and equitable for all children and youth:

- The test must be administered in the student's native language or by another mode of communication.
- The test must be validated for the purpose of its use.
- The test must be administered by a trained examiner and must conform with instructions from the test publisher.
- The assessment should yield not merely an intelligence quotient but also additional information about the student's educational needs.
- The assessment of students with impaired sensory, manual, or speaking skills must be completed with tests that are selected and administered to reflect the student's aptitude or achievement level (or another factor) accurately. The tests should not reflect the student's impaired sensory, manual, or speaking skills (except where these skills are the factors that are being measured).
- No single test should be used to determine a student's eligibility for special education services.
- The student must be assessed in all areas related to the suspected disability, including, where appropriate, health, vision, hearing, social and emotional status, general intelligence, academic performance, communicative status, and motor abilities.
- The assessment must be made by a multidisciplinary team, including at least one member with knowledge in the suspected area of disability.

Source: Adapted from IDEA 34 C.F.R., Sec. 300.532.

additional information, including the educational goals and the steps that describe how the student will meet them. Working together, a team of individuals develops the IEP. The members of the team include:

- the student's parents;
- at least one regular education teacher;
- at least one special education teacher;
- a person who is qualified to provide or supervise specially designed instruction to meet the unique needs of children with disabilities and is knowledgeable about the availability of resources and the general curriculum;
- a person who can interpret the instructional implications of evaluation results;
- other individuals who have knowledge or special expertise regarding the child, including related services personnel as appropriate; and
- the student, if appropriate.

School personnel make every effort to ensure that the parents or guardians of the student are present at the IEP meeting. Parents should be notified early that a meeting will be scheduled, and a mutually agreed-on time and place should be established. School personnel can conduct an IEP meeting without a parent in attendance, but the school is required by IDEA to maintain a record of the attempts to contact the family.

Principle 4. Least Restrictive Environment

The principle of the least restrictive environment is based on the requirement that schools must offer a variety of settings that provide the most appropriate placement options for students with disabilities and from which these students can benefit. These include general education classes, resource rooms, special classes, special schools, and homebound or hospital placements.

The IEP team must consider accommodations and modifications to the general education curriculum before removing a student with a disability from the regular classroom. A student is not removed from a general education classroom unless the student cannot be educated there successfully even after the school has provided accommodations, modifications, aids, or supports. Moreover, a student with a disability cannot be required to demonstrate specific levels of performance before being considered for a regular class placement. IDEA states that students with disabilities must be "placed in settings based on the student's needs and not on such factors as the student's classification, availability of space, or administrative convenience" (Sec. 300, Part 300, App. A, Quest. 1). If the IEP team decides that a student cannot benefit from the general education class, the team identifies the least restrictive setting that is appropriate for the student and from which the student can benefit.

Principle 5. Procedural Safeguards

IDEA specifies procedural safeguards to ensure that the rights of parents and children are protected during the assessment process and the delivery of services. These procedures are sometimes referred to as *due process* and are outlined in Figure 1.3. Due process also guarantees parents or personnel in schools or agencies the right to an impartial hearing conducted by a hearing officer when disagreements occur. Either a parent or school personnel can request a hearing if differences cannot be resolved informally.

Principle 6. Parent and Student Participation in Decision Making

Several of the previous principles described ways that parents and students can participate with teachers and other professionals during the process of planning, imple-

---

Figure 1.3   **Procedural safeguards described by IDEA**

Procedural safeguards include:

- Parents must provide consent for their child to participate in any assessment activity, including a preplacement evaluation.
- Parents have the right to review their child's records regarding the assessment and educational placement.
- Parents must receive written notice before the school initiates or changes the identification, evaluation, or education placement of their child. The notice must be written in language understandable to the general public or provided in the native language of the parent or mode of communication used by the parent.
- Parents must have the opportunity to participate in meetings with respect to the identification, evaluation, and education placement of their child.
- Parents may obtain an independent evaluation of their child by a qualified examiner who is not employed by the school. The evaluation is at no cost to the parent and is paid for by the public school.

Source: Adapted from IDEA 34 C.F.R., Secs. 300.500–517.

Parent and student participate in the IEP team meeting.

menting, and evaluating services for the student. Parents and students bring added knowledge about the student's problem and expertise in helping to create solutions. Their participation brings shared ownership to the student's IEP and encourages the student to take responsibility for the outcomes.

REHABILITATION ACT AMENDMENTS OF 1998

The Rehabilitation Act, first authorized in 1973, has been amended and reauthorized numerous times, much like IDEA. The Rehabilitation Act Amendments of 1998 (P.L. 105-220) provide a far-reaching mandate regarding accessibility and employment for individuals with disabilities. In the following, we focus on Sections 504 and 508 of the act.

Section 504

Section 504 of the Rehabilitation Act of 1998 protects the rights of students with disabilities in programs and activities in public schools and other programs that receive federal financial assistance from the U.S. Department of Education. The provisions of Section 504 and IDEA work well together in helping to provide a range of services for students. Much like a large net, Section 504 casts a wide circle to assist students who need services but are not eligible to receive special education services under IDEA (Figure 1.4).

Similar to IDEA, Section 504 requires FAPE for eligible students, including individually designed instruction (Sec. 104.33); however, Section 504, as well as the Americans with Disabilities Act, uses a broader definition of individual disability areas

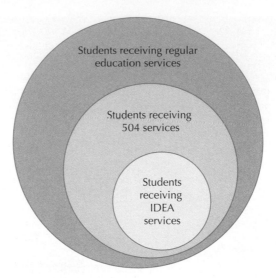

Figure 1.4   **General student body in a public school**
Source: Adapted from *Student Access: A Resource Guide for Educators* (p. 6), Council of Administrators of Special Education, n.d., Arlington, VA: Council for Exceptional Children. Reprinted by permission.

and other conditions. Examples of other conditions that are typically covered under Section 504 include:

- communicable diseases such as tuberculosis;
- medical conditions such as allergies and heart disease;
- temporary medical conditions due to an illness or accident;
- behavioral difficulties; and
- drug or alcohol addiction.

Because of the broader definition provided by Section 504, students who do not meet the criteria for a specific disability under IDEA may be eligible to receive services and accommodations under Section 504 (Table 1.2).

When school personnel decide that a student needs services under Section 504, they meet to write a plan, commonly referred to as a *504 Plan*. In developing a 504 Plan, teachers work with students and their parents to identify and list ideas that will help the student succeed in the classroom. For example, the teacher might begin by encouraging the student to think about what helps the student learn (Blazer, 1999). Then the teacher might identify a low-distraction work area, provide more opportunities for physical activity such as allowing the student to move around, or break assignments into short, sequential steps (Booth, 1998). From these suggestions and by working with the parents, educators develop the 504 Plan (Figure 1.5).

Section 508

Section 508 of the Rehabilitation Act of 1998 requires federal agencies to make their electronic and information technology accessible to people with disabilities.

Table 1.2	Disability Areas Described by Section 504 of the Rehabilitation Act Amendments of 1998 and the Americans with Disabilities Act
Physical or mental impairment	1. any physiological disorder or condition, cosmetic disfigurement, or anatomical loss affecting one or more of the following body systems: neurological; musculoskeletal; special sense organs; respiratory, including speech organs; cardiovascular; reproductive; digestive; genitourinary; hermic and lymphatic; skin; and endocrine; or 2. any mental or psychological disorder, such as mental retardation, organic brain syndrome, emotional or mental illness, and specific learning disabilities.
Major life activities	Functions such as caring for oneself, performing manual tasks, walking, seeing, hearing, speaking, breathing, learning, and working.
Record of impairment	Has a history of, or has been classified as having, a mental or physical impairment that substantially limits one or more major life activities.
Regarded as having an impairment	1. has a physical or mental impairment that does not substantially limit major life activities but is treated by a recipient as constituting such a limitation; 2. has a physical or mental impairment that substantially limits major life activities only as a result of the attitudes of others toward such impairment; or 3. has none of the impairments defined but is treated by a recipient as having such an impairment (such as a person who has a significant birthmark on the face which does not limit any major life activity but [that] the person feels does result in being discriminated against).

Source: Adapted from IDEA 34 C.F.R., Part 104.3 and H.R. Sec. 101.

All federal agencies must comply with Section 508 when they develop, procure, maintain, or use electronic and information technology (Rehabilitation Act Amendments, Sec. 794[d]). This applies to software; Internet-based information systems; telecommunication products; video and multimedia products; self-contained, closed products such as information kiosks, calculators, and fax machines; and desktop and portable computers.

AMERICANS WITH DISABILITIES ACT OF 1990

The Americans with Disabilities Act (ADA) of 1990 (P.L. 101-336) is a civil rights law patterned on Section 504 of the Rehabilitation Act. ADA prohibits discrimination on the basis of disability in employment, programs, and services. Today, the integration of people with disabilities into the mainstream of society is fundamental, due

Figure 1.5   Example of a 504 plan

SOUTH SCHOOL DEPARTMENT

504 ACCOMMODATION PLAN

Date of Meeting: *November 19, 20xx*   Review Date: *November 18, 20xx*

Student name: *Terri Bennet*   DOB: *02/21/xx*   Grade: *8*   School: *Memorial*   Case Manager: *Lonnie Hyer*

Describe nature of handicap: *Altered elimination status—urinary and bowel.*

Describe how this handicap affects a major life activity: *Frequent urinary tract infections due to reconstructed bladder.*

Describe evaluations utilized to determine eligibility: *School attendance, academic performance.*

Team Members:

Susan McIver, school nurse	*Terri Bennet, student*	*Sarah Bennet, parent*
Phyllis Lane, guidance counselor	*Alan Jenkins, principal*	*Helen Folsum, teacher*
		Stephen St. Pierre, teacher

Area(s) of Difficulty	Accommodations	Start Date
Due to frequent medical absences, Terri is missing the important interconnectedness of learning; i.e, in science she misses the vocabulary and experiments and their daily interconnectedness to the next level of learning.	*Tutor 3 days per week. Terri will come to school for tutoring when she has been out unless she is too ill for tutoring.*	*11/19/xx*
	Grades are modified in all areas based on classes attended and tutorial help provided.	*11/19/xx*
Colostomy (occasional appliance detachment)	*Parent or designee will be called when necessary to allow Terri to go home to shower and change.*	*11/19/xx*
Need for daily catheterization	*Terri will use the staff or student bathroom for self-catheterization as she wishes.*	*11/19/xx*

I give consent for this plan to be implemented. I understand that my consent is voluntary and may be revoked at any time.

Sarah Bennet	*November 19, 20xx*
Parent signature	Date

in part to this law. Under the ADA, an individual with a disability is defined in the same way as under Section 504 (Table 1.2).

CARL D. PERKINS VOCATIONAL AND APPLIED TECHNOLOGY EDUCATION ACT AMENDMENTS OF 1998

The Carl D. Perkins Vocational and Applied Technology Education Act Amendments of 1998 (P.L. 105-332) describe a vision of vocational and technical education that includes improving student achievement and preparing the student for further learning and for postsecondary education and career preparation. This legislation promotes reform and innovation in vocational and technical education to assist students in acquiring the skills and knowledge to meet state and national academic standards and industry-recognized skill standards. Secondary students with disabilities need to be able to make connections between their academic and vocational classes. This federal law assists teachers in linking academic, vocational, and technical instruction in secondary and postsecondary classrooms by encouraging students to obtain experiences in all aspects of an industry, involving parents and employers, and providing links between secondary and postsecondary education.

NO CHILD LEFT BEHIND ACT OF 2001

The No Child Left Behind Act (P.L. 107-110), designed to improve student achievement, began a sweeping overhaul of educational practices. This legislation puts renewed emphasis on many areas, including:

- early childhood education and the development of language skills and pre-reading skills
- assessments that align with state academic content and achievement standards
- ongoing assessments each year in Grades 3 to 8 and at least once during Grades 10 to 12
- detailed report cards to parents concerning their child's progress

Before the No Child Left Behind Act was passed, there were few mandates for putting research into practice. This legislation puts special emphasis on the need to implement educational programs and instruction that can demonstrate their effectiveness. Today educators carefully review research findings to help inform classroom practices. Throughout each chapter in this textbook, you will read about relevant research related to teaching and learning and students with disabilities. One important line of research relates to the digital divide.

CHARTER SCHOOLS AND SPECIAL EDUCATION

Although much of our discussion so far has focused on federal legislation and the responsibilities of public schools, more and more students with and without disabilities are attending public charter schools. Public charter schools provide alternatives to local public schools and have increased dramatically in number since the first charter schools appeared in the 1990s. They offer some degree of independence from the rules and regulations that apply to traditional public schools. However, charter schools must follow all federal civil rights laws including IDEA (Sec. 300.312), Section 504 of the Rehabilitation Act, and the ADA (Ahearn, 2002).

STUDENTS WITH DISABILITIES AND HIGH ACADEMIC STANDARDS

As both charter schools and traditional schools strive for excellence for all students, teachers emphasize improving learning so that all students can meet high academic standards. These standards may be tied to school-based, state, or national curriculum standards in

Research to Practice

The Digital Divide

The *digital divide* refers to technology and the people who use it. According to a national study (Lenhart, 2003), people with disabilities have among the lowest levels of Internet access in this country:

- 38% of people with disabilities go online, compared to 58% of all Americans.
- 28% of people with disabilities say their disability makes it difficult or impossible for them to go online (p. 5).

Questions for Reflection

1. What might make Internet access difficult for people with disabilities?
2. What are some methods that help people with disabilities access the Internet and other technologies?

 To answer these questions and learn more about applying research to practice, go to the Companion Website at www.prenhall. com/cohen, select Chapter 1, then choose Research to Practice.

literacy, mathematics, science, social studies, and other curriculum areas. To help students meet these standards, general and special education teachers specify the knowledge and skills students will attain and be able to demonstrate. If the IEP team decides that content or performance standards need to be altered for a student with a disability,

- the alternate standards should be challenging yet potentially achievable;
- these should reflect the full range of knowledge and skills that the student needs to live a full, productive life; and
- the school system should inform parents and the student of any consequences of these alterations. (McDonnell, McLaughlin, & Morison, 1997, p. 9)

PLANNING THE INDIVIDUALIZED EDUCATION PROGRAM

The IEP provides a framework for teaching a student with a disability. Based on assessment information gathered by team members, the IEP includes specific information about the student's current level of functioning, strengths, and needs. The team uses this information to plan the IEP and, later, to determine the extent of the progress and the student's accomplishments.

QUESTIONS THE TEAM CONSIDERS

When the IEP team convenes, there is much to talk about. In this section, we will look at how team members begin planning the student's IEP and some of the questions they consider. Figure 1.6 illustrates these questions and provides the reference link to IDEA.

Figure 1.6   The IEP team must consider many questions

1. What are the results of classroom observations and other assessments?
2. What are the current strengths and concerns of the parents for enhancing the education of their child?
3. What special education needs to be provided to ensure access to the general curriculum? What accommodations and modifications are necessary?
4. Does the student need assistive technology?
5. Does the student need appropriate positive behavioral interventions and strategies?
6. Does the team need to consider special factors such as Braille, sign language, supports for behaviors that impede learning, communication needs, or language needs?
7. What related services need to be provided to ensure access to the general curriculum?
8. Does the student require supplementary aids, services, program modification, or supports for school personnel?
9. Does the student need services during the summer months?
10. Beginning at age 14 or younger if appropriate, what transition services are needed?

Source: Adapted from IDEA 34 C.F.R., Secs. 300.309, 300.346, 300.347, and 300.532.

LINKING ASSESSMENT WITH INSTRUCTION

 During the IEP team meeting, parents provide information about their child's strengths and interests as well as areas of concern. The student may participate by sharing reflections on past work, current difficulties, and aspirations for the future. Other members of the team report the results of classroom observations and other assessments, including the student's current strengths and needs. They also discuss the results of the initial or most recent evaluations and information about the student's performance on any general statewide or districtwide assessments. This information provides the team with a base to establish the student's current level of functioning in the areas of concern and to determine if the student requires (or continues to need) special education services.

Specially Designed Instruction

As the team plans the student's IEP, members address any specially designed instruction that should be used to meet the special needs of the student. Specially designed instruction may include specific teaching methods, instructional strategies, identifying and implementing appropriate accommodations or modifications, instructional materials and equipment, and/or teaching and learning resources.

Accommodations and Modifications

The IEP team also identifies the appropriate **accommodations** and **modifications** needed by the student [IDEA 34 C.F.R., Sec. 300.346(c)]. Accommodations refer to changes to the education program that do not substantially alter the instructional level, the content of the curriculum, or the assessment criteria; modifications involve changes or adaptations of the education program that alter the level, content, and/or assessment criteria. If the student will not participate in some or all of the general education classes, even after considering accommodations and modification, team members write an explanation of the extent to which the student will not participate. If the student will need accommodations or modifications to participate in state or districtwide assessment of achievement, team members include a description of the accommodations or modifications.

In a survey of teachers, both elementary and secondary educators reported that providing individual assistance to a student with a learning disability was the most effective accommodation to help the student succeed in the class. Elementary teachers ranked open book exams as least effective; secondary educators felt that having another student or teacher aide take notes for students was least effective (Bryant, Dean, Elrod, & Blackbourn, 1999). Figure 1.7 illustrates the accommodations frequently used in the general education classroom.

Assistive Technology

As the team considers the student's education program, they also must consider the student's assistive technology (AT) needs and services (IDEA 34 C.F.R., Sec. 300.5). For example, they raise questions such as: "What do we want the student to be able to do within her IEP that she is currently not able to do because of her learning disability?" "Would AT enable this student to meet this goal(s)?" "What has been tried to meet her special learning needs in the past?" "Is it working?" "Is it providing her with the least restrictive environment?"

AT helps a student with a disability participate in the regular education classroom.

Figure 1.7   Accommodations frequently used in the general education classroom

Accommodations

Teacher aide dictates answers on tests

Teacher aide reads test items to students

Student takes test in resource room or special education classroom

Teacher provides review opportunities before a test

Teacher provides individual assistance to student

Teacher divides assignment into smaller tasks

Teacher provides student aids (e.g., hints, cue cards, spelling lists, calculators)

Teacher aide or volunteer takes notes for student

Teacher initiates contact with parents when assignments are not completed

Teacher uses homework folders that parents must sign

Teacher provides study carrel

Modifications

Teacher does not lower the grade due to spelling errors

Teacher arranges a buddy system for in-class assignments

Source: Adapted from "Rural General Education Teachers' Opinions of Adaptations for Inclusive Classrooms: A Renewed Call for Dual Licensure," by R. Bryant, M. Dean, G. F. Elrod, and J. M. Blackbourn, 1999, *Rural Special Education Quarterly, 19*(1), pp. 5–11.

Assistive technology devices include a variety of technology, tools, software, or equipment that can be purchased or specially designed. These materials are used to increase, maintain, or improve the functional capabilities of an individual with a disability (Sec. 300.5). IDEA also provides for **assistive technology services,** which include any service that directly assists a child with a disability in the selection, acquisition, or use of an AT device. AT services include evaluation of the needs of the child, including a functional evaluation of the child; acquiring the device; selecting, designing, fitting, customizing, adapting, applying, maintaining, repairing, or replacing the device; coordinating and using other therapies or services; and training the child, family, and professionals (Sec. 300.6).

Positive Behavioral Intervention, Strategies, and Support

The general education teacher, along with other IEP team members, assists in determining positive behavioral interventions and strategies for the student (IDEA 34 C.F.R., Sec. 300.346). For example, the team discusses the student's need to develop positive interactions with peers through social skill instruction. The regular classroom teacher discusses how this instruction can be transferred to the general education classroom. The school psychologist might be identified as a support person in helping to prevent the student's recurring problem behaviors, if any exist.

Using Technology

Assistive Technology Devices

AT includes both simple, low-cost materials and high-cost digital equipment. Low-cost devices include a wide-tip marking pen or highlighting tape to indicate key concepts in a textbook. More expensive devices include a handheld (or PDA), a touch screen, or a smart keyboard with word processing software. Sometimes software is considered an AT device when it provides the means for a student to access the general education curriculum. For example, a student with a learning disability may use specialized word processing software with word prediction. Word prediction is a feature of the program that predicts words based on the first letter that the student types. This specialized software helps many students with short-term memory difficulties, word retrieval problems, and spelling difficulties.

Questions for Reflection

1. What are some examples of AT devices that might help a student who is having difficulty learning, reading text, writing papers, or organizing assignments?
2. How do team members determine what AT needs a student has?

 To answer these questions and learn more about using technology to support learning, go to the Companion Website at www.prenhall.com/cohen, select Chapter 1, then choose Using Technology.

Consideration of Special Factors

Depending on the needs of the student, the IEP team considers special factors:

- use of Braille for students who have a visual impairment unless the IEP team determines after an evaluation of the child's reading and writing skills that instruction in Braille or the use of Braille is not appropriate
- use of a sign language interpreter so that a deaf or hard-of-hearing student can participate in the general curriculum
- use of strategies including positive behavioral intervention and supports, for students whose behaviors impede their own learning or the learning of others
- communication needs of the student. For students who are deaf or hard of hearing, the team considers the student's language and communication needs, as well as opportunities for direct communication with peers and professional personnel in the child's language and communication mode, including direct instruction in the student's language and communication mode
- language needs of the student with limited English proficiency as they relate to the student's IEP (IDEA 34 C.F.R., Sec. 300.346)

Summer Months

The team also considers whether a student with a disability needs services during the summer months. This right to summer school services is called **extended school year (ESY) services.** These services are not limited to particular categories of disability

(IDEA 34 C.F.R., Sec. 300.309). When a team considers ESY services, it usually considers a variety of factors, including the likelihood of regression of skills and abilities that occurs when a student does not receive services.

Related Services

After considering specialized instruction, the team discusses the **related services** that are required to assist the student to benefit from special education services. These services are offered by professionals in disciplines other than education. IDEA provides for a variety of related services such as occupational therapy, rehabilitation counseling, and social work services (Sec. 300.24). These services are identified and are written into the student's IEP. Table 1.3 lists all the related services mandated by IDEA.

Supplemental Aids and Services

To assist the student in being involved in and making progress in the general education curriculum, the team may identify **supplemental aids and services.** These are provided in the regular education classroom or in another education-related setting to enable children with disabilities to be educated with children without disabilities to the greatest extent possible (IDEA 34 C.F.R., Sec. 300.28).

Table 1.3	Related Services Mandated by the Individuals with Disabilities Education Act

Related services include services that are required to assist a student with a disability to benefit from special education services. These services are identified in the student's IEP and may include one or more of the following:

- audiology
- counseling services
- early identification and assessment of disabilities in children
- medical services
- occupational therapy
- orientation and mobility
- parent counseling and training
- physical therapy
- psychological services
- recreation
- rehabilitation counseling
- school health services
- social work services in schools
- speech-language pathology
- transportation services

Source: Adapted from IDEA 34 C.F.R., Sec. 300.24.

Transition Services

Beginning at age 14 (or younger, if determined appropriate by the IEP team), each student with a disability must have an IEP that includes a statement of **transition services** (IDEA 34 C.F.R., Sec. 300.29). Transition services ensure that the student makes a successful transition to living and working within the community and may include such services as advanced placement courses, vocational programs, supported work, or community living. Beginning at age 16 (or younger, if determined appropriate by the IEP team), each student's IEP must have a statement of needed transition services and interagency responsibilities, if appropriate. This requires interagency planning with other professionals joining the IEP team, such as a rehabilitation counselor, a job training specialist, or an independent living counselor.

INDIVIDUALIZING THE INDIVIDUALIZED EDUCATION PROGRAM

According to IDEA, the IEP must include specific information concerning the student's present level of education performance; the annual goals that the student will accomplish, how they will be measured, and how parents will be informed; and a description of the special education and related services, including their frequency, location, and duration (Sec. 300.347; see Figure 1.8).

Annual Goals

Based on the student's needs, team members write annual goals. These must be measurable and stated so that the student can accomplish them within the program year (IDEA 34 C.F.R., Sec. 300.347). Goals are written for each area in which the student will receive services and are individualized so that they provide a realistic outcome that the student can achieve. Goals may be tied to general education curriculum outcomes or to an individual state's learning standards.

Figure 1.8   Requirements of an IEP described by IDEA

- A statement of the student's present levels of education performance, including how the student's disability affects involvement and progress in the general education curriculum. For preschool children, the IEP must describe how the disability affects the child's participation in appropriate activities.
- A statement of measurable annual goals, including benchmarks or short-term objectives.
- A statement of special education and related services and supplementary aids and services including a statement of the program modification or supports for school personnel that will be provided for the student to:
  - advance appropriately toward attaining the annual goals,
  - be involved and progress in the general curriculum, and
  - participate in extracurricular and nonacademic activities.
- An explanation of the extent, if any, to which the student will not participate with students without disabilities in the regular class.
- A statement of any individual modifications in the administration of state or districtwide assessments of student achievement.
- The projected date for the beginning of the services and modifications, and the anticipated frequency, location, and duration of those services and modifications.

Source: Adapted from IDEA 34 C.F.R., Sec. 300.347.

Considering Diversity

A Wealth of Classroom Experiences and Expectations

In preparing to teach, educators must consider the wealth of classroom experiences and expectations that children bring. Students come from diverse cultural, ethnic, racial, economic, and linguistic backgrounds. In fact, 20% of the students ages 5 to 17 enrolled in elementary and secondary schools today have at least one foreign-born parent, and almost 10 million speak a language other than English at home (Harper, 2003). Students from diverse backgrounds are represented in both general and special education settings. The U.S. Department of Education (2002) reports that 15.8% of students with disabilities are Hispanic, 18.3% are African American, 1.4% are Asian American, and 1.4% are American Indian.

Students bring to their schools rich experiences and expectations. Folktales, dances, music, and family traditions enrich the teaching and learning experience for all students and their teachers. Students can celebrate diversity in the classroom because their teachers promote cultural competence. Diversity perspectives involve being responsive to students, their families, and their communities—a theme that you will find in each chapter of this book.

Diversity perspectives play an important role in the process of obtaining special education services. When the IEP team meets, members must be aware of not only the student's first language but the student's home language(s) as well. For example, how will the team gather assessment information about a student who speaks four languages but is just learning English?

In the past, many students with disabilities were inappropriately placed in separate and special classes based on the results of standardized tests given in English. When working with students who are English language learners, teachers must ensure that the assessment approaches used measure the extent of the disability rather than the child's English language skills. IDEA states that tests and other evaluation procedures must not discriminate on a racial or cultural basis and mandates that assessments must be provided and administered in the child's native language or another mode of communication unless it is clearly not feasible to do so (Sec. 300.532).

Questions for Reflection

1. Consider the students in the schools in your community. Does your community reflect the diversity of families in your state? In the nation?
2. What materials and other resources does your state department of education provide for families of students with disabilities? Other than English, in what other languages are the materials available?

 To answer these questions and deepen your understanding of diversity in schools and communities, go to the Companion Website at www.prenhall.com/cohen, select Chapter 1, then choose Considering Diversity.

Short-Term Objectives or Benchmarks

Short-term objectives, or benchmarks, describe a standard that the student will work to meet. Each short-term objective includes the following required components:

- behavior that is described in terms that can be observed
- the criteria for successful performance
- the method for evaluating the behavior
- the time period for which the objective will be reviewed

Distribution of the Individualized Education Program

The team chairperson, or another designated staff person, arranges for the student's IEP to be available to each regular education teacher, special education teacher, related service provider, and any other service provider who is responsible for its implementation. Parents, too, receive a copy of their child's IEP (IDEA 34 C.F.R., Sec. 300.345).

Teachers and other professionals working with the student must report progress to parents in report cards, in progress notes, or in other ways at least as often as parents of students without disabilities receive report cards. This progress report enables parents to learn about the progress of their child and the extent to which that progress will enable the child to reach the IEP goals by the end of the program year.

ENVIRONMENTS WHERE SPECIAL EDUCATION TEACHERS WORK

Since IDEA provides for a continuum of special education services in the least restrictive environment, special education teachers work in many different settings. Some teachers have their own classrooms; some teachers have no classroom of their own (but consult or coteach in the general education classroom); some teachers spend at least some of the school day traveling among students in different schools or hospital settings. The following sections describe the continuum of environments and how they affect the teaching responsibilities of the special education teacher.

CONSULTING IN THE GENERAL EDUCATION CLASSROOM

By consulting with the general education teacher, special education teachers provide support to students with disabilities in the regular classroom. In the consulting model, the special education teacher meets with the general education classroom teacher on a regular basis to discuss the needs of students, types of supports, accommodations, and modifications. They talk about how a particular teaching strategy is helping (or not helping) and brainstorm about other techniques to use. The consulting teacher has many other responsibilities, including coordinating services and resources and locating special materials or adapted equipment that individual students with disabilities need to participate in classroom activities.

———————— ❖ *VISITING WITH VICENTE PAJARO* ❖ ————————

Vicente Pajaro, a special educator at Suncook School, begins the day with an early morning meeting with the first-grade classroom teacher. They discuss their concerns about one of the students, Lou Traforti, who has problem behaviors. Over the past month, Lou has begun to interrupt other students during classwork and is generally disrespectful. Vicente listens carefully as the teacher describes her frustration concerning Lou and the reaction of other students. Together, they brainstorm several interventions to manage Lou's behaviors. Lou has not been referred for special education services yet, and both teachers are hoping that changes in teaching strategies may help to support positive student behaviors. Together they decide that during the next few days, the teacher will develop with the students a set of guidelines for classroom and playground behavior. Students as well as the teacher will be responsible for ensuring that all students in the classroom follow the guidelines.

COTEACHING IN THE GENERAL EDUCATION CLASSROOM

Teachers who coteach divide up the work and share the teaching load with their regular education colleagues, including planning, teaching, modifying instruction, and assessing progress. Sometimes they work with groups of students, each guiding small-group discussions. At other times, one of the teachers assumes the role of lead teacher while the other teacher moves around the classroom, assisting students both with and without disabilities on an as-needed basis. Their roles may be reversed, depending on the teachers' preferences and their individual strengths in one or more areas of the curriculum. In the following vignette we meet Joy Lu, whose job involves coteaching in the general education classroom.

❖ VISITING WITH JOY LU ❖

Joy Lu stops at her office to look for her social studies folder and project notebook for the fifth-grade class. She hurries down the corridor to the classroom where she will be coteaching and assisting students with disabilities in their civics unit. Today, the classroom teacher will lead the class in a discussion of the reading assignment while Joy provides a graphic organizer of the discussion for Tony, a student with attention deficit hyperactivity disorder. Joy will monitor Tony's progress and be ready to offer support and encouragement as needed, because Tony frequently becomes distracted and has difficulty completing activities. Later, the students will move into small groups for an activity, and Joy and her coteacher will move among the groups assisting individual students as needed.

PROVIDING INSTRUCTION IN THE RESOURCE ROOM

Special education teachers may work in a separate classroom, called the *resource room,* where they provide special instruction and materials to students who are not able to participate all day in the regular classroom. Some students with disabilities come to the resource room for extra classroom support in one or more curriculum areas. The resource room teacher works closely with the general education classroom teacher to provide tutorial support and teaching geared to students' needs in reading, mathematics, or other areas of the curriculum.

Other students with disabilities come to the resource room for special instruction. The special instruction may include adapted or special materials and/or a specific teaching strategy. For these students, the special educator plans and implements instructional activities in social skills, reading, writing, mathematics, science, or social studies, for example. To monitor student progress and achievement, the special educator uses a variety of assessment approaches. In Chapter 4, we will look more closely at how teachers link instructional activities with assessment and discuss the various ways teachers assess student progress.

——————— ❖ *VISITING WITH JOHN BATES* ❖ ———————

John Bates scans the schedule posted near the desk. Managing the activities in the resource room requires good organizational and coordination skills. He plans instructional activities for each student, meets with his teaching assistant to review the day's activities, and arranges time to meet with the classroom teachers. His morning begins today with a group of three students with learning disabilities who come to the resource room for reading. In an hour, these students will leave to return to their regular classrooms and then several students from two other classrooms will arrive. Throughout the day there may only be 3 to 10 students at a time, but they include third, fourth, and fifth graders who have different needs and strengths. John needs to carefully organize each student's assignment and make sure that each person understands the work. John arranges time to help some students directly while others work on specially designed assignments. During the day he will work with students in the areas of mathematics, science, literacy, and study skills. Several of the students have behavior and attention disorders in addition to learning problems, so John needs to consider how to promote positive behaviors as well as academic skills.

TRAVELING AND ITINERANT TEACHING

Schools sometimes share a special education teacher. For the teacher, this means traveling among different schools, carrying materials back and forth, working with complicated schedules, and perhaps having more than one supervisor. Special education teachers with expertise in AT or individuals who work in rural areas find that schools cannot hire a full-time professional but can pool their resources to offer the special education services that children need.

——————— ❖ *ON THE ROAD WITH MARIA PEREZ* ❖ ———————

Maria Perez checks the trunk of her car to make sure she has all the AT devices for the students she will visit today. She is an itinerant AT specialist and covers the school districts in her region of the state. When the IEP team determines that a student may need AT, the team coordinator contacts Maria and makes arrangements for her to visit the school. With her combination of training as a special educator and an assistive technology specialist, she is qualified to work with team members to help determine the assistive technology needs of a student with a disability. With access to AT devices through the regional AT center, she brings a variety of devices to the school. Working with the student, parents, and other team members, Maria assists in determining the most appropriate device(s) and arranges for the students to borrow the device from the AT center for a trial period. Maria also works with team members to arrange training for students, family members, and teachers, if needed. She makes plans to return once the trial period is over to help team members assess the effectiveness of the device and to work with the IEP team to locate funding sources to purchase it. When the device is not satisfactory, she suggests an alternative device and continues to work with the student and IEP team members to determine the best technology solution for the student.

Like John, Maria works with students and teachers across different grade levels and curriculum areas. Today she will be observing a student with learning disabilities in a middle school science class, and then she will meet with the IEP team to discuss problems that the student is having in accessing the general science curriculum. Later, Maria will visit another school and provide one-to-one training for a student with mental retardation who is learning how to use specialized software for writing assignments.

TEACHING IN THE SPECIAL EDUCATION CLASSROOM

Special education teachers who work in special education classrooms in public schools teach children who have difficulty learning in the regular classroom for a majority of the day. Teachers in these settings have the responsibility of planning and implementing specially designed instruction in all areas of the curriculum that the student does not receive in the general education setting. Teachers adapt content and/or delivery of instruction to address the unique needs of the student.

Like special educators who work in resource rooms, teachers who work in special education classrooms use a variety of assessment approaches to monitor student progress, developing skills, and achievement. Assessment activities are ongoing and provide both teacher and student with valuable feedback regarding their work. The teacher uses the assessment information not only to determine how students are progressing but also to modify practice. When a student is not making expected gains, the teacher will consider a number of questions. For example, what additional instructional activities does the student need? Is the teaching method effective? Is the student grouping effective?

❖ VISITING WITH JACOB HOLLINGS ❖

Jacob Hollings is a special education teacher who has his own classroom at Birchview High School. Assisting Jacob in the classroom are two teacher assistants, one who provides one-to-one instruction to a student with autism. Another teacher assistant helps Jacob in providing assistance to several students with moderate mental retardation who need extra help in locating materials, completing class activities, and using the library. Each Friday two volunteer students from the 10th-grade classroom join the class during the last hour of the day. This socialization time gives Jacob's students a chance to visit with their peers while completing a project that the group has chosen. Last week the students decided that they wanted to build a bird feeder. Jacob helped them identify the materials that they would need and how to obtain them. Earlier in the week, Jacob used this project to help his students in mathematics by reviewing money and making change; later he made arrangements for them to go to the hardware store to use these skills.

WORKING IN A DAY OR RESIDENTIAL TREATMENT PROGRAM

Special education teachers who are employed by special day or residential treatment programs work with students who all have similar disabilities. For example, the school may be designed for students with moderate disabilities including significant behavior or learning problems or students with autism spectrum disorders. Special education teachers are responsible for planning and implementing the specialized instruction and assessing student progress. Teachers who work in special schools typically teach a class where students are of similar age and ability. Special-purpose schools may provide day or residential programs.

―――――――――――――― ❖ *VISITING GREENWAY* ❖ ――――――――――――――

Greenway is a small private school. Like many special private schools, Greenway specializes in a program to help students who have a specific disability. Students attend the school daily but live at home. The school employs special education teachers who work in a classroom setting. Each special educator teaches a small class, usually no more than 15 students who are grouped by age. The special education teacher is responsible for planning, teaching, and assessing student progress across the curriculum for the grade level.

―――――――――――― ❖ *VISITING KNIGHT'S HILL* ❖ ――――――――――――

Knights Hill is a residential school where students live on campus and attend school. This type of program provides not only academic instruction for students with moderate disabilities but also a comprehensive program of extracurricular and social activities. Special education teachers who work in these settings may also live on campus and be involved in carrying over instruction in daily living and adaptive behavior skills during trips into the community.

PROVIDING HOME INSTRUCTION

Special education teachers who work with students in their homes spend much of their day traveling among students. Like itinerant teachers, home teachers work with a wide range of students in terms of age and ability who are temporarily homebound and will be returning to their special education program in school. For example, a student with Down syndrome who has a heart condition may have an acute medical crisis that involves hospitalization and several weeks of recuperation at home. Teachers providing home instruction focus on assisting students to maintain their educational progress.

―――――――――――― ❖ *TRAVELING WITH DAWN HILL* ❖ ――――――――――――

Dawn Hill works with students on an individual basis. Her students are homebound due to an illness, an accident, or a chronic condition such as acquired immune deficiency syndrome (AIDS). Many of Dawn's students have an educational diagnosis of "other health impairment" and will return to their school program once their condition improves or stabilizes. Because they may range from elementary to high school students, Dawn must be knowledgeable about a wide range of curriculum areas.

WORKING IN A HOSPITAL-BASED PROGRAM

Similar to home instructors, special education teachers who provide instruction in hospitals typically work with an individual student for a short period of time. Students

Using Technology
Keeping Current

Educators working with students with disabilities must be knowledgeable about current federal laws on education, especially those addressing special education services. To check current legislation, they can access Thomas Legislative Information on the Internet, a site provided by the U.S. Congress that allows the visitor to read the full text of any law passed since 1992. This site provides the most thorough coverage of legislation related to individuals with disabilities and the field of special education.

The U.S. Department of Education maintains a home page with current and fast-breaking news. This site also has a searchable database for information regarding changes to federal laws. From this site you may link to the Office of Special Education and Rehabilitative Services website. The Office of Hearing and Appeals provides a searchable database of decisions involving the U.S. Department of Education and recipients of federal education funds.

Questions regarding federal and state requirements for the education of students with disabilities can be answered at the EDLAW website, a rich source of legal information for parents and professionals.

Questions for Reflection

1. Explore several government websites to view the information posted. Which sites did you find easiest to use? Which sites would you recommend to a new teacher?
2. Locate your state department of education website and browse the information posted. What information did you think was most interesting? Share your findings with your colleagues.

 To answer these questions and learn more about using technology to support learning, go to the Companion Website at www.prenhall.com/cohen, select Chapter 1, then choose Using Technology.

with disabilities may be hospitalized for an acute condition or accident and will eventually be discharged. Other students with chronic conditions, such as leukemia, will be in and out of the hospital several times over the course of the year. In both situations, the hospital-based teacher helps students keep up with work that they would otherwise miss.

❖ VISITING WITH CRAIG O'KEEFE ❖

Craig enjoys his work because he must work closely with the student as well as the hospital staff and the student's family. In planning for students who will be hospitalized for several weeks, Craig also works closely with staff at the student's community school. He finds that he must build and maintain a collection of materials at his office at the hospital, as sometimes he is not able to obtain copies of materials that the student was using before the hospitalization.

SUMMARY

- Preparing to be a special education teacher begins by understanding the requirements of federal legislation related to children and youth with disabilities.
- IDEA describes a comprehensive system for educating students with disabilities and emphasizes the student's involvement in the general education curriculum.
- Sometimes known as *disability civil rights legislation,* Section 504 of the Rehabilitation Act and the ADA provide additional assurances that individuals with disabilities will be able to work and live in their communities.
- Section 508 of the Rehabilitation Act of 1998 provides for finding information via AT devices and technologies that are accessible, including computers, handhelds, and other communication devices. This law mandates that information on all federal websites must be accessible to individuals with disabilities who use AT devices such as screen readers or keyboard controls (rather than mouse navigation).
- Special education teachers assist parents in understanding their rights as described by these laws.
- Special education teachers encourage students to become more aware of their learning needs, assist students in articulating to others how they learn best, help students attain high standards, and support students in identifying and planning realistic career goals.

EXTENDING LEARNING

1. Arrange to visit a general education classroom that includes children with and without disabilities. What types of accommodations and modifications to the classroom did you observe? Interview the classroom teacher to learn about additional accommodations and modifications that are being used.
2. Interview a special education teacher. Find out what specially designed instruction is offered to the students with disabilities in the school.
3. Contact your state department of education. Obtain a copy of your state's special education regulations that describe how your state carries out IDEA. Working with a small group of other students, identify the sections in your state regulations that will be most helpful for you as a teacher.
4. Using an Internet search engine, locate and bookmark the websites of the following organizations:
   the U.S. Department of Education
   your state department of education
   Compare and contrast the information presented. How might you use some of the information to help you in working with parents? With students with disabilities? With other professionals?
5. Working with a small group of classmates, make a list of all the AT devices with which you are familiar. What devices would you like to know more about?
6. Using the information that you identified in the previous question, consider how you would locate additional information about AT. Find the location of the nearest AT resource center. What services does it provide? Alternatively, conduct an Internet search to locate four or five websites that you would recommend. Share your findings with the class.

REFERENCES

Ahearn, E. (2002, Summer). Charter schools and special education: Balancing disparate visions. *Counterpoint, 4.*

American Association on Mental Retardation. (2002). *Mental retardation* (10th ed.). Washington, DC: Author.

Americans with Disabilities Act (Pub. L. No. 101-336). (1990). Washington, DC: U.S. Government Printing Office.

Blazer, B. (1999). Developing 504 classroom accommodation plans: A collaborative, systematic parent-student-teacher approach. *Teaching Exceptional Children, 32*(2), 28–33.

Booth, R. C. (1998). *List of appropriate school-based accommodations and interventions.* Retrieved July 16, 2002, from the National Attention Deficit Disorder Association website: http://www.add.org/content/school/list.htm

Bryant, R., Dean, M., Elrod, G. F., & Blackbourn, J. M. (1999). Rural general education teachers' opinions of adaptations for inclusive classrooms: A renewed call for dual licensure. *Rural Special Education Quarterly, 19*(1), 5–11.

Carl D. Perkins Vocational and Applied Technology Education Act (Pub. L. No. 99-347). (1998). Washington, DC: U.S. Government Printing Office.

Council of Administrators of Special Education, Inc. (n.d.). *Student access: A resource guide for educators.* Arlington, VA: Council for Exceptional Children.

Harper, J. (2003). *U.S. school system continues to grow.* Retrieved August 13, 2003, from the *Washington Times* website: http://www.washingtontimes.com/national/20030811-100201-6119r.htm

Individuals with Disabilities Education Act Amendments (Pub. L. No. 105-17). (1997). Washington, DC: U.S. Government Printing Office.

Kupper, L. (Ed.). (2000). *A guide to the individualized education program.* Retrieved July 16, 2002, from the Office of Special Education Programs website: http://www.ed.gov/parents/needs/speced/iepguide/index.html

Lenhart, A. (2003). *The ever-shifting Internet population: A new look at Internet access and the digital divide.* Retrieved August 10, 2003, from the Pew Internet and American Life website: http://www.pewinternet.org

McDonnell, L. M., McLaughlin, M. J., & Morison, P. (Eds.). (1997). *Educating one and all.* Washington, DC: National Academy Press.

National Information Center for Children and Youth with Disabilities. (2002). *Six principles of IDEA.* Retrieved August 22, 2003, from http://www.nichcy.org/Trainpkg/toc.htm

No Child Left Behind Act (Pub. L. No. 107-110) (2001). Washington, DC: U.S. Government Printing Office.

ORBIS Associates. (1996). *Comprehensive planning: Guidance for educators of American Indian and Alaska Native students.* Charleston, WV: Author. (ERIC Document Reproduction Service No. ED400145)

President's Commission on Excellence in Special Education. (2002). *A new era: Revitalizing special education for children and their families.* Retrieved July 16, 2002, from http://www.ed.gov/inits/commissionsboards/whspecialeducation/index.html

Rehabilitation Act Amendments (Pub. L. No. 105-220). (1998). Washington, DC: U.S. Government Printing Office.

U.S. Department of Education. (2002). *Twenty-third annual report to Congress on the implementation of the Individuals with Disabilities Education Act.* Washington, DC: U.S. Government Printing Office.

2

Chapter

Knowing Students with Mild and Moderate Disabilities

Learning Disabilities, Attention Deficit Hyperactivity Disorders, and Other Health Impairments

After completing this chapter, you should be able to:

❖ Describe how students with disabilities come to receive special education services.

❖ Describe the range of student characteristics that involve mild to moderate disabilities.

❖ Describe the causes and characteristics of specific disabilities, including learning disabilities, attention deficit hyperactivity disorder, and other health impairments.

❖ Discuss the characteristics of and considerations for students from diverse cultures and English language learners who have mild to moderate disabilities.

❖ Identify technology resources for educators.

INDIVIDUAL CHARACTERISTICS

Each of us, whether or not we have a disability, has a unique combination of individual characteristics; indeed, characteristics are what make each of us special individuals. The term **characteristics** encompasses broad areas that define the individual, including the individual's knowledge; motivation; academic skills; physical, social, and emotional attributes; and the environments in which the individual lives, works, and plays. Many factors influence a person's characteristics; for example, having opportunities to learn affects student knowledge; living in poverty affects physical health and well-being; being in an abusive environment frequently affects emotional health and self-esteem. Factors that influence an individual's characteristics also include the absence or presence of a disability and the type of disability. In the classroom, educators observe a cluster of student characteristics that may indicate that the student has a disability.

For example, a learning disability or an attention deficit can affect the ability to acquire, process, or retain information. A student misunderstands the unwritten code of what teenagers believe to be acceptable behavior in the hallways or frequently misinterprets what others say. A student who is constantly distracted because of attention deficit hyperactivity disorder (ADHD) has difficulty following a class discussion. Students with health impairments may miss classroom discussions altogether because of repeated absences due to limited strength or a chronic health condition that requires hospitalization.

Disabilities such as learning disabilities, ADHD, and other health impairments exist along a continuum. At one end, educators consider them mild disabilities because students experience limited difficulties in academic or behavioral areas. For example, a student with a mild disability may experience difficulty in learning how to read or how to interact with others. The student has an IEP that targets these needs and describes how the student will work toward reading achievement or developing appropriate social skills. Another student may have the same educational diagnosis, but the disability affects the student's educational functioning to a more significant degree. Some disabilities such as emotional disturbance, mental retardation, and autism spectrum disorders present great difficulties in learning or acquiring positive behaviors. The degree of difficulties would fall on the other end of the continuum, and the student would be considered to have a moderate disability.

In this chapter, we will examine student characteristics that generally fall on the mild end of the continuum. Our discussion will focus on students with learning disabilities, ADHD, and mild other health impairments. In the following chapter, we will study the characteristics of other disabilities, including emotional disturbance, mental retardation, and autism spectrum disorders. These disabilities often fall on the moderate end of the continuum. We will use the disability categories as defined by IDEA, although individual states may use different terms to describe disability categories and some states may not use a categorical system at all.

Many educators feel that using mild or moderate categories provides a helpful way to describe a student's needs because the category generally implies the degree of difficulty that the student is experiencing. Simply knowing that a student has a learning disability or mental retardation does not provide that level of information. Too, educators who work with students with mild disabilities often use common teaching methods and strategies across disability areas. In Chapters 6 and 7, we will examine research-based teaching methods and strategies for working with children and youth with mild disabilities.

Because some mild disabilities affect development and acquisition of certain skills, they are more likely to be exhibited and identified at certain age levels. For example, when children enter elementary school, teachers are often the first to observe problems in attention, listening, and learning to read, write, and understand mathematics. Later, teachers may observe difficulties in understanding concepts or synthesizing information. Students entering middle school need to manage rotating schedules, work with team teachers, and juggle multiple assignments. During these years, observant teachers can identify students who are experiencing difficulty with organizational skills. In high school, students are expected to take more personal responsibility, to identify goals to further their education or training, and to develop skills for living and working within the community. Transition periods are difficult times for all teenagers; for students with disabilities, transitions may be even more difficult because of problems in learning, conforming to the demands of the school environment, or challenges in overcoming physical or social barriers.

Knowledge of the characteristics of students with mild disabilities assists special educators in identifying students who may have a disability and who should be referred for special education services. Understanding these characteristics helps

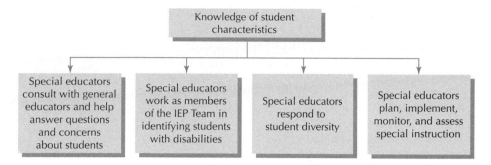

Figure 2.1   **Special educators use knowledge of student characteristics to assist in their work with other teachers, with team members, and with students and their families**

special educators address student strengths and limitations, develop and implement instruction, plan accommodations or modifications, and monitor and evaluate IEPs (Figure 2.1). Special educators also use knowledge of characteristics of students with mild disabilities to help answer questions and deal with concerns about students.

WHEN STUDENTS EXPERIENCE DIFFICULTIES: THE PREREFERRAL PROCESS

Some schools use a prereferral intervention process to identify and address academic and behavioral problems before educators refer a student to special education services (Figure 2.2). This process involves general and special educators who work together as a student assistance team. When a teacher has questions and concerns about a student, team members collaborate to pinpoint the difficulties and to brainstorm possible solutions. They provide the teacher with intervention ideas to consider. After

Figure 2.2   **The prereferral intervention process**

Educators use the prereferral process to work together to:

- document difficulties a student may be having with instruction and determine possible reasons for the problems,
- provide and document classroom interventions and teaching strategies,
- assess interventions to ensure that they are appropriate and successful,
- monitor the student's progress for a significant period of time, and
- identify students for whom the learning and/or behavioral difficulty persists in spite of suggested interventions.

Source: Adapted from *"Addressing Over-Representation of African American Students in Special Education,"* National Alliance of Black School Educators and IDEA Local Implementation by Local Administrators Partnership, 2002, Arlington, VA: Council for Exceptional Children.

Using Technology

Internet-Based Professional Resources

Internet resources provide educators with a wealth of information about working with students with disabilities. When teachers would like to know more about specific disabilities, they can log on to the American Medical Association website. There they can search for information on specific disabilities and disorders by keyword and browse the latest medical journals. A searchable database, AMA Physician Select, provides information on over 650,000 physicians in the United States by name or specialty. Another excellent source of information on disabilities is the website of the National Information Center for Children and Youth with Disabilities

(NICHCY), which provides information on common as well as low-incidence disabilities. At this site one also can find links to organizations dealing with disabilities of children and youth.

When teachers are searching for professional articles on various disabilities, a good place to start is the website of the ERIC Clearinghouse on Disabilities and Gifted Education. At this site they can browse through a vast library of short articles on topics for educators across disability areas. This site also includes information on students with disabilities from diverse cultures.

In addition to professional websites, teachers can find many resources that are helpful in working with students and their families. One of our favorite sites is Family Village. This is a popular site where students can communicate with others who have common problems and challenges. Visitors can post questions and examine resources.

Questions for Reflection

1. Take some time to explore the professional resources described above. What information did you find most helpful to you?
2. What other professional websites would be helpful to new teachers? Share your ideas with your colleagues.

Internet-based resources provide educators with a wealth of information for working with students with disabilities.

To answer these questions and learn more about using technology to support learning, go to the Companion Website at www.prenhall.com/cohen, select Chapter 2, then choose Using Technology.

deciding on the intervention(s) to implement, the classroom teacher documents the student's progress. If the problems persist even after the teacher has tried several interventions, the teacher completes a referral to the multidisciplinary team. Prereferral systems help to reduce inappropriate referrals and build effective interventions within the general education classroom.

❖ PROFESSIONAL PERSPECTIVES ❖

Yi-Nan Chen, a special educator at Brookville Elementary School, meets us at the school entrance and invites us in to visit her school and to talk about her work with students with disabilities. After a short tour of the classrooms, Yi-Nan takes us to the Teachers' Room, where we ask her to explain how teachers are alerted to the fact that a student may have a disability. She begins, "Each week, the teachers in my building come together to discuss students who are not doing well academically or who have problem behaviors. We address difficulties that students are experiencing in the classroom and brainstorm solutions. Sometimes our collective ideas provide teachers with helpful suggestions that they might not have considered otherwise. When teachers feel that a student continues to experience problems, they refer the student to the multidisciplinary team, sometimes called the *child study* or *child assistance team,* to see if in fact the child has a disability and is eligible to receive special education services.

"Let me give you an example of a recent situation. One of the third-grade teachers—we affectionately call her 'Mrs. B.'—is concerned about a student in her class named Tasha. At our weekly meetings, we have discussed Tasha's difficulties and offered suggestions for Mrs. B. to try in the classroom. Tasha is showing little progress in learning how to read. She is experiencing some difficulty in mathematics this year, and she seems to have difficulty in finding and organizing her materials. Lately she is showing a lack of interest in school in general, and her attendance has been poor. Mrs. B. has been providing some individual help to Tasha while other students work in reading groups. She arranged for a volunteer to tape some stories, hoping to increase Tasha's interest and motivation. She also contacted Tasha's parents about her concerns. It seems that they, too, were worried about their child's progress. She has complained about school and lately has been refusing to go. When Mrs. B. discussed referring Tasha to the multidisciplinary team, her parents wanted to know more about the process that Tasha would go through and what services might be available for her."

THE SPECIAL EDUCATION PROCESS

REFERRAL

When a student continues to have difficulty with the general education curriculum, even after teaching interventions, the parent is notified and the general education teacher completes a written referral form. The referral form describes the classroom interventions that have been tried, the results of the interventions, and the learning, social, or behavior problems that persist (Figure 2.3). Other individuals, such as a parent, the school nurse, or the school psychologist, can complete a referral too. Sometimes a student fills out a self-referral.

DETERMINING ELIGIBILITY

A referral is forwarded to a facilitator or coordinator of the special education services team, a multidisciplinary team that is responsible for assessing the student and determining eligibility for special education services. Depending on the types of concerns

Figure 2.3   Written referral

Brookville Elementary School Child Study Team Referral Form

Student's name: *Tasha*   Date of birth: *November 12, 19xx*

Grade: *3*   Teacher: *Mrs. B.*

Parent/guardian: *Aisha Brown*

Home address: *1003 Highway 10, Brookville Station*

Reason for referral: *Tasha continues to have a great deal of difficulty in learning how to read and she is also having difficulty in understanding math this year. She has a lot of problems in keeping school materials organized and in finding her assignments and homework. I am concerned that she seems to be losing interest in school. Lately I have observed that she does not participate well with the other students in our class learning groups.*

Describe the classroom interventions tried and the outcome of each: *I have provided her with individual help in both reading and math but I don't feel that I can provide enough assistance on a regular basis. To keep up her interest in reading, I arranged for a volunteer to tape some nature stories, a topic that is of interest to her. This effort has been mildly successful but I am concerned that she is not developing the necessary literacy skills.*

Other relevant factors involving the referral: *I have spoken with the parent who also is concerned. Her attendance has been poor lately and her mother stated that Tasha has been refusing to come to school.*

and the difficulties that the student is experiencing, the multidisciplinary team members may identify other professionals such as the school counselor, nurse, speech and language pathologist, occupational therapist, or physical therapist who should be involved. Before a student's assessment can begin, the parent or guardian must provide consent for an initial evaluation of their child and all assessments must be completed within a reasonable time [IDEA 34 C.F.R., Sec. 300.343(b)].

Sometimes team members meet first to clarify the questions to be answered during the assessment process and to discuss what types of assessment should be completed. For example, Tasha was referred to the team because of academic learning problems and poor attendance. After reviewing the referral form, team members decided to ask the school counselor to join the team because of Tasha's irregular school attendance. Once all the members were assembled, the team discussed which standardized tests and other types of assessment should be conducted to gather additional information. The special education teacher might be asked to conduct several classroom observations and gather information using formal and informal assessment instruments, along with other team members. In Tasha's case, the school counselor conducted a parent interview and the general education teacher provided samples of Tasha's work. The school psychologist and the special education teacher, in addition to conducting observations, administered standardized norm-referenced tests. A **norm-referenced instrument** is a commercially published test that compares a student's test performance with that of similar students who have taken the same test.

Once all the assessment information has been assembled, the team meets to discuss the results. Team members consider the following: Does the student have a disability that adversely affects the student's educational performance? Team members follow state and federal laws and regulations to answer this question.

In Tasha's case, the referral focused on learning problems and low attendance. The team wondered if her learning problems were related to a learning disability or if they were the result of her irregular school attendance. The team members decided to use several different resources, such as classroom observations, assessments of achievement, and psychological assessment, to determine why Tasha was experiencing learning problems. The assessment information indicated that she had a learning disability. Once the team has determined that a student is eligible for special education services, team members begin the process of planning the IEP.

PROGRAM PLANNING

If the multidisciplinary team determines that a student is eligible for services, the team members convene to develop the IEP. This IEP team often includes the members of the multidisciplinary team but may also include additional professionals with unique expertise, such as a parent advocate. The IEP team facilitator, usually an administrator, is responsible for coordinating all team meetings at the school or district level. In Chapter 5, you will learn more about how teachers and other members of the IEP team plan a student's IEP.

MONITORING PROGRESS

Special educators and related service personnel continuously monitor the student's IEP once services begin. The teacher knows the student's current level of performance, what the student can do in each academic area, and what other needs the student has, such as the need to improve social skills or decrease problem behaviors. The teacher tracks progress through regular observation, student work samples, demonstrations, and formal and informal tests. Monitoring the IEP on a regular basis allows the teacher to make adjustments in the specially designed instruction when necessary.

EVALUATING PROGRESS

Evaluating Individual Student Progress: Annual Review

At the end of the program year, or more frequently if needed, the IEP team reconvenes to discuss the student's progress. Has the student met the IEP goals? The special education teacher, as well as other school personnel who have assisted in providing special education and related services described in the student's IEP, report on the student's progress and on measures of achievement. These measures include various assessments of student performance such as portfolios, observations, curriculum-based assessments, and norm-referenced instruments. The team determines what services the student continues to need, if any. For students who need continuing services, the team plans the program for the coming year.

Evaluating Overall Special Education and Related Services

Along with evaluating individual student progress, program evaluation should address the success of the overall special education program provided by the school. Are students with disabilities making progress in the special education program? Special education programs must be able to demonstrate that students who receive services are making progress and gaining new skills and knowledge. Are parents satisfied with the special education services? Are students with disabilities pleased with the services? As consumers of special education services, students and parents should be given regular opportunities to provide feedback to special education teachers and administrators. Program evaluation can include interviews, checklists, surveys, or formal program evaluation instruments, and information can be collected from special education teachers, parents, and students themselves. Special education teachers strive to provide high-quality, effective services. To that end, these services must be evaluated on a regular basis and changes made, if indicated. Now, let's turn our attention to the students with whom special educators and other members of the IEP team work.

STUDENTS WITH LEARNING DISABILITIES

Students with learning disabilities have average to above-average intellectual abilities but experience difficulty in one or more academic areas. According to the federal definition of learning disabilities that is presented in IDEA:

> This disorder is in one or more of the basic psychological processes involved in understanding or in using language, spoken or written, and may manifest itself in an imperfect ability to listen, think, speak, read, write, spell, or to do mathematical calculations. The term includes such conditions as perceptual disabilities, brain injury, minimal brain dysfunction, dyslexia, and developmental aphasia. The term does not apply to children who have learning problems that are primarily the result of visual, hearing, or motor disabilities; of mental retardation; of emotional disturbance; or of environmental, cultural, or economic disadvantage. (Sec. 300.7)

When learning disabilities are not identified early, students may become frustrated and lose interest in achievement. For example, Tasha, the third grader at Brookville Elementary School whom we met at the beginning of this chapter, continues to have difficulty in reading. She quickly loses interest in looking at books and listening to stories that the teacher reads aloud to the class. During free time Tasha enjoys working at the science table, and at home she has an extensive insect collection. In the classroom, her frustration builds and Tasha develops problem behaviors, becoming disruptive. The Brookville multidisciplinary team meet to discuss these concerns.

Determining whether a student has a disability is the responsibility of this multidisciplinary team after it has gathered information through observation and formal and informal assessments. According to the federal definition described in IDEA, the team decides that a child has a specific learning disability if:

1. The child does not achieve commensurate with his or her age and ability levels in one or more of the areas (listed below) if provided with learning experiences appropriate for the child's age and ability levels and (2) the team finds that a child has a severe discrepancy between achievement and intellectual ability in one or more of the following areas:

   Oral expression
   Listening comprehension
   Written expression

Basic reading skill
Reading comprehension
Mathematics calculation
Mathematics reasoning (Sec. 300.451)

Many states use a discrepancy formula to determine the "severe discrepancy" described in the IDEA criteria. This mathematical formula calculates the difference between ability, as determined by an intelligence test, and achievement. Yet this procedure has caused much debate and concern among professional organizations and researchers in the field of learning disabilities who question the use of an IQ-achievement discrepancy as an identification procedure for determining the presence of a learning disability (President's Commission on Excellence in Special Education, 2002).

Moreover, some states incorporate slightly different criteria in determining eligibility, not only for learning disabilities but for other disability areas as well. In addition, some states do not use categorical definitions of eligibility at all but focus on the intensity of services that a student requires. Although we will examine the federal criteria described in IDEA, you may wish to examine the criteria that your individual state's regulations describe to determine whether a student is eligible for special education services.

CAUSES OF LEARNING DISABILITIES

Scientists now believe that several factors contribute to learning disabilities. Research findings in neuroscience, the discipline that studies the structure and function of the brain and the central nervous system, continue to expand our knowledge of the medical aspects of learning disabilities. Because learning disabilities often occur in multiple family members, another line of research has examined genetic factors. A large body of findings presents strong evidence that, for some students, severe reading disabilities are inherited (studies by DeFries, Stevenson, Gillis, & Wadsworth, 1991; Lubs et al., 1991; Pennington, 1995; Pennington, Smith, Kimberling, Green, & Haith, 1987, as cited in Learner, 2000). Additional lines of research have examined other possible causes such as childhood illnesses, loss of oxygen due to accidents or near drownings, or traumatic brain injury.

CHARACTERISTICS OF STUDENTS WITH LEARNING DISABILITIES

Early Signs of Learning Disabilities in Preschool and Early Elementary Children

Let us examine some of the early signs of learning disabilities that a teacher might observe in a preschooler. One of the first areas that a teacher may observe is the child's speech and use of language. The child's speech may be garbled and difficult to understand. The child may display problems in using and understanding language and may have difficulty with word retrieval. For example, the child may know that a glass holds milk but may be unable to come up with the word *glass* when the teacher asks the children to name various objects in a picture. The child may have difficulty in discriminating letters and numbers, confusing the names of letters or numerals.

Some preschool children show difficulties in attention, such as hyperactivity, inattention, or impulsivity. A teacher may observe that the child has difficulty sitting still during circle time or is easily distracted during the reading of a story. Later the child may begin an activity at one center and then go to a second center before completing the first activity.

Preschool children who later are identified as having learning disabilities acquire fine motor skills after other children typically have mastered them. For example, the child experiences difficulty in learning how to dress and use buttons and zippers. While these skills take time for all children to learn, the child with a learning disability continues to find these tasks frustrating and easily gives up trying. Other fine motor activities such as drawing shapes or writing letters with a pencil, using scissors to cut paper, and completing a puzzle may be difficult and frustrating for the child.

In outside play, the child may display awkwardness in gross motor activities. The child has difficulty throwing or catching a large ball. Jumping and hopping, which require a certain degree of coordination, may present problems for the child.

Although educational diagnosticians and other professionals can identify many disabilities in very young children, these professionals usually do not identify children with learning disabilities during the preschool years. There are many reasons for the lack of early identification where a learning disability is concerned. Many of the early signs of learning disabilities also are associated with overall developmental delays or lack of opportunity. Thus, educators may have difficulty determining whether the young child's problems are the result of an actual disability, lack of appropriate early education experiences, or poor environmental conditions. An accurate diagnosis is difficult, at best, and may be impossible to determine.

Usually, a learning disability is not identified until the child reaches the early elementary grades and experiences difficulty in learning how to read, write, or acquire concepts in mathematics. But there are several early signs that can alert the astute teacher that a child may have a learning disability. When a teacher recognizes these signs, he or she can arrange additional support and instruction so that the child does not experience additional frustrations and lag further behind classmates.

Characteristics of School-Age Students with Learning Disabilities

Similar to students without disabilities, school-age students with learning disabilities do not fit a single profile. Some students have difficulty with short-term memory tasks, others have accompanying attention problems, and still others have difficulties in activities involving motor skills. The one common denominator, though, is an academic achievement problem in literacy, including reading and writing, language use, or mathematics.

Since students with learning disabilities exhibit a broad range of academic achievement problems, special education teachers must identify and plan appropriate educational programs for a diverse group of students. Students typically show uneven patterns of academic performance. Some students have problems in just one area of achievement, whereas others have difficulty in several areas. Within an academic area, students may have some knowledge, but other relevant knowledge, typical of most students at that grade level, is missing.

A student with a learning disability may experience difficulty in learning how to read and comprehend.

For students with learning disabilities, their achievement may not be accurately reflected in standardized test scores. In fact, students with learning disabilities often receive low scores on standardized tests. As with students without disabilities, skills, knowledge, and achievement can be represented in a variety of other ways such as performance-based assessment and portfolios, assessment approaches that we discuss in Chapter 4.

Reading. One of the most difficult areas for many students with learning disabilities is learning how to read and comprehend what has been read. In fact, about 80% of students with learning disabilities have a disability in reading (President's Commission on Excellence in Special Education, 2002). Teachers can identify early signs of learning disabilities by observing problems in phonological awareness in the early grades. Phonological awareness involves understanding and identifying the individual sounds that make up a word. For example, a kindergarten teacher might ask the children, "Who can tell me the sound you hear at the beginning of the word *bat*?" Children who have not developed phonological awareness cannot identify the separate sounds or **phonemes** of words (Torgesen, 1998). Long after other students in the class have learned sound–symbol relationships, students who have learning disabilities may continue to have difficulty remembering the sounds that go with individual letters and how to blend sounds to make whole words.

Older students who have mastered decoding, the reading of printed text, may not develop fluency in reading. They may have difficulty recognizing words quickly or reading longer passages in a manner that permits understanding the material and making connections. In other words, students can read the words but have difficulty answering questions, identifying key concepts, or summarizing and interpreting the main points of the text.

Mathematics. Some students with learning disabilities may demonstrate difficulty in computing mathematics, understanding word problems, or using problem-solving strategies. Students may confuse place value in computation or make consistent errors in combining sets. Word problems create difficulties not only in reading and understanding the problem but also in knowing how to proceed with problem solving. Students must be able to (a) recognize what the problem is asking, (b) decide on the appropriate strategy, (c) remember all the steps in carrying out the strategy, and (d) complete the operation correctly. Students with learning disabilities may have difficulties with each step along the way.

Written language. The content of written language and the mechanics of writing, including spelling, grammar, and punctuation, may be affected by a learning disability. Many children with learning disabilities labor over writing tasks, barely having a few words down when other students are finishing their first draft. Their handwriting is often illegible. Their fine motor difficulties could have been observed during the early years, perhaps when they tried to use markers and crayons or were learning how to print.

Spelling may present special challenges, especially for students who cannot recognize sound–symbol relationships. They may have few sight words, or words that they can read without sounding out and can spell quickly. Other students may produce written text that lacks organization. They may use incorrect grammatical structures and incorrect word meanings but have wonderful, creative ideas.

Oral language. Oral language can be thought of as encompassing three areas. First, *expressive language* is the language used to communicate with others. Second, *receptive language* refers to understanding the language of others. Finally, *inner language* involves the use of language during thinking, planning, organizing, or other thought processes. Students with learning disabilities frequently exhibit impairments in one or more of these areas.

Oral language may be difficult for some students to interpret. Students with auditory processing difficulties can hear what the teacher says but have difficulty understanding. For example, a teacher provides an overview of what the students will be doing during social studies class: "Today we are going to continue our exploration of what it was like to live in the 1700s. Some of you may choose to work in a group that focuses on city life; others may select a group that focuses on living in a rural farming community." A student with an auditory processing problem may miss all or parts of the introduction and may not realize that the task will be to work in a group with other students.

In the classroom, teachers observe

- difficulty in understanding verbal explanations or discussions,
- misinterpretation of a fast-paced group conversation, and
- difficulty in maintaining concentration in an environment that is over-stimulating.

Understanding and using spoken language, often referred to as *pragmatics,* provides individuals with the skills to engage in the give-and-take of everyday conversation. **Pragmatics** includes three areas: (a) using language to achieve communicative goals, (b) using information from contextual clues (such as bringing the topic to a close when the listener uses body language to show lack of interest), and (c) knowing how to use conversational skills (Lahey, 1988). Learning to be a careful listener and to check for understanding prevents miscommunication. Knowing when to add a comment to encourage further conversation, when to change the subject, or when to stop talking are skills necessary for building and maintaining friendships and being successful in many types of jobs. Students with learning disabilities may not keep the conversation going or may make irrelevant comments. Their IEPs will include goals to increase skills in understanding and using conversational language.

Content areas. Students with learning disabilities frequently have difficulty with tasks and assignments in the content areas. For example, a middle science book uses the following new vocabulary words in a chapter on astronomy: *axis, revolution, galaxies, asteroids, pulsars,* and *satellites*. Although the teacher will introduce the new words to all students, a student with a learning disability may not be able to remember them when the student sees them again. In addition, the student may lack the reading skills that other students have developed to figure out the new word. Students may be asked to draw on other skills, too. In this science unit, they will be asked to compare and contrast distances and the time required to travel those distances on Earth. Students will need to draw on mathematical understandings and mathematical skills to complete unit assignments.

When teachers use original source materials in the content areas to heighten student interest and motivation, students with learning disabilities may have difficulties. For example, a social studies teacher wanted to help students deepen their understanding of the American Civil War. The teacher located a number of rich Web resources that included a diary written by an individual who lived during the mid-1800s, plus maps, photographs, and other original documents. Although the information was fascinating, the reading was difficult because none of the text was controlled for vocabulary and contained a number of new words and unfamiliar concepts.

Students with learning disabilities may have difficulty completing assignments. Because a learning disability can affect a student's abilities in written language, an assignment that requires a student to produce a written or oral report presents challenges beyond the planning and gathering of information for the report. The student may experience difficulties in organizing and synthesizing information. The learning disability may affect language and memory skills, such as word retrieval and thought processes, in writing or in giving the oral report. Special educators design specialized instruction, and other members of the IEP team provide services so that the student can be successful and achieve in the classroom while maintaining high expectations. In later chapters of this book, we will discuss how special educators use teaching methods, instructional strategies, and technology to help students become successful learners.

Motor skills and coordination. Motor skills and coordination of large and small muscles present difficulties to some students. Some students with learning disabilities may appear clumsy and awkward and experience difficulty in coordination that hinders them in playing team sports, whereas others may be active team players. Physical therapists refer to these difficulties as *gross motor problems* and work with students to improve their skills. Students with small muscle problems or fine motor difficulties often work with occupational therapists. For example, Ti and Gerri both have learning disabilities. Ti, a fifth grader, has gross motor problems—difficulty in catching and throwing a ball on the playground and problems with coordination during physical activities. Gerri, a first grader, experiences difficulty with fine motor skills such as starting the zipper on her jacket and learning to write letters. Their teachers regularly confer with the therapists to discuss progress and obtain suggestions for transferring therapeutic interventions to the classroom.

Memory. Each of us holds many different types of memories. For example, we can recall melodies of favorite songs or the look on a friend's face when we saw each other after a long absence. During various types of learning and recall activities, researchers have been able to view and study the brain through positron emission tomography scans and functional magnetic resonance imaging. After extended work, they believe that they have been able to identify specific brain areas where different types of memories are labeled (Sprenger, 1999). Table 2.1 illustrates the different types of memory and these corresponding areas of the brain.

Table 2.1	Memory and the Brain: Research Findings	
Type of Memory and Description	**Location in the Brain**	**Description of Brain Activity**
Semantic memory: information learned from words, as in books, discussions, and other classroom activities	Hippocampus	When incoming sensory information is factual, it is sent to the hippocampus, the file cabinet for semantic memory. This memory lane is difficult to use for learning because it takes several repetitions of the learning to cement it in place. The hippocampus has an unlimited capacity to store new information and uses associations to retrieve factual information that has been stored.
Episodic memory: contains information that we remember because it is related to a location, sometimes referred to as *spatial memory*. For example, where were you and what were you doing when you learned about the terrorist attacks of September 11, 2001? Episodic memory is important to consider in teaching because the context of the environment becomes part of the memory.	Cerebellum	This is similar to semantic memory because episodic memory is also factual.
Procedural memory: involves "muscle	Cerebellum	When an individual is trying to remember a procedure such as using a

		Memory and the Brain: Research Findings *continued*
Type of Memory and Description	**Location in the Brain**	**Description of Brain Activity**
memory," or the processes of balance and posture that an individual engages in to complete a task. When a procedure such as driving a car or using a PIN becomes routine, it is stored in the cerebellum of the brain.		PIN, placing a hand in the original position on a keypad helps to trigger this memory.
Automatic memory: contains information that you may have seen, heard, or practiced repeatedly, such as a foreign language or the multiplication tables	Cerebellum	Certain stimuli automatically trigger the memory of this information. For example, if someone begins counting to 10 in a language that you studied several years earlier, you could complete the sequence.
Emotional memory: information containing all sorts of experiences that made you happy or sad, angry or disappointed. These memories take precedence over any other kind of memory.	Amygdala (located in the forebrain next to the hippocampus)	When the emotional memory lane is opened, this area of the brain employs the stress response. The release of stress hormones may interrupt transmission of information in the brain, thus making it impossible to think clearly.

Source: Adapted from *Learning and Memory: The Brain in Action* (pp. 50–54), by M. Sprenger, 1999, Association for Supervision and Curriculum Development, Alexandria, VA.

In contrast, some researchers believe that because experiences are usually composed of several aspects, the brain stores them in more than one area for later retrieval. According to David Sousa (2001a), "Which sites to select for storage could be determined by the number of associations that the brain makes between the new learning and past learnings. The more connections that are made, the more understanding and meaning the learner can attach to the new learning, and the more likely it is that it will be stored in different networks. This process now gives the learner multiple opportunities to retrieve the new learning" (p. 81).

There are three different stages of memory: immediate, working, and long-term memory (Sousa, 2001a). Whereas immediate memory is temporary, working memory can last for hours and allows one to retain relevant information while completing a task. Students with learning disabilities frequently have difficulty with working memory. For example, Tasha begins to write a short story but, while pausing to look up the spelling of a word, forgets what she had planned to say.

Much more remains to be learned about the role of various areas of the brain, how they work together, and how various types of experiences are stored and later retrieved. Students with learning disabilities frequently have difficulty learning and retaining certain types of information. As research in neuroscience continues to inform our practice, educators will be able to apply this information to understanding more about learning disabilities and enhancing teaching and learning opportunities in the classroom.

Research to Practice

Brain-Based Research

Recent developments in brain research have led to renewed interest in cognitive science and its implications for teaching and learning. Some of the research findings have been translated into general classroom recommendations that are helpful to students both with and without disabilities. For example, to promote memory and recall, educators should chunk ideas rather than covering material in small bits, arrange information in a structured and meaningful way, cover the whole and then the parts, and conduct oral or written reviews frequently (Jensen, 1998).

In addition, recent research findings have led to greater understanding of the impact of disability on learning. An extensive review of the literature (Bigler, Lajiness-O'Neill, & Howes, 1998) examined the research on brain imaging technologies and individuals with learning disabilities. Functional magnetic resonance imaging, a process that allows the brain to be seen through imaging techniques, indicates that there may be anatomical and functional differences between the brains of children with learning disabilities and the brains of children who do

not have learning problems. To provide a closer look at brain activity during cognitive processes, investigators use electrophysiological and metabolic imaging techniques. These brain maps have identified a number of brain irregularities and inconsistencies in individuals with learning disabilities (Hynd, Semrud-Clikeman, & Lyytinen, 1991; Sousa, 2001a, 2001b). Although much more research is needed to inform teaching practices, these findings provide insight into the causes of learning disabilities and the difficulties that these students experience.

Questions for Reflection

1. What have you learned about brain-based research in other classes? How might the findings affect your work in the classroom?
2. In what ways are teachers incorporating brain-based research in the classroom?

To answer these questions and learn more about applying research to practice, go to the Companion Website at www.prenhall. com/cohen, select Chapter 2, then choose Research to Practice.

Organizational skills. Keeping track of classes, assignments, extracurricular activities, part-time work schedules, and obligations at home and in the community requires good organizational skills. Students who have difficulty with organization frequently

- misplace assignments.
- cannot locate materials such as textbooks, pencils, or zip disks.
- do not allow enough time to complete an assignment.
- do not know when assignments are due.

Teachers can help students develop organizational strategies by showing them, for example, how to prioritize their work or keep a schedule planner. In Chapter 15 we will examine additional ways teachers help students develop good organizational skills.

Behavioral problems. Students with learning disabilities frequently have compounding behavioral problems. These problems may be the result of experiencing frustrating academic work; difficulty in understanding and interpreting information; misplacing materials, assignments, and books; or misinterpreting social situations and conversations. For example, teachers observe students

- acting out.
- being physically and/or verbally aggressive toward others.
- being disrespectful.
- lacking motivation.

Attention and hyperactivity. Teachers often refer to students with learning disabilities as *having a short attention span* or *being overactive*. These characteristics actually comprise another disability, ADHD, which is sometimes associated with a learning disability. A student who only has characteristics of inattentiveness or hyperactivity does not necessarily have a learning disability. Later in this chapter, we will look more closely at ADHD.

❖ MEET JARED ❖

"I'm a ninth-grade student and I have a learning disability. I remember back a few years ago, I didn't think that I would ever learn to read. It was pretty hard for me because all my friends didn't seem to have any trouble and I just couldn't seem to learn. There were these books about a boy named Harry Potter, who was a wizard. Everybody in my school was walking around with a copy of the latest book, and everybody was talking about it. I walked around with a copy of the book too. I didn't want to be different, but I couldn't read it.

"That same year, I worked with a new special education teacher who knew a lot about teaching students with learning disabilities. I really wanted to learn to read, and every day I worked with that teacher. He had some neat books that we read, and he even taped some of Harry Potter for me. I still don't read as well as a lot of people my age but, hey, I know that I have to continue to work hard if I want to continue my education after high school."

MEET JARED'S FATHER

"Raising Jared has been a challenge. His teachers would call me to talk about some of the problems he was having—like learning how to read. I remember that when I was in school I also had a difficult time with reading. But I hoped that things would be different for Jared. When the school people tested Jared, they found out that he had a learning disability. Now we knew what was causing his problems. The teachers have worked really hard to help him, and I'm so pleased with his progress now. His interest in school has increased, and he's starting to think about a career."

Using Technology
Learning More About Learning Disabilities

Professional websites help educators, other professionals, parents, and students learn more about learning disabilities. A good way to begin is with the Division for Learning Disabilities, one of the divisions of the professional organization for special educators, the Council for Exceptional Children. The Division for Learning Disabilities website focuses on information and resources for teaching students with learning disabilities. Along with obtaining resources for understanding learning disabilities and teaching tips, educators can join discussion groups with colleagues and experts.

Another good resource, the International Dyslexia Association, maintains a website that includes a wealth of information for educators and individuals with learning disabilities, including sections for children, college students, adults, and parents. This site provides an option to display information in English or Spanish. Incidentally, the International Dyslexia Association is one of the oldest and best-known organizations in the field of learning disabilities in this country.

There are a number of other national organizations, such as the Learning Disabilities Association of America (LDA), which maintains affiliates in each state. On the LDA website, one can link to the website of every state affiliate to discover regional activities, information, and resources. The National Center for Learning Disabilities provides a variety of helpful information, including a special section for teens and adults and a special section that features research on strategies and instruction.

Along with recognized national organizations, the Internet itself has spawned at least one resource that is available only online. LDOnline is an extensive website with excellent discussions of the IEP, IEP team meetings, instructional strategies, articles, and research related to learning disabilities. A favorite section for children with learning disabilities is the Kidzone.

Questions for Reflection

1. After exploring several of these sites, compare and contrast the information available in terms of content and usefulness. Which sites do you think would be most helpful to first-year teachers?
2. What additional professional resources on learning disabilities can you find? Share the results of your search with your colleagues.

 To answer these questions and learn more about using technology to support learning, go to the Companion Website at www. prenhall.com/cohen, select Chapter 2, then choose Using Technology.

STUDENTS WITH ATTENTION DEFICIT HYPERACTIVITY DISORDER

Students both with and without disabilities have difficulty paying attention at times, but for students with ADHD, this behavior is a regular occurrence. ADHD is characterized by a persistent pattern of inattention that is more frequent and severe than is typically observed in children and youth at comparable levels of development (American Psychiatric Association [APA], 2000, p. 85). Children and youth who are identified as having ADHD can receive special education services under IDEA, even though there is no separate category for this disorder. These students fall under the category "other health impairments." ADHD will also be mentioned when we discuss students with other health impairments later in this chapter.

Because IDEA does not define a separate disability category for ADHD, we will include the criteria described in the *Diagnostic and Statistical Manual of Mental Disorders (DSM-IV-TR; APA, 2000)* that psychologists use in identifying a child with ADHD:

A. Either (1) or (2):

   1. six (or more) of the following symptoms of **inattention** have persisted for at least 6 months to a degree that is maladaptive and inconsistent with developmental level:

   Inattention

   a. often fails to give close attention to details or makes careless mistakes in schoolwork, work, or other activities
   b. often has difficulty sustaining attention in tasks or play activities
   c. often does not seem to listen when spoken to directly
   d. often does not follow through on instruction and fails to finish schoolwork, chores, or duties in the workplace (not due to oppositional behavior or failure to understand instructions)
   e. often has difficulty organizing tasks and activities
   f. often avoids, dislikes, or is reluctant to engage in tasks that require sustained mental effort (such as schoolwork or homework)
   g. often loses things necessary for tasks or activities (e.g., toys, school assignments, pencils, books, or tools)
   h. is often easily distracted by extraneous stimuli
   i. is often forgetful in daily activities

   2. six (or more) of the following symptoms of **hyperactivity** and **impulsivity** have persisted for at least 6 months to a degree that is maladaptive and inconsistent with developmental level:

   Hyperactivity

   a. often fidgets with hands or feet or squirms in seat
   b. often leaves seat in classroom or in other situations in which remaining seated is expected
   c. often runs about or climbs excessively in situations in which it is inappropriate (in adolescents or adults, may be limited to subjective feelings of restlessness)

    d. often has difficulty playing or engaging in leisure activities quietly

    e. is often "on the go" or often acts as if "driven by a motor"

    f. often talks excessively

Impulsivity

    g. often blurts out answers before questions have been completed

    h. often has difficulty awaiting turn

    i. often interrupts or intrudes on others (e.g., butts into conversations or games)

B. Some hyperactivity-impulsive or inattentive symptoms that caused impairment were present before age 7 years.

C. Some impairment from the symptoms is present in two or more settings (e.g., at school [or work] and at home).

D. There must be clear evidence of clinically significant impairment in social, academic, or occupational functioning.

E. The symptoms do not occur exclusively during the course of a pervasive Developmental Disorder, Schizophrenia, or other Psychotic Disorder and are not better accounted for by another mental disorder (e.g., Mood Disorder, Anxiety Disorder, Dissociative Disorder, or a Personality Disorder).*

CAUSES OF ATTENTION DEFICIT HYPERACTIVITY DISORDER

ADHD occurs in approximately 3% to 8% of American students, and boys are twice as likely to have it as girls (Barkley, 2003; Verner, 2001). Several lines of research are investigating the cause(s) of ADHD. Investigators working in the area of heredity have found that a student with ADHD often has one or more relatives with the same characteristics. Baren (1994) reports that approximately one out of three individuals with ADHD has relatives who also have ADHD.

    In another area, brain-based research continues to increase our understanding of anatomical differences and imbalances in the brain and how neurological dysfunction affects one's ability to learn and attend. Using high-resolution magnetic resonance imaging, researchers have found differences in the areas of the brain linked to attention and impulse control in children with ADHD. In a comparison of the magnetic resonance imaging scans of children and adolescents with and without ADHD, they found that children with ADHD had changes in brain structure in regions controlling attention and impulses (Reuters, 1995).

CHARACTERISTICS OF STUDENTS WITH ATTENTION DEFICIT HYPERACTIVITY DISORDER

Although students with ADHD primarily exhibit difficulties in attention, hyperactivity, and impulsivity, they may also have co-occurring problems. Frequently students with ADHD also have learning disabilities. Other students with ADHD are diagnosed with oppositional defiant disorder, conduct disorder, depression, and other mood problems, anxiety problems, and tics (Kollins, Barkley, & Dupaul, 2001). Although

*Reprinted with permission from the *Diagnostic and Statistical Manual of Mental Disorders,* Text Revision, pp. 92–93, Copyright © 2000, American Psychiatric Association.

American educators frequently observe characteristics of ADHD, this disorder also occurs in other parts of the world, although the prevalence of ADHD in other countries varies, probably due to different diagnostic practices (APA, 2000).

Early Signs of Attention Deficit Hyperactivity Disorder in Preschool and Early Elementary Children

Observing and recognizing early signs of ADHD in young children requires a solid knowledge and understanding of child development. Young children who are developing typically often show limitless energy. Yet, by the time children are 3 years of age, they enjoy sitting and engaging in tabletop activities or listening to a story. Unlike their peers, young children with ADHD have difficulty sitting still long enough to play with play dough or markers or to maintain attention to a short story. According to *DSM-IV-TR* (APA, 2000), parents may observe excessive motor activity in children as young as toddlers. Later these children will be identified as having ADHD.

Usually ADHD is identified once children enter school. In the classroom, teachers expect children to follow rules such as "inside voices" and "walking feet." As the classroom routine becomes more structured, educators often identify children who are having difficulty managing their bodies and attending to the teacher's directions and expectations.

Characteristics of School-Age Students with Attention Deficit Hyperactivity Disorder

Academic areas. The characteristics of hyperactivity and inattention affect students' achievement across the curriculum. These academic difficulties stem from a poor attention span; from inability to sit still, follow directions and complete tasks; and from impulsive behavior. For example, similar to students with learning disabilities, students with ADHD may have difficulty in learning how to read and, as they become older, in comprehending what they are reading. In using written language, students with ADHD often are distracted and forget what they set out to write once they begin writing. Searching the Internet to conduct research in specific content areas may result in exploration of an interesting but very different topic from the one they began.

Behavior: Attention, hyperactivity, and impulsivity. Children with attention problems are easily distracted. General classroom noise, a student passing nearby, or remembering the lyrics of a favorite song may quickly and unexpectedly draw the student's attention away from the teacher who is providing instruction. Once the student has identified the source of the noise or the other distraction, this inattention has prevented the student from receiving important information from the teacher. Missing one or more of the instructional steps that the teacher was explaining prevents the student from understanding the directions or expectations of the assignment.

Another behavior problem associated with ADHD is hyperactivity. The types of hyperactivity usually vary, depending on the age of the student. In the early grades, much of the hyperactivity consists of gross motor activity such as running, jumping, and climbing; as the child becomes older, the hyperactivity behaviors become more subtle, consisting of fidgeting, pacing, or general restlessness (APA, 2000). As the student becomes older, he or she may have difficulty concentrating, may be easily distracted, and may have difficulty staying in one place.

Using Technology
Learning More About Attention Deficit Hyperactivity Disorder

You can use the Internet to find out a lot more information about ADHD. You might begin with the website of the National Institute of Mental Health. This site provides a broad range of information about ADHD for the public as well as for professionals.

You will also want to visit the website of one of the most well-known organizations on ADHD, Children and Adults with Attention Deficit Hyperactivity Disorder (CHADD). This organization provides research-based information about ADHD and serves as a focal point for education, research, leadership, advocacy, and support. Its website provides both print and Web-based materials.

LDOnline also contains a wealth of information about ADHD. You can find articles and documents from the U.S. Department of Education. At this site, too, you can exchange ideas with other professionals, adults with ADHD, or parents of children with ADHD on the ADHD bulletin board.

Questions for Reflection

1. After exploring several of these sites, compare and contrast the information available in terms of content and usefulness. Which sites do you think would be most helpful to first-year teachers?
2. What additional professional resources on ADHD can you find? Share the results of your search with your colleagues.

To answer these questions and learn more about using technology to support learning, go to the Companion Website at www.prenhall.com/cohen, select Chapter 2, then choose Using Technology.

In the classroom these behaviors may include the following:

- getting up every few minutes to sharpen a pencil or get a drink of water
- not completing an activity
- talking to others rather than listening when someone else is talking
- not following directions

Impulsivity is another behavioral characteristic of ADHD. Being impulsive may mean acting without thinking or saying the first thing that comes to mind. Impulsive behaviors cause many difficulties including taking risks that could result in physical harm for the student as well as for others. Impulsive behaviors often interfere with relationships and create social problems with peers. Children with ADHD have more difficulty in identifying the emotions of others than do children without ADHD (Novilitus, Cases, Brookier, & Bonello, 2000). Further, impulsive behaviors prevent a student from maintaining high academic achievement in the classroom.

Students who do not learn how to manage ADHD can experience difficulties in childhood, adolescence, and adulthood. Some research indicates that adolescents and young adults with ADHD are at greater risk for substance abuse disorder. Among individuals who were in a clinic for substance use disorder, such as alcohol and/or cocaine use, 32% met the criteria for ADHD and 35% of those inpatients had a diagnosis of ADHD in school (Clure, Brady, Johnson, Wiad, & Rittenburg, 1999). Untreated problem behaviors often observed in children and adolescents with ADHD such as oppositional/aggressive behaviors may have long-term consequences. For example, Curran and Fitzgerald (1999) report that 9% of young adult prisoners have ADHD compared to 2.5% of young adults in the general population.

ADHD is not a condition that can be cured; rather, a student must learn how to live with and manage it. A large body of research indicates that three general approaches to treating ADHD have received the most attention: pharmacological approaches, behavioral/psychosocial approaches, and a combination of the two (Kollins et al., 2001). With supportive educational interventions, students can use their high activity and energy level to advantage, resulting in positive outcomes. For example, curiosity, divergent thinking, and risk taking can result in inventive solutions and the ability to manage multitasking and complex operations. These characteristics can lead to creative ideas and outcomes when other individuals are focused more on what is inside the box!

❖ MEET DAVE ❖

"Hey! My name is Dave and I'm in fifth grade. I like my teachers a lot this year. I mean, I feel like they really understand me. I can get up and go over to the learning center whenever I need to. Last year the teacher made me sit at my desk all the time, and that was so hard. I mean, can you imagine having to sit in one place when you feel like getting up—and the more you try to sit, the worse you feel? She got really mad at me sometimes, and I didn't know why. Well, I have ADHD, and last year I had to do a lot of tests and then they found out what was the matter. Sometimes I work with a special teacher, Mrs. Young, in another room, but mostly I just stay here in my classroom. I really like the cool way we do things this year—like learning to solve geometry problems. We have a lot of blocks and cubes that we can use, and each person sets up the problem. I'm learning a lot, and I think I'm getting really good with volume and area and stuff like this."

MEET DAVE'S MOTHER

"As a little boy he never seemed to sit still for long, and this was difficult to manage here at home. Later, when he started school and began riding home on the bus, he started having problems. He was always getting into trouble on the bus. I know that ride is difficult after being in school all day. In the beginning he was always jumping up and moving about—and the bus driver would get so mad. Today, he still gets into trouble on that bus. Like the other day, he started throwing somebody's hat and got a lot of other kids to join in on the game. A whole bunch of them got in trouble. He just doesn't think things out sometimes. I mean the other kids are really mad at him now, and he doesn't understand why.

"Dave keeps me on my toes. I mean, he tries to be good but he's just got so much energy. We've tried to get him involved with sports, hoping that this might help. The first year he played soccer and ice hockey—and he's stuck with it. In fact, this year he is looking forward to playing on the travel team."

STUDENTS WITH OTHER HEALTH IMPAIRMENTS

Sometimes students have disabilities that are considered under a broad category called *other health impairments*. These impairments are often associated with a medical

Considering Diversity

English Language Learners

Sometimes educators wonder if the classroom difficulties an English language learner is experiencing are related to learning a new language or to a disability. Which characteristics alert educators to consider the possibility of a disability in a student who is linguistically and culturally diverse? Let us take a closer look at some useful suggestions.

According to Roseberry-McKibbin (1995), an educator may observe that the student uses nonverbal aspects of language that are culturally inappropriate or does not express basic needs adequately. The student may rarely initiate verbal interaction with peers or may respond sporadically or inappropriately when peers initiate interaction. Sometimes the student replaces speech with gestures, communicating nonverbally when talking would be appropriate and expected.

The student may experience difficulty in conveying thoughts in an organized, sequential manner that is understandable to listeners. For example, the student may skip from one topic to the next or have word-finding difficulties that go beyond typical second language acquisition patterns. The student may fail to provide significant information, leaving the listener confused, or may have difficulty with conversational turn-taking skills. The student may perseverate on a topic even after the topic has changed, may fail

to ask and answer questions appropriately, or may need to hear things repeated even when they are stated simply (Roseberry-McKibbin, 1995).

In meeting the needs of students, many of whom may be newcomers to this country, educators learn to observe individual student characteristics. When the teacher has concerns, the parents should be invited and encouraged to come to school so that the concerns can be discussed. Finally, when concerns persist, the student should be referred to the multidisciplinary team to determine whether the student has a disability. If so, the student should receive special education services.

Questions for Reflection

1. What additional information is helpful for educators to know about students who have language disabilities?
2. Can you identify several Web-based resources concerning characteristics of various disabilities that are available in languages other than English?

To answer these questions and deepen your understanding of diversity in schools and communities, go to the Companion Website at www.prenhall.com/cohen, select Chapter 2, then choose Considering Diversity.

condition that may be either acute (short-lived) or chronic (long-lasting). IDEA identifies a sample of medical conditions that fall under this term:

> Other health impairment means having limited strength, vitality, or alertness, in- cluding a heightened alertness to environmental stimuli, that results in limited alert- ness with respect to the education environment that (1) is due to chronic or acute health problems such as asthma, attention deficit disorder or attention deficit hy- peractivity disorder, diabetes, epilepsy, a heart condition, hemophilia, lead poison- ing, leukemia, nephritis, rheumatic fever, and sickle cell anemia; and (2) adversely affects a child's educational performance. (Sec. 300.7)

CAUSES OF OTHER HEALTH IMPAIRMENTS

Other health impairments include a wide variety of conditions that may be traced to prenatal causes (conditions during pregnancy); perinatal causes (conditions that re- sulted during the baby's birth); postnatal causes (conditions that resulted in the first months of life); or environmental causes during the early years. For some medical conditions, the causes may be unknown. Two of the most common health impair- ments in children and youth are asthma and diabetes.

Asthma

Asthma is one of the most common pulmonary disorders among children, with an incidence rate that is rapidly growing (Ladebauche, 1997). Although the exact cause of asthma is not known, medical professionals believe that a primary triggering event leads to inflammation of the lining of the bronchial tubes, causing the tubes to nar- row. This narrowing of the airway makes it difficult to move air in and out of the lungs, resulting in wheezing and coughing. There may be a genetic factor; the child inherits the tendency for inflammation of the lung airway, which then triggers bronchial muscle hyperreactivity (Feldman, 1996).

Allergens, or conditions that cause the inflammation of the airway lining, may be either inhaled or ingested. For example, some people are affected only when they come in contact with certain environmental allergens such as cats and dogs or pollen from grasses, trees, and weeds. Sometimes asthma is exacerbated by cold air or envi- ronmental pollutants. For some students, physical exercise in class or participation in a sports activity can be a triggering event. Others may experience a strong reaction from nuts or milk.

Diabetes

Diabetes is another common disorder among children and youth. There are two types of diabetes: type I and type II. Type I is insulin-dependent diabetes, one of the most common metabolic disorders of childhood. In this condition the student lacks insulin production, which leads to disturbances in carbohydrate, protein, and fat metabolism. Researchers are not sure what specifically causes type I diabetes, but there appears to be a genetic susceptibility.

Up to a few years ago, individuals who developed type II diabetes were usually more than 30 years of age and were often overweight. Today a national epidemic of type II diabetes is following the epidemic of obesity in children and youth (Cincinnati

Children's Hospital Medical Center, 1996; Williamson, 2000). Not only has obesity affected what children can physically accomplish, it has drastically affected their health. Being overweight decreases the body's sensitivity to insulin. This decrease in insulin sensitivity is a primary factor in the development of type II diabetes. In one study, researchers from the fields of nursing, medicine, and public health found that 7% of a sample of 700 school-age children had already developed three of the leading risk factors for heart disease and type II diabetes. These factors included a high insulin level, high blood pressure, and either elevated levels of fats or not enough of the "good cholesterol" (Williamson, 2000).

CHARACTERISTICS OF STUDENTS WITH OTHER HEALTH IMPAIRMENTS

Students with other health impairments generally have medical conditions that require ongoing monitoring and attention (Table. 2.2). Some students need to be hospitalized at times, whereas others only have reduced stamina that prevents them from following the busy routine of a typical school day. The characteristics of the individual impairment can interfere with the lowered or elevated level of alertness, such as those of students with ADHD.

Early Signs of Other Health Impairments in Preschool and Early Elementary Children

Irregular school attendance is one of the indicators that children are not functioning well. In class, children with other health impairments do not always perform at a level equal to that of their peers. When children and their families first learn about an unexpected medical condition that will be long-lasting, they may have many questions, fears, and feelings of anger that they have to deal with. During this time, the child's doctors may need to experiment with various types of medications and dosages before finding the one that meets the child's needs.

Sometimes physicians ask parents and teachers to make careful observations of the child's behavior. Noting periods in the day when the child is very active or very passive may be helpful to physicians as they make decisions about treatment options. More often than not, the treatment decisions include identifying an effective medication and regulating the dosage. Educators work closely with the school nurse when medications must be stored and administered at school.

Asthma. When a young child has asthma, the triggers, or conditions that cause it, may not be known. Finding out just what triggers the inflammation is often a process that occurs as medical professionals work with the family. To compound the difficulties, some children may have a specific trigger, whereas for others, a combination of triggers brings on the condition (Hill, 1999). Parents are valuable resources, informing the school about their child and what factors may bring on an asthma attack. Teachers use knowledge of a child's triggers in considering the classroom environment and in planning learning activities. For example, if a child is not able to tolerate tree pollen, a teacher will arrange a class field trip before or after the time when the pollen is most prevalent.

Teachers also need to be aware of typical childhood illnesses. Children with asthma are affected to a much greater degree than other children by common viruses

| Table 2.2 | Examples of Disabilities Considered Under Other Health Impairments and Their Characteristics |

Disability	Description	Characteristics
Asthma	Inflammation of the bronchial tubes	Coughing and wheezing; decreased ability to run or jump; difficulty completing work or attending to tasks
Attention deficit hyperactivity disorder	A disorder that affects an individual's behavior	Inattention, hyperactivity, and impulsivity
Diabetes, type I	A chronic disorder that results from lack of insulin	Faintness, headache, excessive hunger, nervousness, increased heart rate, cold hands and feet
Diabetes, type II	A chronic disorder that results from obesity and the decrease in the body's sensitivity to insulin	Leads to a wide variety of long-term complications, including heart disease
Epilepsy	Discharge of abnormal electrical activity to one or more areas of the brain	Twitching of a body part, flushing, vomiting, olfactory hallucinations, a feeling of fear. In generalized seizures, consciousness is lost
Hemophilia	A group of lifelong bleeding disorders	Fatigue, severe bleeding episodes
Lead poisoning	Caused by repeated inhalation, ingestion, or absorption through the skin of lead or lead compounds	Anemia, distractibility, hyperactivity, hyperirritability, impulsiveness, lethargy, listlessness
Leukemia	A malignant disease of the blood-making (hematopoietic) system of the body	Anemia, susceptibility to infection, bruising of the skin, often without any noticeable cause, increased incidence of nosebleeds
Nephritis	Inflammation of the kidney associated with infection	Decreased ability of the kidneys to remove waste efficiently
Rheumatic fever	Inflammatory disease that develops after an infection and can involve the heart, brain, joints, or skin	Fever, joint pain or swelling, skin rash, or cardiac problems such as shortness of breath or chest pain
Sickle cell anemia	Abnormal shape of red blood cells, which decreases the oxygen-carrying capacity of the blood	Anemia and decreased ability to participate in physical activity during a sickle cell crisis; periods of intense pain

(Feldman, 1996). Whereas other children may have a cold, the virus in children with asthma stimulates the airway lining, resulting in inflammation and restricted breathing.

Characteristics of School-Age Students with Other Health Impairments

By the time students reach the upper elementary grades, they may need the emotional support of those around them who understand their fears and anxieties and, in some cases, their anger. Teachers, naturally, are anxious too, especially if the condition is complex and unfamiliar. With adequate assistance from health care professionals, educators can plan appropriate educational programs that allow children and youth to be with their friends and to continue their education.

Asthma. Working with the family, educators can learn the results of medical tests that have identified the child's triggers and plan accordingly. For example, if an educator knows that the student has inhaled-induced asthma to certain cleaning agents, the school will need to eliminate this trigger. If the student has exercise-induced asthma, the teacher will need to provide a choice of mild to moderate activities.

If the child has mild asthma, a physician usually prescribes medication to prevent airway lining inflammation. This medication is typically given through an inhaler. For children with moderately severe asthma, the physician may recommend an anti-inflammatory medication that the child takes on a regular basis to control lining inflammation. In addition, the child may need to supplement this regimen with an inhaler. The severity of the asthma at any one time will affect the child's stamina and ability to participate in the regular classroom routine and outside activities such as recess or special field trips.

--- ❖ *MEET AMANDA* ❖ ---

"My name is Amanda, and I am in kindergarten. Sometimes I have trouble breathing. When it gets bad, my daddy says I am having an asthma attack. This is very scary and I don't like it. One time my daddy had to take me to the hospital. I don't remember that, but he does. He says he was very scared too. When I have an asthma attack, I have to use my inhaler and then I feel better."

MEET AMANDA'S MOTHER

"Our daughter, Amanda, has asthma. She experiences shortness of breath and has trouble breathing, like she can't get all the air out of her lungs. The doctor says that her triggers are colds, allergies, certain weeds, perfumes and hairspray, and smoke. Once we were walking through the perfume section of a department store, and she had such a bad reaction that she almost stopped breathing. I got her out of that store fast. Now we always walk on the other side of the mall to avoid passing by that store. Recently, we learned that there are several early warning signs; one of them is a feeling of tightness in the chest.

"I think that it is important to know what an attack can feel like and what are some of the best things one can do for someone during an attack. During her attacks, Amanda can't catch her breath. It is the sort of feeling that you get when you have run too much and are out of breath. We find that during an attack, the best thing someone can do for her is stay calm, get her a glass of water for her coughing, and talk to her. The person should make sure that she uses her inhaler. The inhaler dispenses medication in a mist that she breathes in, relieving some of the airway obstruction. Having an attack is scary because the person has no control of the situation. After an asthma attack, she often has an increased appetite and experiences a rapid heartbeat. She may shake for hours and get very "hyper," followed by extreme fatigue" (adapted from A. Cooke, personal communication, 2000).

STUDENTS WITH MILD DISABILITIES

We have examined the characteristics of students with learning disabilities, ADHD, and other health impairments. Although students in a single classroom may have different educational or medical diagnoses such as these, they most likely have similar needs. Their teachers will be working to increase their academic knowledge, communication

---

Using Technology
Learning More About Other Health Impairments

Sometimes educators need more information about the medical condition of a student. MEDLINEplus is an online medical encyclopedia that provides extensive resources on disorders and disabilities. Written in everyday language, it presents information on various disorders, their causes, symptoms, treatment, and prognosis.

For beginning educators, the Council for Exceptional Children, Division for Physical and Health Disabilities provides a good website to start learning more about educational services for students with other health impairments who receive services in schools, in hospitals, or at home. More information about particular medical conditions can be found at specific websites. For example, the Asthma and Allergy Foundation of America provides a wealth of information about asthma, including facts and frequently asked

questions. The American Diabetes Association website contains information about both type I and type II diabetes and about ways to encourage good heath.

Questions for Reflection

1. After exploring several of these sites, compare and contrast the information available in terms of content and usefulness. Which sites do you think would be most helpful to first-year teachers?
2. What additional professional resources on one or more of the health impairments listed in Table 2.2 can you find? Share the results of your search with your colleagues.

To answer these questions and learn more about using technology to support learning, go to the Companion Website at www. prenhall.com/cohen, select Chapter 2, then choose Using Technology.

skills, appropriate behaviors, social skills, attention, organization, or self-advocacy. In learning to teach students with mild disabilities, special educators must not only understand the characteristics of a specific disability but also understand and address the common needs of all students.

SUMMARY

- Knowledge of the characteristics of specific disabilities enables teachers to work with parents and students to find services through the special education process.
- Being able to discuss the causes and characteristics of specific disabilities, including learning disabilities, ADHD, and other health impairments, provides special educators with a foundation for working with students with mild disabilities.
- Developing an understanding of these general characteristics allows special educators to address the academic, social, and behavior problems of students.
- Special educators must develop awareness and skills in working with students who are English language learners and who have disabilities.
- Knowing how to use technology assists educators in locating and retrieving additional information about mild disabilities.
- No two students with mild disabilities are alike. Each student has unique skills, knowledge, abilities, gifts—and needs. Understanding the characteristics of the learner is one of the cornerstones for creating successful teaching and learning experiences.

EXTENDING LEARNING

1. Individuals can be described in terms of their knowledge, motivation, skills, and physical, social, and emotional attributes. How would you describe your characteristics?
2. Working with a small group of students in your class, identify the characteristics of learners whom you have observed with learning disabilities, ADHD, or other health impairments. What additional information would you want to know about these students? What resources can you identify that would assist you in working with these students?
3. Arrange to visit a classroom at the elementary, middle, or secondary school level. Observe the students to see if you can identify the characteristics of students who may have learning or behavior problems. Can you observe differences and similarities among students at these different grade levels? What characteristics are more typical of younger students? Of older students?
4. Interview a special education teacher about the students with disabilities with whom the teacher works. What types of disabilities do the students have? What are some of their characteristics?
5. Select one area of disability discussed in this chapter and search the Web to locate additional information on student characteristics. Share your findings with the class.

REFERENCES

American Psychiatric Association. (2000). *Diagnostic and statistical manual of mental disorders* (4th ed., text revision). Washington, DC: Author.

Baren, M. (1994). *Hyperactivity and attention disorders in children.* San Ramon, CA: Health Information Network.

Barkley, R. A. (2003). Attention-deficit/hyperactivity disorder. In E. J. Mash & R. A. Barkley (Eds.), *Child psychopathology* (2nd ed., pp. 75–143). New York: Guilford Press.

Bigler, E. D., Lajiness-O'Neill, R., & Howes, N. L. (1998). Technology in the assessment of learning disability. *Journal of Learning Disabilities 31*(1), 67–82.

Cincinnati Children's Hospital Medical Center. (1996). *Children's study identifies emerging adolescent health problem.* Retrieved November 21, 2003 from http://www.cincinnatichildrens. org/about/news/release/1996/5-diabetes.htm

Clure, C., Brady, K. T., Johnson, D., Wiad, R., & Rittenburg, M. (1999). Attention deficit/hyperactivity disorder and substance use: Symptoms, pattern, and drug choice. *American Journal of Drug and Alcohol Abuse, 25*(3), 441–448.

Curran, S., & Fitzgerald, M. (1999). Attention deficit hyperactivity disorder in the prison population. *American Journal of Psychiatry, 156*(10), 1664–1665.

DeFries, J. C., Stevenson, J., Gillis, J., & Wadsworth, S. J. (1991). Genetic etiology of spelling deficits in the Colorado and London twin studies of reading disability. *Reading and Writing, 3,* 271–283.

Feldman, W. (1996). Chronic illness in children. In R. H. A. Haslam & P. J. Valletutti (Eds.), *Medical problems in the classroom* (pp. 115–123). Austin, TX: PRO-ED.

Hill, J. L. (1999). *Meeting the needs of students with special physical and health care needs.* Upper Saddle River, NJ: Merrill/Prentice Hall.

Hynd, G. W., Semrud-Clikeman, M., & Lyytinen, H. (1991). Brain imaging in learning disabilities. In J. E. Obrzut & G. W. Hynd (Eds.), *Neuropsychological foundations of learning disabilities* (pp. 475–511). San Diego, CA: Academic Press.

Individuals with Disabilities Education Act Amendments (Pub. L. No. 105–17). (1997). 20 U.S.C. Secs. 1400 *et. seq.* Washington, DC: U.S. Government Printing Office.

Jensen, E. (1998). *Teaching with the brain in mind.* Alexandria, VA: Association for Supervision and Curriculum Development.

Kollins, S. H., Barkley, R. A., & Dupaul, G. J. (2001). Use and management of medications for children with attention deficit hyperactivity disorder (ADHD). *Focus on Exceptional Children, 33*(5), 1–24.

Ladebauche, P. (1997). Managing asthma: A growth and development approach. *Pediatric Nursing, 23,* 37–44.

Lahey, M. (1988). *Language disorders and language development.* Upper Saddle River, NJ: Merrill/Prentice Hall.

Learner, J. (2000). *Learning disabilities.* Boston: Houghton Mifflin.

Lubs, H. A., Rabin, M., Carland-Saucier, K., Wen, X. L., Gross-Glenn, K., Dura, R., Levin, B., & Lubs, M. L. (1991). Genetic bases of developmental dyslexia: Molecular studies. In J. E. Obrzut & G. W. Hynd (Eds.), *Neuropsychological foundations of learning disabilities* (pp. 49–77). San Diego, CA: Academic Press.

National Alliance of Black School Educators and IDEA Local Implementation by Local Administrators Partnership. (2002). *Addressing overrepresentation of African American students in special education*. Arlington, VA: Council for Exceptional Children.

Novilitus, J. M., Cases, R. J., Brookier, K. M., & Bonello, P. J. (2000). Emotion appraisal in children with attention-deficit/hyperactivity disorder and their parents. *Journal of Attention Disorders, 4*(1), 15–26.

Pennington, B. (1995). Genetics of learning disabilities. *Journal of Child Neurology, 10*(Suppl. 1), S69–S77.

Pennington, B., Smith, S., Kimberling, W., Green, P., & Haith, M. (1987). Left-handedness and immune disorders in familial dyslexics. *Archives of Neurology, 44*, 634–639.

President's Commission on Excellence in Special Education. (2002). *A new era: Revitalizing special education for children and their families*. Retrieved July 16, 2002, from http://www.ed.gov/inits/commissionsboards/whspecialeducation/index.html

Reuters News Service. (1995). *Brain scans shed light on ADHD*. Retrieved November 22, 2003, from the MSNBC website: http://msnbc.msn.com/id/3541411

Roseberry-McKibbin, C. (1995, Summer). Distinguishing language differences from language disorders in linguistically and culturally diverse students. *Multicultural Education*, 12–16.

Sousa, D. A. (2001a). *How the brain learns* (2nd ed.). Thousand Oaks, CA: Corwin.

Sousa, D. A. (2001b). *How the special needs brain learns*. Thousand Oaks, CA: Corwin.

Sprenger, M. (1999). *Learning and memory: The brain in action*. Alexandria, VA: Association for Supervision and Curriculum Development.

Torgesen, J. (1998). Catch them before they fall. *American Educator, 22*(1&2), 32–41.

Verner, K. (2001). *Making connection in the classroom: Brain-based learning*. Retrieved November 15, 2003, from the Penn State Division of Developmental Pediatrics and Learning website: http://www.lablion.org/cbe.htm

Williamson, D. (2000). *New study of NC children presages upcoming epidemic of type II diabetes*. Retrieved November 21, 2003, from the University of North Carolina website: http://www.unc.edu/news/newsserv/archives/nov00/harell81113000.htm

3

Chapter

Knowing Students with Mild and Moderate Disabilities

Emotional Disturbance, Mental Retardation, and Autism Spectrum Disorders

❖ Discuss the needs of students who have moderate disabilities.

❖ Describe the causes and characteristics of specific disabilities, including emotional disturbance, mental retardation, and autism spectrum disorder.

❖ Discuss cultural identity and how educators can be responsive to students from diverse cultures who have mild to moderate disabilities.

❖ Identify technology resources for educators.

STUDENTS WITH MODERATE DISABILITIES

Students with moderate disabilities, similar to students with mild disabilities, experience a range of characteristics that fall along a continuum. Students with moderate disabilities generally have extensive needs in one or more areas. For example, a student experiences difficulty in academic work because of long periods of absence due to an emotional disturbance. The student's diagnosis, clinical depression, also interferes with other aspects of the student's life. The student has difficulty sleeping and eating. Concentrating on assignments is difficult when thoughts of suicide keep recurring.

Describing a student in terms of moderate disabilities provides a starting point for educators in terms of making connections and having conversations. However, overreliance on labels causes misunderstandings and leads to erroneous conclusions. Special educators know that students with moderate disabilities learn, grow, and achieve when given appropriate learning opportunities, support, and experiences that address their needs and abilities. Special educators know the importance of considering the cultural context of the communities from which students come and of helping students to make meaningful connections between home and school. Students can then increase their academic knowledge, communication skills, appropriate behaviors, social skills, attention, organization, or self-advocacy.

Some moderate disabilities, such as emotional disturbance, interfere with motivation, behavior, and interaction with others. Moderate mental retardation and autism affect a student's social skills, communication with others, and adaptive behaviors. Students with chronic health impairments, such as hemophilia or cancer, may be too sick for periods of time to participate in an education program. These impairments impact not only on the student's health, physical strength, and stamina but also on the student's attitude and emotional well-being. Many students with moderate disabilities need to learn skills to cope daily with the physical and

Considering Diversity

Conceptual Framework of Cultural Competence

Working toward a greater understanding of others and obtaining a degree of cultural competence is important for each of us in the 21st century. The National Center for Cultural Competence at Georgetown University has gathered a library of resources and has developed a vision for individuals who wish to begin this process. The Center views cultural competence as a continuum in which individuals acquire different levels of awareness, knowledge, and skills. This framework requires that schools (and other organizations):

• have a defined set of values and principles, and demonstrate behaviors, attitudes, policies, and structures that enable

them to work effectively in a cross-cultural environment
• have the capacity to (a) value diversity, (b) conduct self-assessment, (c) manage the dynamics of difference, (d) acquire and institutionalize cultural knowledge, and (e) adapt to diversity and the cultural context of the communities they serve
• incorporate the above in all aspects of policy making, administration, practice, and service delivery and involve systematically consumers, key stakeholders, and communities.

Source: National Center for Cultural Competence, 1999–2002.

emotional challenges that chronic disabilities bring. Students also need to learn how to live independently, such as learning how to care for themselves and work with others. They may need to learn functional mathematics and literacy, skills needed to use an ATM to make deposits and withdrawals, and to acquire a basic reading vocabulary.

In diagnosing moderate disabilities, the IEP team may use both educational criteria described in IDEA and criteria outlined in the *Diagnostic and Statistical Manual of Mental Disorders (DSM)*. Used by psychiatrists and psychologists, this manual includes diagnostic categories with criteria and descriptions to aid clinical judgment in classifying a wide range of disorders related to learning, behavior, and mental health. Some of the disabilities that are included in *DSM-IV-TR* (APA, 2000) are disruptive behavior disorders, including oppositional defiant disorders and conduct disorders; eating disorders; mood and anxiety disorders; mental retardation, including mild, moderate, severe, and profound types; autism; and other pervasive developmental disorders. In this chapter we will examine *DSM-IV-TR* criteria frequently used in characterizing these students whom we will discuss in the sections that follow.

STUDENTS WITH EMOTIONAL DISTURBANCE

When is student behavior a problem? In educational settings, students may exhibit a range of acceptable behavior, depending on individual teacher expectations, classroom rules, and school policies. Students with problem behaviors, such as acting out or aggression, are easily identified; however, students who are quiet, withdrawn, or depressed may not be recognized as quickly. Behavior problems such as these are troublesome and sometimes challenging but are frequently considered to be disabilities on the milder end of the continuum. In contrast, students with more moderate disabilities have long-term chronic mental health conditions. The federal definition of emotional disturbance, defined in IDEA, states that a student has:

> A condition exhibiting one or more of the following characteristics over a long period of time and to a marked degree that adversely affects a child's educational performance:
> a) An inability to learn that cannot be explained by intellectual, sensory, or health factors.
> b) An inability to build or maintain satisfactory interpersonal relationships with peers and teachers.
> c) Inappropriate types of behavior or feelings under normal circumstances.
> d) A general pervasive mood of unhappiness or depression.
> e) A tendency to develop physical symptoms or fears associated with personal or school problems.

> The term includes schizophrenia. Emotional disturbance does not apply to children who are socially maladjusted, unless it is determined that they have an emotional disturbance. (Sec. 300.7)

CAUSES OF EMOTIONAL DISTURBANCE

Professionals rarely are able to identify one determining factor to explain why students act or behave as they do. Many factors contribute to causes of emotional or behavioral problems, such as biological, educational, economic, familial, learning, psychological, and societal factors. For example, biological conditions may include the following:

- genetics
- biochemical and neuropsychological imbalances
- temperament characterized by less adaptability to change and a more negative mood

Educational conditions may include the following:

- low teacher expectations
- limited connections between the school and the student's family and community members
- lack of caring and respect among peers

Economic, familial, and societal factors of poverty, abuse, lack of caring adults, poor housing, and overcrowding put children at risk. Psychological factors such as difficulty in bonding and attachment disorders contribute to behavior problems and the ability to form strong relationships.

CHARACTERISTICS OF STUDENTS WITH EMOTIONAL DISTURBANCE

Early Signs of Emotional Disturbance in Preschool and Early Elementary Children

Frequently, teachers observe behavior problems in preschoolers and children in the early elementary grades. Because young children often experience behavior difficulties

Young children often display problem behaviors.

as they learn how to share with others, to respect other children's property and space, and to follow a teacher's directions, how do teachers know when a child's behaviors indicate a more serious problem and what do these behaviors look like? Early childhood educators (Froschl & Sprung, 1999; Marion, 1997; Thompson, 1998) describe some of the typical problems that a teacher may observe:

- frequent crying or sulking
- actively resisting by physically or verbally defending a position (or possessions)
- displaying aggressive revenge by physically or verbally retaliating against another child or an adult
- seeking out an adult for comfort to a degree beyond that of other children

Young children often display problem behaviors; in fact, early childhood teachers generally spend much time using child guidance strategies to teach children socially constructive ways to express feelings (Marion, 1997). When these problem behaviors persist for a long period of time in spite of a teacher's intervention, they may be significant, prompting the teacher to complete a referral to the multidisciplinary team.

For preschool children, some states follow the federal definitions of eligibility for special education services as described in IDEA. In other words, teachers look for behaviors that have occurred over a long period of time and that are affecting other areas of the child's development. Some states employ regulations that differ slightly from those defining the emotional disturbance category and the definition in the federal law, whereas other states serve preschool children under the noncategorical term

Figure 3.1   **Young children may receive services under the category**
developmental delay

A developmental delay is a delay in one or more of the following:

• Physical development, including fine and gross motor
• Cognitive development
• Communication development
• Social or emotional development, or
• Adaptive development

Source: From IDEA 34 C.F.R., Sec. 300.7.

developmental delay. This broad term covers five developmental domains (Figure 3.1). Thus, young children with serious behavior problems may receive services under different labels at the individual state's discretion.

Characteristics of School-Age Students with Emotional Disturbance

Students with emotional disturbance demonstrate a wide range of strengths and needs. Many students are resourceful, energetic, and resilient. They frequently complete high-quality academic work; yet, their problem behaviors interfere with their successful achievement, self-image, and interpersonal relationships.

Reading. Students with emotional disturbance vary greatly in their achievement level. Some students may be proficient readers, demonstrating a high level of achievement in the classroom, whereas others are avid readers when they are able to choose an area of interest. On the other hand, students with emotional disturbance may have associated learning disabilities that interfere with reading achievement. Learning to read may add to the stress and frustration that the student is experiencing already. Along with lack of achievement, the student may be absent or truant on a regular basis, thus further impeding progress.

Mathematics. Similar to reading achievement, students with emotional disturbance vary greatly in achievement in mathematics. Some students excel in mathematics, whereas others struggle. For students to develop mathematical understandings, educators plan instructional sequences that build on information presented in prior lessons. A student who is absent frequently or truant misses key information that is needed to grasp the major concepts and ideas.

Oral language. Most students develop expressive and listening skills naturally, with little direct instruction. However, students with emotional disabilities often need instruction in using language in a functional way, according to a set of rules, or pragmatics. They may have difficulty in using turn-taking skills in conversation, entering into a conversation, or interpreting the meaning of the speaker.

Content areas. Content area subjects may be areas of strength for students. For example, science activities that involve hands-on work with materials, tools, and laboratory equipment provide active ways to learn. Social studies that involve projects with flexibility in demonstrating achievement provide students with important choices and control over their learning. Sometimes students have special interests, such as designing graphics or building small engines, that teachers can capitalize on as part of a social studies or science unit.

When students do not attend school on a regular basis, however, absence or truancy creates problems in the content areas. When students are asked to demonstrate achievement through performance-based tasks, irregular attendance may result in the student missing information regarding the task, how it will be assessed, or how it should be performed. Students will have missed opportunities to add materials to their portfolio or to see examples of what the teacher expects.

Behavior. Problem behaviors can be described as falling into one of two broad categories: (a) disruptive and antisocial behaviors and (b) inhibited or withdrawal behaviors. Disruptive and antisocial behaviors present challenges to teachers because they are persistent and difficult to manage. These behaviors include:

- acting out,
- using inappropriate language,
- displaying physical and verbal aggression, and
- defying authority.

Students with inhibited or withdrawal behaviors are at great risk of dropping out of school. Their problems typically go unrecognized if they choose to sit in the back of the class and remain quiet. Some of the symptoms include:

- low achievement,
- low level of participation with peers,
- nonassertive behaviors,
- problems with self,
- rejection by peers, and
- social withdrawal.

Students with moderate disabilities who carry the educational diagnosis of "emotional disturbance" may carry a more specific *DSM* diagnosis according to their psychological or psychiatric report. Oppositional defiant disorder and conduct disorder represent these types of diagnoses. Oppositional defiant disorder includes disobedience and opposition to authority figures; conduct disorder is more serious.

To be diagnosed with oppositional defiant disorder, a student must show a recurrent pattern of negative, defiant, disobedient, and hostile behavior toward authority figures for a period of at least 6 months (APA, 2000). In the classroom, a teacher may observe behavior such as resisting directions, unwillingness to compromise with others, and stubbornness that is not age-appropriate. Students may be argumentative and defiant and use verbal aggression.

A student who is diagnosed with conduct disorder has a chronic condition consisting of behavior patterns that violate the basic rights of others or school rules and norms of the community. Conduct disorders may be diagnosed in children 10 years of age or younger. Children and youth with conduct disorders often initiate bullying and intimidating behavior. They frequently are involved in fights and use weapons that can cause physical harm. Students with conduct disorders destroy the property of others and can be extremely cruel to people or animals. They frequently are absent from

Figure 3.2   Continuum of conduct disorders and significant behaviors

Continuum of conduct disorders

Mild		Moderate	Severe
Serious Violation of Rules *Example:* Lying and truancy	**Deceitfulness or Theft** *Example:* Stealing without confronting	**Nonaggressive Conduct That Causes Property Loss or Damage** *Example:* vandalism	**Aggressive Conduct That Causes or Threatens Physical Harm to People or Animals** *Examples:* Forced sex, physical cruelty; use of a weapon; stealing while confronting a victim; breaking and entering

Source: Adapted from *DSM-IV-TR* (p. 87), American Psychiatric Association, 2000, Washington, DC: APA.

school for periods of time for no good reason. Students with conduct disorder show little concern for and understanding of others (APA, 2000). Figure 3.2 represents a continuum of severe behaviors typical of students with conduct disorders.

DSM-IV-TR (APA, 2000) cautions clinicians to consider specific culture, age, and gender features before making a diagnosis of conduct disorder. For example, an individual who lives in a high-crime area may have assumed some of the characteristic behaviors of conduct disorder as a protective defense. A new student from a war-torn country may have a long history of aggressive behaviors that were necessary to survive. Yet in neither of these cases are the behaviors symptomatic of individual dysfunction; rather, they are a reaction to the social environment in which the student is or was living.

Students who engage in aggressive and other antisocial behaviors and are convicted of crimes are placed in the juvenile justice system. In fact, a large percentage of juvenile offenders are students with learning and behavior problems, although their disability may not be identified. Children and youth who are placed in correctional institutions, special-purpose schools, or treatment facilities are entitled to the same referral, assessment, and special education and related services under IDEA as all children and youth.

Eating disorders. Eating disorders include severe problems associated with eating. Both anorexia and bulimia are diagnosed using *DSM* criteria because they have established psychological or behavioral syndromes. Anorexia is a condition in which an individual refuses to maintain a healthy body weight. Bulimia is characterized by binge eating followed by behaviors that attempt to purge the body of food, such as excessive exercise or self-induced vomiting. Anorexia usually begins during early adolescence, between ages 13 and 18 years (APA, 2000).

Mood disorders. Mood disorders include a family of disorders, defined by *DSM-IV-TR,* that are divided into depressive disorders, bipolar disorders, disorders due to a general medical condition, and mood disorders that are substance induced. Children and youth who experience depression may be sad or irritable. Their symptoms also include changes in appetite, weight, or sleep, decreased energy, difficulty thinking or concentrating, or recurrent thoughts of death or suicide (APA, 2000). Depression

Research to Practice

Cultural Identity

Cultural diversity continues to grow in public schools across the United States. Sometimes the differences among cultures contribute to misunderstandings on the part of educators. Several research findings provide information to assist educators in becoming more responsive to the needs of all students.

Sometimes a teacher's understanding and style of classroom management come into conflict with students' cultural differences. Many teachers lack the skills to use interpersonal communication and problem solving with diverse student populations (Lane-Garon, 2001). In an attempt to deal with cultural differences, one study found that teachers focused on surface behaviors and misbehaviors and imposed inconsistent discipline (Sheets, 2002). Schwartz (2001) wrote that before disciplining a student, educators should demonstrate respect for the student's concerns by considering the reasons for the perceived misbehavior and then identify a consequence appropriate to the misdemeanor.

In a study that examined American Indian and Alaska Native students and their attitudes toward school, Jacobs and Reyhner (2002) found that their families resisted pressure from schools to assimilate the students into the school culture. This family resistance was a factor in the students' ambivalent attitudes toward their education and in supporting antischool and oppositional identities. This study further explored ways of reaching these students through a constructivist or experiential approach. You can read more about teaching methods based on constructivism in Chapter 6.

 To learn more about applying research to practice, go to the Companion Website at www.prenhall.com/cohen, select Chapter 3, then choose Research to Practice.

---

may include a panic attack or separation anxiety in children. A **panic attack** consists of a specific period in which the individual experiences sudden and intense apprehension, fearfulness, or terror, often associated with a feeling of impending doom in the absence of real danger (APA, 2000). Other symptoms that accompany a panic attack include sweating, trembling, a feeling of smothering, or a feeling of losing control. The attack begins suddenly and builds, lasting for about 10 minutes. **Separation anxiety** occurs when a child expresses excessive anxiety concerning separation from home or from the primary care giver(s) beyond that expected of children of that age. The disturbance lasts for at least 4 weeks (APA, 2000).

Bipolar disorders are characterized by manic episodes in which the individual experiences an elated or irritable mood for at least a week or mixed episodes. Frequently the individual also experiences a combination of elated or irritable and depressive episodes (APA, 2000). Students may be truant or experience school failure during these periods.

Mood disorders related to a general medical condition include a persistent depressed mood or irritability that is due to the physiological effects of a general medical condition (APA, 2000). This mood disorder may accompany chronic or incurable diseases such as cancer, spinal cord injury, or AIDS. For many individuals, thoughts of suicide may be present. In contrast, substance-induced mood disorders are due to the physiological

Using Technology
Learning More About Emotional Disturbance

Educators working with students with problem and challenging behaviors use the Internet to access a wide range of professional information. A good place to begin is with the Division for Children with Behavioral Disorders, part of the professional organization of the Council for Exceptional Children.

One of the best sites for beginning teachers is the National Association of School Psychologists website, where visitors can download useful pamphlets, read position papers, and join a listserv. For educators working with students with mental illness, the American Psychiatric Association is a helpful resource. This is a national medical organization whose members specialize in the diagnosis and treatment of mental and emotional illnesses and substance abuse disorders.

Questions for Reflection

1. After exploring several of these sites, compare and contrast the information available in terms of content and usefulness. Which sites do you think would be most helpful to first-year teachers?

2. What additional professional resources on problem and challenging behaviors can you find? Share the results of your search with your colleagues.

 To answer these questions and learn more about using technology to support learning, go to the Companion Website at www. prenhall.com/cohen, select Chapter 3, then choose Using Technology.

effects of drug abuse, a medication, or a toxin (APA, 2000). Characteristics of this type of mood disorder depend on the nature of the substance and when it was used.

According to *DSM-IV-TR* (2000), an individual's culture and ethnicity influence both the experience of mood disorders and the way an individual describes feelings. In some cultures, individuals experience depression in terms of physical symptoms rather than sadness. For example, people from Latino and Mediterranean cultures complain of nerves or headaches; individuals from Asian cultures speak of weakness or "imbalance"; and those from Middle Eastern cultures speak of problems of the heart.

◆ *MEET JUANITA* ◆

"I'm in the tenth grade, and for as long as I can remember, it's been hard for me to make friends. I used to feel sad and I would try really hard, but then I would say something and they'd take it the wrong way. I mean, sometimes I don't really know what to say or how to say it.

"Mr. D is my favorite teacher, but I know that I give him a hard time. I don't know why I do this—it just seems to happen. Sometimes he's really nice and shows me some cool computer stuff—like how to use this drawing program. He says that I am really good in art and design. Maybe I'll be an architect some day. But he says I've got to get my act together."

MEET JUANITA'S FOSTER PARENTS

"Juanita lived with several different families before coming to us about 5 years ago. Her mother is serving time in prison for drug dealing, and her grandmother is no longer well enough for Juanita to live with her. Previous foster placements have not worked out for Juanita. We are grateful for the state agency that has worked closely with us to help define appropriate rules and expectations while making our home a good place for Juanita. Juanita loves animals and spends a lot of time with our two dogs and several cats. As part of her chores, she is responsible for feeding and brushing them. They stand by the window, waiting each day for her to come home from school. But we also worry about Juanita. She rarely receives any messages from other teenagers in spite of our attempts to encourage her to participate in after-school activities."

STUDENTS WITH MILD AND MODERATE MENTAL RETARDATION

Students with mild and moderate mental retardation experience difficulty in the areas of academics and adaptive behaviors. Students with mild mental retardation typically experience delays in learning new information, compared to their classmates, and receive specially designed instruction that addresses their academic needs. On the other hand, students with moderate mental retardation experience substantial difficulties both academically and behaviorally. With additional support and instruction, most students acquire basic academic skills, self-help, and social skills associated with personal independence and the appropriate use of these skills to participate and be contributing members of the community.

IDEA defines mental retardation as "a condition in which there is significant subaverage general intellectual functioning, existing concurrently with deficits in adaptive behavior and manifested during the developmental period, that adversely affects a child's educational performance" (Sec. 300.7).

The *DSM* criteria further define mental retardation as occurring before age 18 and state that, in addition to subaverage intellectual functioning, an individual must have significant limitation in adaptive function in at least two of the following areas: communication self-care, home living, social/interpersonal skills, use of community resources, self-direction, functional academic skills, work, leisure, health, and safety (APA, 2000).

General intellectual functioning is assessed using one or more standardized tests that are administered to the student. School psychologists typically use the Wechsler Intelligence Scales for Children–III (Wechsler, 1991), which assesses the intellectual ability of children 6 to 16 years of age, or the Stanford-Binet Intelligence Scale (4th ed.) (Thorndike, Hagen, & Sattler, 1986). Scores on intelligence tests are reported as an intelligence quotient (IQ). Students without mental retardation, that is, students who have typical cognitive development for their age, score in the average range of 70–130 when they take an IQ test; students who have significantly subaverage functioning score 70 or below. *DSM-IV-TR* describes four degrees of severity of mental retardation based on IQ level (APA, 2000):

Mild retardation:	IQ level 50–55 to approximately 70
Moderate retardation:	IQ level 34–40 to 50–55
Severe retardation:	IQ level 20–25 to 35–40
Profound retardation:	IQ level below 20 or 25

The American Association on Mental Retardation (AAMR) (2002) defines mental retardation as ". . . a disability characterized by significant limitations both in intellectual functioning and in adaptive behavior as expressed in conceptual, social, and practical adaptive skills. This disability originates before 18" (p. 8).

The AAMR definition does not use levels of severity but rather encourages the gathering of more functional information such as supports that an individual must have. One of the criticisms, however, has been that the severity levels provide useful ways for educators, psychologists, and adult-service providers to classify individuals with mental retardation (AAMR, 2002).

Assessing a student's adaptive functioning usually includes a developmental and medical history as well as a standardized assessment that a special educator or another professional on the IEP team administers. Examples of common instruments include the Adaptive Behavior Scales and the Scales of Independent Behavior. The Adaptive Behavior Scales: School Edition: 2 (Lambert, Nihira, & Leland, 1993) assesses personal independence, coping skills, and daily living skills and may be used with children 3 to 18 years of age. The Scales of Independent Behavior-Revised (Bruininks, Woodcock, Weatherman, & Hill, 1996) assesses adaptive and problem behavior in individuals from young childhood to adulthood.

CAUSES OF MENTAL RETARDATION

Mental retardation may result from one or more factors such as chromosomal disorders, societal problems, or difficulties during pregnancy and the birth process. Chromosomal disorders may be genetic or may result from a random error during the embryo's development. In most cases, a screening test during pregnancy can identify a chromosomal disorder such as Down syndrome. Problems during pregnancy, such as the use of drugs and alcohol, can cause mental retardation. Prematurity, low birth weight, brain damage, lack of oxygen, or environmental hazards also cause mental retardation. Yet, more frequently than not, the cause of a student's mental retardation is unknown.

CHARACTERISTICS OF STUDENTS WITH MENTAL RETARDATION

Mental retardation is one of the most common disabilities; as many as 3 out of every 100 Americans have it (NICHCY, 2002). Students with mild mental retardation comprise the largest subgroup of children with mental retardation. These students develop appropriate social and oral communication skills during preschool and the early elementary grades. In fact, any limitations may not be obvious at first. In later grades, students with mild mental retardation experience more difficulties, especially in academic areas, and are slower than other children in learning new information and in acquiring new skills.

Students with moderate mental retardation comprise only about 10% of students with mental retardation (APA, 2000). Acquiring skills at a slower pace, most students with moderate mental retardation eventually develop adequate oral communication skills, functional reading, and functional mathematics. Academic work typically focuses on practical and concrete skills and knowledge. A student's IEP also includes developing and enhancing adaptive behavior skills. These skills include a collection of conceptual, social, and practical skills that all individuals need to function in their daily lives (AAMR, 2002). A student's IEP might include, for example, understanding money concepts (conceptual), avoiding victimization (social), and meal preparation (practical).

Early Signs of Mental Retardation in Preschool and Early Elementary Children

Young children with mild mental retardation may not be readily identified or may be identified as having general developmental delays, whereas children with moderate mental retardation typically exhibit significant delays across developmental areas. Infants attain developmental milestones, such as turning over, sitting, and pulling to stand, several months after the typical period for children without disabilities. In addition to motor delays, young children with moderate mental retardation develop language and self-help skills at a much slower rate. A student with moderate mental

Students with mental retardation learn best using hands-on materials.

Table 3.1	Developmental Areas Typical of Children at 6 Years of Age
Cognitive	• Sorts items on more than one dimension, such as color and shape • Identifies most letters and numerals • Counts by rote to 10 • Demonstrates beginning understanding of hour and daily routine (school begins at 9 a.m.)
Motor	Gross • Skips with alternating feet • Hops for several seconds on one foot Fine • Cuts out simple shapes • Copies own first name • Draws a person with a head, trunk, legs, arms, and features • Shows established handedness • Completes puzzles with up to 15 pieces
Social-emotional	• Engages in cooperative play
Adaptive	• Dresses self • Brushes teeth independently
Communication	• Uses pronouns, plurals, verb tenses • Uses complex sentences to carry on a conversation

Source: Adapted from *Developmental Profiles* (3rd ed.), by K. E. Allen and L. R. Marotz, 1999, Albany, NY: Delmar.

retardation who enters school often has received **early intervention services** for several years. Early intervention consists of a variety of services such as infant stimulation and developmental programs that provide parents with special assistance and show them how to encourage their child's development. As part of the program, an early intervention specialist may work with the parents in a specific area of self-help skills such as feeding and dressing or demonstrating ways to increase language development. Some early intervention programs provide center-based services whereby an early intervention specialist facilitates a toddler play group that encourages social skills, language, and cognitive development. Infants and toddlers with disorders or hereditary conditions that cause mental retardation do not receive early intervention services under the IDEA disability category *mental retardation* until they reach age 3 or older. Rather, similar to students who will later be identified as having emotional disturbance, very young children and their families receive services based on the eligibility category of *developmental delay*.

Table 3.1 illustrates the five developmental domains for young children and typical skills for children at age 6. In the early elementary grades, children with mental retardation still will be working on these skills, which other children have long since mastered. These areas usually include:

- self-help skills such as toileting, dressing, working independently, and taking responsibility for putting away materials after use;
- language development and using words to communicate;
- fine motor skills such as using scissors, markers, and crayons;
- learning colors and shapes; and
- social skills such as turn taking and sharing.

Characteristics of School-Age Students with Mental Retardation

As students with mild mental retardation advance in school, they experience decreased ability in keeping up academically and demonstrate difficulties in acquiring appropriate social and practical behaviors. Students with moderate mental retardation show significant lags in academics compared to other children of the same age. Similar to students without disabilities, though, students with mild mental retardation do not fit any one category. Some of these students may have concomitant conditions such as speech or language impairments, visual impairments, or hearing loss. Approximately one third of the children with Down syndrome have heart problems, most of which are surgically correctable (Aspen Reference Group, 1998).

Additionally, many students with mental retardation may experience poor muscle tone that, in turn, affects oral language, gross motor, and fine motor skills. Muscle strength and endurance also affect a student's physical fitness. Many children with mental retardation are overweight. Whereas one third of all Americans are overweight, almost one half of all individuals with mental retardation are overweight (Rimmer, 1996).

Academic areas. Many students with mental retardation become functional readers, learn mathematical skills, and participate in science, social studies, and other areas of the curriculum. As students advance through the grades, though, delays become more noticeable. Mental retardation decreases an individual's ability to achieve in common classroom activities such as:

- recalling previously learned material,
- explaining why an event happens,
- estimating amounts,
- predicting consequences,
- applying learned material to new situations,
- analyzing relationships, and
- comparing and contrasting two or more ideas.

To assist a student, the IEP team usually identifies one or more **supports.** Supports include other people, such as one or more students who provide friendship activities, or a teacher aide who provides behavioral support, or modifications to the environment that the IEP team identifies. Although the purpose of the support(s) is to reduce the discrepancy between the person and the environmental requirements (AAMR, 2002), educators must ensure that a person providing support does not create a situation of learned dependence. As students with mental retardation enter middle school and then secondary school, they, like their classmates without disabilities, must learn to function as independently as possible.

Figure 3.3   Skills involved in adaptive behavior

Area of Adaptive Behavior	Skill Areas
Conceptual	Language Reading and writing Money concepts Self-direction
Social	Interpersonal Responsibility Self-esteem Gullibility Naiveté Following rules Obeying laws Avoiding victimization
Practical	Activities of daily living Instrumental activities of daily living Occupational skills Maintaining safe environments

Source: Adapted from *Mental Retardation* (p. 82), American Association on Mental Retardation, 2002, Washington, DC: AAMR.

Special educators working with students with mental retardation present lessons in concrete ways. They demonstrate and provide the students with as many hands-on materials and experiences as possible. Frequently they break new tasks into small steps, teaching one step at a time. They provide demonstrations and assistance when needed. Educators also provide immediate feedback to the students regarding attempts and progress.

Adaptive behavior skills. Students with mild and moderate mental retardation have concomitant limitations in adaptive behavior skills involving three general areas: conceptual, social, and practical (AAMR, 2002). Figure 3.3 illustrates the skills involved in each of these general areas of adaptive behavior.

To meet the needs of students with moderate mental retardation, special educators need to focus on practical knowledge and skills in each of the areas of adaptive behavior. Instruction for elementary school students may include, for example, healthy food preparation, keeping the body safe from harm, and learning how to use the public transportation system. The curriculum at the high school level may include effective money management, developing good consumer skills, and obtaining medical care.

Improving the health of persons with mental retardation is a national concern. Following a national conference in 2001, a document entitled *Closing the Gap: A National Blueprint to Improve the Health of Persons with Mental Retardation* was issued that details public concerns. Compared to people without mental retardation, children, adolescents, and adults with mental retardation experience poorer health and more difficulty in finding appropriate care (p. 2). To address these concerns, the Health Resources and Services Administration, the March of Dimes, the American Academy of Pediatrics, and Family Voices are promoting a 10-year plan for appropriate community-based services for children and youth with special health care needs.

Emotional disorders. Educators and other individuals often describe students with mental retardation as happy and content. This is far from the truth. Similar to students without cognitive impairments, students with mental retardation are at risk for emotional disorders. In fact, some researchers have found a higher rate of depression in individuals with mental retardation (McBrien, 2003), and particularly depression in individuals with Down syndrome (Khan, Osinowo, & Pary, 2002).

Motor coordination. Both fine and gross motor activities require an individual to maintain a certain level of muscle tension, or muscle tone, in the legs, arms, or fingers. Some disorders that result in mental retardation have associated low muscle tone or other physical conditions that impact a student's motor skills. Lack of muscle tone affects not only handwriting but also other fine motor tasks such as pouring a solution into a beaker during science class or using a mouse to select the desired Web choice.

Gross motor skills may be affected too. Low muscle tone makes it difficult to run and play competitive games. Lack of opportunity, combined with lack of success, frequently creates conditions in which students are discouraged from pursuing interests that involve high levels of activity. In school, being clumsy and awkward may make it difficult to walk carefully around a crowded classroom without bumping into or knocking over materials.

Speech and communication. Students with mental retardation frequently have difficulty in producing and using the sounds of oral language. In fact, speech and language impairments are frequently associated with mental retardation. Some students have articulation disorders, making it difficult to produce the correct sounds. Because the tongue is a muscle, students with low muscle tone frequently have difficulty in articulating many speech sounds.

Being able to produce speech, though, doesn't imply that a student understands and can apply the "social rules" or pragmatics of language. Special education services often include instruction on learning conversational skills to be a friend and a good worker. Instruction may include areas such as sharing, showing consideration for others, and appropriate ways to refuse a request.

Some students with moderate mental retardation have significant difficulties in using expressive language to communicate with others. Their education program may include using an augmentative or alternative communication system. The special educator will work closely with the speech and language pathologist to assist the student in learning how to use the communication system in the classroom, at home, and in the community.

Attention and memory. Students with mental retardation experience attention and memory problems. They may have difficulty maintaining concentration or they may attend to the wrong thing during classroom teaching and learning activities. Students also have difficulty remembering information. Memory difficulties include not only short- and long-term memory problems but also the ability to maintain current information in working memory to complete a task or activity. In later chapters, we will examine teaching methods and strategies that educators use to help students with mental retardation.

Using Technology
Augmentative or Alternative Communication Systems

Some students with moderate mental retardation require augmentative or alternative communication systems (AAC) because of difficulties or delays in the use of expressive language. An AAC may be as simple as a card with letters or words that a student uses by pointing to the symbols to communicate a thought or request. Other AAC systems use digitized speech to produce a real voice and dynamic displays to access and store hundreds of words, phrases, and sentences. Words + and DynaVox are two examples of AAC devices. AACs are considered AT. As with other AT devices, the student's IEP team can recommend an AAC during the annual IEP meeting. By using a Web search engine, you can locate a wealth of information about AACs.

Questions for Reflection

1. What websites would you recommend for educators who wish to learn more about AAC devices? Share your information with your colleagues.
2. What websites would be helpful for parents?

To answer these questions and learn more about using technology to support learning, go to the Companion Website at www. prenhall.com/cohen, select Chapter 3, then choose Using Technology.

❖ MEET KEISHA ❖

"My name is Keisha. I am in the ninth grade. I like my teachers. I like cheering. I am a cheerleader manager. I like to eat at McDonald's."

MEET KEISHA'S MOTHER

"As you can see from Keisha's comments above, she is brief and to the point when someone asks her a question. She is so excited about being a team manager for the cheering squad this year. She goes to all the games, both home and away, and wears the team jersey everywhere. The boys and girls give her plenty of 'high fives' during the games. It's been a great experience for her.

"I am pleased with her work in school this year. She is continuing to work on her reading and writing skills, and she can recognize many signs out in the community now. She works with the special education teacher for much of the school day, but she takes food services with all the other ninth graders who have chosen this elective. I hope that someday when she finishes school, she can find a job working in one of our local restaurants. We have started planning the skills that she will need to obtain and keep a job during the IEP team meetings. Finding a good job after school and a place to live on her own is what worries me the most now."

Using Technology
Learning More About Mental Retardation

Teachers working with children with disabilities frequently come across diagnoses with which they are not familiar. When one first-year teacher learned that one of his students had Turner's syndrome, he turned to the Internet for more information about this condition. There are many professional organizations where educators can learn more about mental retardation.

First, the Council for Exceptional Children, Division on Developmental Disabilities, provides information on publications and conferences as well as a large collection of links to other organizations on developmental disabilities. Next, one of the best-known national organizations, the AAMR, is an excellent overall resource. The Arc of the United States, another national association, focuses on both children and adults with mental retardation.

When educators begin planning transition services, they often start with the National Transition Alliance for Youth with Disabilities. Its website provides resources that promote the transition of youth with disabilities from school to the community, including employment, postsecondary education and training, and independent living. Parents often find this site helpful, too. Another excellent resource for transition planning is the National Institute on Life Planning for Persons with Disabilities. At its website, visitors can learn more about person-centered planning for persons with disabilities and their families.

Questions for Reflection

1. After exploring several of these sites, compare and contrast the information available in terms of content and usefulness. Which sites do you think would be most helpful to first-year teachers?
2. What additional professional resources on mental retardation can you find? Share the results of your search with your colleagues.

 To answer these questions and learn more about using technology to support learning, go to the Companion Website at www. prenhall.com/cohen, select Chapter 3, then choose Using Technology.

STUDENTS WITH AUTISM SPECTRUM DISORDERS

Students with autism spectrum disorders exhibit a range of neurological disorders characterized by significant impairment in several areas of development, including social interaction and communications skills. A symptom may be mild in one child and severe in another. Professionals identify autism spectrum disorders during a child's first 3 years. According to IDEA, autism is "a developmental disability significantly affecting verbal and nonverbal communication and social interaction, generally evident before age 3, that adversely affects a child's educational performance (Sec. 300.7).

According to *DSM-IV-TR*, autism is considered to be a *pervasive developmental disorder,* an umbrella term that also includes Rett syndrome, Asperger's syndrome, and pervasive developmental disorder not otherwise specified (PDD-NOS) (Table 3.2). Each of these disorders has specific diagnostic criteria (APA, 2000).

The *DSM* diagnostic criteria for autism include significantly impaired development in social interaction and communication and markedly restricted activities and interests (APA, 2000). In most cases, children with autism have associated mental retardation. These children also have a range of behaviors, including hyperactivity, short

| Table 3.2 | **Autism and Other Pervasive Developmental Disorders** |

	Age of Onset	**Characteristics**
Autism	Delays or abnormal functioning in social interaction, language, or symbolic or imaginative play by age 3.	Marked difficulty in social interaction, communication, and development of interests.
Asperger's Syndrome	Onset often recognized in school.	Similar to autism but no significant delays in language or cognitive development. Difficulties in social interaction may be noted in school.
Childhood Disintegrative Disorder	After age 2 (and a period of typical early childhood development) but before age 10.	Similar to autism and usually associated with severe mental retardation.
Pervasive Developmental Disorder Not Otherwise Specified	Later age of onset than autism (often used for *atypical autism* because of later age of onset or atypical symptoms).	Similar to autism.
Rett Syndrome	Onset by age 4 after a period of typical early childhood development.	Stereotyped hand movements, lack of coordination, severe impairment in expressive and receptive language development, usually associated with mental retardation.

Source: Adapted from *DSM-IV-TR,* 4th ed. (pp. 69–84), American Psychiatric Association, 2000, Washington, DC: APA.

attention span, aggressiveness, and self-injurious behavior. They may be oversensitive to sounds, light, odors, or touch. In adolescence, children with autism who have the intellectual capability of insight and self-understanding may become depressed when they realize the seriousness of their disorder (APA, 2000).

Autism is the most common pervasive developmental disorder, affecting 1 to 2 people in every 1,000; its incidence is growing rapidly, at a rate of 10–17% a year (Autism Society of America, 2003). Although no one knows why the United States and other countries are experiencing a rise in autism, the increase will continue to impact our schools for years. Interestingly, autism is three to four times more common in boys than in girls. Girls with the disorder, however, tend to have more severe symptoms and decreased cognitive skills (National Institute of Mental Health, 1997).

Individuals with autism may have concomitant disorders that create additional educational programming challenges. These include ADHD, depressive disorders, obsessive-compulsive disorder, and anxiety disorders. About one third of children and adolescents with autism develop seizures (National Institute of Mental Health, 2001).

CAUSES OF AUTISM

Although much remains to be learned about autism spectrum disorders, most experts accept that these disorders are caused by abnormalities in brain structure or function (National Institute of Mental Health, 1997). Researchers at the National Institute of Mental Health are investigating how the brain differs in people with and without autism. One line of research is focusing on defects that occur during initial brain development. Other research is examining abnormalities in brain structures such as the amygdala, which is known to regulate aspects of social and emotional behavior (National Institute of Mental Health, 1997).

CHARACTERISTICS OF STUDENTS WITH AUTISM

Early Signs of Autism in Preschool and Early Elementary Children

Early warning signs of autism may be recognized in very young children. Infants may avoid eye contact and may not respond to a parent's voice. As toddlers they do not develop language. Young children may appear fixated on a toy or activity, rock, or flap their hands. Like other young children we have read about in this chapter, children with autism frequently come to kindergarten having received several years of early intervention services. These services may involve in-home support or therapeutic interventions in an early-care or education program. Some young children may attend a special-purpose preschool program prior to coming to public school.

Characteristics of School-Age Students with Autism

Students with autism often are obsessed with sameness or routine. They may treat others in ritualized ways. They may be able to remember long lists, such as bus schedules or the exact words of a variety of commercials, but the information tends to be repeated over and over, even in situations that are not appropriate.

Social skills. Students with autism have difficulty developing relationships and communicating with others. Their continued lack of eye contact and delayed language skills are often misinterpreted by others and affect their ability to make and keep friends; they prefer to be left alone. Students with autism do not relate well to others. For example, they may

- prefer solitary activities,
- lack awareness of others,
- lack social skills to develop friendships, and
- show little interest in and enjoyment of others.

Communication. Students with autism usually have difficulty with both spoken language and nonverbal skills such as gestures and eye contact. Students with milder forms

Students with autism, like students without disabilities, enjoy using technology to build literacy skills.

of autism may use speech but rarely initiate a conversation with other students. Their speech is characterized by lack of rhythm and intonation. Middle and secondary students lack an understanding of the use of social language and of how to make and keep a friend.

Students with more involved autism usually have a delay in the use of expressive and receptive language. They respond inconsistently; they appear to hear at some times but not at others. They may not be able to understand simple directions or questions, and their speech is characterized by repetitive language that is difficult to understand. Students who have even more involved autism not only do not develop speech, they do not communicate without specific intervention.

Thus, one of the goals of the IEP is to teach the student how to communicate. Special educators work closely with other team members, such as the speech and language pathologist and the consulting school psychologist, to design, develop, and implement a student's communication program. For example, children and youth with autism learn how to use a picture exchange communication system (PECS). Using picture cards, a student learns to communicate by selecting a card to indicate a desired activity, thought, or idea. Research findings (Kravits, Kamps, Kemmerer, & Potucek, 2002; Schwartz, Garfinkle, & Bauer, 1998) indicate that children with autism not only can learn to use PECS quickly and effectively but can also generalize the use of PECS to untrained settings.

Restricted repertoire of behaviors and interests. Restricted and repetitive behaviors and a persistent preoccupation with an object or activity are often seen when students with autism are left alone. In the classroom, teachers see stereotyped body movements such as hand flapping, toe walking, rocking, or preoccupation with parts of objects such as the top of a pen or a frayed corner of a book. Students generally prefer (and may insist on) a routine.

❖ MEET RAUL'S BROTHER ❖

"Raul's my brother, and since he can't speak, I'll tell you a little about him. He has autism. That means that I have to help him a lot. He's 5 years old and goes to my school, but he's in a special class. His teacher is real nice, and she is helping him learn. She's teaching him how to use these pictures to let her know what he wants, and she sends the pictures home with Raul in his backpack. Raul likes to watch me play games on the computer and I try to show him how to use the mouse, but usually he just likes to look at the screen."

MEET RAUL'S MOTHER

"When Raul was a baby, I wondered why he seemed to be so different from his older brother. When he didn't start talking, I spoke to the pediatrician about my concerns. He examined Raul and told me that sometimes children take a little longer to achieve these milestones than others. But I couldn't stop being a little worried. At home, Raul would scream at times and it was so hard to comfort him. I didn't know if he was sick or if he was trying to tell me something. My next visit to the pediatrician, I talked again about how worried I was, and the doctor decided to make arrangements for us to go to an evaluation clinic to get Raul tested. I think Raul was about 2½ years old then.

"The testing lasted many hours, and several different people saw Raul. I remember having to fill out a lot of forms and answer a lot of questions. Afterward, one of the doctors who had done some of the testing sat with me and explained that Raul had many characteristics of autism. I hardly knew what autism was, but the doctor was very patient and answered a lot of my questions. At first, I didn't know what to do. I didn't know how I was going to tell our relatives, and I was afraid of how they would react. It was very hard on everyone.

"But we started to learn all we could about autism. I spent days on the Internet searching for information, and then I met another parent who also has a son with autism. That has helped a lot—to be able to talk with someone who understands what we are going through. Then Raul started to receive special early intervention services. That was the best thing. A teacher came to our house and taught me ways to help Raul when he started screaming.

"Later, Raul was enrolled in an early education program at our elementary school. He loves his teacher and is learning so much. We are very excited that he is learning how to communicate by using a picture exchange communication system. The teacher calls this *PECS.*"

CHARACTERISTICS OF STUDENTS WITH ASPERGER'S SYNDROME

Students with Asperger's syndrome have characteristics that generally fall on the mild end of the autism spectrum. As with autism, there is a higher prevalence of boys than girls with Asperger's syndrome; yet, unlike children with other forms of autism, children with Asperger's syndrome are identified after age 3. Young children experience typical cognitive development and no marked delays in language development. However, they often have difficulty with pragmatics, or the use of social language. For example, they do not understand the social cues and give-and-take of conversation.

Similar to students with autism, students with Asperger's syndrome may have repetitive and restrictive behaviors. For example, they often have obsessive routines, such as where food is placed on the plate. They may be preoccupied with a particular subject, wishing to talk about it incessantly. Often the parent is the first to observe these behaviors or language concerns and raises questions with the child's doctor. To diagnose Asperger's syndrome, psychologists use the following *DSM-IV-TR* criteria:

A. Qualitative impairment in social interaction, as manifested by at least two of the following:
 1. marked impairment in the use of multiple nonverbal behaviors such as eye-to-eye gaze, facial expression, body postures, and gestures to regulate social interaction
 2. failure to develop peer relationships appropriate to developmental level
 3. a lack of spontaneous seeking to share enjoyment, interests, or achievements with other people (e.g., by a lack of showing, bringing, or pointing out objects of interest to other people)
 4. lack of social or emotional reciprocity
B. Restricted, repetitive, and stereotyped patterns of behavior, interests, and activities, as manifested by at least one of the following:
 1. encompassing preoccupation with one or more stereotyped and restricted patterns of interest that is abnormal either in intensity or focus
 2. apparently inflexible adherence to specific, nonfunctional routines or rituals
 3. stereotyped and repetitive motor mannerisms (e.g., hand or finger flapping or twisting, or complex whole-body movements)
 4. persistent preoccupation with parts of objects
C. The disturbance causes clinically significant impairment in social, occupational, or other important areas of functioning.
D. There is no clinically significant general delay in language (e.g., single words used by age 2 years, communicative phrases used by age 3 years).
E. There is no clinically significant delay in cognitive development or in the development of age-appropriate self-help skills, adaptive behavior (other than in social interaction), and curiosity about the environment in childhood.
F. Criteria are not met for another specific Pervasive Developmental Disorder or Schizophrenia.*

Many students with Asperger's syndrome have exceptional skills or talents but are considered strange by their peers. As the years go on, these characteristics become more obvious and eccentric. As a result, students with Asperger's syndrome are often at risk for being bullied and teased.

*Reprinted with permission from the *Diagnostic and Statistical Manual of Mental Disorders,* Text Revision, p. 84, Copyright © 2000, American Psychiatric Association.

Using Technology

Learning More About Autism Spectrum Disorders

The Autism Society of America promotes opportunities for individuals across the autism spectrum and their families through advocacy, public awareness, education, and research. Its website is a rich source of information about autism, early intervention, educational placements and IEPs, transition, and various specialized instructional techniques and interventions.

The National Institute of Mental Health has a number of print and online publications with the latest research and information about this disability. The materials are well written and useful for beginning teachers or for families of students with autism. This site has extensive links to other resources.

Autism Resources is a website that allows the user to search for information by state. The site provides links to organizations and specialized techniques for working with students with autism. If you are interested in the global nature of this disability and worldwide resources, the National Autistic Society provides links to national and international organizations for children, adolescents, and adults with autism throughout the world.

For individuals who are looking for more in-depth information, MedLine Plus Health Information is a rich source of information about the other disorders associated with autism spectrum disorders, including Rett and Asperger's syndromes.

Questions for Reflection

1. After exploring several of these sites, compare and contrast the information available in terms of content and usefulness. Which sites do you think would be most helpful to first-year teachers?

2. What additional professional resources on autism spectrum disorders can you find? Share the results of your search with your colleagues.

 To answer these questions and learn more about using technology to support learning, go to the Companion Website at www.prenhall.com/cohen, select Chapter 3, then choose Using Technology.

❖ MEET SIDNEY ❖

"I am in the sixth grade. My favorite subject is math. I am in the math club at school. I like doing math. Numbers add up. Numbers and patterns. I want to go to college and maybe go into computer science. My hobby is playing the drums. I've been playing since I was 7 years old. Drums and music. I like that. Sometimes kids make fun of me, but they don't understand about drums and music."

MEET SIDNEY'S MOTHER

"Shortly before Sidney's fourth birthday, he was diagnosed with Asperger's syndrome. Sidney was not a cuddly baby, and as a toddler and preschooler he seemed more clumsy than the other children. Today he's still uncoordinated—but maybe this is just part of preadolescence.

"Sidney participates in the regular sixth-grade class and works with the special educator for about an hour each day on social skills. We hope that this will help him interact more appropriately with other students. Sidney has a few rituals that sometimes other children don't understand. For example, he likes to line up the books in the classroom library a certain way. As a result of this behavior, some of the children have said mean things and bullied him on the playground. Last week I had another meeting at school to discuss these concerns. On the other hand, Sidney is so smart in math. The other day he and I went grocery shopping, and before the clerk had run the items through the checkout, he had calculated the total in his head.

"One organization that has helped us greatly is the Asperger Syndrome Coalition of the United States. This organization has helped us connect with other families and understand more about Sidney's condition. Through the organization, Sidney, too, has been able to meet other students with Asperger's syndrome."

SUMMARY

- Knowledge of the causes and characteristics of specific mild and moderate disabilities, including emotional disturbance, mental retardation, and autism spectrum disorders, provides special educators with a foundation for assessing student skills and knowledge and for planning instruction.
- Developing an understanding of these general characteristics allows special educators to address the academic, social, and behavioral problems of these students.
- Special educators must develop awareness and skills in working with students from diverse cultures who have both mild and moderate disabilities.
- No two students are alike. In fact, each student has unique skills, knowledge, abilities, gifts—and needs. Understanding the characteristics of the learner is one of the cornerstones for building successful teaching and learning experiences. A vast array of Web sources assist beginning educators in developing greater understanding of students with mild and moderate disabilities.

EXTENDING LEARNING

1. Investigate how your state identifies students with moderate disabilities. Are students identified by a specific disability category? If so, what terms do special educators use? If not, describe the process that special educators use.

2. With a small group of classmates, make arrangements to interview special educators who work with children or youth who have moderate disabilities in various schools. What types of disabilities do the students have? What are some of the characteristics? Collect and collate your information across age levels. Present your findings to the class.

3. Identify the characteristics of learners whom you think would present the greatest challenges to you as a teacher. What additional information would you want to know

about these students? What resources can you identify that would assist you in working with students with moderate disabilities?

4. Select one area of disability discussed in this chapter and search the Internet for additional information on student characteristics. Share your findings with the class.

5. Students with moderate disabilities may use PECS. Collect more information about PECS by interviewing professionals such as a speech and language pathologist or a special educator and conducting an Internet search.

REFERENCES

Allen, K. E., & Marotz, L. R. (1999). *Developmental profiles* (3rd ed.). Albany, NY: Delmar.

American Association on Mental Retardation. (2002). *Mental retardation* (10th ed.). Washington, DC: Author.

American Psychiatric Association. (2000). *Diagnostic and statistical manual of mental disorders* (4th ed., text revision). Washington, DC: Author.

Aspen Reference Group. (1998). *Caregiver education guide for children with developmental disabilities.* Gaithersburg, MD: Author.

Autism Society of America. (2003). *What is autism?* Retrieved August 6, 2003, from http://www.autism-society.org/site/PageServer?pagename=whatisautism

Bruininks, R. H., Woodcock, R. W., Weatherman, R. F., & Hill, B. K. (1996). *Scales of independent behavior–revised.* Itasca, IL: Riverside.

Closing the gap: A national blueprint to improve the health of persons with mental retardation. (2001). Retrieved December 3, 2003, from the National Institute of Child Health and Human Development website: http://www.nichd.nih.gov/publications/pubs/closingthegap/sub5.htm

Froschl, M., & Sprung, B. (1999). On purpose: Addressing teasing and bullying in early childhood. *Young Children, 54*(2), 70–72.

Individuals with Disabilities Education Act Amendments (Pub. L. No. 105–17). (1997). 20 U.S.C. Secs. 1400 *et. seq.* Washington, DC: U.S. Government Printing Office.

Jacobs, D., & Reyhner, J. (2002, January). *Preparing teachers to support American Indian and Alaska Native student success and cultural heritage.* Charleston, WV: ERIC/CRESS. (ERIC Document Reproduction Service No. ED459990)

Khan, S., Osinowo, T., & Pary, R. J. (2002). Down syndrome and major depressive disorder: A review. *Mental Health Aspects of Developmental Disabilities, 5*(2), 46–52.

Kravits, T. R., Kamps, D. M., Kemmerer, K., & Potucek, J. (2002). Brief report: Increasing communication skills for an elementary-aged student with autism using the picture exchange communication system. *Journal of Autism and Developmental Disorders, 32*(3), 225–230.

Lambert, N. H., Nihira, K., & Leland, H. (1993). *Adaptive behavior scales—school edition: 2.* Austin, TX: PRO-ED.

Lane-Garon, P. (2001). *Classroom and conflict management.* Paper presented at the annual meeting of the Association of Teacher Educators, Denver, February 2–6, 2001. Charleston, WV: ERIC/CRESS. (ERIC Document Reproduction Service No. ED465716)

Marion, M. (1997). Guiding young children's understanding and management of anger. *Young Children, 52*(7), 62–67.

McBrien, J. A. (2003). Assessment and diagnosis of depression in people with intellectual disability. *Journal of Intellectual Disability Research, 47*(10), 1–13.

National Center for Cultural Competence. (1999–2002). *Conceptual frameworks/models, guiding values and principles.* Retrieved November 21, 2003, from the Georgetown University website: http://gucchd.georgetown.edu//nccc/framework.html

National Information Center for Children with Disabilities. (2002). *Mental retardation.* Retrieved December 3, 2003, from http://www.nichcy.org/pubs/factshe/fs8txt.htm

National Institute of Mental Health. (1997). *Autism* (NIH Publication No. 97-4023). Washington, DC: Author.

National Institute of Mental Health. (2001). *Unraveling autism* (NIH Publication No. 01-4590). Washington, DC: Author.

Rimmer, J. H. (1996). *Physical fitness in people with mental retardation.* Retrieved December 3, 2003, from the Arc website: http://thearc.org/faqs/fitness.html.

Schwartz, I. S., Garfinkle, A. N., & Bauer, J. (1998). The picture exchange communication system: Communicative outcomes for young children with disabilities. *Topics in Early Childhood Special Education, 18*(3), 144–159.

Schwartz, W. (2001). *School practices for equitable discipline of African American students.* New York: ERIC Clearinghouse on Urban Education. (ERIC Document Reproduction Service No. ED423096)

Sheets, R. (2002). You're just a kid that's here: Chicano perception of disciplinary events. *Journal of Latinos and Education, 1*(2), 105–122.

Thorndike, R. L., Hagen, E. P., & Sattler, J. M. (1986). *Stanford-Binet intelligence scale* (4th ed.). Itasca, IL: Riverside.

Wechsler, D. (1991). *Wechsler intelligence scale for children* (3rd ed.). San Antonio, TX: Psychological Corporation.

How Teachers Teach

4

Chapter

Assessing Students with Mild and Moderate Disabilities

CHAPTER OBJECTIVES

After completing this chapter, you should be able to:

❖ Discuss the assessment approaches that special educators use to plan, monitor, and evaluate instruction for students with disabilities.

❖ Compare and contrast contemporary assessment approaches for linking instruction with assessment.

❖ Identify and explain the scoring systems used with curriculum-based assessment, probes, error analysis, teacher-developed quizzes and exams, performance-based assessments, and portfolios.

❖ Discuss reliability and validity considerations.

❖ Discuss ways educators use technology in linking instruction with assessment.

❖ Demonstrate understanding of diversity perspectives related to assessment practices.

Good teaching always begins with an understanding of what the student already knows and can do. Before special educators start to plan specific instruction, they identify questions and gather information about the student's knowledge, skills, and abilities. For example, the teacher will want to know what information the student already knows and what skills the student has and can use independently.

This practice continues during instructional activities and, later, at the end of the activities or instructional unit. By linking assessment with instruction, an educator can use student assessment information to make decisions regarding the need for planning new content instruction, providing additional instruction, or modifying content. In other words, the assessment information helps inform teaching practices.

Finally, assessments that are closely aligned with the curriculum provide a special educator with helpful information in monitoring student progress. By examining this assessment information, the educator can identify areas of mastery and areas of progress. Conversely, assessment information also indicates areas in which the student needs attention, signaling the teacher that adjustments should be made in instruction.

According to Shepard (as cited in Olson, 2002, p. 2), "We have strong evidence that high-quality classroom assessment improves learning tremendously, possibly more effectively than any other sort of teaching intervention." Today educators can select from a variety of assessment approaches, implement the assessment, and then use the assessment information to continually inform instruction. In this chapter, we will examine the ways that a special educator links assessment with instruction to help each student with a disability meet high academic standards, develop positive behaviors, and demonstrate effective social skills.

CONTEMPORARY VIEWS OF LEARNING

Learning about assessment involves understanding contemporary views of learning and knowledge of professional standards in educational assessment. Contemporary views of learning have influenced both our teaching and assessment practices. A basic belief is that learning is a developmental process in which students construct knowledge and new understandings based on past learning and experiences. As children grow, new understandings are influenced by their society and culture. Contemporary writers describe learning and the important role that the social milieu and culture play. Lee and Smagorinsky (2000) describe the acquisition of knowledge as internally constructed and socially and culturally mediated.

Other individuals, especially peers, greatly influence learning. In fact, working with peers, children and youth can construct knowledge through collaborative efforts with others (Lave & Wenger, 1991; Pea, 1993). Learning with others can positively affect motivation, enthusiasm, optimism (Covington, 1998; Slavin & Madden, 2001), self-esteem, self-concept, and expectations.

PROFESSIONAL STANDARDS IN EDUCATIONAL ASSESSMENT

Because assessment is closely linked to instruction, special educators have an obligation to meet the standards for teacher competence in educational assessment. Developed by several professional organizations (the American Federation of Teachers, the National Council on Measurement in Education, and the National Education Association), these professional standards describe the skills and knowledge that educators should have regarding assessment practices. Figure 4.1 illustrates these educational assessment standards for all educators. In becoming skilled in assessment, beginning teachers learn about various assessment approaches and their advantages and limitations. They learn how to use assessment to make instructional decisions and how to communicate the results to students and their parents.

LINKING ASSESSMENT WITH INSTRUCTION

 Linking assessment with instruction is an ongoing process that begins before instruction. For example, Tory Sadler, a special educator, uses the results of classroom assessments to identify the learning goals within each curriculum area for the student. During instruction, he uses assessment information to plan additional instruction or to move on to new content. Prior to, during, and after instruction, Tory collects information about student achievement, skills, or behaviors. This information is then given as feedback to students, parents, and other team members.

Figure 4.1   Standards for teacher competence in educational assessment of students

1. Teachers should be skilled in choosing assessment methods appropriate for instructional decisions.
2. Teachers should be skilled in developing assessment methods appropriate for instructional decisions.
3. The teacher should be skilled in administering, scoring, and interpreting the results of both externally-produced and teacher-produced assessment methods.
4. Teachers should be skilled in using assessment results when making decisions about individual students, planning teaching, developing curriculum, and school improvement.
5. Teachers should be skilled in developing valid pupil grading procedures which use pupil assessments.
6. Teachers should be skilled in communicating assessment results to students, parents, other lay audiences, and other educators.
7. Teachers should be skilled in recognizing unethical, illegal, and otherwise inappropriate assessment methods and uses of assessment information.

Source: From *Standards for Teacher Competence in Educational Assessment of Students,* by the American Federation of Teachers, National Council on Measurement in Education, and the National Education Association, 1990.

Special educators must also acquire knowledge of the assessment requirements for students with disabilities as mandated by IDEA. In this chapter, we will begin by examining the federal requirements regarding assessing students to determine eligibility for special education services. Next, we will examine the various assessment approaches that special educators and other team members use to plan instruction, monitor, and evaluate student progress. Then we will see how special educators select various assessment approaches to measure learning outcomes.

FEDERAL MANDATES: ASSESSMENT AND STUDENTS WITH DISABILITIES

IDEA requirements specify assessment procedures and time lines, including the criteria for eligibility for special education services, how the services will be determined, and how student progress will be reviewed. These regulations also describe parents' rights and opportunities during the assessment process (Figure 4.2) and ensure that students with disabilities will have the services that they require.

REFERRALS AND INITIAL EVALUATIONS

IDEA mandates a referral and assessment process that we will discuss in the following section. However, many schools go beyond the minimum requirements of the law, such as adding a prereferral process before a student is referred to the multidisciplinary team that you read about in Chapter 2. The prereferral process helps some students and they do not require further interventions, whereas at other times, some students will continue to have difficulty. We pick up the process here.

When a student continues to have difficulty with the general education curriculum over a period of time, even with teaching interventions, the parent is notified and the general education teacher completes a written referral form. Concerned parents or the student may also complete a written referral to the IEP team (IDEA 34 C.F.R.,

Figure 4.2   Parents' rights and opportunities during the assessment process

Parent rights:

- Written notice must be given before the school initiates or changes (or refuses to initiate or change) the identification, evaluation, or educational placement of the child.
- Written notices must be provided in the native language of the parent or via another mode of communication used by the parent unless it is clearly not feasible to do so.
- A copy of procedural safeguards must be given
  - upon initial referral for evaluation,
  - upon each notification of an IEP meeting, and
  - upon reevaluation of the child.
- Parents may request an independent educational evaluation of their child at public expense.

Parent consent must be obtained:

- Before conducting an initial evaluation or reevaluation.
- At initial provision of special education and related services.

Parent opportunities:

- Inspect and review all educational records with regard to identification, evaluation, and educational placement of their child.
- Participate in meetings with regard to the identification, evaluation, and educational placement of their child.

Source: From IDEA 34 C.F.R., Secs. 300.503, 300.504, 300.343, and 300.501.

Sec. 300.16). Team members can include the student, parents, or other family members, and professionals in many disciplines, such as education, social work, psychology, health, speech and language pathology, physical therapy, or occupational therapy. Upon receiving a referral, team members review any existing assessment information, including student records, information provided by the parents of the student, current classroom-based assessments, and observations by teachers and related services providers. Based on this information and on input from the student's parents, the team identifies any additional information that they need to determine whether or not the student has a disability.

If the team decides that additional student assessment is needed, they must consider the student's native language. According to IDEA, evaluation of the student is conducted in the language normally used by the student (Sec. 300.19). No matter what assessment approaches are used, the IEP team should be able to ensure that the procedures are responsive to diversity (Figure 4.3).

DETERMINING THE PRESENT LEVEL OF PERFORMANCE

When the team determines that a student is eligible for special education services, members identify and gather any additional information to determine the student's

Considering Diversity

Representation of Culturally Diverse Groups

For many years, educators have been concerned that students from some racial and ethnic groups are being disproportionately identified as needing special education services. Unfortunately, many of these concerns continue to exist today. According to a report issued by the National Academy of Sciences (Donovan & Cross, 2002), many inequities continue to exist across the states and within individual school districts associated with the process of referring students and determining eligibility for special education services. To address overrepresentation, the National Alliance of Black School Educators and the IDEA Local Implementation by Local Administrators Partnership (2002) recommends:

- establishing an appropriate prereferral intervention process to provide students with support that keeps them participating and progressing in the general education curriculum,
- understanding the effect of school climate on educational progress, and
- involving families and learning from them how to understand and respect their child's unique learning strengths, needs, and cultural background.

Questions for Reflection

1. Compare and contrast two or more forms used to refer students to the multidisciplinary team. How do they differ?
2. Using an Internet search engine, locate information about how a school determines eligibility for special education services. Make a chart depicting how different schools in different locations use similar and different procedures.

 To answer these questions and deepen your understanding of diversity in schools and communities, go to the Companion Website at www.prenhall.com/cohen, select Chapter 4, then choose Considering Diversity.

Figure 4.3   Ways that team members can ensure the cultural competence of the special education assessment process

- Team members identify and use multiple assessment tools and strategies that are research-based and culturally competent.
- Team members receive training in the administration of assessment tools and methods that consider the student's culture and background.
- Professionals who are knowledgeable about students' cultures conduct assessments with those students.

Source: Adapted from *Addressing Over-Representation of African American Students in Special Education,* the National Alliance of Black School Educators and IDEA Local Implementation by Local Administrators Partnership, 2002, Arlington, VA: Council for Exceptional Children.

present level of performance. The special educator and other team members use a variety of assessment approaches to determine the student's knowledge of academic content areas, skills, abilities, and behaviors. The special educator, for example, may assess the student's reading level and comprehension, the student's skills in solving word problems, the student's ability to use a graphing program, and the student's behaviors in working cooperatively with peers. IDEA specifies requirements for these tests and other assessments (Sec. 300.532; see Figure 4.4).

USING ASSESSMENT INFORMATION IN THE INDIVIDUALIZED EDUCATION PROGRAM

IEP team members use information collected by various assessment approaches in developing, reviewing, or revising the student's IEP. For example, they gather information about the student's behaviors or social skills using informal assessment,

Figure 4.4   IDEA requirements for tests and other evaluation materials used to assess a student to determine eligibility for special education services

1. Tests and other evaluation materials used to assess a child
   • Are selected and administered so as not to be discriminatory on a racial or cultural basis; and
   • Are provided and administered in the child's native language or other mode of communication, unless it is clearly not feasible to do so.
2. Materials and procedures used to assess a child with limited English proficiency are selected and administered to ensure that they measure the extent to which the child has a disability and needs special education, rather than measuring the child's English language skills.
3. A variety of assessment tools and strategies are used to gather relevant functional and developmental information about the child, including information provided by the parent, and information related to enabling the child to be involved in and progress in the general curriculum.
4. Any standardized tests that are given have been validated for the specific purpose for which they are used and are administered by trained and knowledgeable personnel in accordance with any instructions provided by the producer of the tests.
5. Tests and other evaluation materials include those tailored to assess specific areas of educational need and not merely those that are designed to provide a single general intelligence quotient.
6. Tests are selected and administered so as to best ensure that if a test is administered to a child with impaired sensory, manual, or speaking skills, the test results accurately reflect the child's aptitude or achievement level rather than reflecting the child's impaired sensory, manual, or speaking skills (unless those skills are the factors to be measured).
7. No single procedure is used as the sole criterion for determining whether a child has a disability.
8. The child is assessed in all areas related to the suspected disability.
9. Evaluation is comprehensive.
10. The school uses technically sound instruments.
11. The school uses assessment tools and strategies that provide relevant information that directly assists persons in determining the education needs of the child.

Source: From Individuals with Disabilities Education Act Amendments, 1997.

such as classroom observations or teacher, parent, and student interviews or commercially published checklists. Other assessments, such as curriculum-based assessments, criterion-referenced tests, and performance-based assessments, provide information about a student's academic knowledge and abilities.

Curriculum-based assessments, sometimes known as *curriculum-based evaluation,* assist teachers in determining a student's strengths and weaknesses in reading, mathematics, science, social studies, or other content areas. Educators also use criterion-referenced tests to measure an area of the curriculum or the student's behavior. **Criterion-referenced tests** measure the student's performance with respect to a specific content domain, such as knowledge of mathematical operations. Teachers also use teacher-made tests that provide feedback to students as well as teachers concerning progress. **Performance-based assessments** enable students to demonstrate their knowledge, skills, and abilities. Student–teacher discussions provide additional information about student understanding and learning.

Team members also examine the results of recent evaluations, including standardized norm-referenced tests, and look for patterns of achievement over time. A **standardized test** is one in which the administration, scoring, and interpretation procedures are strictly followed. Aptitude and achievement assessments are examples of standardized tests. **Norm-referenced instruments** are commercially published tests that compare a student's test performance with that of similar students who have taken the same test. Finally, the IEP team considers the results of the student's performance on any general district- or statewide assessment programs (IDEA 34 C.F.R., Sec. 300.346). Comprehensive assessment information helps team members as they develop the IEP and determine the type and amount of special education services the student needs. Team members also use assessment information in reviewing and revising a student's IEP to determine if the special education services are effective or if they need to be changed.

DISTRICT AND STATEWIDE ASSESSMENTS

Teachers must measure students' progress in meeting state and national content standards in general education. According to IDEA, children and youth with disabilities must be included in state- and districtwide assessment programs (Sec. 300.138). Many states have developed assessments that school districts throughout the state must use. These assessments measure the student's progress in the academic content areas and, in some states, are used to determine whether a student should pass to the next grade, attend a summer school program, or receive a high school diploma.

The student's IEP team alone is responsible for making decisions regarding student participation in these assessments. During this process, team members consider questions such as "Will the student need accommodations or modifications to take the district- (or statewide) assessment?" If the IEP team determines that the student needs accommodations or modifications to participate in the assessment, team members identify and describe them in the student's IEP. Typically, students use the same accommodations or modifications for district- and statewide assessments as they do in the classroom when taking quizzes and exams. For example, a student may use a laptop

Figure 4.5   Common accommodations used in large-scale assessments

Presentation
  Braille
  Clarify directions
  Computer administration
  Cueing
  Dictionary
  Examiner familiarity
  Format
  Interpreter
  Interpreter for instructions
  Large print
  Paraphrasing
  Read aloud
  Read directions
  Signed administration
  Simplified language
  Student read aloud
  Visual cues

Response
  Calculator
  Computer administration

Dictated response
Interpreter
Mark answer in test booklet
Point to response
Speech recognition system
Tape recorder
Signed response
Spell checker
Verbalized problem solving
Word processor

Setting
  Study carrel
  Separate room

Timing/scheduling
  Frequent breaks
  Extended time
  Multiple day

Source: Adapted from *Special Topic Area: Accountability for Students with Disabilities,* National Center on Education Outcomes, 2003.

computer to complete written answers or have a teaching assistant record the answers. Figure 4.5 lists common large-scale assessment accommodations that students with disabilities frequently use.

Research (Johnson, Kimball, Brown, & Anderson, 2001; Karkee, Lewis, Barton, & Haug, 2003) regarding the use of accommodations in statewide assessments indicates that more accommodations were provided for elementary school students than for students in middle school. These research findings raise many questions. Why are older students receiving fewer accommodations? If they do not use accommodations in statewide assessments, do older students have access to accommodations in the classroom? Much additional research is needed in this area as students with disabilities strive to meet high academic standards.

PREPARING FOR DISTRICT AND STATEWIDE ASSESSMENTS

How can a special educator assist a student with a disability in preparing to participate in district- or statewide assessments? First, special educators must become

Research to Practice

Large-Scale and High-Stakes Assessment

Federal legislation including IDEA and the No Child Left Behind Act of 2001 require that all students, both with and without disabilities, participate in large-scale assessments. Many advocates view these requirements as equal opportunity and access for students with disabilities (National Center on Educational Outcomes, 2003). Analyzing results from large-scale assessments such as districtwide assessment of student achievement can help improve teaching, learning, and equality of educational opportunity (Heubert & Hauser, 1999). Educators analyze these results to monitor student achievement in reading, mathematics, and other areas of the curriculum. They also use the results to make improvements in the districtwide curriculum. These assessments provide a measure of accountability of how well all students—both with and without disabilities—are meeting curriculum standards.

But sometimes large-scale assessments include a high-stakes component. **High-stakes assessment** is the process of using test information, such as test scores, to make important decisions about individuals. These decisions have important consequences for each student. A student's scores can be used in making decisions about tracking or assigning a student to a particular level. A student may be promoted to the next grade or retained in the same grade for another year. Sometimes a school uses high-stakes assessment scores to determine which students will receive a high school diploma.

Because accountability is becoming more important at the national, state, and local school district levels, large-scale assessment results may trigger rewards for schools and staff when student scores are high; other schools may receive sanctions when student scores are below expected levels. These consequences have gener-

ated much controversy as to whether students with disabilities should be included in the scoring; many educators do not want to be held accountable for students who do not reach expected levels (National Center on Educational Outcomes, 2003).

Some research suggests that students with disabilities tend to score lower on large-scale assessments than students without disabilities. For example, during field testing of the New York State Regents Comprehensive Examination in English, researchers found that students with disabilities scored roughly one standard deviation below students without disabilities and did very poorly on open-ended response questions (Koretz & Hamilton, 2001).

Some evidence suggests that in order to ensure that their students do well on these tests, teachers change the curriculum based on the assessment and spend time teaching to the test content and format (Langenfeld, Thurlow, & Scott, 1997). Teaching to large-scale assessments takes away valuable instruction time from students with disabilities. Much research remains to be completed concerning the effects of high-stakes assessment, instruction, and students with disabilities.

Questions for Reflection

1. What information is available from your state department of education regarding statewide assessments and students with disabilities?

2. How have large-scale assessments affected the work of special educators?

 To answer these questions and learn more about applying research to practice, go to the Companion Website at www.prenhall.com/cohen, select Chapter 4, then choose Research to Practice.

informed of any district and statewide assessments that students take, including the grade levels at which the assessments are given. Special educators should then review examples of test items, including not only the content but also the types of questions that are asked. For example, questions in the mathematics section may not require the student to actually calculate the answer but only to describe the steps that would be used to find the answer. This way of responding may be very different from the response that is expected of the student in the general education classroom or resource room.

Examining the assessment also includes looking at the figures and diagrams involved. If a student receives specialized instruction in a content area covered by the assessment, the special educator must be sure that the student is familiar with and has opportunities to interpret information displayed in figures and diagrams. This does not mean that special educators take valuable instruction time to teach to the test, but rather that they expose students to similar experiences within the context of the curriculum.

Over time, students with disabilities frequently experience difficulties in taking quizzes and exams or large-scale achievement tests. These experiences lead to diminished self-confidence and lower expectations on test performance. In addition, students with disabilities may miss the explanations general educators provide other students in the classroom who are preparing to take the district- or statewide assessment. For these reasons, special educators often work with students with disabilities to help them understand, prepare, and demonstrate their best effort.

To ensure that all students have the same access to information about the assessment, the special educator must work closely with the general educator to see what information is presented in class. Next, the special educator will discuss and review the information with the student with a disability. When students in the general education classroom have opportunities to take practice tests, the special educator will need to be aware of scheduling so that the student with a disability will have those opportunities as well.

Sometimes educators use classroom discussions, demonstrations, or practice tests to teach students test-taking strategies. These strategies may include previewing the test times, organizing the time spent on each section of the test, or following specific rules in answering a test item. For example, students are taught that they should answer only questions in which they can eliminate two of the five possible answers. In later chapters, you will learn more about teaching test-taking strategies.

Finally, special educators can talk with students about the test, encouraging them to develop confidence and realistic expectations. For example, a teacher can explain, "On the mathematics section, you will find some questions that seem relatively easy to you. Other questions may require more thought, and you will need to follow the steps to solving problems that we have learned in class. Since this assessment is designed for a large number of students, you will find some questions that you don't know how to do. Don't spend time worrying about these." Figure 4.6 summarizes how special educators help students with disabilities prepare for district and statewide assessments.

Figure 4.6   **How special educators help students with disabilities prepare for district- and statewide assessments**

Special educators help students by developing their own knowledge of district- and statewide assessments, including an understanding of:

- general content
- types of question formats
- expectations for student responses

Special educators work with students to:

- build self-esteem and confidence
- share information in general discussions
- teach test-taking strategies

Even with accommodations and modifications, some students with disabilities are unable to participate in large-scale assessments. Team members will discuss questions such as "Can the student demonstrate skills and knowledge by taking the district (or state) assessment using accommodations?" When the IEP team agrees that the answer to this question is no, they decide that the student should take an alternative assessment. The state department of education or the local school then takes responsibility for developing a specially designed alternative assessment to measure individual progress (IDEA 34 C.F.R., Sec. 300.138). According to Thompson and Thurlow (2000), who conducted a national survey of alternative assessments for students with disabilities, the most common alternative approach is a performance-based assessment that measures indicators of progress toward state standards or a set of separate standards not linked to general education standards.

LINKING ASSESSMENT WITH INSTRUCTION

 Selecting and planning instruction begins with assessing students to identify where instruction should begin and what the instructional outcomes will be. Linking instruction with assessment also includes gathering information concerning student progress and telling students how their work will be assessed. Teachers use various assessment approaches to measure student progress in academic achievement, improving behaviors, and developing skills. Many of the traditional assessment practices, such as teacher-developed quizzes and standardized achievement tests, focus on content knowledge. These assessment approaches require students to recall or identify information. By contrast, contemporary assessments focus not only on knowledge but on process skills and work habits as well. Students may be asked to compare, analyze, and evaluate information in these types of assessments.

Using Technology
District and Statewide Assessments, Students with Disabilities, and Assistive Technologies

Mariah is an eighth-grade student who has cerebral palsy and a learning disability that affects her written language and organizational skills. Like many of her classmates, she completes all her writing assignments using her laptop and word-processing software. However, for Mariah, the technology is essential because her learning disability affects her ability to write legibly. Word processing allows her to record her ideas and display the information with adequate spacing between words and lines so that she can read what she wrote more easily. Tools such as a spell checker help her identify words that she has difficulty spelling.

When her IEP team met earlier in the year, they discussed Mariah's participation on the statewide assessment for all eighth-grade students in the school district. After careful consideration, her team decided that Mariah will need to use her laptop and word processing, the same accommodations that she is using in the general education classroom, when she participates in the districtwide assessment in the spring. The IEP team facilitator noted this decision on Mariah's IEP.

Laptops and software are not the only ATs that support the participation of students with disabilities in taking district- and statewide assessments. Depending on a student's needs, the IEP team may decide that a student needs one or more AT devices. Some examples include the following:

- pencil grip: supports and helps a student maintain a correct grasp on a pencil or marking pen
- place finder: marks the current line of text (An inexpensive place finder can be a ruler.)
- mask: blocks out additional material on the page (An inexpensive mask can be a page-length piece of light cardboard with a window cut out to view a section of text. Some software programs have a masking option that the user selects, such as to view one sentence or paragraph at a time. The masking option blocks out other text on the screen so that the student is not distracted and can focus on the relevant text.)
- electronic dictionary: allows the user to type in a word and select an option to hear the word spoken, to hear the definition, or to find a word with a similar meaning.

Questions for Reflection

1. What information does your state department of education provide educators and parents regarding district- and statewide assessments, students with disabilities, and the provision of AT?
2. If you were a member of an IEP team for a student with writing and organizational problems, what other inexpensive AT devices might you recommend?

To answer these questions and learn more about using technology to support learning, go to the Companion Website at www. prenhall.com/cohen, select Chapter 4, then choose Using Technology.

A student with a disability uses her computer and specialized software as an accommodation in school assignments.

SELECTING APPROPRIATE ASSESSMENT APPROACHES

Each of the assessment approaches discussed in this chapter has its own strengths and limitations, as described in Table 4.1. Some approaches are best used as an integral part of instruction. Curriculum-based assessments, probes, error analysis, and selecting artifacts for a portfolio are examples of assessments that occur before and during instruction, or **formative assessments.** Formative assessments provide students with ongoing information about their work and progress. For teachers, formative assessments provide information about what students can do and enable teachers to reflect on what methods and strategies are most effective in supporting student learning (Darling-Hammond & Ancess, 1996).

Other approaches, referred to as **summative assessment,** occur at the end of instructional units or marking periods to show student growth and progress. Student performances and teacher-made exams are examples of summative assessments. Although summative assessments provide students time to develop understandings, sometimes students have to wait a long time to receive feedback. In Chapter 8, you will learn more about another valuable assessment approach, student observations, used in both formative and summative assessments. We will examine various ways of conducting observations, including anecdotal records, running records, event recordings, duration recordings, intensity recordings, latency recordings, and interval recordings.

Because teachers use a variety of assessment approaches to make informed decisions, the assessment approach and the scoring procedure must be both reliable and valid. Teachers want to have confidence in the results. The **reliability** of a test refers to the "scoring procedure that enables the examiner to quantify, evaluate, and interpret behavior or work samples. Reliability refers to the consistency of such measurements when the testing procedure is repeated on a population of individuals or groups" (American Educational Research Association, American Psychological Association, & National Council on Measurement in Education, 1999).

The **validity** of a test refers to the "degree to which evidence and theory support the interpretations of test scores entailed by the proposed tests" (American Educational Research Association, American Psychological Association, & National Council on Measurement in Education, 1999). An educator who needs information about a student's reading comprehension or a student's ability to solve a mathematical problem must have confidence that the assessment approach will provide that information.

CURRICULUM-BASED ASSESSMENT

Curriculum-based assessment (CBA) provides valuable information to special educators about what students know and are able to do. Because CBAs consist of items that address specific areas of student knowledge or skills, a teacher can use the assessment results to pinpoint a student's actual skill levels. This information allows the teacher to develop appropriate instructional and learning activities and to focus instruction on what the student needs to master. Special educators frequently use the results of CBA to determine a student's progress toward school district or state curriculum standards.

Table 4.1	Advantages, Limitations, and Pitfalls of Alternative Types of Classroom Assessment Techniques

Formative Assessment Techniques

Assessment Alternative—Conversations and comments from other teachers.

Advantages for Teachers: (a) Fast way to obtain certain types of background information about a student; (b) Permit colleagues to share experiences with specific students in other learning contexts, thereby broadening the perspective about the learners; (c) Permit attainment of information about a student's family, siblings, or peer problems that may be affecting the student's learning.

Disadvantages for Teachers: (a) Tend to reinforce stereotypes and biases toward a family or a social class; (b) Students' learning under another teacher or in another context may be quite unlike their learning in the current context; (c) Others' opinions are not objective, often based on incomplete information, personal life view, or personal theory of personality.

Suggestions for Improved Use: (a) Do not believe hearsay, rumors, biases of others; (b) Do not gossip or reveal private and confidential information about students; (c) Keep the conversation on a professional level, focused on facts rather than speculation and confidential so it is not overheard by others.

Assessment Alternative—Casual conversations with students.

Advantages for Teachers: (a) Provide relaxed, informal setting for obtaining information; (b) Students may reveal their attitudes and motivations toward learning that are not exhibited in class.

Disadvantages for Teachers: (a) A student's mind may not be focused on the learning target being assessed; (b) Inadequate sampling of students' knowledge; too few students assessed; (c) Inefficient: students' conversation may be irrelevant to assessing their achievement.

Suggestions for Improved Use: (a) Do not appear as an inquisitor, always probing students; (b) Be careful so as not to misperceive a student's attitude or a student's degree of understanding.

Assessment Alternative—Questioning students during instruction.

Advantages for Teachers: (a) Permits judgments about students' thinking and learning progress during the course of teaching; gives teachers immediate feedback; (b) Permits teachers to ask questions requiring higher-order thinking and elaborated responses; (c) Permits student-to-student interaction to be assessed; (d) Permits assessment of students' ability to discuss issues with others orally and in some depth.

Disadvantages for Teachers: (a) Some students cannot express themselves well in front of other students; (b) Requires education in how to ask proper questions and to plan for asking specific types of questions during the lesson; (c) Information obtained tends to be only a small sample of the learning outcomes and of the students in the class; (d) Some learning targets cannot be assessed by spontaneous and short oral responses; they require longer time frames in which students are free to think, create, and respond; (e) Records of students' responses are kept only in the teacher's mind, which may be unreliable.

Advantages, Limitations, and Pitfalls of Alternative Types of Classroom Assessment Techniques *continued*

Suggestions for Improved Use: (a) Be sure to ask questions of students who are reticent or slow to respond. Avoid focusing on verbally aggressive and pleasant "stars"; (b) Wait 5–10 seconds for a student to respond before moving on to another; (c) Avoid limiting questions to those requiring facts or a definite correct answer, thereby narrowing the focus of the assessment inappropriately; (d) Do not punish sudents for failing to participate in class question sessions or inappropriately reward those verbally aggressive students who participate fully; (e) Remember that students' verbal and nonverbal behavior in class may not indicate their true attitudes/values.

Assessment Alternative—Daily homework and seatwork.

Advantages for Teachers: (a) Provide formative information about how learning is progressing; (b) Allow errors to be diagnosed and corrected; (c) Combine practice, reinforcement, and assessment.

Disadvantages for Teachers: (a) Tend to focus on narrow segments of learning rather than integrating large complexes of skills and knowledge; (b) Sample only a small variety of content and skills on any one assignment; (c) Assignment may not be complete or may be copied from others.

Suggestions for Improved Use: (a) Remember that this method assesses learning that is only in the formative stages. It may be inappropriate to assign summative letter grades from the results; (b) Failure to complete homework or completing it late is no reason to punish students by embarrassing them in front of others or by lowering their overall grade. Learning may be subsequently demonstrated through other assessments; (c) Do not inappropriately attribute poor test performance to the student not doing the homework; (d) Do not overemphasize the homework grade and overuse homework as a teaching strategy (e.g., using it as a primary teaching method).

Assessment Alternative—Teacher-made quizzes and tests.

Advantages for Teachers: (a) Although primarily useful for summative evaluation, they may permit diagnosis of errors and faulty thinking; (b) Provide for students' written expression of knowledge.

Disadvantages for Teachers: (a) Require time to craft good tasks useful for diagnosis; (b) Focus exclusively on cognitive learning targets.

Suggestions for Improved Use: (a) Do not overemphasize lower level thinking skills; (b) Use open-ended or constructed response tasks to gain insight into a student's thinking processes and errors; (c) For better diagnosis of a student's thinking, use tasks that require students to apply and use their knowledge to "real-life" situations.

Assessment Alternative—In-depth interviews of individual students.

Advantages for Teachers: (a) Permit in-depth probing of students' understandings, thinking patterns, and problem-solving strategies; (b) Permit follow-up questions tailored to a student's responses and allow a student to elaborate on answers; (c) Permit diagnosis of faulty thinking and errors in performances.

continued

Table 4.1	Advantages, Limitations, and Pitfalls of Alternative Types of Classroom Assessment Techniques *continued*

Disadvantages for Teachers: (a) Require a lot of time to complete; (b) Require keeping the rest of the class occupied while one student is being interviewed; (c) Require learning skills in effective educational achievement interviewing and diagnosis.

Suggestions for Improved Use: (a) If assessing students' thinking patterns, problem-solving strategies, etc., avoid prompting student toward a prescribed way of problem solving; (b) Some students need their self-confidence bolstered before they feel comfortable revealing their mistakes.

Assessment Alternative—Growth and learning progress portfolios.

Advantages for Teachers: (a) Allows large segments of a student's learning experiences to be reviewed; (b) Allows monitoring a student's growth and progress; (c) Communicates to students that growth and progress are more important than test results; (d) Allows student to participate in selecting and evaluating material to include in the portfolio; (e) Can become a focus of teaching and learning.

Disadvantages for Teachers: (a) Requires a long time to accumulate evidence of growth and progress; (b) Requires special effort to teach students how to use appropriate and realistic self-assessment techniques; (c) Requires high level knowledge of the subject matter to diagnose and guide students; (d) Requires the ability to recognize complex and subtle patterns of growth and progress in the subject; (e) Results tend to be inconsistent from teacher to teacher.

Suggestions for Improved Use: (a) Be very clear about the learning targets toward which you are monitoring progress; (b) Use a conceptual framework or learning progress model to guide your diagnosis and monitoring; (c) Coordinate portfolio development and assessment with other teachers; (d) Develop scoring rubrics to define standards and maintain consistency.

Assessment Alternative—Attitude and values questionnaires.

Advantages for Teachers: (a) Assess affective characteristics of students; (b) Knowing student's attitudes and values in relation to a specific topic or subject matter may be useful in planning teaching; (c) May provide insights into students' motivations.

Disadvantages for Teachers: (a) The results are sensitive to the way questions are worded. Students may misinterpret, not understand, or react differently than the assessor intended; (b) Can be easily "faked" by older and testwise students.

Suggestions for Improved Use: (a) Remember that the way questions are worded significantly affects how students respond; (b) Remember that attitude questionnaire responses may change drastically from one occasion or context to another; (c) Remember that your personal theory of personality or personal value system may lead to incorrect interpretations of student's responses.

Advantages, Limitations, and Pitfalls of Alternative Types of Classroom Assessment Techniques *continued*

Summative Assessment Techniques

Assessment Alternative—Teacher-made tests and quizzes.

Advantages for Teachers: (a) Can assess a wide range of content and cognitive skills; (b) Can be aligned with what was actually taught; (c) Use a variety of task formats; (d) Allow for assessment of written expression.

Disadvantages for Teachers: (a) Difficult to assess complex skills or ability to use combinations of skills; (b) Require time to create, edit, and produce good items; (c) Class period is often too short for a complete assessment; (d) Focus exclusively on cognitive outcomes.

Suggestions for Improved Use: (a) Do not overemphasize lower level thinking skills; (b) Do not overuse short-answer and response-choice items; (c) Craft task requiring students to apply knowledge to "real life."

Assessment Alternative—Tasks focusing on procedures and processes.

Advantages for Teachers: (a) Allow assessments of nonverbal as well as verbal responses; (b) Allow students to integrate several simple skills and knowledge to perform a complex, realistic task; (c) Allow for group and cooperative performance and assessment; (d) Allow assessment of steps used to complete an assignment.

Disadvantages for Teachers: (a) Focus on a narrow range of content knowledge and cognitive skills; (b) Require great deal of time to properly formulate, administer, and rate; (c) May have low interrater reliability unless scoring rubrics are used; (d) Results are often specific to the combination of student and task. Students' performance quality is not easily generalized across different content and tasks; (e) Tasks that students perceive as uninteresting, boring, or irrelevant do not elicit the students' best efforts.

Suggestions for Improved Use: (a) Investigate carefully the reason for student's failure to complete the task successfully; (b) Use a scoring rubric to increase the reliability and validity of results; (c) Do not confuse the evaluation of the process a student uses with the need to evaluate the correctness of the answers; (d) Allow sufficient time for students to adequately demonstrate the performance.

Assessment Alternative—Projects and tasks focusing on products.

Advantages for Teachers: (a) Same as 2(a), (b), and (c); (b) Permits several equally valid processes to be used to produce the product or complete the project; (c) Allows assessment of the quality of the product; (d) Allows longer time than class period to complete the tasks.

Disadvantages for Teachers: (a) Same as 2(a), (b), (c), (d), and (e); (b) Students may have unauthorized help outside of class to complete the product or project; (c) All students in the class must have the same opportunity to use all appropriate materials and tools in order for the assessment to be fair.

continued

Table 4.1	**Advantages, Limitations, and Pitfalls of Alternative Types of Classroom Assessment Techniques** *continued*

Suggestions for Improved Use: (a) Same as 2(a), (b), (c), and (d); (b) Give adequate instruction to students on the criteria that will be used to evaluate their work, the standards that will be applied, and how students can use these criteria and standards to monitor their own progress in completing the work; (c) Do not mistake the aesthetic appearance of the product for substance and thoughtfulness; (d) Do not punish tardiness in completing the project or product by lowering the student's grade.

Assessment Alternative—Best work portfolios.

Advantages for Teachers: (a) Allow large segments of a student's learning experience to be assessed; (b) May allow students to participate in the selection of the material to be included in the portfolio; (c) Allow either quantitative or qualitative assessment of the works in the portfolio; (d) Permit a much broader assessment of learning targets than tests.

Disadvantages for Teachers: (a) Require waiting a long time before reporting assessment results; (b) Students must be taught how to select work to include as well as how to present it effectively; (c) Teachers must learn to use a scoring rubric that assesses a wide variety of pieces of work; (d) Interrater reliability is low from teacher to teacher; (e) Requires high levels of subject-matter knowledge of evaluate students' work properly.

Suggestions for Improved Use: (a) Be very clear about the learning targets to be assessed to avoid confusion and invalid portfolio assessment results; (b) Teach a student to use appropriate criteria to choose the work to include; (c) Do not collect too much material to evaluate; (d) Coordinate portfolio development with other teachers; (e) Develop and use scoring rubrics to define standards and maintain consistency.

Assessment Alternative—Textbook-supplied tests and quizzes.

Advantages for Teachers: (a) Allows for assessment of written expression; (b) Already prepared, save teachers time; (c) Matches the content and sequence of the textbook or curricular materials.

Disadvantages for Teachers: (a) Often do not assess complex skills or ability to use combinations of skills; (b) Often do not match the emphases and presentations in class; (c) Focus on cognitive skills; (d) Class period is often too short for a complete assessment.

Suggestions for Improved Use: (a) Be skeptical that the items were made by professionals and are of high quality; (b) Carefully edit or rewrite the item to match what you have taught; (c) Remember that you are personally responsible for using a poor quality test. You must not appeal to the authority of the textbook.

Assessment Alternative—Standardized achievement tests.

Advantages for Teachers: (a) Assess a wide range of cognitive abilities and skills that cover a year's learning; (b) Assess content and skills common to many schools across the country; (c) Items developed and screened by professionals, resulting in only the best items being included; (d) Corroborate what teachers know about pupils; sometimes

Advantages, Limitations, and Pitfalls of Alternative Types of Classroom Assessment Techniques *continued*

indicate unexpected results for specific students; (e) Provide norm-referenced information that permits evaluation of students' progress in relation to students nationwide; (f) Provide legitimate comparisons of a student's achievement in two or more curricular areas; (g) Provide growth scales so students' long-term educational development can be monitored; (h) Useful for curriculum evaluation.

Disadvantages for Teachers: (a) Focus exclusively on cognitive outcomes; (b) Often the emphasis on a particular test is different from the emphasis of a particular teacher; (c) Do not provide diagnostic information; (d) Results usually take too long to get back to teachers, so are not directly useful for instructional planning.

Suggestions for Improved Use: (a) Avoid narrowing your instruction to prepare students for these tests when administrators put pressure on teachers; (b) Do not use these tests to evaluate teachers; (c) Do not confuse the quality of the learning that did occur in the classroom with the results on standardized tests when interpreting them; (d) Educate parents about the tests' limited validity for assessing a student's learning potentials.

Source: From *The Educational Assessment of Students,* 4th ed. (pp. 115–117), by A. J. Nitko, © 2004. Reprinted by permission of Pearson Education, Inc., Upper Saddle River, NJ.

Sometimes special educators use a variation of CBA called curriculum-based measurement. **Curriculum-based measurement (CBM)** (Deno, 1985; Deno & Fuchs, 1987; Shinn, 1998) not only assesses specific areas of the curriculum but also uses graphing of assessment information to make instructional decisions and implement interventions. When using CBM, educators assess weekly and graph the student's

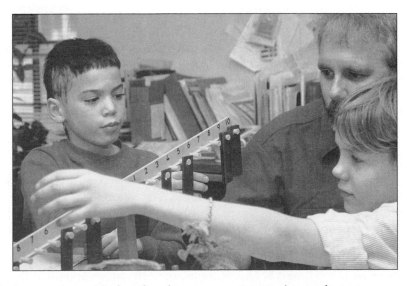

Special educators use curriculum-based measurement to monitor student progress.

Considering Diversity

Using Appropriate Assessment Practices

Throughout the school year, educators identify learning goals and link instruction with appropriate assessment activities. Teachers provide many opportunities for students to perform meaningful tasks and create quality products that demonstrate their progress. Because educators must be sensitive to classroom diversity, they take into account students' cultural and ethnic heritages, home languages, and prior knowledge and experiences during the instructional planning process. In delivering instruction, educators incorporate diversity perspectives and viewpoints, and they consider diversity preferences as they carefully review assessment approaches to make sure that they are appropriate.

Sometimes performance differences lie not only in the task itself but also in how individuals interpret the task (Garcia, 1994). When educators begin planning a performance-based task, they may identify an individual from the community who can provide a perspective on the community's diversity. This individual can give advice on cultural interpretations of various assessment tasks and review performance tasks to ensure cultural sensitivity.

Questions for Reflection

1. What are some of the historical problems with assessment of students from nondominant cultures?
2. What criteria would you use to evaluate the appropriateness of an assessment approach in terms of diversity perspectives?

To answer these questions and deepen your understanding of diversity in schools and communities, go to the Companion Website at www.prenhall.com/cohen, select Chapter 4, then choose Considering Diversity.

performance. They use this weekly information to monitor a student's progress and make changes in instruction when the assessment results indicate that the student is continuing to experience difficulty. The usefulness of CBM is well supported by research findings (Busch & Espin, 2003; Fuchs & Fuchs, 1993; Fuchs, Fuchs, Hamlett, & Stecker, 1991; Tilly & Grimes, 1998).

Developing a Curriculum-Based Assessment

1. *Identify the content area and performance objectives.* By identifying performance objectives, educators define the behaviors that the student must demonstrate in order to indicate progress. Since a CBA focuses on specific areas of the curriculum, educators begin by carefully examining the curriculum area and identifying the specific information or skills they wish to assess. Educators consider what kinds of information students should know: facts, concepts, rules, and/or strategies (Howell & Nolet, 2000). *Facts* are information that the student

has memorized, such as the temperature at which water freezes or capitals of various countries. *Concepts* involve more than memorizing and recall; they require the student to understand and distinguish the attributes of one concept from another. *Rules* and *strategies* involve both memorizing and identifying situations in which the rule or strategy applies. A well-constructed CBA typically assesses two or more types of information.

2. *Decide on the question and response format.* Before educators begin writing the actual test questions, they will need to decide if the assessment will be a paper-and-pencil assessment or if it will be available as a digital file accessible by computer. Educators can construct assessment items that require students to use their laptops to respond in a text or voice note or on a traditional answer sheet.

Educators address other considerations as well, including what question formats to include in the assessment and how students will be asked to respond (Hargrove, Church, Yssel, & Koch, 2002). Question formats include total recall, fill-in, multiple-choice, and matching. Students with cognitive disabilities and short-term memory difficulties may have more difficulty with some question formats than others.

3. *Write the test questions.* In this step, educators develop the specific test questions that correspond to the performance objectives. The content of the test questions should be closely aligned with the curriculum. This will help to ensure that the assessment is valid.

4. *Develop scoring procedures.* Educators must decide how test items will be scored and how educators will determine student progress. For example, a question could be scored as right or wrong, or a certain number of points could be assigned based on the student's response.

5. *Organize and interpret the information.* Educators consider how best to organize the assessment information so that it can be interpreted easily. They frequently create a bar or line graph. By using graphs, educators as well as the student and family members can observe a student's progress.

6. *Link assessment and instruction.* Linking assessment and instruction provides teachers with a procedure for using critical information to design and implement effective instruction. Educators begin by using an assessment approach to identify what students know and do not know. Using this information, they plan appropriate instruction. During instructional activities, they assess and monitor student progress. By analyzing this information, teachers may decide to reteach a concept or to plan additional instruction. When the student's assessment information indicates progress, the teacher carefully records this information and then begins the process again.

Using Curriculum-Based Assessments

Special educators frequently use CBAs to determine the instructional level and to monitor student progress. For example, in reading, special educators construct CBAs to assess reading accuracy as well as reading comprehension. To assess reading accuracy, the teacher selects a 100-word passage and records the number of errors that the student made. The teacher subtracts the number of errors from the number of words read (100) to calculate the number of words read correctly and completes the following formula (Idol, 1996). Thus, if the student made five errors in the 100-word passage, this formula may be used to calculate reading accuracy:

$$\text{Accuracy} = \frac{\text{number of words correct}}{\text{number of words incorrect}} \text{ or } \frac{95}{100} = 95\%$$

This student had a 95% reading accuracy rate.

To assess reading comprehension, special educators identify not only questions that will allow students to gather information directly described in the story (literal-level questions) but also questions to encourage students to interpret and apply information. These expectations involve student understanding of the story, such as the characters and their traits, the setting, the author's purpose in writing the story, and lesson(s) the student learned. Figure 4.7 illustrates a teacher-made CBA to assess reading comprehension. Which questions do you think are literal-level questions? Which are inferential-level questions? Which are application-level questions? (The answers are found at the end of this chapter.)

Graphing the CBA results helps to organize the information. Bar graphs illustrate the number and types of questions that a student completes successfully each week and allow the teacher and student to track progress (Figure 4.8). Bar graphs are useful when the teacher wishes to display the assessment information in terms of the number of correct answers and compare progress in two or more areas.

Line graphs are useful when the teacher wishes to display the assessment information, plotting trends over time. For example, Figure 4.9 illustrates reading accuracy or the percentage of words read correctly on a weekly CBA.

Additional Considerations: Curriculum-Based Assessments

When CBAs produce reliable and valid assessment information, special educators have specific and useful information to use in designing instruction to help students with disabilities attain high levels of achievement. However, developing good CBAs requires a broad base of curricular knowledge. Educators must have not only a strong background in the assessed curriculum but also knowledge of prerequisite skills needed to demonstrate the performance objectives. Developing a CBA can be a time-consuming process.

Figure 4.7   Teacher-developed CBA

1. Who was the main character in this story?
2. What problems did the main character face?
3. How were these problems solved?
4. Where did the story take place?
5. Describe a similar event that happened to you or someone you know.
6. What do you think the author's purpose was in writing this story? What did you learn?

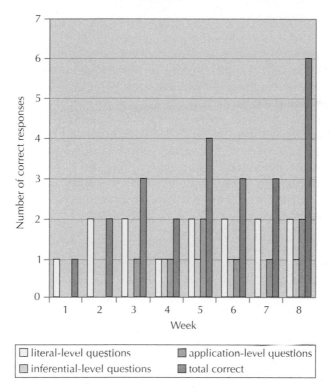

Figure 4.8 Curriculum-based reading comprehension assessment results showing improvement in the student's reading comprehension

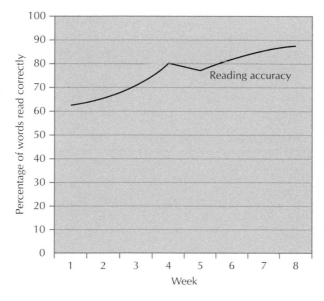

Figure 4.9 Percentage of words read correctly on the weekly CBA

PROBES

Probes are teacher-developed questions or informal test items that provide a quick estimate of a specific skill. Typically, a probe is administered when a teacher meets individually with a student to assess achievement or diagnose areas of weakness in mathematics, reading, written language, science, social studies, or other content areas. For example, at the beginning of the year, a special educator wonders if a student with a learning disability will be able to read and comprehend the science supplements used in the general classroom. The special educator introduces the material and asks the student to read aloud several paragraphs, noting the words that present difficulty. The special educator also checks for understanding using a series of guided questions or probes. This information will be helpful in making decisions about instructional strategies and how much support the student will need.

Developing Probe Sheets

Sometimes a teacher develops a probe sheet to provide a written record regarding mastery or accuracy of specific skills. Probe sheets can be used to assess a student's beginning reading skills or ability to compute mathematical operations. One special educator developed a probe sheet to assess a student's ability to use regrouping in subtraction (Figure 4.10). Sometimes teachers use a probe sheet to check on the retention of information learned earlier in the year. Using the information gained, the special educator planned a number of specially designed instructional activities for the student.

ERROR ANALYSIS

Error analysis is a diagnostic assessment technique in which teachers examine student work to identify patterns of errors. Error analysis may be used across the curriculum but is particularly effective when students make repeated errors in their work such as in mathematics and reading.

Figure 4.10   Teacher-developed probe sheet

Name:_____

38	73	24	61	57	22
−29	−25	−15	−48	−38	−14

45	30	66	81
−26	−18	−39	−36

Number correct _____

When studying errors in reading, teachers sometimes refer to this process as **miscue analysis.** A **miscue** is a word that a student substitutes for the actual word when reading aloud. Although we all make miscues at times, accomplished readers tend to make miscues that retain the underlying meaning of the text; less proficient readers make miscues that make little sense in the context of the passage (Learner, 2000). By analyzing the types of miscues a student makes, the special educator can make adjustments in instruction or plan additional instructional activities.

❖ PROFESSIONAL PERSPECTIVES ❖

Maria Hernadez uses error analysis in her work with students with disabilities. Today, as she works with a student, she asks the student to read aloud a passage from the text. Following along in the teacher copy, Maria notes any miscues that the student makes. For example, the student might read, "The snow melted quietly because the sun was so warm." Because many of Maria's students have learning disabilities, the miscues they make often reflect letter substitutions that result in the sentence's not making sense. By using the information in error analysis, Maria can plan instructional activities to help the student check to make sure that the sentence makes sense. Error analysis allows her to monitor the student's progress closely and to link the assessment information with instructional activities.

TEACHER-CONSTRUCTED QUIZZES AND EXAMS

In addition to collecting diagnostic information about students through probes and error analysis, teachers collect information by using quizzes and exams that focus on student knowledge. This information helps teachers to determine the instructional level, assess student progress, and modify instruction if needed.

Developing Classroom Quizzes and Exams

Teachers develop quizzes and exams to assess what students know and their ability to apply knowledge. Classroom quizzes and exams are different from standardized achievement tests and large-scale statewide achievement tests that are designed to sample a broad range of achievement. Teacher-developed tests link directly to classroom learning.

Developing items for a quiz or test takes thought and practice. Teachers consider the following:

- What content is important for the student to know?
- How will this content be assessed?
- Should students be able to recognize the correct answer or should the question be open-ended?

- Should students be asked to apply what they know?
- Are the test format and the method of student response designed so that they are accessible for students with disabilities in the classroom?

Selected-response questions. Teachers develop **selected-response questions** when they want students to be able to recognize and select the correct answer. True/false and multiple-choice questions are examples of selected-response questions. These questions are designed to focus on reading and thinking skills in the content areas (such as literature, social studies, or science) rather than writing or computational skills. Students respond to these questions by circling or checking the correct response.

One of the disadvantages of selected-response questions is that students may identify the correct answer even if they do not know it or have only partial knowledge. In completing true/false questions, students have a 50% chance of guessing the correct answer; in completing multiple-choice questions, students have a 25% chance (if there are four possible answers) of guessing correctly.

Constructed-response questions. **Constructed-response questions** provide a format for students to demonstrate what they know by using their own words, mathematical reasoning, or illustrations to construct the answer. Short-answer and essay questions are examples of constructed-response questions. For example, a teacher may want students to compare and contrast characters, settings, and plots in the stories that they have read recently. Or a teacher may want students to demonstrate that they can synthesize knowledge about a time in history by explaining the key conditions in society that contributed to a major event.

Constructed-response questions assess understanding and the ability to communicate, even if the teacher does not give credit (or take it off) for organization, logical development, spelling, and grammar. These questions also require students to organize their thoughts and to hold them in memory while completing the answer. The requirements of constructed-response questions may pose difficulties for some students with disabilities, especially those with language-based learning disabilities.

Ensuring Test Validity

Validity is a critical concept in teacher-constructed tests because it refers to the usefulness of test scores. In designing classroom quizzes and exams, care must be taken so that a student's score reflects the student's knowledge of curriculum content and not the level of disability. For a student with a disability, validity concerns can focus on (a) reading and understanding the test items, (b) processing and organizing an answer, and (c) communicating a response.

A student's disability can affect the ability to read and understand. When teachers assess achievement in subjects other than reading by requiring students to read test questions, validity may be compromised. Tests and quizzes in mathematics, science, or social studies that require students to read may not accurately assess student knowledge. For example, a 10-question science quiz would yield a score of not only knowledge of science but also of reading ability. To ensure that the quiz is testing only knowledge of science, the teacher could have a teacher aide read the questions aloud to the student or create a digital file of the quiz so that the student could use text-to-speech software to "read" the quiz. Of course, if the quiz were designed to test reading ability, the student would be required to read the questions independently. Generally, modifications (such as having a different set of questions) and accommodations (such as having a reader or text-to-speech software) to a student's program are listed in the student's IEP.

A student's disability also can affect the ability to process information and organize a response. Constructed-response questions require a student to use short-term memory in formulating answers. For a student with a learning disability, holding information in short-term memory may be very difficult. The resulting test score, then, will reflect not only the student's level of knowledge but also the student's ability to organize and remember.

Students with disabilities may need alternative ways to compose a response. Some of the ways that a student can respond to test items include marking the correct item, writing an answer by using pencil and paper, typing an answer by using a keyboard, selecting an answer by touching a computer screen, or telling the answer to a person who is acting as a recorder. Deciding how a student can respond to classroom quizzes and exams should be part of the IEP team's meeting agenda, or a teacher can meet with the student to discuss individual preferences.

Additional Considerations: Teacher-Constructed Quizzes and Exams

Like other assessments, teacher-constructed quizzes and exams may have errors. For example, they may be difficult to score accurately, because a teacher may be inconsistent in scoring students' papers; this will affect test reliability. The wording of test items may be ambiguous, resulting in misinterpretation. **Rater drift** describes the occurrence of shifting criteria or a change of emphasis from those originally held by the teacher when the grading of papers began. Personal bias, or a teacher's impressions of a student, affect the teacher's judgment and grading of constructed-response questions as well.

In addition to guarding against errors that are associated with grading student quizzes and exams, teachers can strengthen these assessments by carefully planning what will be tested. Developing a test involves clarifying what is expected in terms of student achievement. Aligned with standards, the test items sample what students should know and be able to do as a result of planned instruction and accompanying activities. Teachers should consider the reading level of students in developing the questions and include enough items to cover the key material. Finally, teachers can ask colleagues to review the test and provide feedback regarding clarity of questions and coverage of content.

STUDENT SELF-REPORTS

Students also can provide information about what they know and are able to do. They can identify areas that continue to present difficulty and suggest ways to help. Information from the student's point of view provides the teacher with a unique perspective.

Using Technology
Digital Grading

Using software to record student grades or anecdotal notes regarding student work assists educators in many ways. Having information available in a digital format allows educators to pose questions and manipulate the data to find answers that would be difficult by simply examining information displayed on paper copy. For example, an educator may wonder if there is a relationship between students who did not meet basic achievement expectations and other school-related factors such as class absences or truancy.

Another advantage of using grading software is that educators can easily tabulate weighed scores or sort students to see if the same students are having difficulty across subject areas. Or the software can show which students attending additional help sessions did better on a class quiz. Further, educators can quickly produce multiple copies of a report.

Questions for Reflection

1. What features of grading software would be important to you in your work in the classroom?
2. Compare and contrast several grading programs. Which one would you recommend and why?

 To answer these questions and learn more about using technology to support learning, go to the Companion Website at www.prenhall.com/cohen, select Chapter 4, then choose Using Technology.

There are several ways that a student can share a self-report. One informal way is through a personal conversation with a teacher. The conversation takes place at a planned time, providing the student an opportunity to think in advance about current achievements, strengths, and difficulties.

In talking with the student, a teacher can probe for additional information using the following questions:

- What are you most proud of in terms of your work in this marking period?
- What has proved to be the most difficult problem?
- What study strategies do you use?
- How do you go about getting help?

In addition, a teacher can use a more structured approach by preparing a set of questions to which the student responds. The teacher may meet with the student to discuss the questions or ask the student to respond to them in writing. By using a consistent set of questions, a special educator can gather the same information across students, which can be helpful in examining common needs among students or in planning group instruction.

PERFORMANCE-BASED ASSESSMENT

Performance-based assessments consist of performance tasks and task assessment lists or checklists. In performance tasks, students construct, demonstrate, or perform tasks

Students demonstrate their achievement.

that provide evidence of their knowledge, skills, and behaviors. Tasks may range from short activities to projects developed over several months or a year. Educators consider these tasks and their assessment as an integral part of student learning.

Performance Tasks

Performance tasks involve students in a variety of work formats such as writing (an autobiography, a children's book, a cartoon, or an essay); drawing and designing (a bulletin board, clothing from a certain period in time, or a technical illustration); composing (music, dance, or a song); developing (a graphic organizer to represent a concept, Web page, or slide show); or problem solving (creating a story problem or making a puzzle). Teachers may identify the task(s) or students and teachers together may identify performance task choices. Frequently, school or grade-level teaching teams identify a set of performance formats that all students will learn to use, ensuring that students will have opportunities to develop a variety of skills across performance tasks, such as speaking, conceptualizing information in a graphic, and writing.

Performance tasks that are completed in a real-life context are referred to as **authentic assessment.** The conditions for authentic assessment, such as task complexity, motivation, and standards, are sometimes quite different from those of other performance tasks. Writing a children's book and sharing it with younger children is an example of an authentic task.

Benchmarks. To help students understand what they will be expected to do, teachers often provide **benchmarks**—examples of performance tasks or products that other students have completed. Teachers use benchmarks to help students understand the types and quality of work that are expected. Over time, teachers can develop a collection of excellent and lower-quality examples of student work to use as benchmarks. Also, teachers can find examples of benchmarks on many national organization websites and other education Internet resources. By seeing examples, students not only develop an understanding of what is expected but can also use benchmarks to evaluate and improve their own work.

Scoring Performance-Based Assessment: Checklists and Task Assessment Lists

Checklists. A **checklist** is a list of the elements, components, or steps that must be present in the performance or product. The student or teacher simply checks off whether the element, component, or step is present. One of the advantages of a checklist is that it can be used to show whether a student has performed a series of steps in the correct order. A checklist used by a student with a disability provides a way of organizing an assignment or a performance. For example, in teaching how to solve a mathematical word problem, the teacher shows the student how to first look for the key words and then to identify the mathematical operation indicated. By putting these steps together, the student and teacher can create a checklist for solving word problems. Later, the student uses the checklist as a guide in completing the homework assignment.

Checklists are useful if the components that make up the performance can be listed or if the performance behaviors are in a sequence (Nitko, 2001). Checklists do not include a description of the quality of a component but simply the presence or absence of the item. Checklists are not appropriate when assessing performances that have a range of qualitatively different levels, such as a piece of writing (Arter & McTighe, 2001).

Task assessment lists. A **task assessment list** not only identifies each component of the performance or product that must be present but also rates the quality of each component, rather than just its presence or absence (as in a checklist). Educators can indicate quality by assigning a number of possible points, such as 10 out of 15, or indicating a numerical score on a rating scale, such as 4 on a scale from 1 to 5. Other rating scales can use graphics, such as a series of pictures or icons, depicting a progression from poor to excellent or qualitative terms such as *beginner, intermediate,* and *expert.*

Teachers share the task assessment list with students so that everyone has a written copy of the performance task and the expectations. Some areas of the assessment task list may be worth more points than others if a teacher is emphasizing certain skills. Alternatively, if the skill relates directly to the student's IEP, a teacher may weight the parts of the performance task according to the special needs of the student. Figure 4.11 illustrates the task assessment list for writing a newspaper article.

Additional Considerations: Performance Tasks and Scoring Procedures

Performance tasks have been criticized for taking a large amount of class time and providing only limited opportunities for students to demonstrate what they know and can do. Much of this criticism is directed at educators who use only a few

Figure 4.11   Task assessment list for a newspaper article

Task Assessment List to Evaluate Your Writing

Task	Possible Points	Peer Rating	Self Rating	Teacher Rating
Interesting headline	10			
First sentence describes main idea of the story	10			
The story includes two or three paragraphs that tell who, when, where, why, and how	30			
The writing includes details and examples	30			
A picture or drawing is included	10			
There are no spelling or grammatical errors	10			

Source: Adapted from *Performance-Based Learning and Assessment,* Educators in Connecticut's Pomperaug Regional School District 15, 1996.

performance tasks for students to demonstrate their work. Incorporating a variety of smaller performance tasks may help reduce these problems.

Performance-based assessment, like other assessment approaches, may have problems of reliability and validity. The components of the performance task may not adequately cover the knowledge, skills, or behaviors that are to be tested. The performance task may be unclear to students. The scoring system may be interpreted in more than one way. Or a teacher's bias toward students can affect the assigned rating. A teacher may assign a higher rating than the student's work indicates because the teacher "feels" that the student is capable; the converse also can be true. This is known as the **halo effect.**

The teacher can address sources of error introduced by tasks that do not reflect the curriculum standards, inadequate rating procedures, or the halo effect by involving other professionals in the assessment. Another educator or a paraprofessional can assist the teacher in rating student performances or products. When their ratings do not match, they discuss their reasons for selecting a particular rating. Sometimes these discussions result in the teacher's refining the description in the performance list or including a description that defines the task or performance in terms that can be observed; all of these measures increase reliability.

The following guidelines help ensure the reliability and validity of performance-based assessments:

- Performance tasks should be aligned with curricular goals or curriculum frameworks.
- Assessment task lists should be designed to reflect the knowledge, skills, and behaviors that students will demonstrate.
- Written scoring criteria should be clear.

- Students should understand what they are expected to do in each part of the performance task and how their performance will be scored.
- Students should have a written copy of the assessment task list with the scoring criteria.
- Students should have access to examples and benchmarks.
- Students should have multiple opportunities to participate in performance tasks throughout each school year.
- More than one teacher should be involved in scoring student performance-based assessments.

PORTFOLIO ASSESSMENT

A **portfolio** is a collection of student work that has been assembled systematically over a period of time (Cohen & Spenciner, 2003). Each of the **artifacts,** or student products placed in the portfolio, demonstrates what the student knows and can do, providing concrete examples of progress. For students with disabilities, portfolio artifacts also can be linked directly to the IEP. The portfolio can be shared at parent conferences and during the IEP team's annual review of the student's program.

Educators use portfolio assessments for different purposes. A *process portfolio* illustrates a student's progress in a specific area of study, such as writing or drawing. A *best works portfolio* contains examples of a student's achievement in various areas of the curriculum assembled during the year, whereas a *cumulative portfolio* may be developed over several years and may be part of the graduation requirements. Usually, the purpose of a cumulative portfolio is to provide evidence that a student has attained a specific achievement or skill level.

Deciding What to Include in the Portfolio

Before portfolio assessment is introduced to students, individual teachers, curriculum teams, and districtwide educators put much thought into the purpose and development of portfolio assessment. Like performance-based assessment, the contents of the portfolio are associated with the school's curricular standards.

For students with disabilities, portfolio assessment provides evidence of student work and progress. If the portfolio is a school requirement, the IEP team will discuss whether the student needs any accommodations or modifications to complete the requirement successfully. Let us visit with the IEP team for Jared to discover how the third-grade teachers are using portfolios and the modifications that they will make based on Jared's needs.

During the IEP meeting, team members discussed the school's portfolio requirements. To address Jared's learning and problems, they decided that they would need to include two modifications in the portfolio sections "Language and Literacy" and "Physical Education." The team added a portfolio section entitled "Social Skills" so that there would be a record of Jared's progress in developing positive behaviors and working with others, described in his IEP goals and objectives (Figure 4.12).

**Figure 4.12   A portfolio for elementary students modified by the IEP team
for Jared**

Thomas Point Elementary School Student Portfolio

Language and literacy
 *1. Audiotapes of child retelling a story
  2. Drawing of a favorite part of the story
  3. Writing samples
 *4. List of favorite books written or dictated by child

Science and mathematics
  1. Paper-and-pencil drawings and written descriptions of mathematics problems
  2. Written log/drawings of child's observations of science experiments
  3. Chart with a series of predictions
  4. Child's graph of group data from the class

Art and music
  1. Paintings and drawings
  2. Audiotape of song/music created by child
  3. Photographs of three-dimensional projects
  4. Copies of projects drawn using software

Community and culture
  1. Student maps of the classroom, school, or community
  2. Copies of student e-mail sent to pen pal in another city or state
 *3. Photographs and teacher-transcribed description of field trips
  4. Copies of student thank-you letters to community speakers

Physical education
 *1. Checklist of child's skills completed by the teacher
 *2. Videotapes of child participating in an activity
  3. List of favorite activities written or dictated by child

*Social skills
  1. Child's evaluation of cooperative learning activities
  2. Copies of peer evaluations of cooperative learning activities
  3. Videotapes of student working with others
  4. Checklists of skills or observations completed by the teacher

*Areas of this portfolio that have been modified by the IEP team for Jared, who has
learning and behavior disabilities.

If a student with a disability is experiencing difficulty in achieving the portfolio requirements, the IEP team should consider what additional services, AT, accommodations, or modifications might be needed so that the student can participate in the portfolio assessment process. Students with disabilities, like students without disabilities, may need additional instruction in reflecting on and judging their work and in understanding the rubric and how their work will be assessed. (Rubrics are defined and discussed further on page 134.) These IEP team decisions must be made early in the school year so that the student's program can be monitored and adjusted if necessary.

One of the advantages of portfolio assessment is that it provides an opportunity for students to reflect on their classroom progress over time. Students become part of the assessment process as they revisit, reflect on, and judge their own work (Airasian, 2000); students learn a great deal as they make selections, assemble, and review products for their portfolio. Teachers work closely with individual students, helping them select artifacts that represent a diversity of skills and achievement. In addition, teachers can discuss and model the process skills of reflecting and judging when students are not familiar with them.

Explaining Why an Artifact Is Included

Educators strengthen portfolio assessments by designing learning activities in which students have enough time to reflect on their work. Assembling a portfolio challenges students to think about their learning and their progress. Using a self-reflection process with each artifact, students should include an explanation of why the particular artifact was chosen. Educators can assist students in reflecting on their works in progress and on their completed works by asking questions such as:

- Why do you consider this an example of your best work?
- How did you accomplish this task?
- What might you do differently if you were to do this again?

Questions that help students to think about their group work might include:

- What were the points made by the group as it reviewed your work?
- Describe your response to each point—did you agree or disagree? Why?
- What did you do as the result of their feedback? (Arter & Spandel, 1992, p. 40)

In addition to recording their reflections, conversations with others regarding their work give students the opportunity to think about what they are learning. Students can discuss their work and share observations and reflections with the classroom teacher, the special educator, and their parents. Parents, too, can share their observations and reflections. Therapists, school counselors, social workers, rehabilitation counselors, and others also add rich perspectives. A student might, for example, share with the counselor a written reflection regarding progress in using appropriate behaviors that are tied to the student's IEP and ask the counselor to add comments (Figure 4.13).

Figure 4.13   Student questions for reflecting on classroom behaviors

Using Appropriate Classroom Behaviors

In each of the following areas, I will explain how I am doing:

Following directions

Managing my time wisely

Using self-control when I am angry

Respecting others' property

Working cooperatively with others

I feel that I have made the most improvement in:

I feel that my biggest challenges continue to be:

I would like to focus my next behavioral goal(s) on:

Teachers' comments:

School social worker's comments:

Rehabilitation counselor's comments:

Source: Adapted from *Implementing Student-Led Conferences* (p. 50), by J. M. Bailey and T. R. Guskey, 2001, Thousand Oaks, CA: Corwin Press.

Discussing Portfolios: Student-Led Conferences

Teachers use portfolios to provide concrete examples of student work in discussions with parents; sometimes teachers involve students in these discussions and conferences. Although the teacher traditionally takes responsibility for planning and conducting conferences, portfolios actively involve students in the parent-teacher conference. Students can participate in conferences by explaining their portfolio artifacts and responding to questions regarding their participation and behaviors.

Teachers may ask students to take the lead during conferences, assisting with conference planning and organization, sharing the contents of their portfolios, discussing their work with their parents, asking for parent feedback, and, finally, evaluating the conference. Bailey and Guskey (2001) describe student-led conferences as one way of increasing student responsibility for learning. When students know that they will be reporting to parents or other significant adults, they see the importance of making a good effort, completing their work, and being able to discuss what their work demonstrates.

Teachers who incorporate portfolios in the classroom often observe positive changes in the learning, behavior, and academic achievement of students (Gordon & Bonilla-Bowman, 1996). In many circumstances, students increase their own awareness of how they are learning. They become more sophisticated in revising and reflecting on their work and progress. They are able to talk about and comprehend their thinking processes. When portfolios are involved, much of the students' assessment is also instruction; as students discuss with teachers the merits of their work, they often learn how the work may be improved.

Assessing Portfolios Through Rubrics

A **rubric** is similar to a task assessment list in that it is an assessment scale that identifies the component(s) of performance and the various levels of achievement. However, rubrics consist of narrative statements, or **descriptors**, that provide detailed information about the quality of each achievement level. Since the areas and descriptors identified in the rubric define what the students should know and be able to do, these areas should be tied directly to the curriculum. Rubrics are used to assess various types of student work and performance, including portfolio and performance-based assessments.

Using an Internet search engine, educators can find examples of rubrics across the curriculum. Having good examples to follow is helpful in developing new rubrics. Teachers may work together in workshops or staff development trainings to develop rubrics for particular curriculum units or they may include students in a classroom activity to create a rubric. Teachers discuss the rubric with students so that they understand the levels of achievement and how their work will be evaluated.

Additional Considerations: Assessments Using Rubrics

The scoring system must be both reliable and valid so that educators, students, and parents can have confidence in the assessment results. Students need to understand how performances and products will be scored. The rubric should include well-written, detailed descriptors that clearly specify each level of achievement. Poorly written rubrics consist of descriptors that are ambiguous and/or unclear. When teachers use poorly written rubrics, student work may be scored inconsistently.

Using rubrics to assess student work and inform instruction takes much practice. Arter and McTighe (2001) offer the following guidelines for effective rubrics:

- The rubric helps teachers think about what it means to perform with high quality.
- The rubric is written so clearly that different teachers would assign the same rating.
- A single teacher would be able to provide consistent ratings across assignments and students over a period of time.
- There are several examples of student work that illustrate each rating or score point.
- The language used in the rubric is appropriate for the variety of students in typical classrooms, including English language learners (adapted from pp. 45–51).

Using Technology
Online Assignments and Products of Student Work

Having information about assignments available on the class website helps all students, especially students with disabilities. Students can check assignment descriptions and due dates. They can review benchmarks that provide examples and review the scoring systems (checklist, task assessment list, or rubric, for example) that will be used. Having this information readily available in one place helps students who have difficulty organizing information. Parents, too, can refer to the information and learn more about the expectations for their child.

Many of the assessment approaches described in this chapter can readily be shared with parents, family members, or individuals within and outside the community. Since the Internet reaches so many individuals, teachers can create classroom websites or sites specific to projects for the purposes of displaying student work. Students believe that by creating Web portfolios, they develop a greater awareness of their own learning and achievement (Chen, Liu, Ou, & Lin, 2001). In using the Internet to display student work, teachers first obtain parental permission and then protect the confidentiality of student information by not placing identifying information about individual students on the site.

At Henry M. Jackson High School, educators teaching music, visual arts, and language arts use the school's Web server to post course projects, student portfolios, teacher comments, and peer reviews. English teachers require students to review and evaluate the work of other students using an online rubric. After reading another student's work, the reviewer scrolls down the screen to the project rubric. Over each rubric row is a slider with values from 0 to 10 where the reviewer can compare and score student work against the standard. At the bottom of the rubric is a text box for further comments. This feedback by the reviewing student is turned in as a review assignment to the instructor. This has two purposes: (a) students are accountable for the quality of their feedback to peers and (b) all students receive thoughtful, constructive comments regarding their work (Duxbury, 2000, p. 30).

Questions for Reflection

1. What are some of the ways schools are coping with confidentiality issues when posting information on the Internet? For example, do school personnel create policy statements?
2. Compare and contrast several examples of online performance-based assessment. What types of information are displayed?

 To answer these questions and learn more about using technology to support learning, go to the Companion Website at www. prenhall.com/cohen, select Chapter 4, then choose Using Technology.

SUMMARY

Closely linking assessment with instruction provides valuable information to both students and teachers.

- Students are encouraged to think about their work, to record their progress using graphs and charts, and to take responsibility for their products and performances. They participate in the process of evaluating and critiquing their work. They consider the steps and the process that they used to produce the work and what they might do differently if they were to do the task again.

- Assessment activities prompt teachers to integrate the curriculum content and learning goals. They consider how students will demonstrate knowledge, skills, and behaviors.
- Linking assessment with instruction enables teachers to reflect on and improve both teaching and learning activities.

EXTENDING LEARNING

1. Consider the various assessment approaches discussed in this chapter. Have you experienced any of these approaches as a student? Select two of the approaches and describe their advantages and disadvantages for you as a learner.
2. Working with a small group of colleagues, develop a set of 10 selected-response and 10 constructed-response questions for the first few chapters of this book. Which types of questions were easier to develop? Exchange your teacher-developed test with that of another group and answer the questions. What were some of the difficulties that you experienced? Score your test. Do you think the scoring system was reliable? What suggestions do you have for improvement?
3. The Internet is a rich source of rubrics across the curriculum. Select an area that is of interest to you and use a search engine to locate examples of rubrics. Print out a copy of one of the rubrics and analyze its components. Do you think that it is a well-developed rubric for that curriculum area? Why or why not?
4. Contact a special education administrator to obtain a copy of a CBA. Review the assessment to determine the curriculum content that is assessed. What question formats are used? How many types of response formats are used?
5. A local parent organization has asked you to make a presentation about the portfolios that students in your class are developing. Some of the parents are concerned about validity and reliability issues. Prepare an explanation of how you will address their concerns.

Answers to the teacher-developed CBA in Figure 4.7:
Questions 1 and 4: literal-level questions
Questions 2 and 3: inferential-level questions
Questions 5 and 6: application-level questions

REFERENCES

Airasian, P. W. (2000). *Assessment in the classroom: A concise approach* (2nd ed.). Boston: McGraw-Hill.

American Educational Research Association, American Psychological Association, & National Council on Measurement in Education. (1999). *Standards for educational and psychological testing.* Washington, DC: American Educational Research Association.

American Federation of Teachers, National Council on Measurement in Education, & National Education Association. (1990). *Standards for teacher competence in educational assessment of students.* Retrieved May 15, 2001, from http://www.unl.edu/buros/article3.html

Arter, J., & McTighe, J. (2001). *Scoring rubrics in the classroom*. Thousand Oaks, CA: Corwin.

Arter, J. A., & Spandel, V. (1992). NCME instruction module: Using portfolios of student work in instruction and assessment. *Educational Measurement: Issues and Practice, 11*(1), 36–44.

Bailey, J. M., & Guskey, T. R. (2001). *Implementing student-led conferences*. Thousand Oaks, CA: Corwin Press.

Busch, T. W., & Espin, C. A. (2003). Using curriculum-based measurement to prevent failure and assess learning in the content areas. *Assessment for Effective Intervention, 28*(3&4), 48–58.

Chen, G., Liu, C., Ou, K., & Lin, M. (2001). Web learning portfolios: A tool for supporting performance awareness. *Innovations in Education and Training International, 38*(1), 19–30.

Cohen, L. G., & Spenciner, L. J. (2003). *Assessment of children and youth with special needs* (2nd ed.). Boston: Allyn & Bacon.

Cole, D. J., Ryan, C. W., & Kick, F. (1995). *Portfolios across the curriculum and beyond*. Thousand Oaks, CA: Corwin Press.

Covington, M. V. (1998). *The will to learn: A guide for motivating young people*. Cambridge: Cambridge University Press.

Darling-Hammond, L., & Ancess, J. (1996). Authentic assessment and school development. In J. B. Baron & D. P. Wolf (Eds.), *Performance-based student assessment: Challenges and possibilities* (pp. 52–83). Chicago: University of Chicago Press.

Deno, S. L. (1985). Curriculum-based measurement: The emerging alternative. *Exceptional Children, 52,* 219–232.

Deno, S. L., & Fuchs, L. S. (1987). Developing curriculum-based measurement systems for data-based special education problem solving. *Focus on Exceptional Children, 19,* 1–16.

Donovan, S. M., & Cross, C. T. (Eds.). (2000). *Minority students in special and gifted education*. Washington, DC: National Academy of Sciences–National Research Council. (ERIC Document Reproduction Service No. ED469543).

Duxbury, D. (2000). Make sweet music with electronic portfolios. *Learning and Leading with Technology, 28*(3), 28–31.

Educators in Connecticut's Pomperaug Regional School District 15. (1996). *Performance-based learning and assessment*. Alexandria, VA: Association for Supervision and Curriculum Development.

Fuchs, L. S., & Fuchs, D. (1993). Effects of systematic observation and feedback on teachers' implementation of curriculum-based measurement. *Teacher Education and Special Education, 16,* 178–187.

Fuchs, L. S., Fuchs, D., Hamlett, C. L., & Stecker, P. M. (1991). Effects of curriculum-based measurement and consultation on teacher planning and student achievement in mathematics operations. *American Educational Research Journal, 28,* 617–641.

Garcia, G. E. (1994). Equity challenges in authentically assessing students from diverse backgrounds. *Educational Forum, 59*(1), 64–73.

Gordon, E. W., & Bonilla-Bowman, C. (1996). Authentic assessment and school development. In J. B. Baron & D. P. Wolf (Eds.), *Performance-based student assessment: Challenges and possibilities* (pp. 32–51). Chicago: University of Chicago Press.

Hargrove, L. J., Church, K. L., Yssel, N., & Koch, K. (2002). Curriculum-based assessment: Reading and academic standards. *Preventing School Failure, 46*(40), 4.

Heubert, J. P., & Hauser, R. M. (Eds.). (1999). *High stakes: Testing for tracking, promotion, and graduation*. Washington, DC: National Academy Press.

Howell, K. W., & Nolet, V. (2000). *Curriculum-based evaluation: Teaching and decision making*. Belmont, CA: Wadsworth.

Idol, L. (1996). *Models of curriculum-based assessment*. Austin, TX: PRO-ED.

Individuals with Disabilities Education Act Amendments (Pub. L. No. 105-17). (1997). 20 U.S.C. Sec. 1400 et. seq. Washington, DC: U.S. Government Printing Office.

Johnson, E., Kimball, K., Brown, S. O., & Anderson, D. (2001). A statewide review of the use of accommodations in large-scale, high-stakes assessments. *Exceptional Children, 67*(2), 251–264.

Karkee, T., Lewis, D. M., Barton, K., & Haug, C. (2003). *The effect of including or excluding students with testing accommodations on IRT calibrations*. Los Angeles: National Center for the Study of Evaluation. (ERIC Document Reproduction Service No. ED478166)

Koretz, D., & Hamilton, L. (2001). *The performance of students with disabilities on New York's revised regents comprehensive examination in English CSE technical report*. Los Angeles: National Center for the Study of Evaluation. (ERIC Document Reproduction Service No. ED455287).

Langenfeld, K., Thurlow, M., & Scott, D. (1997). High stakes testing for students: Unanswered questions and implication for students with disabilities (Synthesis Report 26). Minneapolis: National Center on Educational Outcomes. (ERIC Document Reproduction Service No. ED415627).

Lave, J., & Wenger, E. (1991). *Situated learning: Legitimate peripheral participation*. Cambridge: Cambridge University Press.

Learner, J. (2000). *Learning disabilities*. Boston: Houghton Mifflin.

Lee, C. D., & Smagorinsky, P. (Eds.). (2000). *Vygotskian perspectives on literacy research: Constructing meaning through collaborative inquiry*. Cambridge: Cambridge University Press.

National Alliance of Black School Educators & IDEA Local Implementation by Local Administrators Partnership. (2002). *Addressing overrepresentation of African American students in special education*. Arlington, VA: Council for Exceptional Children.

National Center on Educational Outcomes. (2003). *Special topic area: accountability for students with disabilities*. Retrieved May 18, 2003, from http://www.education.umn.edu/NCEO/Default.html

Nitko, A. J. (2001). *Educational assessment of students* (3rd ed.). Upper Saddle River, NJ: Merrill/Prentice Hall.

Olson, L. (2002). Up close and personal. Retrieved June 24, 2002, from the Education Week website: http://www.edweek.org/ew/newstory.cfm?slug=37assess.h21

Pea, R. D. (1993). Practices of distributed intelligence and designs for education. In G. Salomon (Ed.), *Distributed cognitions: Psychological and educational considerations* (pp. 47–87). Cambridge: Cambridge University Press.

Shinn, M. R. (Ed.). (1998). *Advanced applications of curriculum-based measurement*. New York: Guilford Press.

Slavin, R. E., & Madden, N. A. (2001). *Success for all: Research and reform in elementary education*. Mahwah, NJ: Erlbaum.

Thompson, S. J., & Thurlow, M. L. (2000). *State alternate assessments: Status as IDEA alternate assessment requirements take effect* (Synthesis Report 35). Minneapolis: National Center on Educational Outcomes, University of Minnesota. (ERIC Document Reproduction Service No. ED447613).

Tilly, W. D., III, & Grimes, J. (1998). Curriculum-based measurement: One vehicle for systematic educational reform. In M. R. Shinn (Ed.), *Advanced applications of curriculum-based measurement* (pp. 32–60). New York: Guilford Press.

5

Chapter

Planning and Organizing Instruction for Students with Mild and Moderate Disabilities

CHAPTER OBJECTIVES

After completing this chapter, you should be able to:

❖ Discuss standards-based education and the IEP.

❖ Describe how special educators and other team members plan the student's IEP.

❖ Discuss the process of planning a unit, lessons, and other instructional activities.

❖ Describe how educators plan and organize student use of accommodations, modifications, and AT devices and services.

❖ Demonstrate understanding of diversity related to planning and organizing instruction.

Students with and without disabilities need to acquire knowledge and skills across all areas of the school curriculum. In fact, IDEA states that students with disabilities must have access to the general education curriculum (Sec. 300.26). Today, special educators are familiar with the general education curriculum, as well as with specialized teaching methods and instructional strategies for students with disabilities. They may join general educators as part of a teaching team, or they may work alone or with other special educators to plan, organize, and evaluate instruction.

To begin, educators ask questions about the students with whom they will be working. What do Tasha, Tony, and Juanita know? In planning and organizing instruction, special educators begin by assessing the academic needs of students with disabilities in the various content areas, such as literacy (including reading and writing), mathematics, science, and social studies. Assessment results help educators to determine where to begin instruction. In Chapter 4 we examined some of the assessment approaches that educators use to link assessment information with instruction. By using assessment information aligned with the general education curriculum, educators can develop learning activities that deepen students' understanding and strengthen their skills while helping them work toward high academic achievement.

What can students do? Special educators also assess student skills and behaviors. They consider prerequisite skills that a student may need. For example, the educator conducts a brief probe to assess whether the student is familiar with the meaning of new vocabulary words. Knowing this information is critical before planning instruction.

Special educators also assess social skills and behaviors. When students need to build appropriate social skills and positive behaviors, educators plan and organize instructional activities to include a social skills component as part of the academic instruction. For example, an educator may plan a lesson in writing that involves working cooperatively with one or more other students to allow a student with a disability to build positive behaviors in working with peers.

Do students require any accommodations or modifications of the education program? Educators will review the students' IEP to determine what accommodations or modifications are described. If a student uses an AT device, educators consider how the student will use it during assessment, instruction, and learning activities. Careful planning and organizing of instruction create successful learning opportunities for *all* students.

Planning and organizing instruction for students with disabilities begins with knowing the characteristics of learners, what they know, and what they can do. In Chapters 2 and 3 you read about the characteristics of students, their abilities, and their diverse needs. In Chapter 4 we discussed the assessment of students to answer questions about their achievement, skills, and behaviors. This chapter builds on that information by examining how special education teachers plan instruction and organize learning experiences.

CLASSROOM ENVIRONMENTS

In planning instruction, we understand that each classroom consists of various environments—physical, social, and learning. The physical environment consists of the space and furnishings that make up the classroom. The social environment comprises the everyday activities, interactions, and relationships that exist in the classroom and their impact on learning. The learning environment consists of the content of the instruction, the methods and instructional strategies that a teacher uses, the learning strategies that a student uses, and the methods the student uses to demonstrate progress and achievement.

PHYSICAL ENVIRONMENT

As we discussed in Chapter 1, special educators work in various settings, such as general education classrooms, resource rooms, special-purpose schools, and other places. The physical environment for learning has received considerable emphasis in regard to students with disabilities. For example, the Americans with Disabilities Act (ADA) ensures that all public classrooms are physically accessible to students with disabilities. But simply creating ramps and wide doorways is not enough; students must have access to meaningful instruction and learning activities.

To participate fully in learning activities, students need physical access to appropriate classroom materials and equipment. For example, a visitor to Mario Stefani's social studies class observes students working in small groups using a variety of materials. One group of four students works together using laptops, whereas another group uses graph paper, pens, colored pencils, and various small cardboard shapes. Tony, a student with a learning disability and ADHD, is an active participant in another

Special educators create positive social environments for students.

group of four students who are using wooden forms to create a model of the social structure of an ancient society. The teacher frequently plans various small-group learning activities involving hands-on use of materials that are stored in accessible locations. His classroom is set up with small tables scattered throughout the room for small-group work.

Additional considerations in the physical environment include lighting, temperature, distractions, and noise level. Lighting should be adjusted so that projectors and computer screens are free from glare, which can make reading difficult. The teacher checks that room displays are not visually distracting. For example, hanging mobiles help a room look attractive, but materials that are visually stimulating may be distracting to some learners. When possible, the teacher arranges seating away from a door, bulletin board, window, or other areas that could distract these students. To create a positive physical environment, the teacher monitors the noise level, making sure that no student work group is loud enough to distract students in other groups. Figure 5.1 illustrates a teacher-made form for observing the physical environment.

SOCIAL ENVIRONMENT

Establishing positive relationships with peers and teachers, as well as building a school community, are important components of the educational program for all students. Yet, for many students with disabilities, these relationships may not develop. Students with disabilities in fourth and fifth grades report that they felt lonely at school (Pavri & Monda-Amaya, 2000). Murray and Greenberg (2001) found that

Figure 5.1　Observing the physical environment

Point Street School
Physical Environment

Student's Name: *Karen S.*　　　　　Date: *3/13*　　　　　Time: *10:35*

Observer: *T. S.*　　　　　Location: *English*

Characteristic	Always	Sometimes	Never
1. Seating Is the student seated properly?			x
Suggestions for improvement:			
2. Lighting Is the lighting appropriate?	x		
Suggestions for improvement:			
3. Noise Is the noise level appropriate?		x	
Suggestions for improvement: *There are times when the noise level seems high. This may make it difficult for Karen and other students to concentrate. Suggest that the teacher and students monitor the noise level.*			
4. Distractions Is the student distracted by activities in the room?		x	
Suggestions for improvement: *While Karen is distracted at times, she is able to refocus on the tasks at hand.*			
5. Temperature Is the temperature of the room appropriate?		x	
Suggestions for improvement: *There are times when the room is too hot. This does not seem to affect Karen's performance. However, this should be monitored.*			
6. General Atmosphere Does the student appear to be comfortable in the environment?	x		
Suggestions for improvement:			

Source: From Cohen, L. G., & Spenciner, L. J. *Assessment of Children and Youth with Special Needs,* 2/e. Published by Allyn & Bacon, Boston, MA. Copyright © 2003 by Pearson Education. Reprinted by permission of the publisher.

students with disabilities in fifth and sixth grades are more dissatisfied with their relationships with teachers and establish poorer bonds with school than students without disabilities.

Research studies such as these suggest that special educators today must plan ways of creating positive social environments for students with disabilities while

Figure 5.2   Observing the social environment

Point Street School
Physical Environment

Student's Name: *Karen S.*   Date: *3/13*   Time: *10:35*

Observer: *T. S.*   Location: *English*

Characteristic	Always	Sometimes	Never
1. Teacher-Student Interactions Are interactions warm and friendly?	x		
Suggestions for improvement:			
2. Disruptions Are disruptions kept to a minimum?		x	
Suggestions for improvement: *Announcements and the public address system interruptions can distract Karen and other students in the class. An effort should be made to reduce these interruptions.*			
3. Behavioral Interventions Are behavioral interventions effective and appropriate?	x		
Suggestions for improvement:			
4. Peer interactions Are peer interactions appropriate?	x		
Suggestions for improvement:			
5. General Atmosphere Does the student appear to be comfortable in the social environment?	x		
Suggestions for improvement:			

Source: From Cohen, L. G., and Spenciner, L. J. *Assessment of Children and Youth with Special Needs*, 2/e. Published by Allyn & Bacon, Boston, MA. Copyright © 2003 by Pearson Education. Reprinted by permission of the publisher.

planning interventions to strengthen relationships between students with and without disabilities. In fact, Hunt (2000) found that teachers were the driving force for the unification of general education and special education programs. These teachers worked together to develop needed curricular adaptations and social supports, often coteaching in the classroom. They implemented a social curriculum and conflict resolution procedures. They respected and valued all students and, in return, expected all students to respect others. Successful teachers also encourage students to attempt new and difficult tasks and to take learning risks. Teachers hold high expectations for all students, and students' attempts are valued. Figure 5.2 illustrates a teacher-made form for observing the social environment.

Research to Practice

Classroom Organization

Multiage classrooms provide an alternative way to organize the social and learning environments. Students in these classrooms are often 2 to 3 years apart in age. Multiage classrooms help increase heterogeneity and provide opportunities for children to learn from each other. Case studies of schools using multiage classrooms find that these settings often promote successful inclusion opportunities for students with disabilities (Aefsky, 1995; Bonilla & Goss, 1997; Treder et al., 1999). In a study of 10 schools, researchers found that students showed an increase in achievement and a decrease in problem behaviors and functional impairment when educators used innovative practices, including team teaching with consulting special educators and multiage classrooms (Treder et al., 1999).

Looping occurs when teachers stay with the same class for 2 years by moving up a grade with their students. Several research studies suggest that looping benefits younger students by improving student-teacher relationships, reducing anxiety, and improving the teacher's

understanding of students' strengths and weaknesses (Chirichello & Chirichello, 2001); for middle school and older students, improvements include student discipline, attitudes, and achievement (Black, 2000; Lincoln, 2000). Reynolds, Barnhart, and Martin (1999) found that looping gave teachers extra time to bring low-performing students up to grade level and to develop more stable, caring relationships with their students.

Questions for Reflection

1. What are some ways in which special educators and general educators might work together in multiage classrooms? What might be some benefits? What barriers might need to be addressed?
2. How do parents react to multiage classrooms and looping?

 To answer these questions and learn more about applying research to practice, go to the Companion Website at www.prenhall. com/cohen, select Chapter 5, then choose Research to Practice.

LEARNING ENVIRONMENT

As noted earlier, the classroom learning environment includes the content of instruction, the instructional strategies that the teacher employs, the learning strategies that students use, and the methods students use to demonstrate progress and achievement. Students bring diverse needs, skills, and abilities to the classroom. How can learning experiences be meaningful and relevant for each student? How can teachers help every student achieve high academic standards? Teachers frequently plan and organize instruction across more than one content area to help students make learning connections. For example, one team of teachers planned an integrated unit in literacy, science, and social studies. Students broadened their understanding of the 1800s not only by studying historical events but also by participating in and writing about activities that illustrate the way of life during that period. They conducted research to learn how people dressed and what foods they ate. They created replicas of simple machines that people used and learned how they worked.

In planning an integrated curriculum, teachers frequently embed the student's IEP goals and objectives within the curriculum unit's objectives. Let us return to Tony, the boy with a learning disability and ADHD whom we met earlier. When planning instructional activities for Tony and the other students, Nelson Barnes, the social studies teacher, decided to design activities that would involve small-group work. Encouraging students to work and learn together enables them to grasp concepts of earlier societies in which work was interdependent. For Tony, learning to work with peers is not only important for understanding these concepts but is also part of his IEP. One of his goals is to increase his skills in working cooperatively with peers. Learning activities that involve both individual and group work support the diverse abilities that students bring to the classroom.

As Nelson Barnes began organizing instruction, he checked the classroom materials to make sure that there were enough of them so that students could make choices in deciding what to use. From experience, the teacher knew that having choices increased students' interest and involvement in learning activities. He thought about how to introduce the different materials from which students could choose, including small blocks of various shapes and sizes; graph paper and a variety of pens and markers; and software on the school server that could be accessed by student laptops. Although manipulating a mouse and computer software might have been physically easier for Tony because of his impulsiveness and difficulty in manipulating small objects, he chose to join the group of students who were creating a three-dimensional model of an ancient society with blocks. Organizing a variety of materials provides multiple ways in which students, both with and without disabilities, can access the learning environment.

In a report that analyzed how planning instruction to meet a wide range of student abilities and standards-based curricula affects students with disabilities, Jorgensen (1997) found that several essential questions challenge and support students both with and without disabilities. Some of these questions include: What is the central unit, problem, or question? What will interest students—for example, serve as a unit "grabber" or kick-off activity? What are the learning experiences? What assessment approaches can be used? What are the culminating projects? Educators must consider many questions such as these in planning and organizing the learning environment. Figure 5.3 illustrates a teacher-made form for considering the learning environment.

Planning and organizing instruction for students with disabilities involves working closely with general education teachers and the general education curriculum so that all students can achieve high standards. For example, Raphael Suazo, the special education teacher, meets regularly with the classroom teachers to consult and coordinate education planning for Tony. Tony participates in the general education classes for history, science, and language arts and receives specially designed instruction for mathematics. Even though Raphael is responsible for delivering mathematics instruction, Tony is expected to work toward high achievement in the general education classroom. His IEP goals and objectives are aligned with the mathematics curriculum for his grade.

Figure 5.3   Observing the learning environment

Point Street School
Learning Environment

Student's Name: *Karen S.*   Date: *3/13*   Time: *10:35*
Observer: *T. S.*   Location: *English*

Characteristic	Always	Sometimes	Never
1. <u>Materials</u> Are a variety of materials available?	x		
Suggestions for improvement:			
2. <u>Manipulatives</u> Are appropriate manipulatives available?			
Suggestions for improvement: *N/A*			
3. <u>Curriculum</u> Does the curriculum reflect recent reform standards?	x		
Suggestions for improvement:			
4. <u>Activities</u> Is instruction oriented toward the use of various materials rather than paper and pencil tasks?		x	
Suggestions for improvement: *Karen performs best when actively involved in projects. Suggest that options for assignments be developed for Karen and other students.*			
5. <u>Instructional Demands</u> How is the student challenged? Are the instructional demands appropriate for the student?		x	
Suggestions for improvement: *Karen needs to have directions for assignments clarified. She should be asked to repeat the directions to make sure that she understands what is expected.*			
6. <u>Accommodations</u> Have modifications been made to instruction to meet the learning needs of the student?	x		
Suggestions for improvement:			
7. <u>Assessment</u> Are a variety of assessment approaches used to provide feedback to the student?		x	
Suggestions for improvement: *The primary assessment activities in Karen's classroom are quizzes and journal writing. Suggest that the teacher be encouraged to include instructional probes to check for understanding and rubrics.*			

Figure 5.3   Observing the learning environment *continued*

8. <u>Grouping</u> If grouping is used, is it appropriate?	*x*		
Suggestions for improvement:			
9. <u>Instruction</u> Are a variety of instructional methods used?	*x*		
Suggestions for improvement:			
10. <u>Pace of Instruction</u> Is the pace of instruction appropriate?		*x*	
Suggestions for improvement: *Karen may need a longer time to complete her readings. Untimed quizzes and tests are recommended.*			
11. <u>Expectations</u> Are teacher expectations appropriate?	*x*		
Suggestions for improvement:			
12. <u>Student Involvement</u> Is the student actively involved?	*x*		
Suggestions for improvement:			
13. <u>Schedule</u> Is the student's schedule appropriate?	*x*		
Suggestions for improvement:			
14. <u>Transitions</u> Are transitions made smoothly?	*x*		
Suggestions for improvement:			

Source: From Cohen, L. G., & Spenciner, L. J., *Assessment of Children and Youth with Special Needs*, 2/e. Published by Allyn & Bacon, Boston, MA. Copyright © 2003 by Pearson Education. Reprinted by permission of the publisher.

CONTENT STANDARDS AND PERFORMANCE INDICATORS

In planning instruction, general education and special education teachers use content standards and performance indicators. **Content standards,** sometimes referred to as *curriculum standards* (language arts, mathematics, science, and so-cial studies, for example), describe the knowledge and skills that students should know. **Performance indicators** describe a level of achievement and indicate what students should be able to demonstrate. Table 5.1 provides an example from the State of Maine content standards in the mathematics area of Algebra Concepts for students pre-K to Grade 12 and student performance indicators for the grade levels. The standard for Algebra Concepts states, "Students will understand and

Considering Diversity

Considering the Physical, Social, and Learning Environments

In considering the physical, social, and learning environments, the teacher plans ways to enable students to connect classroom learning with their homes and communities. Learning experiences and instructional activities should be culturally relevant and meaningful. Diversity perspectives should be embedded when planning units of instruction. For example, in planning a nutritional unit, the teacher plans and organizes instructional activities for students to learn about foods from various cultural groups that are part of the community. Meaningful learning experiences are included in the unit, such as inviting students to bring in a recipe from home to create a classroom cookbook.

Teachers create culturally responsive social environments, too in the table below. They arrange collaborative groups to encourage student learning. They work to connect prior experiences with new learning. Students engage in a variety of activities that allow them to move about the classroom. What should a teacher consider in planning and organizing instruction that is effective for all students? After extensive research, the Center for Research on Education, Diversity, and Excellence has developed five principles for effective pedagogy that are applicable across K–12 grade levels (Dalton, 1998):

1. Joint productive activity
   Teacher and students producing together
   The teacher designs instructional activities

Planning a Culturally Responsive Classroom

What Teachers Do	What Teachers Do Not Do
Encourage social involvement	Emphasize individual competition over collaborative work
Ensure that multiple stimuli and movement are part of each day	Tolerate only low levels of physical movement and stimulation
Emphasize experiential relevance	Do not connect tasks to personal experiences or interests
Encourage cooperation	Discourage students from talking to others while working on a task
Maintain flexibility	Maintain rigid time schedules

Source: Adapted from *Creating Culturally Responsive Classrooms*, by B. J. Shade, C. Kelly, and M. Oberg, 1997, Washington, DC: American Psychological Association.

requiring student collaboration to accomplish a joint product. . . . [The teacher] organizes students in a variety of groupings, such as by friendship, mixed academic ability, language, project, or interests, to promote interaction. [The teacher] plans with students how to work in groups. . . . (p. 11)

2. Developing language and literacy across the curriculum
   The teacher listens to students talk about familiar topics such as home and community. . . . [The teacher] assists written and oral language development through modeling, eliciting, probing, restating, clarifying, questioning, praising, etc., in purposeful conversation and writing. [The teacher] interacts with students in ways that respect students' preferences for speaking that may be different from the teacher's, such as wait-time, eye contact, turn-taking, or spotlighting. . . . [The teacher] encourages students' use of first and second languages in instructional activities. (p. 17)

3. Making meaning
   Connecting school to students' lives
   The teacher . . . designs instructional activities that are meaningful to students in terms of local community norms and knowledge. [The teacher] acquires knowledge of local norms and knowledge by talking to students, parents, or family members, community members, and by reading pertinent documents. . . . [The teacher] plans jointly with students to design community-based learning activities. . . . (p. 22)

4. Teaching complex thinking
   The teacher assures that students—for each instructional topic—see the whole picture as a basis for understanding the parts. . . . [The teacher] designs instructional tasks that advance student understanding to more complex levels. . . . [The teacher] gives clear, direct feedback about how student performance compares with the challenging standards. . . . (p. 26)

5. Teaching through conversation
   The teacher . . . has a clear academic goal that guides conversation with students. [The teacher] ensures that student talk occurs at higher rates than teacher talk. [The teacher] guides conversation to include students' views, judgments, and rationales using text evidence and other substantive support. . . . (p. 30)

Questions for Reflection

1. Consider the students in your community schools. To develop language and literacy across the curriculum (see recommendation 2), what children's books and folk tales can you locate that would help you in working with these students?

2. To become more knowledgeable about the culture and traditions of the students in your community schools, what online resources would be helpful?

 To answer these questions and deepen your understanding of diversity in schools and communities, go to the Companion Website at www.prenhall.com/cohen, select Chapter 5, then choose Considering Diversity.

| Table 5.1 | Example of Content Standards and Preference Indicators in Mathematics |

H. ALGEBRA CONCEPTS

Students will understand and apply algebraic concepts. Students will be able to:

ELEMENTARY GRADES Pre-K–2

1. Make drawings for problem situations and mathematical expressions in which there is an unknown, using a variety of tools and approaches.
2. Use language and symbols to express numerical and other relationships.

EXAMPLE

- Show all the ways to make 10 (e.g., $2 + x = 10$, $3 + x = 10$, and so forth) by using blocks or othe objects to demonstrate the mathematical statements.

ELEMENTARY GRADES 3–4

1. Develop and evaluate simple formulas in problem-solving contexts.
2. Find replacements for variables that make simple number sentences true.

EXAMPLE

- Plot points on a coordinate graph according to the convention that (x,y) refers to the intersection of a given vertical line and a given horizontal line.

MIDDLE GRADES 5–8

1. Use the concepts of variables and expressions.
2. Solve linear equations using concrete, informal, and formal methods which apply the order of operations.
3. Analyze tables and graphs to identify properties and relationships in a practical context.
4. Use graphs to represent two-variable equations.
5. Demonstrate an understanding of inequalities and non-linear equations.
6. Find solutions for unknown quantities in linear equations and in simple equations and inequalities.

EXAMPLES

- Study the steepness of wheelchair ramps and stairs.
- Solve for x: $3x - 5 = 23 - x$.

SECONDARY GRADES

1. Use tables, graphs, and spreadsheets to interpret expressions, equations, and inequalities.
2. Investigate concepts of variation by using equations, graphs, and data collection.
3. Formulate and solve equations and inequalities.
4. Analyze and explain situations using symbolic representations.

EXAMPLES

- Use measurements from shopping carts which are nested together to find a formula for the number of carts that will fit in a given space and a formula for the amount of space needed for a given number of carts.
- Solve the following problem: Given the formula for height of an object thrown upward with velocity v: $h = h_o + vt + (1/2) gt^2$, use quadratic functions and the quadratic formula to answer questions about the motion of projectiles and falling objects.

Source: State of Maine Learning Results, 1997, p. 10. Used with permission.

apply algebraic concepts." For children pre-K through Grade 2, one of the performance indicators is:

- Make drawings for problem situations and mathematical expression in which there is an unknown, using a variety of tools and approaches (*State of Maine Learning Results,* 1997, p. 10).

The performance indicator is written in general terms so that teachers can create a variety of learning experiences for children to demonstrate what they can do. In general, individual state content standards reflect the standards developed by the professional organizations listed in Table 5.2.

Content standards and performance indicators are part of standards-based reform, an education movement that began when many educators, policy makers, and politicians became concerned about the lack of student achievement. The No Child Left Behind Act mandated that each state develop standards and assessments for students at various grade levels across the curriculum. Student performance must be reported, and if students do not make adequate progress, the school is held accountable. The standards movement in each state has become a catalyst for changes in instruction and assessment for all students, including those with disabilities.

Outcomes must be achievable for all students; at the same time, teachers need to maintain high expectations. Students come to the classroom with a range of strengths, attitudes, abilities, skills, and motivation levels. The diversity of their experiences and needs must be addressed by teachers and the IEP team. Failure to give students access

Table 5.2	Curriculum Standards Developed by Professional Organizations
Curriculum Area	**Web Search Key Word/URL**
English language arts	National Council of Teachers of English http://www.ncte.org/homepage
Mathematics	National Council of Teachers of Mathematics http://www.nctm.org/
Geography	National Council for Geographic Education http://www.ncge.org/
Science	National Science Teachers Association http://www.nsta.org/
Social studies	National Council for the Social Studies http://www.ncss.org/
Technology	International Society for Technology in Education http://www.iste.org/

Using Technology
Content Standards

In designing lessons and learning activities, special educators and general educators keep content standards in mind as they plan and organize instruction. Because standards are so important to educators, each state has developed a website with information about curriculum and instruction, including standards by subject and grade level area. Knowing how to locate this information and how it is organized helps beginning teachers. Developing Educational Standards is an extensive website that provides links to each state department of education and individual state standards.

Questions for Reflection

1. How do special educators in your local schools use content standards in planning instruction?
2. What lessons and activities have you observed that address performance indicators in mathematics or other subject areas?

To answer these questions and learn more about using technology to support learning, go to the Companion Website at www. prenhall.com/cohen, select Chapter 5, then choose Using Technology.

to standards-based education violates the No Child Left Behind Act, as well as the Americans with Disabilities Act, Section 504 of the Rehabilitation Act, and the IDEA (Ordover, 2001).

Ensuring that a student has access to the general education curriculum and the same standards as students without disabilities is part of the special education process. The IEP must address how the student will access the general education curriculum, and the student's progress toward achieving content standards is documented by local and state assessments. The following section describes this process.

THE SPECIAL EDUCATION PROCESS
PLANNING THE INDIVIDUALIZED EDUCATION PROGRAM

Once the multidisciplinary team determines that a student is eligible for special education services, the IEP team convenes to develop the IEP. The IEP includes specific information about the student's current level of functioning, strengths, and needs, as illustrated in Figure 5.4. The student's IEP must be completed within 30 days. During the IEP meeting, team members consider a number of questions, such as "Based on the assessment information, what specially designed instruction does the student need?" "Does the student need any related services?" "What annual goals need to be developed and aligned with curriculum standards?" "In considering AT needs, what does the student need to do in the education program that the student is currently unable to do?" "If the student needs an AT device(s), what AT services are

Figure 5.4   Tasha's IEP

Brookville Consolidated School District: Individualized Education Program   MEETING

PART A: INFORMATION SECTION

Date: *04/10/xx*
Type:

1. *STUDENT INFORMATION*

Student Name: *Tasha Brown*   Identification Number: [^X ^]   Review #
Birth Date: *11/12/xx*   Age: *10*   Grade: *3*   Primary Language: *English*   [ ]   Reevaluation
Address: *1003 Highway 10, Brookville Station*   Home Telephone: *207-555-2765*
School Name/Address: *Brookville Elementary School*
School Telephone: *207-555-3489*

Date: *04/10/xx*
Type:
[ ]   Initial Eval.
[^X ^]   Review #
[ ]   Reevaluation

2. *PARENT INFORMATION*

Information below pertains to: [^X ^] Parent   [ ] Foster Parent   [ ] Guardian
                                       [ ] Educational Advocate   [ ] Student

Name: *Aisha Brown*   Name:
Address: *204 Southfork Road*   Address:
Town/State/Zip: *Brookville Station*   Town/State/Zip:
Home Telephone: Home Telephone:
Cell: *207-555-3372*   Other Telephone:
Primary Language of Home: *English*   Primary Language of Home:

3. *INITIAL EVALUATION AND REEVALUATION INFORMATION*

Prereferral Activities (for initial evaluation only)
Prereferral activities were implemented: [^X ^] Yes, documented in student record   [ ] No
If no, explain:

Eligibility Determination: Learning disabilities
Existence of disability: [^X ^] Yes   [ ] No
Student is making effective progress in regular education: [ ] Yes   [^X ^] No
Eligible for special education services: [^X ^] Yes   [ ] No

If student is not eligible for special education, complete Parts C & D on last page of IEP form. If student is eligible for special education, complete the IEP form.

4. *IEP INFORMATION*

Liaison Name: *Croteau, L.*   Position: *Resource Room 4–5*   Telephone: *207-555-7321*
IEP Period: *04/10/xx to 04/10/xx*   Next Scheduled Annual Review Date: *04/10/xx*
Cost share placement: [ ] Yes   [^X ^] No
If yes, participants:

PART B: STUDENT'S SECTION

1. *STUDENT PERFORMANCE PROFILE*

Describe: (a) student's areas of strength; (b) student's area(s) of need; and (c) the current level(s) of performance for each area of need that corresponds to the attached goal(s) and objectives.

Tasha is a friendly, outgoing student. She is currently experiencing some difficulties with self-esteem related to her ongoing problems in reading, math, and written language. Her academic work (reading and written language) is currently two grade levels below standard.

continued

Figure 5.4   Tasha's IEP *continued*

2. STUDENT INSTRUCTIONAL PROFILE

Describe: (a) student's approach to learning; and (b) any necessary accommodations or modifications in the classroom and other settings that will facilitate successful education for the student, including any necessary assistive technology.

Tasha demonstrates decreased effort in completing classroom assignments. Assistive technology devices that could help Tasha with reading in the content areas and in written language should be explored. The IEP chairperson will contact the assistive technology specialist to arrange for a consultation with Tasha and her teachers.

3. PARTICIPATING IN STATE AND DISTRICTWIDE ASSESSMENTS

Tasha will participate with her classmates.

4. GOALS AND OBJECTIVES

Objectives and Evaluation Procedure and Schedule

Tasha will demonstrate number, operation, and measurement concepts commensurate with the third-grade mathematics curriculum by the end of the program year.

1. *Given 5 two-step word problems (addition, subtraction, multiplication, division), Tasha will generate and accurately organize the information, compute, and explain the results in four out of five instances, as measured by teacher observation. To be reviewed: December 20.*
2. *Given at least two sets of data, Tasha will construct representative graphs (bar or line graph) and correctly interpret the information, as measured by a classroom performance-based assessment. To be reviewed: December 20.*
3. *Given an actual situation, Tasha will use a ruler to correctly solve measurement problems concerning length and perimeter in four out of five trials, as measured by teacher observation. To be reviewed: March 20.*

Progress Report Information

Progress reports shall be at least semiannual. For students in collaborative and private school placements, progress reports shall be quarterly. The annual review meets the requirements for the annual progress report.

5. SPECIAL EDUCATION SERVICE DELIVERY

School District Cycle: [*x*] 5 day cycle [   ] 6 day cycle [   ] 10 day cycle [   ] Other:
A. Consultation (Indirect Services to School Personnel and Parents)

Type of Service	Focus on Goal #	Person(s) Responsible	Start Date	Freq./Duration per Day/Cycle	Total Time	Comments (if applicable)
Couns. Monitor		*Psychologist*	*04/10/xx*	*Up to 150*	*2.50*	
					0	
					0	
					0	

Figure 5.4   Tasha's IEP *continued*

B. Special Education and Related Services in Regular Education Classroom (Direct Services)

Type of Service	Focus on Goal #	Person(s) Responsible	Start Date	Freq./Duration per Day/Cycle	Total Time	Nature of Service (if applicable)
					0	
					0	
					0	
					0	
					0	
					0	

C. Special Education and Related Services in Other Setting (Direct Services)

Type of Service	Focus on Goal #	Person(s) Responsible	Start Date	Freq./Duration per Day/Cycle	Total Time	Location
Acad. Support	1–3	Resource Room	04/10/xx	30 x 35	2.50	Reg. Class/ Resource Rm
					0	
					0	
					0	
					0	
					0	

PART C: PARTICIPANTS IN TEAM MEETING SECTION

Persons Present at Meeting	Role/Assessment Responsibility
Laura Croteau	Chairperson/Administrator of Special Services
Aisha Brown	Mother
Patricia Bloomberg	Grade 3/Teacher
Nina Fellows	Special Educator
Tasha Brown	Student

Sources of Additional Written Input

Name	Role
Jerri Fischer	Psychologist

PART D: RESPONSE OPTIONS/SIGNATURES SECTION

Parent Response and Signatures

[x]   I have received a copy of the Parents' Rights Brochure

In the space below, check the option(s) of your choice, sign and date this form, and make any comments you wish. You may request an independent evaluation* under the following circumstances: if you postpone a decision, if you reject the IEP in full, if you reject the finding of no eligibility for special education, if you reject any portion(s) of the IEP.

continued

Figure 5.4   Tasha's IEP *continued*

[x] I accept the IEP in full.

[   ] I accept the finding of no eligibility for special education.

[   ] I postpone a decision until the completion of an independent evaluation.

[   ] I request an independent evaluation.

[   ] I reject the IEP in full.

[   ] I reject the finding of no eligibility for special education.

[   ] I reject the following portions of the IEP with the understanding that any portion(s) that I do not reject will be considered accepted and implemented immediately. Rejected portions are as follows:

_____

_____

_____

[   ] I request a meeting to discuss the rejected IEP or rejected portion(s).

Signature: *Aisha Brown* _____   Date: *04/10/xx*
(Parent/Foster Parent/Guardian/Educational Advocate/Student 18 and Over)

School Personnel Response and Signatures
I certify that the goals in this IEP are those recommended by the TEAM and that the indicated services will be provided.

Jeffrey Kister _____   *4/10/xx*   *Laura Croteau* _____   *4/10/xx*
(Principal Signature/Date)   (Special Education Administrator Signature/Date)

If placement outside the local education agency is recommended, I certify that services stated in the IEP will be provided at:

_____   _____
(Facility Name/Address)   (Director of Accepting Facility Signature/Date)

*The right to an independent evaluation at school committee expense shall continue for sixteen (16) months after the initial evaluation or reevaluation with which the parent disagrees. A school committee shall not be required to pay for an independent evaluation requested or obtained after that time.

needed?" "What accommodations are indicated?" "Does the student need modifications?" "What would be the most appropriate setting for services?" "How will we evaluate the specially designed instruction and related services?"

According to IDEA, the IEP team is responsible for developing annual goals in each area where special education services will be provided. For example, the team determines that Tasha, a student with a learning disability, requires specially designed instruction in reading, language arts, and mathematics. The team decides that the phonemic awareness instruction for Tasha will consist of individualized reading instruction with the special education teacher in the resource room on a daily basis. She will be included in the general education classroom for language arts and mathematics instruction, receiving one-to-one support from the special education teacher.

Next, the team identifies and agrees on the necessary related services such as physical therapy, speech and language, and psychological services. Goals and objectives for these services are included in the student's IEP too. For Tasha, the team decides that no related services are needed at this time because her needs are solely academic.

During the development of the IEP, team members consider if the student will need classroom accommodations; if so, they determine which ones are appropriate. In

The IEP team is responsible for planning the student's individualized education program.

providing accommodations, teachers expect the same level of achievement for students with disabilities as for students without disabilities. *Accommodations* refer to changes to the education program that do not substantially alter the instructional level, the content of the curriculum, or the assessment criteria; *modifications* involve changes or adaptations in the education program that alter the level, content, and/or assessment criteria. For example, because Tasha has difficulty reading material at her grade level, she will need an accommodation regarding her social studies book. Her IEP team will need to determine what this will be. They may consider specialized software that will allow Tasha to use her laptop to listen to the text while following along as the text is displayed on the screen. This accommodation provides an alternate format, but the level of difficulty of the assignment is not changed. If the team decides to recommend the specialized software, they will need to arrange training on its use for Tasha and her special education teacher. The general education teacher and the special education teacher will meet weekly to consult and plan additional accommodations, such as breaking long assignments into multiple short ones and providing short-term feedback to support her achievement in the content areas.

The team also considers classroom modifications that the student will need. Modifications decrease the difficulty of the task or limit the number of required tasks. When a student with a disability needs modifications, teachers make changes in the student's expected level of achievement. In Tasha's case, no modifications are necessary. However, another student who needs modifications might require the support of a teacher aide who would read the social studies text aloud, substituting easier vocabulary and interpreting some of the content.

When accommodations and modifications are made for a student during instruction, the same accommodations and modifications must be made during assessment of the student's progress. In Tasha's case, her teacher will arrange for Tasha to use her laptop and specialized software to complete quizzes in social studies. In the spring, her class will be taking the statewide assessments required by the No Child Left Behind Act. This federal law mandates yearly assessment for all students in Grades 3 to 8 and at least once during Grades 10 to 12. As you may recall from Chapter 1, students with disabilities must participate in statewide assessments or the IEP team must identify an alternative assessment(s), according to IDEA. These assessments measure students' progress toward meeting the standards in each area of the curriculum. Because Tasha uses her laptop and specialized software as a classroom accommodation in reading material for the content areas, she will be allowed to use this software during the online statewide assessment for each subject area except, of course, for reading. This will allow her to participate fully in the statewide assessment along with her classmates.

Identifying Performance Levels

The IEP team identifies the student's current level of performance in each area of need. These performance levels provide the basis for the yearly evaluation of the IEP to determine whether the student made progress and continues to require special education and related services. Thus, accurate and complete information is critical. A student's level of performance should be defined by observable, measurable descriptive information. For example, Tasha's classroom teacher uses standardized assessment and the classroom curriculum, which is based on the school's English Language Arts Standards, to provide a description of her present level of performance in reading:

▦ *Present Level of Performance:* Reading ▦
Her reading achievement is considerably below that of other students in the class (15th percentile on the districtwide assessment). She lacks strategies for decoding new words. She is unable to summarize what she has read and frequently cannot restate the information.

Tasha's present level of performance, based on the school's mathematics curriculum standards, is described:

▦ *Present Level of Performance:* Mathematics ▦

1. Demonstrates number concepts 1 to 25
2. Identifies different coin combinations to make 15 cents
3. Uses measurement tools to identify feet and inches
4. Completes patterns (for example: ABAB, ABBA, AABB)

Juanita is a student who has an emotional disturbance, including general inattention and aggressive behaviors.

▦ *Present Level of Performance:* Behavior ▦
Juanita attends for a short period of time, generally no longer than 3 minutes, during teacher-directed activities. She is argumentative with other students and is quick to settle disputes by pushing and hitting others.

Celia has mild mental retardation and receives special education services in academic areas and adaptive skills.

⊞ *Present Level of Performance:* Adaptive (Self-Help) Skills ⊞

Celia takes full responsibility for adaptive skills in the area of self-care. She needs help in creating and following a schedule and in other areas of self-direction and social skills. Her current attention span is about 5 minutes.

WRITING ANNUAL GOALS

Annual goals describe what the student will accomplish during the school year while receiving specially designed instruction and related services. They address the student's academic achievement toward the district content standards in the general education classroom, as well as social and behavioral goals. Since annual goals provide an estimate of what the student will know and be able to do, the team considers several factors in developing accurate goals. The factors that help determine what a student will achieve include the student's past performance and current level of performance, as well as the student's interests, abilities, skills, goals, and motivation.

Team members develop annual goals in academic areas, and in other areas if needed. For example, they may develop goals in behavior and social skills, in communication, in adaptive behavior, or in fine and gross motor domains. Tasha's team developed the following annual goal for mathematics:

- *Mathematics:* "Tasha will demonstrate number, operation, and measurement concepts commensurate with the third-grade mathematics curriculum by the end of the program year."

Juanita, the student with problem behaviors, who receives special education services under the criteria of emotional disturbance, has several goals in addition to academic goals, including the following one:

- *Behavior:* "Juanita will improve her personal social skills by demonstrating positive behaviors and working cooperatively with peers by the end of the program year."

Celia, the student with Down syndrome who receives special education services under the criteria of mental retardation, has the following goal for adaptive skills:

- *Adaptive Skills:* "Celia will increase responsibility and attention skills to age-appropriate levels by June 20."

WRITING SHORT-TERM OBJECTIVES

Short-term objectives describe specific steps of achievement that enable the student to meet the annual goal. When a short-term objective is written, the following areas are included:

1. the behavior, which is described in terms that can be observed (level of proficiency)
2. the criteria for successful performance (degree of accuracy that is required)

3. the method of evaluating the behavior
4. the time period for review

Special educators use knowledge of a student's short-term objectives to plan instruction. For students, short-term objectives are those toward which they work. Let us take a closer look at these objectives. Tasha's short-term objectives below specify problem solving, graphing, data analysis, and using measurement indicators that will enable her to demonstrate her mathematics goal.

- *Mathematics goal:* "Tasha will demonstrate number, operation, and measurement concepts commensurate with the third-grade mathematics curriculum by the end of the program year."

Short-term objectives

1. Given 5 two-step word problems (addition, subtraction, multiplication, division), Tasha will generate and accurately organize the information, compute the answer, and explain it in four out of five instances, as measured by teacher observation. To be reviewed: December 20.
2. Given at least two sets of data, Tasha will construct representative graphs (a bar or line graph) and correctly interpret the information, as measured by a classroom performance-based assessment. To be reviewed: December 20.
3. Given an actual situation, Tasha will use a ruler to correctly solve measurement problems concerning length and perimeter in four out of five trials, as measured by teacher observation. To be reviewed: March 20.

Short-term objectives allow the teacher to describe, observe, and measure performance. For example, the terms *accurately organize, construct,* and *use* describe behaviors that can be observed. Words such as *know, understand,* or *learn* should be avoided because they are not specific in terms of describing behaviors.

The behaviors described in Tasha's objectives reflect the fact that, given specially designed instruction, she can achieve without prompting from her teacher. Her objectives also indicate that she will complete her work with 100% accuracy as she works toward achieving the mathematics standards expected of all third-grade students.

By contrast, Celia's teacher believes that she will need classroom supports, such as prompting or cueing, to help her achieve her annual goal.

- *Annual goal:* "Celia will increase her responsibility and attention skills to age-appropriate levels by June 20."

Short-term objectives

1. Given prior verbal/physical prompts, Celia will make a successful transition from one activity to another six out of six times during the school day for 5 consecutive days, as measured by teacher observation. To be reviewed: March 20.
2. Celia will follow classroom rules, with no more than one daily reminder, for 2 consecutive weeks, as measured by event recording. To be reviewed: June 20.

Using Technology
Individualized Education Program Software

IEP software allows special educators to plan, organize, and manage special education forms and paperwork, decreasing time-consuming, repetitive tasks. Software incorporates easy-to-use data entry, report-writing, and forms-generation capabilities. After student information is inserted in the on-screen form, the program can check all areas of a completed IEP to ensure that the information is complete and meets federal and state guidelines.

Teachers can create customized reports for parents or other staff members. An educator can also transfer a single student record from one staff member to another. In addition, software programs can check each student's record and provide an alert on when to issue meeting notifications. Programs track student progress on IEP goals and objectives. Over time, software can track a student through the entire special education process from initial referral to evaluation of the student's program.

Questions for Reflection

1. What features are important to you in a software program that helps organize and manage the paperwork required of special educators?
2. Preview several software programs, comparing and contrasting key features.

To learn more about using technology to support learning, go to the Companion Website at www.prenhall.com/cohen, select Chapter 5, then choose Using Technology.

Celia will accomplish her objectives with the support of teaching strategies such as prompting and fading. Eventually, her teacher will expect Celia to demonstrate these behaviors independently, and her subsequent IEP short-term objectives will reflect this achievement.

Short-term objectives provide descriptions of behaviors and criteria for successful performance so that teachers, family members, and the student know how the annual goal can be achieved. Short-term objectives include the method that will be used to evaluate the behavior and the time period for review. Knowledge of short-term objectives helps the teachers and student understand what needs to be accomplished to meet the goals. Objectives help teachers plan and monitor the individualized instruction. Finally, by using terms to describe what the student should know and be able to do, the teachers, parents, and student can readily determine whether the objectives are being met.

Special education teachers can ensure that students with disabilities have opportunities to develop higher-order thinking skills by including the skills in writing IEP goals and objectives (Figure 5.5). For example, teachers foster skills such as applying, analyzing, or synthesizing by encouraging students to work together in classroom communities of practice (Wenger, 1998). By studying Tasha's objectives above, can you determine what higher-order thinking skills her teacher is encouraging?

PLANNING INSTRUCTION

Planning instruction for students both with and without disabilities involves identifying where instruction should begin (linking assessment with instruction); planning large blocks of instruction (units) and smaller blocks, lessons, and instructional activities;

Figure 5.5　Ways of knowing and illustrative verbs for writing IEP short-term objectives

Knowledge: Recall of a wide range of material, from specific facts to theories and procedures.

Suggested verbs for stating IEP short-term objectives:
Defines, describes, identifies, labels, lists, matches, names, outlines, reproduces, selects, states.

Comprehension: The ability to grasp the meaning of material. For example, a student translates a word problem in math into numbers and mathematical operations; a student interprets a reading by explaining in his own words; a student estimates future trends based on a graph.

Suggested verbs for stating IEP short-term objectives:
Converts, defends, distinguishes, estimates, explains, extends, generalizes, gives examples, infers, para-phrases, predicts, rewrites, summarizes.

Application: The ability to use learned material in new and concrete situations.

Suggested verbs for stating IEP short-term objectives:
Changes, computes, demonstrates, discovers, manipulates, modifies, operates, predicts, prepares, produces, relates, shows, solves, uses.

Analysis: The ability to break down material into its component parts so that its organizational struc-ture can be understood. For example, a student identifies the parts of a simple engine and states how one part relates to the working of other parts.

Suggested verbs for stating IEP short-term objectives:
Breaks down, diagrams, differentiates, discriminates, distinguishes, identifies, illustrates, infers, out-lines, points out, relates, selects, separates, subdivides.

Synthesis: The ability to put parts together to form a new whole. For example, a student plans, researches, develops, and delivers a speech.

Suggested verbs for stating IEP short-term objectives:
Categorizes, combines, compiles, composes, creates, devises, designs, explains, generates, modifies, organizes, plans, rearranges, reconstructs, relates, reorganizes, revises, rewrites, summarizes, tells, writes.

Evaluation: The ability to make judgments based on certain criteria.

Suggested verbs for stating IEP short-term objectives:

Appraises, compares, concludes, contrasts, criticizes, describes, discriminates, explains, interprets, justifies, relates, summarizes, supports.

Source: Adapted from *Measurement and Evaluation in Teaching*, by N. E. Gronlund and R. L. Linn, 1990, New York: Macmillan.

using accommodations or modifications; integrating the student's AT device(s) into the classroom activities; and considering student grouping. In the following sections, we will look at each of these areas in more detail.

LINKING ASSESSMENT WITH INSTRUCTION

Linking assessment with instruction involves gathering, synthesizing, and analyzing information about students' achievements, skills, and behaviors before planning instruction. The assessment process can be informal and does not depend on standardized assessments. In the previous chapter, you learned about the many different assessment approaches educators use, including curriculum-based and criterion-referenced assessments, performance-based assessments, student interviews, and parent conferences. Using several of these approaches allows educators to gather specific information not only about what the student knows and will do, but also about the knowledge, skills, and behaviors that the student has not yet attained. After the information is obtained, the educator must synthesize and analyze it. By linking assessment with instruction in this way, educators can begin planning instruction that allows students to build on previous knowledge. As teachers begin planning instruction, they consider how it will help the student work toward one or more content area standards and their IEP objectives.

PLANNING UNITS

Teachers typically begin planning instruction at the unit level, identifying topics within the unit and then developing learning experiences and instructional activities. Special educators who are coteaching with general educators work with them in planning units. In planning at the unit level, teachers consider the content of the unit, its purpose or goal, and how these are aligned with state standards. Teachers think about how they will encourage students to demonstrate knowledge, skills, and complex thinking. Planning instruction includes not only content that reflects facts and concepts but also content that allows students to develop complex or higher order thinking and to demonstrate understanding by, for example, analyzing and evaluating information. To address the needs of all learners, teachers consider how the unit will allow students to build on previous knowledge, extend concepts, and deepen understanding.

Teaching for understanding involves developing insights and the ability to use them effectively (McTighe & Wiggins, 1999), as well as identifying the different aspects of learning. One of the first people to think about understanding in this way was Benjamin Bloom, who developed a classification system for cognitive skill development and understanding (Bloom, 1954). Others have continued to build on Bloom's taxonomy and the importance of the hierarchy of skills that comprise understanding.

McTighe and Wiggins (1999) describe understanding in terms of the following skills:

1. Explanation: Students are able to provide thorough, supported, and justifiable accounts of phenomena, facts, and data.
2. Interpretation: Students tell meaningful stories and can provide historical or personal dimensions to ideas and events. They can make them personal or accessible through images, anecdotes, analogies, and models.
3. Application: Students can effectively use and adapt what one knows in diverse contexts.
4. Perspective: Students see points of view through critical eyes and ears. They can see the big picture.
5. Empathy: Students find value in what others might find odd, alien, or implausible.
6. Self-knowledge: Students are aware of what one does not understand, of why understanding is hard, and of how one comes to understand. (p. 10)

These different dimensions of understanding provide a framework for planning instruction. Sometimes special education teachers work with general education teachers in planning, implementing, monitoring, and evaluating a unit; at other times, although this is not the best practice, special educators may be solely responsible for the unit because it is taught in the resource room or another special education setting. A unit may focus on one curriculum area, such as social studies, or it may be integrated across curriculum areas. We think of planning the unit as a process involving several steps:

1. First, teachers identify students' knowledge and skills by using various assessment approaches. If a teacher has been monitoring students' achievements closely, the teacher will already know this information.
2. Next, teachers identify the knowledge, skills, and understandings that students will acquire and be able to demonstrate as a result of learning the unit. These are aligned with content and performance standards.
3. Teachers write a brief description of the unit.
4. Teachers decide how student achievement will be measured. Teachers may identify performance tasks, work samples, quizzes, or tests as evidence of students' understanding. They develop criteria such as a rubric, checklist, grading system, or another method that will be used for evaluation.

To help keep in mind the "big picture" of planning a unit, some teachers prefer to work with a graphic organizer that illustrates the unit (Figure 5.6). Other teachers often find that a form including each component of the process works best (Figure 5.7). Which do you prefer?

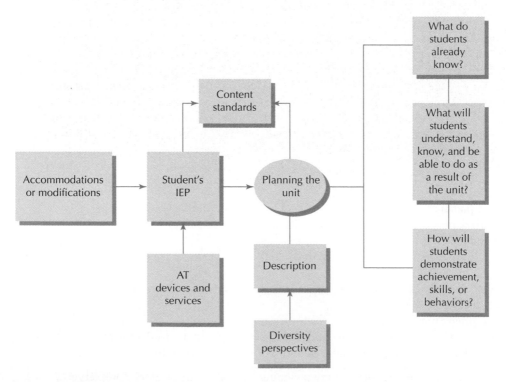

Figure 5.6   **Graphic organizer illustrating planning a unit**

Figure 5.7   Worksheet for unit planning

Planning Guide for Developing a Unit

1. Identify the skills and knowledge that students already have.

2. What greater understandings, knowledge, and skills will students acquire as a result of this unit?

3. Write a brief general description of the unit.

4. How will students demonstrate achievement?
   - Demonstrations
   - Journals
   - Performance tasks
   - Tests
   - Quizzes
   - Work samples
   - Other

5. How will students demonstrate improvement in behavior?
   - Demonstrations
   - Reflective writings
   - Performance tasks
   - Other

6. Describe how the content addresses diversity perspectives.

7. Content standards linked to this unit:

Using Technology
Web Resources for Planning Instruction

The Internet contains a vast array of resources for planning instruction. Educators can design a unit or an individual lesson by accessing video, text, audio, or software from the World Wide Web, or they can locate examples of challenging classroom activities, view peer-reviewed materials such as student projects, and learn about various teaching methods and instructional strategies by watching video clips. For additional information you can begin by visiting one or more of the following sites:

- **PBS TeacherSource:** This site contains over 4,000 free lesson plans and activities in arts and literature, health and fitness, mathematics, science, and social studies (http://www.pbs.org/teachersource).
- **ISTE K–12 Teacher Resources:** The International Society for Technology in Education maintains a vast array of curriculum resources, including art, biology, chemistry, environment, economics, foreign languages, general science, geology, history, language arts, mathematics, music, physical education, physics, social studies, and space (http://www.iste.org/resources/curriculum/k-12/index.cfm).
- **The Teacher's Corner: Multidisciplinary Classroom Activities:** This site,

created by NASA, contains a variety of lesson plans and other resource materials, primarily for educators at the middle and secondary levels (http://imagine.gsfc.nasa.gov/docs/teachers/teachers_corner.html).

- **Federal Resources for Educational Excellence:** This website is constantly being updated with teaching ideas and resources. One may search for resources in various curriculum areas, including arts, educational technology, foreign languages, health and safety, language arts, mathematics, physical education, science, social studies, and vocational education (http://www.ed.gov/free).

Questions for Reflection

1. Explore several of the websites presented above. Which ones would be most helpful to you in your teaching? Why?
2. Using a search engine, find several additional teacher resources that you can use in planning instruction, and share them with your colleagues.

 To answer these questions and learn more about using technology to support learning, go to the Companion Website at www.prenhall.com/cohen, select Chapter 5, then choose Using Technology.

PLANNING LESSONS AND INSTRUCTIONAL ACTIVITIES

Instructional activities and learning experiences enable students to integrate new learning with prior knowledge and experiences. During the planning process, both special and general educators keep content standards in mind, aligning instruction with standards and performance indicators. One team of educators developed a learning activity they called "Alphabet and Animal Problem" (Maine Mathematics & Science Alliance, 2001–2003) that focuses on understanding algebra concepts. Figure 5.8 illustrates the

Figure 5.8   Fourth-grade learning activity assigned with algebra content standard and performance indicator

The Alphabet and Animal Problem

Sometimes a letter or symbol can stand for (be equal to) a numerical value. Maybe you have worked with codes or solved equations. This task asks you to figure out a mathematical code and to use the code in some different ways.

Rose's teacher listed the following equations on the board:

$A = 1, B = 2, C = 3, D = 4, E = 5$ and so on all the way to $Z = 26$

The teacher explained that she would write the names of certain animals on the board and that the students would be asked to figure out a number value for each animal using the same process that she had used in the following examples:

$$CAT = 24, \quad DOG = 26, \quad BEE = 12, \quad BAT = 23, \quad FROG = 46$$

1. Make a complete listing of all letters of the alphabet and the value that each is worth.

2. Using the same method as the teacher, find the value for the following animals: (Show all your work/equations.)

SQUIRREL =

ELEPHANT =

OCTOPUS =

continued

Figure 5.8   **Fourth-grade learning activity assigned with algebra content standard and performance indicator** *continued*

3. Is it possible to have a value of 90 or more for an animal that has exactly three letters in its name? How do you know?

4. Name a different animal than those listed before that has a value of more than 40. What is the value of the animal you just named? Show your work.

Figure 5.8   **Fourth-grade learning activity assigned with algebra content standard and performance indicator** *continued*

TEACHER NOTES WORKSHEET

Aligned Content Standards & Performance Indicators

H. Algebra Concepts

1. Develop and evaluate simple formulas in problem-solving contexts.

National Standards Link: NCTM S-2, G-2, pp. 160–161.

Description of targeted skills and knowledge

Substituting numerical values for alphabet letters and finding sums.

Suggestions for prior instruction, associated resources, etc.

Similar work at an introductory level
May use calculator—be sure to mark on entry slip.
Make sure to remind students to show their equations even if they use a calculator.
Example:
DOG = 26   4 + 15 + 7 = 26

*It is highly recommended that you do not photocopy the students' task on back-to-back pages, as it makes the transposing of letter values more difficult.

Source: Maine Assessment Portfolio, Maine Mathematics and Science Alliance, 2001–2003, Maine Department of Education. Used with permission.

student activity and the teacher notes worksheet. Note that in the worksheet the teachers reference the content standard, Algebra Concepts, illustrated earlier in Table 5.2, and the performance indicator to which this lesson is aligned.

Teachers also consider the use of AT, student groupings, and materials that will provide opportunities for students to succeed. One special educator developed a form to facilitate planning and organizing instruction, as illustrated in Figure 5.9. She also brainstormed a list of ways that students could access information through a variety of sources, including print materials, digital text, video, and audiotapes (Figure 5.10).

Sometimes educators structure learning activities to tap the special capabilities of technology. Harris (2000–2001) suggests a framework for planning that includes telecollaborative activities (interpersonal exchange), teleresearch activities (information collection and analysis), and sequences of student actions (problem solving) (Figure 5.11). Within each of these areas, an educator can plan to use various activity structures that emphasize different skills. For example, an educator who is planning learning activities that will build skills in writing examines the activities described

Figure 5.9   Specially designed instruction plan

Specially Designed Instruction Plan for _____
Date:
Objectives:
(What will the student be able to demonstrate after completing the instructional activity?)

Link to standard:_____

Links to Student's IEP:
(How does the experience/activity link to IEP short-term objectives?)

Materials Needed:
(What books, visual aids, equipment, and other resources will you need for the experience/activity?)

Procedure:
(What is the content and what will be covered? What teaching method and strategies will be used?)

Accommodations and Modifications:
(What accommodations or modifications will be needed for students with disabilities?)

Assisitive Technology:
(How will the student's use of assistive technology be supported?)

Student Grouping:
(Will students work independently or in groups? What are the student responsibilities?)

Teacher Role:
(Is the teacher the primary source of information or will the teacher be a facilitator of learning?)

Assessment:
(What approaches will be used to determine if the objectives have been met?)

Figure 5.10   Using alternative formats

Teachers can choose from a variety of alternative formats so that material is accessible to *all* students.

- Audiotape of book
- CD of book
- Videotape of book
- Videotape with closed captioning
- Large-print copy of book
- Software version of book
- Raised or highlighted graphs or diagrams of drawings in book

under *interpersonal exchange*. Which activity in Figure 5.11 would you select if you wanted to create enthusiasm for student writing?

PLANNING FOR ACCOMMODATIONS AND MODIFICATIONS

As teachers plan instruction, they refer to the individual student's IEP to check on the accommodations or modifications that are described. The teacher may need to plan changes to the lesson or activity based on this information. For example, if the IEP describes modifications needed by the student, the teacher will need to plan adaptations to the lesson or activity that alter the level, content, and/or assessment criteria.

Organizing instruction involves paying attention to details.

Figure 5.11   Specific activity structures categorized by genre and learning processes

Genre	Activity Structure	Learning Process Emphasis
Interpersonal Exchange	Keypals	Longer-term, interest-driven, one-to-one written communication is based on emergent topics of conversation. Can be used to motivate students to communicate in writing.
	Global Classrooms	Longer-term, group-to-group discussion in writing of structured or semi-structured topics. Can be used to help students research and hone their assertions and arguments.
	Electronic Appearances	Short-term communication "event" with someone special by virtue of reputation and/or expertise. Good way to pique interest in a particular topic or event.
	Telementoring	Longer-term communication by writing in a mentor–protégé format. Rich possibilities for long-term professional/ personal relationships/modeling.
	Question & Answer	Very short-term written communication to clarify or complete understanding of a complex topic.
	Impersonations	Variable-term written communication necessitating deep-level, actively applied understanding of a historical period or literary work. Impersonation format is usually quite motivating.
Information Collection and Analysis	Information Exchanges	Variable-term communication in which similar information is compared and contrasted. Especially effective when students are comparing locally generated information that differs across collection sites.
	Database Creation	Previously accumulated information is analyzed deeply enough so that it can be classified and organized for others to use to form higher-level understanding.
	Electronic Publishing	Fruits of learning efforts are formatted so that others can benefit from perusing them. Good for both learning closure and public relations.

Figure 5.11   Specific activity structures categorized by genre and learning processes *continued*

	Telefield Trips	People (and less frequently, animals) are shadowed while they are active so that their experiences can be vicariously apperceived.
	Pooled Data Analysis	Similar information is pooled from multiple sites so that overarching patterns can be discerned. A higher level of thinking than information exchanges.
Problem Solving	Information Searches	Information-searching skills are honed.
	Peer Feedback Activities	Multiple sources of feedback are provided and received so that successive drafts of student work can be prepared.
	Parallel Problem Solving	Different problem-solving strategies applied to the same challenge are compared, contrasted, and appreciated. Good for helping students realize that there are "many right answers" to a problem.
	Sequential Creations	Collaboration on a common product that occurs sequentially rather than simultaneously. Deeper-level understanding of what has been created before is necessary if the work is to continue in a consistent manner.
	Telepresent Problem Solving	Real-time brainstorming and problem-solving skills are exercised using text chat and/or videoconferencing. Good vehicle for use of previously researched information and/or prepared questions.
	Simulations	Immersion in a content-rich, individualized or collaborative context for learning produces in-depth, experiential understanding of the problem situation being explored.
	Social Action Projects	Authentic commitment to assisting others is coupled with authentic learning about a current, often global problem.

Source: Reprinted from *Learning & Leading with Technology,* Vol. 28, No. 4, copyright © 2000–2001, ISTE (International Society for Technology in Education), 800-336-5191 (U.S. & Canada) or 541-302-3777 (Int'l.), iste@iste.org, www.iste.org. All rights reserved. Reprint permission does not constitute an endorsement by ISTE.

PLANNING FOR INTEGRATING ASSISTIVE TECHNOLOGY

The student's IEP also describes the AT devices and services that the student needs. Planning instruction involves considering how the student can use AT in the classroom to work more efficiently or more effectively. For a student who has difficulty reading for meaning in the content areas, specialized software allows the student to listen to material that has been scanned into the computer, such as a supplemental booklet or teacher handout. For a student who has difficulty organizing information, specialized software such as Kidspiration and Inspiration provide areas for brainstorming and creating outlines. For a student who has limited keyboarding skills, speech-to-text software allows the student to create written text by speaking. For a student who has difficulty spelling and producing a piece of writing, word processing with word prediction provides word prompts and requires fewer keystrokes.

Planning for integrating AT involves checking that the specialized software and necessary hardware are installed and working. Planning also includes considering how the student will use the AT device during instructional activities or learning experiences. In later chapters, we discuss specific examples of AT and how teachers plan instruction that allows students with disabilities to use these technology tools.

PLANNING STUDENT GROUPINGS

All students should have opportunities to work collaboratively with others. Sometimes educators plan an activity that depends on two students working together, either as partners or one as the tutor and one as the tutee. Or a teacher might set up a problem-solving partnership with two to three students, a cooperative team with three to four students, or a collaborative group with three to six students (Table 5.3). In planning and organizing group work, teachers can enhance the effectiveness of student groups by including these common characteristics:

> Work done in groups is challenging and meaningful. The teacher is always actively involved in the students' learning process, serving as a resource person, questioner, guide, evaluator, and coach. Learning goals and timelines are clearly understood by the students and monitored by the teacher. Groups are heterogeneous, and all students are actively involved. Cooperation is valued over competition. Students have a sense of being able to accomplish more learning together than they can alone. The group process provides a comfort level for discussion and airing questions. Student interaction and social skills are required, but the purpose of grouping is not primarily social. Group time is not "free time" for student (or teacher). Multiple means of assessment are possible (rubrics, portfolios, quizzes, interviews, presentations, etc.). Evaluation can be of the individual student, of the group, or a combination of these. (Damian, 2001, p. 27)

———————— ❖ PROFESSIONAL PERSPECTIVES ❖ ————————

In the fifth-grade classroom at Central School, the general and special education teachers work together in planning and organizing a science unit they named "Endangered Species," illustrated in Figure 5.12. Their unit will cover several weeks of lessons as they follow four phases. In phase one, the teachers will establish the

Table 5.3	Using Student Groups to Assist Learning

Three Learning Group Strategies

Problem-Solving Partnerships	Cooperative Teams	Collaborative Groups
Two to three students per group	Three to four students per group	Three to six students per group
The duration of group work is short (part of a class period to a few days).	The duration of group work ranges from several days to several weeks.	The duration of group work can be short (days) or longer (weeks or even months).
The specific task or problem to solve is limited in scope (a single problem or question or a limited set) and is usually a challenge or practice activity for students to apply recent learning.	The problem or task is clearly defined by the teacher.	The task or problem is open-ended and may cover large amounts of course content.
Multiple approaches to solving the problem are encouraged. There is no single "right" way to solve most problems, and all reasonable solutions or answers to the problem are honored.	A team plan of operation and goals is specified, and teams are highly structured. Each student has a clearly defined role in the team such as recorder, questioner, reporter. The teacher takes time to teach each student role.	Student roles are flexible and may change throughout the project or assignment. Students observe (and help with) other students' work, and critique, evaluate, explain, and suggest ways for improvement.
Individual students have an opportunity to explain and discuss their suggested solutions as well as their misconceptions.	Team members share leadership within the framework of specific roles.	Open communication and multiple approaches are emphasized. All students are involved in honest discussion about ideas, procedures, experimental results, gathered information, interpretations, resource materials, and their own or other students' work.
New understandings are developed by the individual, by the team, and, finally, by the whole class.	All team members must contribute or the team cannot progress. (Teams "win or lose together.") The end product represents the entire team.	
Group and class discussions (and solutions) provide immediate feedback to the student.	The team focus is on cooperation as well as on achievement of goals. Awareness of the group process is as important as completing the task.	Students are constantly aware of the collaborative communication process, as well as the product or goals. They know they can change direction to meet goals.

Source: Excerpted from Damian, Carol. (2001). *Student Learning Groups That Really Work. ENC Focus 8*(2), 25–29. Reprinted with permission of Eisenhower National Clearinghouse; visit ENC Online (http://www.enc.org/).

Figure 5.12   Thematic unit: Endangered species

	Unit Plan	Considerations During *Teacher Collaboration in Planning for Universal Design for Learning*
Goals	Students will develop awareness of both natural and man-made causes that impede endangered species of our world. Students will use this knowledge to convince human forces to change.	**Evaluate:** Define instructional goal(s) for all learners, separating the means from the goal and aligning the lesson to the standard(s).
	Guiding questions:	
	1. Who or what is responsible for the endangerment of various plant and animal species throughout our world? What problems have remained consistent over time?	
	2. What global changes can be made to protect the vulnerable animals at risk of extinction?	
	3. How much control do we really have?	
	4. What ways can we make ourselves heard?	
	5. Where do we go from here?	
Materials	**Resources:**	**Consider multiple means of access.**
	• *Rain Forest Rap*—video by World Wildlife Fund	• Make accessible with text information in format different from print using:
	• *The Great Kapok Tree* by Lynne Cherry	– Text-to-speech
	• Local or national newspaper clippings about animals in danger of extinction	– Enlarged font, greater color contrasts, etc.
	• *Ranger Rick* magazines, *Nature Conservancy* and *Sierra Club* newsletters	– Enhanced graphics
	• Houghton Mifflin Grade 5 Reading Anthology Theme Unit on "Operation Wildlife"	– Alternative tags
		• Assure that video is available with captioned sound track for students with hearing challenges.
	• Internet resources such as World Wildlife Fund (wwf.com) for current information on endangered species throughout the world	• Access newspapers/journals/magazines electronically available.
	• Other research resources: Encyclopedias on CD, nonfiction picture books of endangered animals	• Assistive technology devices as necessary
	• "Rain Forest Live" unit sponsored by Ocean Challenge, Inc.	– Toggle switches
		– Pointers
		– Response recording
		– Keyboarding alternatives

Tools:

- *Inspiration* software by Tom Snyder
- Projection unit for computer on classroom screen
- Computers with word processing software
- Pens, pencils

Procedures		
Phase 1	**Introduction: Purpose, Motivation, Exploration, Gathering**	
	- The unit is introduced to the whole class using oral presentation. - Focus students' attention on the purpose of the lesson. - Motivate student interest. - Offer exploration of the topic. - Emphasize information gathering as a foundation for application.	- Student engagement can be optimized with the use of graphic organizers as visual aids. - Consider prior knowledge students bring to the unit (e.g., rain forest, endangered, habitat, species). - Identify students for whom it is appropriate to pre-teach concepts if not covered in previous units. - Consider supports for listening and hearing during lecture presentation.
	Thinking Cap Question (local term used to engage children in reflective thinking): Can we be optimistic about the situation in our rain forests today? Why or why not?	
	Activity 1	
	Students view the video "Rain Forest Rap," by World Wildlife Fund, includes footage of rain forest either being burned or cut down. When left alone, the rain forest is thriving, it is home to hundreds and thousands of species. A six-minute clip, with musical interlude, a rap song about the tropical rain forest, offers optimism as more people become aware and proactive.	- Universally designed videos are closed-captioned and verbally described to benefit a full range of students, including visually and hearing-impaired children. - Provide scaffolds with note-taking devices to assist students in recalling important information. - Offer scaffolds such as pre-video questioning for learners to hear or see for specific information during the viewing.

continued

Figure 5.12   Thematic unit: Endangered species *continued*

Unit Plan	Considerations During *Teacher Collaboration* in Planning for Universal Design for Learning
Activity 2 Teacher and students discuss reactions, concerns, and feelings about what was learned from the video. A discussion regarding why animals are endangered (i.e., loss of habitat) and add to the K-W-L chart "Why Animals Are Endangered."	• Positioning of students in front of the display screen to optimize viewing for students with low vision or hearing impairments in need of speech reading/sign language. • Positioning to prompt students with attention issues. • K-W-L charts help children be focused, organized and engaged. • Some students may require individual charts to follow the flow of group problem solving and discussion.
Activity 3 Teacher reads aloud the story *The Great Kapok Tree*, by Lynne Cherry. Children pay attention to the various and numerous kinds of animals, plants and insects that are indigenous to the tropical rain forest. Ask children to choose one animal and respond to the **thinking cap question** in writing: "If you were an animal in this forest and had the opportunity to give the story character Senhor a message, what would you say?" Option for students to share their messages with the class.	• Class "read aloud" provides students with a model of oral fluency and prompts students with comprehension difficulties to listen with purpose. • Provide options for creating different responses to question (e.g. screen readers, voice recognition) to support this activity. • Students with written or expressive language difficulties could note message using a range of modes (e.g., PowerPoint and synthesized speech).
Activity 4 From a collection of sources (Scholastic newspapers, *Boston Globe* articles, and *Nature Conservancy/Sierra Club* newsletters), the teacher will share information about animals that are extinct, endangered, and those returning to the wild. Consider jigsaw cooperative groups of four, so each group will become an expert storyteller of one animal's fate or fortune.	• Make available a broad selection of articles in digital format for students with disabilities. • The formation of expert cooperative groups requires a distribution of roles within each group to examine the literature & develop a story to tell about their particular animal. • Students cooperate to study available resources and gather information (photos, drawings and text).

Phase II

Experience: Active Involvement and Personal Relevance—Application and Further Analysis

Actively involve students and encourage them to raise concerns, consider issues, develop questions, or seek solutions using active participation and interactive processing.

- Monitor to assure engagement in activities.
- Provide multiple means to respond and express ideas and information about the topic.

Activity 11

Develop an awareness of words that persuade.

- Demonstrate meaning of persuasive and not persuasive language.
- Students identify sentences that use persuasive language. e.g., "People searching for oil and minerals threaten to destroy the polar bear's environment," or "People searching for oil and minerals are changing the polar bear's environment."

- Provide multiple means of representation when presenting sentences or words.
- Consider starting exercise with single words and moving to sentence level.
- Scaffold from easy to more difficult the discrimination between sentences.
- Consider more than two sentences to make task more complex, make less complex by providing simpler sentence structure.

Activity 12

Students apply use of persuasive language in communications.

- Students brainstorm words in the English language that are persuasive, especially action words.
- Teacher introduces concept of bias in writing
- Individual students record word list in their research folder.

- Scaffold with examples/counter-examples of persuasive words.
- Consider computer software as a tool—*Inspiration*—use as a tool to record brainstorming.
- Offer multiple means for students to record and store their lists of persuasive words.
- Provide background language information, i.e., action words, bias, persuasive.

continued

Figure 5.12   Thematic unit: Endangered species *continued*

	Unit Plan	Considerations During *Teacher Collaboration* in Planning for Universal Design for Learning
Phase III	**Experience:** Construction of Meaning: Understanding Whole Class and Individual Activities	• Provide students with options for responding, reacting, demonstrating knowledge.
	The students will individually choose one of the four options that are presented here for Application, Synthesis, and Evaluation. Provide students with the opportunity to construct meaning from knowledge and experience. Emphasize critical and creative thinking.	• Provide options to engage that promote self-determination and focus attention.
		• Provide supports for decision-making and options selection.
	Option 1: Persuasive Commercial with Artistic Expression	• Provide structures for demonstrating knowledge in a persuasive structure and to prepare learners for audience. For example:
	Create a persuasive commercial containing the following elements:	— Be prepared to answer questions.
	A written script from the point of view of the animal containing:	— Memorize the script in order to be videotaped.
		— Plan to be dressed as your animal.
	____ Information about the animal itself	• Consider options for presentation mode. Traditionally, we think of standing in front of the class and speaking. Options:
	____ Reasons for its risk of extinction	— Prepare computer slide presentation.
	____ Ways to prevent extinction or to help save the animal	— Make and show video.
		— Create a poster session.
	____ Script must be persuasive, with appropriate language so that viewers commit to efforts	• Provide scaffolding of persuasive presentation components.
	Be prepared to answer questions; memorize the script in order to be videotaped, and plan to be dressed as selected animal.	— State position.
		— Present facts and opinions to support position.
	Artistic Expression	— Present alternate arguments.
	Choose one idea brainstormed in class to present during videotaping.	— Argue why alternate positions are not good.
		— Present concluding statement of position.

Option 2: Create a Set and Role Play

Put on a skit complete with background.

- Create a background set, props, etc. to depict an accurate image of your endangered animal in its habitat.
- Emphasize unique characteristics (beyond its being "cute").
- Describe importance in our ecosystem.
- Demonstrate problems facing this animal.
- Address how enthusiasts can join the cause.
- Provide specific information on how to protect animal.
- Invite classmates to play a part in production.
- Skit to be word processed so that work may be reviewed.

- Provide options for methods to create materials to enhance presentation.
  - Draw
  - Computer images
  - Collage
  - Projected image versus paper
- Provide scaffolds for students to prepare a play set
- Provide scaffolds to put on a play/skit
- Consider options for skit script other than word processing (e.g., recorded, concept map, drawings)

| *Phase IV* | **Closure: Debrief, Conclude, Culminate** |

Teacher, complete the objectives of lesson and relate findings to concepts.

Debrief

- Students will complete the K-W-L chart in a whole class discussion.
- Students will openly discuss satisfaction about progress our world is making in helping endangered species to survive.

- Effective strategies include: open discussion, small group processing, written comments, student presentations, Q/A discussion, "what-if" questions, and written evaluation.

continued

Figure 5.12 Thematic unit: Endangered species *continued*

Unit Plan	Considerations During *Teacher Collaboration in Planning for* Universal Design for Learning
Conclude	Options for display of projects:
• Facilitate students' sharing of products and results, drawing conclusions about concepts, or developing new problems to study.	• School library • Endangered Species Awareness breakfast for families • Student body • Showcase brochures • Show the persuasive commercials • Display graphs and letters (and any responses) to representatives • Skit backdrops can form display
• As visitors view the displays, they may opt to hear nonfiction stories. The children will read their book to listeners.	
• Opportunities to pair up with a student from another class will be provided to give students the opportunity to read before a live audience.	
Culminate	
• Offer opportunity to do creative, independent activities, extending knowledge into creative production.	
• Students establish long-term commitments to endangered animals and seek opportunities to remain involved.	
• Discuss/brainstorm ways students could continue learning.	
• Introduce "Rain Forest Live," by Ocean Challenge, Inc. link to the School for Field Studies (SFS) Center for Rain Forest Studies in Queensland, Australia. Newsletter about discoveries and new information. Students may write questions at any time throughout the year.	

Source: From *Teacher Planning and the Universal Design for Learning Environments,* by R. Jackson and K. Harper, 2001, National Center on Accessing the General Curriculum. Reprinted with permission.

purpose and motivation for learning through student exploration. Phase two will actively involve students by making the topic personally relevant. Phase three will help students construct meaning and achieve understanding. Phase four will provide closure by guiding students to analyze their learning and share their products, which demonstrate what they know and are able to do. Their plans include considerations during teacher collaboration in planning for a wide range of student abilities. Carefully review the teachers' plans illustrated in Figure 5.12. What additional suggestions could you make?

ORGANIZING INSTRUCTION

After teachers plan instruction, it is time to get ready for students. Organizing instruction involves attention to many details: materials, equipment, outside resources, and room arrangement, for example. The teacher reviews the materials that will be needed for instruction and assembles them. Materials must be well organized and labeled. Unless they are potentially dangerous, such as lab materials, they should be easily accessible for student use. If the teacher has not previously used the materials in the planned activity, the teacher should conduct a practice activity using the materials to ensure that the activity will go as planned.

The teacher checks all equipment to make sure that it is working properly. If this is the first time the teacher is using it, conducting a practice session including the equipment will allow the teacher to troubleshoot any problems before using it with students. Equipment that must be obtained from the computer lab or equipment resource center should be ordered well in advance. If the learning activity involves equipment with which some students are not familiar, the teacher will have to organize classroom space so that these students can learn and practice using the equipment without disturbing the other students.

Organizing the classroom space is another detail that the teacher considers. If the planned instruction involves small-group work, the teacher organizes work space for the students by combining desks or identifying small classroom tables for use. If the activity involves all of the students, the teacher organizes seating to promote positive student behaviors. For example, the teacher may plan to separate two students or place one student near another one who provides a good role model. Figure 5.13 illustrates a teacher-created checklist for organizing instruction.

PROFESSIONAL STANDARDS FOR TEACHERS

This chapter began by discussing content and performance standards for students, but there are also standards for teachers. The Council for Exceptional Children, the national professional organization for teachers who work with students with disabilities, outlines a set of professional standards that special educators follow in planning instruction. Table 5.4 illustrates these standards, which ensure a quality education for students with disabilities.

Figure 5.13   A teacher-created checklist for organizing instruction

My To-Do List

Materials needed

- Dry erase markers and eraser
- Highlighters
- Markers
- Pens/pencils
- Software

Equipment needed

- Data projector—working
- Computers—working

Outside resources needed

- _____
- _____

Room arrangement

- Desks
- Tables

Table 5.4	Council for Exceptional Children Standards for Professional Practice: Instructional Responsibilities

Special education personnel are committed to the application of professional expertise to ensure the provision of quality education for all individuals with exceptionalities. Professionals strive to:

1. Identify and use instructional methods and curricula that are appropriate to their area of professional practice and effective in meeting the individual needs of persons with exceptionalities.
2. Participate in the selection and use of appropriate instructional materials, equipment, supplies, and other resources needed in the effective practice of their profession.
3. Create safe and effective learning environments which contribute to fulfillment of needs, stimulation of learning, and self-concept.
4. Maintain class size and case loads which are conducive to meeting the individual instructional needs of individuals with exceptionalities.
5. Use assessment instruments and procedures that do not discriminate against persons with exceptionalities on the basis of race, color, creed, sex, national origin, age, political practices, family or social background, sexual orientation, or exceptionality.
6. Base grading, promotion, graduation, and/or movement out of the program on the individual goals and objectives for individuals with exceptionalities.
7. Provide accurate program data to administrators, colleagues, and parents, based on efficient and objective record keeping practices, for the purpose of decision making.
8. Maintain confidentiality of information except when information is released under specific conditions of written consent and statutory confidentiality requirements.

Source: From *What Every Special Educator Must Know: The International Standards for the Preparation and Certification of Special Education Teachers,* Council for Exceptional Children, 2003, Arlington, VA: Council for Exceptional Children. Reprinted with permission.

Using Technology
Technology Standards for Teachers

The International Society for Technology in Education describes national educational technology standards and performance indicators for teachers. These technology standards include Performance Profiles (ISTE, 2000) that have been developed to correspond to the four phases of typical teacher preparation programs:

1. General Preparation
2. Professional Education
3. Student Teaching/Internship
4. First-Year Teacher

Each of these phases includes several performance profiles that beginning teachers should be prepared to meet. Some of the standards are particularly relevant to working with students with disabilities.

Questions for Reflection

1. Considering the national educational technology standards and performance indicators for teachers, how well prepared do you feel? To learn more about these standards, visit the International Society for Technology in Education website (http://www.iste.org).
2. Which standards do you think are most relevant for educators working with students with disabilities?

To answer these questions and learn more about using technology to support learning, go to the Companion Website at www. prenhall.com/cohen, select Chapter 5, then choose Using Technology.

SUMMARY

- Special educators work with other team members to develop a student's IEP, which is aligned with the school's curricular content standards.
- The IEP describes annual goals and objectives for the student and guides educators in planning and organizing specialized instruction.
- Planning instruction begins with identifying what the student knows and is able to do. Teachers gather this information using a variety of assessment approaches.
- Educators develop blocks of instruction, including units, activities, and learning experiences. When a student's IEP describes a list of accommodations or modifications, the teacher includes them in the instruction, in the learning experiences, and/or in the assessment activities. In addition, if the student's IEP describes AT that the student requires, the teacher plans its integration into the instructional activities or learning experiences and into the assessment activities.
- Teachers plan a variety of activities to help students work independently as well as collaboratively with small groups of other students.
- Linking assessment with instruction gives students many opportunities to demonstrate what they know and can do.
- Finally, teachers measure their own growth by using standards and performance indicators developed by professional organizations.

EXTENDING LEARNING

1. Visit a local school and observe the classroom environments. How would you describe the learning environment? The social environment? The physical environment? What is the impact on student learning?

2. What are the content standards or curriculum frameworks for your state? Determine if this information is available on your state department of education's website and download a copy.

3. Plan to interview two educators at different grade levels about one or more of the units they are implementing in their classroom. How do they use district or state standards in their curriculum planning?

4. Using one of the units from the previous activity, work with a small group of peers to brainstorm what students may already know about the topic. Develop a brief description of the unit. What do you want the students to know and understand as a result of learning this unit? Brainstorm learning experiences and instructional activities. What accommodations would you implement for a student with a learning disability? For a student with mental retardation? Would modifications be needed? If so, describe them.

5. Obtain a lesson plan from one of the teachers. Compare it with those gathered by other students in the class. How are they alike? Different? What types of information would be most helpful for you to include in your own lesson plans?

6. Do a Web search for examples of student IEPs. Print copies and share them. Working with a small group of other students, compare how the IEPs are written. What suggestions can you make?

7. Carefully review the technology standards for teachers. Identify ways you can demonstrate your own achievement in working toward these standards.

REFERENCES

Aefsky, F. (1995). *Inclusion confusion: A guide to educating students with exceptional needs.* Thousand Oaks, CA: Corwin Press.

Black, S. (2000). Together again: The practice of *looping* keeps students with the same teachers. *American School Board Journal, 187*(6), 40–43.

Bloom, B. S. (1954). *Taxonomy of educational objectives.* New York: Longman.

Bonilla, C. A., & Goss, J. (1997). *Public (K–12) education's hot jalapenos.* Stockton, CA: ICA, Inc. (ERIC Document Reproduction Service No. ED405684)

Chirichello, M., & Chirichello, C. (2001). A standing ovation for looping: The critics respond. *Childhood Education, 78*(1), 2–9.

Cohen, L. G., & Spenciner, L. J. (2003). *Assessment of children and youth with special needs.* Boston: Allyn & Bacon.

Council for Exceptional Children. (2003). *What every special educator must know: The international standards for the preparation and certification of special education teachers.* Arlington, VA: Author.

Dalton, S. S. (1998). *Pedagogy matters: Standards for effective teaching practice.* Retrieved June 24, 2002, from Research Reports from the National Research and Development Centers website: http://research.cse.ucla.edu/

Damian, C. (2001). Student learning groups that really work. *ENC Focus, 8,* 25–29.

Gronlund, N. E., & Linn, R. L. (1990). *Measurement and evaluation in teaching.* New York: Macmillan.

Harris, J. (2000–2001). Structuring Internet-enriched learning spaces for understanding and action. *Learning and Leading with Technology, 28*(4), 51–55.

Hunt, P. (2000). "Community" is what I think everyone is talking about. *Remedial and Special Education, 21*(5), 305–317.

International Society for Technology in Education. (2000–2001). *National educational technology standards for teachers.* Eugene, OR: Author.

Jackson, R., & Harper, K. (2001). *Teacher planning and universal design for learning environments.* Retrieved August 8, 2002, from the CAST website: http://www.cast.org/ncac/reports/tpractice2.rtf

Jorgensen, C. M. (1997). *Curriculum and its impact on inclusion and the achievement of students with disabilities.* CISP Issue Brief, 2(2). Pittsburgh: Allegheny Singer Research Institute. (ERIC Document Reproduction Service No. ED409684)

Lincoln, R. D. (2000). Looping at the middle school level: Implementation and effects. *ERS Spectrum, 18*(3), 19–24.

Maine Mathematics and Science Alliance. (2001–2003). *The alphabet and animal problem, Maine Assessment Portfolio.* Retrieved January 3, 2004, from the Maine Assessment Portfolio (MAP) website: http://www.maptasks.org/docs/107282787110927.pdf

McTighe, J., & Wiggins, G. (1999). *Understanding by design.* Alexandria, VA: Association for Supervision and Curriculum Development.

Murray, C., & Greenberg, M. T. (2001). Relationships with teachers and bonds with school: Social emotional adjustment correlates for children with and without disabilities. *Psychology in the Schools, 38*(1), 25–41.

National Center on Educational Outcomes (1994). *Students with disabilities and educational standards: Recommendations for policy and practice.* Retrieved April 28, 2004, from http://www.education.umn.edu/NCEO/onlinepubs/Policy2.html

Ordover, E. L. (2001). *Education rights of children with disabilities: A revised and updated primer for advocates.* Washington, DC: Center for Law in Education.

Pavri, S., & Monda-Amaya, L. (2000). Loneliness and students with learning disabilities in inclusive classrooms: Self-perceptions, coping strategies, and preferred interventions. *Learning Disabilities Research and Practice, 15*(10), 22–33.

Reynolds, J. C., Barnhart, B., & Martin, B. N. (1999). Looping: A solution to the retention vs. local promotion dilemma. *ERS Spectrum, 17*(2), 16–20.

Shade, B. J., Kelly, C., & Oberg, M. (1997). *Creating culturally responsive classrooms.* Washington, DC: American Psychological Association.

State of Maine learning results. (1997). Augusta: Maine Department of Education.

Treder, D., Kutash, K., Duchnowski, A. J., Calvanese, P. K., Robbins, V., Oliveria, B., & Black, M. (1999). School and community study: Exemplary school models and student outcomes over time. Tampa: University of South Florida. (ERIC Document Reproduction Service No. ED445461)

Wenger, E. (1998). *Communities of practice: Learning, meaning, and identity.* Cambridge: Cambridge University Press.

6

Chapter

Methods for Teaching Students with Mild and Moderate Disabilities

After completing this chapter, you should be able to:

❖ Discuss contemporary theories of learning.

❖ Identify and describe research-based teaching methods for students with disabilities.

❖ Compare and contrast two or more teaching methods.

❖ Demonstrate an understanding of diversity perspectives when considering methods for teaching.

❖ Describe ways educators use technology to support teaching methods.

Educators implement instruction in a variety of ways, referred to as teaching methods. A **teaching method** is a broad approach based on theory, research, educational preparation, experiences, and/or philosophy. Sometimes referred to as an *instructional method*, a teaching method consists of a general plan that teachers follow to introduce new material, assist student learning, and provide feedback to students regarding their achievement. Some methods emphasize a teacher centered, structured approach to delivering instruction and high levels of student responses, whereas other methods focus on the importance of working and learning with peers or expert learners and mentors. Which method is best for students with disabilities? Unfortunately, there is no simple answer. In this chapter, we will explore the characteristics of several contemporary methods for teaching and examine the research findings related to students with disabilities.

THEORIES OF LEARNING

Learning is the change in what students are capable of doing as the result of formal and informal experiences (Parsons, Hinson, & Sardo-Brown, 2001). Through these experiences, such as teacher-planned lessons and instructional activities, students learn new skills, acquire new knowledge, and develop deeper understandings. To examine important requirements for learning to occur, let us explore several theories of learning that form the basis for methods of instruction. The major theories of learning include cognitive, behavioral, and social learning. Each theory views the student and the teacher through a slightly different lens, and each emphasizes different factors believed to be critical for learning to occur. Figure 6.1 illustrates these learning theories and their connections to various teaching methods that you will read about later in this chapter.

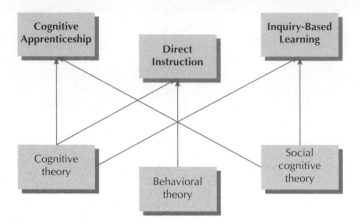

Figure 6.1   Learning theories and their relationships to methods of teaching

COGNITIVE THEORIES

Cognitive theories address how students think, process information, and remember (Ausubel, 1968; Barsalou, 1992; Benjafield, 1992; Bruner, 1966; Byrnes, 1996; Dixon-Krauss, 1996; Farnham-Diggory, 1992; Gagne, 1985; Mayer, 1998). They focus on the role of information processing, or how the learner takes in knowledge, stores it, and retrieves information. **Short-term memory** is memory that holds information temporarily. Individuals can keep information active in short-term memory by using various learning strategies, such as creating a mnemonic, a word that helps the individual to remember a set of steps or a series of words. The teacher's role is to enable students to learn by organizing and structuring new information. For example, in showing a student how to use a mnemonic, the teacher chunks information by grouping individual bits of information in a meaningful way. In Chapter 7 you will learn more about strategies such as this that educators use to help students. **Long-term memory** is memory in which information is permanently stored. Cognitive theorists such as David Ausubel describe how teachers can promote classroom learning.

Ausubel's Cognitive Theory

Ausubel (1977; Ausubel, Novak, & Hanesian, 1978) believes that teachers promote learning by planning well-organized, structured lessons and activities linking new information to familiar information selectively. At the beginning of each class, the teacher presents lesson objectives to students so that they know what they will learn and do as a result of the lesson. Instruction proceeds from general topics to specific ones and from familiar to new information.

—————— ❖ *USE OF COGNITIVE THEORY* ❖ ——————

Sean Bellaire, a high school special educator who coteaches a history class, begins each lesson by giving students a handout that lists the lesson objectives and an outline of the material to be covered. He begins today's discussion by talking about a general topic, familiar to the students, and then moves to the specific topic of today's lesson. As students settle into their seats, he asks, "How many of you have ever moved to a new neighborhood or a new community?" Sean encourages students to share their experiences, sometimes probing with questions such as "How did you prepare for the move?" and "How long did it take to get settled?" After students have a chance to share their experiences, Sean and his coteacher introduce the new unit on the movement west and some of the early settlers who traveled west in wagon trains. The teachers use a graphic that represents the overall unit and includes questions to pique students' interest, such as "Why did some travelers elect not to go through the Donner Pass?" Then the teachers move to the next step, a lecture and an explanation of how the settlers began their movement. After they present this information, they pass out a written follow-up activity for each student to complete and end the class with a brief review of what they covered that day. For a student with a mild to moderate disability, such instructional activities that are well organized and structured are helpful in imparting new information.

Constructivism

Similar to Ausubel's cognitive theory, constructivism (Carter, Ensrud, & Holden, 1997; Fosnot, 1996; Hwangbo & Yawkey, 1994; Wadsworth, 1996) views learning as a process in which students create new knowledge by building on their own past experiences and constructing knowledge as they interact with their teachers and peers. However, the constructivist approach focuses on student-centered activities rather than on more structured, teacher-directed lessons and activities.

—————— ❖ *USE OF CONSTRUCTIVISM* ❖ ——————

Morgan Lindstrom, an elementary special educator, works with a fourth-grade teacher in planning to introduce a new science unit on temperature. They want the children to make discoveries and generate ideas that they can prove—or disprove—during class time. Much as in Sean Bellaire's classroom, the teachers decide to introduce the unit with a question, but then their methods differ considerably. Morgan and her colleague decide to ask the students to consider the question "What are the characteristics of heat?" During the beginning class discussions, they encourage students to draw on their past experiences to help formulate the answer. Students mention that a stove, an oven, a microwave, and a radiator give off heat.

Then someone says that heat comes from coats and mittens. When the other children agree, the teachers decide to put aside other activities and help the children construct an experiment, observe the results, and correct the misconception. They begin by wrapping several thermometers in a coat and mittens. When the temperature does not rise, they discuss the findings and brainstorm ideas. They decide to seal the thermometers and clothing in plastic bags and continue to collect data. The class analyzes the results and brainstorms possible reasons for their findings. When there is still no change in the temperature, the teacher facilitates student discussions by writing down key concepts and drawing a picture to illustrate them. By organizing the class discussion in this way, the teachers help the students draw the conclusion that clothing merely holds the heat in when someone wears it. Through this unit, they hope that students will develop a better understanding of energy (Watson & Konicek, 1990).

Metacognition

Often students with disabilities have difficulties because they do not know how to learn, solve problems, or complete assignments even though they have the facts and information. They do not readily achieve proficiency in problem solving and higher order thinking skills, which are characteristics of successful learners. Many educators feel that these **metacognitive skills** should be taught along with the curriculum. Others believe that selected thinking skills should be integrated within the curriculum.

Metacognition involves learning how to learn and think. Flavel (1985) defines three types of metacognitive knowledge. First, learners hold beliefs about themselves as learners. For example, a student believes that listening to music is helpful when studying. Second, a learner has task knowledge, or an understanding of procedures that must be followed to complete a task. In mathematics, this type of knowledge is important when completing operations (for example, to add two different fractions, change the denominators to a common number). Third, a learner has strategic knowledge, or an understanding of selecting and using various approaches to solving a problem. In mathematics, strategic knowledge helps the student know how to begin to solve a word problem.

Multiple Intelligences

Some contemporary psychologists (Armstrong, 2000; Gardner, 1983, 1999) have written that multiple intelligences (MI) play a critical role in learning. Howard Gardner developed a complex theory of MI and described each intelligence, such as linguistic intelligence, musical intelligence, logical-mathematical intelligence, spatial intelligence, bodily-kinesthetic intelligence, interpersonal and intrapersonal intelligence, naturalist intelligence, and possibly others.

Gardner theorized that each intelligence is relatively independent of the others but that frequently more than one intelligence is involved during the learning process. For example, a learner first observes and then imitates the actions performed by the teacher in learning a new skill. According to MI theory, a learner can use spatial, bodily, and interpersonal intelligences. Linguistic intelligence may be involved to a minor degree (if at all). By contrast, when the teacher presents new information during a classroom lecture, the learner needs to use mostly linguistic knowledge and some bodily-kinesthetic knowledge in note taking.

BEHAVIORAL THEORY

Behavioral theory (Kazdin, 1994; Mahoney, 1974; Skinner, 1974) examines learning in terms of observable behaviors. Behavioral theorists believe that learning occurs by association. When two events occur together often, they are linked, and learning occurs. For example, when the teacher turns the lights off and signals the students to be quiet, they learn that turning off the lights means that they are to stop talking. Next time, the teacher should be able to simply turn off the lights to restore quiet.

Theorists believe that reinforcement is the primary mechanism for changing behavior if the type of reinforcement is desired and meaningful. To increase desired student behaviors, educators use a set of rules, or principles of reinforcement (Walker & Shea, 1998). The first principle is to reinforce only the target behavior, or the behavior that the student should exhibit, when it occurs. Second, the target behavior is reinforced immediately after it is exhibited. Third, the student receives reinforcement every time the target behavior is exhibited. Finally, as the target behavior becomes more consistent, the student is reinforced only intermittently.

Educators use various types of reinforcement, including consumable, activity-based, manipulative, possessional, and social reinforcement (Martin & Pear, 2002). Consumables consist of food that the student likes, such as crackers, fruit, or juice. Activity reinforcers are opportunities to engage in an activity that a student enjoys, such as listening to music, sending an e-mail message, or talking with friends. Manipulative reinforcers include activities that involve drawing, painting, or fixing a machine, for example. Possessional reinforcers include a chance to sit in a desired location, wear a favorite cap, or temporarily use an item that belongs to another. Social reinforcers include verbal praise, a high five, a smile, or a glance that indicates social approval. For reinforcers to be effective, teachers must determine what types of items a student likes or desires. This information can be gathered by asking the student to complete a checklist or talking informally with the student.

Positive reinforcement can be highly effective in helping students to change problem behaviors. But unless educators and other school staff use the principles of reinforcement carefully, this intervention can have many pitfalls. Sometimes school staff inadvertently strengthen undesirable behaviors. In fact, many undesirable behaviors are due to the social attention that they evoke from aides, nurses, peers, teachers, parents, doctors, and others (Martin & Pear, 2002, p. 39).

Teachers can have a dramatic effect on the way students with disabilities learn and behave in the classroom by understanding and applying concepts associated with behavior theory through applied behavior analysis. **Applied behavior analysis** is a systematic procedure that involves identifying and describing the behavior in observable terms, assessing the frequency of the behavior, the antecedent conditions, and the consequences following the behavior, developing an intervention(s) designed to change the behavior, and observing and recording data regarding the effect of the intervention.

Lionel Roy, a resource room teacher, uses applied behavior analysis in his work with students with problem behaviors. When a student is experiencing difficulties, Lionel begins by collecting critical information. He looks for antecedent conditions and consequences. **Antecedent conditions** are events, or triggers, in the environment that occur just before the behavior and can be adjusted by the teacher, who carefully observes any changes in student behavior. **Consequences** are events that occur directly after the behavior and, similar to antecedent events, can be adjusted by the teacher. Both antecedent conditions and consequences directly influence the recurrence of the behavior. Lionel also uses functional behavioral assessment to observe students and their environments to determine when, where, and why problem behaviors do and do not occur. **Functional behavioral assessment** involves assessment approaches that focus on identifying biological, social, affective, and environmental factors that initiate, sustain, or end the behavior in question (Center for Effective Collaboration and Practice, 1998). In Chapter 9 you will read more about functional behavioral assessment.

SOCIAL COGNITIVE THEORY

Social learning theory (Bandura, 1969, 1977, 1986; Glasser, 1990) focuses on how individuals acquire social behaviors and the effects of these behaviors on learning. Teachers can be effective models if they consider four interrelated factors (Bandura, 1986). First, the teacher must get the students' attention. Second, retention of learning occurs when students rehearse or practice learning. Third, students must have opportunities to perform the task. Finally, motivation influences observational learning.

Teaching methods based on social learning theory create ways to support peer tutors and opportunities for collaborative teams of students to work together. In fact, group support and cooperation among students are keys to facilitating learning. Students acquire social behaviors by observing and modeling other students. The classroom becomes a learning community that supports each member, and teachers design activities to foster a sense of belonging. For example, at the beginning of the year, special educator consultant Ti Lang encourages the development of class spirit by asking the students to develop a class nickname or logo. Later in the marking period, he plans a special celebration after all the students complete a research project on the social, economic, and political divisions in the United States.

Learning how to work together with others, sharing successes, and belonging to a group of peers are lifetime skills that help each of us to be contributing members in our communities. For students with learning and behavior problems these skills are essential, yet their disabilities may have interfered with the acquisition of them. Teachers who consider teaching methods based in part on social learning theory believe that they can assist students to acquire collaborative skills in working with others.

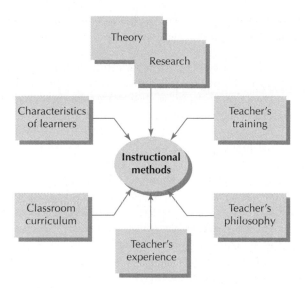

Figure 6.2   **Factors that influence selection of an instructional method**

RESEARCH-BASED TEACHING METHODS

Teachers often select a teaching method that is compatible with their own professional training, philosophy of education, or theoretical perspectives. Other factors such as the characteristics of the learners, the classroom curriculum, and the teacher's experience influence the selection of a teaching method (Figure 6.2).

Learning to be an effective teacher also includes developing knowledge of research-based methods of teaching. Although a teaching method may appeal to the teacher intuitively, if it does not have a strong research base, there is no assurance that it is effective for students with disabilities. The following section explores three contemporary teaching methods: cognitive apprenticeship, direct instruction, and inquiry-based learning.

COGNITIVE APPRENTICESHIP

The **cognitive apprenticeship** method is designed to engage students in authentic tasks and then show them how to generalize the knowledge that they gain (Collins, Brown, & Newman, 1989). Teachers develop units and design learning experiences and instructional activities that provide opportunities for learners to observe, engage in, and discover expert strategies in context. Teaching involves breaking the problem into parts and working alongside students, encouraging them and helping to make thinking explicit, much like a traditional apprenticeship (Collins, Brown, & Holum, 1991).

Cognitive apprenticeship uses many of the components of a traditional apprenticeship. For example, in a traditional apprenticeship, the novice observes the entire process of the task, such as building a cabinet. The novice watches and helps the expert carpenter, perhaps beginning with sanding the wood to a smooth, polished surface by using graduated weights of sandpaper. As the novice gradually assumes some of the duties, the expert provides feedback and suggestions. As the novice builds skills, the mentor carpenter encourages the novice to take on more and more of the tasks of cabinet construction.

As a teaching method, cognitive apprenticeship incorporates elements of more than one learning theory (Figure 6.1). It draws from cognitive theories in focusing on well-organized instruction. Educators design instructional activities that encourage students to construct their own knowledge as they interact with peers and teachers. This method also draws on social cognitive theory. Educators plan and implement ways that students observe and model others to acquire new knowledge and skills.

Like traditional apprenticeship, cognitive apprenticeship includes instructional strategies to help students learn through observation and guided practice. Modeling involves the novice's observing the expert; but, unlike traditional apprenticeship, which focuses on concrete, observable skills, cognitive apprenticeship emphasizes symbolic and thinking skills taught in combination with physical skills (Rojewski & Schell, 1994). For example, a teacher might show students how to solve a math problem by verbalizing her thoughts out loud as she demonstrates the problem-solving process. Coaching involves the novice's carrying out the task while the teacher offers hints and reminders. Scaffolding involves the novice's carrying out the task while the teacher provides supports. Scaffolding requires the teacher to accurately diagnose the student's current skill level and to provide an intermediate step at the appropriate level of difficulty to carry out the activity (Collins et al., 1991). Gradually, the teacher will fade the support. Teachers use the cognitive apprenticeship method to teach thinking and problem-solving skills across the curriculum (Figure 6.3).

Figure 6.3   What does cognitive apprenticeship consist of?

In preparation the teacher:
- develops the learning problem and sets up the environment

The teacher begins by:
- posing questions to motivate students to consider the problem
- assisting in defining the problem

The teacher uses class time to:
- link a novice learner with an expert

Experts assist novice learning by:
- coaching and offering hints
- providing feedback
- offering a reminder
- asking the student to reflect on the thinking process or problem-solving skill being used
- gradually handing control of the learning process to the student

Source: Adapted from "Cognitive Apprenticeship: Teaching the Craft of Reading, Writing, and Mathematics" (pp. 453–494), by A. Collins, J. S. Brown, and S. Newman, 1989, in *Knowing, Learning, and Instruction: Essays in Honor of Robert Glaser* (L. B. Resnick, Ed.), Hillsdale, NJ: Erlbaum.

Novice and expert learners work together.

Novice and Expert Learners

Novice learners are apprenticed to experts to learn new skills. Novice and expert learners differ in important characteristics. Compared to novices, experts are more easily able to detect meaningful patterns of information, organize their knowledge around important ideas and concepts, retrieve information flexibly, and understand how they acquire and retrieve knowledge. A student may be a novice learner in one or more areas of the curriculum and an expert learner in other areas.

Other experts include teachers, parents, and individuals in the community who serve as models for imitative learning and provide connections between past and new learning experiences (Berryman, 1991). Through lessons designed by teachers, experts model strategies needed to solve problems and complete projects. Experts gradually reduce assistance and modeling as novice learners build skills.

Sometimes a teacher is a novice learner in the classroom. For example, there are many case studies in which scientists and teachers are involved in joint creation of curriculum and lesson plans. Scientists begin as content experts only and teachers begin as pedagogical experts only, and each learns from the other (Hawkins & Battle, 1996).

❖ A VISIT WITH JAN BROWSKI ❖

Jan Browski greets us enthusiastically outside one of the eighth-grade classrooms. "Come on into our classroom! Our teaching team and the students are anxious to show you our semester-long project called 'Discover Our City' and tell you about our teaching and learning environments. Our team consists of teachers in math, science, history, a special educator (that's me), and a language arts teacher. We hope to increase student motivation, effort, and achievement by providing a learning environment that is sensitive to individual needs, interests, and abilities."

She continues, "Basically, the classroom teaching focuses on giving students the general skills that they need while working on the project. For example, a few weeks ago the students heard that a local construction company would be demolishing several old buildings to create a new shopping center. The students wondered about the history of the buildings and what would be lost as a result of the construction. They decided to conduct community interviews to gather information about the old buildings and the city's plans for removal. In the classroom, we discussed how to develop an interview and collect the data. Two of the students, along with the teacher, had some experience in developing interview questions, and they became our expert learners for this aspect of the project. They each worked with small groups of novice learners to help them refine their questions.

"Each teacher, as a member of our teaching team, coaches students in writing and public speaking skills. We take turns doing group presentations, smaller seminars, one-on-one coaching, and independent work in the library. You'll see the students working in a two-hour block of time today. Will Engart, the language arts teacher, is going to be working with one of the groups. They have read a historical pamphlet that was written a number of years ago about our city."

As we sit in on the group discussion, we hear students asking:

"What viewpoint is this written from?"

"How do we know this?"

"How is this connected to what we learned in our interviews with senior citizens?"

"If the old store is demolished, what aspects of the period will be lost to the community?"

Will leads the students in thinking about their interpretations. Students with strong higher order thinking skills are our expert learners in this learning community, modeling various ways of connecting the information. Novice learners have ample opportunities to observe expert learners by listening and participating in the discussion. We leave the classroom realizing that novice and expert learning has enabled all students to deepen their understanding of complex renovation and preservation issues faced by this community (adapted from Collins et al., 1991, pp. 9–14).

What Does the Research Say About Cognitive Apprenticeship?

A number of studies of cognitive apprenticeship report increased competencies in literacy (Lee, 1995), mathematical reasoning (Derry, Levin, Osana, & Jones, 1998; Lajoie, Jacobs, & Lavigne, 1995), and science (Roth & Bowen, 1995). For example, students in the early elementary grades who were considered at high risk in literacy made significant gains in reading comprehension (Knapp & Winsor, 1998; Yekovich, Yekovich, & Nagy-Rado, 1999). Seventh-grade students with learning disabilities improved their expository writing and took more responsibility for their own writing (Hallenbeck, 1999). Middle and high school students acquired a variety of skills that are important for career success but are not typically emphasized in the school curriculum, such as interpersonal skills (Berryman, 1991), motivation (Collins et al., 1991), and a deeper understanding of multiple perspectives (Ertmer & Cennamo, 1995). Coupled with a technology-rich environment, some research shows that this teaching method not only enabled students to stay on task but even directed some students toward task orientation (Jaervelae, 1998), and behavior problems decreased significantly (Collins et al., 1991).

DIRECT INSTRUCTION

Direct instruction is a systematic method that can be used to teach, practice, and reinforce specific skills (Adams & Engelmann, 1996; Carlson & Francis, 2002; Kroesbergen & van Luit, 2003; Minskoff & Allsopp, 2003; Rosenshine, 1983). Teachers use direct instruction to assist students in learning skills or demonstrating certain knowledge. As a teaching method, direct instruction incorporates elements of more than one learning theory (Figure 6.1), much as cognitive apprenticeship does. One of the cornerstones of direct instruction is well-organized and structured lessons and activities. In addition to cognitive theories, direct instruction draws from behavioral theory, including the use of reinforcement. Educators use positive comments, high fives, and other types of reinforcement to aid student learning.

Teachers use direct instruction to assist students in learning skills and demonstrating knowledge.

Figure 6.4   **Characteristics of direct instruction**

Teachers using direct instruction:

- establish specific sequential instructional objectives
- teach prerequisite skills, if necessary
- teach specific skills and strategies that promote learning
- provide immediate and corrective feedback
- use praise and rewards for correct responses
- provide opportunities for independent practice
- examine the previous day's work and reteach, if necessary
- use reflective practices
- conduct frequent reviews and assessments in order to monitor student progress

Educators begin direct instruction planning by determining the sequence of skills in the curriculum area. The curricula and the sets of skills, sometimes referred to as a **scope and sequence,** are frequently part of a school's curricular guide. Criterion-referenced assessments are good resources, too, because they provide a broad range of curricula and sequences of skills within curricular areas such as reading, mathematics, spelling, and writing. To assess student knowledge and areas of weakness in one or more areas of the curriculum, special educators frequently use curriculum-based and criterion-referenced assessments. They analyze assessment information to determine how much students have mastered and what they do not know within the sequence of skills. This is the point at which they design and implement instruction.

By knowing what students can and cannot do, the teacher focuses on helping each one to succeed by offering instruction in a systematic, organized fashion (Figure 6.4). Direct instruction, sometimes referred to as *mastery learning,* can be used in general education classrooms and settings where students receive special education services.

Using the direct instruction method, the teacher tells students what they will be learning, the reasons for each lesson, and how these reasons relate to previous lessons. All students use the same materials and are involved in the same activity. The teacher serves as the principal source of information.

Since the purpose of direct instruction is to teach the students specific material, lessons are highly structured. Instruction usually involves teacher-directed discussion, readings, and classroom activities. The teacher checks frequently to make sure that each student is making progress toward the desired outcome. The progress checks provide valuable information and allow the teacher to make adjustments during the lesson if students are having difficulty. The teacher can provide correction and reteach some of the lesson, or can allot additional instructional time or suggest extra learning materials. Since students learn at different rates, the teacher also plans enrichment activities. Thus, students who complete their work before other students have an opportunity to deepen and extend their knowledge. When students demonstrate that

Figure 6.5   What does direct instruction consist of?

In preparation, the teacher:
- prepares lesson materials and activities

The teacher begins class by:
- collecting and reviewing homework
- discussing what the students will be doing and what they will learn

The teacher instructs by:
- presenting information to be learned
- proceeding in small steps
- maintaining a quick pace
- using many examples and illustrations
- encouraging involvement and active responding
- asking questions to check for understanding
- repeating major points to remember

The teacher assists student learning by:
- providing teacher-guided whole-class practice
- providing feedback and reteaching to eliminate misunderstandings
- providing independent practice
- monitoring work to keep students involved and assisting in eliminating errors
- assigning related homework

they have met the learning objectives, the class moves on to the next lesson (Figure 6.5).

Teachers spend time after the class reflecting on the lesson. For example, they might ask themselves: Were the objectives clear to the students? Was the lesson presented clearly? Did the students have enough time to practice? How could I improve the feedback that I gave to the students? After thinking about the instruction, a teacher may decide to make changes for the following day. Reflection provides teachers with a way to improve instruction. Reflective teaching is dynamic and powerful.

❖ *A Visit with Gabe Cerino* ❖

Gabe Cerino, a special educator at an elementary school, invites us to observe a lesson in the resource room. For the next 45 minutes this morning he will be working with Juan, a first grader. One of Juan's IEP goals is to increase reading comprehension. To plan and monitor his specially designed instruction in reading, he uses a chart that lists the skills in developing phonemic awareness. Gabe keeps a daily check sheet of Juan's progress.

When Juan comes in, he joins Gabe at the table, and together they look at a short letter that his teacher has written him (Figure 6.6). Gabe reads it aloud as Juan follows along. When he comes to a word missing the beginning or ending sound of *s*, he pauses and Juan writes in the corresponding letter.

After reading the book Gabe has promised, Juan begins work on a set of picture cards. He pronounces the name of each picture and decides which pictures belong in the pile beginning with an *s* sound. Before going back to his classroom, he completes a drawing of objects beginning with the *s* sound. Afterward, he and Gabe go over his work together, correcting any errors.

What Does the Research Say About Direct Instruction?

Many research studies present evidence that direct instruction is effective in helping students with disabilities learn new skills and increase academic achievement across the curriculum. Swanson and Hoskyn (1998) examined 180 research studies that included students with learning disabilities. In synthesizing their findings, they reported that direct instruction was one of the pervasive influences in remediating the academic difficulties of children with learning disabilities. In a second meta-analysis of 58 interventions, Swanson (1999a) found that direct instruction and strategy instruction were the most effective techniques for adolescents with learning disabilities. Additional studies describe the benefits of direct instruction on achievement in reading (Engelmann, 1999; Gardill & Jitendra, 1999; Spiegel, Vickers, & Viviano, 1999; Swanson, 1999b; Swanson, Carson, & Sachse-Lee, 1996), mathematics (Butler, Miller, Lee, & Pierce, 2001), building social skills (Bendt & Nunan, 1999; Bertone, Boyle, Mitchel, & Smith, 1999), increasing listening skills (Engraffia,

Figure 6.6   Juan's letter

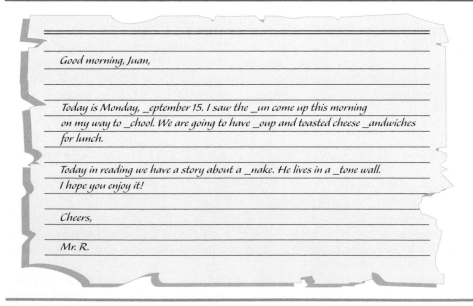

Good morning, Juan,

Today is Monday, _eptember 15. I saw the _un come up this morning on my way to _chool. We are going to have _oup and toasted cheese _andwiches for lunch.

Today in reading we have a story about a _nake. He lives in a _tone wall. I hope you enjoy it!

Cheers,

Mr. R.

Source: Adapted from *The Act of Teaching,* 2nd ed. (p. 229), by D. R. Cruickshank, D. L. Bainer, and K. K. Metcalf, 1999, Boston: McGraw-Hill.

Research to Practice

Direct Instruction

Probably no other teaching method has such a wide research base as direct instruction. Numerous research studies focus on the effectiveness of direct instruction for students with learning disabilities, behavior disorders, mild to moderate mental retardation, and autism. In fact, the effectiveness of direct instruction is not restricted to a particular disability, age group, or skills area (White, 1988).

Direct instruction is one of the most effective classroom interventions. In a review of 24 meta-analyses concerning various types of intervention used with students with disabilities, Forness (2001) found that direct instruction, mnemonic strategies, reading comprehension strategies, and behavior modification were the most effective methods.

Questions for Reflection

1. Carefully review two or more online lesson plans. Do the plans include components of direct instruction? If not, what suggestions could you provide?
2. What was Project Follow Through, often referred to as the "largest controlled comparative study of teaching methods in human history" (Association for Direct Instruction, 2003)? Discuss how these research findings impact on classrooms today.

 To answer these questions online and learn more about research to practice, go to the Companion Website at www.prenhall.com/cohen, select Chapter 6, then choose Research to Practice.

Graff, Jezuit, & Schall, 1999), and developing skills in language arts such as spelling (Berninger et al., 1998) and writing (Anderson & Keel, 2002).

INQUIRY-BASED LEARNING

Inquiry-based learning relies on the teacher to create experiences from which students derive their own knowledge and meaning. Jerome Bruner (1966) believed that inquiry-based learning helps students take responsibility for their own learning and remember important information. Inquiry-based learning, sometimes referred to as *discovery learning*, is built on the theory of constructivism. Elements of social cognitive theory such as group work and cooperation among students play a role in inquiry-based learning, too. But organization of student activities should not be the only principle; inquiry is also characterized by the teacher's mode of participation (Wells, 2000). The teacher begins by planning a broad purpose, or goal, and helping students generate their own questions and topics. The teacher gathers information about the topics and makes sure that students have access to needed resources. Inquiry-based learning uses objects and ideas that encourage students to manipulate and compare. The teacher provides questions to capture students' attention (Table 6.1) and encourage higher order thinking or ways of knowing that were discussed in Chapter 4. Students are encouraged to make guesses based on available information and to find

Table 6.1	Knowledge and Questions That Promote Learning Through Inquiry	
	Form of Knowledge	**Questions That Promote Learning Through Inquiry**
	Facts	What is the average pulse rate? What happens when blue and red mix? Who discovered the moon?
	Concepts	What is a rainbow? What is luck? What is rap music?
	Generalizations	How are families different today than in the 1800s? How is technology changing our lives? Should students go to school year round?
	Rules and laws	Why do certain objects float? How are words divided into syllables? How are fractions divided?

Source: Adapted from *The Act of Teaching*, 2nd ed. (p. 219), by D. R. Cruikshank, D. L. Bainer, and K. K. Metcalf, 1999, Boston: McGraw-Hill.

Figure 6.7   What does supported inquiry-based learning consist of?

In preparation, the teacher:
- identifies the broad purpose and objectives.
- collects information resources.

The teacher begins by:
- capturing and holding the students' attention with a high-interest question.
- presenting a situation that is challenging or baffling.
- assisting students in phrasing the problem.
- providing a safe environment for expressing emerging ideas.

The teacher uses class time by:
- posing questions to help students think about information resources and how to access them.
- holding high expectations while assisting students as needed.
- encouraging students to reflect on their learning. Teachers include questions and challenges that make explicit links between students' concrete experience and the underlying concept.
- assisting students to draw conclusions. Supported inquiry-based learning emphasizes group conversations for helping students coconstruct meaning from hands-on activities.
- providing opportunities for students to use the information.

Source: Adapted from "Supported Inquiry Science: Teaching for Conceptual Change in Urban and Suburban Science Classrooms," by B. Dalton and C. C. Morocco, 1997, *Journal of Learning Disabilities, 30*(6), pp. 670–685.

Special educators use supported inquiry-based learning to encourage inductive thinking.

ways of solving problems. The teacher acts as a guide, providing basic information and encouraging students to determine the best way to organize new and familiar information, but is careful not to provide too much guidance that would interfere with self-direction and discovery (Figure 6.7). General educators often use inquiry-based learning in the general education classroom in the belief that students learn best through active involvement. Science educators, for example, emphasize doing science by focusing on the following student activities: designing experiments, predicting results, manipulating materials, recording observations, and summarizing their findings. These activities are quite different from other teaching methods, such as a more direct instruction approach in which the educator performs the experiment while students watch and then discuss the results.

Students are required to use inductive thinking in many inquiry-based activities. Inductive thinking requires students to consider their observations and then develop a general rule based on their findings or discoveries. Thus, the students "construct" knowledge as a result of their own observations and thinking.

Supported Inquiry-Based Learning

Because students with mild and moderate disabilities often have difficulty with inductive thinking (Mastropieri & Scruggs, 1997), special educators often support them through the use of prompted coaching and supported inquiry methods. In the following dialogue (adapted from Mastropieri & Scruggs), notice how the teacher uses questioning during prompted coaching to help a student with a disability to draw inferences:

EDUCATOR: Anteaters have long claws on their front feet. Why does this make sense?
STUDENT: I don't know.

EDUCATOR: Well, let's think. What do you know about anteaters? For example, what do they eat?

STUDENT: Anteaters eat ants.

EDUCATOR: Good. And where do ants live?

STUDENT: They live in holes in the ground.

EDUCATOR: Now, if anteaters eat ants, and ants live in holes in the ground, why do you think that anteaters have long claws on their front feet?

STUDENT: To dig for ants.

EDUCATOR: Good. To dig for ants.

Sometimes in supported inquiry-based learning, the educator provides the general rule to the students first. Then students are prompted and questioned to apply the rule (Woodward & Noell, 1992). Educators also embed assessment in instruction, including performance tasks as well as questions that students respond to in drawing and writing (Dalton & Morocco, 1997).

◆ *A VISIT WITH KAYLA HENNESEY* ◆

Kayla Hennesey, a special educator in a small K–8 community school, has invited us to join her and her students for the day. One of the first things we see when entering her resource room is a large glass terrarium on a table. Several students are gathered around the table this morning, some with handhelds (such as PDAs) and others with notebooks. The students are using these to record their daily observations. As we move closer, we see a cocoon hanging from a branch. On the table is a variety of magnifying glasses. The students are following the life cycle of two caterpillars they found earlier. Each week they record their observations and take a digital picture to add to the class website.

Kayla introduced the unit by leading a discussion about two different caterpillars she had brought to class. Most of the students knew that caterpillars metamorphosed into butterflies. But the teacher continued to probe, hoping that the additional questions she posed would create interest among the students. Do you think that all caterpillars have the same life cycle? What kinds of butterflies will metamorphose from these caterpillars? The students were hooked! Can we find out? Once the students had accepted the challenge, Kayla helped them decide how to conduct their observations and collect their data. She provided multiple ways, including both text and digital formats, for drawing or sketching and recording their observations. Working with the school librarian, she located resource books at different reading levels and identified community resource people with whom students could discuss their ideas.

What Does the Research Say About Inquiry-Based Learning?

Research studies supporting the benefits of inquiry-based learning have focused on the importance of insight and discovery to learning (Parsons et al., 2001). Students report that inquiry-based learning is enjoyable (Algava, 1999; Romeo & Young, 1997). Teachers using an inquiry-based, hands-on-science curriculum have found that students with learning disabilities learn and comprehend more information than students taught from textbooks (Scruggs, Mastropieri, Bakken, & Brigham, 1993). Research findings suggest that coaching students with learning disabilities to draw inferences regarding science principles results in higher levels of recall and understanding (Scruggs, Mastropieri, Sullivan, & Hesser, 1993; Sullivan, Mastropieri, & Scruggs, 1995) and that supported inquiry is more effective than an activity-based science approach alone (Dalton & Morocco, 1997; Sasaki & Serna, 1995). These studies are part of a small but growing body of research that focuses on inquiry-based learning and higher order thinking not only in science but also in reading, writing, and mathematics (Carnine, 1991; Englert & Thomas, 1987; Montague, 1988).

HIGH-PERFORMING SCHOOLS

In high-performing schools *all* students demonstrate high academic achievement. The Consortium for Policy Research in Education (Miles & Darling-Hammond, 1997) sponsored an in-depth examination of urban elementary and secondary school programs, with high concentrations of students living in poverty, to see what common elements could be discovered. What did their research find, and what might a visitor observe in these classrooms?

ELEMENTARY SCHOOLS

In each of the elementary schools, special education resources were pooled to increase the number of special educators who worked in regular classrooms to support heterogeneous grouping of students. One school used Success for All as a catalyst for including special education teachers and students in the regular classroom.

> By the third year of the program, special education students and teachers from previously self-contained classrooms and resource rooms spent most of their time in heterogeneous groups. . . . Special education teachers team taught with regular education teachers. . . . Special education teachers spent approximately one-quarter of their time either performing individual assessments or working with regular education or special education students who needed targeted help outside the regular classroom. (Miles & Darling-Hammond, 1997, p. 25)

Results of the study indicated that teachers used student grouping in strategic ways according to students' needs. Teachers also created more personal relationships. At one school, professional staff, including the classroom teacher, the afterschool director, and the social worker, met to discuss strategies and problem-solve solutions. Elementary teachers at these high-performing elementary schools also had more common planning time.

An example of a school development program that includes both school and systemwide intervention is the Comer School Development Program (SDP; see Comer, Ben-Avie, Haynes, & Joyner, 1999). This program focuses on healthy child development as the cornerstone for high achievement. The SDP school community recognizes

Research to Practice

Teaching Methods and Specific Content Focus

Some teaching methods, specific to a curriculum area, also have a wide research base that demonstrates their effectiveness for students with disabilities. For example, **strategic instruction,** often used in middle and secondary programs, is an approach that focuses on providing students with rules or guidelines so that they can approach learning activities or assignments more effectively and efficiently, with greater independence. In Chapter 8 we will examine the Strategic Instruction Model (Deshler & Lenz, 1989) and the research findings based on this teaching method.

Another example of a curriculum-specific teaching method is **MathWings** (Madden, Slavin, & Simons, 2002), tied to the national mathematics standards developed by the National Council of Teachers of Mathematics. MathWings involves students in problem solving in real situations using cooperative groups and literature, science, art, and other subjects, as well as the students' personal experiences. Students are encouraged to use calculators for developing mathematical concepts, explain and defend their solutions orally, and write regularly in their individual logbooks. Research studies indicate that students involved in MathWings, including students in poverty, made substantial gains in mathematical achievement. The following table describes other methods and models that research studies have been shown to be effective with students with disabilities.

Research-Based Methods for Working with Students with Disabilities

Name	Contact Information	Grade Levels	Features	Subject Area Materials
Accelerated Schools	National Center for Accelerated Schools Project University of Connecticut 2131 Hillside Road Unit 3224 Storrs, CT 06269	K–8	Teachers offer enriched curricula to all students	All
Carbo Reading Styles Program	Carbo Reading Styles Program P.O. Box 737 Syosset, NY 11791	K–12	Teachers diagnose students' strengths and use a range of reading strategies	Reading/ language arts
Co-nect	Co-nect 37 Broadway Arlington, MA 02474	K–12	Authentic problems, practical applications, and interdisciplinary projects	Literacy program
Direct Instruction	National Institute for Direct Instruction P.O. Box 11248 Eugene, OR 97440	K–8	Scripted instruction, highly interactive lessons presented to small groups of students	Reading, language arts, spelling, mathematics, and other subjects

Name	Contact Information	Grade Levels	Features	Subject Area Materials
Expeditionary Learning Outward Bound	Expeditionary Learning Outward Bound 100 Mystery Point Road Garrison, NY 10524	K–12	Experiential learning, interdisciplinary projects	All
High/Scope	High/Scope Education Research Foundation 600 N. River St. Ypsilanti, MI 48198	K–3	Active learning, learning stations, hands-on materials	Key experiences in language, literacy, mathematics, science, movement, and other areas
Success for All	Success for All Foundation 200 West Towsontown Blvd. Baltimore, MD 21204	PreK-8	Schoolwide reading curriculum, cooperative learning, family support team	Reading/ language arts
Success for All/Roots and Wings	Success for All Foundation 200 West Towsontown Blvd. Baltimore, MD 21204	PreK-6	Cooperative learning, one-to-one tutoring, family support team	Reading, mathematics, science, and social studies
Talent Development High School with Career Academies	Talent Development High School 3003 North Charles St. Suite 200 Baltimore, MD 21218	9–12	Ninth-grade success academy, career academies for Grades 10–12, alternative after-hours program	Strategic reading, student team literature, and transition math

Questions for Reflection

1. Working with a small group of colleagues, select two of the research-based models in the table to explore in more depth. Report your findings to the class.
2. What other research-based methods have you learned about in previous classes? Have you observed one or more of these methods in the classroom?
3. What resources are available to teach educators more about research-based methods?

 To answer these questions and learn more about applying research to practice, go to the Companion Website at www.prenhall. com/cohen, select Chapter 6, then choose Research to Practice.

Considering Diversity

Research-Based Teaching Methods and Latino Students

What teaching methods work best for newcomer students, or students who have recently arrived in this country, and students from diverse cultural and linguistic backgrounds? In an extensive review of the research concerning Latino students, Fashola, Slavin, Claderón, and Durán (2002) found a number of replicable programs for elementary and middle schools that are proven to meet the needs of these students. These programs include the instructional methods that we discussed in this chapter, such as complex instruction and direct instruction, and a very effective instructional strategy, cooperative learning, that you will learn more about in Chapter 7. Success for All, a program that uses cooperative learning, one-to-one tutoring for students who have difficulties, and family support to build positive home-school relations, shows very positive results, too. Latino students who participated in the program made substantial gains on standardized tests compared to Latino students who did not participate (Fashola et al., 2002). Yet Fashola et al. also found large gaps in the knowledge base concerning the teaching of reading and language arts, and particularly in approaches designed for Latino or English language learners. Furthermore, no studies addressed newcomer students with disabilities.

Questions for Reflection

1. What teaching methods do educators in other countries use?
2. What Web-based resources might a first-year teacher find helpful for designing instruction?

To answer these questions and deepen your understanding of diversity in schools and communities, go to the Companion Website at *www.prenhall.com/cohen,* select Chapter 6, then choose Considering Diversity.

six developmental pathways that are critical to a child's development: physical, cognitive, psychological, language, social, and ethical. In Comer schools, teachers focus on much more than cognitive development alone.

High Schools

Four key findings described high-performing high schools. First, specialized programs were reduced so that resources could focus on academic subjects. All teachers, including special educators, taught several interdisciplinary courses. Special educators also helped students with regular classroom work. Second, flexible student grouping allowed all teachers to provide coaching and support for independent study. Third, school arrangements such as teaching teams allowed all teachers to provide academic and advisory support to students and their families. Longer and more varied blocks of instructional time helped students explore content and develop deeper understandings. Finally, all teachers used more common planning time or engaged in staff development.

Using Technology

Tablets, Laptops, and Handheld Computers: Tools or Obstacles?

In considering a teaching method, tablets, laptops, and handheld computers provide exciting possibilities for enhancing teaching and learning activities because each student can access an enormous amount of information from the desktop or small-group work area. These technology tools enable students to develop skills in working with others and to enhance self-esteem and self-sufficiency while working on content knowledge. Students also can use software to help them organize their school schedule and assignments as well as other aspects of their daily lives. Technology tools may allow some students with disabilities to access and use information more efficiently and more accurately than traditional materials.

However, for some students with disabilities, using tablets, laptops, and handheld computers may create major problems. Some students may not be able to see text on the screen, either because it is too small or because they are not able to read text written at that level. Laptops, tablets, and handheld computers may not be compatible with specialized software that students with disabilities need to access text information or they may not support the use of voice input as a keyboard alternative. For students who have

difficulty in keyboarding or who are not physically able to use a keyboard, accessing the computer directly using speech recognition software allows them to find and use information. For students with fine motor difficulties, the reduced keyboard size of some laptops, buttons on tablets, and mini-keyboards or thumb keyboards may be too small or too complicated, or may require too high a degree of fine motor control to operate.

Questions for Reflection

1. Carefully examine two or more laptops from different manufacturers. What are some of the difficulties that the keyboard or screen might present to a student with a disability?
2. Preview a tablet or handheld computer. What are some advantages of these technologies? How easy or difficult is it to learn to use them? What problems might they present to a student with a disability?

 To answer these questions and learn more about using technology to support learning, go to the Companion Website at www.prenhall.com/cohen, select Chapter 6, then choose Using Technology.

SUMMARY

- Teachers select instructional methods based on their training and experience, personal philosophy of education, demands of the curriculum, student characteristics, and knowledge of research findings.
- When the objectives are to encourage the use of thinking and problem-solving skills across the curriculum, teachers design learning activities in which novice learners are apprenticed to experts to learn new skills.

- When the curriculum focuses on teaching specific skills or facts, direct instruction works well.
- When the emphasis is on relationships of concepts and events, inquiry-based learning is effective.
- Technology tools, including tablets, laptops, and handheld computers, hold much promise for all students, including students with disabilities. In selecting technology tools, educators must be sure that all students can access the information and that a student's disability does not interfere with or prevent the student from using the technology. To uphold the right to information access for all students, educators may need to play many roles, such as teacher, advocate, investigator, and leader.

EXTENDING LEARNING

1. Working with another colleague, choose two or more theories of learning and create text descriptions or diagram the theories' main aspects. Which instructional methods best support these theories?
2. Consider the methods discussed in this chapter. Which methods would you identify as teacher-directed? Student-directed?
3. Identify the methods that your instructors use most frequently. Work with your classmates to create a collective chart of the methods and their frequency. Which method(s) do you prefer as a learner? Why?
4. Consider a recent classroom observation or visit that you have completed. What instructional method(s) did you observe?
5. Contact a local special educator to discuss the teaching methods that are typically used in the classroom. Share your findings with the class.
6. Using the information collected in the previous question, analyze the methods used by classroom level. Compare and contrast the methods used in elementary classrooms with those used in middle and secondary classrooms. Are there similarities? Differences?

REFERENCES

Adams, G., & Engelmann, S. (1996). *Research on direct instruction: 25 years beyond DISTAR.* Seattle: Educational Achievement Systems.

Algava, A. (1999). Animated learning. *Educational Leadership, 56*(5), 58–60.

Anderson, D. M., & Keel, M. C. (2002). Using "reasoning and writing" to teach writing skills to students with learning disabilities and behavioral disorders. *Journal of Direct Instruction, 2*(1), 49–55.

Armstrong, T. (2000). *Multiple intelligences in the classroom* (2nd ed.). Baltimore: Association for Supervision and Curriculum Development.

Association for Direct Instruction. (2003). *Scientific methods.* Retrieved August 9, 2003, from http://www.adihome.org/phpshop/di/science.php

Ausubel, D. P. (1968). *Educational psychology: A cognitive view*. New York: Holt, Rinehart & Winston.

Ausubel, D. P. (1977). Facilitation of meaningful verbal learning in the classroom. *Educational Psychologist, 12*, 162–178.

Ausubel, D. P., Novak, J. D., & Hanesian, H. (1978). *Psychology: A cognitive view*. New York: Holt, Rinehart & Winston.

Bandura, A. (1969). *Principles of behavior modification*. New York: Holt, Rinehart & Winston.

Bandura, A. (1977). *Social learning theory*. Upper Saddle River, NJ: Prentice Hall.

Bandura, A. (1986). *Social foundations of thought and action: A social cognitive theory*. Upper Saddle River, NJ: Prentice Hall.

Barsalou, L. W. (1992). *Cognitive psychology: An overview for cognitive scientists*. Hillsdale, NJ: Erlbaum.

Bendt, L., & Nunan, J. (1999). *Enhancing academic achievement through direct instruction of social skills*. Chicago: Master's Action Research Project, St. Xavier University. (ERIC Document Reproduction Service No. ED434299)

Benjafield, J. G. (1992). *Cognition*. Upper Saddle River, NJ: Prentice Hall.

Berninger, V. W., Vaughan, K., Abbott, R. D., Brooks, A., Abbott, S. P., Rogan, L., Reed, E., & Graham, S. (1998). Early intervention for spelling problems. *Journal of Educational Psychology, 90*(4), 587–605.

Berryman, S. E. (1991). *Designing effective learning environments: Cognitive apprenticeship models*. New York: Columbia University. (ERIC Document Reproduction Service No. ED337689)

Bertone, L., Boyle, J., Mitchel, J., & Smith, J. (1999). *Improving prosocial behavior through social skill instruction*. Chicago: Master's Action Research Project, St. Xavier University. (ERIC Document Reproduction Service No. ED434296)

Bruner, J. S. (1966). *Toward a theory of instruction*. Cambridge, MA: Belknap Press.

Butler, F. M., Miller, S. P., Lee, K., & Pierce, T. (2001). Teaching mathematics to students with mild-to-moderate mental retardation: A review of the literature. *Mental Retardation, 39*(1), 20–31.

Byrnes, J. P. (1996). *Cognitive development and learning in instructional contexts*. Boston: Allyn & Bacon.

Carlson, C. D., & Francis, D. J. (2002). Increasing the reading achievement of at-risk children through direct instruction: Evaluation of the Rodeo Institute for Teacher Excellence (RITE). *Journal of Education for Students Placed At-Risk, 7*(2), 141–166.

Carnine, D. (1991). Curricular interventions for teaching higher order thinking to all students: Introduction to the special series. *Journal of Learning Disabilities, 24*, 261–269.

Carter, M., Ensrud, M., & Holden, J. (1997). The Paideia Seminar: A constructivist approach to discussions. *Teaching and Change, 5*(1), 32–49.

Center for Effective Collaboration and Practice. (1998). *Addressing student problem behavior: An IEP team's introduction to functional behavioral assessment and behavior intervention plans*. Retrieved June 4, 2001, from http://www.air.org/cecp/fba/default.htm

Collins, A., Brown, J. S., & Holum, A. (1991). Cognitive apprenticeship: Making thinking visible. *American Educator, 6*(11), 38–46.

Collins, A., Brown, J. S., & Newman, S. (1989). Cognitive apprenticeship: Teaching the craft of reading, writing, and mathematics. In L. B. Resnick (Ed.), *Knowing, learning, and instruction: Essays in honor of Robert Glaser* (pp. 453–494). Hillsdale, NJ: Erlbaum.

Collins, A., Hawkins, J., & Carver, S. H. (1991). *A cognitive apprenticeship for disadvantaged students*. (CTE Technical Report Issues No. 10). Retrieved from the Center for Children and Technology, Education Development Center, Inc. website: http://www.edc.org/CCT/Ccthome/reports/tr10.html

Comer, J. P., Ben-Avie, M., Haynes, N. M., & Joyner, E. T. (Eds.). (1999). *Child by child: The Comer process for change in education*. New York: Teachers College Press.

Cruickshank, D. R., Bainer, D. L., & Metcalf, K. K. (1999). *The act of teaching* (2nd ed.). Boston: McGraw-Hill.

Dalton, B., & Morocco, C. C. (1997). Supported inquiry science: Teaching for conceptual change in urban and suburban science classrooms. *Journal of Learning Disabilities, 30*(6), 670–685.

Derry, S. J., Levin, J. R., Osana, H. P., & Jones, M. S. (1998). Developing middle-school students' statistical reasoning abilities through simulation gaming. In S. P. Lajoie (Ed.), *Reflections on statistics: Learning, teaching, and assessment in grades K–12* (pp. 175–195). Mahwah, NJ: Erlbaum.

Deshler, D. D., & Lenz, B. K. (1989). The strategies instructional approach. *International Journal of Disability, Development and Education, 36*(3), 203–224.

Dixon-Krauss, L. (1996). *Vygotsky in the classroom*. White Plains, NY: Longman.

Engelmann, S. (1999). The benefits of direct instruction: Affirmative action for at-risk students. *Educational Leadership, 57*(1), 77–79.

Englert, C. S., & Thomas, C. C. (1987). Sensitivity to text structure in reading and writing: A comparison between learning disabled and nondisabled students. *Learning Disability Quarterly, 10,* 93–105.

Engraffia, M., Graff, N., Jezuit, S., & Schall, L. (1999). *Improving listening skills through the use of active listening strategies*. Chicago: Master's Action Research Project, St. Xavier University. (ERIC Document Reproduction Service No. ED433573)

Ertmer, P. A., & Cennamo, K. S. (1995). Teaching instructional design: An apprenticeship model. *Performance Improvement Quarterly, 8*(4), 43–58.

Farnham-Diggory, S. (1992). *Cognitive processes in education* (2nd ed.). New York: HarperCollins.

Fashola, O. S., Slavin, R., Calderón, M., & Durán, R. (2002). *Report no. 11: Effective programs for Latino students in elementary and middle schools*. Retrieved June 24, 2002, from Research Reports from the National Research and Development Centers website: http://research.cse.ucla.edu

Flavell, J. H. (1985). *Cognitive development*. Upper Saddle River, NJ: Prentice Hall.

Forness, S. R. (2001). Special education and related services: What have we learned from meta-analysis? *Exceptionality, 9*(4), 185–197.

Fosnot, C. T. (1996). Construction: A psychological theory of learning. In C. T. Fosnot (Ed.), *Constructivism: Theory, perspective, and practice* (pp. 8–33). New York: Teacher College Press.

Gagne, R. (1985). *The conditions of learning and instruction* (4th ed.). New York: Holt, Rinehart and Winston.

Gardill, M. C., & Jitendra, A. K. (1999). Advanced story map instruction. *Journal of Special Education, 33*(1), 2–17, 28.

Gardner, H. (1983). *Frames of mind*. New York: Basic Books.

Gardner, H. (1999). *Intelligence reframed: Multiple intelligences for the 21st century*. New York: Basic Books.

Glasser, W. (1990). *The quality school: Managing students without coercion*. New York: Harper & Row.

Hallenbeck, M. J. (1999). Taking charge: Adolescents with learning disabilities assume responsibility for their own writing. *Learning Disabilities Quarterly, 25*(4), 227–246.

Hawkins, I., & Battle, R. (1996). *Science on-line: Partnership approach for the creation of internet-based classroom resources.* New York: American Educational Research Organization. (ERIC Document Reproduction Service No. ED394498)

Hwangbo, Y., & Yawkey, T. (1994). Constructivist schooling at early and middle grades: Some key elements that work. *Contemporary Education, 65*(4), 207–210.

Jaervelae, S. (1998). Socioemotional aspects of students' learning in a cognitive apprenticeship environment. *Instructional Science, 26*(6), 439–472.

Kazdin, A. E. (1994). *Behavior modification in applied settings* (5th ed.). Pacific Grove, CA: Brooks/Cole.

Knapp, N. F., & Winsor, A. P. (1998). A reading apprenticeship for delayed primary readers. *Reading Research and Instruction, 38*(1), 13–29.

Kroesbergen, E. H., & van Luit, J. E. H. (2003). Mathematics interventions for children with special education needs: A meta-analysis. *Remedial and Special Education, 24*(2), 97–114.

Lajoie, S. P., Jacobs, V. R., & Lavigne, N. C. (1995). Empowering children in the use of statistics. *Journal of Mathematical Behavior, 14*(4), 401–425.

Lee, C. D. (1995). A culturally based cognitive apprenticeship. *Reading Research Quarterly, 30*(4), 608–630.

Madden, N. A., Slavin, R. E., & Simons, K. (2002). *Report no. 17: MathWings: Early indicators of effectiveness.* Retrieved June 24, 2002, from the Research Reports from the National Research and Development Centers website: http://research.cse.ucla.edu

Mahoney, M. J. (1974). *Cognitive behavior modification.* Cambridge, MA: Ballinger.

Martin, G., & Pear, J. (2002). *Behavior modification: What is it and how to do it* (7th ed.). Upper Saddle River, NJ: Prentice Hall.

Mastropieri, M. A., & Scruggs, T. E. (1997). How effective is inquiry learning for students with mild disabilities? *Journal of Special Education, 31*(2), 109–112.

Mayer, R. E. (1998). *The promise of educational psychology.* Upper Saddle River, NJ: Merrill/Prentice Hall.

Miles, K. H., & Darling-Hammond, L. (1997). *Rethinking the allocation of teaching resources: Some lessons from high-performing schools.* Retrieved June 24, 2002, from the Research Reports from the National Research and Development Centers website: http://research.cse.ucla.edu

Minskoff, E., & Allsopp, D. (2003). *Academic success strategies for adolescents with learning disabilities.* Baltimore: Paul H. Brookes.

Montague, M. (1988). Strategy instruction and mathematical problem solving. *Reading, Writing and Learning Disabilities, 4,* 275–290.

Parsons, R. D., Hinson, S. L., & Sardo-Brown, D. (2001). *Educational psychology: A practitioner-researcher model of teaching.* Belmont, CA: Wadsworth/Thomson Learning.

Rojewski, J. W. A., & Schell, J. W. (1994). Cognitive apprenticeship for learners with special needs. *Remedial and Special Education, 15*(4), 234–244.

Romeo, L., & Young, S. A. (1997). *Fifth graders' perceptions of their interactions while using literacy play centers.* Scottsdale, AZ: Presented at the annual meeting of the National Reading Conference. (ERIC Document Reproduction Service No. ED429286)

Rosenshine, B. V. (1983). Teaching functions in instructional programs. *Elementary School Journal, 83,* 335–351.

Roth, W. M., & Bowen, G. M. (1995). Knowing and interacting: A study of culture, practices, and resources in a grade 8 open-inquiry science classroom guided by a cognitive apprenticeship metaphor. *Cognition and Instruction, 13*(1), 73–128.

Sasaki, J., & Serna, L. A. (1995). FAST Science: Teaching science to adolescents with mild disabilities. *Teaching Exceptional Children, 27*(4), 14–16.

Scruggs, T. E., Mastropieri, M. A., Bakken, J. P., & Brigham, F. J. (1993). Reading vs. doing: The relative effectiveness of textbook-based and inquiry-orientated approaches to science education. *Journal of Special Education, 27*, 1–15.

Scruggs, T. E., Mastropieri, M. A., Sullivan, G. S., & Hesser, L. S. (1993). Improving reasoning and recall: The differential effects of elaborate interrogation and mnemonic elaboration. *Learning Disability Quarterly, 16*, 233–240.

Skinner, B. F. (1974). *About behaviorism*. New York: Alfred A. Knopf.

Spiegel, G., Vickers, L., & Viviano, J. (1999). *Improving reading comprehension*. Chicago: Master's Action Research Project, St. Xavier University. (ERIC Document Reproduction Service No. ED433496)

Sullivan, G. S., Mastropieri, M. A., & Scruggs, T. E. (1995). Reasoning and remembering: Coaching thinking with students with learning disabilities. *Journal of Special Education, 29*, 310–322.

Swanson, H. L. (1999a). Intervention research for adolescents with learning disabilities. In *Two decades of research in learning disabilities: Reading comprehension, expressive writing, problem solving, self-concept. Keys to successful learning: A national summit on research in learning disabilities*. New York: National Center for Learning Disabilities. (ERIC Document Reproduction Service No. ED430365)

Swanson, H. L. (1999b). Reading research for students with LD: A meta-analysis of intervention outcomes. *Journal of Learning Disabilities, 32*(6), 504–532.

Swanson, H. L., Carson, C., & Sachse-Lee, C. M. (1996). A selective synthesis of intervention research for students with learning disabilities. *School Psychology Review, 25*(3), 370–391.

Wadsworth, B. J. (1996). *Piaget's theory of cognitive and affective development*. White Plains, NY: Longman.

Walker, J. E., & Shea, T. (1998). *Behavior management: A practical approach for educators*. Columbus, OH: Merrill.

Watson, B., & Konicek., R. (1990). Teaching for conceptual change: Confronting children's experience. *Phi Delta Kappan, 71*, 680–685.

Wells, G. (2000). Dialogic inquiry in education. In C. D. Lee & P. Smagorinsky (Eds.), *Vygotskian perspectives on literacy research: Constructing meaning through collaborative inquiry* (pp. 51–85). Cambridge: Cambridge University Press.

White, W. A. T. (1988). A meta-analysis of the effects of direct instruction in special education. *Education and Treatment of Children, 11*(4), 364–374.

Woodward, J., & Noell, J. (1992). Science instruction at the secondary level: Implications for students with learning disabilities. In D. Carnine & E. Kameenui (Eds.), *Higher order thinking: Designing curriculum for mainstreamed students* (pp. 39–58). Austin, TX: PRO-ED.

Yekovich, F. R., Yekovich, C. W., & Nagy-Rado, A. (1999). *A formative evaluation of the TRALE (Technology-Rich Authentic Learning Environments) project*. Philadelphia: Mid-Atlantic Lab for Student Success. (ERIC Document Reproduction Service No. ED429123)

7

Chapter

Selecting Instructional Strategies

CHAPTER OBJECTIVES

After reading this chapter, you should be able to:

◆ Explain how teachers can support the learning of all students.

◆ Describe specific instructional strategies for promoting learning.

◆ Consider the influence of diversity on instruction.

◆ Identify ways in which technology can be integrated into instruction.

In a second-grade classroom, Deborah and James, two students with learning disabilities, were assigned to work together by their teacher, Tim Downs. Deborah and James selected a book to read. Deborah has excellent reading comprehension, whereas James struggles with reading. He recognizes some sight words but still must laboriously sound out words as he reads them. Deborah's reading lacks fluency.

In an eighth-grade classroom, Andres has always had difficulty focusing on his classroom work. Despite his best intentions, his concentration wanders. He has trouble sitting still for very long. However, during the past few years, his attention has increased and his hyperactivity has decreased because his teachers and family have implemented a variety of strategies that support Andres' learning. Strategies that have been successful include providing Andres with a structured schedule, seating him in a quiet area where distractions have been reduced, and teaching him to stop and think before responding. Today, he is in science class, where his teacher, Allana Gabrielli, has announced that the class will be starting a new unit on environmental pollution.

As these educators teach these students, they ask themselves: What instructional strategies will maximize each student's learning? How can each student be successful?

Teaching consists of complex interrelated activities that involve designing, planning, implementing, and assessing instruction. Knowledge of learners' characteristics as well as up-to-date information on teaching and learning, curriculum development, instructional practices, and assessment and evaluation approaches will help you be a skilled professional.

The use of various instructional strategies is sometimes referred to as *differentiated instruction*. Differentiated instruction (Hall, n.d.-a) means that instructional strategies vary according to the strengths, abilities, and needs of individual students. Differentiation involves flexibility, accommodations, modifications, and multiple options. Cornerstones of differentiated instruction include flexible grouping students, effective classroom management approaches, frequent use of multiple assessment approaches, and engagement of all learners.

In Chapter 6, you learned that an instructional method is a broad perspective based on theory, research, preparation, experiences, and philosophy. An **instructional strategy** is a specific teaching routine in which steps, techniques, and actions are grouped together in a logical, orderly arrangement to develop or reinforce learning. Teaching the meaning of words in context is an example of a strategy. When using this strategy, the teacher points out pictures that provide clues to the word, tells the student to look at the beginning letters of the word, and asks the student to read the words before and after the new word. Skilled teachers have a repertoire of instructional strategies such as the ones described in this book.

STRATEGIES THAT SUPPORT THE CONSTRUCTION OF MEANING

❖ ALLANA GABRIELLI'S CLASSROOM ❖

Allana Gabrielli, the teacher you met at the beginning of this chapter, was ready to begin a unit on environmental pollution. Using a curriculum based on state and national science standards, Allana intended to introduce the students to Lake Baikal, which is located in southeastern Siberia. Lake Baikal is the oldest existing freshwater lake on earth and the deepest continental body of water. Pollution of Lake Baikal from industrial wastes continues to be a serious environmental problem.

Allana recognized that few students in her class would be familiar with Lake Baikal. However, she knew that most students had some knowledge of air and water pollution. Realizing that she wanted to enable her students to develop a deeper understanding of environmental pollution, Allana asked them to share what they already knew about pollution and give examples. Once students had a common understanding of pollution, Allana planned to introduce activities that would help them construct a deeper meaning of the concept. Preteaching, coaching, cueing, modeling, monitoring, scaffolding, sequencing, shaping, reciprocal learning, and guided practice are instructional strategies that support the construction of meaning.

PRETEACHING

Preteaching is a useful process when students have limited background knowledge or experiences on a topic. Preteaching orients learners to a new topic, vocabulary, and concepts. Strategies used in preteaching include recollection of prior experiences and prior knowledge, use of advance organizers and concept maps, and teaching new vocabulary. These methods can be used during various activities including discussions, field trips, experiments, simulations, role plays, and use of multimedia.

Allana Gabrielli implemented several preteaching methods. She asked students to share what they already knew about pollution. She taught them the meaning of new vocabulary terms such as *contamination, pollutant, hazardous waste*, and *solid waste*. Finally, she showed the students how the unit was organized using an outline, a graphic organizer, and a schedule of science activities for the week.

COACHING

Coaching involves providing hints or suggestions to students so that they can acquire knowledge and skills, perform a task, or demonstrate a behavior. Coaching allows students to become involved in their own learning. For example, Allana Gabrielli could suggest that a student check a particular website for specific information about the temperatures of Lake Baikal and could ask a thought-provoking question such as "How could you predict the long-term effects of pollution on humans and animals?"

In another classroom, Seth, an eighth-grade prealgebra student in Kyle MacLeod's class, needed coaching to help him discover the process of finding the rate of a car going X miles for three quarters of an hour. Kyle asked, "How fast would the car be going if it went 20 miles in 1 hour?" Seth responded, "Twenty miles per hour." Kyle then inquired how fast the car would have to go to travel the same distance in only half an hour. Seth thought and then answered, "It would have to go twice as fast, 40 miles per hour." Kyle next asked Seth to think about how he arrived at the answers of 20 miles per hour and 40 miles per hour for the two examples. Seth replied that he divided the distance by the time it took the car to travel.

A teacher coaching a student on using appropriate learning.

CUEING

Cueing provides a cue, clue, hint, stimulus, or reminder that helps students elicit the correct response. Cueing can be physical, social, or verbal. Physical cuing can be a touch or tap by a teacher. An arrow placed on a student's worksheet can indicate where the student should begin work. A teacher's nod can tell a student when to begin reading.

Cueing can be used to aid students who have difficulty remembering steps for solving problems. The letters **K-W-L**—*K* (what you know), *W* (what you want to know), *L* (what you learned) (Ogle, 1986)—can be put on cards in order to provide written hints. Here are the cues that Allana Gabrielli's students generated at the beginning of the unit on environmental pollution:

What We Know
There are many causes of pollution.
Pollution has a long-term impact on the environment.

What We Want to Know
Which lakes are the most polluted?
What are the causes of environmental pollution?
What are the impacts of pollution on people?

What We Learned
What people have done to stop polluting lakes.
What policies have been developed to curb pollution.

Key questions can serve as cues. These questions include:

- Who is the story about?
- What are the important details?
- Where did the events occur?
- When did the events occur?
- What is your interpretation?

MODELING

Modeling is a process in which a person who is skilled demonstrates to a less skilled person how to do a task, engage in a process, or provide a response. Modeling includes good examples or exemplars of how experts solve problems. For example, modeling can be used to demonstrate how fluent readers read a text, scientists arrive at conclusions, or mathematicians solve a problem.

A teacher can model how to find the answer to the problem "$6 \times 9 = ?$" by using manipulatives such as blocks or cuisenaire rods. The teacher shows students how to count off nine blocks. Next, the teacher arranges six groups of nine blocks. Finally, the teacher shows the students how to calculate 6×9 using the groups of blocks.

MONITORING

Monitoring is a process in which the teacher and/or students are engaged in continuous evaluation of a student's work, behavior, and activities in order to determine areas of problem, concern, difficulty, or strength. Once problem areas are identified, the teacher develops and implements strategies that address the areas of concern. Monitoring involves careful observation. When monitoring, the teacher checks to see whether students:

- understand and follow directions
- understand vocabulary
- need cueing, prompting, or modeling
- need additional instruction in strategies, processes, or skills
- need additional materials

SCAFFOLDING

Like the scaffolding used in construction, instructional **scaffolding** refers to teaching strategies that support students as they acquire knowledge and skills. As learners take more responsibility for their learning, the structures, supports, and scaffolds can be faded and learners can work independently. In order for scaffolding to be effective, it should be:

- relevant and related to the task, response, or behavior that the student is asked to do
- provided when needed
- diminished or faded over time

Tim Downs knows that he needs to scaffold the reading process of his students as they improve their reading and tackle more difficult materials. He models fluent reading, helps them to figure out words that are difficult for them, and reviews the content of what they have read to help increase their understanding. As the students become skilled readers, the need for support from their teacher will fade.

Scaffolding Strategies

The following strategies can be used when scaffolding instruction:

- Encourage students to think and engage in problem solving.
- Ask students to recognize rather than recall.
- Ask questions that encourage students to make predictions and solve problems.
- Ask, "What do you think might happen next?"
- Allow enough wait time for an answer. Silence can be productive and may mean that students are thinking. When students do respond, ask, "How did you come up with that answer?"
- Restate students' questions in order to encourage responses.
- Ask students what is known before offering an explanation.
- Avoid questions that can be answered with one word, such as "yes" or "no."
- Make comments, ask questions, and provide clues that help students figure out how to read or write a new letter or word or remember what happened in a story that has been read aloud.

- Offer genuine praise for efforts and accomplishments. Notice small successes as well as large ones: "I see you wrote a *P* on your picture. That's the first letter in your name, 'Peter.'" "You're on the right track."
- Encourage students to take risks and learn from mistakes. Be specific in your feedback (adapted from Koralek & Collins, 1997).
- Use *think-alouds* to model problem-solving strategies. The teacher verbalizes the approach to problem solving or verbalizes specific strategies that were used to read words, use context clues, use illustrations to figure out the meaning, or comprehend the text.
- Preview the text with students by using background knowledge, making predictions, anticipating events, and following the story line.
- Cue students to where the answers can be found.
- Be sure to use explicit and clear instructions when asking students to do tasks.

SEQUENCING

Sequencing involves breaking down a larger task, response, or behavior into its components so that a student can complete one component at a time. Breaking down a writing assignment into components that include brainstorming a topic, selecting reference materials, organizing and developing paragraphs, and drawing conclusions is an example of sequencing. Breaking a task into smaller steps that can be completed one at a time enables students to perform each smaller task successfully.

Paolo Gomez, a high school history teacher, wanted his students to better understand how to use abstract thinking as part of the research process. For a unit on the development of countries, he decided that his students would do best if he sequenced the tasks for them instead of just assigning a research paper. This is the sequence of tasks that he assigned his students:

- Students and teacher select readings and resources from a prepared list.
- Students read and explore resources on the development of two countries, one modern and one ancient.
- Students create a double time line that includes facts from both countries.
- Students construct Venn diagrams that compare the similarities and differences of several key resources. Figure 7.1 is an example of a Venn diagram.
- Using the information that they generated, the students write their reports.

SHAPING

Shaping involves successive approximations of a target behavior. Teaching the target behavior, such as dressing oneself, using eating utensils, or writing one's name, is broken into successive steps that build on each other. The student is rewarded for close approximations of the target behavior.

A student who is learning to tie her shoes may be rewarded when she is able to make the loops and attempt to finish the tying process. In later attempts, she will be praised and rewarded when she completes more of the steps in tying her shoes.

Figure 7.1   **Venn diagram.** This chart can be used to analyze, compare, and contrast characteristics, items, ideas, and information.

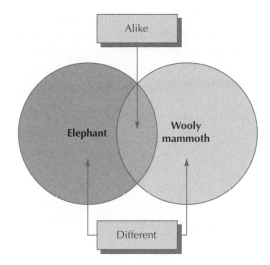

In this way, her behavior is shaped by the rewards and praise that she receives for each step.

Another teacher of a student with a learning disability could employ this strategy while the student is developing the skills needed to write his name. The teacher accepts and praises the student's attempt to form the first letters of his name. As the student's skills are refined, the teacher rewards and accepts closer approximations until he can write all the letters of his name.

RECIPROCAL LEARNING

Reciprocal learning (Hyerle, 1996; Rosenshine, 1997) occurs when a teacher or peer models a process and provides coaching, cueing, or scaffolding as students engage in a task. Reciprocal learning helps students:

- learn important skills or information
- increase understanding or application of new ideas
- improve cooperative skills
- develop listening and positive feedback skills

As students become expert, the teacher or peer phases out the supports and students assist each other in learning the task. The teacher monitors the progress of students and provides assistance when appropriate. Collaboration, cooperation, and interdependence are at the heart of reciprocal learning.

Tim Downs planned a reciprocal learning activity for his students to help increase their comprehension of a story they were reading. He asked each student to develop three questions about the story, with one student taking the role of coach and one student taking the role of a player. The player begins by reading a passage from the story, developing a question about what has been read, and finally answering the question aloud. The student who is the coach listens to the answer and determines if the answer is correct. If it is correct, the coach provides praise; if it is incorrect, the coach provides clues to lead the player to the correct answer. After the first player answers several questions in a row, the roles are reversed. While the students engage in reciprocal teaching, the teacher monitors the comprehension of the story and acts as a super coach (a coach of the student coaches), consulting with the coaches about the answers given.

GUIDED PRACTICE

In **guided practice,** students, working alone, with other students, or with a teacher, engage in a set of activities that involve organizing, reviewing, rehearsing, summarizing, comparing, or contrasting tasks, behaviors, responses, or processes. During guided practice, students receive feedback and instructional support based on close monitoring of activities. These practice activities are related to the outcomes that the teacher is trying to teach and assist students in minimizing errors as they master new skills and information. Guided practice activities are structured and include work assignments, strategy practice, and peer interactions such as cooperative learning, peer tutoring, and partner work (Kemp, Fister, & McLaughlin, 1995).

For guided practice after a lesson on the effects of pollution on Lake Baikal, Allana Gabrielli paired students and asked each pair to brainstorm a list of the effects of pollution and develop a graphic that demonstrates these effects.

TEACHING PROBLEM SOLVING

Directly teaching specific problem-solving skills to students with special needs can improve their ability to solve problems. Strategies that can improve problem solving include the following:

- Teachers and expert peers model how to solve problems.
- Students break a problem into its parts.
- Students describe how they solve problems and receive feedback from expert peers or the teacher in specific content areas such as mathematics, science, and social studies.
- Students learn to solve problems in multiple settings.
- Students identify and use metacognitive strategies.

A science teacher used the following problem to help students think through the effects of pollution on wildlife populations: "During a vacation by the sea, you see dead fish on the beach. People on the beach are picking up the fish and placing them in a bucket. As you walk by, you hear them talking about what a great dinner they will have. Why isn't this a good idea?" The teacher asked the students to identify the issues involved. The students said that not knowing why the fish died was the main issue. They then formulated questions to which they would need to know the answers in order to determine if eating the fish was safe. Some of the questions were: "What kinds of industries are in the area?" "Is there any known natural cause for the death of fish populations?" "Do boats or swimmers pose a threat to the fish populations that could cause them to die?" "How long could a fish be dead and still be safe to eat?" Students then worked in teams to try to answer the questions raised. A discussion of their findings followed. Then the teacher helped them summarize what they had learned to answer the problem question (West, 1992).

STRATEGIES IN ACQUIRING, UNDERSTANDING, AND INTERPRETING INFORMATION

Organizers of information assist learners in acquisition and retrieval of information, understanding of information, and integration of new information (Rosenshine, 1997). An outline is an example of an organizer. Organizers help learners categorize and recall information, explain complex relationships using a minimum of text, clarify and explain concepts, and demonstrate how concepts change as new ideas develop. They help to structure knowledge. Teachers can model the use of organizers and ask students to develop their own.

Graphic organizers, sometimes known as *visual tools,* can be used to generate, analyze, organize, synthesize, and evaluate meaning (Hyerle, 1996). According to Hyerle, visual tools

> are symbols graphically linked by mental associations to create a pattern of information and a form of knowledge about an idea. These linear or nonlinear forms are constructed by individual or collaborative thinkers on paper, board, or computer screen. (1996, p. 24)

Types of organizers include concept maps, webs, and graphic organizers. Graphic organizers help to make abstract concepts concrete, make relationships between concepts explicit, promote learning, and facilitate creation and application of knowledge.

Graphic organizers can be very helpful to students who are deaf, have limited English proficiency, have learning disabilities, or have cognitive disabilities. The graphic depiction of ideas and concepts allows students to express themselves with less dependence on language. Figures 7.1 through 7.4 illustrate different types of graphic organizers. A Venn diagram (Figure 7.1) is used to analyze, compare, and contrast characteristics, items, ideas, and information. Using a concept map, students can brainstorm key factors associated with a central concept or main idea, such as weather (Figure 7.2). A T organizer (Figure 7.3) organizes a main idea with

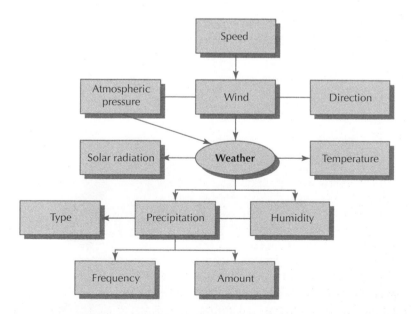

Figure 7.2   **Concept map.** Concept maps help to make abstract concepts concrete.

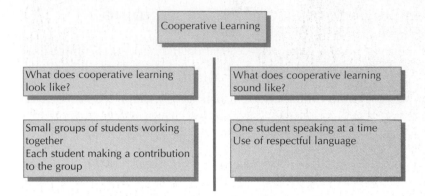

Figure 7.3   **T organizer.** The main concept is at the top of the T, with subtopics and examples underneath.

subtopics and examples. Finally, a mind map (Figure 7.4) organizes and categorizes items in a list.

Inspiration and Expression are two types of software that can be used to develop concept maps and graphic organizers. Ideas about using and developing graphic organizers can be found at the websites The Graphic Organizer and Inspiration.

SUPPORTING ALL LEARNERS

COOPERATIVE LEARNING

Cooperative learning strategies focus on structuring learning situations cooperatively so that students work together while gaining academic knowledge and social skills. The model builds on the premise that when students work together in small groups, they maximize their own and each other's learning. To master skills required

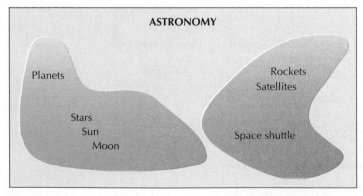

Figure 7.4   **Mind Map.** This mind map begins as a simple list. Students brainstorm items in the list, then group and label items.

Research to Practice

Wait Time

Wait time is the amount of time between a teacher- or student-initiated question and the response or next question. Research (Tobin, 1987) shows that when wait time is used:

- students' responses increase and nonresponses decrease
- students offer more evidence to support their responses
- students' answers are more complex
- student confidence increases
- student-to-student interactions increase

When using wait time, be sure to wait at least 5 seconds between asking the question and acknowledging students' responses. Teachers may find it useful to count the seconds as "one-one thousand," "two one thousand," "three-one-thousand," and so on. They should tell students to raise their hands or signal when they have a response and say that they will call on students after at least 5 seconds have elapsed. Silence is a productive aspect of wait time, and teachers should not be uncomfort-

able when it occurs. During silence, teachers can check students' faces for evidence of confusion, misunderstanding, and comprehension.

If there are no responses after 5 to 10 seconds of wait time, teachers can:

- repeat the question
- rephrase the question
- ask a student to attempt to rephrase the question
- break the question down into parts
- ask students what it is about the question that they are finding difficult

Questions for Reflection

1. Explain why wait time is an important instructional strategy.
2. Develop wait time guidelines for students to use with each other.

 To answer these questions and learn more about applying research to practice, go to the Companion Website at www.prenhall.com/cohen, select Chapter 7, then choose Research to Practice.

for living and working in their communities, students must learn to work cooperatively with others. Cooperative learning results when students:

- work together in small groups;
- work together interdependently;
- maintain individual accountability;
- use positive interpersonal skills such as communication, trust, leadership, decision making, and conflict resolution; and
- promote positive interactions among all learners (Johnson & Johnson, 1989; Johnson, Johnson, & Holubec, 1993)

Teachers use a variety of preteaching and teaching strategies in assisting students to work together cooperatively. First, the teacher clearly communicates the learning outcomes to students before the cooperative learning activity begins. The teacher

These students are engaged in a cooperative learning activity.

models positive interpersonal skills such as turn taking and listening while others talk. The teacher communicates respect for all members of the group and encourages students to help, share, and encourage others.

Types of Cooperative Learning Activities

Planning cooperative learning activities shifts the emphasis from assignments that require students to complete individual work to small-group assignments that require students to work cooperatively while maintaining individual accountability. Before beginning a cooperative learning activity in the classroom, teachers thoroughly plan instruction so that students know and understand interpersonal skills in working with others and have opportunities to practice them. During the course of the year, teachers use instructional time to teach skills in the following areas:

- listening
- taking responsibility
- leadership
- communication
- building trust
- decision making
- conflict management (Johnson et al., 1993)

There are many different ways to form cooperative learning groups, depending on the purpose of the lesson. If one of the learning outcomes is for students to gain specific knowledge or skills, the learning group will be configured to foster peer tutoring. On the other hand, if one of the outcomes is to investigate a topic, the learning group will be designed to share responsibility for gathering information.

Circle of knowledge. In the **circle of knowledge,** the task of the students is to develop as many possible solutions as they can to a problem posed by the teacher. The teacher divides the students into small circles or groups. One student in the group is assigned to be the recorder and reporter of circle activities. The activity concludes with each circle reporting its answers (Kline, 1995).

Complex instruction. **Complex instruction** (Cohen & Lotan, 1997), originally developed for Spanish bilingual classes, is used in many classrooms across the country. It involves group activities that are organized around a central concept or big idea. The teacher provides students with multiple opportunities to work on the big idea so that the concept is understood in different settings and in multiple forms. The tasks, designed for students with diverse backgrounds and differing levels of abilities, are open-ended and require students to make meaningful contributions by working interdependently. Using cooperative learning techniques, students manage their own groups and the teacher provides specific feedback. Both the group and the individual are accountable for the final product. The program builds a positive self-image by reinforcing the idea that all children have different abilities and by making sure that all students have opportunities to be the group expert.

Jigsaw. **Jigsaw** activities are lessons designed to help all students learn a certain body of material. The activity begins with each team member being assigned the responsibility for learning a specific part of the assignment and becoming the expert for the group's team. After meeting with members of other groups who are becoming expert in the same area, the experts return to their own groups and share what they have learned. The teacher monitors the progress of the teams, provides assistance when appropriate, and informally assesses individual knowledge of the whole assignment (Slavin, 1994).

Learning together. **Learning together** activities consist of students working cooperatively in small, teacher-assigned groups on common tasks. Students create a single group product, making sure that each member of the group contributes suggestions and ideas. The teacher monitors the progress of the group and provides assistance when appropriate. The group, rather than individual members, is rewarded for its accomplishments (Johnson & Johnson, 1989).

Student teams-achievement divisions. **Student teams-achievement divisions (STAD)** involve activities to develop a team spirit, in addition to academic and team work skills. STAD involves teacher introduction of content, team study, individual accountability, team recognition, and opportunity for all students to succeed. The teacher forms student groups of four or five members, including high, middle, and low achievers, and presents the new information to the whole class. Then the teamwork begins. Team members study and practice the material in their groups. All team members are responsible for their own learning as well as the learning of the other team members. They complete worksheets and practice exercises, discuss the material, and quiz one another. The teacher monitors the progress of the team and provides assistance when appropriate. At the end, the teacher administers a quiz that students complete individually. After computing individual scores, the teacher adds individual points to the total team points. Students who show improvement or who receive a perfect score secure the most points for their team.

Teams-games-tournaments. **Teams-games-tournaments (TGT)** activities also involve developing a team spirit in addition to academic and teamwork skills, but the teacher does not use quizzes to test student knowledge. After team members work and practice together, a tournament is held in which individual students compete as representatives of their team. The teacher matches individuals from each team based on their prior performance.

❖ A VISIT WITH JERRY NOVAK ❖

Jerry Novak is a high school special educator. Over the past few weeks, he and the ninth-grade school social studies teacher have been coteaching a unit on the U.S. government. Today they will be focusing on the three branches of government: the legislative, judicial, and executive. Let us join their classroom to observe the lesson.

Jerry greets us and offers an overview of what we will be seeing. "During planning time last week, we decided to use a type of cooperative learning activity called jigsaw. Yesterday we assigned students to groups of four, and each student in the group was given a different section of the material to be learned. Today you'll see how each group member is responsible for learning the information and for teaching it to the other members of the group. In other words, each individual is responsible for learning all the assigned material."

As the students enter the classroom and assemble in their small groups, Jerry begins, "Now that you have formed your groups and you each have a section of the material, let's review the steps for doing a jigsaw." (He reviews the steps.)

A special educator monitors students' work.

Bill and Jody, a student with Down syndrome, check that they have the same material and then begin reading silently at first. After a few minutes, Jody turns to Bill and asks, "Hey, what's this word?" Bill helps Jody and then softly finishes reading the material out loud.

"Okay, let's see if you can summarize what I read," says Bill. Jody begins and then checks his material to find the rest of his answer.

"Now it's your turn," says Bill, and Jody carefully follows his page, checking what Bill says. They decide to repeat this process.

After completing their summary, Bill asks, "Okay, are we ready to underline the important parts?" They each grab a colored marker and check each other as they mark their papers. They add some ideas from the day before as notes in the margin.

"Now we have to write down the main ideas and the supporting detail," says Bill, going to the computer. Jody dictates his ideas while Bill types them in and then adds several of his own. Bill repeats them aloud as he types so that Jody has a chance to see and hear them.

Jody slips in front of the keyboard and prints out two copies, one for each of them to take back to their group. Before they leave, they go over their plans on how to teach the material to other group members.

What Does the Research Say about Cooperative Learning?

Research on cooperative learning indicates many benefits for students both with and without disabilities. Cooperative rather than competitive and individual learning can lead to increased achievement, high levels of productivity, supportive relationships among learners, and increased self-esteem. Students with disabilities show increases in mathematics achievement (Xin, 1998), literacy (O'Connor & Jenkins, 1995), science achievement (Farlow, 1994; Mastropieri & Scruggs, 1997; Natal, 1997; Salend, 1998), social studies (Okolo & Ferretti, 1998), and higher order thinking skills across the curriculum (Ibler, 1997).

PEER TUTORING AND PEER TEACHING

Peer tutoring or **peer teaching** is a process in which a skilled student, with a teacher's guidance, helps one or more students at the same grade level learn a skill, concept, or behavior. **Cross-age tutors** are students who work with other students who are either younger or older than themselves. Peer tutoring, in addition to influencing achievement, has important benefits for both the tutor and the tutee, including:

1. learning positive attitudes, values, and skills;
2. learning to share, help, comfort, and to empathize with others; and
3. developing identity and autonomy (Benard, 1990; Thomas, 1993).

Using Technology
Cooperative E-Learning

Cooperative e-learning involves small groups of students who are located at a distance and teacher-designed learning experiences that allow the students to work interdependently by using technologies such as e-mail, listservs, and the Internet. As in traditional forms of cooperative learning, students focus not only on content but also on the process of working with others. During scheduled online learning activities, students share their knowledge and debate with their peers and experts in real time (Andrews & Marshall, 2000). Participating in a virtual classroom, students collaboratively select multidisciplinary topics, conduct research using online databases, and create oral and multimedia presentations.

To build learning communities in cyberspace, Palloff and Pratt (1999) describe several basic steps that should be taken:

- Define the purpose of the group.
- Create a distinctive gathering place for the group.
- Define norms and a clear code of conduct.
- Allow for a range of member roles and
- Allow for and facilitate subgroups (p. 24).

In many ways, cooperative e-learning is very much like working with others in the traditional classroom. The teacher identifies the knowledge area to be studied and the purpose of the group. Since group members may not have face-to-face meetings, the teacher needs to consider the e-meeting place and how to make it inviting. For example, a teacher and students could create a website "playground," an "overlook," or "a library lounge." Students may also share e-mail and agree on other ways to "meet" and work together.

Questions for Reflection

1. Consider the ways in which you have participated in traditional and cooperative e-learning activities, either as a student or as a teacher. What tasks were asked of you as a learner? What was the role(s) of the educator? In what ways did these activities enhance your learning? In which knowledge areas do you think cooperative e-learning works best?

2. Consider two or more different grade ranges at the elementary, middle, or secondary level. How are educators using cooperative e-learning in these classrooms?

To answer these questions online and learn more about technology perspectives, go to the Companion Website at www.prenhall.com/cohen, select Chapter 7, then choose Using Technology.

Developing a Peer Tutoring Program

When developing a peer tutoring program, teachers should consider the following:

1. Start with students who are eager to participate and who make a commitment to tutoring.
2. Train tutors by giving them an overview of tutoring, its importance and goals, and how to structure a tutoring session.
3. Identify activities that lead to success.
4. Model a tutoring session.

5. Provide time for tutoring.
6. Evaluate the peer tutoring program to determine its success.

EXPLICIT OR CONSPICUOUS INSTRUCTION

The National Center on Accessing the Curriculum has synthesized the research on explicit or conspicuous instruction (Hall, n.d.-b). Explicit instruction combines the visible delivery of group instruction, intense teacher and student interactions, and instructional design principles. It includes design components and delivery components.

Explicit instruction has six instructional design components:

Big ideas. Big ideas are the concepts, principles, and heuristics that promote the acquisition of knowledge. For example, when teaching an interdisciplinary unit on myths that involved literature, music, art, and science, Tim Downs, the teacher whom you met at the beginning of this chapter, identified the following two big ideas: myths help us to understand ourselves and others, and myths reflect culture and the world around us.

Conspicuous strategies. Instructional strategies are most helpful when they are made conspicuous, obvious, and evident to learners. The underlying assumptions are that conspicuous strategies should be well designed and thoughtful. For example, Tim Downs chose to use teaching strategies such as cooperative groups, concept mapping, and modeling.

Mediated scaffolding. Scaffolding involves teaching strategies that support students as they acquire knowledge and skills. Mediated scaffolding means that levels of complexity have been tailored to meet the needs of individual students. It necessitates customization of steps, tasks, materials, and supports. For example, Tim Downs customized instructional strategies for Deborah and James, two students with learning disabilities. He modeled research strategies, asked the students to practice them, and provided frequent feedback as they worked on the unit.

Strategic instruction. Strategic instruction consists of the integration of big ideas in new and complex ways. It involves curriculum design and content integration across curriculum areas. Strategic instruction supports the learning and application of new knowledge across curriculum areas. For example, Tim Downs met with the English, music, art, and science teachers in order to integrate the unit's ideas, concepts, and themes. By reading myths, viewing paintings and drawings, listening to music, and engaging in hands-on projects, students were able to demonstrate their understanding of how myths influence culture and development around the world.

Judicious review. Judicious review means that learning is transferred at different times in various contexts. During this phase, new learnings are monitored, practiced, reviewed, and reinforced. For example, as the students continued their learning, Tim Downs reinforced concepts and skills that the students learned and designed opportunities to demonstrate their knowledge in new contexts.

Primed background knowledge. Primed background knowledge involves tapping or stimulating knowledge that students already have about a topic. During this phase, students are encouraged to integrate what they already know with new knowledge and skills that will be acquired. For example, Tim Downs began the unit by asking

Considering Diversity

Being Responsive to All Students

Appropriate instruction is teaching that is responsive to individual students. Teachers respect and value all students as they develop deep understandings, new skills, attitudes, and beliefs. This means that teachers should:

- respect all learners;
- create meaningful learning opportunities adapted to diverse learners;
- understand and use a variety of instructional strategies;
- hold high expectations for all learners;
- be sensitive to individual students' characteristics;
- assist students in using communication techniques that nurture active inquiry, collaboration, and positive interactions; and
- consider individual students' characteristics when developing, organizing, and delivering instruction.

All students should have equitable and meaningful access to high-quality education. The final outcome of equitable, high-quality, meaningful access to school curricula is the education of all students to their highest potential.

Teachers can promote high-quality, meaningful access to education for all students by:

- participating in professional development programs;

- being involved in activities that address equity, diversity, and meaningful access to high-quality curricula in all classrooms;
- aligning curricula, teaching strategies, and assessment;
- using instructional materials that are responsive to diverse student populations;
- using assessment instruments that are free of bias;
- engaging in personal interactions that reflect mutual respect; and
- gearing school programs to high-quality access to meaningful participation for all students.

Questions for Reflection

1. How can high standards support the learning of all students?
2. Write a description of equitable classroom instruction. What types of activities will observers see?
3. What assessment instruments and strategies should be used with diverse learners?

To answer these questions and learn more about diversity, go to the Companion Website at www.prenhall.com/cohen, select Chapter 7, then choose Considering Diversity.

students about myths, family stories, and traditions with which they were familiar. Students were asked to write, draw, or represent their background knowledge and share it with others.

UNIVERSAL DESIGN

Shaped by the vision of universal environments, educators conceptualize classrooms in which instruction can be universally designed. **Universal design** in education means that physical, social, and learning environments are designed so that individuals with a wide range of abilities can have meaningful access to and participation in general education. Universal design in education involves flexibility of materials, strategies, approaches, and technology. It should guide developers, educators, users, and others in developing and implementing environments that support diverse users, regardless of their abilities.

To ensure meaningful access to and participation in general education, attention must be given to the physical, social, and learning educational environments. Focus on the physical environment means that accessible and adjustable tools and surroundings are available. A universally designed social environment means that appropriate social supports, structures, and communities have been created and facilitated. A learning environment that is universally designed is one that contains many natural options, structures, and supports for constructing and expressing knowledge, concepts, and skills.

The concept of universal design in education is evolving. Universal design is an appealing goal. It can guide teachers as they work to make their teaching and learning activities appropriate and accessible to a wide range of learners. Using the concepts of universal design as a framework reduces the necessity of singling students out for specific instructional accommodations and modifications. Making teaching and learning accessible to everyone strengthens educational outcomes for all students.

IMPROVING LEARNING OUTCOMES

Technology can provide rich teaching and learning opportunities. In the following chapters, you will learn about technology applications in content areas. Technology contributes to improved learning outcomes in several ways:

- Interactivity of computer technology and networks promote collaboration and cooperation.
- Computer networks provide distributed learning and knowledge by allowing students to share their knowledge with others.
- Specialized technology allows customization and individualization to meet specific student needs.
- Hypertexts and multimedia add depth and elaboration to learning by associating visual, audio, video, and electronic texts.
- Telecommunication and Internet-based resources provide access to databases, real, virtual, and simulated experiences, and resources (McNabb, Valdez, Nowakowski, & Hawkes, 1999).

ASSISTIVE TECHNOLOGY

In Chapter 1, you learned that IDEA requires that students with disabilities be provided with AT devices and services if the IEP team decides that the student needs them as part of the specially designed instruction. For many students with mild and moderate disabilities, AT and specialized software are essential learning tools. Specialized software enables students to complete tasks and classroom assignments more efficiently. Using a word processing program that includes word prediction features, a student selects a word from among several choices after typing only the first few letters of the word. Deborah and James, the students you met at the beginning of this chapter, use AT to support their learning. They use an electronic version of the book they are reading, which allows them to follow along while a cursor highlights each word in yellow as the computer reads the text. After reading the text together, they collaborate on the development of a story map using software that allows them to sequence the events in the book.

ELECTRONIC TEXTS

Electronic texts (e-texts) are the digital forms of text. Digital text is all around us and enriches our ability to access information (e.g., website resources, library databases) and communicate with each other (e.g., via e-mail and word processing). What you may not have realized is that digital text can easily be transformed into other types of media (Rose & Meyer, 2002). Text in digital form can be converted into:

> Braille
> Synthesized speech
> Digital audio books
> Large-print books

Imagine how text in digital formats might transform learning experiences for students. Digital text provides support for students with learning and reading disabilities, enabling individuals who read at beginner literacy levels to access text.

Using text-to-speech software, students can listen to the digital text as well as follow the text on the monitor. When using digital text, a student can change the computer display to provide various text sizes, spacings, and colors. Text-to-speech software can be critically important for individuals who have learning disabilities or reading difficulties and for those who are blind or have low vision. This software converts text into human speech. The text may come from e-mail, Web browsers, word processors, electronic files, or scanned texts. A number of software companies produce text-to-speech software.

Digital-Format Books

Commercial resources are available online from which textbooks in digital format can be downloaded. At netLibrary (http://www.netlibrary.com) users can browse an e-book online, check out and read an e-book online, or download and read an e-book offline. The collection includes popular works such as best-sellers, trade books such as classic works, and college textbooks in digital format. Interestingly, netLibrary detects if you are logging in from a university server and reconfigures its home page to offer customized resources. WizeUp Digital Textbooks (http://www.dhrnewmedia.com/WU_corp/homeuse.htm) works with leading publishing companies to create digitally enhanced versions of college textbooks. Interactive features of their textbooks include search tools and the ability to import notes and hyperlinks.

E-Text Collections on the Internet

The Internet is host to a growing number of e-books. Web-based collections and digital libraries are provided by many libraries, universities, and educational organizations, allowing access to a wide variety of resources ranging from children's books to government documents.

Bookshare.org

Bookshare.org (http://www.bookshare.org) enables book scans to be shared, thereby leveraging the collections of thousands of individuals who regularly scan books, eliminating significant duplication of effort. Bookshare.org takes advantage of a special exemption in the U.S. copyright law that permits the reproduction of publications in specialized formats for persons with disabilities. For books in the public domain, membership is not required. For copyright books, an annual membership fee is charged.

SUMMARY

- Teachers should know and be able to understand and demonstrate a wide range of instructional strategies that can promote and support instruction.
- Using the concept of universal design, many of the strategies discussed in this chapter can be implemented with all learners, allowing teachers to respect and be responsive to all students.
- Instruction can be supported using technology. AT, specialized software, and Internet accessibility are powerful resources for teaching and learning.

EXTENDING LEARNING

1. Identify three teaching strategies discussed in this chapter. Compare and contrast the strengths and limitations of each.
2. Summarize the teaching strategies described in this chapter using a graphic organizer.
3. Develop three cues that can be used to help you remember and understand how to use teaching strategies.
4. Describe several ways in which e-texts can help improve teaching and learning.
5. Locate and describe Web-based electronic (e-text) centers. How can these centers be used to support teaching and learning activities?
6. You have been asked to work with a general education teacher in developing and teaching a unit for several students with disabilities. These students have difficulty with reading and written communication. Choose a curriculum area and grade level. What strategies could you suggest that the teacher consider?
7. Explore the concept of universal design in education. Suggest teaching and learning strategies that can be implemented with a wide range of learners.

REFERENCES

Andrews, K., & Marshall, F. (2000). Making learning connections through telelearning. *Educational Leadership, 58,* 53–56.

Benard, B. (1990). *A case for peers.* Portland, OR: Northwest Regional Educational Laboratory. (ERIC Document Reproduction Service No. ED327755)

Cohen, E. G., & Lotan, R. A. (1997). *Working for equity in heterogeneous classrooms.* New York: Teachers College Press.

Farlow, L. J. (1994). *Cooperative learning to facilitate the inclusion of students with moderate to severe mental retardation in secondary subject area classes.* Boston: American Association on Mental Retardation. (ERIC Document Reproduction Service No. ED375541)

Hall, T. (n.d.-a). *Differentiated instruction.* Peabody, MA: National Center on Accessing the General Curriculum.

Hall, T. (n.d.-b). *Explicit instruction.* Peabody, MA: National Center on Accessing the General Curriculum.

Hyerle, D. (1996). *Visual tools.* Alexandria, VA: Association for Supervision and Curriculum Development.

Ibler, L. S. (1997). *Improving higher order thinking in special education students through cooperative learning and social skills development.* Chicago: St. Xavier University. (ERIC Document Reproduction Service No. ED410732)

Johnson, D. W., & Johnson, R. T. (1989). *Cooperation and competition: Theory and research.* Edina, MN: Interaction.

Johnson, D. W., Johnson, R. T., & Holubec, E. J. (1993). *Cooperation in the classroom* (6th ed.). Edina, MN: Interaction.

Kemp, K., Fister, S., & McLaughlin, P. (1995). Academic strategies for children with ADD. *Intervention in School and Clinic, 30*(4), 203–210.

Kline, L. W. (1995). A baker's dozen: Effective instructional strategies. In R. W. Cole (Ed.), *Educating everybody's children* (pp. 21–45). Alexandria, VA: Association for Supervision and Curriculum Development.

Koraleck, D., & Collins, R. (1997). *On the road to reading: A guide for community partners.* (ERIC Document Reproduction Service No. ED417017)

Mastropieri, M. A., & Scruggs, T. E. (1997). How effective is inquiry learning for students with mild disabilities? *Journal of Special Education, 31*(2), 199–212.

McNabb, M. L., Valdez, G., Nowakowski, J., & Hawkes, M. (1999). *Technology connections for school improvement.* Oak Brook, IL: North Central Regional Laboratory.

Natal, D. (1997). *The use of cooperative group management software for hands-on science activities to improve communication between students with disabilities and their peers.* (ERIC Document Reproduction Service No. ED420142)

O'Connor, R. E., & Jenkins, J. R. (1995). *Cooperative learning for students with learning disabilities.* (ERIC Document Reproduction Service No. ED390189)

Ogle, D. M. (1986). K-W-L: A teaching model that develops active reading of expository text. *The Reading Teacher, 39*(6), 564–570.

Okolo, C. M., & Ferretti, R. P. (1998). Multimedia design projects in an inclusive social studies classroom. *Teaching Exceptional Children, 31*(2), 50–57.

Palloff, R., & Pratt, K. (1999). *Building learning communities in cyberspace. Effective strategies for the online classroom*. Baltimore: Jossey-Bass.

Rose, D., & Meyer, A. (2002). *Teaching every student in the digital age: Universal design for learning*. Alexandria, VA: Association for Supervision and Curriculum Development.

Rosenshine, B. (1997). Advances in research on instruction: In J. W. Lloyd, E. J. Kameanui, & D. Chard (Eds.), *Issues in educating students with disabilities* (pp. 197–221). Mahwah, NJ: Erlbaum.

Salend, S. J. (1998). Using an activities-based approach to teach science to students with disabilities. *Intervention in School and Clinic, 34*(2), 67–72.

Slavin, R. (1994). *Student team learning* (4th ed.). Baltimore: Johns Hopkins Learning Project.

Thomas, R. L. (1993). *Cross-age and peer tutoring*. Retrieved March 24, 2004, from http://www.ericfacility.net/extra/index.html (ERIC Document Reproduction Service No. ED350598)

Tobin, K. (1987). The role of wait time in higher cognitive level learning. *Review of Educational Research, 57,* 69–95.

West, S. A. (1992). Problem based learning—a viable addition for secondary school science. *School-Science Review, 73*(265), 47–55.

Xin, F. (1998). *The effects of computer-assisted cooperative learning in mathematics in integrated classrooms for students with and without disabilities*. (ERIC Document Reproduction Service No. ED412696)

8

Chapter

Developing and Enhancing Social Skills

CHAPTER OBJECTIVES

After completing this chapter, you should be able to:

- ❖ Identify and describe social skills that students need to be successful.

- ❖ Compare and contrast research-based teaching methods for building and enhancing social skills.

- ❖ Demonstrate an understanding of student diversity and the development of social skills.

- ❖ Describe how educators use technology to support the development of social skills.

- ❖ Describe the link between creating safe classrooms and social skills instruction.

Developing and enhancing social skills involves helping students to manage frustration, resolve conflicts, and develop respect and appreciation for individual differences. In the classroom, special educators work with a wide range of students who have different educational diagnoses such as learning disabilities, emotional disturbance, mental retardation, or autism but who have similar needs in learning and developing good social skills. Social skills instruction is an essential component in building interpersonal relationships and in becoming an effective communicator and a good citizen.

PLANNING SOCIAL SKILLS INSTRUCTION

In planning social skills instruction, special and general educators may work together to plan whole-class activities. At other times, special educators work with individuals or small groups of students with disabilities on targeted social skills. These targeted skills are described in the student's IEP, which mandates social skill instruction for the student with a disability.

LINKING ASSESSMENT WITH INSTRUCTION

Assessing Students' Strengths and Needs

Planning instruction for students begins with assessing their strengths and needs. A special educator typically uses a variety of assessments, including observations, questionnaires, checklists, self-reports, and rating scales.

Special educators gather valuable information about social skills through observation.

For instance, the special educator may begin by making several observations of the student in the classroom, in the cafeteria, and, for younger children, on the playground. Information can be gathered by talking with the student, the parents, and classroom teachers. The special educator will synthesize the results and carefully review the assessment information before planning instructional activities.

Conducting observations. Conducting observations involves a systematic process of gathering information by watching the student's behavior across school environments. Educators must identify the assessment question(s), specify the location(s) for the observations, and decide what method to use in recording observation data (Cohen & Spenciner, 2003). Educators select one or more of the following recording methods, depending on the assessment question:

1. *Anecdotal records.* When teachers want to record an unanticipated event, they often use an **anecdotal record.** This is a brief written account that describes the event(s) after it has occurred.

2. *Running records.* When teachers are interested in the sequence of behavior(s), they complete a **running record,** a description of the event as it occurs. Running records are useful when a teacher believes (or hypothesizes) that one or more antecedent conditions affect behavior. By studying the observational data, the teacher can confirm (or deny) the hypotheses.

3. *Event recordings.* When teachers want to know how frequently an event is demonstrated, they use **event recording,** which records the event each time it occurs. Students also can record their developing skills.

4. *Duration recordings.* Sometimes teachers want to know how long an event or behavior persists. **Duration recording** is used to measure this.

5. *Intensity recordings.* If the assessment question focuses on the degree or strength of a behavior, the teacher uses intensity recording. **Intensity recording** measures various degrees of behavior such as low, medium, or high. Because the ratings depend on the observer's judgment, this method of observation can be subjective and unreliable unless the observer develops descriptors of each of the various levels (Figure 8.1).

6. *Latency recordings.* When teachers want to know the amount of time between a request and the occurrence of a behavior or event, they use **latency recording.** To do this, a teacher uses a stop watch and records the time between the request and the initiation of the behavior.

7. *Interval recordings.* If the assessment question is whether a behavior occurred at various times throughout a class period or in another prespecified time period, a teacher selects interval recording. **Interval recording** consists of dividing the observation period into equal time segments, such as 30-second or 1-minute intervals, and marking the interval if the teacher observes the behavior during that time period. Sometimes educators combine event and interval recording by marking each event as it occurs within the time period, thereby noting the frequency of the behavior during each time segment and developing a record of the frequency of behaviors over time.

Using self-report forms and rating scales. Educators also gather information about student progress from other teachers, parents, and the student by using standardized instruments such as the Conners' Rating Scales—Revised (Conners, 1997) or the Social Skills Rating System (Gresham & Elliott, 1990). The Behavior Rating Profile-2 (Brown & Hammill, 1990) includes six norm-referenced rating scales that are completed by the student, parent, teachers, and the student's peers.

Figure 8.1   **Teacher-developed descriptors for assessing student participation in small-group work (intensity observation recording)**

Degree of Student Involvement in Group Activity

1_____2_____3_____4_____

1. *High involvement:* The target student participated fully in the activity and showed great interest through interactions with other students, body language, and general overall affect.

2. *Medium involvement:* The target student joined the other students in the activity but showed little interest in the progress of the activity, either by lack of interactions or lack of affect.

3. *Low involvement:* The target student primarily watched the other students, occasionally providing words of encouragement, or added comments to the activity.

4. *No involvement:* The target student did not watch other students or comment on the activity.

Source: Adapted from *Assessment of Children and Youth with Special Needs,* 2nd ed., by L. G. Cohen and L. J. Spenciner, 2003, Boston: Allyn & Bacon.

Making Instructional Decisions Based on Assessment Information

Is the instruction effective? Do classroom activities enhance students' social skills? Teachers use observations, self-reports, and rating scales to collect information, to inform instruction, and to monitor student progress. For example, the teacher may decide to conduct several observations of the student across school settings, such as the cafeteria, the general education classroom, or the school gym. This information can be compared to observations that were gathered before instruction began. Figure 8.2 illustrates an observation form that a special educator and a student developed to track the student's progress in staying out of fights. By using information on the observation form, the teacher can probe further regarding the student's perception of the events leading up to fighting. This information is gathered on a regular basis throughout the school year and is sometimes referred to as *formative assessment*.

Based on the information collected during formative assessment, educators decide whether to make adjustments in the instruction and learning activities. For example, the teacher may reteach a skill or may spend more time modeling it, thus providing opportunities for students to practice before moving on to a new area of instruction. If the assessment information indicates that the student is making adequate progress, the teacher begins planning and implementing the next set of instruction and learning activities, thus completing the full cycle of assessing the student's skill level, identifying outcomes, planning, carrying out the instruction, providing learning activities, reassessing the student's outcomes, reteaching, or moving on with the instruction.

Figure 8.2   **Teacher-student–developed interval observation form**

Daryl's Recording Form: Staying Out of Fights ☑

Week of October 1

Monday	Tuesday	Wednesday	Thursday	Friday
Period 1 ☑	Period 1 ☑	Period 1 ☑	Period 1 ☑	Period 1 ☑
Period 2 ☑	Period 2 ☑	Period 2 ☑	Period 2 ☑	Period 2 ☑
Period 3 ☑	Period 3	Period 3	Period 3	Period 3 ☑
Lunch	Lunch	☑ Lunch	Lunch	Lunch
Period 4	Period 4	Period 4	Period 4	Period 4 ☑
Period 5 ☑	Period 5 ☑	Period 5	Period 5	Period 5 ☑

Daryl's comments:

I've had a lot of difficulty this week. Joanie always is bugging me at lunch and then someone makes a dig and then I lose it.

Demonstrating Achievement

Summative evaluation consists of assessment approaches that the educator and student use at the end of the unit or marking period to show the student's growth and progress. To indicate strengths and developing social skills, students can assemble a collection of artifacts in a portfolio such as video clips to illustrate cooperative group work, self-reflections, and teacher-written comments on their behaviors. Or students may complete several performance tasks. Scores that the students assigned themselves, as well as teacher scores and comments on their performance task assessment lists, can illustrate individual skill levels.

The teacher also can collect information about the student's achievements by asking the student to complete a standardized rating scale or questionnaire. Parents and general educators can offer their perspectives through rating forms, notes, e-mail, or face-to-face conferences. Special educators and other team members present summative assessment information at the annual IEP meeting.

SELECTING SOCIAL SKILLS TO TEACH

Generally, individual social skills are grouped by categories that include basic classroom skills; communicating with others, including building friendships; working with others, including collaborative skills; problem solving, including dealing with feelings; and self-control. Figure 8.3 illustrates another way of categorizing social skills and provides a detailed list of skills.

Basic Classroom Skills

By the time most students finish the primary grades, they have learned the behaviors necessary to succeed. They know how to listen and follow a teacher's directions, they ask questions when they don't know or don't understand, and they ask for help when needed.

Students with learning and behavior problems may not acquire these basic classroom skills as readily. Students with language-based learning disabilities and behavior problems sometimes have difficulties using language that is appropriate to the situation, knowing when to speak and when to listen, and understanding what is being said. Some students with learning disabilities have difficulties interpreting nonverbal messages, such as the way a person uses a facial expression or positions the body. Some students with disabilities have difficulty observing what is acceptable in one situation and not in another.

Oppositional behavior, language-based learning disabilities, hyperactivity, and inattention often affect a student's ability to learn these skills without direct instruction. Thus, special educators frequently design learning activities to teach specific skills to individual students. In preparing to teach a skill, special educators usually begin with a **task analysis,** which identifies the steps or behaviors that comprise the skill. For example, a teacher identified the following steps in teaching a student how to make good choices:

1. Stop and think.
2. What choices do I have?

Figure 8.3   Some of the social skills that special educators teach

Group I. Classroom Survival Skills

1. Listening
2. Asking for help
3. Saying thank you
4. Bringing materials to class
5. Following instructions
6. Completing assignments
7. Contributing to discussions
8. Offering help to an adult
9. Asking a question
10. Ignoring distractions
11. Making corrections
12. Deciding on something to do
13. Setting a goal

Group II. Friendship-Making Skills

14. Introducing yourself
15. Beginning a conversation
16. Ending a conversation
17. Joining in
18. Playing a game
19. Asking a favor
20. Offering help to a classmate
21. Giving a compliment
22. Accepting a compliment
23. Suggesting an activity
24. Sharing
25. Apologizing

Group III. Skills for Dealing with Feelings

26. Knowing your feelings
27. Expressing your feelings
28. Recognizing another's feelings
29. Showing understanding of another's feelings
30. Expressing concern for another

31. Dealing with your anger
32. Dealing with another's anger
33. Expressing affection
34. Dealing with fear
35. Rewarding yourself

Group IV. Skill Alternatives to Aggression

36. Using self-control
37. Asking permission
38. Responding to teasing
39. Avoiding trouble
40. Staying out of fights
41. Problem solving
42. Accepting consequences
43. Dealing with an accusation
44. Negotiating

Group V. Skills for Dealing with Stress

45. Dealing with boredom
46. Deciding what caused a problem
47. Making a complaint
48. Answering a complaint
49. Dealing with losing
50. Showing sportsmanship
51. Dealing with being left out
52. Dealing with embarrassment
53. Reacting to failure
54. Accepting no
55. Saying no
56. Relaxing
57. Dealing with group pressure
58. Dealing with wanting something that isn't mine
59. Making a decision
60. Being honest

Source: From *Skillstreaming the Elementary School Child: New Strategies and Perspectives for Teaching Prosocial Skills,* rev. ed. (pp. 88–89) by E. McGinnis and A. P. Goldstein, 1997, Champaign, IL: Research Press. Copyright 1997 by E. McGinnis and A. P. Goldstein. Reprinted by permission.

3. What might happen if I select choice 1? Choice 2?
4. Choose the best option.
5. Evaluate the choice. What happened as a result of my choice? Was this the best choice to make?

After identifying all the steps, the teacher plans how to teach these skills to students. For example, this teacher plans to begin the instruction by talking with the student about a situation between two students that the teacher observed. The teacher feels that this example will spark the student's interest and involve the student in an actual problem. The teacher encourages the student to identify other choices that could have been made. After their discussion, the teacher introduces the list with the steps above; the student will keep it for later reference.

In the following days, the teacher plans to create a role-playing scenario in which the student is required to use these steps in making decisions. Or the teacher may model one of the steps and ask the student to identify the step and what would follow. The teacher will be alert for *teachable moments* to encourage the student to practice decision-making skills in real situations.

Sometimes educators develop learning activities that include goals for individual students and for the class as a whole. In these activities, the class is rewarded with free time, extra recess, or other rewards if all of the members reach the goal. An example of an activity designed for both individual students and the whole class is the Good Student Game (Center for Effective Collaboration and Practice, 1999), described in the following case study.

❖ PROFESSIONAL PERSPECTIVES ❖

Jen Perry's classroom includes several students with learning and behavioral problems, and classroom management is a constant struggle. Students have trouble following directions and completing assignments. Many students have difficulty during independent work times. Jen wants to improve this situation and discusses the problem with the special education consultant, Laurie Franchette. Laurie tells her about the Good Student Game to keep students on task. First, they identify the behaviors that Jen wants to see in the classroom. They make sure that the behaviors are stated in positive terms that describe what the students are to do. Jen decides to address the problems during independent work time. Here is the list of student behaviors that the teachers develop:

- Stay seated.
- Raise your hand if you have a question.
- Work quietly.
- When you finish, pass in your work.
- Use any remaining time to work on your next project.

Next, the teachers set performance goals and rewards. They decide that all students should be able to follow the list of expectations throughout the day during each of the several times they are expected to work independently. Next, the teachers identify the reward. If all students demonstrate the appropriate behaviors, they

Figure 8.4   Daily student checklist

Period: _____	Period: _____
Did I:	Did I:
☐ Stay seated	☐ Stay seated
☐ Raise my hand if I had a question	☐ Raise my hand if I had a question
☐ Work quietly	☐ Work quietly
☐ When finished, pass in my work	☐ When finished, pass in my work
☐ Use any remaining time to work on my next project	☐ Use any remaining time to work on my next project
Period: _____	Period: _____
Did I:	Did I:
☐ Stay seated	☐ Stay seated
☐ Raise my hand if I had a question	☐ Raise my hand if I had a question
☐ Work quietly	☐ Work quietly
☐ When finished, pass in my work	☐ When finished, pass in my work
☐ Use any remaining time to work on my next project	☐ Use any remaining time to work on my next project

will receive 10 minutes of free time at the end of the day. Because students routinely ask for free time, the teachers feel confident that they will value this reward.

Finally, they develop a checklist that the students can use to monitor their own behavior. Jen believes that encouraging students to monitor their own behavior helps them develop more independent work skills and greater pride in their accomplishments. Figure 8.4 illustrates this self-monitoring checklist.

Jen Perry teaches the Good Student Game procedures to students in a 20-minute session. To set the context, she begins by having students discuss the relationship between good behavior and classroom success. She then presents the behaviors, models them, and gives students ample opportunities to practice them. Finally, she shows students how to monitor their own behavior by using the checklist. Over time, Jen observes that students internalize the appropriate behavior (adapted from Center for Effective Collaboration and Practice, 1999, p. 6).

Communicating with Others

For many students, from the moment they board the school bus or walk onto the school grounds, they become engaged with others in conversation. "Hey, how's it goin'?" "What's up?" Other students may be greeted by no one. No one will slide over on the bus seat to make room. The small group of students talking in the hall will not move aside to let them join the conversation. Not being accepted often leads to further interpersonal difficulties such as acting out or withdrawing further from other students.

Other students get into difficulty because of what they say to others or because of the tone and inflection that they use. Often these students are not aware of the effect they are having on others—until it is too late. Some of these difficulties may be the result of impulsive behavior or inability to read the more subtle signals of context clues. In Chapter 2 we referred to these difficulties in understanding and following the social rules of language as *pragmatics*.

Special educators provide direct instruction to enable students to acquire the social skills for communicating with others. For example, the teacher begins an instructional activity by discussing a situation in which some students experienced difficulties in dealing with group pressure. Together they discuss possible reasons why group members may want to coerce another individual. They brainstorm possible consequences and the difficulty of resisting pressure from other students. The educator leads the discussion about other alternatives, such as suggesting a list of more acceptable group activities (adapted from McGinnis & Goldstein, 1997a, p. 147). Special educators also use specially designed curricula to help students acquire communication skills. For example, the ACCESS Program (Walker, Todis, Holmes, & Horton, 1988) is designed for adolescents.

Working with Others

Working with others involves taking turns, collaborating, building trust with others, participating in group decision making, and working to resolve conflicts. While some students with learning disabilities, ADHD, behavioral problems, emotional disabilities, and other disabilities that affect language and impulse control develop collaborative skills by observing peers and participating in classroom experiences, others may need specific instruction, modeling, rehearsal, feedback, and repeated opportunities to build these skills.

Problem Solving

Teachers can introduce social problem solving through classroom meetings. A teacher might begin by identifying the concern. For example, an elementary teacher gathers the students together for their weekly class meeting, saying, "I observed a problem at recess today, and I'm wondering if anyone else observed it, too." The students quickly identify the problem: some students pushed others aside while getting in line. As the problem is discussed, the teacher acknowledges students' ideas and affirms their insights. "Yes, Sasha, each person has a 'personal space' that other people need to respect." The teacher continues, "Does anyone have an idea how we could help people remember about personal space?" Social problem solving is more successful if the teacher doesn't attempt to formulate a solution but rather encourages the students to identify possible solutions and then choose one that they are willing to try (Powell, McLaughlin, Savage, & Zehm, 2001). At the conclusion, the teacher may ask students to sign an agreement indicating their commitment to trying the solution.

Using Technology
Personal Digital Assistants in the Classroom, Part I

At Marysville High School, students with disabilities use Palm handhelds (PDAs) as a component of AT in developing skills in academics, organization, working with others, and self-control. During the first period, they work with the resource room teacher to check their schedules and revise their to-do lists, which are saved to the handheld. The teacher writes reminders on the board, and students enter the tasks. During other class periods, the students attach standard-sized keyboards to input notes directly into their PDAs. If a student misses a class or some of the notes, another student's notes can be beamed into the student's PDA. Later, the student pops it into the cradle and "hot syncs" the file to a desktop computer to print out and study. The teachers find that the beaming capability helps students work together and share information.

Students use PDAs in many ways throughout the school day. In mathematics class, these devices become graphing calculators. The simple buttons on the Palm make learning graphing procedures easier than using more complex graphing calculators. This helps to eliminate frustrating situations. In current events, students download a copy of a national daily newspaper. In physical education, the handheld becomes a stopwatch. According to staff at Marysville High School, "When you make sharing information easier, collaboration becomes possible. Because the students enjoy working with the handheld, it is easier to get them to work as a team: kids can beam their work to each other and share seamlessly, without photocopying, scribbling in notebooks, or circular discussions" (Marysville High School, 2002, pp. 1–3).

Questions for Reflection

1. What are some ways that you and your colleagues use PDAs? What would you say are the greatest benefits of using them? The greatest difficulties?
2. How are educators using handhelds in the classroom?

 To answer these questions and learn more about using technology to support learning, go to the Companion Website at www.prenhall.com/cohen, select Chapter 8, then choose Using Technology.

Self-Control

Self-control, sometimes referred to as **self-regulation,** is the ability to monitor and adjust one's behavior or language in response to a situation. As individuals develop, they learn how to respond to new situations by using past experiences and reflections. They may think or say things to themselves to try to direct their responses. Research suggests that students with learning disabilities use less task-relevant self-talk or inner speech than students without disabilities (Harris, 1986; Richman & Lindgren, 1981). Special educators help students with learning disabilities, ADHD, behavioral disorders, and emotional disabilities develop self-control by using direct instruction and instructional strategies such as modeling, coaching, prompting, and providing constructive feedback.

Sometimes educators teach learning strategies to students. A **learning strategy,** sometimes referred to as *strategy instruction*, consists of a set of steps to help a

A special educator helps a student develop self-control by providing constructive feedback.

student develop and use appropriate social skills or complete an academic assignment. Teachers who help students acquire learning strategies teach them how to be responsible for their own behavior. Figure 8.5 illustrates the eight steps that teachers can follow in teaching a learning strategy. Teachers can encourage middle school and high school students to produce their own strategies by following a

Figure 8.5   Steps in teaching a learning strategy to students

1. Pretest the student on the task to determine strengths and challenges (for example, managing frustration). Discuss with the student the need for a more effective strategy and ask for the student's commitment to try a new strategy.

2. Break the strategy into smaller parts. Describe each part to the student and discuss why it is important.

3. Model the new strategy for the student, using thinking aloud as the strategy is modeled.

4. Ask the student to rehearse each step verbally until the self-instruction is error-free.

5. Arrange for the student to practice the new strategy using a controlled situation. Provide positive and corrective feedback.

6. Arrange for practice in a less controlled or real situation.

7. Posttest the student and give specific feedback regarding performance gains.

8. Help the student continue to generalize the strategy by careful planning and monitoring. Help the student to identify where and under what condition the strategy would be useful. Continue periodic follow-up.

Source: Adapted from *Basic Training: Presenting Learning Strategies,* by J. Tollefson and J. Neduchal, 2000, Center for Research on Learning.

Research to Practice

Teaching Social Skills

Frequently special educators incorporate social skill instruction into ongoing academic instruction using direct instruction or cooperative learning. A number of research studies point to the effectiveness of these two methods in developing and enhancing social skills. Elbaum and Vaughn (1999) conducted a research synthesis of school-based interventions designed to enhance the self-concept of students with learning disabilities. They found that a key component of successful academic interventions was an emphasis on having students work collaboratively with their classmates, as in cooperative learning activities, and receiving feedback from their peers on their progress.

Results of a number of research studies support both direct instruction and specific instruction of learning strategies (Bulgren, Hock, Schumaker, & Deshler, 1995; Duchardt, Deshler, & Schumaker, 1995; Scanlon, Deshler, & Schumaker, 1996). In a meta-analysis of 272 research studies, Swanson (1999) examined the

outcomes for students of average intelligence who were diagnosed with learning disabilities. The analysis showed that the most effective form of instruction combined components of direct instruction (teacher-directed lecture, discussion, and learning from books) with components of strategy instruction.

Questions for Reflection

1. What is strategy instruction and how can you learn more about it?
2. Identify two or three learning strategies you have used (or observed in the classroom). Search the literature to see which strategies have a research base. Share your findings with the class.

To answer these questions and learn more about applying research to practice, go to the Companion Website at www.prenhall. com/cohen, select Chapter 8, then choose Research to Practice.

procedure such as the SUCCESS strategy (Figure 8.6). However, teachers should use caution in requiring a student to remember too many acronyms and self-monitoring phrases because many students with learning disabilities have difficulty with short-term memory.

Self-Advocacy

Students with learning disabilities, behavioral problems, and emotional disabilities must have opportunities to learn how to advocate for conditions that will help them succeed. The special educator can provide direct instruction, encourage students to join peer support groups in the community, connect students with websites maintained by students with disabilities, and arrange for students to hear from successful community members who have disabilities. Learning how to become a successful self-advocate takes time. It is a process that should begin in elementary school and extend through Grade 12.

Figure 8.6   Steps for students to use in developing their own learning strategies

---

SUCCESS

S = Select the problem.

U = Understand by identifying trouble spots.

C = Cash in on what you have used in the past: strategies and experiences.

C = Create a strategy for solving the problem.

E = Echo (try) your strategy.

S = See how well your strategy works in different situations.

S = Save your strategy.

Source: Adapted from "Teaching Adolescents with Learning Disabilities to Generate and Use Task-Specific Strategies," by E. S. Ellis, D. D. Deshler, and J. B. Schumaker, 1989, *Journal of Learning Disabilities, 22*(2).

PREPARING LESSONS AND ACTIVITIES

Interventions should match the types of social skills that students need. Based on a meta-analysis of the research on social skills training and students with high-incidence disabilities, Gresham, Sugai, and Horner (2001) recommend that educators consider how social skills will be taught, depending on the student's needs. For example, when students must *acquire skills,* instruction should include modeling, coaching, behavioral rehearsal, and performance feedback. When students display inappropriate *performance of previously acquired skills,* interventions should address antecedent conditions or manipulation of consequences. Educators might change the antecedent conditions by arranging for peer tutoring or use **incidental teaching,** an instructional strategy that involves using an event or a situation as it occurs to develop or teach a specific skill. Changing the consequences could include contingency contracting, differential reinforcement, or a group-oriented contingency contract. **Contingency contracts** are written agreements between a student and the teacher that describe what the student should do, the behavior(s) that should occur, and the consequence or reinforcement that the student will receive.

SOCIAL SKILLS INSTRUCTIONAL FRAMEWORK

Instruction in social skills can be integrated into the standard classroom curriculum. Warger and Rutherford (1996) developed an instructional framework that can be used across the curriculum by K–8 special and general education teachers. It consists of three phases in planning and implementing social skills instruction. The first phase consists of identifying and defining the social skill to be taught. The definition should be observable and measurable. First-grade teachers in Louisiana came up with the following steps for listening:

1. Getting ready to listen
   - Eyes on the speaker.
   - Hands still.

- Feet on the floor.
- Lips quiet.

2. Letting the speaker know that you are listening
   - Get ready to listen.
   - Lean forward.
   - Nod or smile in agreement with what the speaker is saying. Use facial expressions to show understanding or confusion.
   - Think about what is being said.

Compare this with the way sixth-grade teachers in Texas defined stating a disagreement:

1. Acknowledge that I disagree.
2. Check my emotions. Relax if necessary.
3. Ask myself, "Is it important to state my disagreement now?"
4. If yes, then state how I disagree.
5. Respond to the person I disagreed with:
   - Compromise.
   - Agree to disagree.
   - Check out information for facts.
   - Accept it and go on. (Warger & Rutherford, 1996, p. 21)

After identifying the social skill and the steps involved, the teacher designs a performance-based assessment to measure the skill. The teacher also collects information about evidence of the skill prior to instruction. Frequently teachers use observations.

> One teacher in Florida decided to assess the students' ability to wait their turn during discussion in her fifth-grade class. At 9:10 a.m. she noted how many students in the first two rows waited their turn to speak. At 9:20 a.m. she repeated this observational scan for rows 3 and 4, and at 9:30 a.m. for the remaining students. She repeated this several times throughout the day until she had a good idea of the group's and each individual's abilities. (Warger & Rutherford, 1996, pp. 21–22)

The second phase of this framework consists of implementing instruction. First, teachers use direct instruction to teach a specific social skill and the steps or behaviors involved. Then teachers use modeling, feedback, and activities to practice the skill. A key component of this phase is that once the initial lesson has been completed, teachers provide continuing opportunities for students to practice their newly acquired skill. They look for examples of students using the skill and provide feedback. They may display prominently a poster of the skill and the specific steps that students should follow.

During the third phase, students take responsibility for keeping track of their own performance. Teachers may ask students to track their progress on a behavior checklist. When more support is needed, teachers may provide the students with a card that lists the steps of the social skill. During this final phase, teachers may develop a list of classroom activities from which students can select as part of a reward system.

Skillstreaming

Skillstreaming (McGinnis & Goldstein, 1997a, 1997b) is a curriculum and a procedure to help students acquire social skills. The curriculum, one for elementary students and one for adolescents, includes a wide variety of social skills, each with a set of three to five behavior steps that students learn to follow. Special educators use Skillstreaming with small groups of students to teach needed social skills by following these nine steps (adapted from McGinnis & Goldstein, 1997a, pp. 57–73):

1. *Define the skill.* The teacher begins by leading a group discussion of the skill to be taught.
2. *Model the skill.* Teachers use at least two examples of each skill demonstrated, selecting examples that are relevant to the students' life experiences.
3. *Establish students' skill needs.* Teachers help students identify current and future need for the skill.
4. *Select a role player.* All members of the group role-play each skill that is taught.
5. *Set up the role play.* The teacher selects a student to be the main actor. This student then chooses another person to play the coactor. The teacher describes the relevant information for the scenario, including the physical setting, the events immediately preceding the situation, and the manner the coactor should portray.
6. *Conduct the role play.* The teacher reminds the main actor to think aloud what would normally be thought silently and reminds the coactor to stay in the role of the other person. The teacher coaches the rest of the students on what kinds of cues to observe (for example, posture or tone of voice). During the role play, the teacher may provide additional instruction. Role playing continues until all group members have played the role of the actor and the coactor.
7. *Provide performance feedback.* After each role play, the teacher provides feedback regarding how well the actor followed the behavioral steps involved. For example, in working on the skill "staying out of fights" (Figure 8.7), a student is taught to follow four main steps.
8. *Assign skill homework.* The teacher asks students to try the skill outside of the classroom setting.
9. *Select the next role player.* Another student is selected to serve as the actor, and the procedures begin anew until all students can demonstrate proficiency in the skill.

The Skillstreaming procedure is widely used by special educators, and recent research studies support its effectiveness with elementary and middle school students with emotional and/or behavioral disorders. In one study, classroom behavior improved after a 12-week implementation period, and students indicated that they enjoyed the social skill instructional group sessions (Seferian, 1999). Another study described how educators matched specific Skillstreaming social skills with Vermont state standards and implemented the program for 8 months with twice-weekly sessions. The results indicated that students who participated experienced a "very substantial reduction in school disciplinary actions" (Leonardi, Roberts, & Wasoka, 2001).

Figure 8.7   Skill 40: Staying out of fights

STEPS	NOTES FOR DISCUSSION
1. Stop and count to 10.	Discuss how this can help the student to calm down.
2. Decide what the problem is.	Discuss the consequences of fighting and whether fighting can solve a problem.
3. Think about your choices:	
a. Walk away for now.	Students should ask to leave the area for a few minutes, if needed.
b. Talk to the person in a friendly way.	Discuss how to "read" the behavior of the other person (i. e., is he/she calm enough to talk with), and evaluate one's own degree of calmness and readiness to talk about the problem. Discuss ways to state the problem inoffensively.
c. Ask someone for help in solving the problem.	Discuss who can be the most help: teacher, parent, or friend.
4. Act out your best choice.	If one choice doesn't work, the student should try another one.

SUGGESTED SITUATIONS

School: Someone says that you did poorly on your schoolwork.

Home: Your brother or sister tells your parents that you did something wrong.

Peer group: Someone doesn't play fair in a game or calls you a name.

COMMENTS

This skill may not be supported at home or "on the streets." Nevertheless, students need to be taught the importance of handling conflict in a peaceful way.

Source: From *Skillstreaming the Elementary School Child: New Strategies and Perspectives for Teaching Prosocial Skills,* rev. ed. (p. 130) by E. McGinnis and A. P. Goldstein, 1997, Champaign, IL: Research Press. Copyright 1997 by E. McGinnis and A. P. Goldstein. Reprinted by permission.

❖ *PROFESSIONAL PERSPECTIVES* ❖

Campbell Steele, a special education consultant, meets regularly with general education teachers regarding students' progress and works weekly with several small groups of students in general education classrooms. The small-group sessions allow the students to practice social skills that they have role-played and discussed in the resource room with Campbell. In working with small groups of students, Campbell expects that they will generalize the skills learned in the resource room to other settings. Campbell also works to promote generalization by using anecdotal recordings to note her own observations of students in general education classrooms. Later she discusses the observations with individual students, providing a opportunity for each student to evaluate the behavior and giving feedback. Campbell also works to promote generalization by asking the classroom teachers to observe students' behavior in response to classroom situations and to provide feedback to the students.

RESEARCH-BASED INTERVENTION PROGRAMS

ELEMENTARY SCHOOL

Many children come to school with behaviors that put them at risk for school failure. Some children may have a diagnosis already, whereas others may be at risk for violent or inappropriate behaviors. Recent research suggests that when young children at risk or with emotional disabilities receive structured social skills training in combination with teacher training in behavior management and instruction of parents in positive discipline, there are socially important outcomes years later (Bullis, 2001). One such structured skills training program is the First Step to Success.

First Step to Success

The First Step to Success (Walker et al., 1997) is a collaborative home and school intervention program for kindergartners who show early signs of antisocial behavior such as aggression, oppositional defiant behavior, severe tantrums, or victimization of others. The program has three components: (a) a screening procedure to identify at-risk students; (b) a school instructional component that includes a consultant-based school intervention involving the child, teachers, and peers; and (c) a parent-training component that focuses on ways parents can support and improve the child's adjustment to school. The primary goal of the program is to teach the child to get along with others, including the teacher and peers, and to complete classroom activities in an appropriate and successful manner. The program teaches six social skills (Walker et al., 1998, p. 69):

- Communication and sharing in school
- Cooperation
- Accepting limits
- Problem solving
- Friendship making
- Developing self-esteem and confidence

Other structured intervention programs for elementary students, similar to First Step to Success, address key social skills and encourage positive, socially appropriate behaviors. CLASS is a program focusing on acting-out students, RECESS is for aggressive students, and PEERS is for students who are socially withdrawn (Bullis, 2001).

What does the research say? Several research studies report that structured social skills training is an effective intervention for elementary students. A 4-year study of First Step to Success, involving 46 children who initially received training in kindergarten, found positive behavior changes and persistent gains in social skills into the primary grades (Walker et al., 1998). In an earlier study of CLASS, Hops (1978) found that students who received training significantly increased their appropriate behaviors and required fewer remedial services and special class placement years later.

Promoting Alternative Thinking Strategies

Promoting Alternative Thinking Strategies (PATHS; see Greenberg, Kusché, & Mihalic, 1998) is a multiyear prevention program consisting of a comprehensive curriculum for promoting emotional and social competencies and reducing aggression and behavior problems in elementary school. Unlike First Step to Success, which screens and identifies students who need social skills intervention, this program is provided to all children. The PATHS curriculum includes systematic lessons, materials, and instruction for teaching:

- self-control
- social competence
- positive peer relations
- interpersonal problem-solving skills

The curriculum consists of 20- to 30-minute lessons three times a week. Teachers are provided with the lessons, materials, and instruction for teaching. Figure 8.8 shows the social skills addressed in PATHS lessons.

PATHS is considered a model program by the Center for the Study of Prevention of Violence in Colorado because it meets a prespecified set of evaluation criteria. These criteria require model programs to have a strong research design and be

---

Figure 8.8   Social skills addressed in PATH lessons

- Identifying and labeling feelings
- Expressing and assessing the intensity of feelings
- Managing feelings
- Delaying gratification
- Controlling impulses
- Reducing stress
- Self-talk
- Reading and interpreting social cues
- Understanding the perspectives of others
- Using steps for problem solving and decision making
- Having a positive attitude toward life
- Self-awareness
- Nonverbal communication skills
- Verbal communication skills

Source: Adapted from *Blueprints for Violence Prevention, Book Ten: Promoting Alternative Thinking Strategies (PATHS)*, by M. T. Greenberg, C. Kusché, and S. F. Mihalic, 1998, Boulder, CO: Center for the Study and Prevention of Violence.

replicable to establish program effectiveness. Model programs also must provide evidence of significant prevention or deterrent effects and demonstrate sustained effects.

What does the research say? PATHS has been field-tested and researched with children both with and without disabilities, including children who have learning disabilities and emotional disturbance. Evaluations of PATHS have demonstrated significant improvements in children both with and without disabilities compared to children in control programs in a number of areas. Students improved their self-control, understanding and recognition of emotions, and thinking and planning skills. They increased their ability to tolerate frustration. One year after the intervention, teachers reported that students with disabilities in special education settings showed decreased sadness, anxiety, and withdrawal symptoms, as well as reduced aggressive and disruptive behavior, while students reported decreased sadness, depression, and conduct problems (Greenberg, Kusché, & Mihalic, 1998).

MIDDLE SCHOOL

In middle school, increased peer pressure and opportunities to make different choices abound: drug and alcohol use, sexual activity, and other risk-taking behaviors. At the same time, middle school students experience increased academic demands and decreased parental supervision. Schoolwide focus programs at this level typically include rule following and academic effort, whereas intense instruction in the resource room or an alternative setting may include anger management, impulse control, and resistance to use of alcohol, tobacco, and other drugs (Bullis, 2001).

Effective Behavioral Support Program and the Second Step Violence Prevention Curriculum

The Effective Behavioral Support (EBS) program (Sprague, Sugai, & Walker, 1998), designed for both elementary and middle school students, is a schoolwide program consisting of training, technical assistance, and evaluation of school discipline and climate. EBS provides a whole-school approach to addressing the problems posed by antisocial students and coping with challenging student behaviors. The program involves clearly defining problem behaviors for students and staff as well as defining appropriate positive behaviors. Students are taught appropriate alternative behaviors and given assistance to acquire the skills to change their behavior. The program includes effective incentives and motivational systems. The staff commits to maintaining the intervention over the long term and monitors, supports, coaches, debriefs, and provides booster training as necessary. Finally, through technical assistance, personnel monitor and measure the interventions (Sprague et al., 2001, p. 498). The Second Step Violence Prevention Curriculum (Committee for Children, 1997), usually used in combination with EBS, provides systematic instruction in interpersonal skills.

What does the research say? EBS, in combination with the Second Step Violence Prevention Curriculum, shows promising results. In a study of nine treatment schools in the Pacific Northwest that used both EBS and Second Step, both elementary and middle schools saw a decrease in the number of office discipline referrals and improvements in students' social skills during the 1-year program (Sprague et al., 2001). In a comparison of six matched schools randomly assigned to the Second Step curriculum and a comparison group, students in the intervention group showed decreased physically aggressive behavior and increased neutral and prosocial behaviors (Grossman et al., 1997).

HIGH SCHOOL

High school students with emotional disorders and those with learning disabilities often fail in school, exhibit antisocial behavior, and face unemployment. They are at high risk for school dropout. Research suggests that these students lack job-related social skills (Bullis, 2001).

Strategic Instruction Model

The Strategic Instruction Model (SIM) for adolescents with learning disabilities was developed over many years at the Center for Research on Learning at the University of Kansas (Deshler & Lenz, 1989; Deshler & Schumaker, 1993; Deshler et al., 2001). Sometimes referred to as the Strategies Intervention Model, it is designed for small-group instruction in learning strategies across the curriculum, including reading, writing, mathematics, test-taking strategies, remembering information, and social interaction. Teachers implementing SIM use direct instruction and specific curriculum materials, including books, CDs, newsletters, and videotapes. The curriculum for social interaction consists of instructional programs in community building and in cooperative thinking strategies (Figure 8.9).

Figure 8.9   Social skills addressed in the SIM

Community building
- Participating respectfully in class discussions
- Following instructions effectively

Cooperative thinking
- Analyzing and resolving controversial issues within a group
- Mastering information
- Sharing ideas
- Complimenting others
- Offering help or encouragement
- Recommending changes nicely
- Exercising self-control
- Working as part of a team
    - Analyzing an assignment and dividing it into tasks
    - Offering and requesting help to complete jobs
    - Asking for and giving feedback to group members
    - Assembling individual jobs into one product
    - Evaluating the process used to complete the project
    - Using a self-advocacy strategy to prepare for and participate in IEP conference

Source: Adapted from *Learning Strategies*, n.d., Center for Research on Learning, University of Kansas.

Considering Diversity

Familiarity, Dissonance, or Disability?

Teachers who have concerns about a student's social skills may not be sure if the problems arise from the student's disability, or the student's lack of familiarity with the skills, or dissonance with the school culture. Teachers should consider the cultural context by asking:

- What do we know about this student's linguistic, ethnic, and cultural background?
- How does the student's family explain the behavior in question?
- Do we notice the same or similar behaviors in other students with similar backgrounds?
- Is there any indication that the student's behavior has a cultural, ethnic, or religious basis?
- Is the student able to function successfully in more than one setting? (adapted from Craig, Hull, Haggart, & Perez-Selles, 2000, p. 10)

Because communication is culturally dependent, family and community members may hold views other than those of school personnel. For example, community and family members may have cultural expectations concerning various forms of social interchange, including oral and written communication, gestures, eye contact, and body language. Good teachers search out school and community resources to learn more about other cultures and traditions. They keep an ongoing file of contact people and organizations. Teaching is a profession in which we never stop learning.

Questions for Reflection

1. Consider the students in your community. What expectations do community members hold regarding the behavior and social interactions of children and young adults?
2. What are the components of the school culture? Are these components similar or different across elementary, middle, and secondary school? How do they compare in schools in various regions of the country?

 To answer these questions and deepen your understanding of diversity in schools and communities, go to the Companion Website at www.prenhall.com/cohen, select Chapter 8, then choose Considering Diversity.

What does the research say? Although much has been written about SIM, research specific to it and to the development of social skills is more limited. Van Reusen, Deshler, and Schumaker (1989) found positive outcomes in training adolescents with learning disabilities to use self-advocacy procedures during the IEP conference compared to the outcomes in a control group of students. Using a multiple-baseline across-subjects design, Lenz, Ehren, and Smiley (1991) found that adolescents improved their completion of project-type assignments. In a review of the research that focused on SIM strategies to improve social skills and generalize their use, Van Nooten (1991) found that SIM appeared to be useful in social skill training. In a further study of the benefits of using SIM, 20 typical sixth-grade students and 4 students with disabilities developed more positive academic and social perceptions over the course of the school year compared to students in the control classroom (Reuter & Erickson, 1995).

CONNECTIONS

CONNECTIONS (Johnson, Bullis, Mann, Benz, & Hollenbeck, 1999) is a curriculum that addresses real-life social interaction in competitive work settings and work experiences through actual job placements or job shadowing. Composed of 33 interrelated lessons, the content covers teamwork, communication, and problem solving. Each lesson takes about 50 minutes. To monitor student progress, CONNECTIONS includes curriculum-based measures, social problem-solving assessment exercises, and a structured job interview with community employers. This curriculum is designed for use with heterogeneous groups of students, including typical students, students considered at risk, and students with disabilities.

What does the research say? When CONNECTIONS was used with small, heterogeneous groups of students (10–15) who were at risk or who had disabilities and typical students, all three groups of students increased their knowledge of job-related social skills in an equivalent manner (Bullis, 2001, p. 81). This curriculum continues to be refined by the authors in the hope of moving CONNECTIONS into the general education curriculum.

CREATING SAFE CLASSROOMS

Enhancing and developing social skills helps the student manage frustration, resolve conflicts, and develop respect and appreciation for others. Yet creating a safe classroom may go beyond planning and implementing social skill instruction for selected students. When students have few positive role models in the home or in their neighborhood, they may resort to inappropriate behaviors or become victims of violent or bullying behaviors. In fact, creating safe, violence-free classrooms has become a national concern. In a nationally representative survey of over 2,000 8th to 11th graders, the American Association of University Women Educational Foundation's report *Hostile Hallways: Bullying, Teasing, and Sexual Harassment in School* found that one student in five fears being hurt or bullied in school. Four students in five have personally experienced sexual harassment, and 54% of the students say that they have sexually harassed someone (AAUW, 2001). Each year, 1 out of 12 high school students is threatened or injured with a weapon (APA, 2002).

Creating safe classrooms involves zero tolerance for violent or bullying behaviors. **Bullying** means that a student is exposed, repeatedly and over time, to negative actions on the part of one or more other students. These actions involve intentionally inflicting, or attempting to inflict, injury or discomfort. The behaviors may include physical (hitting, kicking, pushing, choking), verbal (name-calling, threatening, taunting, spreading rumors), or other behaviors such as making faces or obscene gestures or intentionally excluding another student from a group (Center for the Study and Prevention of Violence, n.d.).

Students who resort to bullying frequently have learned to use aggressive behaviors to obtain what they need or want. More often than not, these behaviors are learned first in the home, where these students have few positive role models. One or both parents often display violent verbal and physical overreactions, later ignoring the child for some time. Little praise or encouragement is given. The child grows up

Research to Practice

The Bullying Prevention Program

The Bullying Prevention Program has been used in a number of countries, including Norway, England, Germany, and the United States. Results of several research studies indicate that student reports of bullying or being bullied drop substantially. Students report better discipline at school, better social relationships, and more positive attitudes toward schoolwork and school (Center for the Study and Prevention of Violence, n.d.). Olweus et al. (1999) describe the first systematic evaluation of this program in the United States, which involved over 6,000 students from schools in South Carolina. Research findings indicated that middle school students showed significant decreases in self-reports of bullying in schools that implemented the program compared to control schools.

Questions for Reflection

1. What other bullying prevention programs have a strong research base documenting their effectiveness?
2. Working with a small group of colleagues, compare and contrast two of these programs. Which would you recommend? Why?

 To answer these questions and learn more about applying research to practice, go to the Companion Website at www. prenhall. com/cohen, select Chapter 8, then choose Research to Practice.

Special educators teach effective communication skills.

Figure 8.10   Warning signs for students: Controlling your own risk of violent behavior

When you are angry, you probably feel:

- muscle tension
- accelerated heartbeat
- a "knot" or "butterflies" in your stomach
- changes in your breathing
- trembling
- goose bumps
- flushed in the face

You can reduce the rush of adrenaline that's responsible for your heart beating faster, your voice sounding louder, and your fists clenching if you:

- Take a few slow, deep breaths and concentrate on your breathing.
- Imagine yourself at the beach, by a lake, or anywhere that makes you feel calm and peaceful.
- Try other thoughts or actions that have helped you relax in the past.

Keep telling yourself:

- "Calm down."
- "I don't need to prove myself."
- "I'm not going to let him/her get to me."

Stop. Consider the consequences. Think before you act. Try to find positive or neutral explanations for what that person did that provoked you. Don't argue in front of other people. Make your goal to defeat the problem, not the other person. Learn to recognize what sets you off and how anger feels to you. Learn to think through the benefits of controlling your anger and the consequences of losing control. Most of all, stay cool and think. Only you have the power to control your own violent behavior, don't let anger control you.

Source: American Psychological Association, n.d., and MTV. Copyright © 1999 by the American Psychological Association. Adapted with permission. For additional information, consult the website http://helping.apa.org/warningsigns

learning that intimidation and brute force are ways to interact with others (Roberts & Morotti, 2000).

The Office of Civil Rights and the Office of Special Education and Rehabilitative Services consider bullying a student with a disability as disability harassment. In addition to the devastating effects this behavior may have on the victim, bullying may violate state and local civil rights, child abuse, and criminal laws (Cantu & Heumann, 2000). Educators and other school staff have a responsibility to respond immediately to disability harassment and take prompt action to end all forms of this behavior.

National organizations have posted information about bullying and violence on the Internet for teachers, parents, and students. The American Psychological Association has excellent Web pages geared to adolescents (Figure 8.10), and the National Crime Prevention Council is a rich resource for teachers, parents, and students (Figure 8.11). Figure 8.12 provides suggestions for teachers in classroom management and ways to create safe classroom environments.

Figure 8.11   Warning signs for teachers

Watch for Signs . . . Take Action

Know signs that kids are troubled and know how to get them help.

- Lack of interest in school
- Absence of age-appropriate anger control skills
- Seeing self as always the victim
- Persistent disregard for or refusal to follow rules
- Cruelty to pets or other animals
- Artwork or writing that is bleak or violent or that depicts isolation or anger
- Talking constantly about weapons or violence
- Obsessions with things like violent games and TV shows
- Depression or mood swings
- Bringing a weapon to school
- History of bullying
- Misplaced or unwarranted jealousy
- Involvement with or interest in gangs
- Self-isolation from family and friends
- Talking about bringing weapons to school

Source: National Crime Prevention Council, n.d. Reprinted with permission from the National Crime Prevention Council.

Figure 8.12   Teacher suggestions for preventing violence

Stopping School Violence: What Teachers Can Do

- With help from students, set norms for behavior in your classroom. Refuse to permit violence. Ask students to help set penalties and enforce the rules.
- Learn and teach conflict resolution and anger management skills. Help your students practice applying them in everyday life. Discuss them in the context of what you teach.
- Teach with enthusiasm. Students engaged in work that is challenging, informative, and rewarding are less likely to get into trouble.
- Incorporate discussions on violence and its prevention into the subject matter you teach whenever possible.
- Insist that students not resort to name-calling or teasing. Encourage them to demonstrate the respect they expect.
- Learn how to recognize the warning signs that a child might be headed for violence and know how to tap school resources to get appropriate help.
- Encourage students to report crimes or activities that make them suspicious.
- Firmly and consistently, but fairly, enforce school policies that seek to reduce the risk of violence. Take responsibility for areas outside as well as inside your classroom.
- Regularly invite parents to talk with you about their children's progress and any concerns they have. Send home notes celebrating children's achievement.

Source: Selected items from National Crime Prevention Council, n.d. Reprinted with permission from the National Crime Prevention Council.

Bullying Prevention Program

One of the most carefully researched and effective programs is the Bullying Prevention Program, first developed in Norway (Olweus, 1993; Olweus, Limber, & Mihalic, 1999). This program, which targets elementary, middle, and junior high school students, is a schoolwide plan to respond to and prevent bullying behavior. It begins by building awareness of the current situation, with adults at school and parents examining the degree of bullying and victimization in their school. Various persons, including a school administrator, a teacher from each grade, a guidance counselor, a parent, and a student representative, form a Bullying Prevention Coordinating Committee.

In the classroom, students can learn strategies to avoid being bullied and ways to stop bullying behavior. Teachers hold regular classroom meetings with students to discuss various aspects of bullying and the agreed-upon classroom rules. During the meetings, students engage in role playing, writing, and small-group discussions to help them understand the harm caused by bullying and what they can do.

UNDERSTANDING BULLYING BEHAVIORS AND DEVELOPING SOCIAL SKILLS

When students are not held accountable for their actions, they may resort to bullying. Bullies must learn that aggression is not acceptable and that they need to use alternative means of dealing with everyday frustrations (Roberts & Morotti, 2000). Along with *learning* about prosocial behaviors, students need to *practice* and *experience success* in using these skills. Effective communication is a primary component of appropriate social behavior. Yet for students with language-based disabilities, effective communication may be a problem. Difficulties in processing and understanding language affect the student's ability to communicate effectively or to read communication signals in others.

─────── ❖ *PROFESSIONAL PERSPECTIVES* ❖ ───────

A team of concerned administrators and educators from the Martinville School District met regularly to study the incidence and degree of school violence and bullying in the schools. They held discussions with parents and community leaders, and surveyed students and teachers. Their efforts helped to build awareness among students, parents, educators, and citizens of the degree and seriousness of the problem. When they analyzed the incidence and rate of bullying, they found that many students had experienced some form of bullying, and that bullying and other forms of harassment occurred frequently. Students, both with and without disabilities, had used bullying behavior and were victims of bullying. Frequently, these students displayed poor social skills. Thus began a multiyear effort to foster student responsibility, develop a code of conduct, and improve discipline for all students, both with and without disabilities.

As part of this effort, the special education teachers were asked to work with the school psychologist to prepare a workshop on promising practices and practical approaches to developing social skills. They decided to ask each participant, "Which skills do you use when you join a group of friends who are engaged in a conversation?" Which skills do you think they identified?

SUMMARY

- Learning how to communicate effectively, work collaboratively, show empathy with others, and resolve conflicts are social skills that are necessary to be a contributing member of the class and a productive citizen as a student moves through school and from school to employment in the community. Many students learn social skills readily as they move through the grades; for others, particularly those with learning and behavior problems, social skills may not be easily acquired.
- Assessment of the student's social skills and specialized instruction should be included in the IEP if the assessment results indicate that such instruction is necessary. For these students, social skills, such as basic classroom skills, communicating with others, working with others, problem solving, and self-control, must be taught.
- Programs such as the Bullying Prevention Program or other prevention programs embedded in the standard curriculum help all students develop and refine their social skills.
- Special educators who teach social skills provide students with a gift for life!

EXTENDING LEARNING

1. Consider your own experiences in school or field experiences that you have completed recently. What learning activities related to social skills have you experienced or observed?
2. Interview an administrator, a school counselor, a school social worker, or a special educator in a local school to find out more about how social skills are addressed in the school curriculum. Be sure to prepare your interview questions in advance. Use a class listserv or class discussion to share your results.
3. Compare and contrast two of the teaching methods for social skills described in this chapter. What learning theories described in Chapter 6 do you think these methods incorporate? Would you consider using one of these methods in your own teaching? Why or why not?
4. Select a social skill and use a task analysis to identify and order its components. Compare your results with those of a classmate.
5. Using the social skill from the previous example, choose a grade level and create a learning activity that would help students develop this skill. Demonstrate your learning activity to the class and then evaluate the results. Did the activity go as you expected? What feedback did your classmates provide? Would you make any changes if you were to do this activity in an actual classroom?
6. Using the SUCCESS learning strategy (Figure 8.6), work with a partner to develop a learning strategy for managing a stressful situation. Share your results with the class. Plan to use your strategy in a real situation and evaluate the results.

REFERENCES

American Association of University Women. (2001). *Hostile hallways: Bullying, teasing, and sexual harassment in school*. Washington, DC: AAUW Educational Foundation Research.

American Psychological Association and MTV. (n.d.). *Warning signs: Controlling your own risk for violent behavior*. Retrieved January 14, 2002, from http://helping.apa.org/warningsigns/controlling.html

Brown, L., & Hammill, D. D. (1990). *Behavior rating profile-2*. Austin, TX: PRO-ED.

Bulgren, J. A., Hock, M. F., Schumaker, J. B., & Deshler, D. D. (1995). The effects of instruction in a paired associates strategy on the information mastery performance of students with learning disabilities. *Learning Disabilities Research and Practice, 10*(1), 22–37.

Bullis, M. (2001). A promise unfulfilled: Social skills training with at-risk and antisocial children and youth. *Exceptionality, 9*(1), 67–91.

Cantu, N. V., & Heumann, J. E. (2000). *Memorandum on harassment based on disability*. Retrieved January 22, 2002, from the U.S. Department of Education website: http://www.ed.gov/PressReleases/07-2000/0726_2.html

Center for Effective Collaboration and Practice. (1999). *Prevention strategies that work*. Retrieved February 13, 2002, from http://www.air.org/cecp/preventionstrategies/Default. htm

Center for Research on Learning. (n.d.). *Learning strategies*. Retrieved January 14, 2002, from the University of Kansas website: http://www.ku-crl.org/htmlfiles/lscurriculum/lsdescription.html

Center for the Study and Prevention of Violence. (n.d.). *History and description of the bullying prevention program*. Retrieved January 15, 2002, from the University of Colorado website: http://www.colorado.edu/cspv/blueprints/model/chapt/BullyExec.htm

Cohen, L. G., & Spenciner, L. J. (2003). *Assessment of children and youth with special needs* (2nd ed.). Boston: Allyn & Bacon.

Committee for Children. (1997). *Second step: Violence prevention curriculum*. Seattle: Author.

Conners, C. K. (1997). *Conners' rating scales—revised*. North Tonawanda, NY: Multi-Health Systems.

Craig, S., Hull, K., Haggart, A. G., & Perez-Selles, M. (2000). Promoting cultural competence through teacher assistance teams. *Teaching Exceptional Children, 32*(3), 6–12.

Deshler, D. D., & Lenz, B. K. (1989). The strategies instructional approach. *International Journal of Disability, Development and Education, 36*(3), 203–224.

Deshler, D. D., & Schumaker, J. B. (1993). Strategy mastery by at-risk students: Not a simple matter. *The Elementary School Journal, 94*(2), 153–167.

Deshler, D. D., Schumaker, J. B., Lenz, B. K., Bulgren, J. A., Hock., M. F., Knight, J., & Ehren, B. (2001). Ensuring content-area learning by secondary student with learning disabilities. *Learning Disabilities Research and Practice, 16*(2), 96–108.

Duchardt, B. A., Deshler, D. D., & Schumaker, J. B. (1995). A strategic intervention for enabling students with learning disabilities to identify and change their ineffective beliefs. *Learning Disability Quarterly, 18*(3), 186–201.

Elbaum, B., & Vaughn, S. (1999). *Can school-based interventions enhance the self-concept of students with learning disabilities?: Executive summary*. Paper presented at the 1999 Keys to Successful Learning Summit. Abstract retrieved January 12, 2002, from http://www.ld.org/research/ncld_self_concept.cfm

Ellis, E. S., Deshler, D. D., & Schumaker, J. B. (1989). Teaching adolescents with learning disabilities to generate and use task-specific strategies. *Journal of Learning Disabilities, 22*(2), 108–119, 130.

Greenberg, M. T., Kusché, C., & Mihalic, S. F. (1998). *Blueprints for violence prevention, book ten: Promoting alternative thinking strategies (PATHS).* Boulder, CO: Center for the Study and Prevention of Violence.

Gresham, F. M., & Elliott, S. N. (1990). Social skills rating system. Circle Pines, MD: American Guidance Service.

Gresham, F. M., Sugai, G., & Horner, R. H. (2001). Interpreting outcomes of social skills training for students with high-incidence disabilities. *Exceptional Children, 67*(3), 331–344.

Grossman, D. C., Neckerman, H. J., Koepsell, T. D., Liu, P. Y., Asher, K. N., Beland, K., Frey, K., & Rivara, F. P. (1997). Effectiveness of a violence prevention curriculum among children in elementary school: A randomized controlled trial. *Journal of the American Medical Association, 277,* 1605–1611.

Harris, K. R. (1986). The effects of cognitive-behavior modification on private speech and task performance during problem solving among learning-disabled and normally achieving children. *Journal of Abnormal Child Psychology, 14*(1), 63–67.

Johnson, M., Bullis, M., Mann, S., Benz, M., & Hollenbeck, K. (1999). *The CONNECTIONS curriculum.* Eugene: Institute on Violence and Destructive Behavior, College of Education, University of Oregon.

Lenz, B. K., Ehren, B. J., & Smiley, L. R. (1991). A goal attainment approach to improve completion of project-type assignments by adolescents with learning disabilities. *Learning Disabilities Research and Practice, 6,* 166–176.

Leonardi, R., Roberts, J., & Wasoka, D. (2001). *Skillstreaming: A report to the Vermont State Department of Education.* Montpelier: Vermont State Department of Education. (ERIC Document Reproduction Service No. ED459553)

Marysville High School. (2002). *Marysville High School: Tell us your story.* Retrieved June 27, 2002, from the Palm website: http://www.palmone.com/us/education/studies/study3.html

McGinnis, E., & Goldstein, A. P. (1997a). *Skillstreaming the elementary school child: New strategies and perspectives for teaching prosocial skills* (rev. ed.). Champaign, IL: Research Press.

McGinnis, E., & Goldstein, A. P. (1997b). *Skillstreaming the adolescent: New strategies and perspectives for teaching prosocial skills* (rev. ed.). Champaign, IL: Research Press.

National Crime Prevention Council. (n.d.). *Stopping school violence: 12 things teachers can do.* Retrieved January 14, 2001, from http://www.ncpc.org/ncpc/ncpc?pg-2088-6154

Olweus, D. (1993). *Bullying at school: What we know and what we can do.* Cambridge: Blackwell.

Olweus, D., Limber, S., & Mihalic, S. F. (1999). *Blueprints for violence prevention, book one: Bullying prevention program.* Boulder, CO: Center for the Study and Prevention of Violence.

Powell, R. R., McLaughlin, H. J., Savage, T. V., & Zehm, S. (2001). *Classroom management: Perspectives on the social curriculum.* Upper Saddle River, NJ: Merrill/Prentice Hall.

Reuter, S. F., & Erickson, C. (1995). *Strategies intervention model: Promoting positive academic and social classroom perceptions in middle school students.* Reston, VA: ERIC Clearinghouse on Disabilities and Gifted Education. (ERIC Document Reproduction Service No. ED412713)

Richman, L. C., & Lindgren, S. D. (1981). Verbal mediation deficits: Relation to behavior and achievement in children. *Journal of Abnormal Psychology, 90*(2), 99–104.

Roberts, W. B., & Morotti, A. A. (2000). The bully as victim: Understanding bully behaviors to increase the effectiveness of the interventions in the bully-victim dyad. *Professional School Counseling, 4*(2), 148–154.

Scanlon, D., Deshler, D. D., & Schumaker, J. B. (1996). Can a strategy be taught and learned in secondary inclusive classrooms? *Learning Disabilities Research and Practice, 11*(1), 41–57.

Seferian, R. (1999). *Design and implementation of a social-skills program for middle school students with learning and behavioral disabilities.* Fort Lauderdale, FL: Nova Southeastern University (ERIC Document Reproduction Service No. ED436863)

Sprague, J., Sugai, G., & Walker, H. (1998). Antisocial behavior in the schools. In S. Watson & F. Gresham (Eds.), *Child behavior therapy: Ecological consideration in assessment, treatment, and evaluation* (pp. 451–474). New York: Plenum.

Sprague, J., Walker, H., Golly, A., While, K., Myers, D. R., & Shannon, T. (2001). Translating research into effective practice: The effects of a universal staff and student intervention on indicators of discipline and school safety. *Education and Treatment of Children, 24*(4), 495–511.

Swanson, H. L. (1999). *Intervention research for students with learning disabilities: A meta-analysis of treatment outcomes: Executive summary.* Paper presented at the 1999 Keys to Successful Learning Summit. Abstract retrieved January 12, 2002, from http://www.ncld.org/Research/osep_swanson.cfm

Tollefson, J., & Neduchal, J. (2000). *Basic training: Presenting learning strategies.* Retrieved March 27, 2004, from the Center for Research on Learning website: http://www.ku-crl.org/archives/pd/basic_ls.html

Van Nooten, N. (1991). *A social skills curriculum.* Reston, VA: ERIC Clearinghouse on Disabilities and Gifted Education. (ERIC Document Reproduction Service No. ED349719)

Van Reusen, A. K., Deshler, D. D., & Schumaker, J. B. (1989). Effects of a student participation strategy in facilitating the involvement of adolescents with learning disabilities in the individualized educational program planning process. *Learning Disabilities, 1*(2), 23–34.

Walker, H. M., Kavanagh, K., Stiller, B., Golly, A., Severson, H., & Feil, E. (1997). *First Step to Success: An early intervention program for antisocial kindergartners.* Longmont, CO: Sopris West.

Walker, H. M., Kavanagh, K., Stiller, B., Golly, A., Severson, H. H., & Feil, E. G. (1998). First Step to Success: An early intervention approach for preventing school antisocial behavior. *Journal of Emotional and Behavioral Disorders, 6*(2), 66–80.

Walker, H., Todis, B., Holmes, D., & Horton, G. (1988). *The Walker social skills curriculum: The ACCESS program (Adolescent curriculum for communication and effective social skills).* Austin, TX: PRO-ED.

Warger, C. L., & Rutherford, R. B. (1996). Social skills instruction: An essential component for learning. *Preventing School Failure, 41*(1), 20–23.

9

Chapter

Promoting Positive Behavior

CHAPTER OBJECTIVES

After completing this chapter, you should be able to:

❖ Discuss a theoretical framework for developing positive behaviors.

❖ Describe a functional behavioral assessment and a behavior intervention plan.

❖ Design a positive behavior support system.

❖ Describe the steps in conflict resolution and mediation.

❖ Demonstrate an understanding of diversity perspectives and how educators can strengthen the link between school and home to promote positive behaviors.

❖ Describe how educators use technology to support the development of positive behaviors.

Students with severe and persistent behavior problems typically have limited academic success, lack of interest in school-related activities, and attendance difficulties (Scanlon & Mellard, 2002). Although these students may be creative and articulate, they are at risk for dropping out of school. Failure to address these problems is a national concern. The National Agenda for Achieving Better Results for Children and Youth with Serious Emotional Disturbance (Chesapeake Institute, 1994) describes a plan for what needs to happen in the classroom, in the school, and in the community that includes expanding positive learning opportunities and results, promoting appropriate assessment, strengthening school and community capacity, collaborating with families, and valuing and addressing diversity. This plan continues to be relevant today. Sections of this chapter discuss each of these areas in detail.

STUDENTS WITH PROBLEM BEHAVIORS

Students with problem behaviors do not fit into any one category. Rather, they exhibit a wide variety of behaviors, from extremely aggressive and oppositional to extremely withdrawn and anxious. Aggressive behaviors may involve acts against other individuals such as fighting, coercion, bullying, negative interactions, and manipulation. Oppositional behaviors include noncompliance and defiance. Students may engage in stealing, lying, drug or alcohol use, and other risky behaviors. In the classroom, students with antisocial behaviors are often the first ones recognized (Figure 9.1).

Figure 9.1   **What we know about students with antisocial behaviors**

- Children as young as age 3 can be identified with antisocial patterns of behavior.
- By the end of Grade 3, children with antisocial behavior patterns are considered to have a chronic condition, much like diabetes. These behaviors cannot be cured but can be managed with the appropriate supports and continuing interventions.
- Students with antisocial behaviors are at severe risk for school dropout, drug and alcohol abuse, vocational adjustment problems, and relationship problems.

Source: Adapted from "Preventing Problems by Improving Behavior," by D. M. Kamps, 2002, in *Preventing Problem Behaviors*, p. 12 (B. Algozzine and P. Kay, Eds.), Thousand Oaks, CA: Corwin Press.

In contrast, students with severe and persistent behavior problems may exhibit forms of behavior not necessarily disruptive to the classroom but definitely disruptive to the student's learning and academic progress. One student may be extremely withdrawn, rarely interacting with others; another student may be very anxious, showing extreme reactions to minor everyday events. Students who carry psychiatric diagnoses, in addition to the educational label of emotional disturbance, may have a form of mental illness such as depression. This condition often makes it difficult to come to school or to stay the entire school day. Lack of physical strength and a feeling of hopelessness often prevent students from working cooperatively with others or completing individual assignments.

Severe behavior problems are not limited to students with a diagnosis of emotional disturbance. Students with other disabilities such as learning disabilities, mental retardation, or autism may have compounding disabilities that include challenging or problem behaviors that persist over time. Whatever diagnosis these students carry, they likely lack many of the basic social skills discussed in Chapter 8, as well as having problem behaviors. They may have limited insight into the feelings of other students or adults. Teachers working with students with severe and persistent problem behaviors find that each student is unique. These teachers must work with other professionals to gather information about the student's behaviors and to develop a behavior plan that meets the student's unique needs.

SETTING EVENTS AND STUDENT BEHAVIOR

Setting events (Gardner, Cole, Davidson, & Karan, 1986; Horner, Vaughn, Day, & Ard, 1996; Wahler & Graves, 1983) affect the physical or emotional state of a student at any given time and play a major role in the classroom each day. A student who had an argument with another student on the bus begins the day in a different emotional state than on another day when a friend invites the student to share a seat. Another student who had little sleep the night before arrives in a different physical state than when the student is well rested. These events not only influence a student's behavior and alter the effects of reinforcement that are part of the student's IEP but can also produce particular behaviors that may go unnoticed unless the educator looks beyond the events immediately preceding problem behaviors (Horner et al., 1996). Figure 9.2 illustrates the effects of different setting events on the behavior of a student. Usually

Figure 9.2   **Effects of setting events on problem behaviors**

Setting Event	Momentary Effect of Setting Event	Antecedent	Possible Behaviors	Consequence
Fighting with peer	Increase value of escaping hard tasks Decrease value of teacher praise	Teacher request to do task	Scream/run Throw materials Ask for a break Ask for help	Escape hard task
Headache	Increase value of escaping hard tasks Decrease value of teacher praise Decrease value of completing task		Hit head Don't respond Refuse to work Tell teacher that head hurts	Reduce headache

Source: Adapted from "The Relationship Between Setting Events and Problem Behavior: Expanding Our Understanding of Behavioral Support," by R. H. Horner, B. J. Vaughn, H. M. Day, and W. R. Ard, 1996, in *Positive Behavioral Support: Including People with Difficult Behavior in the Community*, p. 383 (L. K. Koegel, R. L. Koegel, and G. Dunlap, Eds.), Baltimore: Paul H. Brookes.

teacher praise carries high value for this student, but because of his earlier fighting (setting event 1) or his headache (setting event 3), the value of teacher praise is reduced because of the setting events.

SELECTED CONTEMPORARY THEORIES THAT SHAPE PRACTICE

"I'm concerned about Emily," a special educator teacher told a colleague. "When I ask her why she doesn't complete her assignments, she complains that she is too 'dumb' to do the work, but she doesn't listen in class and doesn't ask for help." Some students don't seem interested in learning. Although most children begin school eager to learn, somewhere along the way certain students lose interest and enthusiasm. By examining motivational theories and current educational research findings, teachers can acquire a framework to plan instruction for all students.

COGNITIVE EVALUATION THEORY

Cognitive evaluation theory (Deci & Ryan, 1980) focuses on intrinsic motivation and an individual's underlying psychological needs. This theory identifies self-determination and competence as the key psychological needs that affect intrinsic motivation. Self-determination and competence are influenced by events that are external to the individual. For students, external events could be planned teacher activities such as using positive feedback (verbal reward), offering tangible rewards, or assigning grades.

According to this theory, individuals perceive external events as either informational or controlling. For the student, informational events provide helpful information or feedback about classroom work and behavior. Informational events help build competence and increase intrinsic motivation. When a student perceives these same external events as controlling, the events serve to lower self-determination and undermine intrinsic motivation.

Cognitive evaluation theory and attention to student motivation have implications for educators who are working to increase positive behaviors. Later in this chapter, we will discuss how special educators participate in a functional behavioral analysis and how professionals generate hypotheses concerning a student's behavior. Student motivations are often the core of these hypotheses.

SOCIAL COGNITIVE THEORY

According to social cognitive theory (Bandura, 1969, 1977, 1986), which was introduced in Chapter 6, individuals learn most social behaviors by observing other individuals, such as friends, teachers, parents, community members, famous athletes, or rock stars. Bandura (1977) focuses on the combination of personal factors, environmental factors, and behavior and their interaction, which affect how children acquire social behaviors. For example, Sam frequently observes older students settling an argument by fighting. These students provide a constant model for aggressive behavior. In disputes with peers, Sam expects other students to react aggressively and acts accordingly. The other students respond to Sam's aggressive behavior by responding aggressively in turn.

Supporters of social cognitive theory emphasize that group support and cooperation among students are the keys to facilitating behavior change. Group members provide good models of needed skills, as well as reinforcement and encouragement for other students as they develop and refine their skills. From this work, various classroom practices have evolved. In this chapter, we will see how special educators use some of the principles of social cognitive theory as they design instruction.

BEHAVIORAL THEORY

Behavioral theory (Kazdin, 1994; Mahoney, 1974; Skinner, 1974), described in Chapter 6, examines learning in terms of association and the events before and after the behavior that influence learning. Behavioral theory describes learning in terms of observable behaviors and principles such as antecedents, consequences, and types of reinforcement that influence behavioral occurrence. From this early work, the field of functional behavioral analysis has evolved. This field focuses on promoting appropriate behavior through behavior change. Educators and other professionals examine the function of the problem behavior in terms of present and past environments, and then develop interventions to change the environment so that more appropriate behavior produces the same function (Repp & Horner, 1999). The following section describes functional behavioral assessment, the starting point for addressing behavioral concerns and for planning effective interventions.

EXPANDING POSITIVE LEARNING OPPORTUNITIES

IDEA AND STUDENTS WITH EMOTIONAL DISTURBANCE

In Chapter 3 we examined the IDEA definition of the term *emotional disturbance* to describe a student with severe, persistent emotional and behavior problems. Sometimes special educators use the term *emotional and behavioral disorders* instead of *emotional disturbance* to refer to students with long-standing problem behaviors.

IDEA requires IEP team members to address behavioral as well as learning problems, not only for students with emotional disturbance but also for all students with disabilities. When students have behavioral problems, the IEP team must conduct a functional behavioral assessment (Sec. 300.520), including one or more assessment approaches that focus on identifying the biological, social, affective, and environmental factors that initiate, sustain, or end the behavior in question (Center for Effective Collaboration and Practice, 1998a). Based on the functional behavioral assessment, team members then develop a **behavioral intervention plan,** which describes the skills that students need, the instruction that will be provided, and how the plan will be evaluated (Sec. 300.520).

According to IDEA, IEP teams must conduct functional behavioral assessments and develop behavioral intervention plans when students with disabilities are suspended or placed in alternative educational settings due to discipline problems. For violation of school rules, school personnel may change the student's placement to an appropriate alternative educational setting on a temporary basis or suspend the student for not more than 10 consecutive days. If the student carries a weapon to school or to a school function, or if the student knowingly possesses, solicits, or uses illegal drugs, school personnel may order an appropriate alternative educational setting for not more than 45 days. Within 10 days after taking disciplinary action, school personnel must convene an IEP meeting to develop an assessment plan to address the behavior that resulted in the disciplinary action by conducting a functional behavioral assessment and developing a behavioral intervention plan. If the student already has a behavioral intervention plan, the IEP team must review the plan and modify it, if necessary, to address the problem behavior (Sec. 300.520).

FUNCTIONAL BEHAVIORAL ASSESSMENT

Educators use **functional behavioral assessment** to examine student behavior and to assist in identifying its function, or what the student obtains or is able to avoid as a result of the behavior. In a review of the research, Choi and Kim (1998) provide compelling evidence of the effectiveness of functional behavioral assessment of students with problem behaviors. The information collected during this assessment helps the IEP team plan intervention and positive behavioral supports that will be written into the student's behavior intervention plan. The behavior intervention plan describes the skills that students need, the instruction that will be provided, and how the plan will be evaluated (Cohen & Spenciner, 2003).

IDEA requires that the IEP team meet to formulate a functional behavioral assessment plan and to develop a behavioral intervention plan within 10 days of a disciplinary action by school personnel for behavior such as carrying a gun to school or possessing illegal drugs. If the student already has a behavioral intervention plan, the team must review and revise it as necessary to ensure that it addresses the problem behavior(s) on which the disciplinary action focused (Sec. 300.520).

Planning a Functional Behavioral Assessment

Identifying the problem behavior. The first step in planning a functional behavioral assessment is identifying the problem behavior in terms that are concrete and observable. When a teacher describes the behavior of a student named Thomas as aggressive, we need to define the behavior further so that it can be measured and recorded. A description such as "Thomas is aggressive" is too vague and does not state the nature of the problem behavior or where it occurs. "Thomas threw a book, knocked over his desk, kicked it, and yelled obscenities at the teacher and other students" is specific and describes his behavior in terms that one can observe. The description also identifies the context in which the behavior was observed.

During the meeting, IEP team members consider the function of the behavior for the student, if the behavior may be linked to a skill need (Figure 9.3), or if the student has the skill but lacks motivation to modify the behavior (Figure 9.4).

Using Various Assessment Approaches

A functional behavioral assessment uses multiple assessment approaches, including standardized instruments, record reviews, interviews, and observations.

Standardized instruments. Commercial behavior checklists and rating scales provide standardized measures for collecting information. Usually the teacher, parent, and student complete similar instruments. Sometimes a student's peers complete them as well. This information provides different evaluations of the student's behavior at home and at school. The examiner can test different diagnostic hypotheses to determine the settings in which behavior problems occur and how serious the behavior is perceived to be by individuals close to the student.

Record reviews. The teacher also examines a student's records. A review of past academic work and disciplinary reports indicate when difficulties occurred and the

Figure 9.3   Is the problem behavior linked to a skill need?

If the team suspects that the student can't perform the skills or has a skill deficit, they can devise a functional behavioral assessment plan to determine the answers to questions such as:

- Does the student understand the behavioral expectations for the situation?
- Does the student realize that the behavior is unacceptable, or has that behavior simply become a habit?
- Is it within the student's power to control the behavior, or does the student need support?
- Does the student have the skills necessary to perform expected, new behaviors?

Source: From *Addressing Student Problem Behavior, Part I: An IEP Team's Introduction to Functional Behavioral Assessment and Behavior Intervention Plans* (p. 5), Center for Effective Collaboration and Practice, 1998, Washington, DC: Publisher.

Figure 9.4   Does the student have the skill but not the desire to modify the behavior?

Students who can but do not perform certain tasks may be experiencing consequences that affect their performance (e.g., their nonperformance is rewarded by peer or teacher attention, or performance of the task is not sufficiently rewarding). If the team suspects that the problem is a result of a performance deficit, it may be helpful to devise an assessment plan that addresses questions such as the following:

- Is it possible that the student is uncertain of the appropriateness of the behavior (e.g., it is appropriate to clap loudly and yell during sporting events, yet these behaviors are often inappropriate when playing academic games in the classroom)?
- Does the student find any value in engaging in appropriate behavior? Is the behavioral problem associated with certain social or environmental conditions?
- Is the student attempting to avoid an uninteresting or demanding task?
- What current rules, routines, or expectations does the student consider irrelevant?

Source: From *Addressing Student Problem Behavior, Part I: An IEP Team's Introduction to Functional Behavioral Assessment and Behavior Intervention Plans* (p. 6), Center for Effective Collaboration and Practice, 1998, Washington, DC: Publisher.

types of interventions that were tried. Attendance records provide information about the number of days absent or tardy and patterns of truancy. The student's heath history provides information regarding conditions that may require medical attention or prescription drugs. The IEP team will need to know about any medical conditions that impact the student's behavior.

Structured interviews. **Structured interviews** consist of a set of questions that the educator or another professional considers and plans before meeting with an individual. Interviews provide unique information from each individual's perspective. Parents can provide information about the student's behavior at home with siblings and friends. A school social worker can describe the student's behavior in small-group interactions. Classroom teachers can describe settings in which the behavior does and does not occur. The student can provide a unique perspective, too. For example, interview questions for Thomas could include "What happened to you to make you feel so angry?"

Observations. Educators and other team members can conduct observations of the student in the classroom, in the cafeteria, or in other school settings. This involves observing and recording not only the student's behavior but also situational factors associated with the behavior. The observer notes events that occurred just before the behavior and the consequences that followed the behavior. Figure 9.5 illustrates an observation form used to collect this type of information. Conducting multiple observations over a period of several days helps ensure that the information is consistent and reliable.

Analyzing and Synthesizing Information

Team members meet to compare and analyze the assessment information. Are there any patterns associated with the behavior? For example, does Thomas resort to throwing materials and shouting obscenities when he is frustrated and unable to complete his assignments? How does his medical condition of Tourette's syndrome affect his behavior? (Behaviors associated with Tourette's syndrome cause Thomas to vocalize

Figure 9.5   Observation form for functional behavioral assessment

THURLOW ELEMENTARY SCHOOL

Observation Recording Form

Student name:_____

Grade:_____

Date: Time:

Description of setting and number of students:

Focus of observation (describe problem behavior in observable terms):

Antecedent conditions	Behavior observed	Consequence conditions

and curse at unexpected times during class and display distracting head jerks.) If the team cannot determine any patterns of behavior, it reviews the approaches used to gather the information and identifies additional ways of assessing the behavior.

Once a pattern of behavior emerges, the team establishes a **hypothesis,** which describes the probable function(s) of the behavior and allows the team to predict antecedent conditions or when the behavior is most likely (and least likely) to occur and the probable consequences that serve to maintain the behavior. For example, Thomas's IEP team hypothesized that his behavior was caused by academic frustration and social ridicule by his classmates. To learn more about conducting a functional behavioral analysis and the process of hypothesis generation, please refer to the Center for Effective Collaboration and Practice's website. In addition to providing extensive information, the site has examples of useful forms for IEP teams to use in conducting a functional behavioral assessment and developing a behavioral intervention plan.

Team members analyze and synthesize assessment information and develop a hypothesis regarding student behavior.

BEHAVIORAL INTERVENTION PLANS

Once the IEP team has completed the functional behavioral assessment and developed a hypothesis concerning the behavior, team members develop (or revise) the student's **behavioral intervention plan.** The plan addresses the function of the problem behavior by teaching the student more acceptable behaviors that address the motivation behind the behavior. Developed by the IEP team, this intervention plan describes the skills that students need, the instruction that will be provided, and how the plan will be evaluated. Researchers have found that a functional behavioral assessment and a behavioral intervention plan help students improve their behavior and prevent more serious behaviors (Ingram, 2003; Kamps & Ellis, 1995; Scott, Liaupsin, Nelson, & Jolivette, 2003).

Planning the behavioral intervention involves team members in working together (Figure 9.6). Based on the information collected during the functional behavioral assessment, the plan:

- addresses the student's skill needs and/or performance needs,
- includes positive strategies,
- describes any classroom environment accommodations,
- describes any program accommodations or modifications,
- describes any curricular accommodations or modifications,
- describes supplementary aids and supports, and
- includes a crisis/emergency plan, if necessary.

Figure 9.6   Considerations for designing behavioral intervention plans

- Teach more acceptable replacement behaviors that serve the same function as the inappropriate behavior, such as asking to be left alone or using conflict resolution skills, or alternative skills, such as self-management techniques, tolerating delay, or coping strategies.

- Teach students to deal with *setting events* (the things that make the desired behavior more likely to occur), such as the physical arrangement of the classroom, management strategies, seating arrangements, or the sequence of academic instruction.

- Manipulate the *antecedents* (the things that happen before the behavior occurs) of the desired behavior, such as teacher instructions or directions or instructional materials.

- Manipulate the *consequences* (the things that happen after the behavior occurs) of the desired behavior, such as precise praise or feedback, keeping in mind the principles of shaping and reinforcing incompatible behaviors.

- Implement changes to the classroom curriculum and/or instructional strategies, such as using multilevel instruction or encouraging oral rather than written responses.

- Begin interventions that offer reinforcement for appropriate behavior, such as student performance contracts or group motivational strategies.

Source: Addressing Student Problem Behavior—Part III: Creating Positive Intervention Plans and Supports (p. 6), Center for Effective Collaboration and Practice, 2000, Washington, DC: Publisher.

Components of a Behavioral Intervention Plan

Addressing skills that students need. Students with behavioral problems often lack skills in communicating effectively with others, such as reading and interpreting body language and controlling anger and disappointment. To address students' skill needs, the special educator may need to teach social skills, positive behavioral skills, and academic skills.

The behavioral intervention plan (Figure 9.7) includes a description of the problem behavior so that team members will recognize its onset. If the student lacks specific skills, the plan describes these skills and/or **replacement behaviors** that must be substituted for inappropriate behaviors. The plan describes specific goals and objectives for obtaining new skills and replacement behaviors and instructional procedures that teachers will use. For example, Thomas's plan states that he will work with the resource room teacher to verbally identify and describe the physical signs that he experiences when he is becoming angry. In time he will learn to recognize when he is becoming angry and seek assistance rather than acting out. The resource room teacher will also teach Thomas replacement behaviors in role-playing situations. If a teacher makes changes in the physical environment, these are described in the plan. Finally, the plan specifies how instruction will be implemented in various settings and the persons responsible. Educators report that teaching positive behavior strategies as part of the regular academic program is particularly effective in teaching replacement behaviors (Center for Effective Collaboration and Practice, 1998a).

After completing all the components of the behavioral intervention plan, the IEP team describes how the plan will be evaluated. Team members describe how, when,

Figure 9.7   Thomas's behavioral intervention plan

Positive Behavioral Intervention Plan
Planning Form

IEP teams can use this form to guide them through the process of developing the positive behavioral intervention plan.

Student _____*Thomas Jones*_____ Age ___*13*___ Sex ___*M*___

Teacher(s) _____*Ms. Gilbow/Team B*_____ Grade ___*6th*___

Case Manager _____*Mrs. Brantley*_____ Date(s) ___*4/17/xx*___

Reason for intervention plan:

Tom's behavior often disrupts class. Yesterday he threw a dictionary across the room, knocked over his desk, kicked it, and began yelling obscenities at the teacher and the other students in the class (LD resource room). The teacher had to call for help from his ED resource room teacher to calm him down and safely remove him from the classroom.

Participants (specify names):

(x) student _____*Tom*_____   ( ) special education administrator _____

(x) family member ___*Mrs. Jones*___   (x) general education administrator ___*Mr. Scott*___

(x) special educator ___*Ms. Gilbow*___   ( ) school psychologist _____

( ) general educator _____   ( ) other agency personnel _____

( ) peer(s) _____   _____

( ) other (specify) _____

Fact Finding

1. **General learning environment:** Describe the student's school class schedule, including any special programs or services.

Tom receives special education to provide support for his emotional difficulties and learning disability in two resource rooms. These classes provide instruction in math, language arts, reading, social skills, and social studies. He is in the regular classroom for specials, lunch, and science. He rides a special bus with a paraprofessional to school.

2. **Problem behavior:** Define the problem behavior(s) in observable, measurable, and countable terms (i.e., topography, event, duration, seriousness, and/or intensity). Include several examples of the behavior.

Thomas has Tourette's syndrome, a learning disability that manifests itself in reading and language arts, and an emotional disturbance. Symptoms of Tourette's lead him to display distracting tics and vocalize curses during the usual course of the day. This sometimes causes his classmates to make uncomplimentary comments. His emotional and learning disabilities often lead to frustrating academic and social situations. When he becomes frustrated he often throws objects (books, book packs, pencils), turns over furniture (chairs or tables), and curses obscenities at the adults and other students present in the classroom.

3. **Setting events:** Describe important things that are happening in the student's life that may be causing the behavior(s) of concern.

Thomas recently started to be mainstreamed more often in the regular classroom. He has begun to take science (as an area of strength and interest) in the general education setting.

continued

Figure 9.7   Thomas's behavioral intervention plan *continued*

4. Review existing data: Summarize previously collected information (records review, interviews, observations, and test results) relevant to the behavior(s).

An examination of Tom's medical records and interviews with his parents and teachers all reveal that due to Tourette's syndrome he has uncontrollable tics that cause his head to jerk to the side. Often during these tics he curses, a behavior that has never been observed in isolation.

A review of his IEP, test results, and interviews with his parents and teachers reveal that he has learning problems that keep him from realizing success in the mainstream classroom and cause him a lot of frustration. He also is frustrated by the many rude comments made by his classmates regarding his tics. During unstructured time (recess, before school, between classes), it has been observed that other students tease him. His parents and teachers report that this really bothers Tom and makes it difficult for him to make friends. He spends most of his spare time with his 4th-grade sister, who walks him to and from class in the mornings and afternoons.

Possible Explanations

5. Identify likely antecedents (precipitating events) to the behavior(s).

> *Academic frustration*
> *Social ridicule by peers*

6. Identify likely consequences that may be maintaining the behavior(s).

When Tom acts out he is removed from the situation. We believe that this behavior allows him to escape a frustrating situation.

7. Identify and describe any academic or environmental context(s) in which the problem behavior(s) does *not* occur.

This problem has never occurred in the resource room for students with emotional disturbance. Parents report that it rarely occurs at home and that Tom did not have the same problem in his 5th-grade class. They also report that Tom was asked not to return to the local YMCA because of his acting-out behavior.

Validation

8. Functional assessment: Do you already have enough information to believe that the possible explanations are sufficient to plan an intervention?

a. If yes, go to Step 9; if no, then what additional data collection is necessary?
   ( ) Review of IEP goals and objectives
   ( ) Review of medical records
   ( ) Review of previous intervention plans
   ( ) Review of incident reports
   ( ) ABC (across time and situations)
   ( ) Motivational analysis
   (*x*) Ecological analysis
   (*x*) Curricular analysis
   ( ) Scatter plot
   ( ) Parent questionnaire/interview
   (*x*) Student questionnaire/interview
   (*x*) Teacher questionnaire/interview (specify who) <u>*Mr. Elliott—5th-grade teacher*</u>
   (*x*) Other (explain) <u>*Talk with director of the YMCA*</u>

b. Summarize data. Attach additional sheets if necessary.

Figure 9.7   Thomas's behavioral intervention plan *continued*

Tom does not seem to have problems in environments that are well-supervised and where he is not expected to perform tasks that are more difficult than his skill level.

- *The YMCA director reported that the other kids teased Tom and that Tom would just "explode." He said that he knew the other kids antagonized Tom, but he was afraid someone would get hurt if Tom was permitted to continue to come to the Y. He told Tom that when his behavior was under control, he was welcome to return.*

- *Mr. Elliott, his 5th-grade teacher, said that at the beginning of the school year he had his class study Tourette's syndrome and had a guest speaker come in to discuss the effects of Tourette's. Tom even led some of the discussion. He felt that once the other students understood what was happening they were more comfortable with the tics, and soon they began to ignore them.*

- *Tom is about 2 years behind his grade peers in reading and written language ability. He is intelligent and can understand grade-level tasks that are presented orally. When he is permitted to respond orally rather than writing an answer, he performs on grade level. If he is asked to read aloud or silently or is asked to fill out worksheets without assistance, he becomes frustrated or distracted and does not complete his work.*

- *Tom does better in structured environments where there is adult supervision. Adults in these environments seem to deter the teasing of his peers and provide him with individual help in academics. Ms. Gilbow, his ED resource teacher, reports that he does well when given independent work on his grade level. She says that he does well in structured cooperative learning groups where he is permitted to respond orally and other team members do the writing and reading aloud. She also reports that Tourette's syndrome was thoroughly discussed at the beginning of the school year and reviewed when new students are placed in her class.*

Planning

9. **Formulate hypothesis statement:** Using the table below, determine why the student engages in problem behavior(s), whether the behavior(s) serves single or multiple functions, and what to do about the behavior(s)

	Internal	External
Obtain Something		
Avoid Something	*Expectation of ridicule about his tics and embarrassment associated with school failure.*	*Avoiding ridicule by avoiding social situations in which peers tease him.*

10. **Current level of performance:** Describe problem behavior(s) in such a way that the team will recognize the onset and conclusion of behavior.

Tom becomes noticeably frustrated and tics increase in response to peer taunting or difficult academic assignments. He hangs his head down low and focuses intently on one thing before a big outburst of aggressive behavior. He becomes nonverbal except for the obscenities associated with Tourette's syndrome.

continued

Figure 9.7   Thomas's behavioral intervention plan *continued*

11. Describe replacement behavior(s) that are likely to serve the same function as the behavior(s) identified in Step 9.

Tom will approach the adult in charge of the setting when he notices himself getting agitated and ask to have assistance—either academic help or counseling. This will allow him to escape the situation without using inappropriate behavior.

12. Measurement procedures for problem behavior(s) and replacement behavior(s):

    a. Describe how (e.g., permanent products, event recording, scatterplot), when, and where student behavior(s) will be measured.

Using event recording, Tom will be taught to count the number of times he becomes frustrated and the number of times he has outbursts vs. how often he asks for help. He will be given a checklist to record this on.

    b. Summarize data by specifying which problem behavior(s) and replacement behavior(s) will be targets for intervention.

Problem behavior: out-of-control anger—throws things, hits or kicks, uses unacceptable language, or makes threatening remarks or actions.

Replacement behavior: appropriately deal with anger—1) he asks for help from an adult or peer when he feels angry and thinks he needs to leave a situation; 2) he will use self-talk and anger management skills to independently deal with his anger.

13. Behavioral intervention plan:

    a. Specify goals and objectives (conditions, criteria for acceptable performance) for teaching the replacement behavior(s).

Working with Ms. Gilbow, the ED resource room teacher, Tom will verbally identify and describe the physical signs that he experiences when he is becoming angry.

Tom will recognize when he is becoming angry and will seek the assistance of an adult rather than acting out 100% of the time.

Tom will contact the director of the local YMCA and report his progress at controlling his temper, and discuss the technique that he uses to manage this. He will ask if he can return to the YMCA and use his skills with the adults that supervise after-school activities there.

    b. Specify instructional strategies that will be used to teach the replacement behavior(s).

The ED resource room teacher will model thinking aloud using a role-play situation in which she becomes angry. She will identify why she thinks she is angry and will discuss all the possible ways to deal with her anger. She will model choosing an option that helps her reduce her anger in acceptable ways.

Tom will role-play situations in which he has a history of becoming angry (e.g., on the recess field, in the classroom, in the hall during passing time) with the ED resource room teacher and other students. He will model his self-talk and will discuss ways of dealing with his anger in acceptable ways (e.g., enlist the help of an adult or trusted peer). He will choose a time when he usually encounters anger and frustration to practice this technique and will report back to his teacher and the class the outcomes of this technique. If the technique was successful he will identify other situations in which it could be used. If it is unsuccessful, he will work with his teacher and peers to identify reasons why it did not work and suggest modifications.

Tom will use the technique in other school and nonschool settings.

Figure 9.7   Thomas's behavioral intervention plan *continued*

    c. Specify strategies that will be used to decrease problem behavior(s) and increase replacement behavior(s).

The adults that work with Tom will be told the signs to look for that indicate that Tom is beginning to feel frustration. They will approach him and ask him if he needs to talk. Any time he asks them if he can speak with the counselor or to them about the way he feels, they will comply immediately or send him to an environment with an adult who can talk with Tom if they are busy with other things.

    d. Identify any changes in the physical environment needed to prevent problem behavior(s) and to promote desired (replacement) behavior(s), if necessary.

    1. Tom will be given the opportunity to respond to academic questions verbally (either aloud or on a tape recorder). Tom will never be asked to read aloud in class unless he asks to. He will be given audio tapes with the written materials read aloud on them, or work in cooperative groups in which other students read the written materials aloud.

    2. Tom's classmates will be taught about Tourette's syndrome and will be given the opportunity to ask questions of experts (including Tom, if he feels comfortable) about the syndrome.

    e. Specify extent to which intervention plan will be implemented in various settings; specify settings and persons responsible for implementation of plan.

This plan will first be implemented in the ED resource room and then in the LD resource room. Once Tom has identified the physical signs that he is becoming angry he will share them with his other teachers (Science) and his parents. The intervention plan will then be implemented in those settings, as well. Once Tom has gone for 2 weeks without having a behavior incident in which he loses control, he will contact the director of the YMCA (with adult support, if he feels it is necessary) to discuss the possibility of his return.

14. Evaluation plan and schedule: Describe the plan and timetable to evaluate effectiveness of the intervention plan.

    a. Describe how, when, where, and how often the problem behavior(s) will be measured.

For the first 3 weeks, Tom and his ED resource room teacher will discuss and chart (percent of appropriate reactions to his anger) his progress daily. They will compare it to the number of outbursts during the previous 2 weeks. If after 3 weeks Tom's behavior has not decreased by at least 50%, the team will meet again to discuss possible changes in the intervention. If after 6 weeks Tom's behavior has not decreased by at least 90%, the team will meet again to discuss possible changes in the intervention. At 8 weeks Tom should have no incidents of outbursts at school.

    b. Specify persons and settings involved.

Initially it will be the responsibility of the ED resource room teacher. The intervention will then be initiated in the LD resource room, Tom's science class, and at home. Once Tom has had no outbursts for 2 weeks, the intervention will be extended to the YMCA (with the director's agreement).

    c. Specify a plan for crisis/emergency intervention, if necessary.

    Should Tom have a behavior outburst the ED resource room teacher will be called in to help.

    d. Determine schedule to review/modify the intervention plan, as needed. Include dates and criteria for changing/fading the plan.

    8 May 20xx   Review/modify if the behavior has not reduced by 50%.
    29 May 20xx   Review/modify if the behavior has not reduced by 99%.
    12 June 20xx Review/modify if the behavior has not reached 0.

continued

Figure 9.7   Thomas's behavioral intervention plan *continued*

15. Describe plan and timetable to monitor the degree to which the plan is being implemented.

Each Friday the ED resource room teacher will contact Tom's other teachers and the recess supervisors to discuss the implementation of the plan. Any time Tom has a behavior outburst, the ED resource teacher will conduct an out-briefing with the adult in charge to discuss the situation and to determine whether the plan was followed as written.

Source: Addressing Student Problem Behavior—Part III: Creating Positive Intervention Plans and Supports (pp. B5–B10), Center for Effective Collaboration and Practice, 2000, Washington, DC: Publisher.

where, and how often they will measure the problem behaviors and identify individuals who will be responsible for the evaluation. They determine a schedule for reviewing or modifying the plan based on the criteria for behavior change.

Including supports. The IEP team also identifies **supports**, or people and/or modifications to the environment that will assist the student to be educated with students without disabilities to the maximum extent appropriate (IDEA 34 C.F.R., Sec. 300.28). Students such as Thomas may need supports, as seen in Figure 9.7, such as a classroom modification and an individual with similar disabilities from the community who can provide mentoring, added to the behavioral intervention plan. Personnel supports can include the school guidance counselor, school social worker, or psychologist who works with the student to improve behavior. Or a student might work with the school mechanic, custodian, or secretary for a class period when the student needs to avoid a structured learning environment such as the classroom. The parent can provide support by assisting the student in organizing school materials and constructing a schedule for after-school activities, including homework. Other students can provide supports, too. For example, the special education teacher made arrangements with a high school student who had similar interests to meet with Thomas on a weekly basis to provide academic encouragement.

Supports also can include modifications to the environment. For example, a teacher might rearrange the room to provide more space for small-group projects. A counter along the back wall could be cleared to allow a student to complete individual assignments while standing at the counter instead of seated at a desk.

Student Crisis/Emergency Plan

Sometimes as part of the behavioral intervention plan, it is necessary for team members to develop a student crisis or emergency plan to address situations in which the student uses self-injurious behavior or hurts others, to safeguard school property, or to deal with an acute disturbance (Figure 9.8). In the student crisis or emergency plan, team members specify the steps to be taken, making sure that the parent understands and approves. When the crisis/emergency plan is used, school personnel and the parent should be notified. Following the incident, team members should write an emergency/crisis report that includes ways to prevent further occurrences of the behavior (Center for Effective Collaboration and Practice, 2000).

Evaluation of the Behavioral Intervention Plan

The IEP team reviews and evaluates the behavioral intervention plan during the annual meeting, but members may review the plan more frequently if necessary. If the student

Figure 9.8   A crisis intervention plan

SAMPLE CRISIS/EMERGENCY PLAN

Student: *Carl Stephens*   Date: *February 24*

School: *Hadley Jr. High School*   Grade: *7th*

Reason for crisis/emergency plan: *repeated verbal threats to physically harm a classmate in retaliation for unknown act ("getting in my face," "putting me down")*

Persons responsible for developing the plan (indicate position): *Mr. Papadolious (Assistant Principal); Ms. Hayes (school psychologist); Mr. Jordan (special education teacher); Ms. Lopez (school counselor)*

Parental Approval

Indicate level of parent/guardian participation and approval of the plan. *Both Mr. and Mrs. S. were involved in creating and approving this plan.*

Parent/guardian signature: *Mr. and Mrs Stephens*

1. Give a full description of the behavior that poses a risk of physical injury to the student or to others, damage to physical property and/or serious disturbance of the teaching/learning process and for which a crisis/emergency plan is required, including both the frequency of occurrence and magnitude of behavior.

   Carl repeatedly verbally threatened to "kick the s—— out of Fred." Verbal threats were very loud, laced with profanity and linked to some provocation; however, the actual provocation(s) was not apparent to the classroom teacher. This very intense verbal threat was the fifth time Carl stated that he was going to physically harm Fred.

2. Give a full description of previous interventions (including those in the student's IEP or existing behavioral intervention plan) that have been applied and have not been successful, including length of implementation.

   The current IEP calls for social skills instruction, including group self-control.
   An office referral was written after the third verbal threat.
   A 2-day in-school suspension was imposed following the fourth verbal threat.

3. Give a full description of the strategies or procedures included in the plan, the times, places, and situations under which the plan may be introduced, person(s) responsible for its implementation, and any potential risks associated with the plan.

   Reduce academic stressors by reducing length and complexity of selected class assignments and rearrange seating arrangement to place Fred at a distance from Carl and any common pathways.

   Preemptive "pull-out" 1:1 instruction with a special education teacher in the school counselor's office to address (a) "perceptual errors"— Carl's misreading of the nonverbal behavior of classmates and (b) use of mnemonics for self-control (FAST) and "self-cueing," for self-reinforcement of appropriate behavior. The teacher will use direct instruction (cognitive modeling—how to "think aloud"), verbal rehearsal, and verbal feedback/reinforcement. Sessions will be about 20 minutes and occur twice a day for 4–5 school days (across one weekend), depending on Carl's cooperation and his ability to learn the strategy.

   Next, small group instruction (two or three classmates, selected on the basis of appropriate behavior and acceptability to Carl) will take place in the classroom when other students are out of the room (at a computer lab) and consist of behavioral rehearsals of the self-control strategy (beginning with simply breaking eye contact and walking away) and use of verbal prompts and positive feedback from peers. Session will be about 20 minutes and occur once a day for 3–4 days, depending on successfulness.

continued

Figure 9.8   A crisis intervention plan *continued*

Follow-up will include periodic "behavioral probes" (after 3 weeks) including role play of original problem/solutions; teachers will observe for other possible triggers.

4. Give a full description of how, when, and where measurement procedures will be used to evaluate the effectiveness of the plan, the criteria against which the plan will be judged, and the timetable for its evaluation.

   Classroom teacher observation and narrative recording of problem behavior incidences, on a sheet with checklist columns for antecedent events, student responses, and consequences.

   Carl will self-count the number of incidences and self-rate his use of self-prompts (self-talk) to use self-control.

   Peers will count the number of incidences, rate Carl's use of self-control, and their own verbal praise.

5. Give the timetable for review of the plan.

   Two weeks.

6. Give a description of the behavior that will be strengthened and/or taught to the student to replace the behavior of concern, including steps to provide frequency opportunities for the student to engage in and be reinforced for the desired behavior.

   Carl will use cognitive strategies and role play to: (a) identify likely problem situations and physical signs of stress/anger (sweating, trembling, flushed feeling in the face); (b) cue for self-control; (c) self-count and reinforcement. Selected peers will be used to strengthen level of appropriate behavior through verbal prompts and reinforcement.

7. Give a full description of the plan for withdrawing the crisis/emergency plan and the less restrictive and intrusive intervention that will replace it, including the timetable for withdrawal of the crisis/emergency plan.

   Given the seriousness of the problem, the plan will be introduced immediately, beginning with the "pull-out:" instruction, for at least 4–5 days, followed by at least 3–4 days for peer training sessions. The special education teacher will judge Carl's acceptance of instruction and ability to fully and accurately "mirror" teacher modeling of the strategy.

   The special education teacher and other team members will observe Carl's behavior (and that of his classmates) across classroom settings and meet formally in 2 weeks to discuss impact of plan and need for any changes. The team will convene immediately following any further serious behavior incidences.

8. Give a full description of the steps that will be taken to eliminate future occurrences of the behavior, including changes in the social/physical environment, teaching of replacement behavior, or both.

   Because of the seriousness of the problem, use of peer supports remain in place. Carl's history teacher will incorporate instruction on the peaceful resolution of conflicts and the special education teacher will introduce a class-wide conflict resolution program.

9. Indicate the person(s) responsible for notifying the parent/guardian when the crisis/emergency plan has been introduced and the way in which that notification will be documented.

   School counselor—Ms. Lopez

10. Indicate the persons(s) responsible for the written report of the outcome of the crisis/emergency plan.

    Special education teacher—Mr. Jordan

Source: Addressing Student Problem Behavior—Part III: Creating Positive Intervention Plans and Supports (pp. D5–D7), Center for Effective Collaboration and Practice, 2000, Washington, DC: Publisher.

Using Technology
Personal Digital Assistants in the Classroom, Part II, Engaging Students in Positive Behavioral Support

In Chapter 8 we learned how students in one high school use Palm handhelds (PDAs) as AT to improve their academic work. PDAs also increase opportunities for students to assume ownership in improving their behaviors. When a student begins working on positive behaviors, a PDA provides an easy, efficient way to record behaviors and monitor daily progress. As part of the behavior support plan, the teacher—or student—sets up a file, perhaps in a word processing or spreadsheet format on the classroom computer, and then downloads the file to a PDA. The student uses the system to record and manage positive behaviors. Aside from the advantages of having a "cool tool," a student can use the PDA at any time during the day, while going to different classes, in the cafeteria, or on the bus. The PDA eliminates the problem of lost pencils or missing paper recording sheets. At the beginning of each school day, the student uploads the data to the classroom computer, where it can be added to a weekly chart.

Questions for Reflection

1. What are some advantages of PDAs over more traditional methods of recording behaviors such as paper-and-pencil charts? What might be some disadvantages?

2. What software is available that might help a student manage and work to improve behavior?

To answer these questions and learn more about using technology to support learning, go to the Companion Website at www. prenhall.com/cohen, select Chapter 9, then choose Using Technology.

has met the behavioral goals and objectives, the plan should be revised to include the new goals and objectives. If the plan does not seem to be effective and there is little change in the student's behavior, team members need to review the plan, decide whether to conduct further assessment, and develop a new plan that will produce positive changes in behavior.

CLASSROOM INSTRUCTION

Gradually, the student assumes more and more responsibility for managing behavior by learning new skills, replacement behaviors, and self-management strategies. The following sections describe how teachers implement instruction by structuring positive classroom environments, teach conflict resolution and mediation, address student motivation, provide clear expectations and teach compliance, understand setting events and student behavior, and use instructional strategies to promote active involvement in instruction.

STRUCTURING POSITIVE CLASSROOM ENVIRONMENTS

Supporting students with severe, persistent behavior problems requires a high level of self-awareness on the part of teachers. Teachers are realistic about their capabilities and know when to request assistance from other team members such as

Figure 9.9   **The stages of frustration and examples of appropriate teacher responses**

Stages of Student Frustration	Examples of Appropriate Teacher Responses
Anxiety: Student sighs or uses other nonverbal cues.	Teacher responds by active listening and nonjudgmental talk.
Stress: Student exhibits minor behavior problems.	Teacher uses proximity control, boosts student interest, or provides assistance with assignments.
Defensiveness: Student argues and complains.	Teacher reminds student of rules, uses conflict resolution, and encourages student to ask for help.
Physical aggression: Student loses control and hits, bites, kicks, or throws objects.	Teacher gets help, escorts student from class, and protects the safety of the other students.
Tension reduction: Student releases tension through crying or verbal venting, or student may become sullen and withdrawn.	Teacher uses supportive techniques to help the student gain insight into feelings and behavior.

Source: Adapted from *Violence and Aggression in Children and Youth*, by M. K. Fitzsimmons, 1998, Reston, VA: ERIC Clearinghouse on Disabilities and Gifted Education.

other teachers, the school social worker or school psychologist, or the building administrator.

In planning instructional activities, teachers are mindful of sources of frustration for students, such as boredom, an irrelevant curriculum, and disorganized learning activities (Fitzsimmons, 1998). Teachers recognize and respond to various stages of student frustration (Figure 9.9). Teachers work to create structured and consistent, yet nurturing and caring environments, establishing trust and rapport with and among students. They hold high expectations for all students and provide high-quality academic instruction in which students are actively engaged. Teachers work to make learning fun and induce a positive mood. For example, at the beginning of the day the teacher might

- sing a silly song that makes children laugh.
- tell students something funny that happened.
- see who can make a comical face (Gorman, 2001, p. 114).
- ask students to create three goals that they would like to achieve during the day.
- select an inspiring video segment to view and briefly discuss.

Providing Choices in the Classroom

Educators can provide many opportunities throughout the day for students to make choices as they complete learning activities and assignments and strengthen appropriate behaviors. Students can choose where to sit during individual or small-group work—or where to stand. They can choose the order in which they will complete two or more assignments or which part of an assignment to complete: all of the even-numbered items or all of the odd-numbered ones. They can also choose which questions of a set to answer or how to demonstrate their achievement from among a list of possibilities.

What does the research say about choice making? An emerging area of research indicates that when educators include opportunities for student choice making during academic instruction, positive results occur. Reviews of the literature (Jolivette, Stichter, & McCormick, 2002; Repp & Horner, 1999) found that when students were allowed to choose the task, their accuracy and completion of academic assignments increased and disruptive behaviors decreased.

TEACHING CONFLICT RESOLUTION

Conflict resolution is a group of positive approaches that a facilitator uses to assist two or more individuals to resolve conflict in daily life. Conflict resolution concepts can be taught alone or within the standard school curriculum. Powell, McLaughlin, Savage, and Zehm (2001) describe three steps of conflict resolution:

First Step: Negotiation. Negotiation is a process whereby students attempt to work out an agreement. The goal is to arrive at a win-win solution, one that benefits both students. The steps in the negotiation process are (Johnson & Johnson, as cited in Powell et al., 2001):

a. Describe what each student wants.
b. Describe what each student feels.
c. Exchange reasons for specifying positions that have created the conflict.
d. Understand each other's position.
e. Invent options for mutual benefit.
f. Reach an agreement that is mutually beneficial.

A special educator uses conflict resolution to help students solve problems.

Second Step: Mediation. When students cannot reach an agreement by themselves, a third party becomes involved. Many schools use **peer mediation,** a process that involves students who are trained in the negotiation process and who act as a third party.

Before mediation begins, a period of time is provided for each student to "cool off"; then each student must agree to make a commitment to the mediation process. The mediator works to keep the discussion focused on the conflict and not become sidetracked. The role of the mediator is to assist the two parties in finding a solution and to facilitate the process so that students can learn how to use it on their own. When an agreement is reached, it is written down and everyone signs it. When an agreement cannot be reached, the process moves to arbitration.

Third Step: Arbitration. Arbitration is a process whereby a solution to the conflict is imposed by a third party, such as a special educator or counselor. Sometimes the arbitrator asks students to submit a written solution to the conflict and explains that the one that is most fair will be selected.

ADDRESSING STUDENT MOTIVATION

Students with behavior problems often engage in inappropriate behavior because they consider this behavior more desirable or acceptable than the appropriate behavior. The student may not be motivated to act or may not see any value in the appropriate behavior. Kamps (2002) identifies a number of possible teacher interventions, depending on a student's motivation for engaging in problem behaviors, including attention-motivated behavior, escape-motivated behavior, access/control-motivated behavior, and sensory/stimulation-motivated behavior.

Attention-Motivated Behavior

Begin by teaching appropriate attention-seeking behaviors. For example, when a student is seeking another person's attention, an educator teaches the student to say the person's name once and wait for the person to look at or acknowledge the student. The educator allows the student a limited number of requests for attention in each class period and keeps a visual tally of the requests, using praise when the student demonstrates the positive behavior. During class, the teacher also uses specific praise and privileges for peers who model appropriate attention-seeking behavior. The teacher avoids verbal reprimands and, only as a last resort, uses timeout. **Timeout** is a procedure whereby a student is removed from the group or activity and placed in a neutral setting for a specified period of time.

Timeout should be used sparingly, for short "cool-down" periods. For example, a teacher may place a student in timeout when the student engages in violent behavior. Since timeout helps protect the safety of the student and other students, it is a helpful procedure; however, when a student is in timeout, valuable classroom learning time is lost. A student should be placed in timeout for only a few minutes.

Escape-Motivated Behavior

The teacher may begin by reviewing current classroom practices and evaluating learning activities to make sure that students have multiple opportunities for hands-on activities. The teacher structures lessons and learning activities so that easier activities are interspersed with more difficult tasks. Students are given opportunities to choose the order in which the learning activities will be completed, and the teacher provides written examples, or exemplars, of well-done activities or tasks.

The teacher encourages students to ask for help in an appropriate manner during the instructional lesson and learning activities and always responds to these requests. The teacher provides additional assistance to the student and monitors the student's performance frequently. By reinforcing the student's on-task behavior at 3- to 5-minute intervals, the teacher helps the student increase self-management. The teacher does not use timeout, as this only serves to reinforce the student's escape-motivated behavior.

Access/Control-Motivated Behavior

Educators begin by teaching the student acceptable ways to interact with others and request access to materials or an activity. Students also learn how to manage disappointment and anger. To control student behavior, teachers may use **contingent statements,** which include the condition that the student must satisfy before engaging in a desired behavior. For example, a teacher announces, "After all the materials are put away, you may have the remaining time to check your e-mail or listen to music. We have 10 minutes before we need to get ready to go home."

Sensory/Stimulation-Motivated Behavior

IEP team members and other professional consultants decide whether to ignore the behavior if it does not disrupt the student's learning or the learning of others. For behaviors that do interfere with learning, teachers interrupt and redirect them. For example, Luis constantly clicked his pen—off-on, off-on. His teacher provided a Koosh ball that allowed him the needed sensory stimulation but was not distracting to others.

PROVIDING CLEAR EXPECTATIONS AND TEACHING COMPLIANCE

Effective approaches for promoting positive behavior begin with preventive measures for minimizing discipline problems (Figure 9.10). Educators communicate clear expectations for student behavior and provide positive and corrective feedback, while students learn to monitor their own behaviors and evaluate their progress. Teachers ensure that students are treated fairly and consistently. This section discusses establishing rules, identifying procedures, and teaching compliance.

Establishing Rules and Identifying Procedures

Special educators, in collaboration with students, construct **classroom rules,** usually written statements, that describe student behavioral expectations. Through words and/ or pictures, the rules illustrate what students should *do,* rather than *not* do, and are written in positive terms. When teachers involve students in developing a set of classroom rules, everyone accepts ownership of the rules. In addition, students are more likely to follow the rules and to help reinforce them with others. Classroom rules are more effective when they are developed at the beginning of the school year. The teacher keeps the list of rules relatively short—no more than five or six—and posts

Figure 9.10   Preventive measures for minimizing discipline problems

- Clear communication of expectations for student behavior. Teachers define acceptable behaviors in a concrete manner.
- Ongoing positive and corrective feedback. Teachers tell students what they are doing correctly and praise them for appropriate behaviors.
- Fair and consistent treatment of students. Rules, consequences, and enforcement procedure are clearly defined and articulated to all students.
- Positive recognition and public acknowledgment of appropriate behavior.
- Engaging in student-centered instruction.
- Collaboration between regular and special educators.

Source: Adapted from *Safe, Drug-Free, and Effective Schools for ALL Students: What Works?* by M. M. Quinn, D. Osher, C. C. Hoffman, and T. V. Hanley, 1998, Washington, DC: Center for Effective Collaboration and Practice, American Institutes for Research.

them in a highly visible place. The teacher begins by demonstrating (or inviting students to demonstrate) each of the rules, and then reviews and refers to them frequently. The teacher is careful to consistently reinforce the classroom rules daily. Sometimes teachers must review classroom rules at the beginning of the school day and reteach them to the group or to individual students as necessary. Martin and Pear (2002) define effective rules as rules that describe deadlines for specific behavior, even when the outcomes are delayed (p. 212).

One first-grade class and their teacher developed the following set of rules and posted them at the front of the classroom for all to see.

In Our Classroom, We . . .

- use quiet voices,
- take out our walking shoes,
- put on our listening ears, and
- keep our hands and feet to ourselves.

Teachers must follow through with consequences when a student does not follow the rules. A **consequence** is the event that follows a behavior and may influence whether the behavior occurs again or how frequently. Students need to understand that there will be consequences when they do not follow classroom rules. Consequences should be posted in a visible place as a reminder.

A fifth-grade teacher posted the following consequences on the classroom wall:

What Happens if I Don't Follow the Rules:

- First time, a teacher or student reminds me.
- Second time, I receive a checkmark by my name.
- Third time, I miss recess.
- Fourth time, a message is sent to my parents.

When students have difficulty following rules, teachers can help them learn to monitor their own behaviors. By using a checklist (Figure 9.11), students can observe

Figure 9.11   Teacher-designed self-monitoring card for students

How Did I Do?

Date:_____

	Homeroom	Science	Math	English	Social Studies
Organized my work space					
Followed directions					
Shared a relevant comment at least twice					
Listened when others spoke					

their own behavior, record it, and evaluate it. Self-monitoring helps students internalize their positive behaviors, and recording sheets or checklists provide a visual reminder of what is expected of them (Center for Effective Collaboration and Practice, 1999).

Sometimes people confuse classroom rules with classroom procedures. **Classroom procedures** describe the steps or components of daily activities that must be followed to complete tasks. For example, a first-grade teacher posts the following classroom procedures on the bathroom wall:

- Please flush the toilet.
- Wash your hands with soap and warm water.
- Turn off the light.

A middle school teacher lists the following procedures on the classroom's Web page regarding homework assignments:

- Carefully read the directions before beginning the assignment.
- Use a spell checker after you complete your draft.
- Pass in your paper or send it as an attached file to your teacher on Friday.

Teaching Compliance

Teachers expect students to follow requests, directions, and classroom rules as they build affective and academic skills. Many students with severe, persistent emotional and behavioral problems demonstrate oppositional, defiant, and noncompliant behaviors. To begin to increase student compliance, a teacher can stand next to the student and state the request in a normal, unemotional voice, allowing a few seconds for compliance to begin and praising the compliant behavior (Kamps, 2002).

However, educators often need to use specific teaching strategies because noncompliance may be a well-learned problem behavior (Table 9.1). Successful teachers use consistent procedures and carry out the teaching strategy firmly and with confidence. Sometimes teachers inadvertently reinforce noncompliant behavior by (a) asking a

Table 9.1	Teaching Strategies for Increasing Student Compliance
Teaching Strategy	**Procedures**
Precision requests: Making appropriate request in a way that maximizes student compliance (Rhode, Jenson, & Reavis, 1992)	1. Teacher explains request and consequences simply and clearly. 2. Request is made up close with eye contact, using "please." 3. Teacher waits 5–10 seconds for compliance. 4. Specific verbal response is given for compliance. 5. For noncompliance, a second request is given "I need . . ." 6. Continued noncompliance requires a preplanned consequence. RULE: Make more start/do requests than stop/don't commands. RULE: Minimum of 4:1 positive-to-negative teacher statements.
Precorrection: Instruction in appropriate behaviors, and reminders before setting/context occurs of expectations (Colvin, Sugai, Good, & Lee, 1997)	1. Identify the context and the predictable problem behavior. 2. Specify the expected behavior. 3. Modify the context. 4. Conduct behavior rehearsals. 5. Provide strong reinforcement. 6. Prompt expected behaviors. 7. Monitor the plan.
Differential attention: Ignoring behaviors that tend to be attention seeking, reinforcing alternative or appropriate behaviors (Rhode, Jenson, & Reavis, 1992; Forehand & McMahon, 1981)	1. Ignore inappropriate behavior (break eye contact, do not speak to student, walk away, engage with an appropriate student). 2. Differentially pay attention to appropriate behavior as soon as possible following misbehavior. 3. Reward appropriate behavior at a high rate. RULE: Ignoring behavior usually results in a quick increase or burst of behavior (student testing): teachers must be prepared to ignore all instances—intermittent attention will have a negative effect. RULE: Ignoring is more effective if peers ignore as well.

Teaching Strategies for Increasing Student Compliance *continued*	
Teaching Strategy	**Procedures**
Behavioral momentum: Requesting 2–3 easy behaviors immediately prior to difficult request to increase compliance (Davis & Reichle, 1996)	1. Identify multiple requests that student is highly likely to follow. 2. Give 2–3 requests with high probability for compliance. 3. Immediately follow high probability request with harder request. EXAMPLE: Pass these papers to your row. Please write numbers 1–10. Write your favorite movie for number 1. Please write the vocabulary words and definition for numbers 2–10.
Compliance games: Reinforcement systems designed to reward student compliance to teacher requests (Rhode, Jenson, & Reavis, 1992)	Sure I Will: 1. Students divided into teams. 2. Teams select specific/unique compliance phrase (e.g., "Sure I will"; "Sure, anytime"; or "No problem"). 3. Students receive points for their team for saying the phrase and complying with requests. 4. Teams earn rewards for reaching compliance goals. Compliance Matrix (Bingo game using compliance as markers.)

Source: From D. M. Kamps, "Preventing Problems by Improving Behavior," in B. Algozzine & P. Kay (Eds.), *Preventing Problem Behaviors,* p. 17, copyright © 2002 by Corwin Press. Reprinted by permission of Corwin Press.

student repeatedly to complete a request (thus teaching that the student doesn't have to follow the direction the first time the teacher asks) and (b) allowing a student to negotiate delaying compliance (no consequence for continuing to play music even though class has begun; adapted from Kamps, 2002, p. 16).

USING INSTRUCTIONAL STRATEGIES FOR ACTIVE RESPONDING

Teachers who use positive behavioral supports and develop learning activities that actively engage students provide an atmosphere conducive to student learning. In the following section, we will examine several instructional strategies that special educators use to support and promote positive behavior in the classroom. After all, high academic expectations and active student engagement complement good classroom support. Students who are actively engaged in learning display positive classroom behaviors and a marked decrease in problem behaviors, whereas inappropriate teaching methods can exacerbate behavior problems in the classroom.

One teaching method that has broad research support for its use and effectiveness with students who have learning and behavior problems is direct instruction, which you read about in Chapter 6. Teachers using direct instruction can include instructional strategies that support a high level of student involvement, as well as frequent and immediate feedback such as choral responding, response cards, and guided notes.

Choral Responding

Choral responding requires students to respond aloud as a group to the teacher's questions. For example, a resource room teacher using choral responding asks the reading group, "What sound do you hear at the beginning of the word *pumpkin*?" Each child replies *puh*. By scanning the group, the teacher can monitor the children's answers. A student who doesn't know the answer hears the correct response. The teacher may say, "Tell me one more time." All students can respond again, including the student who didn't know the answer.

Response Cards

Like choral responding, response cards involve students actively. Each student uses response cards to indicate the answer to a teacher's question. Response cards can be as simple as "yes" and "no" color-coded cards. The teacher might use these cards during shared-book time to provide an opportunity for each child to predict what will happen next as the children listen to a story. "Do you think that Heather will go down into the cave?" The children decide by holding up a "yes" or a "no" response card.

The teacher can use paper, cut in 3 × 5 inch pieces, to provide each student with a set of blank response cards. Students can write their answers on the cards and hold them up in response to the teacher's questions. Or students can use individual wipable white boards with markers.

Research findings support the use of response cards for increasing academic achievement in both elementary and secondary students with disabilities (Cavanaugh, Heward, & Donelson, 1996; Gardner, Heward, & Grossi, 1994; Narayan, Heward, Gardner, Courson, & Omness, 1990). Teachers who used response cards during classroom review sessions in an earth science class with secondary students, some of whom had mental retardation or learning and behavior disabilities, found that all students, including those with disabilities, achieved higher test scores (Cavanaugh et al., 1996).

Teachers who used response cards to encourage class participation found that the frequency of active student response was greater than when students raised their hands to participate (Gardner et al., 1994; Narayan et al., 1990). Students reported that they preferred using the cards to raising their hands (Narayan et al., 1990).

Guided Notes

To help students become more actively involved in lesson activities, a middle school or high school special educator can prepare guided notes that outline the lesson material. The guided notes can include new vocabulary words, important dates, and the key ideas that the teacher wants the students to know. The teacher distributes a copy

Research to Practice

Dropout Prevention

Students with mild and moderate disabilities are at high risk for dropping out of school before high school graduation. To address this concern, educators have examined ways of reaching students with disabilities at the middle school level. Research on these dropout prevention programs shows promising results (Christenson, Sinclair, Evelo, & Thurlow, 1995; Edgar & Johnson, 1995; Thornton, 1995). The Achievement for Latinos through Academic Success (ALAS) program is a research-based dropout prevention program for high-risk Mexican youth, including those with disabilities, who live in high-poverty urban neighborhoods.

The Belief Academy (Edgar, Parker, Siegel, & Johnson, 1994) emphasizes accelerated acquisition of basic skills. The program also provides social support and family case management to address out-of-school issues that affect learning (medical care, housing, family counseling). Both this and the ALAS program include the following components: maintaining persistent, long-term contact with students; adapting school rules; establishing discipline procedures and policies for students; and facilitating student participation in school-sponsored activities.

Questions for Reflection

1. What are some other ways schools are working on dropout prevention?
2. What are the current statistics on school dropouts among students with and without disabilities?

 To answer these questions and learn more about applying research to practice, go to the Companion Website at www.prenhall. com/cohen, select Chapter 9, then choose Research to Practice.

---

of the guided notes to each student prior to the lesson, either through e-mail or as a hard-copy handout. During the lesson, students complete the outline provided in the guided notes by listening carefully to the lecture and writing down the information.

Research studies indicated that the use of guided notes improved academic achievement for adolescents with learning and behavior problems (Hamilton, Seibert, Gardner, & Talbert-Johnson, 2000; Lazarus, 1991, 1993; Sweeney et al., 1999). Furthermore, students reported that they preferred using guided notes rather than their own notes (Hamilton et al., 2000; Sweeney et al., 1999).

STRENGTHENING SCHOOL AND COMMUNITY CAPACITY

❖ *PROFESSIONAL PERSPECTIVES* ❖

Administrators and educators at John Fuller Elementary School are in the third year of implementing a schoolwide positive behavior support system. The first year, teachers agreed on a schoolwide **code of conduct** (Figure 9.12). A code of conduct

Figure 9.12   Schoolwide code of conduct from the John Fuller Elementary School

Schoolwide Code of Conduct

Respect: I will be courteous, appreciative, and accepting of individual differences.

Citizenship: I will obey rules, respect authority, and conserve natural resources.

Responsibility: I will accept responsibility to take care of myself and be a dependable member of the community.

Caring: I will show kindness, sharing, and compassion.

Source: Adapted from *Research Connections: Emerging Models* (pp. 1–4), Center for Effective Collaboration and Practice, 1997, Washington, DC: Publisher.

defines the behavior that teachers, administrators and other school staff, and parents expect of students. Sometimes students, along with teachers and other school personnel, sign their names to a public display of the school's code of conduct. When students do not follow the code, teachers use a standard set of schoolwide disciplinary procedures. When the behavior escalates beyond typical minor classroom violations, the procedures include a social cognitive problem-solving component that asks the students, in writing, to

- describe what happened.
- describe what the student did.
- identify which conduct principles were violated.
- explain the effect on the student and others.
- specify what needs to happen.
- articulate the consequences.
- plan how to prevent the transgression from happening again.

In the second year, to assist students in learning **self-discipline,** a process that involves learning how to exert self-control and manage one's own behaviors, the teachers established a schoolwide behavioral support system in which students have the chance to earn points for good behavior and can exchange the points for the privilege of being a *self-manager*—a role that allows student to carry out special tasks such as running errands. As part of the Self-Manager Program, teachers give students a "Caught You" award when they catch a student exemplifying one or more of the behaviors in the code of conduct. The teacher writes a brief description of the positive behavior observed on the "I got caught" sticker, which can be worn by the student or displayed in the classroom or hallway.

During the third year, the teachers developed social skills lessons for classroom instruction and focused on strategies for dealing with the needs of students with chronic behavioral problems. They created crisis prevention strategies and family support networks. Educators and administrators are pleased with having a consistent, efficient process that supports both students and teachers (adapted from Center for Effective Collaboration and Practice, 1997).

SCHOOLWIDE BEHAVIOR SUPPORT SYSTEMS

Because many students need positive behavior instruction, schools are reexamining traditional discipline procedures and providing opportunities for students to learn self-discipline. There are several common features of schoolwide behavioral support systems:

- total staff commitment to managing behavior, whatever approach is taken
- clearly defined and communicated expectations and rules
- consequences and clearly stated procedures for correcting rule-breaking behaviors
- an instructional component for teaching students self-control and/or social skill strategies
- a support plan to address the needs of students with chronic, challenging behaviors (Center for Effective Collaboration and Practice, 1997, p. 1)

WORKING WITH PROFESSIONALS IN COMMUNITY AGENCIES

Special educators work closely with professionals in local and regional community agencies. For example, social workers, mental health counselors, psychologists, and consulting psychiatrists may be involved, along with special educators, occupational therapists, physical therapists, and speech and language pathologists, in delivering services in outpatient mental health treatment centers. Let us take a closer look at how these professionals would work together to help Jake, who is 15 years old.

——— ❖ EVALUATION AND TREATMENT OF JAKE ❖ ———

Staff at the intensive outpatient mental health treatment center are evaluating Jake while providing crisis stabilization and treatment. This is the third outpatient treatment for Jake, who has episodes of aggressive behavior and has been diagnosed with intermittent explosive disorder. According to *DSM-IV-TR* (2000), this disorder involves discrete episodes in which the individual is unable to resist aggressive impulses that result in serious acts of violence or destruction of property (pp. 663–667). Jake has a history of violent, aggressive, and oppositional behavior at home. After threatening to hurt his mother with a knife, Jake was referred to the center, and school personnel have been working with Jake's outreach social worker and psychiatrist.

As part of Jake's evaluation, the center is using a **strength-based assessment.** This assessment approach measures skills, achievements, and characteristics that create a sense of personal accomplishment, contribute to satisfying relationships, and help the individual to deal with adversity and stress (Rudolph & Epstein, 2002).

Once Jake's initial evaluation was completed, a team meeting was arranged. The team consisted of Jake, his mother and grandmother, his primary therapist at the treatment center, a child protective service caseworker, the school counselor, Jake's best friend, his favorite special educator, and his math teacher.

The team initially focused on how to promote Jake's strengths. After reviewing Jake's intrapersonal and academic strengths, team members made several recommendations to support Jake in pursuing his interests, including joining the school's intramural basketball team, becoming a peer tutor in math, pursuing volunteer work, and structuring free time with peers through participation in supervised community activities.

The team then addressed areas for skill development, including improving interpersonal and affective skills as well as increasing family involvement. The team agreed to work on the affective skills through Jake's participation in an intensive anger management program for youth and their families. Jake also agreed to meet with the school counselor, to discuss difficulties he may be having with peers, and to establish concrete goals in an effort to increase his understanding of the consequences of his actions.

The team planned to provide support to Jake's mother in developing behavior support, problem-solving, and communication skills through in-home Family Preservation Services, a division of the state's department of mental health. Jake's family agreed to plan a meal together at least three times per week and hold meetings at least once a week to build family communication (adapted from Rudolph & Epstein, 2002).

TAPPING COMMUNITY MENTORS

A valuable resource for educators is the development of community mentors who can be linked with students. A mentor is typically an older, established member of the business community or a retired person who makes a commitment to be a young person's guide over a period of time (Waller, 2002). The mentor can be a continuous presence in the student's life, "seeing potential, challenging, encouraging, demonstrating, as well as providing resources and access" (p. 14).

What Does the Research Say About Mentoring?

Peer mentors can reduce behavior problems and absenteeism among elementary students who are transitioning to middle school (Leland-Jones, 1998). Sixth graders were matched to a mentor/tutor, meeting twice weekly to become better acquainted and to work on academic and other concerns. Each person kept a journal detailing the problems, discussions, and possible solutions for each meeting. After the 8-month intervention project, teachers reported fewer student requests for assistance and fewer referrals for behavior problems and absenteeism.

Aaron Kipnis (1999) relates a number of personal stories of young men who had a history of violence, substance abuse, inadequate educational experiences, and physical and sexual abuse. A number of these individuals were considered violent, and some had been incarcerated as adolescents. Their personal accounts describe effective programs, including mentoring and its effect, in helping them overcome these behaviors to become productive adults.

COLLABORATING WITH FAMILIES

Educators can draw on *natural mentors,* too. Mentoring is a long-established aspect of many families. Siblings, parents, grandparents, and aunts and uncles may have provided a support system since the student was a young child. In some cultures, such as among the Navajos of the southwestern United States, people believe that mentoring is a birthright, and each person is expected to fulfill individual responsibilities to relatives.

❖ UNCLE TELES ❖

Among the Dine (Navajo) people, the maternal uncle mentors his sisters' children. In many families, his responsibilities include shepherding his nieces and nephews through their education. Teles, for example, is a young attorney and a college professor in a large metropolitan area in the Southwest, several hours' drive from his tribal home on the Navajo reservation. Since his six nieces have been in grade school, Teles has inspired them to set goals and achieve in school. He challenges them and provides them with both emotional and material support as they progress through each phase of their educational development. Guided by Teles, the three oldest girls graduated from their border town (the town adjacent to the reservation) high school a year early and subsequently moved to the city where Teles lives. Currently, four of his nieces, one of whom has an infant, live with Teles in his home in the city. Heather, an eighth grader, is continuing her education via home schooling as she undergoes her second round of chemotherapy for bone cancer (adapted from Waller, 2002, p. 14).

Educators search out and create culturally relevant educational experiences.

Considering Diversity

Creating Culturally Relevant Educational Experiences

Behavioral expectations are an integral aspect of the culture that surrounds us. Some families may expect children to respect and not question authority figures, while others encourage children to be assertive and "speak up" to make their opinions and wishes known. Thus, for some students, the culture of the school, home, and community all hold similar behavioral expectations, while other students find a marked contrast in cultural expectations as they move from home to school to "hanging out" in their neighborhoods.

The factors in schools that exacerbate inequities include curriculum and pedagogy (Nieto, 1996), as well as behavioral expectations and communication styles. Teachers can work to create culturally responsive educational experiences by building on students' interests while providing high-quality academic instruction. Educators search out and provide information related to students' lives and place instructional information in a context that is familiar to students. They respect and model an appreciation of individual differences and similarities and provide students with positive examples of role models. The Center for Research on Education, Diversity,

and Excellence is an excellent resource that assists teachers in responding to classroom diversity. Their website includes research findings and standards for pedagogy.

Questions for Reflection

1. Explore the Center for Research on Education, Diversity, and Excellence website. What information regarding culturally relevant education did you find most helpful?
2. Consider the home culture of a student with whom you have worked. What instructional activities would you create to provide a relevant learning experience for the student?
3. WebQuests, inquiry-oriented activities in which students use Web-based information, often build on students' interests while providing high-quality academic instruction. Describe the qualities you might find in a WebQuest that would create a relevant learning experience for students with whom you have worked.

 To answer these questions and deepen your understanding of diversity in schools and communities, go to the Companion Website at www.prenhall.com/cohen, select Chapter 9, then choose Considering Diversity.

SUMMARY

- Special educators work closely with other professionals in the school and in the community to promote positive student behavior.
- Many school districts develop codes of conduct that all students are expected to follow.
- Special educators create a positive classroom environment by specifying expectations for student behavior. They work closely with other IEP team members to assess student behavior by using a functional behavioral analysis and writing a behavioral intervention plan that specifies the skills or replacement behaviors that the student needs. The plan includes a description of the instructional strategies and details on how the plan will be evaluated. When the intervention plan is not working, the team meets to revise it, monitoring student progress carefully.

EXTENDING LEARNING

1. Arrange to interview the director of special education services in a local school to discuss how crisis and emergency situations are handled. Does the school have a policy? What training is offered to the staff?

2. Working in small groups, identify questions you might ask a special educator regarding developing, implementing, or evaluating behavioral intervention plans. Use e-mail or a classroom visit with a teacher to gather your information and share it with the class.

3. As a new teacher, you want the year to get off to a good start by working on positive behavior support. With a small group of others, role-play a discussion that you might have with your students on developing a set of classroom rules. What questions will you ask the students? How will you encourage them to identify the most important rules? What rules might you and the students identify? Remember, your list should contain no more than five or six rules. Write down the rules that were generated and evaluate the results. Would these rules be appropriate for the age level of your students? Would you make any changes in your list?

4. Based on your classroom observations or experiences, identify four or five problem behaviors in the classroom. List the behaviors in a column and brainstorm with other classmates the possible functions that each behavior might have for a student. What replacement behaviors might you suggest?

5. Create a learning activity for the class (using one of the topics that you have covered in this course). Include one instructional strategy described in this chapter to encourage active responding. After conducting the activity, evaluate the effectiveness of the strategy.

6. Work with a small group of peers to develop your own case study. Describe the behavior in observable terms. What assessment questions do you have, and what approaches would you suggest for gathering additional information? What suggestions might you offer regarding the function of the student's behavior?

7. Research the use of codes of conduct in area schools. Share your findings with the class.

REFERENCES

American Psychiatric Association. (2000). *Diagnostic and statistical manual of mental disorders* (4th ed., text revision). Washington, DC: Author.

Bandura, A. (1969). *Principles of behavior modification*. New York: Holt, Rinehart & Winston.

Bandura, A. (1972). *Social learning theory*. Upper Saddle River, NJ: Prentice Hall.

Bandura, A. (1986). *Social foundations of thought and action: A social congnitive theory*. Upper Saddle River, NJ: Prentice Hall.

Cavanaugh, R. A., Heward, W. L., & Donelson, F. (1996). Effects of response cards during lesson closure on the academic performance of secondary students in an earth science course. *Journal of Applied Behavior Analysis, 29*(3), 403–406.

Center for Effective Collaboration and Practice. (1997). *Research connections: Emerging models*. Retrieved February 13, 2002, from http://www.air.org/cecp/resources/recon/art2.htm

Center for Effective Collaboration and Practice. (1998a). *Addressing student problem behavior—Part I: An IEP team's introduction to functional behavioral assessment and behavior intervention plans.* Retrieved June 4, 2001, from http://www.air.org//cecp/fba/problembehavior/main.htm

Center for Effective Collaboration and Practice. (1998b). *Addressing student problem behavior—Part II: Conducting a functional behavioral assessment* (3rd ed.). Retrieved June 4, 2001, from http://cecp.air.org/fba/problembehavior2/main2.htm

Center for Effective Collaboration and Practice. (1999). *Prevention strategies that work.* Retrieved February 13, 2002, from http://www.air.org/cecp/preventionstrategies/Default.htm

Center for Effective Collaboration and Practice. (2000). *Addressing student problem behavior—Part III: Creating positive behavioral intervention plans and supports.* Retrieved February 13, 2002, from http://www.air-dc.org/cecp/fba/problembehavior3/text3.htm

Chesapeake Institute. (1994). *National agenda for achieving better results for children and youth with serious emotional disturbance.* Retrieved February 13, 2002, from the Center for Effective Collaboration and Practice website: http://www.air.org/cecp/resources/ntlagend.html

Choi, J., & Kim, U. (1998). Research digest: Functional assessment for individuals with problem behaviors. *Diagnostique, 23*(4), 277–282.

Christenson, S., Sinclair, M., Evelo, D., & Thurlow, M. (1995). *Tip the balance: Practices and policies that influence school engagement for youth at high risk for dropping out.* Minneapolis: Institute on Community Integration. (ERIC Document Reproduction Service No. ED398673)

Cohen, L. G., & Spenciner, L. J. (2003). *Assessment of children and youth with special needs* (2nd ed.). Boston: Allyn & Bacon.

Colvin, G., Sugai, G., Good, R., & Lee, Y. (1997). Using active supervision and precorrection to improve transition behavior in an elementary school. *School Psychology Quarterly, 12,* 344–363.

Davis, C., & Reichle, J. (1996). Invariant and variant high-probability requests: Increasing appropriate behaviors in children with emotional behavior disorders. *Journal of Applied Behavior Analysis, 29,* 471–482.

Deci, E. L., & Ryan, R. M. (1980). The empirical exploration of intrinsic motivational processes. In L. Berkowitz (Ed.), *Advances in experimental social psychology* (Vol. 13, pp. 39–80). New York: Academic Press.

Edgar, E., & Johnson, E. (1995). *Relationship building and affiliation activities in school-based dropout prevention programs: Rationale and recommendations for action.* Minneapolis: Institute on Community Integration. (ERIC Document Reproduction Service No. ED398672)

Edgar, E., Parker, W., Siegel, S., & Johnson, E. (1994). Staying in school: A technical report of three dropout prevention projects for middle school students with learning and emotional disabilities. *Preventing School Failure, 38*(2), 7–13.

Fitzsimmons, M. K. (1998). *Violence and aggression in children and youth.* Reston, VA: ERIC Clearinghouse on Disabilities and Gifted Education. (ERIC Document Reproduction Service No. ED429419)

Forehand, R., & McMahon, R. (1981). *Helping the noncompliant child.* New York: Guilford Press.

Gardner, W. I., Cole, C. L., Davidson, D. P., & Karan, O. C. (1986). Reducing aggression in individuals with developmental disabilities: An expanded stimulus control, assessment, and intervention model. *Education and Training of the Mentally Retarded, 21*(1), 3–12.

Gardner, R., III, Heward, W. L., & Grossi, T. A. (1994). Effects of response cards on student participation and academic achievement: A systematic replication with inner-city students during whole-class science instruction. *Journal of Applied Behavior Analysis, 27*(1), 63–71.

Gorman, J. C. (2001). *Emotional disorders and learning disabilities in the elementary classroom.* Thousand Oaks, CA: Corwin Press.

Hamilton, S. L., Seibert, M. A., Gardner, R., III, & Talbert-Johnson, C. (2000). Using guided notes to improve the academic achievement of incarcerated adolescents with learning and behavior problems. *Remedial and Special Education, 21*(3), 133–140.

Horner, R. H., Vaughn, B. J., Day, H. M., & Ard, W. R. (1996). The relationship between setting events and problem behavior: Expanding our understanding of behavioral support. In L. K. Koegel, R. L. Koegel, & G. Dunlap (Eds.), *Positive behavioral support: Including people with difficult behavior in the community* (pp. 381–402). Baltimore: Paul H. Brookes.

Individuals with Disabilities Education Act Amendments (Pub. L. No. 105–17). (1997). 20 U.S.C. Sec. 1400 et seq. Washington, DC: U.S. Government Printing Office.

Ingram, K. L. (2003). Comparing the effectiveness of indicated and contra-indicated based functional behavioral assessment interventions (Doctoral dissertation, University of Oregon, 2003). *Dissertation Abstracts International, 63*(8-A), 2833.

Jolivette, K., Stichter, J. P., & McCormick, K. M. (2002). Making choices—improving behavior—engaging in learning. *TEACHING Exceptional Children, 34*(3), 24–29.

Kamps, D. M. (2002). Preventing problems by improving behavior. In B. Algozzine & P. Kay (Eds.), *Preventing problem behaviors* (pp. 11–36). Thousand Oaks, CA: Corwin Press.

Kamps, D. M., Ellis, C., Mancina, C., Wyble, J., Greene, L., & Harvey, D. (1995). Case studies using functional analysis for young children with behavior risks. *Education and Treatment of Children, 18*(3), 243–260.

Kazdin, A. E. (1994). *Behavior modification in applied settings* (5th ed.). Pacific Grove, CA: Brooks/Cole.

Kipnis, A. (1999). *Angry young men: How parents, teachers, and counselors can help "bad boys" become good men.* San Francisco: Jossey-Bass.

Lazarus, B. D. (1991). Guided notes, review, and achievement of secondary students with learning disabilities in mainstream content courses. *Education and Treatment of Children, 14*(2), 112–127.

Lazarus, B. D. (1993). Guided notes: Effects with secondary and postsecondary students with mild disabilities. *Education and Treatment of Children, 16*(3), 272–289.

Leland-Jones, P. J. (1998). *Improving the transition of sixth-grade students during the first year of middle school through a peer counselor mentor and tutoring program.* Fort Lauderdale, FL: Nova Southeastern University. (ERIC Document Reproduction Service No. ED424911)

Mahoney, M. J. (1974). *Cognitive behavior modification.* Cambridge, MA: Ballinger.

Martin, G., & Pear, J. (2002). *Behavior modification: What it is and how to do it* (7th ed.). Upper Saddle River, NJ: Prentice Hall.

Narayan, J. S., Heward, W. L., Gardner, R., III, Courson, F. H., & Omness, C. K. (1990). Using response cards to increase student participation in an elementary classroom. *Journal of Applied Behavior Analysis, 23*(4), 483–490.

Nieto, S. (1996). *Affirming diversity* (2nd ed.). White Plains, NY: Longman.

Powell, R. R., McLaughlin, H. J., Savage, T. V., & Zehm, S. (2001). *Classroom management: Perspectives on the social curriculum.* Upper Saddle River, NJ: Merrill/Prentice Hall.

Quinn, M. M., Osher, D., Hoffman, C. C., & Hanley, T. V. (1998). *Safe, drug-free, and effective schools for ALL students: What works?* Washington, DC: Center for Effective Collaboration and Practice, American Institutes for Research.

Repp, A. C., & Horner, R. H. (1999). *Functional analysis of problem behavior*. Belmont, CA: Wadsworth.

Rhode, G., Jenson, W., & Reavis, H. K. (1992). *The tough kid book: Practical classroom management strategies*. Longmont, CO: Sopris West.

Rudolph, S. M., & Epstein, M. H. (2000). *Empowering children and families through strength-based assessment*. Retrieved February 13, 2002, from the Center for Effective Collaboration and Practice website: http://cecp.air.org/interact/expertonline/strength/sba.htm

Scanlon, D., & Mellard, D. F. (2002). Academic and participation profiles of school-age dropouts with and without disabilities. *Exceptional Children, 68*(20), 239–258.

Scott, T. M., Liaupsin, C. J., Nelson, C. M., & Jolivette, K. (2003). Ensuring student success throught team-based functional behavioral assessment. *TEACHING Exceptional Children, 35*(5), 16–21.

Skinner, B. F. (1974). *About behaviorism*. New York: Alfred A. Knopf.

Sweeney, W. J., Ehrhardt, A. M., Gardner, R., III, Jones, L., Greenfield, R., & Fribley, S. (1999). Using guided notes with academically at-risk high school students during a remedial summer social studies class. *Psychology in the Schools, 36*(4), 305–318.

Thornton, H. (Ed.). (1995). *Staying in school: A technical report of three dropout prevention projects for middle school students with learning and emotional disabilities*. Minneapolis: Institute on Community Integration. (ERIC Document Reproduction Service No. ED398674)

Wahler, R. G., & Graves, M. G. (1983). Setting events in social networks: Ally or enemy in child behavior therapy? *Behavior Therapy, 14*(1), 19–36.

Waller, M. (2002). Family mentors and educational resilience among native students. *The Prevention Researcher, 9*(1), 14–16.

10

Chapter

Partnering with Educators, Professionals, Paraprofessionals, and Families

CHAPTER OBJECTIVES

After completing this chapter, you should be able to:

- ❖ Describe knowledge, skills, and strategies for developing effective partnerships.

- ❖ Discuss ways of working with other professionals in arrangements such as collaborative teaming and consulting.

- ❖ Discuss strategies for working with paraprofessionals.

- ❖ Identify ways to communicate effectively with parents and other team members.

- ❖ Demonstrate an understanding of diversity perspectives.

- ❖ Identify technology tools for enhancing communication and seeking resources for parents.

Special educators develop working partnerships with many individuals colleagues, parents, professionals from other agencies, and community members. They work closely with classroom teachers to plan and implement appropriate teaching and learning activities, and they work with paraprofessionals such as teaching aides or assistants, supervising their work with small groups or individual students. To support the carryover of skills to classrooms, they also meet regularly with therapists such as speech and language pathologists, occupational therapists, physical therapists, and therapeutic recreational therapists. Special educators work closely with parents, too, regarding their child's progress and changes in performance. They also work with other professionals, such as rehabilitation counselors and job counselors, in planning and implementing transition activities and community-based instruction. In addition, they may develop close partnerships with members of the community who volunteer to work in the classroom or mentor individual students.

MODELS FOR WORKING WITH OTHERS

Depending on their training and experience, special educators may follow one of the contemporary models for collaboration or they may use an eclectic approach such as a combination of models. Models of collaboration typically used in schools today include the mental health consultation model, the behavioral model, and the collaborative model. Each model has a separate theoretical base, goals, and responsibilities for team members. For example, a special education teacher who follows the mental health model takes responsibility for gathering information about a problem and then works with the teacher (or student or parent) to cope with, create, or implement solutions together. A special education teacher who uses a behavioral perspective may encourage mutual problem solving but primarily acts as an expert consultant. Educators using the collaborative consultation model assume shared ownership in solving learning and behavior problems, with general and special educators bringing their own discipline-specific competencies to the situation.

Various consultation models for understanding the perspectives of others are well documented (Gallessich, 1982; Heron & Harris, 2001; Stewart, 1971; West & Idol, 1987). We like the rich metaphor and the vision of working from a bridge (Trumbull, Rothstein-Fisch, Greenfield, & Quiroz, 2001). From a bridge, one can see both sides simultaneously, enhancing one's perspective and allowing one to travel back and forth between points of view. "The bridge is more than just knowledge of each cultural framework. It is an expansion of understanding cultures beyond that which can be seen only from one side or the other" (Trumbull et al., 2001, p. 131).

KNOWLEDGE, SKILLS, AND STRATEGIES

To develop strong partnerships, special educators need to have a tool box of knowledge, skills, and strategies. In the following sections we will examine confidentiality of information, trust as a basic skill in developing partnerships, and collaboration with others. Next, we will examine ways to problem solve and resolve conflicts using both nonconfrontational and confrontational solutions. Finally, we will see how teachers continue to work to improve their skills.

CONFIDENTIALITY

Strong partnerships involve open and honest communication as information is shared with other professionals, paraprofessionals, and parents. But are there limits and, if so, how are they observed? Special educators and other professionals working with students and their families have a legal and an ethical responsibility to ensure that the information is used appropriately. All individuals need to agree that the information being shared is for the purpose of assisting the student in the education program. One should discuss a particular student only with individuals who need to know the information and with whom the family has agreed the information may be shared. Discussions about a student are exchanged in appropriate places where only the individuals who need to know the information are present; never where others may overhear the conversation. Educators share information that is relevant to the classroom and to student learning. For example, a special educator might share with the teacher aide information about the student's new medication and possible side effects of which the teachers need to be aware.

An educator gains trust by using empathy and by accepting the skills and competence of others.

All written information is subject to the Family Educational Rights and Privacy Act (FERPA) (Public Law 93-380). This federal law gives the family the right to review all records kept on their child and to challenge any of the information in the records. FERPA also states than no educational agency (such as a public school) may release student information without written consent from the parents. When information is released, school personnel must maintain records on when it was released and to whom, as well as send a copy of the records that were released to the student's parents.

GAINING TRUST

Team members gain trust by using empathy; by accepting the skills, competencies, and experiences of other team members; and by believing that other team members are competent (DeBoer, 1995).

❖ JOSH AND DANIELLE ❖

Two teachers, Josh and Danielle, have gained a sense of trust while working together during the school year. After Danielle confided to Josh, "I want Rafael to be able to do well, but I'm not sure how best to help him," Josh replied, "Yes, I know how you feel. I had that same feeling last year when Rafael came to our school. He was so far behind the other students in his grade, and his motivation was low. We found that he responded well to working with another student or in small groups. I think that your plans for student work groups for the project will help Rafael get a good start. And using heterogeneous grouping of students is a good instructional strategy." Josh showed that he understood Danielle's concerns, but he also wanted Danielle to know that he recognized and appreciated her skills as a classroom teacher. Josh continued, "Since Rafael has been having difficulty with map reading, let's plan when I could provide one-to-one instruction in the resource room so that he doesn't get left behind on this. I'd also like to have him try a new writing program that may help in completing the interview assignment."

Collaborating

Collaborating is a process in which two or more individuals share their own experiences, skills, and knowledge. It involves feelings of mutual respect, equality, and personal value. Educators create collaborative learning environments by the ways they interact with students, parents, other educators, and other professionals. A collaborative relationship connotes parity, reciprocity, mutual problem solving, shared resources, responsibility, and accountability (Heron & Harris, 2001).

Collaboration among educators or other professionals also involves having a colleague to assist in navigating unfamiliar or challenging situations (Klein & Chen, 2001). While new teachers use collaboration and outreach to other professionals to establish a support network, they bring fresh insights and skills to more experienced teachers.

What does the research say about collaboration and student achievement? Researchers found changes in classroom practices and increased student performance when teachers worked in teams in a predominantly African American middle school located in a low socioeconomic status neighborhood (Trimble & Peterson, 2000). Collaboration as part of a learning community distinguishes a high-performance, high-poverty school from other high-poverty schools (Bell, 2001). Development of school-based collaborative partnerships among families, community members, school personnel, and students enhanced family and community involvement in education and was self-sustaining over time (Rudo, Achacoso, & Perez, 2000).

Problem Solving

Teaching students with learning and behavior problems involves both working independently and working with others to solve problems. A special educator may work with a small group of students in promoting positive behavior but consult on a weekly basis with the school psychologist regarding instructional strategies and student progress. Sometimes special educators and other team members use a problem-solving sequence, such as the one illustrated in Figure 10.1, that keeps the team focused on a vision and how to achieve it.

Figure 10.1   Steps to creative problem solving

1. Develop a vision.
   a. What will the student be able to do by the end of this program year?
   b. What are our future hopes for the student?
2. What are the student's gifts and strengths?
3. What are the student's challenges and learning needs?
4. Use collaborative problem solving.
   a. Describe the problems.
   b. Where do the problems occur most frequently?
   c. When do they usually occur?
   d. With whom do they usually occur?
   e. Why do they occur?
   f. What is the student's usual response?
5. Prioritize student needs.
6. Plan the intervention.
   a. Brainstorm.
   b. Evaluate and select.
   c. Develop an action plan.
      If developing an IEP, identify goal(s) and objectives or benchmarks.
      How will the plan be implemented?
      Who will be responsible?
      When will the student's progress be reviewed?
7. Implement the plan.

Source: Adapted from "Creating a Sense of Ownership in the IEP Process," by S. D. Kroeger, C. K. Leibold, and R. Ryan, 1999, *TEACHING Exceptional Children, 32*(1), pp. 4–9.

Problem solving begins with team members developing a shared vision of what the student will be able to do. This keeps the team centered on a common positive goal. To help members focus on the problem, an effective facilitator uses a flip chart or graphic organizer software and records comments so that all team members can see the results of their work. The facilitator invites participation, valuing and supporting contributions by commenting: "That's a good point." "I am glad that you raised that question." "How can we build on Danielle's suggestions?"

Once team members identify the vision or possible solutions, they list the student's strengths, challenges, and needs. Each participant contributes to the discussion. Identifying not only problem areas and concerns but also what the student does well ensures that positive aspects of the student's performance are not forgotten. Later, when members identify the plan of action, the student's strengths will be the foundation of the design.

To communicate effectively, members do not merely exchange messages but also use substantive, analytical communication (Heron & Harris, 2001). During problem solving, individuals may describe other problems and pinpoint information regarding where, when, and with whom the problems most frequently happen. By describing the problems in detail, the members will be able to build the framework of the action plan while identifying the area of concern.

When the student is part of the team, problem solving can become a powerful process. Not only does the student have a unique perspective, but listening to other team members often brings new insights to the student. A student who listens and participates with adult team members sees a group that is interested in progress and achievement. Through participation, a student can become invested in the action plan.

Problem-Solving Techniques

Educators use various techniques to help solve problems. The following sections examine brainstorming and the nominal group technique.

Brainstorming. At some point, each of us has used the problem-solving technique of brainstorming, which involves generating as many ideas as possible. Usually one person acts as the recorder, writing down the ideas. No idea is rejected. In fact, a basic tenet of brainstorming is to not judge any idea until all the ideas are listed. Once this is done, participants can review the list, discussing and eliminating ideas until they decide which solution to implement.

Nominal group technique. Sometimes group members do not agree on a solution or the priority of items. Sometimes groups do not function in a manner that allows each member to have an equal voice. The **nominal group technique** is a decision-making process in which all members' voices are equally represented. During the process the group generates a collective ranking of all the items/solutions being considered. This technique consists of the following steps (adapted from Friend & Cook, 1992):

1. Each person is given the same number of index cards, each card corresponding to one of the items/solutions (as many as 10 ideas and 10 cards), and then writes one idea on each card.
2. Each person then ranks the cards from high (thus assigning a "10" for the most important of 10 cards) to low.
3. A facilitator gathers the cards and records all participants' votes for the ideas.
4. If a clear preference emerges, the procedure is complete; if not, additional discussion ensues and then the group participates in a second vote.

RESOLVING CONFLICTS

Teachers and others who approach partnerships with a "can do" attitude can be successful team players. Positive attitudes are contagious. But sometimes teachers with upbeat attitudes find themselves in situations that are difficult to resolve.

When professionals work closely with others, conflicts may arise over misunderstandings or lack of success in carrying out a student's IEP. Some conflicts may be resolved in a nonconfrontational manner, while others may require direct confrontation.

❖ NONCONFRONTATIONAL SOLUTIONS ❖

A nonconfrontational solution involves working around the problem and modeling the desired behavior (Snell & Janney, 2000). The problem is resolved without directly confronting the person. For example, during the school year, a special educator became more and more frustrated over the classroom teacher's seeming lack of effort to support Yolanda, a student with learning and behavior problems, in her attempts to make friends. The special educator decided to address the situation by joining the classroom teacher for recess duty. On the playground, the special educator observed the students, waiting for the right opportunity. When Yolanda picked up one of the kick balls from the storage box, the special educator went over to her and began talking. "What game would you like to play with the kick ball?" Yolanda decided on a popular game, "Call Out." As the special educator scanned the playground, she observed a couple of children who were watching. She suggested to Yolanda, "Anne and Jodi look like they're trying to find something to do. Why don't you invite them to play?" The special educator stayed with Yolanda to support the beginning of the game. Then, once the children were engaged, she stepped back. By modeling intervention strategies on the playground and then discussing them informally with the classroom teacher who was on playground duty, the special educator did not address her concerns directly. She worked around the problem by providing an opportunity for the classroom teacher to observe an effective way of helping the student join and participate with a group of classmates.

CONFRONTATIONAL SOLUTIONS

Sometimes a situation calls for immediate action followed by a discussion with the other person. The individual who is concerned plans the meeting and identifies a quiet space where there will be no interruptions. At the beginning of the meeting, the individual states the specific concerns, using "I" messages to explain feelings. The individual listens to the other person's reaction. Together they discuss alternatives for the future.

Let us return to the special education teacher who was concerned about Yolanda to see how this approach works. The special educator contacted the classroom teacher in order to schedule a meeting. "A concern with Yolanda has come up that I would like to discuss. Would you have about a half hour sometime this week in which we can sit down and talk?" On the day of the meeting, the special educator thanked the classroom teacher for taking the time to meet and then continued, "I want to share a concern about Yolanda's lack of friends on the playground and see if we can come up with some strategies to address the situation. When the class has recess, Yolanda is having a great deal of difficulty with some of the other girls. The group that uses the swings has been refusing to let her join them. They tell her to go away and refuse to share equipment. The girls who usually play soccer seem to have chosen sides and will not let her play with them. I feel that it is important to address this situation because it is affecting how Yolanda feels about herself."

After using the "I" messages, the special educator paused and listened to the classroom teacher's reply. "Well, I have noticed that Yolanda does not seem to be playing

with the other children but, to be honest, I am so busy during recess duty settling argu-
ments and making sure that everyone is safe that it's difficult to worry about just one
child." After both teachers had a chance to talk about their concerns, they discussed
possible solutions. They decided to try two of the ideas. During Yolanda's scheduled
time in the resource room, the special educator would provide social skills instruction
in learning ways to join a group of classmates. The classroom teacher would use the
class morning meeting time to talk about the school community and the responsibilities of each student in this community, both in the classroom and at recess.

EVALUATING PERSONAL SKILLS

Good teachers continually reflect on and evaluate their own actions and behavior.
After a collaborative meeting, coteaching activity, or consultation, a teacher may
spend a few minutes reflecting on the work. The teacher identifies what went well and
what needs to be improved. To assist in evaluating personal skills, a teacher can use
reflective journals or opportunity thinking. **Opportunity thinking,** a conversation
that one has with oneself as one reflects on events that happened during a particular
situation, allows individuals to evaluate and improve their actions.

Reflective Journal

A **reflective journal** is a personal record of the teaching process from the educator's
perspective. The journal provides an opportunity to record a summary of interactions,
including exchanges that went well, problems that were encountered, and strategies
that were used. Teachers may record ideas that can be tried another time or questions
to consider. A special educator recorded the following passage during her first year of
teaching:

> ### October 2
>
> I met with Dylan's aunt and uncle this afternoon. They have cared for him the
> last 6 to 7 months since he was removed from his biological parents. The uncle
> was very open when talking about the situation. But many times I had to redi-
> rect the uncle back to the actual questions that I posed. He provided a lot of
> detail—because I used a lot of open-ended questions?—but I was able to gather
> information about their concerns and they were looking for some help in
> knowing what to do. They both asked many questions about some of Dylan's
> behaviors and what the child should be doing in school. For next time: I need
> to review typical development for 7-year-olds. Check on community resources
> that are available?

Opportunity Thinking

"I don't know if I'll ever finish this assignment," you may have thought. Or perhaps
you looked at the situation this way: "I'm halfway through . . . I'm doing pretty well."

Many of us engage in a conversation with ourselves as we reflect on a situation. These conversations can be considered opportunity thinking (Manz, 1992, as cited in Cramer, 1998). To examine opportunity thinking more closely, you may want to examine your self-talk:

1. Observe and record your self-talk.
2. Reflect on your observations.
   a. Analyze the thoughts on which your self-talk is based by looking at how functional and constructive your thoughts are.
   b. For each self-talk sentence (or underlying thought) that is defeating, substitute a self-talk sentence or thought that is more functional or constructive.
3. Change your actions.
   a. Substitute your new, more constructive thoughts in difficult situations.
   b. Continue to monitor your self-talk, and the accompanying, underlying thoughts. (Adapted from Neck & Barnard, 1996, p. 26, as cited in Cramer, 1998, p. 193)

WORKING WITH EDUCATORS AND OTHER PROFESSIONALS

❖ PROFESSIONAL PERSPECTIVES ❖

Per Lysaker, an elementary special educator, and Tina Young, a speech and language pathologist, were reviewing the language strategies that Tina would be demonstrating once the children arrived in the resource room. "I'll be using a couple of different techniques to increase language," said Tina. "One strategy is called *expansion*. You'll see me restating some of the students' words and then adding words or more complex phrases. I'll also be using an open-ended questioning technique. This type of questioning moves students away from simple yes/no responses and requires them to think more deeply about their responses." They planned that, first, Tina would work with the students, modeling expansion and questioning while Per observed. Then Per would try out the strategies while Tina observed. She would provide coaching and feedback while Per developed his skills in using these techniques with students.

COLLABORATIVE TEAMING

Collaborative teaming is a process in which two or more individuals work together to enable students to develop their skills and abilities. The IEP team is an example of a team that should be collaborative, but not all collaborative teams are IEP teams. Collaborative teams can include two or more individuals such as special educators, general educators, paraprofessionals, therapists, parents, counselors, adapted physical education specialists, nurses, and others, depending on the needs of the student. Members of collaborative teams discuss problems, assess students' needs, identify solutions, implement plans, and evaluate outcomes.

Snell and Janney (2000, p. 6) describe the characteristics of collaborative team members:

- Support each other, and readily share ideas and resources
- Understand other team members' roles and talents
- Learn to communicate effectively
- Identify and resolve concerns
- Reach consensus on decisions
- Develop trust

Collaborative teaming often leads special educators to consider coteaching.

Coteaching

Coteaching involves collaborating with other professionals in planning and implementing learning activities with students. Coteaching usually takes place in the general education classroom. A special educator may coteach with a classroom teacher or, depending on the needs of students, may coteach with the speech and language pathologist, physical therapist, or occupational therapist. From the literature, Heron and Harris (2001) identify eight components that contribute to coteaching: interpersonal communication, physical arrangement of the classroom, familiarity with the curriculum, curriculum goals, and modification, behavior management, instruction presentation, grading and evaluation, and instructional planning. When professionals plan coteaching activities, they often use one or more different structures such as complementary instruction or role exchange.

Complementary instruction. **Complementary instruction** involves two or more professionals who coteach, each complementing the role of the other, based on individual skills, knowledge, and abilities. During complementary instruction, one individual may assume the lead, with the other playing a supportive role. Later, the roles are reversed. Usually, the general educator maintains primary responsibility for teaching the subject matter and the special educator assumes responsibility for addressing students' specific needs. Figure 10.2 shows the complementary roles of an English teacher and a special education teacher in a high school English class.

Complementary instruction can be a rewarding experience. Educators often report that they gain new ideas for instructional activities and classroom management by working closely with a colleague (Snell & Janney, 2000). Complementary instruction also provides rich opportunities for reflection and self-improvement (Figure 10.3).

However, complementary instruction is not without challenges. Based on a series of observations and interviews with more than 70 general education/special education teams, Vaughn, Schumm, and Arguelles (1997) identified several areas that teachers must address if this method is to be successful:

- *Whose students are these?* The general education teacher is responsible for all of the students in the class, but how do these responsibilities change when the special education teacher is in the room? Who is responsible for the students with special needs in the general education classroom, and when do these responsibilities change?
- *Who evaluates students' performances and assigns grades?* General educators are accustomed to grading based on a uniform set of expectations. Making joint decisions and developing guidelines for grading, such as a joint reporting system, will reduce potential problems.

Figure 10.2   Coteaching complementary roles in a high school English class

The English Teacher:	The Special Education Teacher:
• Reviews the past 2 days	• Takes roll silently
• Introduces discussion of questions completed on homework	• Gives student locker pass
• Locates materials for a student	• Assists student in locating materials
• Leads discussion of each question, including reading the question, calling on students for the answers, probing for more in-depth responses, reinforcing students for their comments, and writing responses on the board	• Walks around room to check for completed homework; makes record in grade book
	• Restates several questions for clarification while checking work
	• Takes over duty of recording answers on board
• Moves around room continuing to question	• Prompts student to read aloud
• Questions a detail that requires students to locate an answer in book	• Locates passage in student's book
	• Prompts student to read aloud
• Calls on student to reread for clarification	• Prompts student to attend to discussion
• Continues to lead discussion of questions, reinforcing students for their answers	• Adds details to discussion
	• Walks around room with eyes on students' books to be sure all are on correct page
• Prompts a student to behave	• Helps a student find the correct page
• Tells students when to expect a turn to answer when several students want to answer a question	• Continues board note-taking: verbally reinforces student
	• Quietly prompts student to behave
• Continues to lead class discussion	• Checks student's notes for clarity
• Wraps up discussion, reinforces everyone's effort	• Restates point from a different perspective
	• Writes assignment on board
• Announces the reading of "Old Demon" for homework	• Prompts student to write down assignment
• Announces quiz on this story	• Writes "QUIZ" on board
• Provides alternative assignments for students who need them	• Reminds teacher that two students need alternate assignments to replace missed assignments
	• Records alternative assignments

Source: Snell, M. E., & Janney, R. (2000). "Teaching Collaboratively." In *Collaborative Teaming: Teachers' Guides to Inclusive Practices* (p. 96). Baltimore: Paul H. Brookes Publishing Co. Reprinted by permission of M. E. Snell and the publisher.

- *Whose classroom management rules are used?* When should the special education teacher step in to assist with classroom management? Coteachers should discuss, negotiate, and agree on ways of managing behavior problems and the roles they would like each other to assume.
- *What are students told?* Do students have two teachers? The students should be informed that they have two teachers and that both teachers have the same authority. Many students who have participated in classrooms where coteaching has occurred report that they like having two teachers rather than one.
- *What are parents told?* Parents should be brought in early as part of the planning process in preparing to coteach.

Figure 10.3   Challenges of coteaching: A teacher's perspective

"The most difficult problem that my coteacher and I faced throughout the year was finding time during the school day to plan, discuss instruction, and collaborate on student progress. We found it necessary to designate a specific time and place each day to meet and limit the time so as not to take time away from other planning responsibilities. Many times we felt rushed and not thoroughly prepared. In addition, I believe that it is absolutely imperative that coteachers believe in the collaborative process and the inclusive setting, as well as have the ability and flexibility to work well with others.

"There were times when we disagreed, and we learned to compromise and sometimes give the final decision to the other teacher. Our classroom management styles were also different, but we learned to find a compromise that worked for both of us. Most important, I think that it was critical to inform our students of what we were doing and why. Our students understood that they would have two teachers, with equal authority and with whom they would have equal opportunities to work. Many of my students expressed that having two teachers is better because everyone gets more help."

Source: Adapted from "A Passion for Action Research," by N. L. Langerock, *TEACHING Exceptional Children, 33*(2), 2000, pp. 26–34. Copyright © 2000 by the Council for Exceptional Children. Reprinted with permission.

• *How can teachers have time to coplan?* Teachers need uninterrupted time each week for planning. Some teacher teams designate a day or a half day every 6 to 8 weeks to plan, identify changes to be implemented, and discuss student progress.

Role exchange. **Role exchange** is a process used during coteaching activities that enables one individual to mentor another in developing new professional skills. The experienced individual works with a group of students to demonstrate a particular teaching strategy while the other person observes. Afterward, they discuss the activity and reverse roles, with the mentor providing coaching and feedback. Special educators may exchange roles with other educators or other professionals. For example, a physical therapist may demonstrate therapeutic positioning for students when they are completing an activity while seated or when sitting on the floor; an occupational therapist may show how to use sensory integration therapy, techniques that help a student focus on the instructional activity during small-group work. In Professional Perspectives on page 335, we saw how Per, the special educator, and Tina, the speech and language pathologist, used role exchange in the resource room.

Consulting

In addition to collaborative teaming, special educators may spend a portion of their time consulting. **Consulting** is an interactive process in which individuals with specific areas of expertise come together for the purpose of generating solutions to mutually defined problems (adapted from Idol, Nevin, & Paolucci-Whitcomb, 2000). They work together to discuss questions and concerns about students with disabilities, to brainstorm ideas, to implement suggestions, and to evaluate their effectiveness. Consulting differs from simple collaboration because here suggestions are generated, implemented, and evaluated. Consulting involves an expert model of problem solving rather than the mutual problem solving used in collaboration. Teachers may use a written form to initiate the request for consultation (Figure 10.4). While most special educators spend at least some of their time consulting with classroom teachers, therapists, and other professionals and paraprofessionals, others work exclusively as consultants.

Figure 10.4 Request for consultation

Request for Consultation

Date: _Nov. 2_

Student's name: _Terri Lindstrom_

Grade: _2_ Date of birth: _February 21_

Referring teacher: _Mr. Ferrachi_

Available times for consultation: _Any Monday or Wednesday after school_

Please mark the appropriate area(s) below. Briefly summarize questions and concerns.

Academic areas	Questions and concerns
❏ Reading	_Terri is having a great deal of difficulty in remembering letter sounds and recognizes only a handful of sight words._
❏ Language arts	_Her printing is very difficult to read, and she has trouble copying some letters. She doesn't seem to understand the use of spacing between words._
❏ Mathematics	
❏ Science	
❏ Social studies	
❏ Art	
❏ Music	
❏ Physical education	

Behavior	Comments
❏ Activity level	_Terri is constantly on the move and is beginning to disrupt the other children during work time._
❏ Adaptability	
❏ Distractibility	
❏ Intensity of emotional reactions	_She is easily distracted._
❏ Mood	
❏ Motivation	_She is beginning to lose interest in reading activities, especially when independent work is expected of the children._
❏ Oppositional behavior	
❏ Self-direction	
❏ Social skills	

Briefly describe the classroom interventions that you have tried and the results.

I have been using peer coaching for reading. By pairing Terri with a friend who is a better reader, I hoped that this would increase her skill level as well as her motivation. Although she likes working with others, I find that she is not making progress. Also, I am concerned about the behaviors that Terri has recently exhibited and how best to address them.

Using Technology
Enhancing Communication

Lack of time to meet on a regular basis, scheduling difficulties, and meetings that feel rushed are all major stumbling blocks in working with others. Busy teachers find that technology can alleviate some of these problems while providing a means of efficient communication. For example, in the course of a typical day:

- The classroom teacher sends an e-mail copy of upcoming student assignments to the special educator.
- A resource room teacher sends the occupational therapist an attached file with observations completed on a student with whom they are both working.
- A team member sends other team members a revised draft of a planned unit through the school's e-mail list.
- A special educator clicks on an electronic planner connected to the

school network to view staff schedules and identify a common meeting day for an IEP meeting.

Questions for Reflection

1. What technologies do you use to communicate with your professors, colleagues, family, and friends? Which technology do you feel most confident using?
2. What technologies do families in your community most commonly use? Are some technologies accessible to most families? Only a few families?

 To answer these questions and learn more about using technology to support learning, go to the Companion Website at www.prenhall.com/cohen, select Chapter 10, then choose Using Technology.

WORKING WITH PARAPROFESSIONALS

Frequently, beginning teachers find that they are working side by side with experienced paraprofessionals or teacher assistants. In fact, both new and experienced teachers may have the responsibility of supervising paraprofessionals' work, providing on-the-job training, and giving and receiving feedback from experienced assistants (Morgan & Ashbaker, 2001). These responsibilities may present difficulties, such as supervising an adult who has more experience in the classroom than the teacher. In the following section, we will examine the research and some strategies that educators use to create positive working relationships with paraprofessionals.

Working with and supervising paraprofessionals involves both administrative and management skills. In a survey of over 500 administrators, teachers, and paraprofessionals, Wallace et al. (2001) identified seven competencies that educators need. Educators need to communicate with paraprofessionals to share student-related information and explain the role of the paraprofessional. They must coordinate schedules, establish goals, set plans, establish time for planning, and consider the strengths and interests of paraprofessionals when aligning tasks. Educators should provide regular feedback regarding each paraprofessional's work performance, support paraprofessionals in providing instruction to students, and

Special educators work with and supervise paraprofessionals.

provide support and direction to paraprofessionals who work in independent capacities. Through modeling, educators demonstrate a caring and respectful manner when interacting with students. Educators should inform administrators, teachers, and parents of the responsibilities and roles paraprofessionals have in the educational program, and should advocate for the paraprofessional regarding training and leave time, modifications of responsibility, involvement in decision groups, and so on. Educators should provide on-the-job training for skill development. Finally, they should maintain regular positive and supportive interactions with paraprofessionals and contribute to the evaluation of paraprofessionals' performance (adapted from Wallace et al., 2001).

PLANNING AND SCHEDULING

Special education teachers have responsibilities for planning and managing instruction for students with disabilities, identifying accommodations and modifications, and participating on the IEP team. According to IDEA, paraprofessionals who are adequately trained and supervised may assist in the delivery of special education and related services [Sec. 300.136 (f)]. To help reduce potential problems, the teacher can ask school administrators and paraprofessionals to meet and discuss teaching and classroom responsibilities. Clarifying roles decreases the likelihood of misunderstandings as the year goes on and strengthens collaboration and teamwork.

Because classrooms are such busy places, teachers and paraprofessionals often have difficulty finding time to plan how they will coordinate their work in the classroom unless it is a scheduled activity. Rueda and Monzó (2000) found that lack of planning time allowed little time for paraprofessionals to ask questions of teachers and for teachers to assist paraprofessionals in developing effective teaching strategies. Both groups indicated that more opportunities for teacher-paraprofessional interaction would be very beneficial. One solution is to identify regular meeting times and to follow a schedule. These meetings help enable communication, joint planning, negotiation, and consensus.

INSTRUCTIONAL SUPPORT

Once the IEP team has met and developed the IEP, the special education teacher and classroom teacher work to implement the program along with paraprofessionals and other professionals. Although paraprofessionals do not participate in writing the IEP, they often are the individuals who work most closely with students and are responsible for carrying out the instruction under the supervision of the teacher.

The special educator or case manager, who may be a special educator, assumes the coordination responsibilities, making sure that paraprofessionals have the knowledge and skills to carry out the instruction. Some schools use a system that places a paraprofessional at a particular level of responsibility, depending on the person's education and/or experience (Table 10.1). These levels are often tied to the paraprofessional's amount of college coursework and salary. Using Table 10.1, select a level and consider how you would coordinate your work and that of a paraprofessional in your classroom.

Once an IEP is written, teachers and paraprofessionals carefully go over the student's goals and objectives to discuss how they will be carried out. On a regular basis, the teacher and paraprofessional confer on the teaching and learning activities, reflecting on strategies that worked well and discussing changes that needed to be implemented. Together, they regularly monitor the student's progress. Let us revisit some special educators we met in Chapter 1 to see what these activities consist of.

❖ VISITING WITH JOY LU ❖

Joy Lu, a special education teacher at Suncreek Elementary School, was working with the fifth-grade teacher on a civics unit. During their weekly planning sessions Joy, the classroom teacher, and the paraprofessional carefully reviewed the planned activities. They discussed the fact that once the small-group activities began, they would move among the groups, assisting individual students as needed. Joy described her concerns about the special needs of Tony, a student with ADHD. She talked about the need to monitor Tony's progress and be ready to offer support, structure, and redirection as needed for him to complete the activities with his group.

❖ VISITING WITH JOHN BATES ❖

When we last visited John's resource room, he was reviewing his schedule for the day. Now let's see what happened next. Before the students arrived, he met with the teaching assistant to review progress notes on the students and to discuss any

Table 10.1	Examples of Paraprofessional Roles and Responsibilities	
Level	**Job Title**	**Typical Classroom Responsibilities**
Level One	Teacher aide	• Prepare materials, set up classroom equipment and learning centers.
		• Assist students with disabilities with personal and hygienic care.
		• Reinforce lessons initiated by the teacher.
		• Escort students from classrooms to resource rooms and other programs.
Level Two	Instructional assistant, teacher assistant	• Tutor individual students using instructional objectives and lessons developed by teachers or other professional personnel. • Assist with supplementary work for students and supervise independent study. • Assist the teacher by observing, recording, and charting information about student performance or behavior. • Implement behavioral management strategies using the same emphasis and techniques as those of teachers and other professional personnel. • Assist teachers with crisis problems and discipline. • Assist with the preparation of materials for use in specific instructional programs. • Attend IEP or staff meetings at the request of teachers or administrative personnel.
Level Three	Instructional assistant, teacher assistant	• Supervise students in community learning environments. • Select and use appropriate instructional techniques, including reinforcement, cueing, prompting, modeling, and fading. • Record and share information about student performance and progress with teachers and therapists. • Organize and schedule classroom activities and maintain a safe environment.

Source: Adapted from *Paraprofessionals in the Education Workforce,* by A. L. Pickett, 1995.

adjustments that should be made to the planned teaching and learning activities for the day. Several of the students had been using laptops for their writing logs but were having difficulty using the speech output features. John turned to the laptop on his desk, and together he and the teaching assistant went over the procedure for using the software program. They decided that the teaching assistant would create cue cards describing each step for the students to use and would work individually with students who continued to have difficulty.

WORKING WITH PARENTS

Parents need access to meaningful information about their child's work and progress (President's Commission on Excellence in Special Education, 2002). Working with parents as partners in their child's education requires educators to have good inter-personal and communication skills. Let us examine how educators can develop these skills.

DEVELOPING COMMUNICATION SKILLS

Interacting with parents and others requires effective communication skills. Communication includes talking and listening, as well as using and interpreting non-verbal messages. Communication also involves writing, such as composing an informal note or e-mail message, which requires skills in written expression to convey a message without the benefit of immediate feedback from the receiver. More formal communications include synthesizing information and composing periodic written reports or end-of-year evaluation summaries concerning student progress.

Teachers communicate with parents to share their observations of the student's academic achievement and behavioral progress, and to notify parents when the student is experiencing problems and having success. Communications should be open, polite, and diplomatic. Effective communicators present their concerns in a clear, precise manner and provide examples. Sensitivity to feelings helps create a positive atmosphere. Use reflection to demonstrate understanding and acknowledgment of a person's feelings: "I understand that this situation is stressful for you." Clarify by restating: "It sounds like you usually observe this behavior in the morning." Use direct language, avoiding educational jargon such as "I'll call the SAT, ASAP."

Seeking Information and Clarifying Interactions

Asking questions is a primary way of seeking more information and clarifying interactions. Teachers use a variety of questions for different purposes. Friend and Cook (1999) identify three different types:

1. *Questions that seek information.* This is the most common type of question. For example, a special educator asks the teacher assistant, "What problem behaviors did you see during free time?" to obtain information about student behaviors while she was out of the room.

2. *Questions that provide information.* A teacher sometimes uses questions to provide information to another individual by attempting to guide action by giving suggestions. A special educator asks, "What do you think would happen if you gave Cindi only one set of directions at a time?"

3. *Questions that clarify or confirm information.* Teachers use this type of question to clarify information that may not be fully understood, such as "What did you mean when you said that you are not in favor of extended school year programming for Jose?"

Questioning Techniques

A teacher's skill in using different questioning techniques greatly affects the amount of information that is provided. Questions may be open- or closed-ended, direct or indirect. Open-ended questions have a large number of possible answers. For example, a special educator says to a new classroom teacher, "I'm so happy that Samantha is going to be in your classroom this year. What are some ways that I could help you?" A small number of answers characterizes closed-ended questions, as in the following example. The special educator says to a new classroom teacher, "Do you want me to help you in planning for Samantha?" Sometimes, though, the situation calls for closed-ended questions. The special educator continues the conversation by saying, "Would you prefer to meet before or after school?"

The questions that have been used so far are examples of direct questions. Indirect questioning can be very useful at times, because the listener is not required to provide an answer. Indirect questions do not put anyone on the spot. For example, "It would be interesting to know if Samantha could participate in the small-group activity without the assistance of the teacher assistant."

Communicating Electronically

Communicating electronically, either through e-mail or through information posted on a class website, involves adopting and practicing effective communication strategies. In electronic communication, word choice can affect meaning, organization can affect clarity, and typographical techniques can emphasize ideas (Schultz, 2000). Using electronic communication involves levels of preparation similar to those of a phone call or face-to-face meeting, as well as additional types of preparation. First, the educator determines the purpose of the message and the information to be conveyed. Once the text has been composed, the educator reviews the information for organization, content, and appropriate tone. Let's take a look at the following e-mail examples composed and sent by a busy educator. What do you think the parent's response will be to message 1? To message 2?

Message 1

Dear Mrs. A.,

Tried to reach you several times by phone today. Need to set time for fall parent conference. Is 3:30 on the 21st or 4:30 on the 22nd best for you?

Ms. S.

Message 2

Dear Mrs. A.,

We are making plans for our annual fall parent conferences the week of the 21st, and I am writing in the hope that you can let me know which of two times would be best for you. The dates available are Monday the 21st at 3:30 or Tuesday the 22nd at 4:30. I look forward to talking with you about Jon's work. Could you let me know as soon as possible which time would be more convenient for you?

Sincerely,
Ms. S.

Active Listening

Being able to express oneself is one aspect of communication; listening is another. Teachers who use active listening send the message that the conversation is important. Active listening consists of hearing and responding to the words that the speaker uses. Individuals who use active listening offer relevant comments to the conversation, and they ask the speaker to provide an example when they are not sure that they understand. Active listening involves putting aside one's own agenda to hear what the other person is saying.

Conducting an effective parent-teacher conference involves preparation and planning.

Table 10.2	Examples of Misconceptions During Communication	
Misconceptions	**Cultural Explanations**	
Parents are passive	May require time to consider and discuss issues	
Do not respond during discussion	Verbal (Yes, um-hmm) or nonverbal (nodding) responses may not be part of culture	
Lack interest or are preoccupied	May not make eye contact due to respect for authority	
Do not ask questions	Sign of respect for school decision making process	
Passively accept suggestions, do not disagree or give personal opinion	Hesitate to practice personal rights	
Show discomfort when complimented	Avoid attention to self	
Appear uncomfortable when greeted	Touching may be unacceptable	

Source: From Alper, Sandra, Schloss, Patrick, and Schloss, Cynthia N. *Families of Students with Disabilities: Consultation and Advocacy.* Published by Allyn and Bacon, Boston, MA Copyright © 1994 by Pearson Education. Reprinted by permission of the publisher.

Positive nonverbal communication helps others feel comfortable and willing to share ideas and concerns. Posture, gestures, eye contact, a tilt of the head, or a brief frown all send messages. The burden of interpretation is on the receiver. Nonverbal communication is often difficult to decipher because it is subtle and culture-bound; yet, with the increasing number of students from linguistically diverse cultures, teachers should acquire sensitivity to these messages as well. Sometimes a nonverbal message can be misunderstood. Examples of common misconceptions among educators include seeming lack of interest or lack of response on the part of the parent when in fact that is not the case (Table 10.2).

CONDUCTING PARENT CONFERENCES

Special educators conduct many parent conferences during the year as they build partnerships with students' families. Some conferences are informal and occur during schoolwide parent conference evenings; other conferences are scheduled because the teacher or parent has concerns about the progress of the student. During parent conferences, teachers share examples of student work, discuss progress, raise concerns, and problem-solve solutions. These conferences allow parents to share their observations, questions, and concerns with their child's teachers, too.

Conducting a parent conference requires preparation and planning. Before the conference, the teacher assembles examples of the student's work and summarizes the academic, social, and behavioral strengths and concerns of the student. For example, a special educator may prepare a written record, create a graph of progress in reading and math, and summarize behavioral observations in a chart.

If the parent requires an interpreter or a translator, arrangements must be made well in advance of the conference. When the parent arrives, the teacher thanks the parent for coming and talks informally before beginning the conference in order to establish rapport. For example, one special educator begins by saying, "Hola [hello], Mrs. Rodriguez, thanks for taking time to come in this afternoon. I have been looking forward to our meeting. Your daughter Maria speaks of you often." If English is not the home language of the family, the teacher may attempt to learn and use a few words in the family's native language.

At the beginning, educators review the conference agenda, including the time limits for the conference, and describe the expected outcomes. Reviewing the conference process relieves stress and helps keep the conference moving in a positive direction. For example, the teacher begins: "First, I am going to ask you to share with me what you have observed about Maria this year that makes you feel good about your child's progress." As the parent conference continues, the teacher will ask the parent to discuss any questions or concerns. Effective listening is especially critical. Listening is a primary way of not only gaining information but also conveying interest in what the parent is saying (Friend & Cook, 1992). Together the teacher and parent review examples of the student's work, and the teacher shares classroom observations of the student. As the conference draws to a close, the teacher summarizes what they discussed, including the next steps, and thanks the parent for coming. The teacher may inquire about the best ways to keep in touch during the year.

More formal conferences are part of the IEP process and involve the IEP team members. These meetings also provide an opportunity to build strong partnerships with parents. Educators can take an active role by greeting family members, making introductions, and helping them feel welcome. Figure 10.5 provides an extensive list of further suggestions for best practice.

Keeping in Touch

Finding the best ways to keep in touch during the school year helps build effective teacher-parent partnerships (Figure 10.6). In addition to planned meetings, teachers use phone calls and written communications such as e-mail or rotating notebooks between home and school to stay in touch.

WORKING WITH COMMUNITY PARTNERS

Special educators often reach outside the classroom to work with community partners. Being an effective teacher involves knowing these community connections. In Chapter 9 we saw how special educators work closely with mental health professionals in local and regional community agencies. For example, when students with severe behavior problems have needs beyond the capacity of the school, special educators work closely with social workers, mental health counselors, psychologists, and consulting psychiatrists.

Figure 10.5   Best practices for IEP conferences

Preconference Preparation

- Appoint a service coordinator to organize all aspects of the IEP conference.
- Solicit information from the family about their preferences and needs regarding the conference.
- Discuss the meeting with the student and consider his or her preferences concerning the conference.
- Decide who should attend the conference and include the student, if appropriate.
- Arrange a convenient time and location for the meeting.
- Assist families with logistical needs such as transportation and child care.
- Without educational jargon, inform the family verbally and/or in writing of the following:
- Explain the purpose of the meeting.
- State the time and location of the conference.
- Give the names of participants.
- Share information the family wants before the conference.
- Encourage the student, family members, and their advocates to visit the proposed placements for the student before the conference.
- Encourage families to share information and discuss concerns with participants before the conference.
- Gather needed information from school personnel.
- Prepare an agenda to cover the remaining components of the IEP conference.

Initial Conference Proceedings

- Greet the students, family, and their advocates.
- Provide a list of all participants or use name tags.
- Introduce each participant with a brief description of his or her role in the conference.
- State the purpose of the meeting. Review the agenda, and ask for additional issues to be covered.

- Determine the amount of time participants have available for the conference and offer the option of rescheduling if needed to complete the agenda.
- Ask if family members desire clarification of their legal rights.

Review of Formal Evaluation and Current Levels of Performance

- Provide family members with a written copy of evaluation results if desired.
- Avoid educational jargon as much as possible, and clarify diagnostic terminology throughout the conference.
- If a separate evaluation conference has not been scheduled, ask diagnostic personnel to report the following:
  - What tests were administered?
  - What were the results of each?
  - What are the options based on the evaluation?
  - Summarize the findings, including strengths, gifts, abilities, and needs.
  - Identify implications of test results for involvement and progress in the general curriculum and extracurricular activities.
  - Ask all participants for areas of agreement and disagreement with corresponding reasons.
  - Proceed with the IEP only when consensus is reached about the student's exceptionality and current levels of performance.

Development of Annual Goals and Objectives

- Encourage the student, family members, and advocates to share their expectations for the student's participation in the home, school (including general curriculum), and community.
- Collaboratively generate appropriate annual goals and objectives for all subject areas requiring special instruction consistent with expectations.
- Discuss annual goals and objectives for future educational and vocational options based on great expectations for the student.
- Identify objectives to expand the positive contributions the student can make to family, friends, and community.

continued

Figure 10.5   Best practices for IEP conferences *continued*

- Prioritize all annual goals and objectives in light of student preferences and needs.
- Discuss and specify transition plans at age fourteen (needs statement), sixteen (needed transition services; inter-agency responsibilities); and at least one year before age of majority (student rights for decision making when student becomes of age).
- Clarify the manner in which the responsibility for teaching the objectives will be shared among the student's teachers.
- Ask family members and advocates if they would like to share in the responsibility for teaching some of the objectives at home or in the community.
- Determine evaluation procedures and schedules for identified annual goals and objectives and how the student's parents will be informed at least as often as parents of students without disabilities are informed.
- Discuss and specify any individual modifications in the administration of state or district assessments of student achievement; if the committee determines the student will not participate in the assessment, state the rationale.
- Explain to family members and advocates that the IEP is not a guarantee that the student will attain the goals; rather, it represents a good-faith effort on the part of school personnel that they will teach these goals and objectives.

Determination of Placement and Related Services

- Discuss the benefits and drawbacks of viable placement options.

- Select a placement option that allows the student to be involved with peers without exceptionalities as much as possible.
- Agree on a tentative placement until the student and family can visit and confirm its appropriateness.
- Discuss and specify the supplementary aids and services that will be provided to enable the student to be successful in the general education curriculum, extracurricular activities, and nonacademic activities.
- Specify the extent the student will *not* be participating in general education curriculum, extracurricular activities, and nonacademic activities.
- Discuss the benefits and drawbacks of modes of delivery for related services the student needs.
- Specify the dates for initiating related services and anticipated duration, frequency, and location of each.
- Share with family members and advocates the names and qualifications of all personnel who will provide services.

Concluding the Conference

- Assign follow-up responsibility for any tasks requiring attention.
- Summarize orally and on paper the major decisions and follow-up responsibilities of all participants.
- Set a tentative date for reviewing the IFSP/IEP document.
- Identify strategies for ongoing communication among participants.
- Express appreciation to all participants for their help in the decision-making process.

Source: From *Families, Professionals, and Exceptionality: Collaborating for Empowerment,* 4th ed. (pp. 271–73), by A. P. Turnbull and H. R. Turnbull, © 2001. Reprinted by permission of Pearson Education, Inc., Upper Saddle River, NJ.

Figure 10.6   Ways of keeping in touch

October 25

Dear *Ms. Thomas,*

I am very pleased to be working with *Jared* this year and I am looking forward to keeping in touch with you concerning his progress. Could you let me know which of the following would work best for you?

Many thanks,

Ms. Campbell Steel

___ I'd like to come to school to meet with you. Days and times that work best for me are:_____

___ I'd like to write in and read a notebook that travels in my child's backpack.

___I'd like phone calls at home. Days and times that work best for me are:_____

___I'd like to use e-mail. My address is:_____

___I'd like to talk when I pick my child up after school. Days and times that work best for me are:_____   _____

___I'd like to visit the classroom. Days and times that work best for me are:_____

Source: Adapted from *Collaborative Teaming: Teachers' Guide to Inclusive Practices* (p. 56), by M. E. Snell and R. Janney, 2000, Baltimore: Paul H. Brookes.

When students enter middle school and to a greater extent high school, special educators work closely with professionals in rehabilitation services. For students who will be transitioning from school to work or postsecondary education, the special educator may work with a job coach or rehabilitation counselor. Together they will ensure that the student makes a successful transition from school.

Using Technology
National Organizations That Support Families

Federally funded parent centers in each state provide training and information to parents of preschoolers, school-age children, and young adults with disabilities. These services, offered at no charge, help parents participate more effectively in their child's education. To reach the parent center in your state, you can conduct an Internet search or contact the Technical Assistance Alliance for Parent Centers (the Alliance), the agency that coordinates the delivery of technical assistance to the Parent Training and Information Centers and the Community Parent Resource Centers through four regional centers located in California, New Hampshire, Texas, and Ohio. Educators and other professionals who work with children with disabilities may also take advantage of information provided by parent centers and other national organizations that support families (Table 10.3).

Table 10.3	National Organizations That Support Families		
	Parent Advocacy Coalition for Educational Rights Center (PACER)	Parent training organization based on parents of children with disabilities helping other parents of children with disabilities	Information on: * general and special education * multicultural services, including those dealing with language and cultural issues * early childhood intervention * transition to adult life
	Technical Assistance Alliance for Parent Centers	Supports parent training and information centers in each state	Information on a wide variety of topics
	National Information Center for Children and Youth with Disabilities (NICHCY)	Provides information to parents, teachers, and administrators	Information on: * specific disabilities * links to people with common concerns * a vast library of downloadable products

Questions for Reflection

1. How would you use the information available through the parent center in your state to assist you in working with families?

2. Compare and contrast the online information available from other national organizations (Table 10.3). What information did you find helpful to you? What information do you think would be of most interest to parents?

 To answer these questions and learn more about using technology to support learning, go to the Companion Website at www.prenhall.com/cohen, select Chapter 10, then choose Using Technology.

Research to Practice

School, Home, and Community Partnerships

For students with disabilities, many research findings attest to the benefits of partnerships and collaboration of school, family, and community (Catalano, Loeber, & McKinney, 1999; Kober, 2002; McEvoy & Welker, 2000; Van Acker & Wehby, 2000). In planning partnerships with families, educators must reach out to both parents. In a study that examined the involvement of fathers in the special education programs of their children (ages 5 to 16), fathers reported that they did not receive the communication from the school or the teacher that they needed (League & Ford, 1996). Partnerships with parents are also important to the students themselves. One study, involving 112 adolescents who were receiving special education services, addressed students' perceptions of home and school partnership practices. Findings of this study indicated that parents' monitoring of and involvement in their children's learning activities predicted students' time spent on homework and students' grades (Deslandes, Royer, Potvin, & Leclerc, 1999).

School partnerships with community groups also increase student achievement. Students with emotional and behavioral disabilities showed a significant improvement in reading achievement over time in schools that were involved in restructuring activities, including the use of mental health services (Kutash et al., 2001).

Questions for Reflection

1. Create a list of examples of school, home, and community partnerships. Share your findings with the class.

2. What might be additional outcomes for students who attend schools with strong home and community partnerships?

 To answer these questions and learn more about applying research to practice, go to the Companion Website at www.prenhall. com/cohen, select Chapter 10, then choose Research to Practice.

Considering Diversity

Community Partnerships

Professional partnerships provide teachers with opportunities to build bridges across cultural communities. Large school districts sometimes employ individuals in the community to work in schools as community–school consultants. These individuals typically help answer questions about community customs, connect a teacher with community resources, or come to the classroom to share information with students.

In smaller school districts, teachers or paraprofessionals may take on this role. Frequently, paraprofessionals live in the cultural community and share common experiences with students. Because teachers and paraprofessionals work closely as a team, the paraprofessional can provide the teacher with information and connections to other community resources.

Paraprofessionals also can serve as a bridge for students between home and school. Rueda and DeNeve (2001) found that paraprofessionals use interesting classroom strategies and provide "comfort zones" to help students learn and develop motivation in the classroom. They observed paraprofessionals using subtle strategies, such as a hand on the shoulder at a strategic moment, and less subtle strategies, such as the use of locally meaningful phrases. For example, a paraprofessional might often call a student "*mijo*," which is an affectionate term often used by Latino parents, meaning "my little one" (p. 5).

Questions for Reflection

1. How might a community consultant assist you in your teaching?
2. What are some of the benefits for schools that employ community consultants?

To answer these questions and deepen your understanding of diversity in schools and communities, go to the Companion Website at www.prenhall.com/cohen, select Chapter 10, then choose Considering Diversity.

SUMMARY

- Teaching students with learning and behavior problems is a shared responsibility.
- Some individuals seem to have a natural talent for solving problems and settling conflicts, but most of us need to practice skills in communicating effectively and resolving conflicts.
- Many of the skills that we must learn must also be taught to our students. They, too, need to communicate effectively with their peers.

EXTENDING LEARNING

1. Working with two or three of your classmates, prepare a list of potential cross-cultural concerns in home–school relationships. What community and national resources are

available to improve educator–parent partnerships? To start your list of resources, you can evaluate the website of the National Network of Partnership Schools.

2. You are beginning a new teaching position and have a paraprofessional to assist you in the classroom. Working with a partner, identify several questions that you will ask the paraprofessional. How will you begin a dialogue about the responsibilities that each of you will assume? With your partner, take turns assuming each role. Afterward, critique your performance and identify changes in your script that you would suggest.

3. Develop several interview questions for a special educator regarding working with others. For example, you might ask the educator to describe a difficult problem and how it was resolved. Arrange to conduct an interview and share the results with the class.

4. Lorrie and Paula, both special educators at Townsend Elementary School, worked in adjoining resource rooms. As a new teacher, Lorrie initially tried to be friendly with Paula but gradually discontinued her efforts as the year went on. Another teacher told Lorrie that Paula had been complaining about her and her work with students, although Paula had not confronted Lorrie with her concerns. If you were Lorrie, what would you do?

5. Plan a parent conference for one of the following students in your classroom: Juan, whose home language is Spanish; Tanya, who recently was adopted from Eastern Europe; or Taylor, who recently transferred to your classroom. Be sure to describe any special considerations.

REFERENCES

Alper, S. K., Schloss, P. J., & Schloss, C. N. (1994). *Families of students with disabilities: Consultation and advocacy*. Boston: Allyn & Bacon.

Bell, J. A. (2001). High-performing, high-poverty schools. *Leadership, 31*(1), 8–11.

Catalano, R. F., Loeber, R., & McKinney, K. C. (1999). School and community interventions to prevent serious and violent offending. *Juvenile Justice Bulletin*, 1–12. Washington, DC: Office of Juvenile Justice and Delinquent Prevention.

Cramer, S. (1998). *Collaboration*. Boston: Allyn & Bacon.

DeBoer, A. (1995). *Working together: The art of consulting and communication*. Longmont, CO: Sopris West.

Deslandes, R., Royer, E., Potvin, P., & Leclerc, D. (1999). Patterns of home and school partnership for general and special education students at the secondary level. *Exceptional Children, 65*(4), 496–506.

Friend, M. P., & Cook, L. (1992). *Interactions: Collaborative skills for school professionals* (3rd ed.). Boston: Addison-Wesley.

Gallessich, J. (1982). *The profession and practice of consultation*. San Francisco: Jossey-Bass.

Heron, T. E., & Harris, K. C. (2001). *The educational consultant* (4th ed.). Austin, TX: PRO-ED.

Idol, L., Nevin, A., & Paolucci-Whitcomb, P. (2000). *Collaborative consultation* (3rd ed.). Austin, TX: PRO-ED.

Klein, M. D., & Chen, D. (2001). *Working with children from culturally diverse backgrounds.* Albany, NY: Delmar.

Kober, N. (2002). *Twenty-five years of educating children with disabilities: The good news and the work ahead.* Washington, DC: American Youth Policy Forum. (ERIC Document Reproduction Service No. ED464450)

Kroeger, S. D., Leibold, C. K., & Ryan, R. (1999). Creating a sense of ownership in the IEP process. *TEACHING Exceptional Children, 32*(1), 4–9.

Kutash, K., Duchnowski, A. J., Kip, S., Oliveira, B., Greeson, M., Harris, K., & Sheffield, S. (2001). *School reform efforts for children with emotional disturbances and their families.* Tampa, FL: Research and Training Center for Children's Mental Health. (ERIC Document Reproduction Service No. ED465251)

Langerock, N. L. (2000). A passion for action research. *TEACHING Exceptional Children, 33*(2), 26–34.

League, S. E., & Ford, L. (1996). *Fathers' involvement in their children's special education program.* Presented at the annual meeting of the National Association of School Psychologists, Atlanta, GA. (ERIC Document Reproduction Service No. ED400632)

Manz, C. C. (1992). *Mastering self-leadership.* Upper Saddle River, NJ: Prentice Hall.

McEvoy, A., & Welker, R. (2000). Antisocial behavior, academic failure, and school climate: A critical review. *Journal of Emotional and Behavioral Disorders, 8,* 130–140.

Morgan, J., & Ashbaker, B. Y. (2001). *A teacher's guide to working with paraeducators and other classroom aides.* Alexandria, VA: Association for Supervision and Curriculum Development.

Neck, C. P., & Barnard, A. W. H. (1996). Managing your mind: What are you telling yourself? *Educational Leadership, 53,* 24–27.

Pickett, A. L. (1995). *Paraprofessionals in the education workforce.* Retrieved October 6, 2001, from http:www.nea.org/esp/resource/parawork.htm

President's Commission on Excellence in Special Education. (2002). *A new era: Revitalizing special education for children and their families.* Retrieved July 16, 2002, from http://www.ed.gov/inits/commissionsboards/whspecialeducation/index.html

Rudo, Z. H., Achacoso, M., & Perez, D. (2000). *Collaborative action team process: Bringing home, school, community, and students together to improve results for children and families.* Final research report. Austin, TX: Southwest Educational Development Lab.

Rueda, R. S., & DeNeve, C. (2001). *How paraeducators build cultural bridges in diverse classroom.* Retrieved October 6, 2001, from http://www.usc.edu/dept/education/CMMR/paraed/Rueda_DeNeve_article.html

Rueda, R. S., & Monzó, L. D. (2000). *Apprenticeship for teaching: Professional development issues surrounding the collaborative relationship between teachers and paraeducators.* Retrieved December 18, 2001, from http://www.cal.org/crede/pubs/research/RR8.htm

Schultz, H. (2000). *The elements of electronic communication. The elements of composition series.* Boston: Allyn & Bacon.

Snell, M. E., & Janney, R. (2000). *Collaborative teaming: Teachers' Guides to Inclusive Practices.* Baltimore: Paul H. Brookes.

Stewart, E. C. (1971). *American cultural patterns: A cross-cultural perspective.* Pittsburgh: Regional Council for International Education.

Trimble, S. B., & Peterson, G. W. (2000). *Multiple team structures and student learning in a high risk middle school.* New Orleans: American Educational Research Association. (ERIC Document Reproduction Service No. ED442892)

Trumbull, E., Rothstein-Fisch, C., Greenfield, P. M., & Quiroz, B. (2001). *Bridging cultures between home and school: A guide for teachers.* Mahwah, NJ: Erlbaum.

Turnbull, A. P., & Turnbull, H. R. (1997). Families, professionals and exceptionality: A special partnership (3rd ed.). Upper Saddle River, NJ: Merrill/Prentice Hall.

Van Acker, R. W., & Wehby, J. H. (2000). Exploring the social contexts influencing student success or failure: Introduction. *Preventing School Failure, 44,* 93–96.

Vaughn, S., Schumm, J. S., & Arguelles, M. E. (1997). The ABCDEs of co-teaching. *TEACHING Exceptional Children, 30*(2), 4–10.

Wallace, T., Shin, J., Bartholomay, T., & Stahl, B. J. (2001). Knowledge and skills for teachers supervising the work of paraprofessionals. *Exceptional Children, 67*(4), 520–533.

West, J. F., & Idol, L. (1987). School consultation (Part I): An interdisciplinary perspective on theory, models, and research. *Journal of Learning Disabilities, 20*(7), 388–408.

Curriculum Areas

III

Part

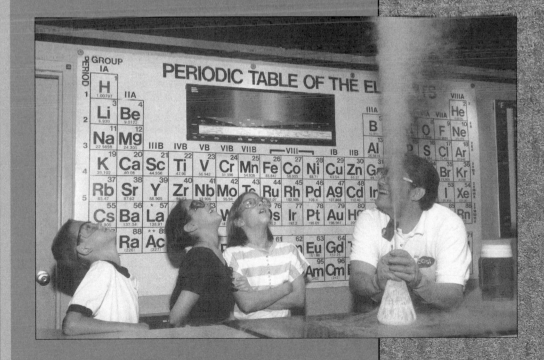

11

Literacy

CHAPTER OBJECTIVES

After completing this chapter, you should be able to:

❖ Describe contemporary perspectives about teaching reading to students with disabilities.

❖ Describe approaches for the assessment of literacy.

❖ Explain how teachers can support students' development of literacy.

❖ Consider the influence of diversity on instruction.

❖ Describe how technology can be used to support reading instruction.

Literacy involves being able to read, write, think, and communicate. Probably no other subject receives as much emphasis in the early grades. As students progress through school, all of them are expected to be literate. In school, literacy is linked to achievement. Once students leave school, the ability to read and write is required in everyday life and is tied to success in many careers, economic level, and personal satisfaction. Yet, many students continue to experience difficulties in learning to be literate.

Reading and writing are reciprocal processes. *Reading* is the process of constructing meaning through interactions that involve the reader's existing knowledge, the text being read, and the context of the reading situation. This chapter focuses on the teaching of reading. Chapter 12 is devoted to a discussion of the teaching of written language.

Contemporary instructional practices stress the link between reading and writing. A great deal is known about how individuals learn to read. Research (Marinak, Moore, Henk, & Keepers, 1997; National Reading Panel, 2000; Snow, Burns, & Griffin, 1998) indicates that reading develops in social situations, involving the interaction of students, educators, and family. Reading requires the restructuring, application, and flexible use of knowledge in new situations. Skilled readers use a range of reading strategies independently and flexibly. Knowledge of phonics, phonemic awareness, semantics, syntax, and pragmatics influences the reading process (National Reading Panel, 2000). **Syntax** refers to the order or pattern of words in sentences and phrases. **Pragmatics** focuses on how people use language, signs, and gestures in social situations. Skilled readers integrate what they learn with background information or prior knowledge and apply knowledge, skills, and strategies in constructing meaning.

Research to Practice

Thinking about Technological Literacy

There has been a shift in the concept of what it means to be literate. New approaches to becoming literate go beyond text-based teaching that relies solely on skill-building activities. Technological literacy means more than just using a word processor and the Internet. It involves using technology to access electronic texts and media, communication, learning, and productivity.

Visual and Information Literacy

According to Smolin and Lawless (2003), individuals who are technologically literate understand technology and are comfortable with its use. Teachers should integrate technologies that support this broader concept of literacy. Smolin and Lawless have described two categories of technological literacy: visual literacy and information literacy. *Visual literacy* involves being able to comprehend and produce visual messages. It can be demonstrated through the use, incorporation, and production of digital images that accompany text. *Information literacy* involves knowing when to find information, as well as identifying, locating, evaluating, and using it.

Questions for Reflection

1. Search for examples of visual literacy in children's picture books or on the Internet. Explain how the use of images enhances the comprehension of texts.
2. Identify several sources of information on the Internet. How can knowledge about information literacy support the evaluation of electronic information?
3. Explore definitions, standards, and competencies related to information literacy. How can knowledge about information literacy guide teaching?

 To answer these questions and learn more about using technology to support literacy instruction, go to the Companion Website at www.prenhall.com/cohen, select Chapter 11, then choose Research to Practice.

READING DISABILITIES

Nine-year-old Joseph is embarrassed because he has so much trouble reading. He recognizes individual letters, but he has trouble blending sounds together to form words. Once he is able to blend sounds together, he guesses or uses trial and error to combine the sounds into words. It takes him so long to figure out each word that he frequently forgets what he has read by the time he gets to the end of the sentence. He reads haltingly and slowly.

Brain-based research has found that many individuals who have reading disabilities have disruptions in their brains (D'Arcangelo, 2003). Brain imaging techniques have provided new insights into reading. For example, when children who are typical readers sound out unfamiliar words, front and back areas of the brain are activated. However, in children and adults who have difficulty reading, these areas are underactivated. The disruptions are evident in early childhood and can continue through adulthood (D'Arcangelo, 2003). As a consequence, reading can be difficult for these individuals throughout their lives.

Characteristics of reading disabilities include difficulty in remembering, using, understanding, and expressing language and problems in the areas of speaking, listening, reading, spelling, and writing. Students who experience reading disabilities often have difficulty expressing themselves verbally, reading sight words, sounding out words, comprehending reading materials, spelling common words, organizing assignments, expressing thoughts in written form, and listening to, remembering, and following directions. Reading disabilities can range from mild to severe.

Various terms have been used to describe reading disabilities. **Dyslexia** refers to a language-based disability in which the student has difficulties in understanding, reading, and expressing language. *Learning disabilities* refers to difficulties in reading, understanding, and communication.

LINKING ASSESSMENT WITH INSTRUCTION

The assessment of reading abilities and skills involves a variety of approaches in order to reflect an understanding of what students know and are able to do. Assessment of reading and writing should reflect integrated activities that evaluate students' ability to think, rethink, construct, and interpret knowledge.

Assessment of reading should be conducted frequently and routinely. Multiple approaches should be used. Many of these approaches have been described in Chapter 4. This chapter addresses assessment approaches that have specific application to reading, including probes, cloze procedure, think-alouds, retelling, informal reading inventories, standardized tests, and observation. Table 11.1 describes reading assessment questions, purposes, and assessments.

A special educator conducting an assessment to determine reading progress.

Table 11.1	Assessment Questions, Purposes, and Approaches		
	Assessment Questions	**Steps and Purposes**	**Approaches**
		Screening	
	Is there a possibility of a disability in reading?	To determine whether students *may* have a disability in reading and should be referred for further assessment	Norm-referenced instruments Curriculum-based assessment Criterion-referenced assessment Observation Checklists
		Eligibility	
	Does the student have a disability? What disability does the student have? Does the student meet the criteria for services? What are the student's strengths and weaknesses? Why is the student having difficulty reading?	To determine if there is a disability To compare the student's performance in reading with the performance of the peer group To determine specific strengths and weaknesses in reading To understand why the student is having difficulty	Norm-referenced instruments Curriculum-based assessment Criterion-referenced assessment Observation Probes Error analysis Interviews Checklists Student, parent, and/or teacher conferences Performance assessment
	Connecting Instruction with Assessment		
		Program Planning	
	What does the student not understand about reading? Where should instruction in reading begin?	To understand what the student knows and does not know To plan the student's program To determine instructional approaches	Norm-referenced instruments Curriculum-based assessment Criterion-referenced assessment Observation Probes Error analysis Interviews Checklists Student, parent, and/or teacher conferences Performance assessment

Assessment Questions, Purposes, and Approaches *continued*		
Assessment Questions	**Steps and Purposes**	**Approaches**
	Program Monitoring	
Once instruction begins, is the student making progress in reading? Should reading instruction be modified?	To understand the strategies and concepts the student uses To monitor the student's program	Curriculum-based assessment Criterion-referenced assessment Observation Probes Error analysis Interviews Checklists Student, parent, and/or teacher conferences Portfolios Exhibitions Journals Written descriptions Oral descriptions

Source: Adapted from *Assessment of Children and Youth,* by L. Cohen and L. Spenciner, 1998, New York: Addison Wesley Longman.

PROBES

The use of probes was introduced in Chapter 4. Probes can provide quick estimates of students' knowledge and skills. They can be used to identify learning difficulties and assist in planning instruction. For example, suppose that a teacher wants to determine whether a student is ready to proceed to a more difficult reading book. The teacher can give the student a selection from the book and observe the strategies that the student uses when reading. The student may be able to read the words on the page but may need some help learning new vocabulary. The teacher may help the student by introducing the new vocabulary and providing background knowledge.

Instructional probes are implemented during the process of instruction. When designing an instructional probe, the following steps can be used:

1. The teacher identifies the area of reading that is to be observed and determines whether the student is able to do the tasks or use certain reading strategies. Examples include recognizing letter patterns, using context clues, retelling a story, and recognizing common warning signs such as *danger* and *keep out*.
2. The teacher uses strategic interventions. For example, to facilitate the recognition of warning signs (e.g., *danger, keep out*) the teacher may have the student say, trace, recognize, and write the words. To assist in retelling, a teacher can ask: "What happened afterward? Tell me more about _____."
3. The teacher determines whether the student can successfully complete the task, use the strategy, or comprehend the passage.

CLOZE PROCEDURE

The **cloze procedure** is usually used to determine whether the reading material is within a student's ability. Generally, the teacher selects a passage to be read and reproduces it, leaving out every fifth word. The assumption is that if the student can fill in the blanks, the reading is within the student's ability. Some alternatives to using the fifth word rule are (Rhodes & Shanklin, 1993):

- The teacher can decide which words to omit.
- The teacher can read orally and ask the student to fill in the missing word.
- Blanks can be left so that various parts of speech are omitted.

For example, the teacher _____ a passage to be _____ and reproduces it leaving _____ every fifth word. The _____ is that if the _____ can fill in the _____, the reading is within _____ student's ability.

THINK-ALOUDS

A **think-aloud** is the verbalization of a student's thoughts about a text before, during, or after reading. Think-alouds provide insight into the student's comprehension abilities and thinking processes. For example, when asked to read a story about immigrants in the United States, the teacher could ask: "What do you think this story will be about?" "What do you already know about immigrants?" During the reading, the student may say, "I don't know that word" or "My mother told me about her parents, who were immigrants." After reading, the student may say, "I didn't understand how the immigrants left their homes" or "That paragraph was hard."

When eliciting think-alouds, teachers can use the following procedures (Rhodes & Shanklin, 1993):

1. Ask the student to think aloud while reading. Explain that thinking aloud will help students to understand the text.
2. Indicate where the student should stop while reading in order to think aloud.
3. Model how a think-aloud is done.
4. While the student is thinking aloud, record the student's comments.
5. Analyze the think-aloud for patterns such as the use of context clues, substitutions, misunderstandings, inferences, use of information, and the addition of information to the text.

RETELLING

Retelling occurs when the student retells as much of a text as can be remembered after reading it. Retelling provides considerable information about comprehension. The following procedures can be used in retelling (Rhodes & Shanklin, 1993):

1. State that when the student has finished reading, a retelling will be requested.
2. Once the student has finished reading, request the retelling.
3. Audiotape the retelling.
4. Once the student has finished the retelling, ask if there is anything else that the student would like to add.

5. At this point, the teacher can choose to ask questions or use prompts to elicit additional information.
6. Use a checklist or record form to analyze the retelling for patterns and trends in the knowledge of story structure, story elements, use of details, and use of language.

INFORMAL READING INVENTORIES

Informal reading inventories (IRI) are frequently used as part of the assessment of literacy. An IRI can be selected from those already published, or a teacher may be interested in developing one. Inventories can aid in assessing students' instructional strengths and needs and provide insight into how instruction should proceed. An IRI can consist of questions relating to the students' knowledge and skills in phonemic awareness, phonics, word recognition, reading comprehension, and other areas.

STANDARDIZED TESTS

Because reading instruction varies considerably throughout the United States, assessment instruments should be carefully selected so that those that best match national and state standards and the curriculum are selected (Cohen & Spenciner, 1998). Table 11.2 lists achievement batteries that assess reading.

Table 11.2	Standardized Reading Tests
Name	**Ages/Grades**
BRIGANCE diagnostic comprehensive inventory of basic skills (Brigance, 1983)	Grades K to 9
Diagnostic achievement battery (DAB-3) (Newcomer, 2001)	Ages 6-0 to 14-0
Kaufman test of educational achievement-II (K-TEA-II) (Kaufman & Kaufman, 2004)	Grades 1 to 12 Ages 6-0 to 18-11
Peabody individual achievement test-R/NU (PIAT-R/NU) (Markwardt, 1997)	Grades K to 12 Ages 5-0 to 22-11
Wide range achievement test-3 (WRAT-3) (Wilkinson, 1994)	Ages 5 to 75
Wechsler individual achievement test-II (WIAT-II) (The Psychological Corporation, 2002)	Grades K to 12 Ages 5-0 to 19-11
Woodcock-Johnson psychoeducational battery III (Woodcock & Johnson, 2001)	Ages 2 to 90 Grades K to 12

OBSERVING STUDENTS IN VARIOUS ENVIRONMENTS

In Chapter 5 you learned about the importance of considering students within physical, learning, and social environments. The interactions between each student and the environment are important assessment considerations.

The physical environment can influence the student's reading performance. The temperature, lighting, and seating arrangements of the spaces used for teaching and learning can affect how well the student performs.

A comfortable learning environment can facilitate the development of reading and writing abilities, positive attitudes, and good habits. The curriculum, instructional methods, books, materials, and assessment procedures are all areas of concern. Students will be willing to engage in reading and writing activities when (a) the activities are challenging; (b) students realize that the assignments and the assessment activities are worth doing; (c) a variety of instructional approaches, books, and materials are used; and (d) multiple assessment procedures are employed.

Relationships with students and teachers can affect performance in reading and writing. The social environment is important to the development of self-concept and self-esteem. These, in turn, contribute to positive attitudes toward literacy development. By observing the social environment, teachers can study the relationships students have with peers and adults.

INSTRUCTIONAL STRATEGIES

Carlos can sound out individual words but does not understand the meaning of sentences. Cherie reads slowly, with little understanding of what she has read. Carlos and Cherie, like other students with reading difficulties, need intensive and specialized instruction in reading comprehension.

Students frequently have difficulty with recognizing sight words, reading unfamiliar words, understanding what they read, writing about what they have read, and spelling. This section describes instructional strategies that can be used when teaching reading to students with disabilities.

Contemporary views of teaching reading (Rhodes & Shanklin, 1993; Routman, 2000; Vaughn et al., 2003) emphasize that students benefit from a wide variety of teaching and learning approaches. This is especially true for students who have reading, writing, or spelling difficulties. Comprehensive reading programs have several important characteristics. In these programs, teachers support students as they construct meaning. Skills are taught as part of the reading process, not in isolation. Students engage in conversations, collaboration, and learning with teachers and peers. Teachers guide, support, coach, and assess progress. A wide variety of materials and strategies are used (Routman, 2000).

Grouping of students for reading instruction is an important factor when focusing on effective reading outcomes. In a study of several grouping formats (Vaughn et al., 2003), three groups of second-grade students with reading difficulties were taught reading using phonological awareness activities, word structures, word patterns, fluency, and comprehension instruction. The researchers demonstrated that students who received 1-to-1 reading instruction achieved at higher levels than those who received 1-to-3 and 1-to-10 instruction; however, there was no significant difference between students who received 1-to-1 instruction and those who received 1-to-3 instruction.

LETTER–SOUND ASSOCIATION

Phonemic Awareness

The **phoneme** is the smallest unit of sound that has meaning in a language. **Phonemic awareness,** which is frequently confused with phonics instruction (phonics involves the use of letter sound correspondence to read or spell words), is the ability to segment and manipulate sounds of speech. Sometimes phonemic awareness is referred to as *phonological awareness,* or the ability to decode words. This text uses the term *phonemic awareness* consistent with the practice of the National Reading Panel, which was commissioned by the National Institute of Child Health and Human Development.

Research conducted by Shaywitz (1996, 2003) has linked certain neurological activities with reading achievement. Shaywitz (2003) has documented the relationship between knowledge of phonemic awareness, also known as *decoding,* and reading skills and advocates the teaching of phonemic awareness activities to struggling readers.

The National Reading Panel (2000) indicated that teaching phonemic awareness, as one part of a student's reading program, can be very effective in improving reading performance. Activities that develop phonemic awareness involve practice with sounds and syllables. The English language has approximately 44 phonemes (Table 11.3) that produce all spoken and written words. For example, the word *bat* consists of three phonemes: *ba, aah,* and *tuh.* (These sounds are represented as |b| |ae| and |t|.)

In the following we discuss some activities that teachers use to teach knowledge about phonemes.

Listening Awareness
The teacher tells the students to close their eyes.
The teacher claps his or her hands, snaps fingers, and stomps feet.
The teacher asks the students to open their eyes.
The teacher says, "First, you heard _____. In the middle, you heard _____. And last, you heard _____."
The students fill in the blanks.
The teacher and students continue the listening game using the following:
animal sounds (moo, oink, quack)
familiar items (tree, grass, truck)
sounds of the alphabet (*c-a-t*)

Rhyming Awareness
The teacher reads and teaches a familiar nursery rhyme such as "Hickory Dickory Dock." The teacher shows how to substitute rhyming words with other familiar words, as in the following example:

"Hickory, Dickory, Dock,
The mouse ran up the _____."
Here, the child can substitute *sock* or other rhyming words for *clock.* Dr. Seuss books, familiar songs, and rhymes can also be used to teach rhyming awareness.

Table 11.3	Phonemes

CONSONANT SOUNDS (Note that consonant phonemes have fewer and clearer spellings than do vowel phonemes)

/b/ big robber
/d/ down called daddy
/f/ if phone differ cough half
/g/ go wiggle ghost
/h/ had whole
/j/ gym job edge gem
/k/come keep back chrome
/l/ let fell ample label pupil
/m/ me swimmer dumb autumn
/n/ no know winner gnaw pneumatic
/p/ pay apple
/r/ read write marry are rhyme
/s/ so cent pass house castle screw
/t/ to fatter debt
/v/ very give of
/w/ we when quite once
/y/ yes
/z/ has zoo please buzz sneeze
/ku/ quit really two phonemes /k/ /w/
/c/ is always /k/ or /s/
/ks/ box—actually two phonemes /k/ /s/

Digraph—single consonant sounds—two letters

/sh/ show motion sure
/th/ thin (unvoiced)
/th/ this (voiced)
/ch/ much nature match
/ng/ song think
/wh/ what when—in English this phoneme and /w/ often overlap

VOWEL PHONEMES

American English uses 18 vowels that have close or overlapping sounds.
The six vowel letters (a e i o u y) are used in 70 different spellings.
Say the a in at, the e in ed, the i in in, the o in on, and the u in up.
These short vowels sound alike and are hard to say in isolation.
Say the oo in too and the oo in book, the au in ball and the ou in out.

Short Vowel Sounds

/a/ am laugh
/e/ end bread many said friend
/i/ in myst
/o/ top
/u/ but touch come was does

Phonemes *continued*

Long Vowel Sounds

/ae/ able make aid day they eight vein
/ee/ she seat bee key piece many chief ceiling
/ie/ find ride by pie high height
/ou/ no note soul boat low door
/eu/ unit use few you

Blended Vowel Sounds

/oo/ too super cube do crew due fluid two soup shoe
/oo/ or /uu/ look put could
/ou/ mouse now drought
/au/ haul talk draw water bought caught
/oy/ oil boy

/r/-Influenced Vowel Sounds*

/ar/ car
/er/ her fur sir work learn syrup dollar
/or/ for ore oar our poor
*/r/ influenced vowels are the most variable speech sounds and are most sensitive to dialects.

Word and Syllable Awareness

Word Clap: The teacher says words of one, two, or more syllables and claps once for each syllable. For example, the teacher says *classroom,* clapping once on *class* and once on *room.* Students repeat the word while clapping once for each syllable. Other words that can be used to teach word and syllable awareness include:

playground	*paper*
sandbox	*kitchen*
crayons	*bedroom*
chair	*bathroom*
friend	*computer*

What's the Word? Game: The teacher says a word, emphasizing each syllable, and students repeat the entire word.

The teacher says, "*di-no-saur.*"

Students say, "*dinosaur.*"

Other words that can be used in this game are:

al-pha-bet
tel-e-vi-sion
win-dow
croc-o-dile
pen-cil
el-e-phant

In a variation on this activity, the teacher shows pictures of familiar people, places, or things, and students clap the syllables while saying the words. For example, the teacher holds up the following pictures while the students clap and say the words:

Word Family Awareness
The teacher selects a word family to practice.
The teacher says, *"c-at.* What's the word?"
The students say, *"cat."*

The teacher continues with the same word family to reinforce rhyming, vowel patterns, and sound blending. The teacher says the words *pan, man, ban, plan,* and so on. Additional word families that can be introduced can be found in Table 11.4.

Phonics

In contrast to phonemic awareness, **phonics** involves knowing how specific spoken sounds relate to particular written letters. For example, the letter *b* makes a *buh* sound. Phonics emphasizes knowledge of letter–sound correspondences. There has been considerable controversy over the place of phonics instruction in reading programs. However, many experts acknowledge that the teaching of phonics is important to beginning reading instruction (National Reading Panel, 2000).

Letter–sound association should be taught both visually to auditorily and auditorily to visually. For example, using spelling words, a teacher asks students to say the sound that each letter makes (visual to auditory). Later, the teacher says a letter sound and asks students to find the spelling word that begins or ends with that sound (auditory to visual). Students must develop knowledge of the blending of

Table 11.4	Word Families						
at	an	it	en	ot	ake	ane	ole
cat	ran	bit	hen	dot	cake	plane	sole
sat	fan	hit	pen	cot	sake	cane	whole
bat	man	sit	ten	tot	rake	lane	mole
fat	clan	fit	men	lot	make	mane	pole

Table 11.5	**Strategies for Teaching Phonics**	
Spelling	With sound	Spell the words you hear.
	Word endings	Spell the new word by adding the ending.
Decoding	Silent letters	Find the missing silent letters in words.
	Decoding patterns	Match sounds in words.
	Sound sort	Sort sounds you hear in words.
	Syllables	Count the number of syllables in each word.
Word building	Scrambles	Rearrange the letters in each word to make another word.
	Word forming	Form as many words as you can using the letters given.
	Compound words	Form compound words from the word given.
Word meanings	Word meanings	Fill in the words to complete the phrases.
	Blends	Find two blended words for each target word.
	Homophones	Find a word with the same pronunciation but with a different spelling and a different meaning.
	Rhyming	Complete sentences with a rhyming pair.
	Prefix/suffix	Create words using clues and using prefixes and suffixes.

Source: Adapted from the Alphabet Superhighway website: http://www.ash.udel.edu/ash/index.html

sounds and letters into words as well as the segmenting of whole words into the individual sounds. The teaching of phonics should not emphasize isolated skills but should be systematically integrated into a balanced literacy program.

Several approaches can be used to systematically incorporate phonics instruction into a balanced literacy program (National Reading Panel, 2000), including analogy phonics, analytic phonics, embedding phonics, phonics through spelling, and synthetic phonics. Strategies for teaching phonics can be found in Table 11.5.

Analogy Phonics. In **analogy phonics,** teachers help students read unfamiliar words by helping them to recognize a familiar segment in the new word—for example, reading *book* by recognizing that *ook* is part of known words *look* and *cook.*

Analytic Phonics. Teachers can teach students to analyze letter–sound correspondences in words already known and apply this knowledge to new words. **Analytic phonics** involves breaking words down into segments and sounds, reading the segments and sounds, and combining them into a whole in order to read the word—for example, reading *smack* when the student can recognize *sm-a-ck.*

Embedded Phonics. Teachers can embed or incidentally include phonics instruction in text reading. This approach, **embedded phonics,** is an implicit or indirect approach and may be more difficult to understand for students who have reading disabilities. For example, instead of providing systematic instruction in phonics, teachers address phonics only when phonics problems arise during reading.

Phonics through Spelling. Teachers teach students to segment words in phonemes and to identify letters for the phonemes. For example, they teach students to segment *book* into /b/ /oo/ /k/ and to associate letters with the phonemes.

Synthetic Phonics. In **synthetic phonics,** teachers teach students to change letters into phonemes and blend the sounds to form words. For example, they teach students to associate the letters *b r i n g* with their corresponding sounds /b/ /r/ /i/ /n/ /g/ to produce *bring.* Table 11.6 summarizes letter–sound relationships in phonics instruction.

SIGHT VOCABULARY

Automatically recognizing printed words that occur frequently allows students to read a text fluently. This **sight vocabulary** builds over time as students have multiple experiences with words in various contexts. Thus, students come to recognize words

Table 11.6	Highlights of Letter–Sound Relationships in Phonics Instruction
	Consonants: *b, c, d, f, g, h, j, l, m, p, r, s, t, w, k, v, y, z*
	Short and long vowels: *a, e, i, o, u, y(e), y(i)*
	Consonant digraphs: *ch, sh, th* (voiced), *th* (unvoiced)
	Major phoneme word families: *ab, all, an, ap, ack, ake, at, eed, ell, en, est, ew, ick, ight, ill, in, ing, it, op, ot, ore, ot, ow, ub, uck, ug, um, ump, unk, ut*
	Consonant blends: *br, cr, dr, fr, gr, pr, tr, wr, bl, cl, fl, gl, pl, sl, sc, sk, sm, sn, sp, st, sw, ch, ph, sh, th, wh, scr, spr, squ, str, thr*
	Vowel digraphs and dipthongs: *ay, ai, aw, ea (long e), ea (short e), ee, oa, oi, oo, ou, ow, ew, ey, ue*
	Consonant/consonant digraphs: *c(s), g(j), ph(f), tch(ch), dge*
	r-controlled schwa: *ar, er, ir, or, ur, oor, ear, our, eer*

Using Technology
Software That Supports Development of Phonemic Awareness and Letter–Sound Recognition

Lexia Phonics Based Reading (Lexia Learning Systems, Inc., 2003a) and Lexia Reading S.O.S. (Strategies for Older Students; Lexia Learning Systems, Inc., 2003b) are software programs for students that provide activities on phonemic awareness, sound–symbol correspondence, and reading comprehension. Lexia Phonics Based Reading is intended for students ages 5 through 8; Lexia Reading S.O.S. was developed for students ages 9 through adulthood. Information about these software programs can be found at http://www.lexialearning.com.

Earobics software programs (Cognitive Concepts, 2003) emphasize phonological awareness, sound blending, segmenting, rhyming, sound discrimination, and phonics skills. They are intended for students ages 4 through 10.

Information about this software program can be found at http://www.earobics.com.

Questions for Reflection

1. Find out more about these software programs and others by visiting the websites of the companies that publish them. What are important features of these programs?
2. How should software programs such as Lexia Phonics Based Reading and Earobics be integrated into instruction?

 To answer these questions and learn more about using technology to support learning, go to the Companion Website at www.prenhall.com/cohen, select Chapter 11, then choose Using Technology.

that occur frequently on sight. Teachers should avoid teaching sight words by themselves or in isolation. Students should be encouraged to find these words in a text and to read them in context. Table 11.7 is a list of frequently used sight words.

A variety of activities can be used to build sight vocabulary, including:

- Say the word in unison, clap the syllables, spell the word aloud, and say the word again.
- Point out unusual features of the word.
- Have students trace the word.
- Cover the word, ask students to spell it, and uncover the word.
- Ask students for rhyming words.
- Ask students to add the word to their personal dictionaries.
- Post words on a classroom bulletin board or word wall.
- Use sight word association cards that allow students to associate the picture with the word (Figure 11.1).

Sight Word Association Cards

When using sight word association cards, the teacher begins by placing the cards in front of the students. The teacher points to the picture and then to the word. The teacher pronounces the word. Students repeat the word. One or two additional cards are placed in front of the students. The teacher repeats the procedure by pointing to

Table 11.7	Sight Words (Ranked in the Order of Their Use in the English Language)		
1–25	**26–50**	**51–75**	**76–100**
the	or	will	number
of	one	up	no
and	had	other	way
a	by	about	could
to	word	out	people
in	but	many	my
is	not	then	than
you	what	them	first
that	all	these	water
it	were	so	been
he	where	some	call
was	when	her	who
for	your	would	oil
on	can	make	now
are	said	like	find
as	there	him	long
with	use	into	down
his	an	time	day
they	each	has	did
I	which	look	get
at	she	two	come
be	do	more	made
this	how	write	may
have	their	go	part
from	if	see	over
101–125	**126–150**	**151–175**	**176–200**
new	great	put	kind
sound	where	end	hand
take	help	does	picture
only	though	another	again
little	much	well	change
work	before	large	off
know	line	must	play
place	right	big	spell
year	too	even	air
live	mean	such	away
me	old	because	animal

Sight Words (Ranked in the Order of Their Use in the English Language) *continued*

101–125	126–150	151–175	176–200
back	any	turn	house
give	same	here	point
most	tell	why	page
very	boy	ask	letter
after	follow	went	mother
thing	came	men	answer
our	want	read	found
just	show	need	study
name	also	land	still
good	around	different	learn
sentence	form	home	should
man	three	us	America
think	small	move	world
say	set	try	high

201–225	226–250	251–275	276–300
every	left	until	idea
near	don't	children	enough
add	few	side	eat
food	while	feet	face
between	along	car	watch
own	might	mile	far
below	close	night	Indian
country	something	walk	real
plant	seem	white	almost
last	next	sea	let
school	hard	began	above
father	open	grow	girl
keep	example	took	sometimes
tree	begin	river	mountain
never	life	four	cut
start	always	carry	young
city	those	state	talk
earth	both	once	soon
eye	paper	book	list
light	together	hear	song
thought	got	stop	leave
head	group	without	family
under	often	second	body
story	run	late	music
saw	important	miss	color

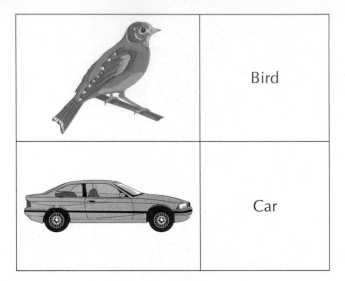

Figure 11.1   Picture and sight vocabulary association cards

each picture and pronouncing the word. Students repeat each word as it is pronounced. The teacher covers one picture and asks the students to pronounce the word that goes with it. This procedure is repeated for each sight word association picture card. Students practice reading the sight words independently using the cards. The teacher and the students identify words that the students consistently are unable to read. Each word is written on an index card and can be stored in a dictionary file. Each word is discussed with these students and written on a separate card. The teacher and the students review the cards daily. Finally, the students are asked to find the words in a text.

Word Walls

A **word wall** is a large section of a classroom wall where important words are posted for use in reading and writing. Teachers can cover a section of a classroom wall, room divider, or easel with colored paper and write directly on the paper, or they can write individual words on colored strips of paper that can be attached to the wall. In the early grades, words that are frequently encountered and words that the teacher identifies are posted in alphabetic order. After posting a word on the word wall, the teacher should provide various strategies that will help students remember, recognize, comprehend, and spell the word. Figure 11.2 illustrates a word wall.

Prompts

Teacher prompts, hints, or reminders can aid students in figuring out how to read words, aid comprehension, shape predictions, and make self-corrections. Examples of teacher prompts are (adapted from Routman, 1994):

1. How does the word begin?
2. A word that rhymes with *that* is _____.

Figure 11.2   Word wall words

a	friends	lot	their
about	from	make	them
after	fun	me	then
all	get	more	there
and	go	my	they
are	good	no	things
as	got	not	this
at	had	of	time
back	has	on	to
be	have	one	too
because	he	or	up
big	her	other	us
but	him	our	very
by	his	out	want
came	home	people	was
can	house	play	we
could	I	said	went
day	if	saw	were
did	in	school	what
didn't	is	see	when
do	it	she	will
don't	just	so	with
down	know	some	would
every	like	that	you
for	little	the	your

3. What word makes sense here?
4. Does that sound right? Try again.
5. Look at the pictures for clues.
6. While the learner follows along in a text, the teacher reads aloud, pausing at key words, phrases, or parts of words so that the learner can fill in the missing text. This type of prompt is known as the *cloze procedure*.

Word Banks and Personal Dictionaries

Word banks and personal dictionaries contain words that students can read. Words can be written on small cards and stored in a student's small file box, notebook, or computer. Students can be asked to identify words that have the same endings and match words in the word bank with words in stories the students read. Cards can be used to make up games such as Lotto, Concentration, or Bingo.

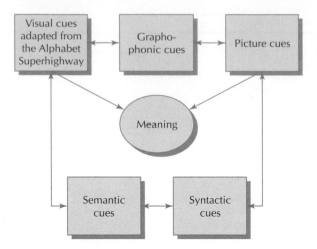

Figure 11.3   **Dynamic interrelationships between cueing systems**

The words can be used to make sentences. Students can share their word banks and dictionaries with other students. Finally, students can write stories using their words.

CUEING

Cueing provides the learner with evidence, hints, and suggestions for letter and word recognition and reading comprehension (Routman, 1994). Skilled readers can efficiently use various types of cues, including visual cues, pictures, syntax, and semantics. Reading instruction must consider the dynamic relationship between cueing systems. Figure 11.3 illustrates this dynamic interrelationship.

Visual Cues

Visual cues refer to the shape or visual configuration features that allow readers to recognize a word or a group of words. The visual configuration allows readers to recognize words automatically. Picture cues or clues can provide hints and suggestions that enable the learner to recognize words. Figure 11.4 shows an example of a visual cue.

Semantic Cues

Semantic cues reflect an understanding of the meaning of language and aid the learner in predicting and reading unknown words from the meaning of other words in a sentence or passage. When teachers ask, "What word makes sense here?" they are asking students to use their knowledge of semantics. Semantic knowledge helps

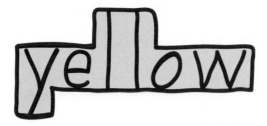

Figure 11.4   Example of using visual cues to promote word recognition.

learners decide the meaning of words. It helps them distinguish the correct meaning of the word *time* in the following sentences: "Tell her what time to come." "She came in record time."

Syntactic Cues

Syntactic cues demonstrate knowledge of grammar and word order. Syntactic knowledge assists learners in predicting unknown words. Reading, "Ariel ran to the _____," the learner applies syntactic knowledge to complete the sentence.

BUILDING COMPREHENSION

Autumn, a fifth grader, is able to word call, or read aloud, most words she sees. However, she struggles with reading comprehension and remembering what she has read. Reading comprehension involves being able to obtain meaning from a text, understand what is read, connect information within the context of a text, and relate what is being read to what is already known. In this section, instructional strategies for developing and enhancing reading comprehension will be described. During the reading process, readers apply knowledge of phonics, phone-mic awareness, semantics, syntax, and pragmatics; they connect background or prior knowledge with a text, constructing meaning and understanding as they proceed.

READING ALOUD TO STUDENTS

Reading aloud to students should be an integral part of all reading programs. Reading aloud helps students to develop positive attitudes toward reading, expands their vocabulary, increases their knowledge, stimulates imagination, sharpens listening skills, and promotes positive social interactions among teachers, peers, and family members (Rhodes & Shanklin, 1993).

There are several important considerations when teachers choose books for reading aloud. When teachers choose a book, they take into account whether the book is enjoyable to themselves, supports and builds on the students' interests and experiences, has attractive pictures that help to convey meaning, is slightly above the students' current vocabulary level, and introduces a new genre or style such as poetry or a folk tale.

Before reading the book aloud to students, teachers should become familiar with it by examining the illustrations so that picture clues can be used, reading the story to themselves, planning ways to vary their voices (tone, volume, pauses) to fit the plot and characters, and collecting dress-up clothes, puppets, or other props related to the story.

When teachers are ready to begin reading aloud to students, they should introduce the author and/or illustrator, talk about other books they and the students have read by the same author and/or illustrator, show the cover and point out details in the illustration, and read the title aloud. They should talk about what type of book it is, such as nonfiction, fiction, autobiography, poetry, essay, or memoir.

Teachers should then describe where and when the story takes place and introduce the setting and the main characters. They should suggest things to look and listen for in the story. They should show a few pages and ask: "What do you think will happen in this book?"

While reading the story, teachers should:

- Vary their voices to fit the characters and the plot.
- Stop frequently to add information that will help students understand what is happening.
- Rephrase words or sentences that might be confusing.
- Explain the meanings of new words.
- Ask students to predict what might happen next.
- Ask students about the story and characters.
- Show and describe the pictures.
- Use the props to enhance the students' enjoyment of the story.
- Encourage participation by inviting students to join in with rhymes and repeated words and phrases.

Finally, after reading the story, teachers should ask students to do the following:

- Recall what happened in the story.
- Relate the story to personal experiences (e.g., "Did you ever _____?").
- Put themselves in the story (e.g., "What would you have done?").
- Act out the story (with or without props).
- Make up a sequel to the story that can be written on a large piece of paper.
- Draw pictures that show the events or characters in the story.
- Learn about the author and/or illustrator.
- Look at other books by the author and/or illustrator (adapted from Koralek & Collins, 1997).

GUIDED READING

The focus of guided reading is on constructing meaning while engaged in problem-solving strategies. Guided reading is based on three beliefs (Fountas & Pinnell, 1996). First, students use their experiences, including formal and informal exposure to texts, to construct meaning. They rely on stories that have been read aloud to them, expectations of others, experiences with books, and adults who model the love of reading, as well as other experiences. Second, language is based on rules. The structure or syntax of a text is based on knowledge of rules that have been learned. Finally, visual information about text is derived from knowledge of the relationship of oral language and the letters that form words.

Guided reading has the following elements (Fountas & Pinnell, 1996):

- A teacher or skilled adult reader works with students individually or in small groups.
- Students, working in small groups, read at a similar level and all students read the same text.
- The teacher introduces each story and supports each reader in developing independent reading strategies.
- Each student reads a complete text.
- The teacher guides by introducing increasingly difficult texts.
- Regrouping and grouping of students occur frequently, depending on the students' use of reading strategies.
- The teacher works closely with students, asking critical questions about what has been read, identifying possible difficulties in reading, and teaching specific reading strategies.

Table 11.8 summarizes the guided reading process.

GUIDED QUESTIONING

Guided questioning, also known as *directed reading,* is a group or individual activity in which learners are asked questions about a text both before and after they read it. They must find the answers in the text by reading it independently and silently. This activity is useful when teaching students how to locate specific information in newspapers, textbooks, and instructional materials. This activity can be combined with writing by having learners write about their answers, using vocabulary found in the text.

Language Experience Approach

The **language experience approach** to teaching reading and writing emphasizes use of the learner's own language, repeated reading, visual configuration of words, sight words, and context clues. This approach is based on what the reader can think about, talk about, write, read, and read what others write (Van Allen, 1976; Van Allen & Allen, 1982).

Instruction involves either suggesting or asking students to describe an experience that is of interest to them. Teachers can use pictures, books, or other materials to help students select the experience. Teachers should begin by talking briefly about the topic and explaining that they will write what each student dictates. As the students dictate, the teacher writes down each student's exact words, including dialect or grammatical variations. Periodically, the teacher should stop and read aloud what has

Table 11.8	Guided Reading		
	Prior to Reading	**During Reading**	**After Reading**
Teacher	• Selects a text that the students can read but that presents several challenges • Introduces the story and pays attention to prior knowledge, skills, and experience of students, new meanings, new word forms, illustrations	• Observes and listens to students • Asks questions • Provides scaffolding • Helps with problem solving • Records use of strategies, skills, successes, and areas needing improvement	• Discusses the text with the students • Uses the text to teach new skills and strategies • Engages the students in conversation about the use of strategies • Evaluates students' progress • Extends the story through activities that reinforce strategies, skills, and concepts
Students	• Ask questions • Find information in the text • Attend to illustrations	• Read the text • Use strategies and skills to construct meaning	• Engage in a discussion of the text with the teacher and peers • Reread the story with a peer • Participate in any extended activities

Source: Adapted from *Guided Reading,* by I. C. Fountas and G. S. Pinnell, 1996, Portsmouth, NH: Heinemann.

been written, pointing to each word. The teacher should ask the student to confirm that the words and ideas are accurate. The teacher leaves space on each page for illustrations that the learner will draw.

When the learner has finished the dictation, the teacher reads the entire story, pointing to each word as the students follow along. Next, the teacher and the learner read the story together, pointing to each word. Students can illustrate the story, make a cover, and write a title. Books can be published by the teacher and added to the class or school library. Additional activities can be developed in which the teacher can check on words the students know, practice unknown words and phrases, and read the story to other students.

REPEATED READING

Repeated reading involves having the learner read a text more than once until fluency is achieved. Repeated reading can be done in a group or as a tutorial activity. To begin, learners choose a story that is approximately 50 to 200 words in length and somewhat easy to read. The skilled reader reads the text at a medium pace while the learner follows along. Next, the skilled reader checks for comprehension by asking several questions about the text. Finally, both the skilled reader and the learner read together, with the skilled reader setting the pace, reading fluently and with expression. As the learner progresses, more difficult texts can be selected. Learners can also read along with an audiotape.

DUET READING

In **duet reading,** the student reads along with a proficient reader, who can be either a peer or the teacher. Reading together helps students to practice reading. First, the two readers sit side by side, using the same book. The skilled reader sets the pace, staying one or two syllables ahead. The skilled reader reads aloud, fluently and with expression. The learner reads along silently and may or may not read aloud. By listening to intonation and pronunciation, the learner's comprehension can be enhanced.

ECHO READING

In **echo reading,** also known as *imitative reading* or *modeled reading,* a skilled reader, such as a teacher or peer, reads a text one sentence at a time. The learner follows along and echoes or imitates the skilled reader. Echo reading helps learners gain confidence in reading aloud, learning sight words, comprehending a text, and reading with phrasing and expression.

SHARED READING

Shared reading is an activity in which a learner or group of learners follows along as a skilled reader, who can be a teacher or peer, reads the text fluently and with expression (Routman, 1994). In addition to being an enjoyable reading experience, shared reading aids learners in making connections between print and speech, builds vocabulary, assists in teaching sight vocabulary, encourages prediction in reading, and aids in the development of fluency and expression in reading. Shared reading is frequently used with beginning readers but does not have to be limited to this group.

The text can be a favorite story, nursery rhyme, or song that has enlarged print, such as a book, or is displayed on a projector. When beginning a shared reading, the teacher introduces the title, illustrations, and story. Next, the teacher reads fluently and expressively, tracking each word with a pointer or highlighter. Then the teacher rereads the text, encouraging everyone to join in by reading certain words or phrases. Following the second or third reading, the learners read the highlighted words or phrases while the teacher reads the other words.

In classes doing shared reading, you will see:

- a teacher introducing a book, identifying the title, author, and cover illustrations.
- big/oversize books that are large enough so that a large group of students can easily see the text.
- stories displayed on large paper or a projector.
- discussions with readers of a story and illustrations prior to reading. During these discussions, the teacher links the story with children's prior knowledge and talks about the title, illustrations, characters, or key events in the story.
- discussions of a story after reading in order to assist comprehension. During these discussions, the teacher reviews the story and connects it to daily experiences.
- the teacher reading or rereading a nursery rhyme or story, tracking each word with a pointer and pausing at key words or phrases so that the students can fill in the missing words.
- the teacher reading or rereading a poem, highlighting with a colored marker the repetitive words, repetitive phrases, or sight words that the learners know.
- students, as a group, reading along with the teacher a story about their recent field trip.

SCAFFOLDING

Scaffolding was introduced in Chapter 7. In this chapter, we will explore how this instructional strategy can be applied to the teaching of reading. Scaffolding is a group of experiences and events that assist learners to successfully read, understand, learn, and enjoy a text (Graves & Graves, 1994).

In this example, Leslie, a third grader, reads a passage from *One Fish, Two Fish* by Dr. Seuss (Geisel, 1981) while his teacher uses scaffolding (adapted from Koralek & Collins, 1997).

LESLIE: One fish, two fish. Red fish, yellow fish. (Stops reading. Looks at teacher.) Yellow doesn't sound right.

TEACHER: That was a good guess, but you're right, it's not yellow.

LESLIE: What is it?

TEACHER: Well, let's take a look. Do you see any clues in the picture?

LESLIE: There's fish in the picture.

TEACHER: What can you tell me about the fish?

LESLIE: There's a red one and a blue one. I know, I know. One fish, two fish. Red fish, blue fish.

TEACHER: How else could you figure out that the word says *blue*?

LESLIE: It starts with a *b*.

TEACHER: More good thinking. Can you read some more?

In this example, the teacher used several scaffolding techniques. The teacher and Leslie worked together to figure out the new word, *blue*. The teacher helped Leslie understand the connections between what was already known about colors and the letter *b*. The teacher was warm and responsive. Praise and acknowledgment of Leslie's success in figuring out the new word were offered. The teacher asked questions and offered clues to help Leslie make discoveries (Koralek & Collins, 1997). Additional suggestions can be found in Table 11.9.

Table 11.9	Learner's Focus and Teaching Strategies

Learner's Focus	Teaching Strategies
Left-to-right and top-to-bottom movement	• Using a finger or pointer, teacher demonstrates that reading progresses from left to right, top to bottom • Teacher points to the starting place • Teacher assists the student's use of a finger, pointer, or place marker to move from left to right, top to bottom

Matching spoken words with written text	• Using a finger or pointer, teacher reads aloud while pointing to each word, matching the spoken and written words
	• Teacher monitors student matching of spoken with written words
	• Teacher uses prompts:
	  • "Use your finger as a pointer while you read."
	  • "Did the spoken words match the written words?"

Self-monitoring	• Teacher explains that the illustrations should help to explain the story
	• Teacher praises student when student self-corrects
	• When student pauses or makes an error, ask:
	  • "How can you figure it out?"
	  • "What did you notice?"
	  • "Does that sound right?"
	  • "Does it make sense?"
	• Teach student how to *know* when understanding is reached by:
	  • Retelling the story
	  • Making notes about the events
	  • Developing a story map
	  • Summarizing the story
	  • Identifying when there are gaps
	  • Identifying connections to other stories
	  • Using what they have read in other contexts

Figuring out words	Teacher uses prompts such as: • "Start the word again." • "Read the word without the vowel." • "This is a word you already know." • "Sound out the word."

continued

Table 11.9	Learner's Focus and Teaching Strategies *continued*
Figuring out words	• "Look at the word again—beginning, middle, ending." • "Read on, and then come back to the hard word and try again." • "Stretch out the letters; take the word apart." • "Think about what would make sense." • "Think about what would sound right."
Building comprehension	Teach the following prompts: • "Reread difficult parts." • "What do you already know about this topic?" • "Omit the difficult word and continue reading." • "Substitute a word." • "Read slowly." • "Skim important information." • "Talk to myself and paraphrase." • "Read aloud to myself." • "Highlight important parts." • "Make predictions about what will happen next."

Source: Adapted from *Conversations,* by R. Routman, 2000, Portsmouth, NH: Heinemann.

DIRECT INSTRUCTION

Direct instruction focuses on highly structured lessons in which the teacher takes an active role and the student is expected to be an involved participant. Direct instruction involves structured lessons that guide students' thinking and performance (Miller, Butler, & Lee, 1998). The primary purpose of direct instruction is to increase both the quantity and quality of learning (Stein & Carnine, 1998). Research has shown that direct instruction is very effective when teaching students with mild disabilities (Swanson, 1999; Swanson, Carson, & Saches-Lee, 1996). While the underlying approach to direct instruction is consistent, there can be variations in the way direct instruction is implemented (Stein & Carnine, 1998).

Direct instruction frequently involves scripted lessons. When this method is applied to reading, the teacher tells students what will be learned, the reasons for each lesson, and how these reasons relate to previous lessons. During direct instruction, the teacher describes the skill or strategy to be learned and then demonstrates or models it. The teacher verbalizes and explains the procedures, asks students to demonstrate the skill or strategy, and actively observes and gives feedback. The teacher provides activities so that students can practice the skill or strategy, always connecting it to a text. The teacher monitors the students' performance, providing corrective feedback as necessary, until students are able to apply the skill or strategy independently. The teacher demonstrates how students can assess their own performance.

What does direct instruction look like in reading? Bernard Carmen, a ninth-grade English teacher, begins by reading a scripted lesson on characters in a story that the students have read. Pausing after each request, Bernard says, "Students, look at the first page of the story. What are the names of the characters? Write down their names. As the story begins on page 1, find out what they are doing. Write it down. Next, draw a picture of what they are doing." The lesson continues in this way, with the teacher pausing, checking, and providing corrective feedback to the students.

FUNCTIONAL READING

Some students with mild and moderate disabilities experience considerable difficulties in learning to read. For these students, **functional reading** should be emphasized. Functional reading is the ability to recognize specific sight words and symbols and use them in daily living activities, in school, at work, and in the community. The focus of functional reading is on specific sight words that have practical use.

Selection and instruction of functional words should be individualized. Considerations should include the student's language, environment, preferences, daily living activities, community activities, and personal safety. Examples of functional words include *stop, go, men, women, caution, fire*, and *exit*. When teaching functional words, teachers can:

- associate pictures and symbols with words,
- teach the shape of the word,
- provide cues that facilitate sight recognition, and
- provide frequent practice in various settings.

SELECTING READING MATERIALS

The sources of reading texts include almost everything that is expressed in text. Thus, posters, signs, newspapers, websites, advertisements, magazines, students' writings, and books can be used to create powerful print-rich environments for students. There are many lists of recommended books for students. Various types of books and materials can be selected for reading, including big books, predictable/pattern texts, basal readers, and series books.

PREDICTABLE/PATTERN TEXTS

Predictable or pattern texts are stories, poems, song lyrics, or other forms of written text that contain repetitious language patterns that can be anticipated or expected by the reader. These predictable features include repetitions of words, phrases, or sentences, rhymes, rhythms, a chain or circular story in which the ending leads back to the beginning and similar questions and answers are repeated throughout the story, a cumulative story in which all previous events are repeated, and familiar sequences such as days of the week, letters of the alphabet, or numbers.

Children enjoy hearing the same word patterns over and over again. As texts are reread over a period of several days or weeks, children begin to predict the language patterns. Teachers can direct their attention to the patterns of phrases, sentences, words, and letters. As children become familiar with the text, they will naturally read along and anticipate word patterns. Predictable stories and collections of poetry can be found in Table 11.10.

Table 11.10	Predictable Texts		
Level	**Title**	**Author**	**Publisher**
Young children and beginning readers	*Aunt Nina, Good Night*	Franz Brandenberg	Greenwillow
	The Cat in the Hat	Dr. Seuss	Random House
	Chicken Soup and Rice	Maurice Sendak	Williams
	Dinosaurs, Dinosaurs	Byron Barton	Crowell
	Goodnight Moon	Margaret Wise Brown	Harper & Row
	Green Eggs and Ham	Dr. Seuss	Random House
	If You Give a Mouse a Cookie	Laura Joffe Numeroff	Harper & Row
	I Know an Old Lady Who Swallowed a Fly	Nadine Bernard Wescott	Houghton Mifflin
	Is It Time?	Marilyn Janovitz	North-South Books
	Is Your Mama a Llama?	Deborah Guarino	Scholastic
	One Bear Alone	Caroline Bucknall	Dial Books

Predictable Texts *continued*

Level	Title	Author	Publisher
	Rosie's Walk	Pat Hutchins	Macmillan
	The Runaway Bunny	Margaret Wise Brown	HarperCollins Publishers
	The Wheels on the Bus	Maryann Kovalski	Little, Brown
	The Teeny Tiny Woman	Margot Zemach	Scholastic
	This Old Man	Pam Adams	Grosset & Dunlap
	Today Is Monday	Eric Carle	
	Whose Mouse Are You?	Robert Kraus	Macmillan
	The Very Hungry Caterpillar	Eric Carle	Philomel
Advanced beginners and emergent readers	*Alexander and the Terrible, Horrible, No Good, Very Bad Day*	Judith Viorst	Atheneum
	The House That Jack Built	Rodney Peppe	Delacorte
	Home for a Bunny	Margaret Wise Brown	Golden
	Millions of Cats	Wanda Gãg	Coward-McCann
	Pinkerton Behave!	Steven Kellogg	Dial
	The Three Billy Goats Gruff	Marcia Brown	Harcourt
	Where the Wild Things Are	Maurice Sendak	Scholastic
	Why Mosquitos Buzz in People's Ears	Verna Aardema	Weston Woods Studio

BASAL READERS

Basal readers are beginning textbooks containing stories and passages that have been developed to progressively reinforce what students are learning. Most major elementary textbook companies publish a series of basal readers.

There is some controversy over the extent to which teachers should rely on basal readers when teaching reading because the language in the readers is very controlled and some stories lack complexity, richness, and detail.

SERIES BOOKS

Books in a series are texts that include similar characters, settings, and plots. Readers become familiar with the author's style and background. Series books can be particularly useful for children who have difficulty reading. Examples of series books include the American Girl, Ramona, Hardy Boys, Nancy Drew, Harry Potter, and Narnia series. A list of series books is presented in Table 11.11.

Table 11.11	**Series Books**		
Level	**Title**	**Author**	**Publisher**
Easy	*Arthur* books	Marc Brown	Little, Brown
	Bear books	Frank Asch	Scholastic
	Clifford books	Norman Bridwell	Scholastic
	Curious George books	H. A. Rey & Margaret Rey	Houghton Mifflin
	Cam Jansen	David Adler	Viking
	Dragon books	Dav Pilkey	Orchard
	Frances books	Russell Hoban	Harper & Row
	Frog and Toad books	Arnold Lobel	HarperCollins
	Little Bear books	Elise Homelund Minarik	HarperCollins
	Oliver Pig books	Jean Van Leeuwen	Dial
	Zelda and Ivy books	Laura McGee Kvasnovky	Candlewick
Transitional	*Anastasia Krupnik* books	Lois Lowry	Houghton Mifflin

Series Books *continued*			
Level	**Title**	**Author**	**Publisher**
	Babysitters books	Ann Martin	Scholastic
	Goosebumps books	R. L. Stine	Scholastic
	Little House books	Laura Ingalls Wilder	Harper & Row
	Ramona books	Beverly Cleary	Morrow
	Time Warp Trio books	Jon Sciezska	Viking
	Young Merlin books	Jane Yolen	Scholastic
Challenging	*Anastasia Krupnik* books	Lois Lowry	Houghton Mifflin
	Animorphs	Katherine Applegate	Scholastic
	Friendship Ring books	Rachel Vail	Scholastic
	Harry Potter books	J. K. Rowling	Scholastic
	Here There Be . . . books	Jane Yolen	Harcourt Brace
	Roll of Thunder, Hear My Cry books	Mildred Taylor	Dial
	Young Merlin books	T. A. Barron	Philomel

CHILDREN'S LITERATURE

Children's literature refers to both fiction and nonfiction stories and books that were developed especially for children. Children's literature includes fairy tales, poetry, mythology, folk tales, and fiction. Examples include *Aesop's Fables, Beauty and the Beast,* and the Harry Potter books. Advantages of using children's literature are that the vocabulary is rich and the stories are engaging. Disadvantages are that new vocabulary words are frequently used and the reading level may make it difficult to match stories to individual learners.

BIG BOOKS

Oversize editions of children's books can be shared with a small group, allowing the text and illustrations to be seen by all students in the group. **Big books** can be useful when doing shared readings. Many books are available in big-book format.

A teacher and her students use big books.

HIGH-INTEREST/LIMITED-VOCABULARY BOOKS

High-interest/limited-vocabulary books address interesting topics and are written at a limited vocabulary level. These books can motivate reluctant or poor readers and provide opportunities to engage in reading. High-interest/limited-vocabulary books are available at many levels for students of various ages.

SPECIALIZED APPROACHES

SUCCESS FOR ALL/ROOTS AND WINGS

There is considerable evidence that Success for All/Roots and Wings can improve reading achievement (Slavin & Madden, 1999). The heart of this program consists of 90 minutes of uninterrupted daily reading instruction. Children are grouped by reading level across classes and grades. Materials that are used include big books, controlled selections of children's literature, and basal readers. Instruction emphasizes direct instruction, cooperative learning, individual tutoring, peer tutoring, phonetic awareness, letter–sound recognition, story structure, metacognition for self-assessment and self-correction, frequent assessments, and family involvement.

In kindergarten and first grade, the emphasis is on integrated units in science and social studies that include language, art, reading, and writing. One component, Story Telling and Retelling (STaR), involves the students in listening to, retelling, and dramatizing children's literature.

Using Technology
Text-to-Speech Software

Text-to-speech software can be critically important for individuals who have learning disabilities or reading and writing difficulties. This software converts text into speech. Text-to-speech software reads aloud electronic texts such as e-mail messages, Web pages, word-processing documents, electronic files, and scanned texts. The software allows users to hear electronic text located on a computer. Using text-to-speech software, students can adjust the size and color of text information on the screen and use the built-in dictionary.

Both Windows and Macintosh operating systems include built-in text-to-speech software. Specialized text-to-speech software programs typically include additional features that built-in programs may not offer.

Two software programs, Kurzweil 3000 and Wynn, are powerful integrated programs that have numerous features, including text-to-speech capabilities, word processing, optical character recognition (OCR), and study skills support. These programs allow students to move to the beginning and end of documents, find the meanings and synonyms of words in talking dictionaries, and highlight each word as the computer reads it. The OCR capability allows these programs to read scanned documents, electronic files, e-mail messages, and the Web.

Questions for Reflection

1. Some text-to-speech software programs are available on the Web as demonstration versions or are free. ReadPlease, one of these programs, is available at readplease.com. Visit the website of this software program or others and try out the software. How does text-to-speech software support reading instruction?
2. Use a text-to-speech software program to read Web pages. Can Web pages be read easily? What problems occur when reading them?

 To answer these questions and learn more about using technology to support learning, go to the Companion Website at www. prenhall.com/cohen, select Chapter 11, then choose Using Technology.

Success for All/Roots and Wings uses minibooks. Minibooks begin with *shared stories*, in which part of a story is presented in a small type size (read by the teacher) and part is presented in a large type size (read by the students). Phonetically controlled vocabulary is used in the students' part. As students progress, the teacher's part becomes brief and the students' portion increases in length until students read the entire book.

READING RECOVERY

Reading Recovery is focused on the lowest achieving students in first grade and provides intense instruction that lasts for approximately 12 to 16 weeks. The teacher works individually with each identified student for about 30 minutes a day. The goal of Reading Recovery is to raise students' reading achievement to the level of their peers. Once they have reached this level, they are dropped from the program. Each

Reading Recovery lesson follows a similar pattern of activities that are designed based on an analysis of students' progress.

Developed by New Zealand educator and psychologist Marie M. Clay, Reading Recovery was introduced in the United States in 1984. A variation on Reading Recovery was introduced by Herman and Stringfield (1997). Pinnell (2000), in a comprehensive review of Reading Recovery, found that many Reading Recovery strategies, especially when used in combination, can improve reading performance. According to Pinnell, Reading Recovery includes elements of phonological awareness (sometimes called *phonemic awareness*), visual perception of letters, word recognition, phonics, decoding skills, comprehension, and early intervention.

Each Reading Recovery lesson has seven elements:

1. The learner and the teacher reread several familiar books. The books are selected from a variety of works with varying levels of difficulty.

2. The student independently rereads a book introduced during the prior lesson while the teacher observes and records the student's reading strategies such as word identification, comprehension, and monitoring.

3. If the student is not able to identify or write upper- and lowercase letters, the teacher guides the student using plastic, magnetic, sandpaper, or other types of letters in various activities such as tracing letters, forming them into words, and making alphabet books.

4. The student writes several sentences, a short message, or a brief story. If the student needs assistance, the teacher may provide feedback. The teacher encourages the student to listen to the sounds, make predictions, and verbally repeat words as the teacher writes and says them. The student reads what has been recorded. Next, the teacher writes the sentences, message, or story and cuts them up into sentence strips.

5. After the sentences, message, or story have been cut up, the student rearranges the sentence strips and compares them to the original.

6. The teacher introduces a new book. The teacher assists the student by connecting the new book to the student's prior or background knowledge and by introducing new information. The teacher gradually increases the difficulty level of the reading and introduces new strategies that guide the student in problem solving. The teacher focuses the reading by encouraging the student to look at illustrations, explaining the framework for the plot, pointing out language that may be unfamiliar, or explaining the use variations on sentence formations.

7. The lesson ends with the teacher and the learner reading the new book.

FERNALD METHOD

Visual-Auditory-Kinesthetic-Tactile (VAKT) is a multisensory approach. Fernald, the developer of this approach (Fernald, 1943), believed that seeing, hearing, feeling, and touching individual words will help students to read and write them. Because research on this approach is lacking, VAKT should not be used in isolation from other strategies discussed in this chapter. It is most commonly used in a tutorial setting with students and has seven steps:

1. The teacher and student identify a word that the student is unable to read and would like to read.
2. The teacher either prints the word or writes it in cursive writing on a strip of paper that measures approximately 4 by 11 inches.
3. The teacher pronounces the word while it is being written.
4. The teacher traces the letters of the word with one finger and pronounces the word again.
5. The student is asked to trace the letters of the word and to pronounce it. This procedure is repeated several times.
6. Once the student is able to pronounce and read the word, the student writes it from memory.
7. The word is filed in a word bank or file box and reviewed by the student and teacher.

ORTON-GILLINGHAM METHOD

The **Orton-Gillingham method** (Gillingham & Stillwell, 1956; Meese, 2001) is an intensive, sequential, phonics-based system that teaches the basics of word formation before word meanings. The method accommodates and uses the three learning modalities, or pathways, through which people learn—visual, auditory, and kinesthetic. Instruction is structured, sequential, and repetitive. This approach, although popular years ago, is used in relatively few schools today.

WILSON READING SYSTEM

The Wilson Reading System (Meese, 2001; Wilson & Hall, 1968) emphasizes the structure of words through decoding words and spelling by moving students through a 12-step program. Based on the Orton-Gillingham approach, instruction emphasizes letter sounds, sound blends, syllabication rules, spelling rules, and reading individual words, words in sentences, and brief stories.

Using a multisensory approach, students listen to sounds, manipulate color-coded sound, syllable, and word cards, use their fingers to tap syllables, write spoken words and sentences, read aloud, and listen to others read aloud.

❖ EXCITED ABOUT AUTHORS! ❖

Using several technology tools, Miriam Gordon's fifth-grade class developed and shared what they learned about their favorite book authors. Collaborating with the school's librarian, Miriam taught the students how to research information about their favorite authors by using author websites, electronic databases, and encyclopedias. Working alone and in small groups, the students selected authors and located information about their lives. Using word processing tools, graphic organizers, and clip art, they developed time lines, posters, a newsletter, and multimedia presentations on their favorite authors.

Using Technology
Multimedia

Multimedia include Web-based resources, CD-ROMs, DVDs, video, and audio. Multimedia incorporate words, pictures, sounds, video, and interactivity. There is considerable evidence that multimedia can promote learning (Mayer, 1999). Accessibility to high-quality, meaningful multimedia is essential for all students with disabilities.

The multisensory characteristics of multimedia add interactivity to otherwise static learning resources and provide a range of teaching and learning situations. Electronic books, Web-based resources, CD-ROMs, and other technologies have transformed reading instruction from a static experience to a multisensory, interactive one. Hypertext links allow print-based texts to be multisensory by associating audio, video, visual, and graphical elements that allow the reader to interact in multiple ways (McNabb, 1999). Accessibility considerations for students with disabilities include using close-captioned television, captioned videos and software, and described images.

Questions for Reflection

1. Visit at least two websites that support literacy using multimedia. What are the key features of these sites? Share this information with others in your course.
2. Review a multimedia literacy resource such as a CD-ROM, DVD, video, or audio tape. How do these resources engage students? Why or why not are they appealing?

To answer these questions and learn more about using technology to support learning, go to the Companion Website at www.prenhall.com/cohen, select Chapter 11, then choose Using Technology.

STRATEGIES FOR INVOLVING FAMILIES IN CHILDREN'S READING

Involving families in reading activities is critical to students' success. Here are some strategies for teachers to share with family members:

- Listen to children and pay attention to their problems.
- Read with them.
- Tell family stories.
- Have books and other reading materials in the house.
- Share favorite poems and songs with them.
- Take them to the library and get them their own library cards.
- Go exploring with them and learn about plants, animals, local geography, museums, or historical sites.
- Find a quiet place for them to study.
- Review their homework.
- Encourage parents of young children to read to their children.
- Welcome parents as volunteer tutors in your classroom.
- Provide lists of recommended children's books.
- Develop book clubs for parents.

Considering Diversity

English Language Learners

Students who are English language learners and who have reading difficulties require special consideration. Successful strategies for teaching reading to English language learners include (Gersten & Geva, 2003):

- explicit teaching that incorporates models, makes relationships evident, provides prompts, and emphasizes key features of concepts;
- strategies that feature visuals, gestures, and facial expressions that teach the meaning of vocabulary;
- dynamic teaching that promotes interactions among students, maximizes student involvement, and incorporates students' ideas and responses; and
- strategies that involve all students, engage struggling learners, and provide additional time, practice, and review.

Teachers can create learning communities and value all students' contributions. High, reasonable expectations should be held for all students. Actively involve students in reading activities. Provide activities and tasks that students can successfully complete. Assign activities that are reasonable, avoiding frustration. Use scaffolding strategies such as think-alouds, story maps, visual organizers, or other aids to help students organize information. Be sure to provide background knowledge. Ask questions that encourage students to elaborate and clarify. Use cooperative learning strategies and small groups to encourage cooperative learning. Use consistent language in order to avoid confusion. Meaningfully incorporate the students' primary language and respect diversity, culture, and family (Jiménez & Gersten, 1999).

Questions for Reflection

1. Think about how you will involve students from diverse backgrounds in literacy instruction. Describe and share with others several resources and strategies that can be used.
2. Search for resources that can be used to teach reading with students whose primary language is other than English. What resources are available in Spanish, Farsi, Somali, Khmer, and other languages?

To answer these questions and deepen understanding about diversity in schools and communities, go to the Companion Website at www.prenhall.com/cohen, select Chapter 11, then choose Considering Diversity.

SUMMARY

- Teaching reading to students with disabilities involves a repertoire of instructional strategies and assessment approaches.
- Research on teaching reading to students with disabilities has yielded important findings. A research base informs instructional practices.
- Incorporating technology into reading instruction can support students as they learn and practice new skills and strategies and can provide access to content areas.

EXTENDING LEARNING

1. Conduct interviews with a general education and a special education teacher. Ask them which reading strategies they find to be most effective. Compare their responses.
2. Select three teaching strategies described in this chapter. Construct a concept map that identifies the key characteristics of each strategy.
3. Obtain three standardized reading tests. Examine the test items on each instrument. How are they alike? Different? How do the findings compare to those obtained in question 2?
4. Yizhong has a severe learning disability. He is a bright, enthusiastic student who loves science and computers. However, he struggles with reading and writing. Although he is in sixth grade, an assessment of Yizhong's reading and writing skills indicates that his work is not up to expectations. Suggest teaching strategies that can be used with Yizhong. How can technology support his learning?

REFERENCES

Brigance, A. (1983). *BRIGANCE diagnostic comprehensive inventory of basic skills*. Billerica, MA: Curriculum Associates.

Cohen, L., & Spenciner, L. (1998). *Assessment of children and youth*. New York: Addison Wesley Longman.

D'Arcangelo, M. (2003). On the mind of a child. *Educational Leadership, 7,* 6–10.

Earobics literacy launch [Computer software, multimedia tools, and books]. (2003). Evanston, IL: Cognitive Concepts.

Fernald, G. M. (1943). *Remedial techniques in basic school subjects*. New York: McGraw-Hill.

Fountas, I. C., & Pinnell, G. S. (1996). *Guided reading*. Portsmouth, NH: Heinemann.

Geisel, T. S. (1981). *One fish, two fish*. New York: Random House.

Gersten, R., & Geva, E. (2003). Teaching reading to early language learners. *Educational Leadership, 7,* 44–49.

Gillingham, A., & Stillwell, B. W. (1956). *Remedial training for children with specific disability in reading, spelling, and penmanship*. New York: Anna Gillingham.

Graves, M., & Graves, B. (1994). *Scaffolding reading experiences*. Norwood, MA: Christopher-Gordon.

Herman, R., & Stringfield, S. (1997). *Reading recovery* [monograph]. *Educational Research Service, 77*–92.

Jiménez, R. T., & Gersten, R. (1999). Lessons and dilemmas derived from the literacy instruction of two Latina/o teachers. *American Educational Research Journal, 36,* 265–301.

Kaufman, A., & Kaufman, N. (2004). K-TEA/NU: *Kaufman test of educational achievement—normative update*. Circle Pines, MN: AGS Publishing.

Koralek, D., & Collins, R. (1997). *America reads challenge*. Washington, DC: Corporation for National Service, U.S. Department of Education, U.S. Department of Health and Human Services.

Lexia Phonics Based Reading [Computer software]. (2003a). Lincoln, MA: Lexia Learning Systems, Inc.

Lexia Reading S.O.S. [Computer software]. (2003b). Lincoln, MA: Lexia Learning Systems, Inc.

Marinak, B. A., Moore, J. C., Henk, W. A., & Keepers, A. (1997). *Reading instructional handbook*. Harrisburg, PA: Pennsylvania Department of Education. Retrieved March 24, 2004 from the Richmond, VA, Public Schools website: http://www.richmond.K12.va.us.

Markwardt, F. (1997). *Peabody individual achievement test—revised/normative update*. Circle Pines, MN: AGS Publishing.

Mather, N., & Woodcock, R. W. (2001). *Woodcock-Johnson III tests of achievement*. Itasca, IL: Riverside.

Mayer, R. E. (1999). Multimedia aids to problem-solving transfer. *International Journal of Educational Research, 31,* 611–623.

McNabb, M. L. (1999). *Technology connections for school improvement. Teacher's guide*. Oak Brook, IL: National Central Regional Educational Laboratory. (ERIC Document Reproduction Service No. ED437907)

Meese, R. M. (2001). *Teaching learners with mild disabilities*. Belmont, CA: Wadsworth/Thompson Learning.

Miller, S. P., Butler, F. M., & Lee, K. (1998). Validated practices for teaching mathematics to students with learning disabilities: A review of the literature. *Focus on Exceptional Children, 31,* 1–15.

National Reading Panel. (2000). *Teaching children to read: An evidence-based assessment of the scientific research literature on reading and implications for reading instruction* (NIH Publication No. 00-4769). Washington, DC: U.S. Government Printing Office. Accessed at http://www.nichd.nih.gov/publications/nrp/smallbook.htm

Newcomer, P. (2001). *Diagnostic achievement Battery (DAB3)*. Austin, TX: PRO ED.

Pinnell, G. (2000). *Reading Recovery: An analysis of a research-based reading intervention*. Columbus, OH: Reading Recovery Council of North America.

Rhodes, L. K., & Shanklin, N. L. (1993). *Windows into literacy*. Portsmouth, NH: Heinemann.

Routman, R. (1994). *Invitations*. Portsmouth, NH: Heinemann.

Routman, R. (2000). *Conversations*. Portsmouth, NH: Heinemann.

Shaywitz, S. (1996). Dyslexia. *Scientific American, 275*(5), 98–105.

Shaywitz, S. (2003). *Overcoming dyslexia: A new and complete science-based program for overcoming reading problems at any level*. New York: Alfred A. Knopf.

Slavin, R. E., & Madden, N. A. (1999). *Success for All/Roots and Wings: Summary of research on achievement outcomes*. Baltimore: Johns Hopkins University, Center for Research on the Education of Students.

Smolin, L. I., & Lawless, K. A. (2003). Becoming literate in the technological age: New responsibilities and tools for teachers. *The Reading Teacher, 56,* 570–577.

Snow, C. E., Burns, M. S., & Griffin, P. (Eds.). (1998). *Preventing reading difficulties in young children*. Washington, DC: National Research Council.

Stein, M., & Carnine, D. (1998). Direct instruction: Integrating curriculum design and effective teaching practice. *Intervention in School and Clinic, 33,* 227–235.

Swanson, H. (1999). Reading research for students with LD: A meta-analysis of intervention outcomes. *Journal of Learning Disabilities, 32,* 504–532.

Swanson, H., Carson, C., & Saches-Lee, C. (1996). A selective synthesis of intervention research for students with learning disabilities. *School Psychology Review, 25,* 370–391.

The Psycological Corporation. (2002). *WIAT-II*. San Antonio, TX: Author.

Van Allen, R. (1976). *Language experiences in communication*. Boston: Houghton Mifflin.

Van Allen, R., & Allen, C. (1982). *Language experience activities* (2nd ed.). Hopewell, NJ: Houghton Mifflin Company.

Vaughn, S., Linan-Thompson, S., Kouzekanani, K., Bryant, D., Dickson, S., & Blozis, S., (2003). Reading instruction grouping for students with reading difficulties. *Remedial and Special Education, 24,* 301–315.

Wilkinson, G. (1994). *Wide range achievement test-3 (WRAT-3)*. Austin, TX: PRO-ED.

Wilson, R., & Hall, M. (1968). *Programmed word attack for teachers*. Upper Saddle River, NJ: Merrill/Prentice Hall.

12

Chapter

Written and Spoken Communication

CHAPTER OBJECTIVES

After completing this chapter, you should be able to:

- ❖ Describe the functions and types of communication.

- ❖ Describe contemporary perspectives on teaching writing to students with disabilities.

- ❖ Describe approaches for the assessment of written language.

- ❖ Explain how teachers can support students' development of written language and foster positive attitudes, beliefs, and expectations about written language.

- ❖ Describe how teachers can support spoken communication and other forms of expression.

- ❖ Identify ways in which technology can be integrated into instruction.

- ❖ Relate how technology can support students' communication needs.

Communication is critical to human growth and development and is a prerequisite to academic learning. It involves the exchange of information between individuals and may involve written language, spoken language, gestures, signs, signals, or other behaviors.

WRITTEN COMMUNICATION

According to the National Joint Committee for the Communicative Needs of Persons with Severe Disabilities (1992), communication is "any act which one person gives to or receives from another person information about that person's needs, desires, perceptions, knowledge, or affective states. Communication may be intentional or unintentional, may involve conventional or unconventional signals, may take linguistic or nonlinguistic forms, and may occur through spoken or other modes" (p. 2).

Contemporary perspectives on teaching and learning stress the link between reading and writing (Indrisano & Squire, 2000). Some teachers stress the close association between the development of reading and writing and view the development of written language as a process. Other teachers focus on topic development, organization, use of details, and language and writing style. Still others emphasize the development of specific skills such as correct spelling, punctuation, capitalization, and grammar.

Table 12.1	Instructional Approaches in the Development of Written Language					
Instructor Variables	**Direct Instruction**	**Explicit Instruction**	**Cognitive Approach**	**Whole Language**	**Schema Theory**	
Orientation to reading and writing	Emphasis is on the teaching of subskills (e.g., punctuation, capitalization, grammar, spelling)	Skills are explicitly taught	Meaning is constructed from the text	Immersion in a print environment; close link between reading and writing activities	Activate prior experiences; interpret, reconstruct, and integrate knowledge; metacognition	
Instruction	Directed by teacher	Directed by teacher	Teacher and student collaborate	Student, with teacher guidance	Teacher as guide, coach, tutor, collaborator	
Instructional materials	Workbooks, worksheets, spelling lists	Worksheets, literature-based program	Literature-based program, small discussion groups, writing projects	Literature-based program, integrated writing, individual and small discussion groups	Literature-based program, integrated writing, individual and small discussion groups	

Source: Adapted from "Does Whole Language or Instruction Matched to Learning Styles Help Children Learn to Read?," by S. A. Stahl and M. R. Kuhn, 1995, *School Psychology Review, 24,* pp. 393–404.

Research has yielded knowledge of teaching written expression to students with mild disabilities. Gersten, Baker, and Edwards (1999), in a review of the research literature, found that specific teaching strategies can increase students' written expression. These strategies involve an emphasis on planning for writing, explicit teaching of the writing process, revision, and providing clear feedback.

By varying the purposes for writing, teachers can provide students opportunities to write for different audiences. Students should be asked to write about what they read because the process of writing facilitates learning to write. Indrisano and Squire (2000) terms this model of writing *writing-to-learn* (p. 223). Writing can become integrated into daily classroom activities in a variety of ways and formats such as journals, summaries, essays, book reviews, plays, reports, stories, poetry, biographies, autobiographies, newspaper articles, letters, invitations, thank-you notes, signs, posters, menus, riddles, directions, and advertisements. Depending on the background and orientation of the teacher, one or more of the instructional approaches discussed in Table 12.1 may be used (adapted from Stahl & Kuhn, 1995).

CLASSROOM CLIMATE

A classroom climate that supports and encourages writing fosters students' engagement in writing. Examples of writing should be evident, including signs, posters, students' work, and books. Time for talking about and sharing writing should be valued. All students should be encouraged to participate. Teachers and students can both share their writing with each other. Students can confer with each other and make suggestions.

WRITING ACROSS THE CURRICULUM

Writing should not be restricted to language arts. The teaching of writing should be integrated with other academic subjects. Research on writing across the curriculum demonstrates that writing assists students in understanding content areas (Indrisano & Squire, 2000). Writing across the curriculum promotes the development of skills needed for various types of writing, including letters, e-mail, reports, biographies, autobiographies, research papers, essays, poetry, and fiction.

Teachers should distinguish between **high-stakes** and **low-stakes** writing assignments and opportunities (Indrisano & Squire, 2000). High-stakes writing assignments involve making judgments about the merits of the writing. For example, district- and statewide assessments are usually considered high-stakes testing because their consequences can have important implications for a student's grades, classroom placement, or graduation. Low-stakes writing assignments usually are early drafts and can be "messy, tentative, and unfinished" (Indrisano & Squire, 2000, p. 219). They are formative in nature and provide opportunities for students to develop and polish their written assignments.

LINKING ASSESSMENT WITH INSTRUCTION

 The assessment of written language abilities and skills should involve a variety of approaches in order to reflect an understanding of students' abilities, developmental levels, maturity, gender, and ethnic and racial backgrounds. The assessment approaches should include standardized testing as well as a variety of other approaches. The assessment questions, purposes, and approaches used in written language assessment are described in Table 12.2.

A fundamental principle is that assessment of written language abilities and skills should be directly linked to reading instruction. Linking instruction to assessment in written language means that:

- Assessment occurs as a normal part of the student's work. Assessment activities should emerge from the teaching and learning situations. Examples of this type of assessment include the use of journals, notebooks, essays, oral reports, homework, classroom discussions, group work, and interviews. These assessment activities can occur individually or in small groups and can take place during one session or over multiple sessions.

Table 12.2	Assessment Questions, Purposes, and Approaches		
	Assessment Questions	**Steps and Purposes**	**Approaches**
		Screening	
	Is there a possibility of a disability in writing?	To determine whether students *may* have a disability in writing and should be referred for further assessment	Norm-referenced instruments Curriculum-based assessment Criterion-referenced assessment Observation Checklists
		Eligibility	
	Does the student have a disability? What disability does the student have? Does the student meet the criteria for services? What are the student's strengths and weaknesses? Why is the student having difficulty writing?	To determine if there is a disability To compare the student's performance in writing with the performance of the peer group To determine specific strengths and weaknesses in writing To understand why the student is having difficulty	Norm-referenced instruments Curriculum-based assessment Criterion-referenced assessment Observation Probes Error analysis Interviews Checklists Student, parent, and/or teacher conferences Performance assessment
	Connecting Instruction with Assessment		
		Program Planning	
	What does the student not understand about writing? Where should instruction in writing begin?	To understand what the student knows and does not know To plan the student's program To determine instructional approaches	Norm-referenced instruments Curriculum-based assessment Criterion-referenced assessment Observation Probes Error analysis Interviews Checklists Student, parent, and/or teacher conferences Performance assessment

Assessment Questions, Purposes, and Approaches *continued*		
Assessment Questions	**Steps and Purposes**	**Approaches**
Once instruction begins, is the student making progress in written language? Should writing instruction be modified?	***Program Monitoring*** To understand the strategies and concepts the student uses To monitor the student's program	Curriculum-based assessment Criterion-referenced assessment Observation Probes Error analysis Interviews Checklists Student, parent, and/or teacher conferences Portfolios Exhibitions Journals Written descriptions Oral descriptions
Has the student met the goals of the IEP in written language? Has the instructional program been successful for the student? Has the student made progress? Has the instructional program achieved its goals?	***Program Evaluation*** To determine whether the IEP goals have been met To determine whether the goals of the program have been met To evaluate program effectiveness	Curriculum-based assessment Criterion-referenced assessment Observation Probes Error analysis Interviews Checklists Student, parent, and/or teacher conferences Portfolios Exhibitions Journals Written descriptions Oral descriptions Surveys

- The conditions for assessment should be similar to the conditions for doing academic tasks. Students should have sufficient time, have access to peers, be able to use appropriate literacy materials, and have the chance to revise their work.
- Assessment tasks should be meaningful and multidimensional. They should provide students with the opportunity to demonstrate a variety of writing abilities and skills.

A teacher explains the results of written language assessment.

- Feedback to students should be specific, meaningful, and prompt and should inform the students about their work.
- Students participate in the assessment process. They help to generate and apply standards or rubrics. Self-assessment and peer assessment are part of the assessment process.

STANDARDIZED TESTS OF WRITTEN LANGUAGE

Standardized norm-referenced tests of written language can be useful in identifying students with writing difficulties, pinpointing strengths and weaknesses, and evaluating programs.

There are several standardized tests of written language. They are listed in Table 12.3.

USING RUBRICS TO EVALUATE WRITING

In Chapter 4, rubrics were introduced. Two types of scoring, holistic and analytic, are used when evaluating writing samples, written products, portfolios, performance assessments, and exhibitions. Each type of scoring uses a rubric or scale to assign points to different levels of performance.

| Table 12.3 | Instruments That Contain Tests of Spelling and Written Language |

Name	Ages/Grades	Group/Individual	Areas
Diagnostic achievement battery (DAB-2) (Newcomer, 1990)	Ages 6-0 to 14-0	Individual	Spelling Grammar Mechanics Written language
Diagnostic achievement test for adolescents-2 (DATA-2) (Newcomer & Bryant, 1993)	Grades 7 to 12	Individual	Spelling Grammar Written language
Oral and written language scales (Carrow-Woolfolk, 1996)	Ages 5 to 21	Individual or small group	Use of conventions Use of linguistic forms Content
Peabody individual achievement test-R (PIAT-R) (Markwardt, 1997)	Grades K to 12 Ages 5-0 to 18-11	Individual	Spelling Written language
Test of adolescent and adult language (TOAL-3) (Hammill, Brown, Larsen, & Wiederholt, 1994)	Ages 12-0 to 24-11	Individual or group	Grammar Written langugage
Test of early written language (TEWL-2) (Hresko, Herron, & Peak, 1996)	Ages 3-0 to 10-11	Individual	Spelling Mechanics Written language
Test of written expression (TOWE) (McGhee, Bryant, Larsen, & Rivera, 1995)	Ages 6-6 to 14-11	Individual or group	Spelling Mechanics Grammar Written language
Test of written language (TOWL-3) (Hammill & Larsen, 1996)	Ages 7-6 to 17-11	Individual or group	Spelling Mechanics Grammar Written language
Test of written spelling (TWS-3) (Larsen & Hammill, 1999)	Ages 1 to 12	Individual or group	Spelling

continued

Table 12.3	Instruments That Contain Tests of Spelling and Written Language *continued*			
Name	**Ages/Grades**	**Group/ Individual**	**Areas**	
Wide range achievement test-3 (WRAI-3) (Wilkinson, 1994)	Ages 5 to 75	Individual	Spelling	
Wechsler individual achievement test (WIAT-II) (Psychological Corporation, 2002)	Grades K to 12 Ages 5-0 to 19-11	Individual	Spelling Written language	
Woodcock-Johnson psychoeducational battery III (Woodcock & Johnson, 2001)	Grades K to 12 Ages 2 to 90	Individual	Spelling Mechanics Written language	

Holistic Scoring

In **holistic scoring** (Figure 12.1), one score is produced in the evaluation of the student's work. It is quick and efficient. The score provides an impression of writing ability. Holistic scoring rests on the assumption that all of the elements of writing, such as organization, mechanics, fluency, and so on, work together in the whole text. This type of scoring may also be useful when the teacher is looking for one or two previously identified characteristics in a student's work. One important disadvantage of holistic scoring is that it does not provide detailed information about the success of the student in specific areas of writing (Spandel & Stiggins, 1990). Another disadvantage is that holistic scoring does not provide detailed information about a student's culture and world perspectives.

Analytic Scoring

Analytic scoring produces a detailed analysis of the written text. The teacher uses a scale or rubric to assign points to different levels of performance in the areas that are assessed. For example, a teacher wants to describe the ability of students to organize, use mechanics, and use paragraphing. The teacher rates the students' writing samples on a scale, from 1 to 5 or 1 to 6, in each of these three areas, and the student receives three separate scores.

Analytic scoring is frequently done by two or more raters, working independently, who rate the same written text. When they have finished, comparisons are made to determine the similarity of the ratings. If the ratings are dissimilar, the raters may discuss why they gave certain ratings or a third teacher may be asked to rate the text. Figure 12.2 is an example of analytic scoring.

Figure 12.1   Example of criteria used in holistic scoring

Holistic Scoring Guide—Writing

Score	Criteria
5	The paper is superb. The ideas are very well developed. If there are any errors in mechanics, grammar, or spelling they are minor. Sentence structure is very clear and varied. There is a clear sense of purpose and audience. Ideas are explained and very well supported.
4	The paper is very good. The ideas are very well developed. There are few errors in mechanics, grammar, or spelling. Sentence structure is clear and varied. There is a clear sense of purpose and audience. Ideas are explained and supported.
3	The paper is good. The ideas are well developed. There are some errors in mechanics, grammar, or spelling. Sentences follow a similar pattern. There is some sense of purpose or audience. Ideas are not always explained or supported.
2	The paper is moderate. Some ideas are developed. There are frequent errors in mechanics, grammar, or spelling. Sentences follow a similar pattern. There may be sentence fragments. There is little sense of purpose or audience. Ideas are infrequently explained or supported.
1	The paper is poor. Ideas are rarely developed. There are many errors in mechanics, grammar, or spelling. Sentences follow a similar pattern. There are sentence fragments. There is no sense of purpose or audience. Ideas are rarely explained or supported.

SELF-ASSESSMENT

Self-assessment provides students with an opportunity to analyze their own writing to reflect on their own learning. Figure 12.3 is an example of a checklist that students can use when assessing their own writing.

ERROR ANALYSIS

Error analysis is important in the assessment of spelling and other skills. Spelling should be evaluated as part of the development of written language rather than as a finished product. Four principles can be used in the evaluation of spelling (Wilde, 1997):

- Spelling should be evaluated on the basis of natural writing rather than by tests of words in isolation.
- Spelling should be evaluated analytically rather than as correct or incorrect.
- Spelling should be analyzed by discovering the strategies that were used in the context of writing.
- The teacher should be informed about language development and language disabilities and how they can affect the development of written language.

PEER ASSESSMENT

When conducting peer assessments, students have an opportunity to reflect on the writing processes, skills, and strategies of their peers as well as those of their own. Figure 12.4 is an example of a checklist that students use when conducting a peer assessment.

Figure 12.2   Analytic scoring rubric

Analytic Scoring—Writing

	1	2	3	4	5
Development of Ideas	Little under-standing of audience; little elaboration of ideas	Some under-standing of audience; some elaboration of ideas	Good under-standing of audience; good elaboration of ideas	Very good understanding of audience; very good elab-oration of ideas	Excellent understanding of audience; superb elaboration of ideas
Organization	No evidence of an organized plan for writing; ideas and paragraphs run together	Some evidence of an organized plan for writing; ideas and paragraphs are loosely organized	Good evidence of an organized plan for writing; ideas and para-graphs are organized	Very good evidence of an organized plan for writing; ideas and paragraphs are well organized	Excellent evidence of an organized plan for writing; ideas are original, and paragraphs are well organized
Fluency	Language is very limited and repetitive; written text is very brief	Language is somewhat limited and repetitive; written text is brief	Language is good, and there are few repetitions; written text has adequate elaboration	Language is very good and varied; there are no repetitions; written text has very good elaboration	Language is excellent and varied; there are no repetitions; written text has excellent elaboration
Spelling	Few words are spelled correctly	Most words are spelled phonetically; most sight words are spelled correctly	Most words are spelled correctly; some errors with homophones and endings	Words are spelled correctly; there are few errors	Words are spelled correctly; errors are minor
Capitalization and Punctuation	No capitaliza-tion or punctuation	Some evidence of correct capitalization and punctuation	Good evidence of capitalization and punctuation	Very good evidence of capitalization and punctuation; few errors	Excellent evidence of capitalization and punctuation; errors are rare

Figure 12.3   Self-assessment checklist

Name	Date
Authentic Writing	**My Comments**
1. I know my audience.	
2. I take risks when I write.	
Rehearsal of Writing	
3. I think or plan ahead when I write.	
4. I consult with my peers.	
5. I use print and nonprint media as sources.	
6. I help others to write.	
Developing the Draft	
7. I feel that I can put my thoughts down on paper.	
8. I have a good attitude toward writing	
9. I am able to spell most words.	
10. I know which words to capitalize.	
11. I know how to use punctuation.	
12. I make changes to my text based on rereading.	
Revising	
13. I incorporate feedback.	
14. I make changes such as beginnings, transitions, and endings.	
Editing	
15. I am willing to edit my draft.	
16. I am able to edit and correct spelling.	
17. I am able to edit and correct punctuation.	
18. I am able to edit and correct capitalization.	
19. I am able to edit and correct grammar.	
20. I am able to edit and correct paragraphing.	

Research to Practice

Teaching Expressive Writing to Students with Learning Disabilities

A great deal of analysis has been done on research studies that have investigated interventions leading to success in expressive writing by students with learning disabilities. According to Baker, Gersten, and Graham (2003), many students with learning disabilities have inadequate writing and spelling skills. In fact, according to the National Assessment of Educational Progress (NAEP), many students in the United States are not able to write at the basic level. Writing problems tend to emerge in the early grades and continue throughout elementary and secondary school. Research has shown that, for writing instruction to be effective, it should have clear objectives, and students should be asked to write about specific topics. Brainstorming helps students to organize information before writing begins. Baker and colleagues found that students use writing strategies when they value what they write, when predictable writing strategies are used, when teachers model writing strategies, and when planning and revision are built into the instructional routine.

Questions for Reflection

1. Find out more about the research base for developing written language. Identify and share key findings from several research-based articles.
2. Learn more about NAEP by visiting the National Center for Education Statistics website at nces.ed.gov. In what ways is the information on this website relevant to teaching writing?

 To learn more about the research base for teaching written language, go to the Companion Website at www.prenhall.com/ cohen, select Chapter 12, then choose Research to Practice.

Figure 12.4   Peer assessment checklist

Student's Name: Peer's Name:	Date:
1. My peer writes for a purpose.	
2. My peer consulted me before writing.	
3. My peer made changes based on my feedback.	
4. My peer conferred with me.	
5. My peer uses transitions.	
6. My peer is able to edit the written text.	

INSTRUCTIONAL STRATEGIES

Joe Gordon, a high school teacher, was concerned about one of his students. Jacob is 15 years old, loves computer games, plays the clarinet, and is considered to be one of the top basketball players in his school. Despite his success outside of school, he struggles with reading and writing. His reads painstakingly, word by word. When asked to write, he has trouble putting his thoughts in writing. He lacks a firm understanding of how to structure paragraphs, grammar, and punctuation. Recently, he has made some gains with intensive support from his teachers. As you read this section, you will learn about strategies that Joe can implement when teaching Jacob and other students who have written communication problems.

FILL IN THE BLANKS

For class reports, use the fill-in-the-blank strategy (Figure 12.5). This strategy is especially helpful for students who are developing skills in writing and for those who have difficulty recalling details and processing language. Teachers can prepare a series of sentences or phrases and leave one or two key words blank in each one. Students are asked to fill in the blanks or select the appropriate words or phrases.

WRITING PROMPT

A **prompt** is what students are asked to do. It can be as basic as "Write a research report about the city in which you live" or "Write a description of a new tool that would make a task easier" or as comprehensive as "Describe your vision of the city of the future." Teachers can use writing prompts to encourage students' responses. The final piece can take various forms, depending on the purpose for writing. For example, the written piece may be a newspaper article, a review of a story, poem, play, or story, or a report (Rhodes & Shanklin, 1993). Examples of writing prompts include:

I had an unusual experience when
I was surprised when
My favorite animal is
I wish that
One of my favorite things
My favorite place in my country of origin

Sometimes students benefit from having focused writing prompts. Rather than leaving a writing prompt open-ended, such as "One of my favorite things," the teacher could add, "What is something that you really like to do? Is it something you do by

Figure 12.5   Fill-in-the-blank strategy

Snakes are _____.
Their bodies can be described as _____ and _____.
Their skins provide camouflage so that _____.

Figure 12.6   Structured guide to help students generate and record ideas

Topic 1	Subtopics
Topic 2	Subtopics
Topic 3	Subtopics

yourself, with friends, or with your family? Is it something that you do frequently or only occasionally? Why is it one of your favorite things?" The teacher could also give more focused directions by adding: "Be sure the paragraph is at least five sentences long. The first sentence should be the introduction. The last sentence should be the summary. The three sentences in between make up the body of your paragraph and elaborate, explain, and provide details. The first word of each sentence is capitalized. Every sentence ends with a period."

STRUCTURED GUIDES

A **structured guide** is a prepared, preplanned organizer such as an outline, semantic web, or concept map that organizes written pieces. Structured guides can help students generate and record ideas (Figures 12.6, 12.7, and 12.8).

INSTRUCTIONAL STRATEGIES THAT SUSTAIN WRITING

MODELING WRITING

Teachers have many opportunities to demonstrate how writing is done. During the school day, they can model writing. Teachers can write directions for completing assignments, classroom rules, letters to parents and class guests, concept maps, signs

Figure 12.7   Structured writing guide

1. Who is the main character?

2. Describe the main character.

3. Who are the other characters?

4. Describe the other characters.

5. What does the main character want to do?

6. What happens to the main character?

7. What happens at the end of the story?

Figure 12.8   Structured outline for book reports

The title of the book I read is _____. It is written by _____. The main character is _____. Several other characters in the story are _____. The story takes place in _____. The main character wanted to _____. The story ended when _____.

I recommend that other students _____.

and charts, and personal communications to students. As they demonstrate writing, teachers can involve students. They can ask students to suggest the next sentence, spell words, look at the word wall for help with spelling, identify the correct punctuation marks, or recommend a title for the story (Routman, 2000).

WRITING ALOUD

In writing aloud, teachers demonstrate and verbalize the writing process. The teacher uses a word processor in which text is projected on a large screen, a large pad, an overhead projector, or the white board. Brainstorming, organizing, planning, developing ideas, and formatting are demonstrated. The teacher can model how spelling, grammar, and punctuation can be checked. The teacher makes the writing process explicit. Next, students can be asked to model their own writing on what has been observed (Routman, 2000).

Students review new vocabulary words.

❖ WRITING A JOURNAL ENTRY ❖

Here's how Jacob's teacher, Joe Gordon, modeled writing a journal entry about the September 11, 2001, attacks on the World Trade Center: "I begin by brainstorming what I know about the attacks on the World Trade Center. I write down several key ideas: airplanes, explosion, fire, towers collapse. Next, I think about how I should organize the journal entry. I consider whether I should describe the events in the order in which they happened or whether I should tell about how shocked and saddened my friends and I were. I decide to write about the events as I remember them and how I felt. I plan to write several sentences about each of these topics. I will write two paragraphs; each one will have a topic sentence that will describe the main idea. After I finish writing, I will read what I wrote and ask myself if I forgot anything. I will add more details, if necessary. I will use the spelling and grammar checkers on my word processing program and will check to make sure that I used correct punctuation." After he finished speaking, Joe listed the steps that Jacob would need to follow on a writing guide that he kept on his desk.

Jacob listened carefully while Mr. Gordon wrote aloud. When Mr. Gordon was finished, Jacob began to think about how he would begin his journal entry. Like his teacher, Jacob began brainstorming a list of key ideas. He knew that he would continue to check with his teacher as he wrote journal entries. Jacob also knew that he could refer to the writing guide on the desk.

SUSTAINED SILENT WRITING

Sustained silent writing provides a separate block of time that is dedicated to written language. During this period, teachers and students can both engage in writing.

When introducing this activity, teachers tell students that a block of time, for example 10 or 15 minutes, will be set aside every day so that students can focus on writing. During this time, students can be asked to write in their journals, respond to written language prompts, or engage in creative writing.

Mr. Gordon, Jacob's teacher, using the preteaching strategies and one of the graphic organizers discussed in Chapter 6, allocated the first part of the lesson to brainstorming, new vocabulary, and development of concepts. Once these areas are discussed, students spend time writing. When engaging in sustained silent writing, be sure to use a predictable writing routine (Routman, 2000). In addition to the steps described here, Routman suggests that students be asked to write the date every time, save all written work, and leave enough space for written comments.

While students are engaged in writing, teachers can move from one student or small group to the next. Teachers can determine which students are having trouble. Do they have a topic? Are they experiencing difficulty getting started? Do they have enough information? Students can also support each other by sharing ideas and what they have written. Routman (2000) emphasizes that sustained silent writing should be guided by the teacher in order to promote engagement and motivation.

Students use technology to support and improve written expression.

PLANNING AND PRACTICING WRITING

Planning means that students know what is expected. They should be able to choose the type of writing that is appropriate for the purpose. Planning can involve drawing pictures, developing semantic webs, taking notes, using an advance organizer, and brainstorming.

REVISING AND EDITING

Students should have numerous opportunities to revise and edit their writing. Writing the first draft involves fluency and rereading. Fluency involves being able to put ideas in writing and having the thoughts flow. Editing allows the student to correct the written piece. Editing involves making the piece conform to writing conventions; revising involves organization and ideas. Revising and editing drafts are important because they allow students to elaborate, clarify, add or delete information, make corrections, and change the sentence or paragraph structure.

Teaching students to systematically proofread their papers can help students during the revision process. Students may object to others making notations on their written work. Sticky notes can be used to edit students' writing and to make comments and suggestions. Some basic copyediting marks that can be taught to students are:

Figure 12.9   Editing checklist

	Checked by Self		Checked by Peer	
	Yes	No	Yes	No
1. Spelling				
2. Grammar				
3. Punctuation				
• periods				
• question marks				
• exclamation points				
• quotation marks				
4. Paragraphing				

¶   begin new paragraph
lc   lowercase
caps capitalize
∧   insert here

Most word processing programs include grammar and spell check features. Figure 12.9 is an example of a checklist that can be used, either alone or in combination with a word processing program.

PROVIDING RESOURCES

Teachers should make sure that students have appropriate resources available when they are writing (Routman, 2000). These resources include:

- *Alphabet aids.* These can help students remember letter–sound associations. Classroom alphabet charts should be posted. Students can have their own alphabet charts or letter strips on their desks.
- *Word walls.* These were described in Chapter 11. Classroom and students' personal word walls are wonderful sources of frequently used words.
- *Dictionaries and other resources.* Both paper and electronic dictionaries, thesauruses, and lists of frequently misspelled words are valuable resources.
- *Spelling and grammar checkers.* Word processing programs should have both types of checkers.

WORD AND IDEA BANKS

Students can use a word or idea bank that provides words and ideas when asked to write about a topic. Words can be written on cards and stored in a student's file box,

Using Technology
Speech-to-Text Software

Speech-to-text software, or voice recognition software, converts spoken language to digital or electronic text. Students can dictate stories, reports, and e-mail as well as read aloud digital text. Once the text has been entered, students can edit, revise, and listen to what they have written. Vocabulary words can be customized for content areas. Dragon NaturallySpeaking (ScanSoft, Inc.) and IBM ViaVoice are two commonly used speech-to-text software programs. Initial training of users is required so that the software gets accustomed to the user's speech. These software programs are relatively easy to use and are available for Windows, Macintosh, and handheld computers.

Questions for Reflection

1. Visit the websites that feature Dragon NaturallySpeaking (ScanSoft, Inc.) and IBM ViaVoice. What are the essential features of these software programs?
2. How can speech-to-text software programs be integrated into content areas such as science and social studies?
3. Explore how speech-to-text software can be used with students who speak various languages. Which languages are supported?

 To answer these questions and learn more about using technology to support learning, go to the Companion Website at www.prenhall.com/cohen, select Chapter 12, then choose Using Technology.

notebook, or computer. Teachers can instruct students to keep track of new words, words that are particularly descriptive, and new ideas. Students can use a cardboard or plastic container, keep a computer file, or put their entries in a journal.

PICTURE AND MULTIMEDIA FILES

Teachers can develop files of pictures, photographs, and multimedia sources that can be used to generate ideas for writing. These files can be kept in cardboard or plastic storage containers or in computer and Web-based archives. Teachers can encourage students to keep files and to bookmark websites that have pictures, photographs, and multimedia. When teaching students, they can use the files to help students develop ideas to write about, begin their writing, sequence written assignments, and describe details. Teachers can use pictures and photographs that they have collected and organized. Students can be asked to develop their own picture files, including pictures they have cut out of magazines, photographs they have taken, and drawings they have collected. The Web contains numerous archives of photos and pictures that can be used to stimulate writing. For example, the websites of the National Geographic Society, the National Aeronautics and Space Administration, and the Library of Congress are excellent sources.

TEACHING SPELLING

Although Cindee is an average reader, she has struggled with spelling in all grades. When writing, she only uses words that she knows how to spell. She knows only a few spelling rules and has few strategies for spelling unknown words. She relies on electronic spell checkers, peers, and adults to identify and correct errors.

Many students who have reading and writing disabilities need assistance with spelling. Correct spelling can be complicated and arduous because it involves memorization, phonemic awareness, phonics, and editing. (Phonemic awareness and phonics were discussed in Chapter 11.) When the focus is on development of fluency and expression of ideas, correct spelling should be de-emphasized.

REFLECTIONS

Teachers can promote students' reflections on spelling by asking them to think about the words that pose difficulty and the strategies that the students use when spelling unknown words (Sipe, Walsh, Reed-Nordwall, Putnam, & Rosewarne, 2002). Students can reflect on the idiosyncrasies in their spelling and the reasons for misspelling. After writing a draft, students can note on a corner of the paper the words they think are misspelled. They can record these words in a spelling log for future reference. After reading students' drafts, teachers can ask students to identify the error patterns. Prompting students to reflect systematically on their spelling can enable them to be strategic spellers.

WORD STUDY

Some teachers rely on the word study approach (Routman, 2000). Although not appropriate for some students with reading and writing disabilities, this approach can be useful. Repetition of the following steps is encouraged until the word has been learned:

1. *Look:* Look at the word. Identify any unusual features.
2. *Say:* Say the word slowly. Say each syllable slowly.
3. *Cover:* Cover the word. Try to visualize it. Remember any unusual features.
4. *Write:* Write the word.
5. *Check:* Check to see that the word has been correctly spelled.

TEACHING SELECTED SPELLING RULES

Spelling rules can be useful to students. Some students may be able to memorize certain rules; others may need to refer to lists of common spelling rules. Table 12.4 illustrates common spelling rules for Spanish and Table 12.5 presents common English spelling rules.

WORD BANKS AND PERSONAL DICTIONARIES

Have students keep an individual word bank, list, or notebook of commonly misspelled words.

Table 12.4	Examples of Spelling Rules for Spanish
	• Las terminadas en *-bundo, -bunda,* y *-bilidad,* como *tremebundo, moribunda* y *amabilidad.* Se exceptúan movilidad y sus compuestos y civilidad. • Todos los tiempos de los verbos *deber, beber,* y *sorber* y sus compuestos. • Todos los tiempos de los verbos cuyos infinitivos terminen en *-aber,* como *haber, saber,* y *caber;* en *-bir,* como *escribir* y *recibir;* y en *-buir,* como *distribuir.* Las únicas excepciones son *precaver, hervir, servir,* y *vivir,* y sus compuestos (*convivir, sobrevivir,* etc.). • Las desinencias o terminaciones *-ba, -bas, -bamos, -bais,* y *-ban* de los pretéritos imperfectos de indicativo correspondientes a los verbos de la primera conjugación, como *lloraba, estudiabas, danzábamos, mirabais,* y *fumaban.*

Word Lists

Provide word lists when studying content areas. Lists can be placed in students' notebooks, taped to their desks, or added to spell check or word prediction software.

High-Frequency Words

Teach words that are most frequently used (Table 12.6 lists high-frequency spelling words). Students can create rebus sentences, form sentences on cards using frequently used words, make wall and student word charts of the words, and create personal spelling dictionaries. (A rebus is a representation of words using pictures. For example, this picture stands for the word *star.*)

Table 12.5	Examples of Spelling Rules for English
	• Nouns that end with *-s, -z, -x, -sh, -ch*: add *-es* (*glass/glasses, buzz/buzzes, box/boxes, bush/bushes, switch/switches*) • Nouns that end in *-o*: add *-es* (*potato/potatoes, echo/echoes, hero/heroes*) (exceptions: *studio/studios, piano/pianos, kangaroo/kangaroos, zoo/zoos*) (either: *buffalo/buffalo(e)s, cargo/cargo(e)s, motto/motto(e)s*) • Nouns that end in a consonant + *-y*: change *-y* to *-i* and add *-es* (*baby/babies, spy/spies, poppy/poppies*) • Nouns that end in *-f* or *–fe*: change *-f* to *-v* and add *-es* (*shelf/shelves, wolf/wolves, knife/knives, wife/wives*)

Table 12.6	High-Frequency Spelling Words		
	about	have	saw
	after	he	see
	all	her	she
	am	here	so
	an	him	some
	and	his	that
	are	if	the
	as	in	their
	at	into	them
	back	is	then
	be	it	there
	because	just	they
	been	like	this
	big	little	to
	but	look	two
	by	made	up
	came	make	very
	can	me	was
	come	more	we
	could	my	well
	day	no	went
	did	not	were
	do	now	what
	down	of	when
	first	off	where
	for	on	which
	from	one	who
	go	only	will
	get	or	with
	going	our	would
	got	out	you
	had	over	your
	has	said	

Using Technology

Portable Keyboards

Portable smart keyboards, such as AlphaSmart, CalcuScribe, and QuickPAD are inexpensive, lightweight computers. They run on batteries, access wireless networks, and connect to more powerful computers so that files can be transferred. Students can easily carry them from one classroom to the next as they work on their writing assignments. These devices have spell checkers and other common utilities. They are inexpensive solutions for students who need computer access for their assignments.

Questions for Reflection

1. Find out more about these portable keyboards and others by visiting the websites of the companies that have developed these programs. Locate and share information about software that can be added to portable keyboards.

2. Brainstorm ways in which portable keyboards can facilitate teaching and learning.

 To complete these activities and learn more about using technology to support learning, go to the Companion Website at www.prenhall.com/cohen, select Chapter 12, then choose Using Technology.

Word Families

Group word lists into word families. A word family is a group of words that have some of the same letter combinations. Word families can be taught using variations of games such as Concentration and Lotto. Table 11.4 in Chapter 11 lists common word families.

USING SPELLING STRATEGIES

Students may be reluctant to write when they do not know how to spell a word. Let students know that there are a variety of strategies to use when they do not know the spelling of words. Students may generate their own strategies as well. Here are some strategies that Routman (2000) has suggested:

- Draw a circle around the word that you think is misspelled and come back to it later.
- Listen for all the sounds of the word as you say it slowly.
- Picture the word in your mind.
- Look around the room, on the word wall, or in a word bank.
- Use a spelling dictionary.
- Use word cards of frequently used words.
- Use sentence strips that have already been created of word phrases.

What strategies work for you?

Using Technology

Using E-Mail and Electronic Discussion Boards to Promote Writing

E-mail and electronic discussion boards can be used to stimulate students' writing. Student-to-student connections can be made between students in the same classroom or school, with other students in the same community, or with students in other countries. Students can post suggestions, questions, and responses. They can contribute in several ways, including posting to existing educational mailing lists, contacting specific websites, writing to other students and teachers they already know, and working on collaborative projects.

Questions for Reflection

1. List and describe ways in which using e-mail and electronic discussion boards can support literacy instruction. Share your ideas with others.
2. Do you use listservs and electronic discussion groups? If so, describe the ones you use and explain why they are useful.
3. How can teachers use e-mail and electronic discussion boards or groups to support learning?

To answer these questions and learn more about using technology to support learning, go to the Companion Website at www.prenhall.com/cohen, select Chapter 12, then choose Using Technology.

SPOKEN LANGUAGE AND OTHER FORMS OF COMMUNICATION

Communication involves the exchange of information between individuals and may involve spoken language, written language, gestures, signs, signals, or other behaviors. According to the National Joint Committee for the Communicative Needs of Persons with Severe Disabilities, communication is "Any act which one person gives to or receives from person information about that person's needs, desires, perceptions, knowledge, or affective states. Communication may be intentional or unintentional, may involve conventional or unconventional signals, may take linguistic or nonlinguistic forms, and may occur through spoken or other modes" (1992, p. 2).

Language is a system that is used to communicate. For most individuals, speech and language develop in a predictable, but not rigid, sequence. Speech and language developmental milestones are presented in Figure 12.10. For some students who have mild and moderate disabilities, the development of speech and language is not typical. These students may have one or more speech or language disorders or a combination of disabilities. For example, Jesse is a middle school student who had severe seizures when he was an infant, leaving him unable to use spoken language. He communicates with his family, teachers, and friends using hand signals, gestures, and a communication device.

Speech is the spoken form of language. Speech disabilities can vary and include dysfluencies such as stuttering, articulation difficulties, and voice disorders such as problems with pitch, volume, or voice quality.

According to the American Speech-Language-Hearing Association (ASHA, 1982), a **language disorder** is an impairment in the use and/or comprehension of spoken or

Figure 12.10 Speech and language milestones

By Age 1

Recognizes name
Says two or three words
Imitates familiar words
Understands simple instructions
Recognizes some words as symbols for objects

Between Ages 1 and 2

Understands "no"
Uses 10 to 20 words
Combines at least two words
Makes the sounds of familiar animals
Gives a toy when asked
Points to his or her toes, eyes, and nose
Brings object from another room when requested

Between Ages 2 and 3

Identifies body parts
Engages in conversation with self, others, and toys
Verbalizes first name
Displays fingers to communicate age
Enjoys hearing the same story repeated
Identifies common pictures and things
Matches three or four colors
Demonstrates the concepts *big* and *little*
Has approximately a 450-word vocabulary

Between Ages 3 and 4

Relates a story
Has a sentence length of four or five words
Obeys simple requests, such as "Put the toy away"
Verbalizes last name
Says name of street on which child lives
Relates several nursery rhymes
Has approximately a 1,000-word vocabulary

Between Ages 4 and 5

Identifies shapes such as triangles, circles, and squares
Poses many questions, such as "who?", "why?", and "what?"
Has approximately a 1,500-word vocabulary

Between Ages 5 and 6

Has a sentence length of five or six words
Understands spatial relations such as *on top, behind, far,* and *near*
Understands *same* and *different*
Counts to 10
Poses questions for information
Has approximately a 2,000-word vocabulary

Source: Adapted from *Speech and Language Milestone Chart,* Learning Disabilities Association of America, 2003.

written language and involves (a) sounds, words, and word order; (b) semantics, or the meaning of language; and (c) pragmatics, or the use of language in various contexts. Students who have language disorders may have difficulty expressing ideas, incorrect grammar, difficulty understanding the meaning of words, or limited vocabulary. They may hear or see a word but be unable to understand its meaning. An example of sound confusion is when a young child confuses the initial sounds of words, saying "I wike T wee" rather than "I like to watch TV." An error in word order can occur when an individual omits words, such as saying "Me car" rather than "I want to go in the car." An error in pragmatics occurs when an individual does not understand how to take turns in a conversation, understand facial expressions such as sad or happy ones, or make eye contact.

INTERVENTIONS

Speech and language therapists and pathologists may work in schools, agencies, or private practice. Frequently, speech and language therapists collaborate with educators to establish goals and implement strategies that address speech and language problems by providing information, assessment, instruction, and consultation. Depending on students' needs, speech and language therapists may provide individual, small-group, or large-group instruction. Teachers may be asked to carry out interventions with students and to incorporate speech and language strategies as part of their instruction. When teachers suspect that a student has a communication difficulty, they are usually asked to complete a referral form or questionnaire. An example of a speech and language questionnaire is presented in Figure 12.11.

CONSIDERATIONS FOR STUDENTS FROM DIVERSE LANGUAGE BACKGROUNDS

When considering students who have speech or language difficulties, it is important to keep in mind that many students have diverse language backgrounds. The native dialect, syntax, word and phrase meanings, forms of expression, gestures, and body language can impact students' language competence. Owens (1998) has pointed out the complex nature of speech and language assessments and interventions for students from diverse language backgrounds. Winzer and Mazurek (1998) and Polloway, Patton, and Serna (2000) indicate that the following steps should be followed: (a) consider the family and the instructional environments, (b) identify the student's preferred language, (c) assess proficiency in the languages that the student speaks, (d) evaluate communication skills, and (e) involve a speech and language professional in determining communication disorders.

AUGMENTATIVE AND ALTERNATIVE COMMUNICATION

Individuals with multiple and complex communication needs may require augmentative and alternative communication (AAC). According to the American Speech-Language-Hearing Association (ASHA, 1991), AAC interventions should emphasize

Figure 12.11 Speech and language questionnaire

Child's name:
Date of birth:
Grade:

	Yes	No
1. Does the student pronounce words or use sounds or words incorrectly?		
2. Does the student have unusual voice quality (such as hoarse or nasal)?		
3. Is the student's speech difficult to understand? If yes, provide examples.		
4. Does the student frequently repeat sounds, syllables, or words? If yes, provide examples.		
5. Is the student able to follow verbal directions?		
6. Does the student have difficulty communicating needs and ideas?		
7. Does the student rely on gestures, utterances, or signals to communicate? Please explain.		
8. Does the student understand gestures and body language?		
9. Has the student had a recent hearing screening?		
Questions for Students Whose First Language Is Not English		
1. Is the student able to communicate adequately in the native language?		
2. Is the student able to follow directions in the native language?		
3. Does the student use sentences that have appropriate structure and grammar?		
4. Does the student have difficulty pronouncing words?		

multiple modalities and should use "the individual's full communication capabilities, including any residual speech or vocalizations, gestures, signs, and aided communication" (p. 10). ASHA emphasized that an AAC system should use "the individual's full communication capabilities, including the symbols, aids, strategies, and techniques used by individuals to enhance communication" (p. 10). Frequently, but not always, AAC involves technology. It can be accessed using a mouse, touch screen, joystick, trackball, head-pointing device, alternate keyboard, Morse code, or switch. Many types of specialized software programs and hardware support communication. Some AAC devices have digitized or synthesized voices that can be customized, depending on the student's age, gender, and personal preferences. AAC allows individuals to communicate and participate in school, employment, and the community.

Augmentative and Alternative Communication Software

EZ Keys by Words+ has word prediction and abbreviation expansion features that save effort by displaying a list of frequently used words when the student begins to type a word. The student chooses the word or phrase, which is then inserted into the page.

Talking Screen by Words+ is a communication program designed for individuals who may not be literate, may not be able to speak, or prefer using pictures or symbols to communicate. Using this software, students can choose pictures and symbols to communicate. They can also choose one of the numerous digitized computer voices to "speak" for them.

Speaking Dynamically Pro by Mayer-Johnson Inc. allows students to use a Macintosh computer as a communication device. Pictures, symbols, and words can be displayed. Digitized voices can be customized.

Augmentative and Alternative Communication Devices

LightWRITER by ZYGO Industries Inc. is a portable text-to-speech communication device. It has dual displays, allowing two students to communicate. One student can see what is being typed; the other student can see the display.

The DynaVox by DynaVox Systems is a dedicated communication device with a touch color screen that displays pictures, symbols, words, and/or phrases. Using a digitized voice, the DynaVox enables an individual to communicate.

The Palmtop Portable Impact by Enkidu is a palm-sized AAC device that has an external speaker and runs on the Windows operating system. The software displays pictures, symbols, words, and/or phrases.

SUMMARY

- Contemporary perspectives on teaching and learning stress the link between reading and writing.
- Assessment of written communication should be linked to teaching strategies. Assessment approaches can include standardized tests, rubrics, self-assessment, and peer assessment.
- There are a variety of strategies that teachers can use to support the development of communication.
- Technology can provide support for students as they develop and use communication skills. Some students may need AT such as smart keyboards, specialized software, or AAC to communicate.

EXTENDING LEARNING

1. Identify three teaching strategies discussed in this chapter. Compare and contrast the strengths and limitations of each.
2. Visit the websites of the National Council of Teachers of English (NCTE) and the International Reading Association (IRA). Develop a list of resources that can be used to support written language instruction.

3. You have been asked to work with a classroom teacher in supporting the written language instruction of students. Several students have learning disabilities, and one student has ADHD. What strategies could you suggest that the teacher consider?

4. Your team has been asked to develop a newsletter for parents that describes students' activities in communication. Choose one or more strategies and write a brief article about it.

5. Steven, an elementary student, has a learning disability. Pat, a student in a high school English class, struggles with writing. Both of these students are enthusiastic learners. You are the special education teacher who consults with classroom teachers on making learning accessible to all students. What teaching strategies could you suggest for either Steven or Pat?

6. Identify at least two different AAC technologies. How do their features assist communication?

REFERENCES

AlphaSmart 3000 user's manual [Computer manual]. Cupertino, CA: AlphaSmart.

American Speech-Language-Hearing Association. (1982). Definitions: Communicative disorders and variations. *ASHA, 24,* 949–950.

American Speech-Language-Hearing Association (1991). Report: Augmentative and alternative communication. *ASHA,* Suppl. 5, 9–12.

Baker, S., Gersten, R., & Graham, S. (2003). Teaching expressive writing to students with learning disabilities: Research-based applications and examples. *Journal of Learning Disabilities, 36,* 109–123.

CalcuScribe [Computer software]. (2000). San Francisco: Author.

Carrow-Woolfolk, E. (1996). *Oral and written language scales.* Minneapolis: American Guidance Service.

Gersten, R., Baker, S., & Edwards, L. (1999). *Teaching expressive writing to students with learning disabilities: A research synthesis.* Eugene: University of Oregon Press.

Hammill, D. D., Brown, V. L., Larsen, S. C., & Wiederholt, J. L. (1994). *Test of adolescent and adult language* (3rd ed.). Austin, TX: PRO-ED.

Hammill, D. D., & Larsen, S. C. (1996). *Test of written language* (3rd ed.). Austin, TX: PRO-ED.

Hresko, W. P., Herron, S. R., & Peak, P. K. (1996). *Test of early written language* (2nd ed.). Austin, TX: PRO-ED.

Indrisano, R., & Squire, J. (2000). *Perspectives on writing.* Newark, DE: International Reading Association.

Larsen, S. C., & Hammill, D. D. (1999). *Test of written spelling.* Austin, TX: PRO-ED.

Learning Disabilities Association of America. (2003). *Speech and language milestone chart.* Accessed November 13, 2003, from http://www.ldonline.org/ld_indepth/speech-language/lda_milestones.html

Markwardt, F. C., Jr. (1997). *Peabody individual achievement test/Normative update.* Circle Pines, MN: American Guidance Service.

McGhee, R., Bryant, B. R., Larsen, S. C., & Rivera, D. M. (1995). *Test of written expression.* Austin, TX: PRO-ED.

National Joint Committee for the Communicative Needs of Persons with Severe Disabilities. (1992). Guidelines for meeting the communication needs of persons with severe disabilities. *ASHA, 33* (Suppl. 5). 18–20.

Newcomer, P. L. (1990). *Diagnostic achievement battery* (2nd ed.). Austin, TX: PRO-ED.

Newcomer, P. L., & Bryant, B. R. (1993). *Diagnostic achievement test for adolescents* (2nd ed.). Austin, TX: PRO-ED.

Owens, R. (1998). *Language disorders: A functional approach to assessment and intervention* (3rd ed.). Upper Saddle River, NJ: Pearson Education.

Polloway, E., Patton, J., & Serna, L. (2000). *Strategies for teaching learners with special needs.* Upper Saddle River, NJ: Pearson Education.

Psychological Corporation. (2002). *Wechsler individual achievement test II.* San Antonio, TX: Author.

QuickPAD [Computer software]. (2002). Mountain View, CA: Author. Retrieved January 22, 2002, from http://www.quickpad.com

Rhodes, L. K., & Shanklin, N. L. (1993). *Windows into literacy.* Portsmouth, NH: Heinemann.

Routman, R. (2000). *Conversations.* Portsmouth, NH: Heinemann.

Sipe, R., Walsh, J., Reed-Nordwall, K., Putnam, D., & Rosewarne, T. (2002). Supporting challenged spellers. *Voice from the Middle, 9,* 23–31.

Spandel, V., & Stiggins, R. (1990). *Creating writers: Linking assessment and instruction.* Boston: Addison-Wesley.

Stahl, S. A., & Kuhn, M. R. (1995). Does whole language or instruction matched to learning styles help children learn to read? *School Psychology Review, 24,* 393–404.

Wilde, S. (1997). *What's a schwa sound anyway?* Portsmouth, NH: Heinemann.

Wilkinson, G. (1994). *Wide range achievement test* (3rd ed.). Austin, TX: PRO-ED.

Winzer, M., & Mazurek, K. (1998). *Special education in multicultural contexts.* Upper Saddle River, NJ: Prentice Hall.

Woodcock, R. W., & Johnson, M. B. (2001). *Woodcock-Johnson psychoeducational battery-III.* Chicago: Riverside.

13

Chapter

Mathematics

CHAPTER OBJECTIVES

After completing this chapter, you should be able to:

❖ Describe contemporary perspectives on teaching mathematics to students with disabilities.

❖ Describe approaches for the assessment of mathematics.

❖ Demonstrate instructional strategies for teaching mathematics to students with disabilities.

❖ Consider the influence of diversity on mathematics instruction.

❖ Identify ways in which technology can be integrated into mathematics instruction.

Although the mathematics performance of most American students is weak, students with mild disabilities frequently achieve at a lower level than peers who do not have disabilities. Students may experience problems in different grades and in different mathematics domains (Kroesbergen & Van Luit, 2003). Contributing to their difficulties in mathematics may also be problems with reading, communication, cognition, motivation, memory, problem solving, strategy acquisition, and social and emotional behaviors (Kroesbergen & Van Luit, 2003; Miller & Mercer, 1997).

The focus of mathematics instruction in general education has shifted from an emphasis on skills and computation to a vision focused on constructivist discovery learning, an approach that is promoted by the National Council of Teachers of Mathematics (NCTM; Woodward & Montague, 2002). Some critics of this approach (Woodward & Montague, 2002) have argued that a constructivist approach will lead to greater failure of students with disabilities in mathematics. Additional research is needed to identify successful teaching strategies that promote a constructivist approach to mathematics instruction for these students (Woodward & Montague, 2002).

Mathematics encompasses several branches. The four basic operations of arithmetic—addition, subtraction, division, and multiplication—are the foundation. In elementary arithmetic, students study two main types of problems. The first type can be solved by counting objects (or by grouping and regrouping whole or natural numbers). The second type can be solved by measuring or comparing quantities (by using fractions: common fractions, decimal fractions, and percentages). Other branches of mathematics include algebra, which uses letters to solve problems when certain numbers are unknown; geometry, which includes plane geometry and solid geometry; trigonometry, which involves computing the relations (ratios) between the sides of a right triangle; analytic geometry, which involves applying algebra to geometry; calculus, which deals with changing quantities and includes differential calculus and integral calculus; probability, which involves the study of the likelihood of events; and statistics, which analyzes large bodies of numbers.

Mathematics instruction should be connected to other content areas, such as science, technology, social studies, history, geography, languages, and literature. Frequently, students should be asked to communicate their understandings of mathematics. Connections and communication provide the relevance, meaningfulness, and real-word examples that are critical to learning mathematics and facilitating students' understanding of the subject. For example, students can be asked to design a playground, prepare a scaled drawing of it, estimate the number of children who will use it, calculate the dimensions and placement of the playground equipment, and calculate the costs involved. They can represent their work in written, verbal, numerical, graphical, or gestural forms and in three-dimensional models.

Teaching mathematics to students with disabilities has received considerable attention in the research literature (Miller, Butler, & Lee, 1998). Instructional strategies, including the use of manipulatives, visualizations, strategy instruction, problem solving, and direct instruction, have been demonstrated to be effective.

LEARNING DIFFICULTIES IN MATHEMATICS

Learning difficulties in mathematics can range from mild to severe and can be manifested in a number of ways. Because these learning problems in mathematics can occur with disabilities in reading and writing (Garnett, 2001; Wright, 2001), students' difficulties may be compounded.

Some students have difficulty memorizing basic number facts. Although they may spend considerable time and effort trying to remember facts, they continue to experience difficulty. These students may count on their fingers, rely on counting objects, or scribble on paper.

Some students may have difficulty doing mathematical calculations. These students may know the mathematical facts, but their calculations are inconsistent. They may not pay attention to operational signs and symbols such as $+$, $-$, $\times$, $/$, $\geq$, and $!$. Other students may have problems understanding mathematical symbols and may have difficulty with abstract concepts.

Students may experience problems with the language of mathematics. They have considerable difficulty with word problems and the use of technical terms such as *axis, variable,* and *square root*. They may not fully comprehend the problem that is presented, have difficulty formulating their responses, and have difficulty communicating their responses to others. To these students, mathematics may seem to be filled with facts, incomprehensible terms, and procedures that do not make sense.

Some students may have difficulty with visual and spatial perception. These students have trouble following directions, giving directions, reading maps, understanding scaled drawings and diagrams, and comprehending quantities, shapes, and three-dimensional models (Garnett, 2001; Wright, 2001).

LINKING ASSESSMENT WITH INSTRUCTION

 The assessment of mathematical abilities and skills should involve a variety of approaches in order to reflect an understanding of students' abilities. Emphasis should be placed on students demonstrating their understandings by solving real-world problems that are interdisciplinary in nature, developing conclusions, understanding relationships, and generating new questions (Marolda & Davidson, 1994).

ERROR ANALYSIS

The purposes of **error analysis** are to (a) identify the patterns of errors or mistakes that students make in their work; (b) understand why students make the errors; and (c) provide targeted instruction to correct the errors. Teachers, peers, and students themselves can conduct error analyses. When conducting an error analysis, the student's mathematics problems are checked and the errors are categorized. The following is a list of errors that students commonly make (Ashlock, 2001).

Addition and Subtraction
- lack of understanding of regrouping
- confusion of 1s and 10s in carrying and writing
- forgetting to carry 10s and 100s
- forgetting to regroup when subtracting 10s and 100s
- regrouping when it is not required
- incorrect operation (the student subtracts when it is necessary to add)
- lack of knowledge of basic number facts

Multiplication and Division
- forgetting to carry in multiplication
- carrying before multiplying
- ignoring place value in division
- recording the answer from left to right
- lack of alignment of work in columns
- lack of knowledge of basic number facts

Fractions
- incorrect cancellation
- failure to reduce to the lowest common denominator
- ignoring the remainder
- incorrect conversion of mixed numbers to fractions

Word Problems
- difficulty in reading
- inability to relate to the context of the problem
- inability to understand the language and vocabulary of the problem
- difficulty in identifying relevant and irrelevant information
- difficulty in identifying the number of steps required to solve the problem
- trouble in doing mathematical operations (addition, subtraction, multiplication, division)

After an error analysis is conducted, the error patterns should be summarized. However, many errors that students make may not fall into a pattern. Conversely, the fact that a pattern emerges does not mean that the problem is serious. Error analysis should be viewed as a preliminary assessment, and further evaluation of the student's work should be conducted.

PERFORMANCE-BASED ASSESSMENT

Performance-based assessment requires students to demonstrate that they can develop a product or to demonstrate an ability or a skill based on an understanding of concepts and relationships. Portfolios and exhibitions are two types of performance-based assessment that can be used to assess mathematics achievement and disposition.

Portfolios

A **portfolio** is a collection of a student's work that demonstrates the student's efforts, progress, and achievement. When used to document and assess mathematical abilities, portfolios can provide information about conceptual understanding, problem solving, reasoning, communication abilities, disposition toward mathematics, creativity, work habits, and attitudes. Mathematics portfolios help students to see that the study of mathematics is more than discrete rules and procedures (Kulm, 1994). Portfolios in mathematics assessment can be used for program planning and evaluation. A portfolio is not just a folder of worksheets or of all the work that the student has completed. The selection of the contents of a portfolio needs to be carefully considered. The following are suggestions for inclusion (Kulm, 1994; National Research Council, 1993):

- photographs of student projects of bridge building using rods of different lengths
- worksheets that involve students in creating new shapes
- projects that involve students in using software to design quilts from squares
- performance tasks that require students to demonstrate knowledge of geometry
- journals in which students record the processes used in problem solving
- experiments with probability
- audiotapes of students collaborating on projects
- videotapes of students constructing structures or demonstrating what they have learned after analyzing data on rainfall

Exhibitions

An **exhibition** is a display of a student's work that demonstrates knowledge, abilities, skills, and attitudes concerning one project or a unit of work. An exhibition provides a student the opportunity to summarize and synthesize what has been accomplished. In mathematics assessment, exhibitions are useful because students can realize that doing mathematics is more than just a series of worksheets or exercises; it also involves conceptual understanding, problem solving, and reasoning. Exhibitions are useful for program planning and evaluation.

A special educator with students using measurement tools to complete a mathematics activity.

OBSERVING THE STUDENT WITHIN THE ENVIRONMENT

In previous chapters you learned about the importance of considering the student within the physical, learning, and social environments. The interactions between the student and the environment are important assessment considerations.

A comfortable, supportive learning environment can facilitate the acquisition of a positive disposition toward mathematics and can contribute to mathematics achievement. The curriculum, instructional methods, materials, and assessment procedures are all areas of concern. Developing a positive disposition toward mathematics is influenced by the learning environment. Students will be willing to do mathematics when (a) mathematics problems are challenging; (b) students realize that mathematics problems are worth doing; (c) mathematics problems are accessible to a wide range of students; (d) a variety of instructional approaches are used; and (e) multiple assessment procedures are used.

Relationships with other students and teachers can affect mathematics achievement. The social environment is important to the development of self-concept and self-esteem. These, in turn, contribute to a positive disposition toward mathematics. By observing the social environment, teachers can study the relationships students have with peers and adults.

STANDARDIZED TESTS

There are numerous norm-referenced, standardized tests that can be used to assess mathematics achievement. Information gathered from standardized tests should always be coupled with assessment information from other sources. Tables 13.1 and

Table 13.1	Standardardized Tests of Mathematics		
Name	**Ages/Grades**	**Group/Individual**
Diagnostic achievement test for adolescents-s (Newcomer, 1993)	Grades 7 to 12	Individual
KeyMath revised-NU (AGS, 1998)	Ages 5–22	Individual
Slosson-diagnostic math screener (S-DMS) (Erford & Boykin, 1996)	Grades 1 to 8, ages 6 to 13	Individual or group
Stanford diagnostic mathematics test (4th ed.) (Harcourt Brace Educational Measurement, 1995)	Grades 1.5 to 13	Individual or group
Test of early mathematics ability (TEMA-3) (Ginsburg & Baroody, 2003)	Ages 3-0 to 8-11	Individual
Test of mathematical abilities-2 (TOMA-2) (Brown, Cronin, & McEntire, 1994)	Grades 3 to 12	Individual

13.2 list commonly used standardized tests of mathematics and tests that include subtests in mathematics.

INSTRUCTIONAL STRATEGIES

Tracy Spear, an eighth-grade student, was intently focused on a problem that she and the other members of her small group were trying to solve. Tracy's teacher, Duane Bunker, had introduced the problem. Duane had explained, "Today, Jasper Woodbury's [Learning Technology Center, 1996] grandfather challenged him to find the cave in which the family's treasured heirloom is hidden. Your group will need to read the directions to the cave, locate the cave on a map, and communicate accurate directions for the rescuers to find the fastest way to the cave. The mathematics that you will do involves whole numbers, fractions, decimals, proportion, and angles."

Tracy has a learning disability in mathematics. She has difficulty understanding the language of mathematics and does not grasp the connection between mathematical facts and procedures. When presented with word problems, she is unable to figure out the steps that should be followed in order to solve the problem. As you read this

Table 13.2	Test Batteries That Contain Mathematics or Mathematics-Related Subtests

Name	Ages/Grades
BRIGANCE Life Skills Inventory (Brigance, 1994)	Vocational Secondary Adult education
BRIGANCE employability skills inventory (Brigance, 1995)	Vocational Secondary Adult education Job training
BRIGANCE inventory of early development-II (Brigance, 1991)	Ages birth to 7
Diagnostic achievement battery (DAB-3) (Newcomer, 2001)	Ages 6-0 to 14-0
Diagnostic achievement test for adolescents—2 (Newcomer & Bryant, 2003)	Grades 7 to 12
Kaufman assessment battery for children (K-ABC-II) (Kaufman & Kaufman, 2004)	Ages 2-6 to 12-6
Kaufman test of educational achievement/NU (K-TEA/NU) (Kaufman & Kaufman, 1998)	Grades 1 to 12, ages 6-0 to 18-11
Peabody individual achievement test-R/NU (Markwardt, 1997)	Grades K to 12, Ages 5-0 to 18-11
Wide range achievement test-3 (WRAT-3) (Wilkinson, 1994)	Ages 5 to 75
Wechsler individual achievement test-II (Riverside, 2002)	Ages 4-0 to 89-0
Woodcock-Johnson psychoeducational battery-III (Woodcock & Johnson, 2001)	Grades K to 12, ages 2 to 90

Research to Practice

What Does the Research Say About Tracking Students in Mathematics?

Haury and Milbourne (2002) examined the research on tracking students in mathematics. Tracking is the practice of sorting students into different courses or course sequences, called *tracks*, based on their achievement level. Although widely criticized, tracking is commonly used in the United States. Frequently, students with disabilities may end up in lower-track mathematics classes. For the most part, when students who have been in lower tracks are assigned to mixed-ability courses, their achievement increases. A slight benefit of tracking is that higher ability students tend to achieve at somewhat higher levels than when they are in mixed-ability classes. Teachers' questioning patterns differ, depending on the track they are teaching. Teachers of higher track students tend to ask questions that require inquiry and higher order thinking, whereas teachers of lower-track students frequently assign textbook reading assignments and worksheets. For the majority of students, Haury and Milbourne recommend that tracking be discontinued and that all students be placed in mixed-ability mathematics classes.

Questions for Reflection

1. Despite the overwhelming evidence that tracking is not beneficial to most students, many schools continue to use this practice. Can you suggest some reasons?
2. Develop an informational letter for parents that conveys the problems and benefits, if any, of tracking.

 To answer these questions and learn more about applying research to practice, go to the Companion Website at www.prenhall. com/cohen, select Chapter 13, then choose Research to Practice.

chapter, you will learn about the strategies that her teacher uses when teaching Tracy and other students who have difficulty learning mathematics.

In this section, instructional strategies for teaching Tracy and other students with mild disabilities are described. Many of the instructional strategies that were discussed in Chapter 7 can also be applied to teaching mathematics.

NUMBERS AND OPERATIONS

One-to-One Correspondence

One-to-one correspondence is the most fundamental understanding of mathematics. It means that one group has the same number of objects as another group and that a number can be associated with each object. Activities that promote the understanding of one-to-one correspondence include passing one cup to each child, using pegs in a pegboard, matching one cube with another, putting one block in each cup, and using a number line to match a number of objects with the corresponding numeral that represents the number.

☺ ☺ ☺ ☺ ☺	3	6	5
☺ ☺ ☺	2	3	5
☺ ☺ ☺ ☺ ☺ ☺ ☺	5	7	6

Figure 13.1 **Students circle the number that corresponds to the number of smiling faces**

Manipulatives can help to make abstract concepts tangible. Manipulatives include Cuisenaire rods, small blocks, unifix cubes, dice, dominoes, trading chips, bottle tops, variously shaped pasta, beads, seeds, or other materials that support student learning. Figure 13.1 illustrates how students can match objects with the corresponding number.

Mathematical Operations

Mathematical operations are addition, subtraction, multiplication, and division. Students may encounter difficulty grouping, spacing numerals, and sequencing operations. Strategies for sequencing and signaling mathematical operations include fewer problems per page, increased spacing between problems, and grouping similar problems on a page. Figure 13.2 illustrates grouping similar problems on a page.

Figure 13.2 **Grouping similar problems on a page**

142 +96	921 +86	78 +76
876 −42	549 −96	989 −47
54 ×67	29 ×58	98 ×33

Figure 13.3   Labeling columns

1,000s	100s	10s	1s
10	4	9	8
9	7	0	7
20	2	0	5

Figure 13.4   Using dotted lines or boxes

Insert dotted lines between columns or use boxes so that the student can put the answer in the correct column.

$$
\begin{array}{r}
1\ 4\ 8 \\
+\quad 4\ 8 \\
\hline
1\ 9\ 6
\end{array}
\qquad
\begin{array}{r}
2\ 9\ 6 \\
-1\ 4\ 2 \\
\hline
\square\ \square\ \square
\end{array}
$$

Labeling columns involves:

- Using different colors for symbols such as −, +, and =.
- Using a highlighter or colored tape to indicate similar problems on a page.
- Using arrows to indicate that problems should be solved from left to right rather than from right to left.
- Using color-coded areas or arrows to indicate when the student should turn the page and the point at which to stop working.
- Labeling columns for teaching 1s, 10s, 100s, 1,000s, and so on. Figure 13.3 illustrates this strategy.

Using dotted lines or boxes involves:

- Inserting dotted lines between columns or using boxes so that the student can put the answer in the correct column. Figure 13.4 illustrates this.
- Rotating lined paper vertically so that the lines form columns.
- Using graph paper to help students organize problems and keep columns straight.

Prompting

Prompts provide cues, hints, or suggestions that students can use to guide their work. Stick-on notes can be used to provide prompts. Tables or charts can be used as mathematics references. As students develop skills, they can compile a small reference book that includes basic mathematics concepts. Figure 13.5 is an example of a multiplication chart that students can use.

Students can keep a number line on their desks to which they can refer when doing mathematical calculations. Here is an example of a number line.

$$-7 \quad -6 \quad -5 \quad -4 \quad -3 \quad -2 \quad -1 \quad 0 \quad 1 \quad 2 \quad 3 \quad 4 \quad 5 \quad 6 \quad 7$$

Figure 13.5   A multiplication chart for students to check their work

1	2	3	4	5	6	7	8	9
2	4	6	8	10	12	14	16	18
3	6	9	12	15	18	21	24	27
4	8	12	16	20	24	28	32	36
5	10	15	20	25	30	35	40	45

Teachers can explain that when adding 2 and 3, start by moving to the number 2 on the number line two units to the right of 0. Then move three units to the right. The student ends up five units to the right of 0. The answer must be 5 as a result of these movements. If asked to add −2 and −4, first move two units to the left of zero. Then move four units farther left. Since there is a total of six units to the left of 0, the answer is −6.

A fraction number line can be used to indicate fractions that are less than 1, greater than 1, or equal to a whole number. Figure 13.6 illustrates this.

Algebra

Algebra promotes an understanding of symbolic reasoning and calculations with symbols. Knowledge of algebra is critical when solving problems and in the study of mathematics and science. Algebra involves the study of concepts such as *rational, irrational,* and *real numbers, reciprocals, roots, exponents, equations,* and *polynominals.* The study of algebra can be started as early as kindergarten and first grade. For example, students can be taught the meaning of the symbols +, −, and =. They can use and create number sentences with operational symbols and expressions to solve problems such as "Jody has some balls. Kia gave her three more for a total of eight balls. How many balls did she have to start with?" Students can write the following equation: ____ + 3 = 8.

A variety of strategies can be used to teach algebra concepts to all students, including teaching specialized vocabulary. Manipulatives, such as blocks or objects, and

Figure 13.6   Fraction line

A fraction number line can be used to indicate fractions that are less than 1, greater than 1, or equal to a whole number.

$3/4 + 3/4 =$

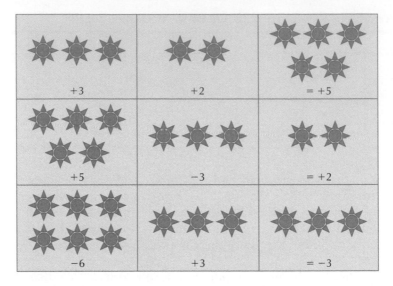

Figure 13.7   **Teaching positive and negative numbers**

number lines can be used to teach positive and negative numbers. Figure 13.7 illustrates this.

The order of mathematical operations should be taught. This means that calculations within parentheses should be done first, then exponents (if any), then multiplication and division (from left to right), and then addition and subtraction (from left to right). A mnemonic for remembering this order is: PEMDAS ("Please excuse my dear Aunt Sally") for Parentheses, Exponents, Multiplication, Division, Addition, and Subtraction.

When teaching algebraic concepts, use multiple representations of problems and their solutions. These include words, tables, graphs, and symbols. Multiple representations support the learning of all students and show students how concepts and their representations are connected.

When computing operations, inequality and equality of operations can be problematic for students. Teach students rules for these operations such as:

Postulates of Inequality

- reflexive property of equality: $a = a$
- symmetric property of equality: if $a = b$, then $b = a$
- transitive property of equality: if $a = b$ and $b = c$, then $a = c$
- addition property of equality: if $a = b$, then $a + c = b + c$
- multiplication property of equality: if $a = b$, then $a \cdot c = b \cdot c$
- substitution property of equality: if $a = b$, then a can be substituted for b in any equation or inequality
- subtraction property of equality: if $a = b$, then $a - c = b - c$

- addition property of inequality: if $a <> b$, then $a + c <> b + c$
- multiplication property of inequality: if $a < b$ and $c > 0$, then $a \cdot c < b \cdot c$; if $a < b$ and $c < 0$, then $a \cdot c > b \cdot c$
- equation to inequality property: if a and b are positive and $a + b = c$, then $c > a$ and $c > b$; if a and b are negative and $a + b = c$, then $c < a$ and $c < b$
- subtraction property of inequality: if $a <> b$, then $a - c <> b - c$
- transitive property of inequality: if $a < b$ and $b < c$, then $a < c$

Postulates of Operation

- commutative property of addition: $a + b = b + a$
- commutative property of multiplication: $a \cdot b = b \cdot a$
- distributive property: $a \cdot (b + c) = a \cdot b + a \cdot c$ and vice versa

GEOMETRY

Geometry involves the study of measurement and relationships of points, lines, angles, surfaces, and shapes. Geometry concepts can be introduced when working with young children and should be integrated with the teaching of science and social studies.

Young children can classify and arrange shapes. Concepts such as *near, far, below, above, up, down, behind, in front of, next to, left of,* and *right of* can be taught. Strategies that promote shape recognition include using a series of pictures and asking students to point out geometric shapes. Once students have identified shapes, they can be asked to match the written name of the shape with the shape. Using textured or rough paper such as sandpaper, students can trace shapes. They can classify pictures according to shape, and can create and describe patterns and shapes. Activities that focus on developing models and constructing geometric figures with manipulatives can be implemented. Students can explore and predict results of combining and changing shapes.

Older or advanced learners can be taught more complex concepts such as how to use formulas and how to calculate the volume of solid shapes such as cones, pyramids, cylinders, and prisms. Students can be asked to solve real-world problems connected to other areas of study. For example, they can create a plan for a park or community open space area. They can apply geometric concepts to the exploration of space and do research on volcanoes.

MEASUREMENT

Measurement involves the understanding of length, width, depth, height, weight, volume, money, temperature, and time. Measurement concepts can be connected to the study of geometry and other areas of mathematics. Strategies for teaching measurement include:

- Before beginning to measure objects, ask students to estimate their dimensions or weight.
- Using either metric or inch rulers, ask students to measure a variety of objects in the classroom such as tables, chairs, blocks, and books. Introduce the

following vocabulary: *square, rectangle, box, wide, width, length, height, measurement, plus, equal, close, closest, long, longest, large, largest, short, shortest, tall, tallest, results.*

- Use three-dimensional models of objects such as cones, pyramids, and spheres to promote understanding of volume.
- Use both analog (clocks with hands) and digital clocks to teach time.
- Use a daily calendar. Use colors to highlight days of the week, changes in the month and season, and holidays.

DATA ANALYSIS AND PROBABILITY

Reading and interpreting charts, graphs, and data are essential skills in being a productive worker and an informed citizen. Students should be able to

1. generate questions that can be addressed with data.
2. select ways to collect data.
3. select and use appropriate methods to organize and display data.
4. develop and evaluate results.
5. generate additional questions based on the data.
6. understand and interpret probability and chance.

Strategies that promote understanding of data analysis and probability are participation in hands-on experiences for collecting, organizing, displaying and interpreting data. For example, students can be asked to collect school-related information on trash that is recycled, beverages that are consumed, the number of students who participate in sports and extracurricular activities, and the number and types of television programs that are watched.

━━━━━ ❖ TEACHER LISA GOLDBERG ❖ ━━━━━

Lisa Goldberg, a special education teacher, was working with a small group of middle school students. She distributed individual packages of colored candies to each student. She told the students that they were members of the sales team for a candy manufacturer and that it was their job to determine if the price for the candy should be increased. One of their first tasks was to determine the number of candies in the individual packages. They counted the total number of candies per package and graphed their results. They presented their results in a bar chart (Figure 13.8).

Lisa asked another group of students to generate a research problem that could be investigated by collecting data. The students felt that a common concern of students is that they worry a lot. They formulated the research question "To what extent does worrying about school increase as students get older?" Next, they constructed a brief questionnaire about worrying that they distributed to other students in their school. They collected and analyzed the data in two ways. First, they presented the data as a scatterplot for all students (Figure 13.9). Scatterplots are very useful in showing the relationships of two variables, such as worrying and age, for

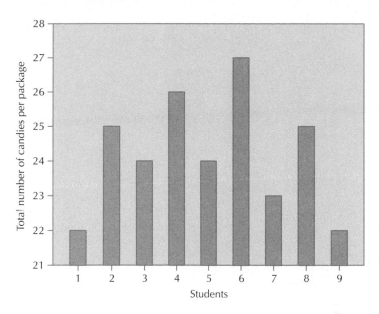

Figure 13.8 Bar chart showing students' tally of the number of candies per package

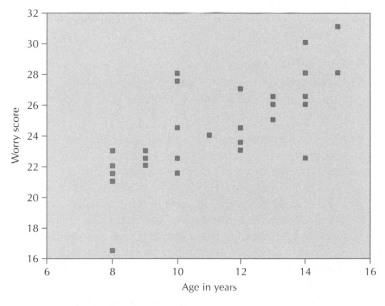

Figure 13.9 Students' scatterplot of worry scores

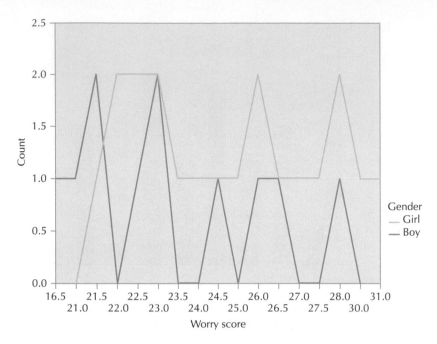

Figure 13.10 **Students' line plot of worry scores for girls and boys**

a group of individuals. Next, they presented the data separately for girls and for boys (Figure 13.10). What did they conclude? Can you suggest the next steps that these students should take?

PROBLEM SOLVING

Solving word problems can be especially tricky for students with learning disabilities or reading problems. The following strategies can be used to help students understand and solve word problems:

- Make sure that the students are able to do the mathematical operations before presenting word problems.
- Teach the meanings of unknown words.
- Read the word problem along with students. Using prompting and guiding, check that they understand what is being asked.
- Use hands-on demonstrations and activities.
- Point out information that is not required to solve the problem.
- Teach abstract concepts using manipulatives, concept maps, drawings, and diagrams.
- Number the steps needed to solve the problem.
- Use a highlighter or colored tape to identify important words.
- Prompt students to restate the question.

Figure 13.11 Breakfast cereal

In this example, a breakfast cereal is used to teach multiplication: $3 \times 7 = 21$.

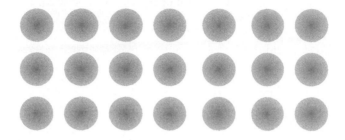

- Ask students to draw a picture of the problem or to use a concept map to visualize the problem.
- Ask students to do the mathematics by using paper and pencil, manipulatives, a calculator, or appropriate software.
- Prompt students to check the mathematics.
- Require students to review the word problem and to check that the answer makes sense.
- Model solving the mathematics problem using verbalizations and manipulatives. In this example, a breakfast cereal is used to teach multiplication: $3 \times 7 = 21$. Figure 13.11 illustrates this.

Use cookies, blocks, or paper circles to indicate fractions. Figure 13.12 illustrates this.

- Teach students the steps to follow when solving word problems. The following steps can be helpful:
- *Read* the question.

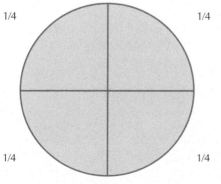

Figure 13.12   **Using cookies, blocks, or paper circles to represent fractions**

- *Restate* the question.
- Use a *concept* map to visualize the problem or *draw* a picture of the problem.
- *Decide* which mathematical operations will be used.
- *Do* the calculations.
- *Check* the work.
- *Review* and check that the answer makes sense.

REASONING AND PROOF

According to the NCTM (2000), "the ability to reason systematically and carefully develops when students are encouraged to make conjectures, are given time to search for evidence to prove or disprove them, and are expected to explain and justify their ideas" (p. 122). Being able to reason mathematically, evaluate, and justify their results enables students to be confident in mathematics.

Inductive reasoning moves from specific observations to generalizations. For example, the general principle is that the sum of the angles in any triangle is always 180°. When evaluating a specific triangle, the students can always work from this general principle. In contrast, deductive reasoning moves from generalizations to specific examples, patterns, or observations. For example, knowing that the month of November has 30 days could lead to the conclusion that all months have 30 days. Although this conclusion is incorrect, this does not mean that inductive reasoning is faulty. Students may use inductive reasoning to discover patterns, to make classifications, or when multiplying by 10 or 100.

Reasoning and proof pervade mathematics. Students use reasoning and proof as they solve mathematics problems, evaluate solutions, learn new skills, and learn new concepts.

CONNECTIONS

Mathematics is an integrated content area that has connections to many domains and disciplines. According to the NCTM (2000), students should be able to understand and identify connections among mathematical ideas and understand how mathematical ideas connect and build on one another. For example, students can apply concepts and skills in geometry, classification, measurement, and algebra as they study patterns of life and the cultures of other countries. Recognizing patterns and shapes can inform the study of science. For example, investigating the patterns of temperature, rainfall, and bird migration can be supported and informed by mathematics.

COMMUNICATIONS

Mathematical communications focus on the organization and communication of clear, logical mathematical thinking, the analysis and evaluation of mathematical thinking and strategies, and the accurate use of the language of mathematics. Providing students opportunities to communicate, in many ways, about mathematics promotes the understanding of mathematics. Students should be involved in reflecting on and communicating what they learn mathematically using the language of mathematics. They should be encouraged to reflect on how to communicate their mathematical thinking across disciplines.

Teachers can promote mathematical communications in a variety of ways. They can encourage students to clarify, explain, and elaborate on their ideas. They should ask students to develop models and representations of their ideas. Activities that promote exploration and application of mathematical concepts can be used. When students collect data on temperature, rainfall, and bird migration, they need to communicate what they did and what they learned. They use mathematical thinking and mathematical language.

REPRESENTATION

Mathematics can be represented in many forms: numerical, fractions, algebraic expressions, equations, graphs, spreadsheets, diagrams, or symbols. This standard focuses on using mathematical representations to organize, record, communicate, use, and interpret mathematical ideas and mathematical representations in order to solve problems. For example, when collecting and analyzing data on temperature, rainfall, and bird migration, students can represent the information in a spreadsheet, table, scatterplot, and bar graph.

Tracy, the student who was introduced earlier in this chapter, and the rest of her classmates in Duane Bunker's class were studying the extent to which paper was recycled in their school. They gathered data on the types and quantity of paper that was placed in recycling bins. After recording their data in a spreadsheet, they represented them in a graph. They summarized and reported their findings in a multimedia format. They then posted their report on their class Web site and shared the information with e-pals.

FUNCTIONAL MATHEMATICS

Functional mathematics prepares students for mathematical topics that they encounter in daily living and work (Forman & Steen, 1999). For most students with mild and moderate disabilities, teaching functional mathematics is essential. Real-life and simulated practical problems are presented to students in order to connect mathematics with daily and work activities. Emphasizing a practical approach, functional mathematics topics can include telling time, identifying money, making change, receiving an allowance, keeping a budget, saving and investing money, using credit cards, and comparison shopping. For example, in a series of lessons on independent living, students can develop and apply mathematics skills when finding out about living costs, including deposits for rent, heat, and utilities, shopping for groceries, and making decisions about entertainment costs. Other students may be asked to develop spending and savings plans for allowances, research the costs of various items by comparison shopping, and calculate the expenses of a small student-owned business such as selling soft drinks, providing pet-sitting services, or doing everyday jobs.

Considering Diversity

Meet Raasfa

Raasfa is an eighth-grade student with a severe learning disability in Dela Devou's class. She is a bright student who works well with others. She has considerable difficulty in reading and writing. The students were studying an interdisciplinary unit on mathematics in Africa. Anchoring the study of mathematics to the standards of the NCTM, Dela connected the unit to literature, geography, technology, and mathematics. Her objectives were to increase the mathematics skills of students and to promote the connection to and communication about the use of mathematics in other cultures. Knowing that the native peoples of southern Africa have a rich history in the use of mathematics, Dela asked the students to investigate the development of ancient mathematics.

Working in a cooperative learning group, Raasfa began her research by searching several digital reference books, including an encyclopedia and an atlas. Next, she and other students in her group met with the school information specialist to decide on a Web search strategy. Once she identified her sources of information, Raasfa used text-to-speech software to read several text excerpts while she followed along as the cursor highlighted each word. Using concept mapping software, she and other members of her group organized their ideas and developed an outline.

Students learn about multicultural mathematics.

Finally, she used word prediction software to write her report.

Raasfa told the other students in the class that a Zulu citizen indicates the number 5 by extending five fingers of the left hand, holding the palm up with the fingers slightly bent; the number 10 is indicated by holding both hands palm up, with the fingers bent and the fingertips of both hands touching (Zaslavsky, 1998).

Ethnomathematics   The study of mathematics can become more meaningful if it is taught in connection with diversity. The term **ethnomathematics** is used to describe the mathematical practices of identifiable cultural groups. Mathematics can be viewed as the development of ideas that involve number, pattern, logic, and spatial configuration in various cultures. Various strategies can be used to promote a multicultural understanding of mathematics:

- Use recipes from other cultures and countries when teaching fractions, ratio, and proportion.
- Incorporate maps when teaching about distance.
- Use a world almanac as a resource for percent problems, graphs, and statistical information.
- Teach games from different cultures that incorporate mathematics.
- Use examples of mathematicians and scientists who have a variety of cultural, racial, or ethnic backgrounds.

- Teach about the contributions of female mathematicians.
- Invite guest speakers from different cultures who can be role models and mentors.
- Encourage and promote the study of mathematics by all students.

The International Study Group on Ethnomathematics has a website with resources and promotes the understanding of the cultural diversity of mathematical practices and the application of this knowledge to education. The Council for African and Americans in the Mathematical Sciences encourages individuals to pursue the study of mathematics.

Questions for Reflection

1. Research number systems that have been developed by other cultures. Share what you learn with your classmates.
2. Conduct research on promoting the participation of girls and women in the study of mathematics. Share what you learn with your classmates.

 To pursue this research and deepen your understanding of diversity in schools and communities, go to the Companion Website at www.prenhall.com/cohen, select Chapter 13, then choose Considering Diversity.

Using Technology
Mathematics Teaching Resources

The websites of the NCTM and the ERIC Clearinghouse for Science, Mathematics, and Environmental Education contain resources for using technology in mathematics instruction, including online multimedia applications, interactive Web-based mathematical activities, lesson plans, and professional resources.

"Ask an expert" websites, such as Dr. Math, allow students to ask mathematics experts questions. There are a variety of "ask a mathematician" websites, including those that focus on algebra, geometry, and statistics.

Web-based software and freestanding programs, such as the following, provide opportunities for direct instruction, tutoring, practice, modeling, and problem solving:

Destination Math (Riverdeep Interactive Learning) is a software series, sequenced from prekindergarten through high school,

that places the study of mathematics in real-life contexts.

Graph Club (Tom Snyder Productions) allows elementary school students to create and explore picture, bar, line, and circle graphs.

IntelliMathics (IntelliTools) for students in kindergarten through eighth grade, uses onscreen manipulatives to solve mathematics problems.

Math Workshop (Broderbund) provides activities for learning in addition, subtraction, multiplication, division, fractions, estimating, and basic geometry.

Millie's Math House (Edmark) is intended for students who are learning basic concepts about numbers, shapes, sizes, quantities, patterns, sequencing, addition, and subtraction.

The Geometer's Sketchpad (Key Curriculum Press) can be used with middle school through college students. It allows students to dynamically construct, explore, and visualize geometric figures.

Questions for Reflection

1. Search for "ask the expert" websites. Describe the resources that are available.
2. Obtain one or more mathematics education software programs. Compare the features. Which software programs would you use as a teacher?

To answer these questions and learn more about using technology to support learning, go to the Companion Website at www. prenhall.com/cohen, select Chapter 13, then choose Using Technology.

A student uses technology to learn mathematics concepts.

SUMMARY

- Contemporary perspectives on teaching and learning stress that mathematics should be integrated into content area teaching.
- There is a range of strategies that teachers can use to support students' mathematics learning. A variety of assessment approaches should be used and linked to teaching and learning activities.
- The term *ethnomathematics* describes the mathematical practices of various cultural groups.
- Mathematics can be viewed as the development of ideas involving number, pattern, logic, and spatial configuration in various cultures.
- Using ethnomathematics as a springboard, teachers can develop interdisciplinary units that integrate the study of mathematics with science, technology, social studies, history, geography, languages, and literature.

EXTENDING LEARNING

1. Identify three teaching strategies discussed in this chapter. Compare and contrast the strengths and limitations of each.
2. Visit the websites of the NCTM. Develop a list of resources that can be used to support mathematics instruction.
3. You have been asked to work with a classroom teacher in supporting the mathematics instruction of students. Several students in the class have learning disabilities, and one student has ADHD. Choose a grade level. What strategies could you suggest that the teacher consider?
4. Your team has been asked to develop a resource guide for parents that describes students' activities in mathematics instruction. Choose one or more resources and write a brief summary of each.
5. Kia, an elementary student, has a learning disability. Mark is a student who is identified as having a disability relating to memory in a high school mathematics class. Both of these students are enthusiastic learners. You are the special education teacher who consults with classroom teachers on making learning accessible to all students. What are several teaching strategies that you could suggest for either Kia or Mark?

REFERENCES

AGS Publishing. (1998). *KeyMath revised/NU*. Circle Pines, MN: Author.

Ashlock, R. (2001). *Error patterns in computation: Using patterns to improve instruction*. Upper Saddle River, NJ: Prentice Hall.

Brigance, A. H. (1991). *BRIGANCE inventory of early development-II*. Billerica, MA: Curriculum Associates.

Brigance, A. H. (1994). *BRIGANCE life skills inventory*. Billerica, MA: Curriculum Associates.

Brigance, A. H. (1995). *BRIGANCE employability skills inventory*. Billerica, MA: Curriculum Associates.

Brown, V., Cronin, M., & McEntire, E. (1994). *Test of mathematical abilities-2*. Austin, TX: PRO-ED.

Destination Math [Computer software]. Novato, CA: Riverdeep Interactive Learning.

Erford, B., & Boykin, R. (1996). *Slosson-diagnostic math screener*. Aurora, NY: Slosson Educational Publications.

Forman, S., & Steen, L. (1999). *Beyond eighth grade: Functional mathematics for life and work*. Portland, OR: Northwest Regional Laboratory.

Garnett, K. (2001). *Math learning disabilities*. Retrieved February 7, 2001, from the LD Online website: http://www.ldonline.org

Geometer's Sketchpad [Computer software]. Emeryville, CA: Key Curriculum Press.

Ginsburg, H. P., & Baroody, A. J. (2003). *Test of early mathematics ability-3*. Austin. TX: PRO-ED.

Graph Club [Computer software]. Watertown, MA: Tom Snyder Productions.

Harcourt Brace Educational Measurement. (1995). *Stanford diagnostic mathematics test*. San Antonio, TX: Author.

Haury, D. L., & Milbourne, L. A. (2002). *Should students be tracked in math or science?* Columbus, OH: ERIC Clearinghouse for Science, Mathematics, and Environmental Education. (ERIC Document Reproduction Service Number EDO-SE-99-04)

IntelliMathics [Computer software]. Pentaluma, CA: IntelliTools.

Kaufman, A., & Kaufman, N. (1998). *Kaufman test of educational achievement/NU*. Circle Pines, MN: AGS.

Kaufman, A., & Kaufman, N. (2004). *Kaufman assessment battery for children-II*. Circle Pines, MN: AGS.

Kroesbergen, E. H., & Van Luit, J. (2003). Mathematics interventions for children with special needs. *Remedial and Special Education, 24,* 97–114.

Learning Technology Center. (1996). *The adventures of Jasper Woodbury* [Videodisc]. Atlanta: Optical Data Corporation.

Kulm, G. (1994). *Mathematics assessment: What works in the classroom*. Baltimore, MD: Jossey-Bass.

Markwardt, F. (1997). *Peabody individual achievement test-revised/normative update*. Circle Pines, MN: AGS.

Marolda, M., & Davidson, P. (1994). Assessing mathematical abilities and learning approaches. In C. Thornton & N. Bley (Eds.), Windows of opportunity: Mathematics for students with special needs (pp. 83–114). Reston, VA: National Council of Teachers of Mathematics.

Miller, S. P., Butler, F. M., & Lee, L. (1998). Validated practices for teaching mathematics to students with learning disabilities: A review of the literature. *Focus on Exceptional Children, 31,* 1–15.

Math Workshop [Computer software]. Novato, CA: Broderbund.

Miller, S. P., & Mercer, C. D. (1997). Educational aspects of mathematics disabilities. *Journal of Learning Disabilities, 30,* 47–56.

Millie's Math House [Computer software]. Cambridge, MA: Edmark.

National Council of Teachers of Mathematics. (2000). *Principles and standards for school mathematics*. Reston, VA: Author.

National Research Council. (1993). *Measuring what counts: A conceptual guide for mathematics assessment*. Washington, DC: Author.

Newcomer, P. (1993). *Diagnostic achievement test for adolescents-2*. Austin, TX: PRO-ED.

Newcomer, P. (2001). *Diagnostic achievement battery-3*. Austin, TX: PRO-ED.

Newcomer, P., & Bryant, B. (2003). *Diagnostic achievement test for adolescents-2*. Austin, TX: PRO-ED.

Riverside Publishing. (2002). *Wechsler individual achievement test-III*. Itasca, IL: Author.

Wenglinsky, H. (1998). *Does it compute? The relationship between educational technology and student achievement in mathematics*. Princeton, NJ: Educational Testing Service. Retrieved from ftp://ftp.ets.org/pub/res/technolog.pdf

Wilkinson, G. (1994). *Wide range achievement test-3*. Austin, TX: PRO-ED.

Woodcock, R., & Johnson, M. B. (2001). *Woodcock-Johnson psychoeducational battery-III*. Chicago: Riverside.

Woodward, J., & Montague, M. (2002). Meeting the challenge of mathematics reform for students with LD. *Journal of Special Education, 36*, 89–101.

Wright, C. C. (2001). *Learning disabilities in mathematics*. Retrieved February 7, 2001, from the LD Online website: http://www. ldonline.org

Zaslavsky, C. (1998). *Math games & activities from around the world*. Chicago: Chicago Review Press.

14

Science and Social Studies

CHAPTER OBJECTIVES

After completing this chapter, you should be able to:

- ❖ Describe contemporary perspectives on teaching science and social studies to students with disabilities.

- ❖ Describe approaches for the assessment of science and social studies.

- ❖ Explain how teachers can support students' understanding of science and social studies and foster positive attitudes, beliefs, and expectations about learning these subjects.

- ❖ Identify ways in which technology can be integrated into science and social studies instruction.

- ❖ Consider the influence of diversity on science and social studies instruction.

SCIENCE

Science is a critically important content area for all students. A major principle underlying contemporary approaches to the teaching of science is that science is for all students. Every citizen should be knowledgeable about science so that informed decisions can be made about current problems such as global warming and sea level change. Science provides exciting and fulfilling career opportunities at a variety of levels. Students need many and varied opportunities to become scientifically literate. Science education should begin in the early grades and continue throughout the school period.

Approaches to teaching science have changed over the years (Table 14.1). The study of science helps students make sense of their world and promotes the development of concepts, problem solving, and critical thinking skills. As citizens who will be asked to make decisions about the world in which they live, students need to be informed. They should have many and varied opportunities for investigating, collecting, sorting, cataloging, observing, understanding relationships, analyzing, and drawing conclusions. For example, they need to know and understand:

- how their environment shapes them,
- how they impact their environment,
- how to keep their minds and bodies healthy,
- life cycles,
- sources of energy,
- how science applies to their daily lives, and
- careers in science.

Table 14.1	Teaching Science: Then and Now	
	Then	**Now**
	All students are taught in the same way.	Teaching responds to individual strengths and needs of students.
	The same curriculum is applied to all students.	The curriculum is selected and modified.
	Learning and memorization of concepts are emphasized.	Student understanding and application of the scientific approach are emphasized.
	Learners work independently. Students compete.	Learning communities and group discussions are established. Students share responsibility for learning.
	End-of-chapter or unit tests are given.	Continuous assessment includes varied methods.

Source: Adapted from *National Science Education Standards,* National Committee on Science Education Standards and Assessment, 1996, Washington, DC: National Research Council.

The teaching and learning of science should be interactive. Active, inquiry-based learning promotes engagement, helps students build concepts, and promotes an understanding of their world. The construction of knowledge is exciting and blends the application of factual information with creativity and imagination. As students inquire about science, they need to be actively involved in their quest for scientific knowledge.

Dr. Larry Scadden, former director of the Program for Persons with Disabilities at the National Science Foundation, is a scientist who is blind. He has offered this advice: "I think the best way to work with a person with a disability is to ask them what they need and allow them to work from that point, rather than doing something for somebody. Give them the tools so that they can do it themselves. In my talks to persons with disabilities, I always just tell them to let their expectations soar, and the people around them should let their expectations soar for someone with a disability and give them the opportunity to succeed" (Scadden, personal communication).

Ridgway, Titterington, and McCann (1999) have identified characteristics of high-quality science education programs for students in elementary and secondary schools:

- Include the vision outlined in the national science standards.
- Allow for students' past experiences.
- Include real-life applications.
- Incorporate hands-on activities.
- Consider individual strengths and needs.
- Use individualized instruction.

- Integrate science education with other content areas using an interdisciplinary approach.
- Incorporate multimedia.
- Include cooperative learning.
- Allow for group discussion.
- Use a problem-solving approach.
- Include ongoing embedded assessment.

 ## *LINKING ASSESSMENT WITH INSTRUCTION*

——————— ❖ *A MIDDLE SCHOOL SCIENCE CLASS* ❖ ———————

You have been invited to accompany a group of middle school students, their teacher, Juan Peres, and two environmental scientists on a visit to a nearby river in order to check on a field experiment that focuses on the destruction of ecological environments. In several parts of the world, including North America, many native frog species have disappeared. Since frogs have permeable skins, they readily absorb toxic substances. The students in the class will be investigating aspects of the environment that may have led to the disappearance of frog species.

Several weeks ago, the students placed frog eggs in screened boxes that allow water to flow over them. On top of several boxes, they placed plastic filters that block ultraviolet radiation. Several other boxes were left uncovered, exposing the eggs to the sun's rays. Today, they were going to discover which of the eggs hatched.

These students are collecting science data.

What do you think that the students discovered when they examined the frog eggs? The eggs that had been shielded from ultraviolet radiation hatched; the uncovered eggs did not. After the students examined the boxes, they engaged in a discussion about the river environment with their teacher and the two scientists.

Juan Peres, the teacher, used a variety of approaches to assess his students' understanding, including assessment rubrics, student journals, and anecdotal observations. Students are required to keep a journal of their observations. Ashley used an adapted keyboard and a software scanning program to record her observations. Paula, Sean, Clara, and Juanita, who have learning disabilities, used concept mapping software to organize their observations before recording them. All students were asked to keep a portfolio that contained their data recording sheets, hypotheses they had developed, and e-mail conversations with students in Costa Rica who were also studying the impact of the environment on frog populations.

Assessment of science instruction should be ongoing. Frequent assessment of student learning provides feedback that instruction is aligned with the curriculum, standards, and benchmarks. Ongoing assessment provides information on students' understanding of scientific concepts and helps teachers adjust or adapt teaching methods to the learning needs of individual students. Assessments should be designed so that they provide feedback about the understanding of rich, complex scientific knowledge, principles, and reasoning. Assessments inform

- students about their achievement, expectations, attitudes, and beliefs.
- teachers about the quality of their science lessons, activities, and programs.
- parents about their child's progress.
- school districts about the effectiveness of science programs.

INSTRUCTIONAL STRATEGIES

— ❖ STUDYING SCIENCE IN SETH ALLEN'S CLASS ❖ —

When teaching a unit on the properties of objects and materials, Seth Allen, a fourth-grade teacher, asks his students what will happen if they place an ice cube in a dish and leave it there until recess. Tami, who is nonverbal, uses an augmentative communication device with speech output to answer. She replies that the ice cube will melt. Seth asks the students what causes the ice cube to melt. Rosa answers that the classroom is warmer than the ice cube and that ice melts when the air around it is warm. Seth groups his students into pairs and gives each pair two disposable cups. One cup contains an ice cube; the other cup contains an ice cube and warm water. He explains that they will perform an experiment to see which ice cube melts faster. Before beginning, Seth asks the students to predict the answer. At the end of the experiment, the students discover that the ice cubes immersed in water melted faster. Seth asks, "Does water or air provide more heat?" The students discuss how they can investigate whether heat is conveyed differently by various substances such as salt water, sugar water, vinegar, and juice. They develop hypotheses and procedures to test them. The next day, they will continue their investigations (adapted from Lowery, 1997).

Many of the teaching strategies such as scaffolding, concept maps, word walls, and infusion of technology that were discussed in previous chapters can also be applied to science education. Considerable evidence demonstrates that when adaptations are made in science classrooms and laboratories, students with disabilities can be very successful (Mastropieri & Scruggs, 1992). Review previous chapters, your notes, and discussions. Which teaching strategies are particularly relevant to teaching science?

TEACHING AND LEARNING FRAMEWORK

A teaching and learning framework supports students in moving from concrete thinking to abstract concepts. It has four steps: preteaching, guided practice, application, and assessment. Each step can take a few days or a few weeks to complete.

1. *Preteaching.* Students engage in hands-on activities that allow them to explore a topic. Activities can be open-ended or guided and include holding discussions that generate informed guesses or hypotheses, conducting observations, collecting data, and analyzing data. Students work in small groups to brainstorm explanations, make predictions, and create experiments that test hypotheses. Preteaching with engaging activities allows students to reflect on what they already know and connect prior knowledge with new experiences and instruction.

2. *Guided practice.* The teacher uses guided practice with one or more students, during which students receive feedback and instructional support based on close monitoring of their activities. This helps students construct their own meaning from the activities. Guided practice activities include direct instruction, demonstrations, simulations, experimentation, and discussions.

3. *Application.* Once students have become familiar with a topic, they can begin to apply it to new situations, make predictions, and develop new hypotheses. When new information is discovered, there can be some overlap between application and preteaching for the next activities. The overlap can help students understand how conclusions from research lead to new research questions, problems, and hypotheses.

4. *Assessment.* Assessment provides feedback to the teacher about instruction and information on what students know and are able to do. The results of assessment help teachers to adjust and individualize instruction.

INQUIRY-BASED INSTRUCTION

Active, inquiry-based, hands-on learning helps diverse learners to construct knowledge, capitalize on each other's strengths, and develop an understanding of scientific concepts. Learning is facilitated when students develop their own ideas and knowledge through high-quality, meaningful learning activities. When students construct their own knowledge, the study of science is exciting. Active, inquiry-based science helps make abstract ideas concrete. As students raise questions, they should be actively involved in their quest for scientific knowledge.

Inquiry-based instruction has the following characteristics:

- Students make connections to previous knowledge.
- Students bring their own questions to learning.
- Students investigate to try out their own ideas.
- Students communicate what they learn in multiple ways, such as journal writing, oral presentations, drawings, and demonstrations.
- Students develop and revise explanations.

The 5E Instructional Model

The **5E instructional model** (Trowbridge & Bybee, 1996) is based on an inquiry-based model of instruction. The model guides the teacher in helping students connect new learning with prior knowledge, redefine, reorganize, elaborate, and build new concepts. The model has five phases: engagement, exploration, explanation, elaboration, and evaluation. Table 14.2 illustrates the teaching and learning activities in the 5E model.

Engagement. In this stage, the teacher engages in a problem, situation, or event. The instructional activities focus on connecting prior learning to new learning experiences.

Exploration. Students are involved in activities that allow them to explore objects, problems, events, or situations as they build new ideas and concepts.

Explanation. Once exploration has occurred, concepts, processes, and skills are explained. Both students and teachers provide explanations, and terms are defined. The goal is to arrive at a clear, concise explanation that connects students' explanations and observations to new learning.

Elaboration. Students are engaged in experiences that extend or elaborate on new learning. New problems may be introduced as a way to test students' understanding and to clarify misconceptions.

Evaluation. Evaluation of student outcomes and feedback on instruction should be obtained. A variety of assessment approaches can be used, including performance-based assessment, portfolios, informal measures, journal entries, interviews, and standardized assessment. Assessment approaches are discussed later in this chapter.

QUESTIONING

The use of questioning, both by students and by the teacher, helps students to understand more deeply, apply what they know, elaborate, and explain what they know. The use of questions promotes inquiry and critical thinking and develops higher order thinking skills. Table 14.3 shows how Bloom's taxonomy can be used as a guide in developing questions.

Table 14.2	5E Instructional Model	
Stage	**What the Teacher Does**	**What the Student Does**
Engage	Develops students' interest in and curiosity about the topic Asks questions Connects instruction with students' prior knowledge and experiences	Demonstrates interest Asks questions
Explore	Provides opportunities for students to work together Observes students and provides feedback Generates questions for further exploration Consults with students	Examines predictions Tests hypotheses Reformulates hypotheses Records observations and ideas
Explain	Connects new explanations with prior learning Asks students for evidence Provides formal definitions and explanations	Connects new explanations to prior learning Provides evidence to explain observations and ideas Incorporates observations in explanations Develops questions about other students' explanations
Elaborate	Asks students to extend and apply what they have learned to new situations Encourages students to incorporate new terms, definitions, examples, and concepts in their explanations Asks students to refer to evidence in their explanations Checks for understanding	Apply what they have learned to new situations Incorporate new terms, definitions, examples, and concepts in their explanations Refer to evidence in their explanations Ask questions based on new information Propose new solutions Draw conclusions
Evaluate	Uses a variety of informal and formal approaches to assess student learning Assesses instructional methods Revises instruction based on informal and formal evaluation	Demonstrates understanding using a variety of approaches Uses self-evaluation techniques

Source: Adapted from *Teaching Secondary School Science,* by L. W. Trowbridge and R. W. Bybee, 1996, Upper Saddle River, NJ: Merrill/Prentice Hall.

Table 14.3	Applying Bloom's Taxonomy		
Level	**Description**	**Verbs Used in Questions**	
Knowledge	The learner recalls factual information.	*describe* *define* *draw* *select* *name* *locate*	
Comprehension	The learner understands what is being communicated.	*explain* *predict* *summarize* *illustrate* *paraphrase* *express*	
Application	The learner uses ideas in specific, concrete situations.	*apply* *change* *interpret* *dramatize* *make* *produce* *solve* *model*	
Analysis	The learner can break down a task into its components, steps, or parts.	*analyze* *classify* *contrast* *infer* *differentiate*	
Synthesis	The learner puts together elements or parts to form a whole.	*combine* *construct* *organize* *formulate*	
Evaluation	The learner makes judgments about the value of material, ideas, or methods within a specific context.	*evaluate* *assess* *critique* *judge*	

Reciprocal Teaching

Reciprocal teaching (Palincsar & Brown, 1984) actively supports students as they construct meaning. Originally developed to aid reading comprehension, reciprocal teaching is especially useful in science because it promotes critical inquiry and can be adapted to demonstrations and laboratory activities.

When introducing reciprocal teaching, the teacher explains and models four steps. Students practice them and take the role of the teacher with each other. Once students are able to use this strategy with each other, the teacher's role involves monitoring, providing feedback, and encouraging independence. Students are encouraged to interact directly with each other.

Students are required to use each step when encountering new material. The four steps are:

1. *Summarizing:* involves recognizing important information and communicating it concisely.
2. *Question generating:* asks students to think about what they don't know, need to know, or would like to know. This step can be useful in forming hypotheses.
3. *Clarifying:* focuses on constructing meaning and learning new concepts.
4. *Predicting:* involves making reasonable guesses or estimations based on information.

Think-Alouds

Thinking aloud helps students focus on a particular problem, remember steps, organize their thoughts, and demonstrate problem-solving strategies. Thinking aloud is particularly useful when teaching science. When first teaching students to think aloud, teachers can model the process.

Think-alouds are actually a form of debriefing. Debriefing strategies (Roth, 1987) can be activities in which students share what they have learned. During debriefing, the teacher can ask questions, encourage, and prompt students. Other debriefing activities include:

- journal writing,
- writing a story in which the student is a major character, and
- developing concept maps.

Using Scaffolding to Support Problem Solving

Consider the following questions: How do we get energy from plants? How do microorganisms enter our bodies through open cuts and sores in the skin? What are the effects on plants and animals when the environmental temperature is below 32 °F? The answers to these questions are complex and require students to integrate previously learned concepts and experiences with newly acquired information.

Chapter 7 described instructional scaffolding as a technique that supports students as they learn new strategies and skills. As learners take more responsibility for

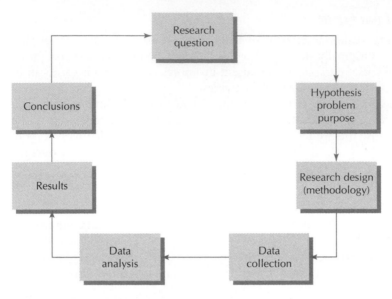

Figure 14.1   Visual organizer of the scientific process

their learning, the structures, supports, and scaffolds can be faded and learners can work independently.

Scaffolded problem-solving strategies provide learners with supports that enable them to solve problems using concepts and information that they already know (but may not be aware that they know!). Here are six steps that can be used in scaffolding experiences in science:

1. With the student, write down information that is provided in a problem.
2. Record what is being asked. What is the question?
3. Recall and record information from prior learning that may be helpful.
4. Develop a plan on how to solve the problem. The student can use drawings, visual organizers, dictation, or narration.
5. Develop a first response or draft to solving the problem using the plan in step 4. Review the accuracy of the solution and make any necessary changes.
6. Review the problem, each of the scaffolding steps, and revise the solution, if necessary (see Figure 14.1).

ACCOMMODATIONS FOR SPECIFIC DISABILITIES

The following lists provide examples of accommodations that can be made when teaching science (Burgstahler & Norse, 1998; Lewi & Sadler, 1999).

STUDENTS WHO HAVE LEARNING DISABILITIES

For students with learning disabilities:

- Use visual, aural, and tactile demonstrations.
- Provide extra time and access to materials.
- Use a computer equipped with speech, large-print output, a spell checker, and a grammar checker.
- Ask another student to be a note taker.
- Provide course and class outlines.
- Use audiotaped and electronic texts.
- Provide cue cards or labels that identify the specific steps of a procedure.

STUDENTS WHO HAVE MOBILITY DISABILITIES

For students with mobility disabilities:

- Provide an accessible laboratory facility with adjustable-height tables and equipment.
- Provide alternative input and output tools such as Morse code, voice, and an alternative keyboard.
- Provide a lab partner or scribe to facilitate participation.
- Use modified scientific equipment that provides access.
- Ensure that field trips are in accessible locations.

STUDENTS WHO HAVE HEALTH IMPAIRMENTS

For students with health impairments:

- Provide flexible scheduling arrangements that allow completion of work.
- Consider that the student may tire easily.
- Use e-mail.

ALL STUDENTS

For all students:

- Use three-dimensional models.
- Use hands-on learning.
- Provide an orientation to laboratory equipment.
- Label equipment, tools, and materials clearly.
- Use color coding for labels and materials.
- Provide copies of notes and overheads.
- Use hands-on, active learning.
- Build background and knowledge of concepts.
- Guide students in their construction of knowledge.
- Use scaffolding to support inductive and deductive thinking.
- Ask clarifying questions to check students' understanding of concepts.
- Directly link assessment with instruction.

Using Technology
Technology for Access

Computers linked to devices that measure temperature, acidity, voltage, and light permit measurements to be made easily. These same computers, when connected to AT devices such as alternative keyboards, speech-to-text, and text-to-speech software, allow students with a wide range of disabilities to participate fully in science.

Mining the Internet for Data

The Internet contains rich resources for teachers and students, especially in science. Students can collect and share data gathered in their own schools with students from around the world. Students can access many Internet sites for real science data. Here are some examples:

- GLOBE, a worldwide science education program, enables students to participate as data collectors and researchers in research relating to the atmosphere, hydrology, soils, and land cover. The GLOBE website (http://www.globe.gov) allows students to access data in such areas as air temperature, humidity, cloud observations, and temperature.
- The Cold Spring Harbor website (http://www.cshl.org), an important resource on the human genome, allows students and others to access DNA databases and develop models of genetic changes over time.
- Earthquake websites provide live data on seismic activity.
- Websites provide data on star charts, space stations, space shuttles, and satellites.

Interacting with Experts

- "Ask an expert" websites allow students to ask real scientists questions, and to learn about other questions that have been posed and scientists' responses to them. There are a variety of such websites, including sites for astronomers, geologists, earth scientists, physicists, and astrobiologists.

NATIONAL SCIENCE FOUNDATION

The National Science Foundation (NSF) sponsors numerous projects that promote and support science education for individuals with disabilities. Check the NSF website (http://www.nsf.gov) for these projects.

Nancy Lightbody, director of Biotechnology Works! and EAST (Eastern Alliance in Science, Technology, Engineering, and Mathematics), described some accommodations and modifications that were implemented during a National Science Foundation–funded summer program:

- In the pre-lab session for each lab, each student and teacher received a notebook with the purpose, list of materials, procedure, and an illustrated flowchart. A large point size, simple font style, and double-spaced lines were used. Large-print versions of flowcharts were also used. Teachers' notebooks included more details than those that were given to the students.

- Using the Web, students can take virtual field trips with scientists. For example, JASON expeditions have explored the Mediterranean Sea, the Great Lakes, the Galapagos Islands, the Sea of Cortez, Belize, and other geographic areas of the world. A Mars Team website allows students to make virtual explorations of Mars and to ask scientists about the planet.

Virtual Science

- Websites provide virtual telescopes and microscopes.
- Websites offer simulations, dynamic modeling, and interactive data manipulations.
- Websites host virtual science fairs.
- On the Web, virtual explorations can be conducted of glaciers, Antarctica, and laboratories.

Teacher Resources

- Web clearinghouses are large sites that provide gateways to other websites. Web clearinghouses frequently organize and categorize resources, lesson plans, and student activities.
- Software companies offer interactive software on a wide variety of science topics.
- Television and video companion sites offer activities and resources that complement science television and video programs.

Questions for Reflection

1. Find out more about several of these resources. Share what you have learned with others.
2. Locate virtual exploration or simulation science websites. How can these websites facilitate the study of science?

 To answer these questions and learn more about using technology to support learning, go to Companion Website at www.prenhall.com/cohen, select Chapter 14, then choose Using Technology.

- All sign language interpreters were given teacher notebooks at the beginning of the week so that they could review some of the technical scientific concepts and vocabulary.
- We used a variety of written formats for explaining the labs: overhead projector, green chalkboard with yellow chalk, cream-colored chart paper with wide black markers, student and teacher notebooks, and Braille.
- Definitions of all terms were posted for everyone to see and were read aloud during the pre-labs. Questions that students or teachers asked during the labs were abbreviated and posted, along with abbreviated answers.
- Test tubes and other laboratory equipment were color-coded whenever possible.
- Braille labels were affixed to laboratory equipment whenever appropriate.
- We worked on keeping the aisles of the classrooms free of clutter for easy accessibility; we planned where the various heating and refrigeration units would be located to maximize traffic flow.

- All overheads for the pre-labs and the actual labs were photocopied on paper and given beforehand to the deaf students, who were then able to take notes more easily as they watched the sign language interpreters.
- A slip-resistant surface (Benchcoat) was used at each lab station.
- "Hot hands" were used to handle hot labware. Another heat-resistant, gripper-type mitt could also be used.
- Large petri dishes and simple templates were used whenever appropriate.
- Liquid level indicators or light sensors with tone oscillators were available for those who were blind for measuring fluids and/or solids.
- Braille readouts on the balance were used for students with visual impairments.
- Flowcharts had representations.
- Everyone tried to be as specific as possible when giving an explanation. The teacher presenters and the lab assistants made a concerted effort to eliminate vague terms and phrases such as *this, over there,* and *just like this one* from their vocabulary.
- Many models and analogies were used to explain the general concepts for each lab. For instance, plates of cooked spaghetti and tomato sauce helped clarify the concept of spooling DNA for DNA extraction.
- We put each lab in context (for instance, using a description of a crime scene or comparing a specific procedure to a pregnancy test) so that there would be a reason for doing each lab.
- We provided many opportunities both inside and outside of classrooms and laboratories for building teams, working together, and sharing responsibilities. These were very important and helped ensure that the labs functioned as smoothly as possible.
- Although pre-lab and lab overheads were photocopied to make note taking easier for deaf students and others, we were not always able to copy notes from outside speakers.
- Students were asked to preview the assignments the night before.
- Audiotaped notes and summaries were made available.

UNIVERSAL DESIGN

Science is a fertile content area for incorporating universal design (Cawley, Foley, & Miller, 2003; Miner, Nieman, Swanson, & Woods, 2001) because many science activities include hands-on, experiential approaches. Universal design involves flexibility in tools, materials, strategies, approaches, assessments, and technology. It incorporates multiple ways of seeing, hearing, and touching, (and perhaps, when safe, tasting and smelling). Coupling technology with science activities allows various means of learning, engagement, and expression.

Cohen, Lightbody, Locke, Langley-Turnbaugh, and Washburn (2003) described the application of universal design to an earth science program in which teachers, scientists, and students with learning disabilities, ADHD, and emotional and behavioral disabilities participated in the study of a salt marsh. The authors wrote that all

Research to Practice

Role Models and Mentors

Using role models and mentors can be a powerful way for students to learn what scientists do. Role models and mentors provide inspiration and promote opportunities for in-depth learning. Research has shown that mentoring encourages students to take advanced science courses and enter science careers. Yet just 48% of students with disabilities who were surveyed said there was someone in their scholarly lives who served as a mentor compared with 60% of students without disabilities (Blackorby & Cameto, 1997). In addition, the research literature documents the effectiveness of using electronic mentoring in science (O'Neill, Wagner, & Gomez, 1996; Schatzman, 1995). Tiered mentoring is a highly effective iterative strategy in which established science professionals mentor graduate and undergraduate students, who in turn mentor high school and elementary students (Absher, 2003).

DO-IT, a program that has received numerous awards for mentoring activities at the University of Washington, has demonstrated the critical role that mentors play in the lives of individuals with disabilities. Sheryl Burgstahler, director of DO-IT, paired students with mentors in biology, computer science, statistics, physics, and engineering. Using personal meetings and e-mail, the mentors and students worked and studied together. Mentoring led to academic, personal, professional, and career achievements.

Questions for Reflection

1. Find out more about role models and mentors. Locate and describe resources for initiating and implementing mentoring with students. What resources are available in your community?
2. Explore the resources available for electronic mentoring. What are the benefits and limitations of this approach?

 To answer these questions and learn more about applying research to practice, go to the Companion Website at www.prenhall. com/cohen, select Chapter 14, then choose Research to Practice.

These educators are discussing strategies for implementing a mentoring program.

Considering Diversity

World of Science

The world of science is diverse, and because of this, science is a natural area for including and supporting different types of learners. Hands-on laboratory and field-based activities, combined with interactivity, can appeal to a wide range of learners.

Important science topics such as AIDS, the quality of the environment, and living creatures are of concern to all of our planet's citizens. Students in Costa Rica can easily share information about frogs with students in North America. Students in Alaska can talk to students in Iceland about global warming. Scientists in Japan can mentor students in Brazil.

The science education standards provide a vision for teaching all students. Teachers, students, families, educators, and citizens are partners in learning communities. Every science program must ensure that all contributions are valued and that equity is assured for every student.

Questions for Reflection

1. Find out more about science education standards. To what extent do they support diversity?
2. Think about teaching strategies that have been emphasized. Which strategies are particularly effective for involving and supporting diversity in the classroom?

 To answer these questions and deepen your understanding of diversity in schools and communities, go to the Companion Website at www.prenhall.com/cohen, select Chapter 14, then choose Considering Diversity.

participants had one common bond: their passionate interest in earth system science, an approach to the study of the earth that emphasizes interactions among the land, atmosphere, oceans, and biosphere. Universal design allowed all students to participate in the study and learn compelling science content.

Components of universal design ranged from solving practical access problems to developing strategies to promote and support complex behaviors. Addressing the needs of students with emotional and behavioral disabilities, teachers collaborated with behavioral specialists to learn how to use positive behavior supports to reduce problem or challenging behaviors. Class sessions involved viewing an insect collection and then gathering a collection in a salt marsh. Other strategies that benefit all learners are:

- Provide clay models of soil structural units (granular, blocky) and of landscape formation.
- Use voice-output versions of scales, digital meters, or probes (temperature, dissolved oxygen, salinity, pH).
- Provide reading materials, directions, definitions, and procedures in multiple formats, including large-print and electronic ones.
- Begin with a graphic organizer with step-by-step laboratory directions.
- Provide a checklist for each part of the lab and lesson. Record progress with check marks.
- Rotate membership in groups. Within the groups, rotate roles and tasks.

- Use analogies and models. For instance, when explaining sea levels, use blue plastic wrap to show the rise of the ocean on a profile drawing of the marsh border, the upper-high marsh, the middle-high marsh (with a pool and a panne), and the lower-high marsh. With the same blue wrap, also show the mean sea level, the mean high tide, and the effects of the extreme spring tide.

SOCIAL STUDIES

The overall purpose of social studies is to enable students to make informed and reasoned decisions as citizens of diverse democratic communities about their nation and the world. Social studies promotes involvement in civic affairs such as election of governmental officials and involvement in community activities. Social studies is cross-disciplinary and integrates anthropology, archaeology, economics, geography, history, law, philosophy, political science, psychology, religion, and sociology. The study of social studies may also involve content from mathematics and the sciences as well as literacy skills.

The study of social studies can involve a great deal of reading and writing, which can cause problems for many students. To compound the difficulty, the primary source material can include textbooks, trade books, articles, primary documents, and literature. Reading and writing strategies that were discussed in Chapters 11 and 12 can be used when teaching content areas. These include metacognitive strategies, guided reading, guided questioning, scaffolding, direct instruction, guided notes, and graphic organizers.

 ## LINKING ASSESSMENT WITH INSTRUCTION

❖ LILY GOLDBERG'S UNIT: ASSESSMENT ❖

Lily Goldberg, a high school social studies teacher, has developed several stimulating assessment opportunities for students as the class studies mountain environments and cultures. She embedded authentic assessment tasks in instruction. Directly linking assessment with instruction creates meaningful opportunities for students to demonstrate what they know and can do. This approach is particularly relevant in a content area such as social studies because of the cross-disciplinary nature of social studies.

Lily's students were allowed to choose from several assessment options, including developing tourism brochures, three-dimensional models, and resource and conservation plans. Lily collaborated with them in providing detailed descriptions, requirements, and rubrics for each assessment task. She had clarified and communicated her expectations to students before beginning the tasks. As the students developed their projects, Lily provided frequent monitoring and feedback, both in writing and verbally. She encouraged the students to ask formative questions and to provide supportive, positive feedback to each other.

Assessment of social studies emphasizes **authentic assessment,** which involves performance tasks that are relevant to real-life contexts. Authentic assessment is particularly appropriate for social studies because of the dynamic nature of the content and the many natural opportunities to use this assessment. The conditions for authentic assessment include task complexity, motivation, and learning standards.

Social studies assessment involves teachers selecting content worth knowing and providing time for students to develop new knowledge, concepts, and skills. Assessment strategies are linked to meaningful learning activities and the most important ideas embedded in the activities.

Nurturing deeper understandings of social studies means that multiple opportunities are provided for students to demonstrate what has been learned. Assessment practices reflect these learning opportunities. Instruction and assessment are varied in order to promote student learning. Traditional pencil-and-paper tests are minimized. Instead teachers use a variety of approaches, including observations, individual and group projects, rubrics, interviews, artifacts, demonstrations, dramatizations, museum displays, and writing samples (Maxim, 1999).

READING STRATEGIES

When children first learn to read, they read fiction. They learn to expect that stories have a specific structure, such as a beginning, middle, and end. When reading fiction, readers expect that the characters develop as the story unfolds. However, reading social studies differs from reading fiction in several important ways (Banks & Banks, 1999).

First, many social studies materials are nonfiction and are written in an expository style. Unlike most fiction, social studies texts are frequently nonlinear and may not have a beginning, middle, and end. Social studies narratives have been described as a series of "embedded outlines" (Banks & Banks, 1999, p. 163). The largest outline is the book or, in some cases, the topic under study. Chapters, subtopics, sections, and units form other outlines. If students read a chapter from beginning to end, main ideas and major headings may be overlooked (Banks & Banks, 1999).

A second way in which reading social studies differs from reading in other content areas is its vocabulary, initials, and acronyms. Social studies involves learning new vocabulary such as *allocation, economic, assets,* and *representative democracy;* new initials such as *UN* for *United Nations;* and new acronyms such as *NATO* for *North Atlantic Treaty Organization.* The meanings of vocabulary terms need to be understood, remembered, and interpreted within various contexts.

Third, social studies frequently is conveyed by concepts such as *markets, allocation of resources, market economy, fiscal policy, ecosystem,* and *cultural geography.* Teachers need to consider the abstractness of the concepts, students' prior knowledge, the number and complexity of the concepts, and how concepts are introduced.

Fourth, the purposes for reading social studies differ from those for reading fiction. Reading social studies involves "reading to learn" rather than "learning to read" (Banks & Banks, 1999, p. 164). The purposes for reading social studies involve identification of ideas; remembering facts, ideas, and concepts; interpreting concepts and ideas; and connecting various ideas and concepts to each other.

Finally, the authors' purposes for writing social studies–related materials differ from the purposes of authors who write fiction. Rather than entertaining readers, social studies authors write to communicate information, concepts, and interpretations. They may write to persuade, convey a point of view, or make comparisons. Students need to identify the authors' reasons for writing and to critically read and evaluate the materials.

Banks and Banks (1999) encourage teachers to show students how texts are structured. They should show students where they can find the table of contents, introduction, purposes, concepts, vocabulary, time lines, index, and glossary. Each of these sources has its own unique structure.

Encyclopedias, almanacs, reference books, dictionaries, websites, and electronic sources also have their own structures. The teacher should provide students with opportunities to examine the structure of these sources and practice how to use them. The study of social studies frequently involves the use of multimedia sources such as audio recordings, videotapes, television programs, media streamed on the Internet, pictures, charts, and artwork. Students should be guided on how to use these media. Teachers should give students an overview of the materials and show how they are organized. They should be clear in their explanations and in what they expect students to do when using the materials.

Social studies may involve the use of primary sources such as diaries, letters, interviews, and artifacts. Students should be told why these materials are being used, how they can be used, how they can be incorporated in their work, and how they can be critically evaluated.

WRITING STRATEGIES

Teaching social studies frequently requires students to express what they have learned in written form. For many students with mild disabilities, writing can be difficult. There are a number of strategies that can be used to incorporate the teaching of writing in social studies (Farris, 2001).

Guided Literature Response Journals

Guided literature response journals enable students to respond to a passage, chapter, or book as they read it. Before assigning a text to be read, the teacher indicates specific categories for response such as person, place, or environment. While students read the text, they make notes, comments, and illustrations within each category. After reading each student's journal entries, the teacher makes comments or asks questions, to which students respond.

RAFT

RAFT (Santa, Havens, & Harrison, 1989) stands for the Role of the writer, the Audience to whom the writing is directed, the Format of the writing, and the Topic of the writing. It allows students to write for a specific audience.

Either with the teacher's help or by themselves, students proceed through each of the RAFT steps. Jared's sixth-grade class was studying the seven wonders of the ancient world: the temple of Artemis, the statue of Zeus, the pyramids of Egypt, the lighthouse at Alexandria, the hanging gardens of Babylon, the mausoleum of Halicarnassus, and the colossus of Rhodes. Here's how Jared proceeded:

Role: Jared said that he would be a citizen of Egypt.
Audience: The audience was described as members of Jared's class.
Format: Jared decided to develop a comparison between an ancient wonder and a contemporary wonder. He would write about and illustrate his topic.
Topic: Pyramids of Egypt and the trans-American pyramid.

Reading and Writing Circles

Reading and writing circles can be used for various purposes, such as reading a specific text or passage, generating questions about the reading, and writing about assigned topics. Three to five students can be arranged in small groups. Each group is given an assignment and asked to work cooperatively. Students are assigned specific roles within the group (Farris, 2001). For example, a discussion leader directs the discussion and summarizes the work of the group, a cartographer develops maps, a word keeper maintains a list of new words and terms encountered and their definitions, an artist renders illustrations, and a historian keeps track of historical events and documents the group's progress.

❖ A READING AND WRITING CIRCLE ❖

Here's how Lewis John, a student with attention and organizational difficulties, worked cooperatively with the members of his five-person group. For the past 2 weeks, Lewis's class has been studying Americans before European contact. Together, the group decided to research the Taino/Arawak, the first Indians Christopher Columbus saw when he landed in the Bahamas. During their first meeting, the group assigned roles. Lewis said that he would be the cartographer because he loved to draw maps. Other students took on the roles of leader, historian, word keeper, and artist. The students assigned tasks and developed a schedule for completing their work. Lewis drew a map that depicted the migration route of the Taino/Arawak group that originally settled along the eastern slopes of the Andes Mountains. They spread down the Amazon River and its tributaries, north into the Orinoco Valley, along the coast of Venezuela to eastern Colombia, and into Guiana, the Antilles, and the Florida Keys. Lewis worked closely with the group's historian in developing and documenting the migration routes.

INSTRUCTIONAL STRATEGIES

❖ AN INTERDISCIPLINARY UNIT ❖

Lily Goldberg, the teacher you met earlier, is teaching an exciting interdisciplinary unit on mountains of the world. The students have begun to investigate how local tourism can be balanced with the protection of mountain environments and cultures by focusing on the Blue Mountains of Australia.

Ms. Goldberg, working with Zeke Raynolds, a special education teacher, has asked student teams to pretend that they are members of the World Conservation Union, the world's largest conservation organization. The students have been asked to investigate the environmental and cultural impact of tourism and to develop a plan that considers natural resource conservation and local community involvement. The student teams will present their plans next week.

Several of the students in the class have ADHD. Two other students have severe disabilities in reading and written language. Mr. Raynolds has worked with the classroom teacher to combine technology with instructional strategies such as scaffolding to make the curriculum accessible to all students. Specifically, he has introduced text-to-speech software, scanned text, and e-text, and provided guidelines for Internet accessibility.

One of the most important changes has been the increased level of accessibility of the Web-based online library catalogs and the general search functions on the Internet. Mr. Raynolds has taught the students many different search strategies. For example, he has shown them how specific search engines return important information, indicate relevant hits quickly with terms in boldface, cache pages in case the website is down, link to highly ranked pages, suggest word or phrase lists in order to refine the first search term, and categorize results into folders by concept, document, and site type. He also has taught the students how to identify credible websites.

LEARNING ROUTINES

The University of Kansas Center for Research on Learning (Deshler & Schumaker, 1999) developed **learning strategy routines** that promote and support students' learning in content areas. These learning routines can be used to support the study of social studies. Several of them are described in this section, including the Survey Routine, the Concept Anchoring Routine, the Concept Mastery Routine, and the Recall Enhancement Routine.

The Survey Routine provides an overview of a new chapter or reading. During this routine, the teacher directs students through a step-by-step process of examining the content of a new chapter. Making notes on a teacher-developed worksheet, students identify the title, major sections, new vocabulary, and relationships between the unit and other chapters, and they reword the introduction and summary of the chapter.

The Concept Anchoring Routine enables teachers to help students connect new concepts to previously learned ones. The routine uses a graphic that anchors the new, difficult concept to concepts with which the student is familiar. The teacher helps students identify the similarities and differences between the concepts.

Somewhat similar to the Concept Anchoring Routine, the Concept Mastery Routine helps students understand and learn essential concepts. This routine uses a graphic that represents a target concept. The graphic shows the placement of the essential concept within a larger framework or scheme, identifies key characteristics, provides both examples and nonexamples, and constructs a definition of the concept.

The Recall Enhancement Routine includes a number of strategies that support students in remembering important facts, ideas, and concepts. Strategies that are included in this routine include using keywords, first-letter mnemonics, visual imagery, and rhymes.

MAPS, MODELS, AND GLOBES

❖ *USING MAPS TO STUDY MATH* ❖

Iris Raade, an elementary school social studies teacher, and David Brown, a special education teacher, had collaborated on a unit that focused on the students' local community. Now they were developing a lesson that integrated mathematics concepts with the study of maps. The teachers wanted to use instructional strategies that could accommodate the learning needs of all students.

Earlier in the week, Ms. Raade took digital photographs of each student in the class. She distributed paper copies of the photographs and addresses of all students. Working in pairs, the students matched the addresses with the picture of each student.

Mr. Brown showed aerial photographs and a commercially published road map of the community in which the students lived. Tracing paper was placed over the aerial photographs, and the students traced over the roads and streets to create a road map. They compared their map with the commercial road map.

The concepts of *near* and *far* were explored. The teachers took the students on a walk to experience the distance of 1 mile. The students walked half a mile away from the school and then returned.

Using symbols for students' homes and the school, the students estimated and then measured the distance between the school and their homes. Students' family members were asked to record the mileage between home and school.

Finally, the students were able to identify where their classmates lived. Using small blocks to represent miles, the students made stacks to represent how many miles the school was from their home. They made a graph that showed the distance each student lived from school (adapted from Michigan Department of Education, 1996).

A storyboard map provides a visual means for conceptualizing and organizing information. A storyboard approach can be used for developing community geoportraits in which students visually present their community's geography with photos, video, or other visual means. Figure 14.2 illustrates how the students in Ms. Raade's class portrayed their community.

Maps, models, globes, and three-dimensional representations enable students to make abstract ideas and concepts concrete. A map is a drawing of, or part of, a surface of an area such as a country, planet, or celestial object that shows the shape and position of different countries, political borders, natural features such as valleys and mountains, and artificial features such as roads, bridges, landmarks, and buildings.

Figure 14.2   Students' community

Three-dimensional models such as landscapes, buildings, and towns can be used, as well as models depicting interactions between physical systems such as the earth's rotation and revolution, volcanoes, and earthquakes.

Tactile graphics were originally developed for use by individuals who are blind to obtain information that sighted individuals get from looking at graphical information. However, tactile graphics can be very useful to students with reading or other learning disabilities because they provide an additional way of presenting information and concepts. The following guidelines (adapted from Osterhaus, 2002) can be used when developing tactile graphics:

- Make the tactile graphic as clear as possible.
- Determine if the original shapes and textures are necessary to convey the concept or whether simple geometric shapes can be used.
- Omit unnecessary parts of the diagram so that the original shapes and textures can be presented on a larger and clearer scale.
- Keep in mind the knowledge level, skill base, and age of the reader.
- Remember to keep graphs simple; unnecessary information and clutter may prohibit the student from gaining relevant information.
- Edit/proofread the graphic with your fingers, not your eyes, before showing it to a student.

Using Technology
Social Studies Software

Tom Snyder Productions has developed several excellent software programs for use in teaching social studies. Software programs can be useful when teaching students with mild and moderate learning and behavior problems because the programs help to make abstract ideas and information concrete, and they assist the organization of ideas, events, and concepts. Several software programs allow multimedia, images, recordings, and historical documents to be incorporated. These programs include the following:

• *Timeliner* allows events to be organized chronologically or thematically. Comparisons across time, cultures, and civilizations can be made. Digital images and multimedia can be incorporated.

These teachers are previewing social studies software.

ADAPTING MATERIALS

For many students with reading and writing disabilities, materials will have to be adapted. Lenz and Schumaker (1999) have identified steps that should be followed when adapting materials.

First, develop a plan for adapting the materials. When developing the plan, consult with administrators and other teachers. Consider that most adaptations can benefit many students and that adaptations are likely to be maintained and supported when they can be implemented with more than one student. Next, when appropriate, involve students, other teachers, counselors, and paraprofessionals in developing and implementing the adaptations. Third, identify specific responsibilities for developing and implementing

- *Mapmaker's Toolkit* contains an extensive library of maps, and it allows students to identify and organize maps according to historical events, current events, and themes such as precipitation, land use, and population. Maps can be customized and symbols can be inserted.
- *Community Construction* enables elementary school students to design historical communities and buildings, cut them out, and construct three-dimensional structures.
- *Africa Inspirer* allows students to explore the African continent as well as specific countries.

Edmark offers software programs that are especially useful with early learners.

- *Trudy's Time & Place House* allows students to explore geography and time through various activities.
- *Travel the World with Timmy! Deluxe* introduces students to the people, places, and cultures of five countries: Argentina, Japan, Kenya, France, and Russia.
- *ThemeWeavers* allows teachers to create theme-based activities by integrating language arts, mathematics, science, social studies, and art.

Internet Sites

There is a treasure trove of Internet sites that provide resources for both educators and students. For teachers, the website of the National Council for the Social Studies provides information on social studies standards and resources for teaching students. Both teachers and students can explore other sites including those of the Library of Congress, the National Geographic Society, the History Channel, Plymouth Plantation, the United Nations, the U.S. Congress, the White House, encyclopedias, and the United States National Archives.

Questions for Reflection

1. Find out more about software programs that support teaching and learning in social studies. Compare the features of the software programs that are mentioned here. Identify additional software programs that can be useful.

2. Explore Internet resources available for teaching social studies to students with disabilities. Identify and describe several resources.

 To pursue these activities and learn more about using technology to support learning, go to the Companion Website at www.prenhall.com/cohen, select Chapter 14, then choose Using Technology.

the adaptations. Fourth, evaluate the success of the adaptations. Make any necessary adjustments. Finally, disseminate the information to other teachers, administrators, and parents. Table 14.4 describes strategies that can be used when teaching social studies.

PROBLEM-BASED LEARNING

Frequently, teachers use an inquiry learning approach known as *problem-based* to teach social studies. **Problem-based learning** requires students to be active learners, conduct research, generate and test hypotheses, evaluate resources, and work cooperatively with other students.

Table 14.4	Strategies for Teaching Social Studies	
	Area of Difficulty	**Strategy**
	Abstractness: Content is too abstract.	Provide concrete examples, interpretations, concept maps, analogies, and experiences.
	Organization: Organization is not clear.	Make the organization explicit. Use outlines, organizers, and reading guides.
	Relevance: Content appears to be irrelevant to students' experiences and interests.	Make clear connections between content and students' experiences and interests.
	Learning strategies: Students lack study and learning strategies.	Teach study skills and learning strategies.
	Prior experiences: Students lack critical background experiences.	Develop background and prior experiences for students. Provide opportunities for students to build relevant prior experiences.
	Complexity: The material is complex or has many steps or parts.	Provide an organizer such as an outline, list, or concept map that shows how each of the parts is connected to the whole. Provide opportunities to scaffold the material so that students experience success as they proceed.
	Quantity: There is a large quantity of information, materials, processes, or steps.	Break the information down into manageable chunks. Provide a summary of the information. Present each step one at a time.

Source: Adapted from *Adapting Language Arts, Social Studies, and Science Materials for the Inclusive Classroom,* by K. Lenz and J. Schumaker, 1999, Reston, VA: Council for Exceptional Children.

For example, Ms. Goldberg, the teacher you read about earlier, extended the work that her students were doing on natural resource conservation and local community involvement. Working with the local chamber of commerce, community leaders, and school officials, she posed a problem for her students that would apply and extend the knowledge and skills they had acquired earlier in the year. Ms. Goldberg explained to her students that community recreation areas were deteriorating and that community leaders were considering closing them. She asked the students to identify specific community concerns, research responses of other communities, construct a plan, and develop a presentation to community leaders on their findings.

Problem-based learning has the following characteristics:

1. Loosely structured problems that do not have one solution. New information is gathered, and solutions are tested in an iterative process.

Using Technology
Digital Resources

There are many excellent websites that provide images, photographs, documents, records, films, and multimedia. For example, the Library of Congress website has rare historical film clips, images, documents, and recordings. The National Aeronautics and Space Administration, the United States Geological Survey, and the National Archives and Records Administration host other websites that contain digital images, maps, and important historical documents. Libraries, historical societies, and colleges and universities around the world also host online digital archives. Many of these resources are in the public domain and can be freely used. For others, permission is required.

Questions for Reflection

1. Find out more about digital resources that can enhance learning. Locate and describe several resources.
2. Identify state and locally developed electronic archives. How can these resources be incorporated into units and lessons that focus on local communities, governments, and issues?

To answer these questions and learn more about using technology to support learning, go to the Companion Website at www. prenhall.com/cohen, select Chapter 14, then choose Using Technology.

2. Teams of students who work together to solve problems.
3. Teachers who act as coaches and facilitators.
4. Student-generated products, including portfolios, websites, multimedia, demonstrations, and presentations. Products demonstrate knowledge and problem-solving skills.

Students with mild disabilities frequently need additional support to participate successfully in problem-based learning experiences. Students must know how to participate as team members. All students are expected to take responsibility and contribute to the work of the group.

Teachers have a unique role when working with students who are engaged in problem-based learning. They develop problems, coach and facilitate learning, teach problem solving, provide frequent feedback, and evaluate learning.

Teachers should ensure that students are taught the appropriate social skills in order to function as effective team members. Organizational, research, and note-taking skills may need to be taught. Teachers should ensure that the problems have enough structure so that students will be able to identify what they should know and do. Problems should be constructed that assist students to learn appropriate skills and knowledge.

ROOTS AND WINGS

Roots and Wings (Slavin & Madden, 1999) is a specialized approach to teaching social studies based on the Success for All reading program described in Chapter 11. At the core of the program are thematic grade-specific units that are integrated with

Considering Diversity

Four Approaches

Social studies is a natural area of study that easily incorporates diversity. In general, teachers use a combination of four approaches when addressing diversity (Banks & Banks, 1997). Level 1, the **Contributions Approach,** emphasizes heroes, heroines, holidays, and selected cultural and ethnic events such as Cinco de Mayo, Kwanzaâ, and Ramadan. Level 2, the **Additive Approach,** incorporates content about diversity into existing curricula. For example, when studying the war in Afghanistan, students are introduced to the religious practices of its citizens. The limitations of these two approaches are that stereotypes can be perpetuated, diversity can be regarded as strange or unusual, and diversity content is viewed through the lens of the mainstream culture.

Level 3, the **Transformative Approach,** infuses diverse perspectives into the curricula. Rather than focusing on the ways various ethnic, cultural, racial, and religious groups have contributed to mainstream society, this approach emphasizes the complex and dynamic interactions among groups. An example of this approach would be interviews with both Israeli and Palestinian families on how the Middle East conflict has changed their lives. Finally, Level 4, the **Social Action Approach,** incorporates Level 3 and involves students in making their own decisions about various issues that they study. For example, in addition to studying the Israeli and Palestinian perspectives, students are asked to collect data, identify the pros and cons of various decisions and actions, synthesize multiple sources of information, and form their own opinions.

Disability and Diversity

Disability is another facet of our diversity, and the study of disability can be incorporated into diversity (Hehir, 2002). Disability studies are interdisciplinary and include history, social action, humanities, and culture. Including disability as part of diversity highlights the idea that persons with disabilities should have full and equal participation in society and that all persons can lead meaningful lives. The contributions of individuals with disabilities can be highlighted. For example, Alexander Graham Bell, the inventor of the telephone, had a learning disability. Richard Radtke is an oceanographer who has multiple sclerosis. Christopher Reeve, the actor, has a physical disability. Individuals with disabilities add unique perspectives and ideas that improve the quality of life for all citizens.

Websites provide resources for learning more about persons with disabilities. Using a Web search engine, websites can be located that convey information about the rise of the disability rights movement, the lives of famous persons with disabilities, resources for learning more about disability studies, movies that portray individuals with disabilities, and books about their lives.

Questions for Reflection

1. How does an understanding of disabilities contribute to the four approaches to diversity?
2. How have persons with disabilities influenced federal and state laws?

To answer these questions and deepen your understanding of diversity in schools and communities, go to the Companion Website at www.prenhall.com/cohen, select Chapter 14, then choose Considering Diversity.

literacy, mathematics, and science activities. In WorldLab, students work in cooperative groups to learn about the world through experiences, simulations, and investigations. Higher order thinking processes are emphasized. Examples of the units include:

1. *BayLab.* Students are citizens of a fictional town called Baytown, where they have a simulated family and occupation. They participate in a series of investigations on problems that affect the bay and how these problems impact their simulated lives.
2. *From Rebellion to Union.* Students play the roles of patriots or loyalists with families and occupations during the American Revolution.
3. *Adventures and Africa.* Students participate in these units consecutively. The units focus on geography, economics, and physical and earth sciences.

WorldLab lessons are structured and consist of the following elements:

1. An initial period of approximately 10 minutes during which the agenda and key concepts for the day are presented.
2. A 20-minute lesson on important concepts that the students will need to know in order to engage in the activities.
3. An activity period of approximately 45 minutes during which students work actively in their teams on simulations and investigations.
4. A debriefing period of approximately 15 minutes during which the teacher encourages higher order thinking about the issues and problems that may have developed as the students worked with their teams. Students are encouraged to discuss problems with team members and to make notes in their journals.

SUMMARY

- Contemporary perspectives on teaching science and social studies to students with disabilities were discussed.
- For some students with disabilities, reading and writing problems can be barriers to successful participation in science.
- Teachers should be familiar with a wide range of strategies and resources so that all students can have opportunities to learn.
- The study of science and social studies involves a great deal of reading, interdisciplinary knowledge, and understanding of abstract concepts.
- Teaching science and social studies requires that teachers use a wide variety of instructional strategies including the strategies that are described in this chapter and in other chapters.
- Assessment of science and social studies should be directly linked to the content. Creating multiple, meaningful assessment opportunities allows students to demonstrate what they know and can do.
- Authentic assessment allows teachers to embed assessment tasks into teaching and learning.

EXTENDING LEARNING: SCIENCE

1. Identify three teaching strategies discussed in the section on science. Compare and contrast the strengths and limitations of each.
2. You have been asked to work with a science teacher in developing and teaching a unit designed for all students. Several students in the class have learning disabilities, and one student has ADHD. Choose a science curriculum area and grade level. What strategies could you suggest that the teacher consider?
3. Visit the websites of the ERIC Clearinghouse for Science, Mathematics, Environmental Education, the National Science Foundation, and the National Science Teachers Association. Identify resources that can be used when teaching science to students with disabilities.
4. Tracy, an eighth-grade student who has a learning disability in reading, is a student in Mr. White's science class. She is a very enthusiastic learner. The class has started on a unit on pollution. You are the special education teacher who consults with classroom teachers on making learning accessible to all students. What are several teaching strategies that you could suggest to Mr. White? How would you advise him to proceed?

EXTENDING LEARNING: SOCIAL STUDIES

1. Identify three social studies concepts. Describe how these concepts can be taught to students at either the elementary, middle, or high school level.
2. Review Chapters 7 and 11. Identify several strategies that can be used to improve teaching and learning in social studies.
3. You have been asked to work with a general education teacher in developing and teaching a unit for several students with disabilities on one of the following topics: addressing urban sprawl, improving urban environments, or addressing concerns in small towns and cities. Choose a curriculum area and grade level. What instructional strategies could you suggest to the teacher to consider?

REFERENCES

Absher, M. (2003, March 4). National Science Foundation plenary session, joint annual meeting, Washington, DC.

Africa Inspirer [Computer software]. Watertown, MA: Tom Snyder Productions.

Banks, J. A., & Banks, C. A. M. (Eds.). (1997). *Multicultural education: Issues and perspectives* (3rd ed.). Boston: Allyn & Bacon.

Banks, J. A., & Banks, C. A. M. (1999). *Teaching strategies for the social studies*. New York: Longman.

Blackorby, J., & Cameto, R. (1997). *A case study of persons with disabilities* majoring in science, engineering, mathematics, and technology. Menlo Park, CA: SRI.

Burgstahler, S., & Norse, S. (1998). *Accommodating students with disabilities in math and science classes*. Seattle: DO-IT.

Cawley, J., Foley, T., & Miller, J. (2003). Science and students with mild disabilities. *Intervention in School and Clinic, 38,* 160–171.

Cohen, L., Lightbody, N., Locke, S., Langley-Turnbaugh, S., & Washburn, K. (2003). Wheelchairs on a saltmarsh. *ENC Focus.* Retrieved March 27, 2003, from the ENC Online website: www.enc.org

Community Construction [Computer software]. Watertown, MA: Tom Snyder Productions.

Deshler, D. D., & Schumaker, J. B. (1999). An instructional model for teaching students how to learn. In J. L. Graden, J. E. Zins, & M. J. Curtis (Eds.), *Alternative educational delivery systems: Enhancing instructional options for all students* (pp. 391–411). Washington, DC: National Association of School Psychologists.

Farris, P. J. (2001). *Elementary and middle school social studies*. Boston: McGraw-Hill.

Hehir, T. (2002). Eliminating ableism in education. *Harvard Educational Review, 72,* 1–32.

Lenz, K., & Schumaker, J. (1999). *Adapting language arts, social studies, and science materials for the inclusive classroom*. Reston, VA: Council for Exceptional Children.

Lewis, B. F., & Sadler, K. L. (1999). *Teaching science to students with hearing impairments: Issues and strategies for inclusion*. Paper presented at the annual meeting of the Association for the Education of Teachers in Science, Austin, TX.

Lowery, L. F. (1997). *NSTA pathways to the science standards,* elementary edition. Arlington, VA: National Science Teachers Association.

Mapmaker's Toolkit Watertown, [Computer software]. MA: Tom Snyder Productions.

Mastropieri, M. A., & Scruggs, T. E. (1992). Science for students with disabilities. *Review of Educational Research, 62,* 377–411.

Maxim, G. M. (1999). *Social studies and the elementary school child*. Upper Saddle River, NJ: Merrill/Prentice Hall.

Michigan Department of Education. (1996), *Michigan curriculum framework*. Lansing, MI: Author.

Miner, D., Nieman, R., Swanson, A., & Woods, M. (2001). *Teaching chemistry to students with disabilities: A manual for high schools, colleges, and graduate programs* (4th ed.). Washington, DC: American Chemical Society.

National Committee on Science Education Standards and Assessment. (1996). *National science education standards*. Washington, DC: National Research Council.

O'Neill, D. K., Wagner, R., & Gomez, L. M. (1996). Online mentors: Experimenting in science class. *Educational Leadership, 53,* 30–42.

Osterhaus, S. (2002). *Math education and Nemeth Code*. Retrieved March 27, 2004, from the Texas School for the Blind and Visually Impaired website: http://www.tsbvi.edu

Palincsar, A. S., & Brown, A. L. (1984). Reciprocal teaching of comprehension-fostering and comprehension-monitoring activities. *Cognition and Instruction, 1,* 117–175.

Roth, J. (1987). Enhancing understanding through debriefing. *Educational Leadership, 45,* 24–27.

Santa, C., Havens, L., & Harrison, S. (1989). Teaching secondary science through reading, writing, studying, and problem solving. In D. Lapp, J. Flood, & N. Farnan (Eds.), *Content area reading and learning* (2nd ed., pp. 137–151). Upper Saddle River, NJ: Prentice Hall.

Schatzman, S. (1995). *Science and mathematics initiatives in education: A model of distance learning program building*. Berkeley: University of California at Berkeley. (ERIC Document Reproduction Service No. ED395722)

Slavin, R. E., & Madden, N. A. (1999). *Success for All/Roots and Wings: Summary of research on achievement outcomes* (Rep. No. 41). Baltimore: Center for Research on the Education of Students Placed at Risk (CRESPAR).

ThemeWeavers [Computer software]. Redmond, WA: Edmark.

Timeliner [Computer software]. Watertown, MA: Tom Snyder Productions.

Travel the World [Computer software]. Redmond, WA: Edmark.

Trowbridge, L. W., & Bybee, R. W. (1996). *Teaching secondary school science*. Upper Saddle River, NJ: Merrill/Prentice Hall.

Trudy's Time & Place House [Computer software]. Redmond, WA: Edmark.

Promoting Independence

15

Chapter

Learning and Study Skills

CHAPTER OBJECTIVES

After completing this chapter, you should be able to:

❖ Describe approaches for the assessment of study skills.

❖ Teach skills that students can use when studying.

❖ Identify and explain instructional strategies that support students in their learning.

❖ Describe how technology can be used to support the development of learning strategies.

❖ Consider the influence of diversity on learning and study skills.

Learning and study skills are essential for school and work success. This chapter introduces skills for gathering, comprehending, and organizing information. The teaching of study skills should begin in elementary school. Their use should be reinforced as students progress through school. Assessment of learning strategies should occur frequently to ensure that students are using the strategies appropriately and to determine if additional strategies should be taught.

Students with disabilities frequently have difficulty with time management, learning how to learn, making representations of what they understand, taking notes, taking tests, and doing homework. These students should be strategic learners (NICHCY, 1997), and they need to know how to study and how to learn. According to the National Information Center for Children and Youth with Disabilities (NICHCY), "knowing that certain techniques and strategies can be used to assist learning, knowing which techniques are useful in which kinds of learning situations, and knowing how to use the techniques are powerful tools that can enable students to become strategic, effective, and lifelong learners" (1997, p. 1). To be efficient learners, students with disabilities should be taught learning and study strategies. This chapter discusses essential skills that students can use when studying, several instructional strategies that can be used to promote student learning, and assessment of study skills.

LINKING ASSESSMENT WITH INSTRUCTION

Assessment of study skills should occur prior to teaching them, during students' practice and implementation of these skills, and then periodically to determine whether students are using them correctly and if additional skills should be taught. A variety of approaches can be used to assess learning and study strategies. These include commercially published tests and teacher-developed instruments.

Figure 15.1   Self-assessment checklist

How Well Did I:
1. Organize my time for the assignment?
2. Take notes?
3. Use visual representations?
4. Read and reread assignments?
5. Use learning strategies?
6. Edit and proofread?

Both teacher- and student-developed instruments can be used. Figure 15.1 is a self-assessment checklist that Ari, a student, developed. Figures 15.2 and 15.3 are checklists that teachers developed.

There are a number of books, articles, and other references that provide teacher-developed questionnaires and checklists for the assessment of learning and study

Figure 15.2   Learning strategies and study skills checklist

Student's Name: _____

Date: _____

Learning Strategies and Study Skills

Time Management
- ❑ Uses a schedule
- ❑ Prioritizes tasks
- ❑ Completes tasks within allowed time

Metacognition
- ❑ Uses mnemonics
- ❑ Uses advance organizers
- ❑ Develops visual representations

Note Taking
- ❑ Uses K-W-L strategy
- ❑ Uses PRR strategy
- ❑ Develops guided notes

Test Taking
- ❑ Applies strategies in preparation for taking tests
- ❑ Uses strategies while taking tests
- ❑ Understands when to select specific strategies

Homework
- ❑ Completes homework on time
- ❑ Prioritizes tasks
- ❑ Allows sufficient time for each task

Figure 15.3   **Note-taking survey**

Student's Name: _____
Date: _____
- ❑ Do you take notes in class?
- ❑ How often does your teacher provide notes for students?
- ❑ How often do you use someone else's notes?
- ❑ Do you use any shortcuts when you take notes? If so, which ones do you use?
- ❑ When you take notes, do you use an outline?
- ❑ When you take notes, do you make lists?
- ❑ Do you use abbreviations for words?
- ❑ Do you write down main ideas?
- ❑ After taking notes, do you review them after class?
- ❑ After taking notes, do you label them?
- ❑ Do you put or file notes in a place where you can find them easily?
- ❑ When you miss a statement or idea, do you follow-up later?
- ❑ Do you date and number the pages?
- ❑ When you quote directly, do you write down identifying information about the author or speaker?

strategies, such as those by Coman and Heavers (2001), Fry (2000), Johson and Johnson (2001), and Meyers (2000).

SUPPORTING STUDENTS' LEARNING AND STUDY SKILLS

ORGANIZATIONAL SKILLS

Students with disabilities need assistance in planning how to use their time, allocating time for specific tasks, and planning ahead. Success in school, transition, vocational education, and post-secondary education can be supported through the use of a range of learning and study skills. There are many resources available, and libraries, schools, training programs, and community organizations frequently offer opportunities and resources that support the development of learning and study skills. Students should be encouraged to seek out resources, select appropriate skills and strategies, and practice using new skills.

Keeping a Schedule

Most individuals do better when they systematically keep track of classes, homework, appointments, and obligations. A daily schedule enables students to keep track of day-to-day activities. Encourage students to use a calendar or an electronic organizer. Commitments, both in and out of school, should be recorded. Block schedules can be helpful. Show students that they can record their activities in blocks, providing time

Figure 15.4   Block schedule

Time	Sunday	Monday	Tuesday	Wednesday	Thursday	Friday	Saturday
6:00–7:00	Free time	Wake up, shower, breakfast	Wake up, shower, breakfast	Wake up, shower, breakfast	Wake up, shower, breakfast	Wake up, shower, breakfast	
7:00–8:00	Free time	Travel to school	Travel to school	Travel to school	Travel to school	Travel to school	
8:00–9:00	Free time	Language arts	Mathematics	Language arts	Mathematics	Language arts	Wake up, shower, breakfast
9:00–10:00	Free time	Mathematics	Language arts	Mathematics	Language arts	Mathematics	Volunteer at local nursing home
10:00–11:00	Free time	Social studies	Science	Social studies	Science	Social studies	Volunteer at local nursing home
11:00–12:00	Free time	Lunch and supervised study	Lunch and supervised study	Lunch and supervised study	Lunch and supervised study	Lunch and supervised study	Volunteer at local nursing home
12:00–1:00	Free time	Physical education	Physical education	Physical education	Physical education	Physical education	
1:00–2:00	Library	Science	Social studies	Science	Social studies	Science	Free time with friends
2:00–3:00	Library	After-school activities	After-school activities	After-school activities	After-school activities	After-school activities	Free time with friends
3:00–4:00	Library	After-school activities	After-school activities	After-school activities	After-school activities	After-school activities	Free time with friends
4:00–5:00	Free time	Return home	Return home	Return home	Return home	Return home	Free time with friends
5:00–6:00	Supper with family	Supper with family	Supper with family	Supper with family	Supper with family	Supper with family	Supper with family and friends
6:00–7:00	Review week's schedule	Homework	Homework	Homework	Homework	Homework	Evening with family

Figure 15.4   Block schedule *continued*

Time	Sunday	Monday	Tuesday	Wednesday	Thursday	Friday	Saturday
7:00–8:00	Complete any unfinished homework assignments	Homework	Homework	Homework	Homework	Homework	Evening with family
8:00–9:00	Homework	Homework	Homework	Homework	Homework	Homework	Evening with family
9:00–10:00	Relaxation	Relaxation	Relaxation	Relaxation	Relaxation	Relaxation	Evening with family
10:00–11:00	Get ready for bed	Get ready for bed	Get ready for bed	Get ready for bed	Get ready for bed	Get ready for bed	Get ready for bed

for classes, basketball practice, work, homework, and leisure activities. Students should include any chores or work that they regularly do at home, such as walking the dog, taking out garbage, and cleaning their room. Figure 15.4 shows a block schedule developed by Ari and his teacher, Mr. White.

Weekly, monthly, and semester schedules enable students to plan for long-term obligations such as writing research reports or completing college applications. Figures 15.4 and 15.5 are examples of weekly and monthly schedules.

Figure 15.5   Monthly schedule

October 200x

Sunday	Monday	Tuesday	Wednesday	Thursday	Friday	Saturday
1	2	3	4	5	6	7
Family time	School	School	School Study group	School	School	Library
Family time	School	School	School Study group	School	School	Visit Aunt Lynne
Visit Aunt Lynne	School	School	School Study group	School	School	Study group
Finalize math project	School	School	School Study group	School	School	Library

❖ *FINE-TUNING A SCHEDULE* ❖

After setting up the weekly schedule, Mr. White checked with Ari several times a week to see if he was having any problems with it. Mr. White verified that Ari was able to better organize his daily activities, prioritize them, and complete tasks on time. There are several strategies that Mr. White can use to fine-tune these time schedules:

1. Entries can be color-coded. For example, items highlighted in yellow can indicate school-related activities, while items highlighted in green can signal leisure time.
2. Encourage students to consider their optimal concentration span, and divide projects into chunks that fit into this period. For example, students who are able to concentrate for only brief periods of time can alternate projects that require a great deal of concentration with activities that require much less.
3. Schedule backward. Identify the date when the project or activity should be completed and plan backward from that date.
4. When making appointments, include contact information, such as telephone numbers or e-mail addresses, alongside the appointment for quick reference.
5. If students need to remember to bring items to appointments, such as equipment or books, a *B* for *bring* can be inserted next to the appointment.
6. Use free time efficiently. Keep track of tasks or phone calls that do not take much time (Morgenstern, 1998).

A teacher assists students in keeping track of their assignments.

Taking Notes

Teaching students strategies to use before, during, and after reading or listening to speakers can greatly improve their performance. There are a number of approaches from which to choose.

Streamlining Note Taking

Coman and Heavers (2001) have developed several strategies that streamline note taking. Abbreviations can be used for words that are commonly used and for words that students have difficulty spelling. For example, *co.* is used for *company, esp.* for *especially,* and *hist.* for *history.* Periods can be omitted from abbreviations, such as *misc* for *miscellaneous* and *ex* for *example.* Finally, symbols can be used for words, such as ~ for *approximately,* & for *and,* and # for *number.*

Outlining

Outlining is the most widely used strategy for taking notes (Coman & Heavers, 2001). It provides a structure for identifying the main idea and supporting details. Outlines follow a basic structure:

I. Main idea 1
   A. Supporting detail about main idea 1
      1. Subpoint about the detail
         a. Supporting detail about the subpoint
   B. Supporting detail about main idea 1
      1. Subpoint about the detail
      2. Subpoint about the detail
   C. Supporting detail about main idea 1

II. Main idea 2
   A. Supporting detail about main idea 2
      1. Subpoint about the detail
         a. Supporting detail about the subpoint
   B. Supporting detail about main idea 2
      1. Subpoint about the detail
         a. Supporting detail about the subpoint

Provide students with opportunities to practice outlining, especially with content area materials. Check students' practice outlines and provide feedback. When making and checking assignments, monitor students' outlines. Encourage them to use this strategy when completing assignments and when studying for tests.

Listing

The listing strategy can be used when outlining appears to be too complex for students or when details are not emphasized (Coman & Heavers, 2001). Listing can be useful in content area classes, especially social studies. For example, the following is a list of major early events in the exploration of the Antarctic (http://www.south-pole.com/p0000052.htm):

1. 1519—Ferdinand Magellan discovers a narrow strait to the Pacific Ocean.
2. 1578—Francis Drake is blown off course and sails around the island of Tierra del Fuego.
3. 1773—Captain James Cook and his crew are the first sailors to cross the Antarctic Circle.
4. 1911—Roald Amundsen, a Norwegian, and four others reach the South Pole. They leave letters for Robert F. Scott and erect a Norwegian flag.
5. 1912—Robert F. Scott, Edward Wilson, Edgar Evans, and Lawrence Oates reach the South Pole, only to find that Amundsen had already been there. They all perish on their return trip.
6. 1915—Ernest Shackleton and his crew abandon their ship, *Endurance,* as it is crushed in the ice of the Weddell Sea.

MARKING THE TEXT

Students should be encouraged to be actively engaged in reading texts. Kiewra and DuBois (1998) encourage readers to be aggressive. They state, "Effective students read aggressively and with purpose, as if they were scrutinizing a treasure map or a rich uncle's will. They mark important 'landmarks' and 'pathways' that reveal the text's structure. They use note-taking strategies that unearth the text's 'treasures' " (p. 218). Kiewra and DuBois provide a marking system that can be used to identify the titles, topics, subtopics, repeatable categories, details, sequences, and lists.

John White and Martha Spatz, two high school teachers, showed students a marking system that can help them read in the content areas. They created a poster of the marking system and placed it on the bulletin board, and they created smaller versions that students could keep on their desks and use when they did homework. They involved students in the creation of additional symbols that could be used. This marking system is illustrated in Figure 15.6.

GLEANING STRATEGY

The **gleaning strategy** involves the use of abbreviations and symbols while taking notes. This strategy is especially efficient for students who do not write or type. Abbreviations consist of brief versions of words that represent the complete word. Hulme (1993) developed the gleaning strategy in which vowels are omitted, words are shortened, and symbols are used to represent the main ideas of the text. Figure 15.7 provides examples of using abbreviations and symbols. The steps in the gleaning strategy are:

1. Read the text.
2. Identify the main ideas.
3. Represent the main ideas in using symbols and abbreviations. Notes can be made on the text, on note cards, or electronically.
4. Review the text by restating the main ideas based on the information recorded.

Figure 15.6   **Marking system symbols**

	Main idea
	Major topic
	Subtopic
	Repeatable category
[details are in brackets]	Detail
1, 2, 3, 4, . . .	Sequence or list

continued

Figure 15.6   Marking system symbols *continued*

Example of Marking Text

THE EMPEROR'S NEW CLOTHES*  title

Hans Christian Anderson

major topic

 details

Many years ago, there was an Emperor, who was so excessively fond of new clothes, that he spent all his money in dress. He did not [trouble himself in the least about his soldiers]; nor did he care to go either to the [theater or the chase], except for the opportunities then afforded him for displaying his new clothes. He had a different suit for each hour of the day; and as of any other king or emperor, one is accustomed to say, "he is sitting in council," it was always said of him, "The Emperor is sitting in his wardrobe."

*Note: Obtained from Project Gutenberg—™ Etexts. Retrieved March 27, 2004, from http://www.gutenberg.net

Source: Adapted from *Learning to Learn,* by K. A. Kiewra and N. F. DuBois, 1998, Boston: Allyn & Bacon.

Figure 15.7   Examples of abbreviations and symbols used in note taking

Symbol or Abbreviation	Meaning
Use common symbols for abbreviations	
+	plus
//	parallel
©	copyright
Σ	sum of
≠	not equal to
√	check
♀	female
♂	male
$	dollars
?	question
i	information
Use abbreviations without periods	
eg for *e.g.*	example
dept for *dept.*	department
NYC for *N.Y.C.*	New York City
Use only the first syllable of a word	
sci	science
math	mathematics
ref	references
Use the entire first syllable and the first letter of the second syllable	
hist	history
beg	beginning

Figure 15.7   Examples of abbreviations and symbols used in note taking *continued*

Symbol or Abbreviation	Meaning
Omit vowels from the middle of words, retaining only enough consonants to provide a recognizable form of the word. *thry* *effct*	theory effect
Form the plural of a symbol or abbreviated word by adding *s* *autos* *bks*	automobiles books
Use *g* to represent *ing* endings *incg* *workg*	increasing working
Leave out unimportant verbs *has* *was*	
Leave out unnecessary articles a an the	
If a term, phrase, or name is initially written out in full during the lecture, initials can be substituted whenever it is used again World Wide Web	WWW
Use symbols for common connective or transition words & w/ w/o vs @	and with without against or versus at
Create your own set of abbreviations and symbols → ★	leading to or results important

Source: Adapted from "Gleaning," by L.D. Hulme, 1993, *Journal of Reading, 36,* pp. 403–404.

SKILLS THAT SUPPORT STUDENTS' READING COMPREHENSION

Chapter 11 addressed methods and strategies for teaching reading. This section describes strategies that students can use when studying. These strategies encourage active engagement with and comprehension of text.

PREVIEW-READ-RECALL

Preview-Read-Recall (PRR) encourages active reading of texts (Kiewra & DuBois, 1998). During the Preview phase, there are a number of steps that should be considered. Students should be taught to ask why they are reading the material and to develop an overview of the main ideas and the organization of the text. They should identify the title, front and back cover information, author's biographical information, publication date, table of contents, introduction, preface, index, and glossary.

During the Read phase, students should identify the introduction, headings, subheadings, topic sentences of each paragraph, diagrams, tables, charts, conclusion, and summary. Encourage them to use the KWHL strategy ("What do you know?", "What do you want to know?", "How will you find out?", "What did you learn?") previously discussed.

Finally, during the Recall phase, teach students to mentally review or verbalize the highlights of what they have read. Address the "L" question of KWHL, "What did I learn?" Students should underline and make marginal notes of the key words or phrases in the section. Underlining after, rather than before, reading is very helpful in remembering what has been read. Show students how to make separate notes, outlines, or representations of what they have read. It is sometimes useful for students to work with other students when using the PRR phases. Figure 15.8 summarizes these phases.

Figure 15.8   Preview-Read-Recall

Preview Phase
Purpose
Organization
  Title
  Front cover information
  Back cover information
  Table of contents
  Introduction
  Preface
  Index
  Glossary
Read Phase
Introduction
Headings and subheadings
Topic sentences
Diagrams, tables, and charts
Summary
Recall Phase
What was learned?

SQ3R Strategy

SQ3R stands for Survey, Question, Read, Recite, and Review (Kiewra & DuBois, 1998). The strategy involves reading a text several times and processing the information in several ways. SQ3R can be used with a variety of reading materials. However, it is not very useful with long or complex texts.

In Survey, the first step, students should begin by quickly looking over the material for clues to the organization of the text. This includes the table of contents, chapter titles, introduction, headings, subheadings, figures, tables, photographs, and conclusions. These clues are used to create a *mental map* of the material. If explicit textual clues are absent, students should attend to paragraph breaks and phrases such as *most important* and *in summary*. Students should be able to identify main ideas.

In the second step, Question, students should be asked to predict questions that can be answered by reading the text. This step encourages active engagement with the text and can also be used to study for tests. Questions can be developed by changing major headings and subheadings into questions and by drawing upon prior knowledge and experiences. Questions that students predict can be compared to those at the end of the chapter.

In the third step, Read, students read the text one section at a time, looking for answers to the questions that have been predicted. While reading, the emphasis should be on jotting down brief notes about the text. Highlighting the text is discouraged because this may be distracting to the student.

In Recite, the fourth step, students should take time to recall the important points. They can verbalize or write them down. Students should review the answers to the predicted questions and summarize the sections. Next, they should review the text one section at a time. Students should refer to the headings and subheadings, the predicted questions, their responses, written notes, text that was underlined or highlighted, and any tables, charts, or visual aids. They should summarize in writing or by recording their verbal responses regarding the purpose and main ideas of the text.

In the last step, Review, students review the entire SQ3R process and return to the text periodically to increase their comprehension.

PQ4R Strategy

PQ4R involves previewing, questioning, reading, reflecting, reciting, and reviewing (Kiewra & DuBois, 1998). The main difference between it and SQ3R is that in PQ4R the student needs to read the text in its entirety before reflecting, rather than section by section, as with SQ3R. The student should carefully read the complete text, recording notes in the margin or underlining information that answers the predicted questions.

SNIPS Strategy

SNIPS is a five-step strategy that focuses on understanding and interpretation of visual aids such as pictures, graphs, charts, maps, time lines, and other visual representations (Kiewra & DuBois, 1998). There are some similarities among SNIPS, SQ3R, and PQ4R. The SNIPS steps are: Start with questions, Note what can be learned from hints, Identify what is important, Plug it into the chapter, and See if you can explain it to someone.

In the first step, students should ask themselves why they are looking at a particular visual aid. Students ask questions to determine the types of information on which to focus, depending on the type of visual aid presented. For example, for graphs and charts the student asks, "What is being compared?" and "What are the similarities and differences?" For maps the student asks, "What type of information is being conveyed?" For time lines the student asks, "What are the dates that are described?" and "Why are these important?"

In the second and third steps of SNIPS, students should note what can be learned from hints and identify hints, clues, or cues that are included in the visual representation. These clues can include the title, labels, color coding, scale, time frame, and main ideas conveyed by the representation. Students are encouraged to apply prior knowledge as they identify clues and interpret their meanings.

The fourth step focuses on relating the visual representation to the text. The final step encourages students to explain the presentation to themselves and others. They should identify how it relates to the text and the information, ideas, or processes that are conveyed.

REAP STRATEGY

The **REAP** (Eanet & Manzo, 1976) strategy is used for making annotations or notes of texts. The steps are Read, Encode, Annotate, and Ponder. The student begins by reading a portion of the text. Next, the student encodes or paraphrases what has been read. Annotating text, the third step, is the major strength of this approach. Annotations are brief notes on a text that summarize, explain, or question the text. Annotating is frequently preferable to highlighting and underlining because annotating promotes active engagement with the text and helps to focus the attention of the learner. Eanet and Manzo described 10 types of annotation. The types that are used depend on the purpose of the assignment or reading.

1. *Summary Annotation.* The student summarizes the meaning of the text. Elaborations on the meaning, such as examples, plot, and supporting details, are not included.
2. *Thesis Annotation.* The student summarizes the main idea of the text.
3. *Question Annotation.* This annotation is written in question form and should ask, "what is the question that the author is trying to answer?"
4. *Critical Annotation.* This indicates the extent to which the student agrees or disagrees with the author. The annotation consists of three sentences. The first sentence restates the author's main idea. The second sentence gives the student's response that critiques the author's position. The third sentence provides supporting details that explain the student's position.
5. *Heuristic Annotation.* The term *heuristic* describes a process in which an individual learns through discovery. In this type of annotation, the student restates the author's main idea and the student's interpretation of it in the student's own words. The author's words are indicated by quotation marks (") and the student's ideas are marked with brackets ([ ]).

6. *Intention Annotation.* The student summarizes the author's purposes or intentions in writing the text based on the student's knowledge about the author, the author's language and writing style, and the student's impression of why the author wrote the text.

7. *Motivation Annotation.* The student hypothesizes or guesses about the author's motivation in writing the text, using clues found in the text as well as prior knowledge and experiences.

8. *Probe Annotation.* The student notes any questions, ideas, or concepts that should be investigated further. The student asks, "What else should I know about this?", "Who also did similar work?", and "Why is this important?"

9. *Personal View Annotation.* The student reflects on personal beliefs, understandings, and opinions of the text. Comparisons are made between the student's reflections and the beliefs and opinions of the author.

10. *Inventive Annotation.* The student develops a new, creative, or different conclusion to the text.

MULTIPASS STRATEGY

The purpose of the **multipass** strategy is to improve reading comprehension, learning acquisition, generalization, and paraphrasing skills (Schumacher, Deshler, Alley, Warner, & Denton, 1982). The student makes three passes through a text, using different strategies during each pass. This method can be used in content areas to improve understanding of a text. The three stages or passes of multipass are:

1. *Survey the Reading.* The student rapidly surveys the title, introduction, headings, visual representations, and summary in order to become familiar with the organization and main ideas of the text. During this phase, the student reflects on the following questions: "What is the general subject of the reading?" "What are the purposes or goals of the author?" "What are the main ideas?" "What is the conclusion?"

2. *Size Up the Reading.* The student carefully reads the text, identifying details and visual representations that support the main idea. Close attention is given to visual representations, statistics, and words in boldface or italic print. The student should identify the main ideas and supporting details and either take notes, make recordings, or develop a visual representation such as a story map, time line, or graphic organizer.

3. *Sort Out the Information.* The student reflects on the text and identifies what was learned and what needs to be learned. The student can use end-of-chapter or end-of-section questions, if available, or can pair up with another student for review of the text.

TEST-TAKING STRATEGIES

There are a number of test-taking strategies that can be of benefit to students. They can be divided into three categories: those used before, during, and after the test. Teachers should explain the test-taking strategies to students, ask them to practice the

These students are practicing test-taking strategies.

strategies during a practice test, have students apply them when taking tests, and, finally, ask students to reflect on which strategies were successful and which ones require further practice. Invite students to suggest additional strategies and to develop their own.

STRATEGIES BEFORE THE TEST

1. Preparation and study well before the test is essential. Last-minute cramming usually is not effective.
2. Keep notes on texts that have been read.
3. Keep notes on class discussions and activities.
4. Organize notes and resources efficiently.
5. Provide sufficient time to practice new skills and processes.
6. Study with one or more partners. Explaining responses, asking questions, and checking responses with others can improve understanding.
7. Obtain a good night's sleep before the test.
8. Get proper nutrition before the test.
9. Get some exercise. This can reduce anxiety and heighten alertness.
10. Arrive early for the test.
11. Select a good seat. Choose a quiet part of the room, sitting away from other students and the door (Kiewra & DuBois, 1998).

STRATEGIES DURING THE TEST

1. Try to stay relaxed and confident. Use deep-breathing exercises to reduce anxiety.
2. Be prepared. Bring all the materials that are needed such as pencils, pens, a calculator, a dictionary, and a watch.
3. Read the directions carefully. Check to see if multiple-choice questions can have more than one correct response, if there is a penalty for guessing, or if more than one essay question should be answered.
4. Preview the items. Look over the test and estimate the amount of time that will be spent on each section.
5. Complete the easy questions first. Next, answer the questions that have the highest point values. Leave the most difficult questions, the ones with lower point values, and the ones that require the greatest amount of writing for last.
6. Use hints from other items. Sometimes, answers to questions are revealed by questions or choices for other items.
7. Ask the teacher questions about directions, vocabulary, or questions that are not understood.
8. Use specific strategies for each type of test item, such as multiple-choice, true/false, and essay questions.
9. Allow enough time for review at the end of the test.
10. Use all of the time that has been given. Do not rush to complete the test.

STRATEGIES AFTER THE TEST

The work of students and teachers is not over once the test is finished. Each test can provide a foundation for preparation for the next test. Once the corrected test is returned to students, the following strategies should be used:

1. Conduct an error analysis of the test results. Identify the items that the student completed successfully and unsuccessfully.
2. Reflect on the strategies that were used. Which ones worked? Which ones did not work?
3. Keep the corrected tests in a safe place for review when studying for unit tests or final exams.

STRATEGIES FOR SPECIFIC TYPES OF TESTS

Multiple-Choice Tests

1. Answer the easy questions first.
2. When unsure of the response, eliminate answers that are incorrect.
3. If there is no penalty for guessing, eliminate obviously wrong answers and make an informed guess.
4. Select the response that contains the same form of the word as the item stem and that makes sense grammatically when the item is read.
5. Use the answers to other questions for hints about the correct answer.
6. Avoid guessing when there is no basis for the choices and if there is a penalty for guessing.

Matching Tests

1. Read the instructions carefully. Some tests allow items to be used only once; others permit multiple use of choices.
2. Matching tests are the same as multiple-choice tests. Use the same strategies for both.
3. Answer easy items first.
4. Cross out items that have been used.

True-False Tests

1. Most true-false tests contain more true answers than false answers. When in doubt, guess *true*. The student has a chance of over 50% of selecting the correct response.
2. Qualifiers such as *no, never, none, always, every, entirely,* and *only* limit acceptable answers and usually imply that the statement is false. Students should be encouraged to circle qualifiers.
3. Qualifiers such as *sometimes, often, frequently, ordinarily,* and *generally* frequently indicate true answers.
4. If a statement seems true, then make sure that every part of the sentence is true.
5. Pay attention to long sentences, groups of words set off by commas, and long strings of words. These sentences can be confusing and are frequently false.
6. Answer easy items first.

Short-Answer Tests

1. Read the instructions and items carefully.
2. Answer easy items first.
3. Answer the entire question, not just part of it.
4. Use hints from other questions. Sometimes answers to questions are revealed by questions or choices from other questions.

Essay Tests

1. Think through the response before writing.
2. Check to see the type of response requested. Be alert for key terms that signal the type of response, such as *compare and contrast, analyze, evaluate, conclude,* and *synthesize* (Kiewra & DuBois, 1998).
3. Develop a brief outline or visual representation of ideas before writing. Plan the order of discussion of the key points, ideas, and concepts.
4. Use topic sentences for paragraphs. State the main point in the first sentence. Make sure that the rest of the paragraph provides supporting details or elaboration on the key point.
5. The first paragraph should provide an overview or introduction to the entire essay.
6. Use specific facts, examples, and quotations to support the details.
7. Summarize in the last paragraph, restating the main ideas and why they are important.

8. Proofread spelling, grammar, and punctuation.
9. If time is short, save time by outlining the response.

Skill Tests

1. Be alert for words that have specific meanings such as *of, mean, sum,* and *is.* Circle key terms.
2. At the beginning of the test, write down specific formulas that will be used.
3. Use visual representations to figure out the steps or processes that need to be followed.
4. Review answers to mathematics problems. Compare the answers obtained with the estimated answers.

INSTRUCTIONAL STRATEGIES FOR DEEPENING UNDERSTANDING AND ENHANCING MEMORY

Metacognition is the awareness of and control over personal learning strategies. Knowing how to identify personal cognitive skills that are used in studying and when and how to use them helps students acquire, use, and retain information. Because metacognition is important to learning, learning materials frequently include summaries, concept maps, and organizers that increase students' understanding. Teachers can support students by calling attention to these aids, teaching students how to develop similar aids for themselves, and demonstrating how to use them efficiently.

Flavell (1976) defines three types of metacognitive knowledge. First, learners hold beliefs about themselves as learners. For example, a student believes that listening to music is helpful when studying. Second, a learner has task knowledge, such as the procedures that must be followed to complete a task. In mathematics, task knowledge is important when completing operations: to add two fractions with different demoninators, the student must first change both denominators to a common number. Third, a learner has strategy knowledge, which is the ability to choose an appropriate strategy to solve a task. In mathematics, strategy knowledge enables the student to know how to begin to solve a word problem.

Telling students to stop, look, and listen and teaching test-taking skills are examples of metacognitive strategies. Asking students to engage in a series of steps in which they describe a problem, discuss how they plan to solve it, and analyze how it turned out is another example of a metacognitive strategy (Mayer & Wittrock, 1996). Other strategies that can enhance metacognition include teaching self-awareness of thinking patterns, self-verbalizations, modeling, self-monitoring, self-reinforcement, self-management, and strategic thinking.

Visual representations facilitate conceptualization by making concepts concrete and by making relationships between concepts explicit. Representations of knowledge are more effective (Kiewra & DuBois, 1998) because they allow similar types of information to be clustered or grouped together, enable missing details to be identified, and provide a quick overview of the topic. Visual representations (Martin, 1999) can increase the speed of communication because visual symbols can be recognized easily and quickly. They can help learners organize and recall information, explain complex relationships using a minimum amount of text, clarify and explain concepts, and demonstrate how concepts change as new ideas develop (Hyerle, 1996). There are several types of representations including graphic organizers, hierarchies, sequences, matrices, and diagrams.

GRAPHIC ORGANIZERS

Graphic organizers help to make abstract concepts tangible and promote the creation and use of knowledge (Bean, Singer, Sorter, & Frasee, 1986). Graphic organizers (Larkin, 1997) can be used to:

- locate and remember key facts and ideas,
- introduce and/or rearrange information,
- organize written and spatial arrangement of information,
- summarize text chapters/units,
- view information as a meaningful whole,
- develop study guides,
- demonstrate interrelationships among ideas, and
- provide alternative test formats.

K-W-L

The K-W-L strategy (Ogle, 1986) was introduced in Chapter 7. This strategy focuses on the goals or purposes of the reading activity. It stimulates the student's prior or

This small group of students is brainstorming test taking strategies.

background knowledge and connects the text to what the student knows and wants to learn. The three stages of the K-W-L strategy are:

1. *K (What You Know).* In this step, students engage in brainstorming in response to a stimulus provided by the teacher or another student. The stimulus can be a word, concept, process, category, or question. For example, when studying astronomy, the teacher could begin by asking, "When you are outside at night, what objects have you seen in the sky?" After students offer their comments, the teacher could continue by asking, "Has anyone seen a comet or a meteor?" The use of visual representations, discussed earlier in this chapter, can be useful during the brainstorming.

2. *W (What You Want to Know).* Next, teachers can build on the students' comments, interests, and curiosity by identifying what else they would like to know about the topic. Students may want to know about the origin of comets and meteors, whether any comets or meteors have landed on Earth, and the orbits of these objects. During the last part of this stage, students should translate what they would like to know into purposes for reading.

3. *L (What You Learned).* Students can identify the main ideas, supporting details, and their conclusions. Additional examples of graphic organizers (Figure 15.9) can be found in Chapter 7.

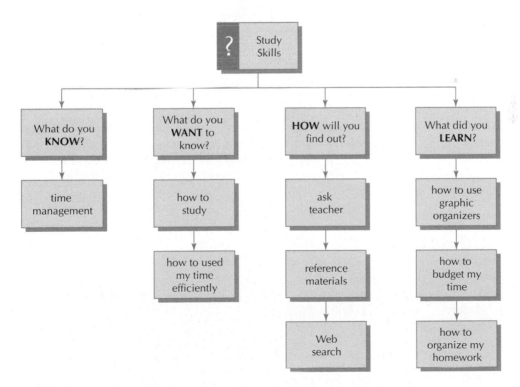

Figure 15.9   **KWHL graphic organizer**

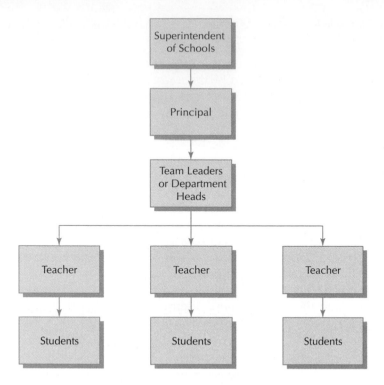

Figure 15.10   **Hierarchy**

HIERARCHIES

A **hierarchy** organizes information into levels and groups. Levels indicate details and characteristics. Hierarchies can support analysis, understanding of structures, and comprehension of attributes. Examples of hierarchies include family trees, organization of the U.S. Supreme Court, and the celestial bodies in the universe. Figure 15.10 is a hierarchy used in education.

SEQUENCES

Sequences organize ideas, steps, events, and stages in chronological or sequential order (Figure 15.11). They can have subsequences or multiple levels. Sequences can be used in all content areas, but they are especially useful in mathematics, literature, and history (Kiewra & DuBois, 1998).

MATRICES

Selene, a student in Martha Spatz's ninth-grade science class, was excited about the new unit on the solar system. She loved to go out at night and look at the twinkling

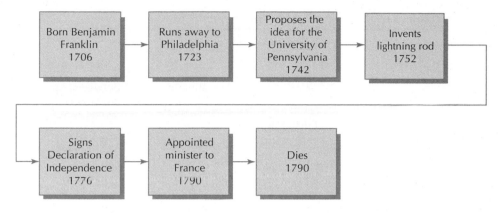

Figure 15.11   **Sequence: Life of Benjamin Franklin**

sky. Sometimes her aunt went outside with Selene and pointed out planets that were visible to the unaided eye such as Venus, Mars, Jupiter, and Saturn. Ms. Spatz's evident excitement about this topic increased Selene's enthusiasm. However, Selene was becoming confused about the new concepts that her teacher introduced. Her teacher, who frequently checked for students' understanding, soon realized that Selene was puzzled about the new terminology and concepts. Ms. Spatz showed her students how to use a learning strategy that would help them organize their new learning.

A **matrix** builds on hierarchies and sequences by including topics, categories, and details. Matrices provide information on levels, groups, and relationships between items in the matrix.

Topics are placed along the top of the matrix. Repeatable categories are placed along the left side. The details or facts intersect the topic and categories (Kiewra & DuBois, 1998). Figure 15.12 is the matrix that Martha Spatz developed with her students to organize new science concepts.

DIAGRAMS

A **diagram** provides a picture that summarizes and organizes information. Diagrams show the most important details or features of an object, function, or process. Frequently, the important features are labeled. Figure 15.13 is an example of a diagram.

Venn Diagram

A Venn diagram is usually made up of two or more overlapping circles. It can be used to show similarities and differences between events, people, situations, ideas, and concepts. Venn diagrams are often used in mathematics to show relationships. They are also useful in other content areas such as language arts, science, and social studies. Figure 15.14 is an example of a Venn diagram.

Figure 15.12   **Matrix: Interplanetary debris of our solar system**

	Material	Composition	Origin	Location
TOPICS				
Repeatable Category	Asteroids	Silicates, iron, nickel	Formation of solar system	Between Mars and Jupiter
DETAILS				
Repeatable Category	Comets	Water, ice, methane, ammonia, carbon dioxide, silicates	Possibly formed from materials from Jupiter and Saturn	Near Jupiter and Saturn
Repeatable Category	Meteors	Silicates	Remains of comets	General orbits of original comets from which they were formed
Repeatable Category	Interplanetary gas and dust	Hydrogen and helium gases, silicates and graphite dust	Debris from comets and asteroids	Throughout the solar system

Advance Organizer

An **advance organizer** is an instructional strategy used to introduce an activity such as a lesson, assignment, reading, or multimedia presentation. It presents a structured introduction to the activity. The following steps can be used in developing an advance organizer:

1. The teacher tells the students that they will be provided with an introduction to the activity.
2. The main and supporting ideas are described.
3. An organizational framework, representation, outline, or list is provided by the teacher.
4. The concepts and new information that are presented are related to prior learning or experiences.
5. Familiar examples and nonexamples are presented.

Concept Ladder

A **concept ladder** enables students to understand how words and concepts are related to each hierarchically. It helps them use their prior knowledge and experiences to

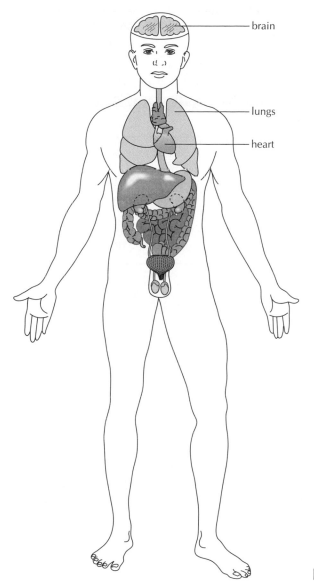

Figure 15.13   **Diagram**

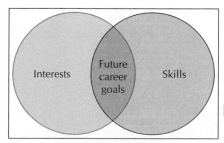

Figure 15.14   **Venn diagram: Future career goals**

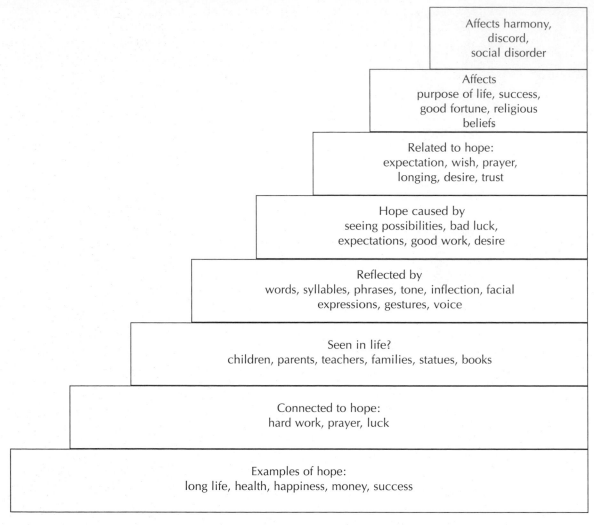

Figure 15.15   Concept ladder—hopes

develop an understanding of abstract concepts. Concept ladders can be used to establish purposes for reading and to summarize how concepts are related. Figure 15.15 is an example of a concept ladder.

THINK-ALOUDS

A think-aloud, as discussed in Chapter 11, is a comprehension monitoring strategy in which learners communicate thoughts while engaging in a task. Thinking out loud can help students focus on a particular problem, demonstrate problem-solving strategies, and provide insight into the problem-solving process. When first teaching students to think aloud, teachers can model it. For example, here is how Raj Jahal, a mathematics teacher, uses think-alouds to teach his students how to solve word problems.

─────── ❖ *THINKING ALOUD ABOUT MONEY* ❖ ───────

Problem: Four students decide to have a party for one of their friends and to share the expenses equally. Carmen buys a cake for $8.00, Ruth buys ice cream for $5.00, Sarah spends $2.00 on decorations, and Julio pays $3.00 for popcorn and $6.00 for soda. If the students share the expenses equally, which students owe money to other students?

Teacher: "Today we are going to look at our first word problem. I am going to take you through the process. I am going to explain my thought processes and think aloud as I work through the problem. From the title of the word problem, I can expect the problem to involve spending money. As I read the problem, I notice that four persons are listed, along with the amounts of money they spent on the party. The first sentence states that the students will 'share the expenses equally.' The end of the problem asks, 'which students owe money to other students?' I need to find out who owes money and who is due money. It seems that I will need to determine the total amount paid so that I can see who overpaid and who underpaid. I remember solving a similar problem where I made a chart to list the names of the people and how much they paid (using prior knowledge to make connections).

Name	Money Spent
Carmen	$8.00
Ruth	$5.00
Sarah	$2.00
Julio	$3.00 + $6.00 = $9.00

"I know that some people paid too much and some underpaid. To figure out how much they overpaid or underpaid, I need to figure out how much each person should have paid. If I add the total amount spent and divide by 4, I'll know how much each person should have paid.

Name	Money Spent	Money Due Back (Overpaid)	Money Need to Pay (Underpaid)
Carmen	$8.00		
Ruth	$5.00		
Sarah	$2.00		
Julio	$3.00 + $6.00 = $9.00		
Total	$24.00		

"The total amount spent was $24.00. This amount divided by four persons equals $6.00. Therefore, each person should have paid $6.00. Now that I know how much each person should have paid, I can determine if they overpaid or underpaid.

Name	Money Spent	Money Due Back (Overpaid)	Money Need to Pay (Underpaid)
Carmen	$8.00	$2.00	—
Ruth	$5.00	—	$1.00
Sarah	$2.00	—	$4.00
Julio	$3.00 + $6.00 = $9.00	$3.00	—
Total	$24.00		

"Using this chart has made it very easy to see who overpaid and who underpaid. To help make this even clearer, I will write what each person needs to do, and then I can answer the question 'which students owe money to other students?' I see that because there are two people paying and two people receiving, there might be more than one solution. Let's see what happens.

Solution 1
Ruth pays $1.00 to Carmen.
Sarah pays $1.00 to Carmen.
Sarah pays $3.00 to Julio.

Solution 2
Ruth pays $1.00 to Julio.
Sarah pays $2.00 to Carmen.
Sarah pays $2.00 to Julio.

"Both solutions work. By making the chart and carefully going step by step, I was able to keep all the numbers straight, and I did not get confused. It also made it easy to see how to solve problems similar to this one" (adapted from Mason, Stacey, & Burton, 1982).

Research to Practice

Mnemonics

Mnemonics is a strategy that can help students remember academic and behavioral tasks (Mastropieri & Scruggs, 1998). Choose a learning or behavioral outcome and list the steps that are required to complete it. Word each step so that a key word begins it. Spell a word that relates to the outcome, using the first letters of each step. An example of mnemonics is the FAST strategy, which is used to aid students in problem solving (McIntosh & Vaughn, 1995):

F	Freeze and think	Stop and define the problem.
A	Alternatives	List alternatives to solve the problem.
S	Solution	What will solve the problem?
T	Try it	Try the solution and see if it works.

Some schools employ this type of mnemonic to denote their silent reading time. They use the letters DEAR to mean "Drop Everything And Read."

Another mnemonic strategy is to make a sentence or word using the first letter of each item in the list that must be remembered. Examples of this are:

- *Roy G. Biv.* The first letters of each word stand for the first letters of the colors of the light spectrum: red, orange, yellow, green, blue, indigo, violet.
- *Homes.* Each letter stands for the first letter of each of the Great Lakes: Huron, Ontario, Michigan, Erie, Superior.
- *My Very Educated Mother Just Served Us Nine Pizzas.* The first letter of each word starts the names of the planets in order from the sun outward: Mars, Venus, Earth, Jupiter, Saturn, Uranus, Neptune, and Pluto.

Questions for Reflection

1. Develop several mnemonics that support learning and study skills. Share these with your classmates.
2. Conduct a Web search and make a list of mnemonics that can be used to support instruction in the content areas.

To perform these activities and learn more about applying research to practice, go to the Companion Website at www.prenhall. com/cohen, select Chapter 15, then choose Research to Practice.

HOMEWORK

According to Bryan and Sullivan-Burstein (1997), students with disabilities have a number of problems with homework, including negative feelings about doing it, distractibility, failure to complete it, need for reminders, boredom, lack of confidence, and a perception that they receive less help and more criticism from parents. Success in homework assignments involves clear communication with students and their families.

TEACHERS' REFLECTIONS ON THEIR ASSIGNMENTS

Teachers should take the time to reflect on their assignments, which will enable them to improve the assignments to optimize student learning. Estimate how long an assignment should take. Ask students to write on a corner of their homework page the amount of time it took them to complete it. Compare your estimated time with the students' actual time.

Explain to students the reasons for assigning difficult or unpopular assignments. If changes are made, provide reasons. Discuss homework assignments with other teachers. Identify the strategies that they have found to be successful and unsuccessful (Bryan & Sullivan-Burstein, 1997).

COMMUNICATION WITH PARENTS

Encourage parents to use strategies that support successful homework completion. Involve parents in homework assignments by encouraging them to do the following (adapted from Bryan & Sullivan-Burstein, 1997):

1. Show that education and homework are important.
2. Set a regular time every day for doing homework.
3. Provide the appropriate books, paper, and tools that the child needs to complete assignments.
4. Provide a quiet place to study.
5. Set a good example by reading and writing.
6. Keep in regular communication with the child's teachers. Meet early in the year with the child's teachers. When a problem arises, communicate with the teacher.
7. Know the teacher's expectations for length of assignments.
8. Know the teacher's expectations for parental involvement.
9. Monitor assignments. See that they are started and completed.
10. Be aware of where your child keeps homework assignments.
11. Provide guidance.
12. Be familiar with how your child learns.
13. Assure structure and organization by providing a calendar and assignments.
14. Provide books, book bag, or folders, if needed.
15. Discuss homework strategies and schedules with the child.

Using Technology
Supporting Learning

Technology, including computers, software, personal organizers, wireless devices, and the Internet, can be of enormous assistance in supporting students' study skills. The World Wide Web offers abundant resources for both teachers and students. Web sites offer calendars, study skills, test-taking strategies, online translations, dictionaries, self-assessment of study skills, presentations, and distance learning courses.

The Web has a number of resources for the assessment of learning and study strategies. A good place to start is to type phrases such as *study skills, how to study, assessment of study skills,* and *time management* into a Web search engine such as Google, Yahoo!, Lycos, Excite, AOL Search, Ask Jeeves, and others.

Many software companies have demonstration programs that can be downloaded from the Web. Downloading programs allows both teachers and students to try out software before purchase. Other software programs are available free. The following software is generally available for demonstration purposes:

- graphic organizer software.
- study strategies described in this chapter, such as SQ3R.
- electronic calendars.
- grammar, spelling, and punctuation checkers are common features of most word processing programs. Students should be encouraged to use these features on a regular basis.
- time management software.
- note-taking software.
- outlining software.
- reading, writing, and vocabulary skills software.
- presentation skills software.
- test-taking skills software.
- translation software.
- foreign language dictionaries.

There have been a number of advances in technology hardware. For example, voice recorders can be used to record and replay assignments and play notes. PDAs, handheld devices, have features that allow students to organize their schedules, prioritize tasks, set alarms for reminders, organize telephone numbers and addresses, keep to-do lists, and take notes.

Questions for Reflection

1. Explore the grammar, spelling, and punctuation checkers built into the word processing software that you use. How can these checkers be customized for students? What features do they have for speakers of languages other than English?
2. Using an Internet search engine, compare several time management software programs. Organize your thoughts using concept mapping software.

 To answer these questions and learn more about using technology to support learning, go to the Companion Website at www. prenhall.com/cohen, select Chapter 15, then choose Using Technology.

Considering Diversity

Modified Paired Storytelling Strategy

Based on a strategy developed by Lie (1994), **modified paired storytelling** is a strategy that can be used to support the language learning of students who speak languages other than English. This strategy has several advantages. It provides students who speak other languages a chance to communicate in English. An important component of this strategy is that communication is contextualized. Partners have the opportunity to practice communication in English. Use its vocabulary, and improve comprehension.

The first step in implementing this strategy is to assign students to partners. After introducing the topic, the teacher asks the students to brainstorm about their prior knowledge of or previous experiences with the topic. Next, the teacher gives a structured assignment to the pairs. The assignment may be to read or write about a character or to develop a visual representation of the characters or events.

Working in pairs, students record their own responses. Next, the members of each pair share their work with their partners. They then provide feedback to their partners by adding details and providing suggestions. Finally, each pair shares their work with the entire class.

Questions for Reflection

1. Consider the modified paired storytelling strategy. Why is it important to be sensitive to diversity when teaching study skills?
2. What other study skills approaches can be used when teaching study skills to diverse learners?

To answer these questions and deepen your understanding of diversity in schools and communities, go to the Companion Website at www.prenhall.com/cohen, select Chapter 15, then choose Considering Diversity.

SUMMARY

- Teaching study skills to students with disabilities involves knowledge of the student's needs and familiarity with learning and study skills, including time management, knowing how to learn, making representations of what students know, taking notes, taking tests, and doing homework.
- Integration of learning and study skills into content areas can provide students opportunities to practice and apply new skills as well as reinforce skills and strategies that have been learned. Study skills should not be taught in isolation; modeling and practicing skills should be an integral part of content area study.

EXTENDING LEARNING

1. Interview a general education and a special education teacher. Ask them about the study skills they teach their students. Compare their responses.
2. Review the study skills described in this chapter. Which ones do you prefer for yourself? Why?
3. After reading the section on note taking, choose two strategies and use them to take notes on several pages of text. Which strategy do you prefer? Why?
4. Review the section on marking systems. Develop additional symbols. Share them with others in your class.
5. Technology can be very useful in supporting study and organizational skills. Develop two examples of how technology can be used. Share these examples with others in your class.

REFERENCES

Bean, T. W., Singer, H., Sorter, J., & Frasee, C. (1986). The effect of metacognitive instruction in outlining and graphic organizer construction on students' comprehension in a tenth-grade world history class. *Journal of Reading Behavior, 18,* 153–169.

Bryan, T., & Sullivan-Burstein, K. (1997). Homework how-to's. *TEACHING Exceptional Children, 29,* 32–37.

Coman, M., & Heavers, K. (2001). *How to improve your study skills.* New York: Glenco McGraw-Hill.

Eanet, M. G., & Manzo, A. (1976). READ—A strategy for improving reading/writing/study skills. *Journal of Reading, 19,* 647–652.

Flavell, J. H. (1976). Metacognitive aspects of problem solving. In L. B. Resnick (Ed.), *The nature of intelligence* (pp. 231–235). Mahwah, NJ: Erlbaum.

Fry, R. (2000). *How to study* (5th ed.). Franklin Lakes, NJ: Career Press.

Hawk, P. (1986). Using graphic organizers to increase achievement in middle school life science. *Science Education, 70,* 81–87.

Hulme, L. D. (1993). Gleaning. *Journal of Reading, 36,* 403–404.

Hyerle, D. (1996). *Visual tools for constructing knowledge.* Reston, VA: Association for Supervision of Curriculum Development.

Johnson, C., & Johnson, D. (2001). *Learning power* (2nd ed.). New York: Simon & Schuster.

Kiewra, K. A., & DuBois, N. F. (1998). *Learning to learn.* Boston: Allyn & Bacon.

Larkin, M. (1997). Graphic organizers. *The Collaborator.* Retrieved October 14, 2003, from the College of William & Mary website: http://www.wm.edu/TTAC/articles/learning/graphic.htm

Lie, A. (1994). Paired storytelling: An integrated approach for bilingual and English-as-a-second-language students. *Texas Reading Report, 16,* 4–5.

Martin, A. (1999). *Using electronic graphic organizers to build reading skills.* Retrieved from the Suite101.com website: http://www.suite101.com/article.cfm/reading

Mason, J., Stacey, K., & Burton, C. (1982). *Thinking mathematically.* Boston: Addison-Wesley.

Mastropieri, M. A., & Scruggs, T. E. (1998). Enhancing school success with mnemonic strategies. *Intervention in School and Clinic, 33,* 201–208.

Mayer, R. E., & Wittrock, M. C. (1996). Problem-solving transfer. In D. C. Berliner & R. C. Calfee (Eds.), *Intelligent tutoring systems: Lessons learned* (pp. 35–57). Hillsdale, NJ: Erlbaum.

McIntosh, R., & Vaughn, S. (1995). Fast social skills with SLAM and KAP. *TEACHING Exceptional Children, 28,* 37–40.

Meyers, J. (2000). *The secrets of taking any test* (2nd ed.). New York: Learning Express.

Morgenstern, J. (1998). *Organizing from the inside out.* New York: Henry Holt.

NICHCY. (1997). Interventions for students with learning disabilities. *NICHCY News Digest, 25.* Washington, DC: Author.

Ogle, D. (1986). K-W-L: A teaching model that develops active reading of expository text. *Reading Teacher, 39,* 564–570.

Schumaker, J. B., Deshler, D., Alley, G., Warner, M. Multipass: A learning strategy for improving reading comprehension. *Learning Disabilities Quarterly, 5,* 295–304.

16

Chapter

Transition

CHAPTER OBJECTIVES

After completing this chapter, you should be able to:

- ❖ Describe the transition process, activities, and services.
- ❖ Discuss federal mandates for transition activities.
- ❖ Describe assessment approaches used in transition.
- ❖ Explain foundational concepts: self-determination, self-advocacy, person-centered planning.
- ❖ Describe career development activities.
- ❖ Identify ways in which technology can be integrated into instruction.

Transition is a process that enables children and youth with disabilities to move easily, efficiently, and successfully from one school grade to another and from school to work and the community. Key points of transition include preschool to early elementary grades; elementary school to middle school or junior high school; middle school or junior high school to high school; and high school to work, postsecondary education, and the community. Transitions can involve moving from a child care setting to a preschool setting, entering kindergarten, changing teachers, moving from one school building to another, moving to new living arrangements, beginning new recreational and leisure activities, moving from high school to postsecondary educational experiences, and starting a job.

Knowledge of postschool outcomes and **transition services** enables educators to support transition planning and transition activities. While transitions occur throughout life, the transition from the school setting to adult life is one that requires careful planning and implementation. This should result in successful outcomes for students with disabilities. An outcome is the end result or consequence of transition activities. Postschool outcomes include postsecondary education, vocational training, continuing and adult education, employment, community participation, and independent living. Table 16.1 depicts postschool outcomes and activities.

More students with disabilities than students without disabilities drop out of school (Babbitt & White, 2002). There are many reasons why students with disabilities have less successful school experiences than their nondisabled peers. Students with disabilities tend to have difficulty with social skills. They frequently need assistance in interpreting and responding to social demands. For example, understanding how to participate in cooperative learning groups may pose difficulties for some students. Self-advocacy, especially in higher education settings, is another area of

Table 16.1	Postschool Outcomes and Activities	
	Outcome	**Activity**
	Postsecondary education	Community college College or university Other postsecondary education
	Vocational training	Vocational technical center Rehabilitation facility Community-based education and training Other vocational training
	Continuing and adult education	Adult basic education Community college Other continuing/adult education
	Employment	Competitive employment Supported employment Sheltered employment Volunteer work Other employment
	Community participation	Specialized recreation/social activities Sports or social clubs Community center programs Parks and recreation programs Hobby clubs Independent activities Other community participation
	Independent living	Financial and income Living arrangements Medical services and resources Personal management Transportation Advocacy and legal services

Source: Adapted from *Developing and Including Transition Services in the IEP,* by L. Love, 1993, Phoenix: Arizona Department of Education.

concern. During their K–12 years, teachers and family members frequently take on advocacy roles. However, once students enter the workforce or higher education, they are expected to advocate for themselves. Students may need assistance in expressing their needs and identifying beneficial resources. Another area of concern is that students with disabilities often have little knowledge of the modifications and accommodations that are beneficial to them. They are frequently unaware of their rights and of

These students will be making a transition from preschool to kindergarten.

the nature and types of support that they need to be successful. Their study, organization, note-taking, and test-taking skills may be deficient (Babbitt & White, 2002).

In previous chapters, you learned that an instructional method is a broad perspective based on theory, research, experiences, and philosophy. A teaching strategy is a specific instructional routine. Teaching strategies discussed in previous chapters can be used to support the transition activities of students.

FEDERAL LEGISLATION

❖ TRANSITION PLANNING FOR KARA ❖

Kara, a student at Washington High School, will be turning 16 next month. She lives at home and loves to be with her friends. Her IEP indicates that she has difficulty with reading and written communication. Kara and her mother recently participated in a team meeting that included Kara's special education teacher, a vocational educator, the school principal, and a job coach, an individual who goes with an employee to a job, learns the essential functions of the job, and provides strategies and supports for the employee to do the job. The team reviewed the plans for making a transition to the community after Kara finishes high school. The priorities that the team identified were developing self-advocacy skills, considering post-secondary educational opportunities in the community, and completing applications for summer employment.

Educational, vocational, and transitional services are mandated in legislation for individuals with disabilities. Current laws call for an interdisciplinary effort to serve these individuals. There are five laws that provide the authorization and the focus for transition services: the Rehabilitation Act Amendments of 1998, the Carl D. Perkins Vocational and Applied Technology Education Act Amendments of 1998, the Workforce Investment Act of 1998, the School-to-Work Opportunities Act of 1994, and the Individuals with Disabilities Education Act Amendments (IDEA).

The Rehabilitation Act Amendments of 1998 state that employment and training programs for all individuals should be coordinated and administered through a state workforce investment system. For individuals with disabilities, this means that they will be able to access services and programs designed to increase employment, skills, retention, and wages. Although the intended outcome is increased employment, the definition of employment is broad enough to include full- and part-time employment, the vocational outcome of supported employment, and other vocational outcomes such as self-employment.

The Carl D. Perkins Vocational and Applied Technology Education Act Amendments of 1998 guarantee equal access to vocational education programs and opportunities for all students. Students who are eligible to receive services under the Perkins Act include individuals with disabilities, individuals from economically disadvantaged families, individuals preparing for nontraditional training and employment, single parents, displaced homemakers, and individuals with other barriers to educational achievement, including those with limited English proficiency. The Perkins Act links students with disabilities to transition services by mandating that each student who has a disability and who participates in vocational education must have equal access to vocational activities; is assessed regarding vocational interests, abilities, and special needs; must be provided with special services; and must receive guidance, career, and transition counseling.

The purpose of the Workforce Investment Act of 1998 is to combine, coordinate, and improve employment, training, literacy, and vocational rehabilitation programs. This act consolidates services through a one-stop delivery system that assists individuals, including those with disabilities. In terms of transition planning, students with disabilities and their families should be able to locate information on employment and vocational training opportunities through this system.

The School-to-Work Opportunities Act of 1994 provides for a national framework (Krieg, Brown, & Ballard, 1995) that supports school-to-work opportunities. The implementation of the school-to-work opportunities system is determined by each state, and the ultimate goal is to link youth to productive employment. Because the implementation of this legislation is determined by each state, the participation of students with disabilities varies from one state to another.

The Individuals with Disabilities Education Act (IDEA) is the major legislation that mandates transition services. The focus is on assisting the individual with a disability to make a smooth transfer from the school to independent adult life. According to IDEA, transition services means:

> with disabilities that is a coordinated set of activities for a student designed within an outcome-oriented process, which promotes movement from school to post-school activities, including post-secondary education, vocational training, integrated employment (including supported employment), continuing and adult education, adult services, independent living, or community participation. (Sec. 300.29)

Research to Practice

Thinking About Youth with Disabilities

Research on American youth has yielded disturbing findings on education and employment. Greene and Kochhar-Bryant (2003) summarized the research and found that, compared with all Americans, almost twice as many students with disabilities do not complete high school. Students with disabilities are also much less likely to complete postsecondary education. Of those students who do participate in postsecondary education, many have a poor self-concept and poor socialization skills, and experience stress and anxiety. These students are reluctant to let instructors know that they need accommodations because they fear that they will be stigmatized. One of the most disturbing findings is that students with disabilities are much less likely to be employed than students without disabilities. A growing number of students with disabilities are applying for Supplemental Security Income (SSI), a federal program that assists persons with disabilities by providing funds to meet basic needs for food, clothing, and shelter each year. Thus, there is an ever-widening gap between persons with and without disabilities in relation to education and income.

Questions for Reflection

1. What are some reasons why so many students with disabilities do not complete high school?
2. Brainstorm strategies that can be used to keep students with disabilities from leaving school.
3. Identify strategies that can foster the employment of persons with disabilities. How can job coaches and mentors be helpful? Share these strategies with your classmates.

 To answer these questions and learn more about applying research to practice, go to the Companion Website at www.prenhall. com/cohen, select Chapter 16, then choose Research to Practice.

A "coordinated set of activities" means that all transition activities must meet the student's needs and complement, not duplicate, each other. Many individuals and agencies are involved in the transition process. The coordinated set of activities described in the preceding paragraph must:

1. be based upon the individual student's needs, taking into account the student's preferences and interests; and
2. include:
   a. instruction,
   b. community experiences,
   c. the development of employment and other post-school adult living objectives, and
   d. if appropriate, acquisition of daily living skills and functional vocational evaluation. [20 U.S.C. 1401(a) (19)]

Although progress has been made, several challenges remain. The National Council on Disability has defined these challenges as (a) increasing secondary school students' access to relevant and rigorous curricula and information technology while at the same time increasing the number of students who successfully complete high school;

(b) expanding the range of options for students who enter employment after graduation from high school; (c) improving access to higher education opportunities; (d) ensuring a wide range of vocational and educational opportunities for individuals with disabilities who do not complete a high school program; and (e) increasing the accountability of government-funded programs that provide postsecondary education, vocational training, and employment (National Council on Disability, 2000).

LINKING ASSESSMENT WITH INSTRUCTION

 The assessment of transition needs and preferences is an outcome-oriented process that should begin as early as elementary school and takes place over an extended period of time. Transition assessment includes the evaluation of vocational, career, academic, personal, social, and living needs.

Collaboration between experts and interagency collaboration are viewed as important to the assessment process. The assessment of transition needs and preferences should be conducted by professionals from a variety of disciplines, such as education, employment, transition services, psychology, and others, along with input from parents, caregivers, and the student. Collaboration among these experts is important to the success of a student's transition.

In order to develop an IEP, information about the individual's present levels of performance can be gathered using transition assessment in the following areas: vocational, career, academic, personal, social, and living needs. Transition assessment has multiple purposes, including (Cohen & Spenciner, 2003):

- recognizing levels of career development
- evaluating self-concept
- evaluating academic, vocational, and career preferences and training needs
- determining life supports
- identifying abilities, interests, strengths, and needs
- matching interests and abilities with training and employment
- analyzing the results of information from previous assessments
- taking part in activities that promote self-discovery of vocational and career interests
- assessing work-related behaviors, skills, and aptitudes
- identifying needs for supported employment
- recognizing the need for continuing education and adult services

Both teacher-developed and published instruments can be used to gather information. These include learning style inventories, classroom observation instruments, curriculum-based assessments, learning environment assessments, physical environment assessments, social environment assessments, future planning questionnaires, interviews with students, interviews with parents and family members, adaptive behavior instruments, behavioral and functional assessments, technology evaluations, and self-determination checklists. The Outcome/Skill Checklist for Transition Planning (Roessler, 1998), an assessment tool that is aligned with Life-Centered Career Education (LCCE), can be found in Figure 16-1.

Figure 16.1   Outcome/skill checklist for transition planning

Student Name_____Date_____Evaluator_____

> **Checklist Orientation and Purpose**
> The purpose of this checklist is to help participants in the IEP meeting review plans for the student's transition into adult roles. Quality transition plans describe both adult outcomes and skill training objectives. This checklist reminds students, parents, teachers, and others of the adult outcomes and life skills that are included in a comprehensive transition plan.

I. Adult Outcomes

How well does the plan specify adult outcomes? If any of the following outcomes are not addressed and no justification is provided, the planning group should continue its work.

A. Are specific transition outcomes listed?

1. Postsecondary education options: Is the setting named *specifically*?

__4-year college
__2-year community college
__Apprenticeship
__Trade/technical school
__Adult continuing education

__GED Program
__Other (specify)_____
__None, no justification
__None, justification

2. Postsecondary employment: Is the setting named *specifically*?

__Full-time employment without support
__Part-time employment without support
__Full-time supported/supervised employment
__Part-time supported/supervised employment
__Adult/work activity center

__Military
__Other (specify)_____
__None, no justification
__None, justification

3. Residential Options: Is the setting named *specifically*?

__Live alone without support
__Live alone with support
__Live with family/relative
__Live with roommate(s)
__Group home-specialized training

__Supervised apartment
__Residential/nursing facility
__Other (specify)_____
__None, no justification
__None, justification

4. Community Involvement: Is the setting named *specifically*?

__School activities
__Parks and recreation
__Churches
__4H/Scouts
__Hobbies/clubs

__Voter registration
__Informal peer activities
__Other (specify)_____
__None, no justification
__None, justification

B. Is each transition outcome consistent with the student's program of study (indirect services, resource, and/or self-contained)?

__Yes   __No (If *no*, the planning group needs to continue its work.)

continued

Figure 16.1   Outcome/skill checklist for transition planning *continued*

II. Life Skills Instructional Objectives

Are life skills instructional objective specified? Does the plan address the life skills the student needs to achieve and maintain adult outcomes? In *Life Centered Career Education, A Competency Based Approach* (Brolin, 1997), life skills are clustered in three areas: (a) Daily Living, (b) Personal/Social, and (c) Occupational Guidance and Preparation. These 3 areas include 21 competencies and 97 subcompetencies.

A. DAILY LIVING SKILLS

1. MANAGING PERSONAL FINANCES

— 1. Count Money and Make Change
— 2. Make Responsible Expenditures
— 3. Keep Basic Financial Records
— 4. Calculate and Pay Taxes
— 5. Use Credit Responsibly
— 6. Use Banking Services

2. SELECTING AND MANAGING A HOUSEHOLD

— 7. Maintain Home Exterior/Interior
— 8. Use Basic Appliances and Tools
— 9. Select Adequate Housing
—10. Set Up Household
—11. Maintain Home Grounds

3. CARING FOR PERSONAL NEEDS

—12. Demonstrate Knowledge of Physical Fitness, Nutrition and Weight
—13. Exhibit Proper Grooming and Hygiene
—14. Dress Appropriately
—15. Demonstrate Knowledge of Common Illness Prevention and Treatment
—16. Practice Personal Safety

4. RAISING CHILDREN AND MEETING MARRIAGE RESPONSIBILITIES

—17. Demonstrate Physical Care for Raising Children
—18. Know Psychological Aspects of Raising Children
—19. Demonstrate Marriage Responsibilities

5. BUYING, PREPARING, AND CONSUMING FOOD

—20. Purchase Food
—21. Clean Food Preparation Areas
—22. Store Food
—23. Prepare Meals
—24. Demonstrate Appropriate Eating Habits
—25. Plan and Eat Balanced Meals

6. BUYING AND CARING FOR CLOTHING

—26. Wash/Clean Clothing
—27. Purchase Clothing
—28. Iron, Mend and Store Clothing
—29. Demonstrate Knowledge of Civil Rights and Responsibilities

7. EXHIBITING RESPONSIBLE CITIZENSHIP

—30. Know Nature of Local, State and Federal Governments
—31. Demonstrate Knowledge of the Law and Ability to Follow the Law
—32. Demonstrate Knowledge of Citizen Rights and Responsibilities

8. UTILIZING RECREATIONAL FACILITIES AND ENGAGING IN LEISURE

—33. Demonstrate Knowledge of Available Community Resources
—34. Choose and Plan Activities
—35. Demonstrate Knowledge of the Value of Recreation
—36. Engage in Group and Individual Activities
—37. Plan Vacation Time

9. GETTING AROUND THE COMMUNITY

—38. Demonstrate Knowledge of Traffic Rules and Safety
—39. Demonstrate Knowledge and Use of Various Means of Transportation
—40. Find Way Around the Community
—41. Drive a Car

Figure 16.1   Outcome/skill checklist for transition planning *continued*

B. Personal-Social Skills

10. ACHIEVING SELF-AWARENESS

___42. Identify Physical and Psychological Needs
___43. Identify Interests and Abilities
___44. Identify Emotions
___45. Demonstrate Knowledge of Physical Self

11. ACQUIRING SELF-CONFIDENCE

___46. Express Feelings of Self-Worth
___47. Describe Others' Perceptions of Self
___48. Accept and Give Praise
___49. Accept and Give Criticism
___50. Develop Confidence in Oneself

12. ACHIEVING SOCIALLY RESPONSIBLE BEHAVIOR

___51. Develop Respect for the Rights and Properties of Others
___52. Recognize Authority and Follow Instructions
___53. Demonstrate Appropriate Behavior in Public
___54. Know Important Character Traits
___55. Recognize Personal Roles

13. MAINTAINING GOOD INTERPERSONAL SKILLS

___56. Demonstrate Listening and Responding Skills
___57. Establish and Maintain Close Relationships
___58. Make and Maintain Friendships

14. ACHIEVING INDEPENDENCE

___59. Strive Toward Self-Actualization
___60. Demonstrate Self-Organization
___61. Demonstrate Awareness of How One's Behavior Affects Others

15. MAKING ADEQUATE DECISIONS

___62. Locate and Utilize Sources of Assistance
___63. Anticipate Consequences
___64. Develop and Evaluate Alternatives
___65. Recognize Nature of a Problem
___66. Develop Goal-Seeking Behavior

16. COMMUNICATING WITH OTHERS

___67. Recognize and Respond to Emergencies
___68. Communicate with Understanding
___69. Know Subtleties of Communication

C. Occupational Guidance and Preparation

17. KNOWING AND EXPLORING OCCUPATIONAL POSSIBILITIES

___70. Identify Remunerative Aspects of Work
___71. Locate Sources of Occupational and Training Information
___72. Identify Personal Values Met Through Work
___73. Identify Societal Values Met Through Work
___74. Classify Jobs into Occupational Categories
___75. Investigate Local Occupational and Training Opportunities

18. SELECTING AND PLANNING OCCUPATIONAL CHOICES

___76. Make Realistic Occupational Choices
___77. Identify Requirements of Appropriate and Available Jobs

___78. Identify Occupational Aptitudes
___79. Identify Major Occupational Interests
___80. Identify Major Occupational Needs

19. EXHIBITING APPROPRIATE WORK HABITS AND BEHAVIORS

___81. Follow Directions and Observe Regulations
___82. Recognize Importance of Attendance and Punctuality
___83. Recognize Importance of Supervision
___84. Demonstrate Knowledge of Occupational Safety
___85. Work with Others
___86. Meet Demands for Quality Work
___87. Work at a Satisfactory Rate

continued

Figure 16.1   Outcome/skill checklist for transition planning *continued*

---

20. SEEKING SECURING AND EMPLOYMENT

___89. Search for a Job

___89. Apply for a Job

___90. Interview for a Job

___91. Know How to Maintain Post-School Occupational Adjustment

___92. Demonstrate Knowledge of Competitive Standards

___93. Know How to Adjust to Changes in Employment

21. EXHIBITING SUFFICIENT PHYSICAL-MANUAL SKILLS

___94. Demonstrate Stamina and Endurance

___95. Demonstrate Satisfactory Balance and Coordination

___96. Demonstrate Manual Dexterity

___97. Demonstrate Sensory Discrimination

III. Interagency Linkages

Who can help? Does the plan make referrals to adult agencies that can help the student at this time or at a later date? Should any of the following agencies be involved that are not already included in the plan?

___Developmental Disabilities

___Division of Rehabilitation Services

___Social Security Administration (SSI, SSDI)

___Social Services

___Adjustment Training Center

___Job Services

___Mental Health Center

___Independent Living Center

___Services to the Blind & Visually Impaired

___Public Health Center

___Guardian/Estate Planning

___Military/Selective Service

___Low Income Housing

___Other (specify) _____

IV. IEP Team Composition/Participation

Has everyone had a say? Is everyone in agreement? Review the list of important participants in the transition planning process. Have appropriate persons had a chance to make their contributions to the plan? Do they agree that the plan adequately meets the student's needs? Identify individuals from whom information is still needed and determine how to involve them in the planning.

___Student

___Mother

___Father

___Guardian

___Other family member

___Special educator

___General educator

___Vocational educator

___School counselor

___Special education supervisor

___Transition specialist

___School psychologist

___Principal

___Assistant principal

V. Student Involvement/Self-Determination

Was the student involved?

___Does the plan include a statement of the student's needs, preferences, and interests?

___Is it clear how the student's preferences were included in the plan?

From *Making the Transition: An Outcome/Skill Checklist for Transition Planning,* by Richard Roessler, 1998, *LCCE Insider,* 3–6. Reprinted with permission of Richard Roessler.

There are a number of published instruments that provide information on transition assessment. However, many of these instruments are outdated and have other limitations. As with all assessment instruments, users should carefully review the technical aspects and administration procedures and consider how the results of the assessment will be applied. In supporting students' preparation for transition, some of these instruments have little relevance and educators need to think about how to collect more relevant information. Tables 16.2 and 16.3 contain lists of commonly used instruments.

Table 16.2	Tests of Work-Related Behaviors, Skills, and Aptitudes	
Instrument	**Individuals**	**Characteristics**
BRIGANCE Employability skills inventory (Brigance, 1995)	All disabilities	Criterion-referenced
Kaufman functional academic skills test (K-FAST) (Kaufman & Kaufman, 1995)	Mild cognitive disabilities, behavioral disabilities	Norm-referenced, standardized test; assesses performance in reading and mathematics applied to daily life situations
Quality of life questionnaire (Schalock & Keith, 1993a)	Mild to severe cognitive disabilities Ages 18+	Assesses levels of satisfaction, productivity, independence, community integration
Quality of student life questionnaire (Schalock & Keith, 1993b)	All disabilities Ages 14 to 25	Assesses levels of satisfaction, well-being, social belonging, and control Interview
Scales of independent behavior-revised (SIB-R) (Bruininks, Woodcock, Weatherman, & Hill, 1996)	All disabilities	Norm-referenced; motor skills, social interaction and communications skills, personal living skills, and community living skills
The arc's self-determination scale (Wehmeyer & Kelchner, 1995)	All disabilities	Student self-report global self-determination, autonomy, self-regulation, psychological empowerment, and self-awareness
Transition behavior scale (McCarney & Anderson, 2000)	All disabilities	Assess work-related behaviors, interpersonal skills, social and community expectations Rated by at least three individuals

continued

Table 16.2	Tests of Work-Related Behaviors, Skills, and Aptitudes *continued*		
Transition planning inventory (Clark & Patton, 1995)	All disabilities		Assesses skills related to employment, education, daily living, leisure, community integration, health communication, interpersonal relationships Rating scale completed by student, parent/guardian, and school personnel
Transition-to-work inventory (TWI) (Friedman)	Severe disabilities		Job analysis, worker analysis, accommodations, and job redesign
Work adjustment inventory (WAI) (Gilliam, 1994)	All disabilities		Norm-referenced Activity, empathy, sociability, assertiveness, adaptability, and emotionality

Table 16.3	Interest Inventories			
Instrument	**Grade Level**	**Reading Level**	**Administration Time**
Kuder career search with person match (Zytowski, 2000)	Grade 7 through adult	Grade 6	30 minutes
Occupational aptitude survey and interest schedule (OASIS-2) (2nd ed.) (Parker, 1991)	Grades 8 to 12	Not reported	30 minutes
Reading-free vocational interest inventory-2 (Becker, 1988)	Grade 9 through adult	No reading required	20 minutes
Strong interest inventory (Campbell & Hansen, 1994)	Grade 8 through adult	Grade 8	60 minutes

When implementing transition assessment, there are several considerations that should be kept in mind (Sitlington, Clark, & Kolstoe, 2000; Cohen & Spenciner, 2003). Assessment instruments should be identified based on the essential questions about the student's transition needs. These questions should be driven by information that is needed to support the individual in making transitions in educational, living, and work environments. Transition assessment should be continuous. Assessment should start early and be ongoing. Multiple types of assessment should be used, including formal and informal tools and procedures. Assessment tools and procedures should be carefully selected. Make sure that they are technically adequate and appropriate for the purposes for which they were intended. Assessment instruments and procedures should be sensitive to gender, culture, race, and language. Assessment information should be carefully recorded and organized. Considerations about person-centered planning, self-determination, and self-advocacy should be integrated in the assessment process.

ASSESSMENT AND SELF-DETERMINATION

The IEP team should identify the experiences, supports, and services that should be in place in order to achieve a successful transition. Achievement of IEP goals and objectives should move the student closer to the transition and to inclusion in the community.

Student self-determination is at the center of transition planning. All activities in the transition process, including assessment, planning, implementation, and evaluation, should include the student as an active participant as fully as possible. Self-determination means that the individual's hopes, dreams, and desires influence the types of assessment that are implemented. Figure 16.2 is an example of a worksheet that may help a student express hopes and dreams. Transition assessment should include and document self-determination skills. Various instruments can be used to assist in the assessment of self-determination skills, including one or more interviews

Figure 16.2 Strengths, needs, opportunities, and worries

Strengths	Needs
What skills have I learned that will help me reach my dreams? Things I can do well are . . .	What do I still need to learn to do to reach my dreams? What skills do I have trouble with? What do I need help with?

Opportunities	Worries
What is helping me now to reach my dreams? Who can assist me concerning my dreams? How can they help?	What worries me when I think about reaching my dreams?

Adapted from *A Transition Planning Guide for Families of Youth and Young Adults with Developmental Disabilities Toolkit*, Southern Maine Advisory Council on Transition, 1997, Portland, ME: Publisher.

with the student, interviews with parents and family members, checklists, and observations (Sitlington, Neubert, Begun, Lombard, & Leconte, 1996). Suggested questions to ask include:

> Does the individual understand the transition planning process?
> Does the individual understand her or his rights under the law?
> Does the individual demonstrate self-advocacy skills?
> Can the individual explain her or his role in the transition planning process?
> Can the individual identify personal interests and preferences?
> Can the individual describe her or his transition goals?

TYPES OF TRANSITION ACTIVITIES

Planning for and implementing transition activities and services should occur well before students anticipate completing school. Transition activities are those actions that lead to successful outcomes. These activities fall into three major categories: those that occur 4 to 5 years before leaving school, 2 to 3 years before leaving school, and at least 1 year before leaving school.

FOUR TO 5 YEARS BEFORE LEAVING SCHOOL

- Identify supports needed to be a successful learner and worker.
- Identify career interests and skills.
- Identify interests, options, and supports for future living arrangements.
- Effectively communicate interests, preferences, and needs.
- Explain the nature of the disability and the supports and accommodations needed.
- Learn and practice informed decision-making skills.
- Learn and practice self-advocacy skills.
- Participate in community activities.

TWO TO 3 YEARS BEFORE LEAVING SCHOOL

- Identify community support services, programs, and independent living arrangements.
- Invite adult service providers, peers, and others to the transition IEP meeting.
- Match career interests and skills with appropriate course work and integrated work experiences.
- Investigate postsecondary programs and/or employment options.
- Identify entrance, admission, application, and financial requirements for postsecondary activities.
- Use and practice appropriate interpersonal communication and social skills.
- Practice independent living skills such as budgeting, shopping, cooking, and housekeeping.
- Identify personal assistant services that are needed and, if appropriate, learn to direct and manage these services.

AT LEAST 1 YEAR BEFORE LEAVING SCHOOL

- The school informs students of their rights 1 year before reaching the age of majority.
- Apply for financial support programs such as Supplemental Security Income, independent living services, personal assistant services, and vocational rehabilitation.
- Make arrangements for postsecondary educational programs.
- Use and practice communication and interview skills.

FURTHER EDUCATION AND TRAINING

- Arrange to meet with the disabilities education coordinator.
- Identify and obtain ATs that will be used.
- Meet with instructors and arrange for any special accommodations that may be needed.
- Review and practice the schedule.
- Arrange for transportation.

TRANSITION SERVICES

The provision of transition services is critical in assisting students with disabilities to prepare for adult life. Although students with disabilities continue to fall behind their typical peers in postschool employment, wages, postsecondary education, and residential independence, gains have been made. The federal government mandates that students with disabilities must be provided with services that will facilitate their transition from school to postschool activities, including postsecondary education, vocational training, integrated employment (including supported employment), continuing and adult education, adult services, independent living, and community participation.

Beginning at age 14 (or sooner if determined by the Pupil Evaluation Team) and updated annually, the IEP team must develop a statement of the transition service needs of the student that focuses on the student's courses of study. At age 16, transition services must be discussed and documented at every IEP meeting until the student leaves school. For some students, it may be appropriate to begin transition services earlier. For example, the preparation and supports necessary for a student with a severe disability may require a long period of time. The responsibility for determining when to begin transition services is left to the IEP team. Figure 16.3 is an example of a transition plan for Dimitri, a 16-year-old student who is interested in working in a restaurant and continuing his education after high school.

LEVEL AND INTENSITY OF SUPPORT

Supports enable persons with disabilities to lead independent lives and assist them to plan for and control their own futures. Successful outcomes for students depend on environmental, social, and personal supports. These supports can vary in degree, strength, amount, and magnitude.

Figure 16.3   Transition Services Plan

Student's Name: _Dimitri Petrozski_   **Current Age:** _16_
Date: _October 21, 20xx_

Transition Planning Areas (check all that apply)	x Instruction x Employment x Community experiences _ Daily living skills _ Related services
Statement of Student/Family Interest/Preferences	Dimitri enjoys being with his family, eating at the local restaurant, and watching television. He would like to continue his education after high school.
Postschool Goals/Objectives	Dimitri would like to work in a restaurant.
Present Level of Performance	Dimitri is able to read simple menus and follow two-step directions.
Statement of Need for Transition Services	Dimitri needs literacy support and vocational guidance and training. He would like to explore options that are available for continuing his education after he graduates from high school.

Graduation Date: _June 20xx_

Needed Transition Services

Target	Activities	Persons Responsible	Begin Date	End Date
Instruction	Reading, writing, and mathematics instruction should focus on functional skills including reading instructions, following directions, taking menu orders, and making change	L. Swett (special education teacher) M. Moste (vocational education teacher)	11/1/xx	6/10/xx
Employment	Interpersonal skills, completing job and postsecondary education applications, following a schedule	M. Moste (vocational education teacher) N. Light (school counselor)	11/1/xx	6/10/xx
Community Experiences	Exploration of community recreation and leisure resources and activities	L. Swett (special education teacher)	11/1/xx	6/10/xx
Daily Living Skills				
Related Services				

Environmental supports include a signal for when it is time to take a break, the use of pictures to show the steps involved in setting the table, and a list of the telephone numbers of sources of additional assistance. Social supports include walking with a friend to work, signals used in taking turns, and a list of conversation starters. Personal supports include verbal prompts for indicating choices, signals that enable students to control their anger, and a caregiver who assists in the development of social skills.

TRANSITION TEAM

Planning and implementation of successful transition services and activities require the collaboration of individuals with a variety of perspectives and expertise. The student and the family are essential team members. IEP team members, such as special education teachers, general education teachers, occupational therapists, physical therapists, speech and language pathologists, administrators, and transition specialists, should also be involved. Other professionals who should be included, when appropriate, are vocational rehabilitation counselors, job coaches, social workers, college counselors, community recreation professionals, technology specialists, employers or potential employers, and professionals who provide services that support independent or residential living (National Information Center for Children and Youth with Disabilities, 1999).

SELF-DETERMINATION, SELF-ADVOCACY, AND PERSON-CENTERED PLANNING

The cornerstones of transition planning include providing for student choice and self-determination, self-advocacy, levels and intensities of support, person-centered planning, and individualizing career development (Algozzine, Browder, Karvonen, Test, & Wood, 2001; Wehman, 2001; West et al., 1999).

STUDENT CHOICE AND SELF-DETERMINATION

Involving students in making decisions about their futures is critical. For students to have direction and control over their own lives, they, rather than service providers, are central to planning for, implementing, and evaluating transition activities. Teaching students to plan and control the direction of their lives is key to a successful transition. Several researchers (Martin et al., 2003) concluded that teaching students to use self-determination, planning, and evaluation facilitates successful transitions. Strategies should be designed and implemented that promote collaboration among the student, employers, co-workers, agency personnel, educators, and community members.

Wehmeyer, Agran, and Hughes (2000) asked special educators teaching in secondary schools about IEP goals and self-determination. They found that 31% of the teachers reported writing no self-determination goals in student IEPs, 47% reported writing goals for some students, and only 22% reported writing goals for all students. Many special educators (41%) reported that they did not have sufficient training or information about teaching self-determination.

A student, along with his person-centered team, updates a transition plan.

Algozzine et al. (2001) conducted a comprehensive review of the literature on interventions that promote self-determination in persons with disabilities. They define self-determination as "the combination of skills, knowledge, and beliefs that enable a person to engage in goal-directed, self-regulated, autonomous behavior" (p. 219). Although much more research needs to be done, Algozzine and colleagues found evidence that self-determination and self-advocacy can be successfully taught to individuals with disabilities and make a difference in their lives. However, research is needed to determine the success and the effects of teaching self-determination and self-advocacy to children with disabilities. Awareness of the lack of an empirical research base is important because our knowledge of strategies and interventions is still evolving.

Morgan, Ellerd, Gerity, and Blair (2000) wrote that for self-determination activities in transition to be successful, certain conditions must be in place. First, the services that will be provided must be accessible, coordinated, and assessed. Second, students who are involved in transition activities must be aware of their needs, be able to advocate for themselves, and be able to set and work toward goals. Students, family members, and key support staff must have sufficient information to make informed decisions.

❖ MIGUEL ❖

Miguel is 13 years old and in the sixth grade. He has been identified as having mild mental retardation and an emotional disability. Miguel's language abilities are well below the range of an average 13-year-old. He often gets frustrated when he is unable to communicate effectively and sometimes responds inappropriately by striking out at others.

Miguel talked about feeling different from his classmates with his special education teacher, Shauna Moore. He stated that feeling different made him angry and sad. When asked what he likes to do, he responded, "I like to play video games and play with my dog." Shauna asked Miguel what career he would like when he is older. Miguel indicated that he would like to be a "vet" (veterinarian). When asked why he wanted to be a veterinarian he said, "animals can understand me."

MIGUEL'S MOTHER

In an interview, Miguel's mother expressed concern about his future. She worried that he would not be able to do the things that other students would be doing, "like drive a car" or "have a girlfriend." She stated that he preferred to play alone or with his dog but had no friends. She did not have many problems understanding her son but knew that he easily became frustrated when he was unable to communicate well with others. When asked about Miguel's future after high school, she thought that he might be able to work as a building custodian as long as he was supervised.

SELF-ADVOCACY

Self-advocacy is an essential concept in providing services to individuals with disabilities (West et al., 1999). Self-advocacy means that individuals with disabilities make informed decisions and take responsibility for them. According to Van Reusen, Bos, Schumaker, and Deshler (1994), self-advocacy can help students get ready to participate as citizens in our society. It involves communication, negotiation, and declaration of individuals' interests, dreams, needs, and legal rights.

Developing self-advocacy has several components, including identifying strategies for teaching self-advocacy, developing self-advocacy objectives for students' IEPs, and selecting self-advocacy skills needed for job interviews (Van Reusen et al., 1994; West et al., 1999).

Strategies for Teaching Self-Advocacy

Students should have opportunities to practice self-advocacy skills. They can rehearse these skills when they:

- develop a class schedule,
- plan to live independently,
- meet with a vocational counselor,
- interview for a job, or
- make decisions at IEP meetings.

Self-Advocacy Objectives on the Individualized Education Program

IEPs can incorporate objectives that involve self-advocacy. These objectives can relate to:

- rights associated with IDEA and other legal mandates,
- information about support services, and
- definition and demonstration of assertive behaviors.

Self-Advocacy Skills Needed for Job Interviews

Students can be taught self-advocacy skills that they will need during job interviews. These skills include:

- completion of a job application,
- development of a resume,
- ability to greet the interviewer,
- ability to use eye contact,
- preparation to answer questions, and
- skill in asking appropriate questions.

PERSON-CENTERED PLANNING

Person-centered planning means that the person with a disability and those who love and care for the individual direct the planning process. Person-centered planning focuses on high-quality, meaningful outcomes, and fosters dignity and respect for the individual with the disability. It is responsive to the individual and involves sustained efforts over a long period of time. Individual needs, values, and interests are identified, and appropriate personal, community, and familial supports are provided.

Person-centered planning means that the student with a disability engages in an active, meaningful way with parents, educators, community members, and others during the assessment, planning, and service delivery processes. It focuses on self-determination, self-advocacy, and the student's hopes, dreams, and desires. Natural supports (the individual's own supports that the general population uses), rather than specialized services, are emphasized. Natural supports include neighbors, employers, clergy, and other community members.

In person-centered planning, students with disabilities are encouraged to take a leadership role during the transition activities. This process should result in a comprehensive plan that addresses educational and employment opportunities, financial and income needs, friendship and socialization needs, transportation needs, health and medical needs, and legal and advocacy needs (Wehman, Everson, & Reid, 2001). Person-centered planning has the following characteristics (Wehman et al., 2001):

1. It focuses on abilities rather than disabilities.
2. It encourages planning that is future oriented.
3. Involvement of community members and organizations is an integral part of the process.
4. Supports, connections, and commitment are emphasized rather than programs and services.
5. Person-centered approaches are tailored to each student's needs and desires. The student and family members provide strong direction for transition planning and implementation activities.

Wehmeyer (2001) described the outcomes of a program designed to foster student-directed transition planning activities, including learning about community resources, jobs, themselves, and legal mandates. He concluded that student involvement in transition planning was positive. After participating in the program, students responded:

Using Technology
Occupational Information Network

The U.S. government's Employment and Training Administration website contains several job-related databases. O*NET (Occupational Information Network) is a database that contains information on job requirements and worker requirements. This website is a gateway to many other employment and training Web resources that are sponsored by the U.S. government.

Web search engines such as Google, Yahoo!, Lycos, Excite, AOL Search, Ask Jeeves, and others enable users to mine the Internet for information. Typing *resume* into a Web search engine will lead to a number of websites that provide support on developing resumes.

The Web, with local, regional, and national job databases, is a rich resource that can assist the job search. Typing in terms such as *jobs* and *careers* will yield a number of websites that contain databases on available jobs. Businesses, institutions, organizations, and government agencies frequently list available openings on their websites. Many newspapers also have websites that contain employment listings.

Questions for Reflection

1. Using a resume-writing tool, develop or revise your own resume.
2. Locate websites that list employment opportunities. Compare the ease of use and features of several of them.

 To learn more about using technology, go to the Companion Website at www. prenhall.com/cohen, select Chapter 16, then choose Using Technology.

"I can be more independent, go out on my own, do more on my own."

"I can go and get help when I need help. People can help give me support."

"I set some goals. My goals after high school are to get my own apartment and a job. My goal is to graduate from high school." (Wehmeyer, 2001, Conclusion section, para 4)

Developing Person-Centered Individualized Education Programs

When developing IEPs that are person-centered, individuals who are part of the student's personal network should be identified. Along with the student and the family, the personal network develops a vision of the student's future. Individuals who can be involved in the person-centered planning process include the student, family members, special educators, general educators, vocational educators, vocational rehabilitation counselors, providers of adult services, and other community members. Each major transition should be connected to a part of the student's dream.

Kara, the student you met at the beginning of this chapter, was preparing to meet with her IEP team. She met with her teacher, and they decided that the IEP meeting would be an appropriate time for Kara to practice her self-advocacy skills. With the encouragement of her teacher, Kara decided to suggest the following goals at the meeting (West et al., 1999):

1. With her school counselor, Kara will complete assessments in order to determine her vocational strengths.

2. With her teacher, Kara will become informed about several community recreation programs.
3. Kara will practice appropriate interpersonal skills in preparation for job interviews.

CAREER DEVELOPMENT

Career development should be individualized for each person with a disability. Social skills training, career awareness, self-advocacy, and career education should be available based on the individual's needs, interests, and aspirations (Wehman, 2001).

Collaboration with business and industry will improve the outcomes for both the individual with a disability and society at large. Collaboration can involve mutual planning, implementation, and evaluation of work-related training and experiences.

For example, Ric, a 16-year-old boy with a traumatic brain injury caused by a severe car accident 3 years ago, was about to begin a student internship at a company that provided training in using computers. The manager of the company wanted to hire a trainee who could eventually take on some of the responsibilities for scheduling new training. Working closely with Ric and his teachers, the manager identified the skills that Ric would need before beginning the internship. Back at school, Ric's teachers planned and implemented a curriculum that would enable him to gain the required knowledge and skills.

CAREER EDUCATION CURRICULUM

Brolin's (1993b) Life-Centered Career Education (LCCE) series includes transition competencies, assessment tools, and IEP planning activities. LCCE focuses on development of daily living skills, personal-social skills, and occupational development. It is based on the following competencies:

Daily Living Skills

1. personal finances
2. household selection and management
3. personal care needs
4. family responsibilities
5. food buying, preparation, and consumption
6. clothing selection and care
7. leisure-time activities
8. local transportation
9. clothing selection and care

Personal-Social Skills

1. self-awareness
2. self-confidence
3. socially responsible behavior
4. interpersonal skills
5. independence
6. decision making
7. communication

These students are sharing career development strategies.

Occupational Guidance and Preparation

1. exploration of occupations
2. occupational planning and selection
3. work habits and behavior
4. employment seeking and selection
5. physical-manual skills
6. occupational skills

The LCCE model conceptualizes transition as a series of four stages that begin in the early elementary years and continue into adulthood. Major points of transition are career awareness, career exploration, career preparation, and career assimiliation.

Wehman (2001) emphasizes the importance of strong involvement by family members, individual choice, self-advocacy, and self-determination. Seven areas of transition are identified: employment, living arrangements, getting around in the community, financial independence, making friends, sexuality and self-esteem, and enjoyment. According to Wehman, transition activities should emphasize family involvement, functional community-referenced skills, person-centered planning, the provision of supports rather than services, paid employment, employment experiences that contribute to a good quality of life, involvement of business and industry, and expanded participation of postsecondary educational institutions.

Considering Diversity

Reaching Out to Latinos

Proyecto Visión (Project Vision) links Latinos who have disabilities with employment services, government agencies, and other organizations. Hosted by the World Institute on Disability (WID), the project's website provides resources, including job banks and information about resume writing, in both English and Spanish. Employers can locate information about transition, accommodations, employment initiatives, and legislation.

WID provides resources on employment and health-related information for individuals with disabilities. There is a special focus on women with disabilities. The vision of WID is "that culture, laws, policies, perceptions and customs throughout the world reflect the full inclusion of all people, including those with disabilities."

Questions for Reflection

1. What strategies can be implemented when supporting the transition of students with diverse backgrounds?
2. Catalog local and state resources that can be used to support the transition of students with diverse backgrounds.

To deepen your understanding of diversity in schools and communities, go to the Companion Website at www.prenhall.com/ cohen, select Chapter 16, then choose Considering Diversity.

SUMMARY

- Transition is a process that enables children and youth with disabilities to move easily, efficiently, and successfully from one school grade to another and from school to work and the community.
- Five major laws guide transition activities: the Individuals with Disabilities Education Act (IDEA), the Carl D. Perkins Vocational and Applied Technology Education Act Amendments of 1998, the Americans with Disabilities Act of 1990, the School-to-Work Opportunities Act of 1994, and the Rehabilitation Act Amendments of 1998.
- Transition activities and supports include postsecondary education, training, employment, adult services, independent living, and community participation.
- Research has shown that transition services and activities increase the postschool outcomes of students with disabilities.
- Transition activities should begin as early as elementary school.
- Students should be involved in all stages of the transition process.
- Educators should guide students in making their own choices, becoming advocates for themselves, and envisioning their own future.

EXTENDING LEARNING

1. The U.S. Department of Education makes a yearly report to Congress on the nation's progress in educating students with disabilities. What progress has been made in increasing the rate of employment and postsecondary education for these students?
2. Interview a special education teacher at a local school to find out what transition activities, services, and supports have been developed and implemented for students with disabilities. Share your results in class.
3. Working with a small group of students in your class, plan an activity that describes the range and types of transition activities
4. Check the activities that your state and community offer as part of the School-to-Work initiative. What types of activities are offered? How do they provide support services for students?
5. Develop a checklist that a teacher could use to assess students' needs for transition supports and services.

REFERENCES

Algozzine, B., Browder, D., Karvonen, M., Test, D. W., & Wood, W. (2001). Effects of interventions to promote self-determination for individuals with disabilities. *Review of Educational Research, 71,* 219–277.

Babbit, B. C., & White, C. M. (2002). R u ready? Helping students assess their readiness for postsecondary education. TEACHING Exceptional Children, *35,* 62–66.

Becker, R. L. (1988). *Reading-free vocational interest inventory—2.* Columbus, OH: Elbern.

Brigance, A. (1995). *BRIGANCE employability skills inventory* (2nd ed.). Billerica, MA: Curriculum Associates.

Brolin, D. E. (1993a). *Life-centered career education (LCCE) knowledge and performance batteries.* Reston, VA: Council for Exceptional Children.

Brolin, D. E. (1993b). *Life-centered career education: A competency-based approach* (4th ed.). Reston, VA: Council for Exceptional Children.

Bruinicks, R. H., Woodcock, R. W., Weatherman, R. F., & Hill, B. K. (1996). *Scales of independent behavior: Woodcock-Johnson psychoeducational battery—R.* Allen, TX: DLM.

Campbell, D. P., & Hansen, J. (1994). *Strong-Campbell interest inventory.* Stanford, CA: Stanford University Press.

Carl D. Perkins Vocational and Applied Technology Education Act Amendments. (1998). Washington, DC: U.S. Government Printing Office.

Clark, G. M., & Patton, J. R. (1995). *Transition planning inventory.* Austin, TX: PRO-ED.

Cohen, L. G., & Spenciner, L. J. (2003). *Assessment of children and youth* (2nd ed.). Boston: Allyn & Bacon.

Gilliam, J. (1994). *Work adjustment inventory.* Austin, TX: PRO-ED.

Greene, G., & Kochhar-Bryant, C. A. (2003). *Pathways to successful transition for youth with disabilities.* Upper Saddle River, NJ: Merrill/Prentice Hall.

Individuals with Disabilities Education Act Amendments. (1997, June 4). Washington, DC: U.S. Government Printing Office.

Kaufman, A., & Kaufman, W. (1995). *Kaufman functional academic skills test (K-FAST)*. Circle Pines, MN: AGS Publishing.

Krieg, F. J., Brown, P., & Ballard, J. (1995). *Transition: School to work.* Bethesda, MD: National Association of School Psychologists.

Love, L. (1993). *Developing and including transition services in the IEP.* Phoenix: Arizona Department of Education.

Martin, J., Mithaug, D., Cox, P., Peterson, L., Van Dycke, J., & Cash, M. (2003). Increasing self-determination: Teaching students to plan, work, evaluate, and adjust. *Exceptional Children, 69,* 431–447.

Miller, R. J. (1992). Review of the reading-free vocational interest inventory—Revised. In J. Kramer, & J. Conoley (Eds.), *Mental measurements Yearbook* (Vol. 11, pp. 752–753). Lincoln: University of Nebraska Press.

Morgan, R. L., Ellerd, D. A., Gerity, B. P., & Blair, R. J. (2000). That's the job I want! *TEACHING Exceptional Children, 32,* 44–49.

National Council on Disabilities. (2000). *Transition and post-school outcomes for youth with disabilities.* Washington, DC: Author.

National Information Center for Children and Youth with Disabilities. (1999). *Transition planning: A team effort.* NICHCY Transition Summary #TS10, 1999. Washington, DC: NICHCY. Retrieved February 7, 2002, from the LD online website: www.ldonline.org

Parker, R. (1983). *Occupational aptitude survey and interest schedule* (2nd ed). Austin, TX: PRO-ED.

Rehabilitation Act Amendments. (1998). Washington, DC: U.S. Government Printing Office.

Roessler, R. (1998). Making the transition: An outcome/skill checklist for transition planning. *LCCE Insider,* 3–6.

Schalock, R. L., & Keith, K. D. (1993a). *Quality of life questionnaire.* Worthington, OH: IDS.

Schalock, R. L., & Keith, K. D. (1993b). *Quality of student life questionnaire.* Worthington, OH: IDS.

School-to-Work Opportunities Act. (1994). Washington, DC: U.S. Government Printing Office.

Sitlington, P. L., Neubert, D. A., Begun, W., Lombard, R. C., & Leconte, P. J. (1996). *Assess for success.* Reston, VA: Council for Exceptional Children.

Southern Maine Advisory Council on Transition. (1997). *A transition planning guide for families of youth and young adults with developmental disabilities toolkit.* Portland, ME: Author.

Sparrow, S., Balla, D., & Cicchetti, D. (1984). *The Vineland adaptive behavior scales.* Circle Pines, MN: American Guidance Service.

Stinnett, T. A. (1992). Review of the social and prevocational information battery—revised. In J. Conoley & J. Impara (Eds.), *Mental measurements yearbook* (Vol. 12, pp. 836–838). Lincoln: University of Nebraska Press.

Van Reusen, A. K., Bos, C. S., Schumaker, J. B., & Deshler, D. D. (1994). *The self-advocacy strategy for education and transition planning.* Lawrence, KS: Edge.

Wehman, P. (2001). *Life beyond the classroom* (3rd ed.). Baltimore: Paul H. Brookes.

Wehman, P., Everson, J. M., & Reid, D. H. (2001). Beyond programs and placements. In P. Wehman (Ed.), *Life beyond the classroom* (pp. 91–124). Baltimore: Paul H. Brookes.

Wehmeyer, M. L. (2001). *Whose future is it anyway?* Retrieved April 30, 2001, from the Arc website: http://thearc.org/sdet/wfarpt.html

Wehmeyer, M. L., Agran, M., & Hughes, C. A. (2000). A national survey of teachers' promotion of self-determination and student directed learning. *Journal of Special Education, 34,* 58–68.

Wehmeyer, M. L., & Kelchner, K. (1995). Measuring the autonomy of adolescents and adults with mental retardation: A self-report form of the Autonomous Functioning Checklist. *Career Development for Exceptional Individuals, 18,* 3–20.

West, L. L., Corbey, S., Boyer-Stephens, A., Jones, B., Miller, R. J., & Sarkees-Wircenski, M. (1999). *Integrating transition planning into the IEP process.* Reston, VA: Council for Exceptional Children.

Workforce Investment Act. (1998). Washington, DC: U.S. Government Printing Office.

World Institute on Disability. (n. d.). Proyecto Visión: National Technical Assistance Center for Latinos with Disabilities. Retrieved June 10, 2002, from http://www.wid.org/pages/WID Projects.htm

Zytowski, D. (2000). *Career search with person match,* Adel, IA: Career Assessment Services.

Accommodations. Changes to the education program that do not substantially alter the instructional level, the content of the curriculum, or the assessment criteria.

Adaptive behavior. According to the American Association of Mental Retardation, adaptive behavior involves three general areas: conceptual, social, and practical.

Additive Approach. An approach in social studies that incorporates content about diversity into existing curricula.

Advance organizer. An instructional strategy used to introduce an activity such as a lesson, an assignment, a reading, or a multimedia presentation. It presents a structured introduction to the activity.

Allergens. Conditions that cause inflammation of the lining of the bronchial tube, resulting in narrowing of the bronchial tube. Allergens may be inhaled or ingested and result in a chronic health condition called *asthma*.

Analogy phonics. A process in which students read unfamiliar words by recognizing a familiar segment in the new word.

Analytic phonics. A process in which students analyze letter-sound correspondences in words already known and apply this knowledge to new words.

Analytic scoring. A scoring system that uses a matrix of narrative statements to describe the achievement level for each area of the rubric. Often used to measure performance-based or portfolio assessments.

Anecdotal record. An observation method consisting of a brief written account that describes the event after it has occurred.

Antecedent conditions. Events, or triggers, in the environment that occur just before the behavior and may be adjusted by the teacher who carefully observes any changes in the student's behavior. Antecedents directly influence the recurrence of the behavior.

Applied behavior analysis. A systematic procedure that involves identifying and describing a behavior in observable terms; assessing the frequency of the behavior, the antecedent conditions, and the consequences following the behavior; developing an intervention(s) that is designed to change the behavior; observing; and recording data regarding the effectiveness of the intervention.

Artifacts. Examples of student work such as video or sound clips, drawings, or writing drafts that are placed in the student's portfolio.

Assistive technology devices. Technology, tools, software, or equipment that is purchased or designed to address a student's individual needs. These materials are used to increase, maintain, or improve the functional capabilities of a student with a disability.

Assistive technology services. A variety of services that directly assist a child with a disability in the selection, acquisition, or use of an assistive technology device.

Augmentative and alternative communication (AAC) interventions. Interventions that emphasize multiple modalities and should use all of the individual's communication capabilities, including any residual speech or vocalizations, as well as gestures, signs, and aided communication.

Augmentative and alternative communication (AAC) systems. Materials, such as a notebook with graphics that represent objects, actions, and ideas, or devices such as a portable system with speech output. Some individuals with disabilities use AACs to communicate with others. The American Speech-Language-Hearing Association emphasized that an AAC system should use "the individual's full communication capabilities, including the symbols, aids, strategies, and techniques used by individuals to enhance communication" (ASHA, 1991, p. 10).

Authentic assessment. Performance tasks that are completed in a real-life context.

Basal reader. Beginning textbooks containing stories and passages that have been developed to progressively reinforce what students are learning.

Bibliotherapy. The careful selection and use of children's literature to help students develop greater self-understanding while addressing specific social skills.

Big books. Oversize editions of children's books that can be shared with a small group and allow the text and illustrations to be seen by all students in the group.

Behavioral intervention plan. Developed by the IEP team, this plan describes the skills that students need, the instruction that will be provided, and how the plan will be evaluated.

Benchmarks. Examples of performance tasks or products that other students have completed.

Bullying. Negative actions by one or more students directed against another student.

Characteristics. Broad areas that define a person's individuality.

Checklist. A list of all of the components that must be present in the performance or the product.

Circle of knowledge. A type of cooperative learning in which the task of the students is to develop as many possible solutions as they can to a question posed by the teacher.

Classroom procedures. The steps or components of daily activities that must be followed to complete tasks.

Classroom rules. Statements, either implicit or written, that describe students' behavioral expectations.

Cloze procedure. A procedure generally used to determine whether the reading material is within a student's ability.

Coaching. Providing hints or suggestions to students so that they can acquire knowledge and skills, perform a task, or demonstrate a behavior.

Code of conduct. Usually adopted as a schoolwide policy, a code of conduct defines the behavior that teachers, administrators and other school staff, and parents expect of their students.

Cognitive apprenticeship. A method of instruction designed to engage students in authentic tasks and then show them how to generalize the knowledge that they gain.

Collaborating. A process in which two or more individuals share their experiences, skills, and knowledge.

Collaborative teaming. A process in which two or more individuals work together to enable students to develop their skills, abilities, and gifts.

Communication. The exchange of information among individuals, which may involve written language, spoken language, gestures, signs, signals, or other behaviors. According to the National Joint Committee for the Communicative Needs of Persons with Severe Disabilities, communication is "any act performed by or received from another person containing information about that person's needs, desires, perceptions, knowledge, or affective states. It may be intentional or unintentional, may involve conventional or unconventional signals, may be linguistic or nonlinguistic in form, and may occur through speech or other forms.

Complementary instruction. A process used in coteaching in which each professional complements the role of the other based on individual skills, knowledge, and abilities.

Complex instruction. A type of cooperative learning in which the teacher creates group activities that are organized around a central concept or big idea. The tasks, designed for students with diverse backgrounds and differing levels of abilities, are open-ended and require students to make meaningful contributions by working interdependently.

Concept ladder. A method of organizing words and concepts hierarchically.

Conflict resolution. A collection of positive approaches that a facilitator uses to help two or more individuals resolve conflict in daily life.

Consequences. Events that follow a student's behavior and may be adjusted by the teacher who carefully observes any changes in behavior. Consequences directly influence the recurrence of the behavior.

Constructed-response questions. Questions on a quiz or test that require students to demonstrate what they know by using their own words, mathematical reasoning, or illustrations to construct the answer. Examples of constructed-response questions include short-answer and essay questions.

Contributions Approach. In social studies, an approach that emphasizes heroes, heroines, holidays, and selected cultural and ethnic events.

Consulting. An interactive process in which individuals with specific areas of expertise come together to generate solutions to mutually defined problems.

Content standards. Sometimes referred to as *curriculum standards,* these standards describe the knowledge and skills that students should have.

Contingency contract. A written agreement between a student and a teacher that describes what the student should do, the behavior(s) that should occur, and the consequence or reinforcement that the student will receive.

Contingent statement. A statement that includes the conditions that the student must satisfy before engaging in a desired behavior.

Cooperative learning. A method of instruction that structures learning situations cooperatively so that students work together while gaining academic knowledge and social skills.

Cooperative e-learning. A method of instruction in which the teacher connects a small group of students who are located at a distance and creates learning experiences that allow the students to work interdependently by using technologies such as e-mail, listservs, and the Web.

Coteaching. Collaborating with another professional in planning and implementing learning activities with students.

Criterion-referenced tests. Commercial tests that measure a student's performance with respect to a specific content domain, such as self-help skills or knowledge of mathematical operations.

Cross-age tutors. Students who work with students who are either younger or older than themselves.

Cueing. A hint, stimulus, or reminder that helps students produce the correct response.

Curriculum-based assessment (CBA). An assessment designed to measure a specific area of the curriculum or the student's behavior. Curriculum-based assessments, sometimes known as *curriculum-based evaluation,* assist teachers in determining areas of student strengths and weakness and in planning instruction.

Curriculum-based measurement (CBM). An assessment approach that includes both assessing student knowledge in specific areas of the curriculum and graphing the results to make instructional decisions and implement interventions.

Descriptors. Narrative statements that provide detailed information about the quality of each achievement level in an assessment rubric.

Developmental delay. Broad term under which young children may receive early intervention or special education services due to delays in one or more of the following developmental areas: cognitive, physical, communication, social and emotional, or adaptive.

Diagram. A snapshot or picture that summarizes and organizes information. Diagrams show the most important details or features of an object, a function, or a process.

Direct instruction. A method of instruction that focuses on highly structured lessons in which the teacher takes an active role and the student is expected to be an involved participant.

Discovery learning. A teaching method that uses students' interests and self-motivation to guide planning and designing of instruction.

Due process. See procedural safeguards.

Duet reading. The student reads along with a proficient reader, who can be either a peer or the teacher.

Duration recording. A method of conducting an observation in which the observer measures the length of time that an event or behavior occurs.

Dysgraphia. A disability in which a student has physical problems in writing letters, words, or sentences.

Dyslexia. A language-based disability in which the student has difficulties in understanding, reading, and expressing language.

Early intervention services. A variety of services such as infant stimulation and developmental programs that provide parents with special assistance and show them how to encourage their young child's development.

Echo reading. In this form of reading, a skilled reader, such as a teacher or peer, reads a text one sentence at a time. The learner follows along and echoes or imitates the skilled reader.

Electronic text (e-text). The digital form of text.

Embedded phonics. Phonics instruction incidentally included in text reading.

Ethnomathematics. A term used to describe the mathematical practices of identifiable cultural groups.

Error analysis. A diagnostic assessment technique in which teachers examine the student's work to identify patterns of errors or miscues that the student makes.

Event recording. A method of conducting an observation in which a behavior or event is recorded each time it occurs.

Exhibition. A display of a student's work that demonstrates knowledge, abilities, skills, and attitudes concerning one project or a unit of work.

Extended school year (ESY) services. Summer school services.

Extinction. Removal of a reinforcer that either sustains or increases the occurrence of a behavior.

5E instructional model. A model based on an inquiry-based model of instruction. The model has five phases: engagement, exploration, explanation, elaboration, and evaluation.

Formative assessment. A procedure of gathering information on a regular basis to inform instruction and to monitor student progress.

Free, appropriate public education (FAPE). One of the individual rights described in IDEA which assures that no child or youth (3 to 21 years of age) can be excluded from an appropriate public education because of a disability, including students with profound disabilities, students with disruptive behaviors, and students with contagious diseases.

Functional behavioral assessment. Assessment approach that focuses on identifying biological, social, affective, and environmental factors that initiate, sustain, or end the behavior in question.

Functional reading. The ability to recognize specific sight words and symbols and use them in daily living activities, school, work, and the community.

Gleaning strategy. A strategy that involves the use of abbreviations and symbols while making notes.

Graphic organizer. A strategy that organizes information in a visual image.

Guided practice. A set of activities that involve organizing, reviewing, rehearsing, summarizing, comparing, or contrasting tasks, behaviors, responses, or processes by a student working alone, with other students, or with a teacher.

Guided questioning. A group or individual activity in which learners are asked questions about a text both before and after they read it.

Halo effect. Assigning a higher rating than the student's work warrants because the teacher believes that the student is capable; the converse also can be true.

Hierarchy. Organization of information into levels and groups.

High-interest/limited-vocabulary books. Books with interesting topics and content written at limited vocabulary level.

High-stakes assignments. Assignments that involve making judgments about the merits of a student's work.

Holistic scoring. A method of assessing the entire work rather than individual areas or a rubric. In holistic scoring, educators assign an overall descriptive rating to the work or performance.

Hyperactivity. An excess of motor behavior, such as fidgeting, talking, running, or climbing, typically not seen in other children of the same age.

Hypothesis. A description of the probable function(s) of the behavior that allows the team to predict antecedent conditions or when the behavior is most likely (and least likely) to occur and the probable consequences that serve to maintain the behavior.

Impulsivity. Behaviors that include interrupting, intruding, and difficulty in waiting.

Incidental teaching. An instructional strategy that involves using an event or situation as it occurs to develop or teach a specific skill.

Informal reading inventory (IRI). Aids in assessing students' instructional strengths and needs and provides insight into how instruction should proceed.

Inquiry-based learning. Use of objects and ideas that encourage students to manipulate and compare while constructing knowledge.

Instructional method. *See* teaching method.

Instructional strategy. A teaching routine in which a logical, orderly arrangement of steps, techniques, and actions are grouped together to develop or reinforce learning.

Intensity recording. A method of conducting an observation that measures various degrees of behavior such as low, medium, or high.

Interval recording. An observation method that measures whether a behavior occurs within prespecified time segments, such as 30-second or 1-minute intervals.

IRI. See *informal reading inventory*.

Jigsaw. A type of cooperative learning in which all students learn a certain body of material. The activity begins with each team member being assigned responsibility for learning a specific part of the assignment and becoming the expert for the group's team. After a meeting with members of other groups who are becoming experts in the same area, the experts return to their own groups and share what they have learned.

KWHL. An information organizer in which K stands for "What do you know?", W stands for "What do you want to know?", H stands for "How will you find out?", and L stands for "What did you learn?"

K-W-L. A study skills strategy in which K stands for "what you know," W means "what you want to know," and L means "what you learned."

Language. A system used in order to communicate. It can consist of spoken words, written words, signs, gestures, signals, or symbols.

Language disorder. An impairment in the use and/or comprehension of spoken or written language, which involves (1) sounds, words, and word order; (2) semantics or the meaning of language; and (3) pragmatics or the use of language in various contexts.

Language experience approach. An approach to teaching reading and writing that emphasizes use of the learner's own language, repeated reading, visual configuration of words, sight words, and context clues.

Latency recording. An observation method that measures the amount of time that elapses between a request and the occurrence of a behavior or event.

Learning. The change in what students are capable of doing as the result of formal and informal experiences.

Learning strategy. A set of steps that enables a student to develop and mobilize appropriate social skills or perform an academic assignment.

Learning strategy routine. Routines that promote and support students' learning in content areas.

Learning together. A type of cooperative learning in which the teacher assigns students to work together cooperatively in small groups on common tasks and students create a single group product.

Least restrictive environment. According to IDEA, this means that "(1) to the maximum extent appropriate, children with disabilities, including children in public or private institutions or other care facilities, are educated with children who are nondisabled; and [that] (2) special classes, separate schooling, or other removal of children with disabilities from the regular educational environment occurs only if the nature or severity of the disability is such that education in regular classes with the use of supplementary aids and services cannot be achieved satisfactorily" [20 U.S.C. 1412(a)(5)].

Literacy. The ability to read, write, think, and communicate.

Long-term memory. Information that is held on a permanent basis in the brain.

Low-stakes assignments. Usually early drafts that do not involve major judgments about students' performance.

Mapping. A learning strategy that helps to make abstract concepts concrete, make relationships between concepts explicit, promote learning, promote creation of knowledge, and promote use of knowledge.

MathWings. A teaching method tied to the national mathematics standards developed by the National Council of Teachers of Mathematics. MathWings involves students in problem solving in real situations using cooperative groups and literature, science, art, and other subjects as well as the students' personal experiences.

Matrix. A learning strategy that builds on hierarchies and sequences by including topics, categories, and details. Matrices provide information on levels, groups, and relationships between items in the matrix.

Metacognition. Awareness and control of personal learning strategies.

Metacognitive skills. Skills that involve knowing how to learn, to solve problems, or to complete multistep assignments.

Method. See teaching method.

Miscue. The word that a student substitutes for the actual word when reading aloud.

Miscue analysis. The process of studying student errors to make adjustments in instruction. Educators look for patterns in the student's substitution of words for the actual words when reading aloud.

Mnemonics. A strategy that can help students remember academic and behavioral tasks.

Modeling. A process in which a person who is skilled demonstrates to a less skilled person how to do a task, engage in a process, or provide a response.

Modifications. Changes to or adaptations of the education program that alter the level, content, and/or assessment criteria.

Modified paired storytelling. A study skills strategy that can be used to support the language learning of students who speak other languages.

Monitoring. A process in which the teacher and/or students are engaged in continuous evaluation of a student's work, behavior, and activities in order to determine problems, concerns, difficulties, or strengths.

Multipass. A study skills strategy used to improve reading comprehension in content areas. It consists of three phases: survey the reading, size up the information, and sort out the information.

Negative reinforcement. Removal of a stimulus that the student perceived as aversive.

Nominal group technique. A decision-making process in which each member's vote is equally represented and the group generates a collective ranking of all the items/solutions being considered.

Norm-referenced instruments. Commercially published tests that compare a student's test performance with that of similar students who have taken the same test.

Obstacle thinking. *See* opportunity thinking.

Opportunity thinking. A conversation one has with oneself while reflecting on events that happened during a particular situation. This is sometimes known as *obstacle thinking*. Opportunity thinking is a reflective activity that educators and other individuals engage in for the purpose of evaluating and improving their actions.

Ordinal scale. A scale in which every point is not necessarily equidistant from every other. For example, the difference between 3 and 4 is not necessarily the same as the difference between 4 and 5. Numbers in ordinal scales *cannot* be mathematically manipulated.

Organizer. An organizer of information assists learners in acquisition and retrieval of information, understanding of information, and integration of new information.

Orton-Gillingham method. An intensive, sequential, phonics-based system that teaches the basics of word formation before word meanings.

Panic attack. A sudden and intense experience of apprehension, fearfulness, or terror, often associated with impending doom.

Pattern texts. Stories, poems, song lyrics, or other forms of written text that contain repetitious language patterns that can be anticipated or expected by the reader.

Peer mediation. A process that involves students who are trained in the negotiation process and who act as a third person, or facilitator, during the process of conflict resolution.

Peer tutoring (or **peer teaching**). A process in which a skilled student, with a teacher's guidance, helps one or more students at the same grade level learn a skill, concept, or behavior.

Performance-based assessment. Assessment designed to provide students with ways to demonstrate what they know and can do by documenting their accomplishments.

Performance indicator. The level of achievement that students should be able to demonstrate.

Person-centered planning. An arrangement in which the person with a disability and those who love and care for the person direct the planning process. Person-centered planning focuses on high-quality, meaningful outcomes and fosters dignity and respect for the individual with the disability.

Phoneme. The smallest unit of sound that has meaning in a language.

Phonemic awareness. The ability to segment and manipulate speech sounds.

Phonics. Knowledge of how specific spoken sounds relate to particular written letters.

Picture cue. A cue or clue that provides a hint or suggestion that enables the learner to recognize words.

Portfolio. A collection of student work that has been assembled systematically over a period of time.

Positive reinforcement. A tangible object or an intangible reinforcer, such as a high-five, a thumbs-up signal, or the comment "great job."

PQ4R. A study skills strategy that involves previewing, questioning, reading, reflecting, reciting, and reviewing.

Pragmatics. Focuses on how people use language, signs, and gestures in social situations.

Predictable texts. See pattern texts.

Preteaching. Orienting learners to a new topic, vocabulary, and concepts. Strategies used in preteaching include recollection of prior experiences and prior knowledge, use of advance organizers and concept maps, and teaching new vocabulary.

Preview-Read-Recall (PRR). A strategy that encourages active reading of texts. During the Preview phase, students ask why they are reading the material and develop an overview of the main ideas and organization of the text. During the Read phase, students identify the introduction, headings, subheadings, topic sentences of each paragraph, diagrams, tables, charts, conclusion, and summary. During the Recall phase, students mentally review or verbalize the highlights of what they have read.

Probe. A diagnostic technique in which instruction is modified to determine whether an instructional strategy is effective.

Problem-based learning. An inquiry approach that requires students to be active learners, conduct research, generate and test hypotheses, evaluate resources, and work cooperatively with other students.

Procedural safeguards. Principles of fairness that are followed by school personnel so that no prejudicial or unequal treatment results during the process of obtaining or receiving special education services.

Prompt. What students are asked to do.

PRR. See Preview-Read-Recall.

Punishment. Taking away a desired object or activity or adding an aversive stimulus.

Rater drift. The shifting of criteria or a change of emphasis from that originally held by the teacher when the grading of papers or an observation of a student began.

REAP. A study skills strategy used for making annotations or notes of texts. The steps are Read, Encode, Annotate, and Ponder.

Reciprocal learning. A learning process in which a teacher or peer models a process and provides coaching, cueing, or scaffolding as students engage in a task.

Reciprocal teaching. A teaching process in which the teacher's role involves monitoring, providing feedback, and encouraging independence.

Reflective journal. A personal record of the teaching process from the educator's perspective.

Related services. Services provided to students with disabilities by professionals in disciplines other than education, including occupational therapy, physical therapy, rehabilitation counseling, or social work services.

Reliability. The consistency of the scoring procedure that enables the examiner to quantify, evaluate, and interpret behavior or work samples.

Repeated reading. A process in which the learner reads a text more than once until fluency is achieved.

Replacement behaviors. Behaviors substituted for inappropriate behaviors when a student lacks specific skills.

Retelling. The student retells as much of a text as can be remembered after reading it.

Role exchange. A process used during coteaching activities that enables one individual to mentor another in developing new professional skills.

Rubric. An assessment scale that identifies the component(s) of performance and the various levels of achievement.

Running record. An observation method that involves writing a description of events as they occur.

Scaffolding. Teaching strategies that support learners as they acquire knowledge and skills.

Scope and sequence. A detailed list of the set of skills that comprise an area of the curriculum.

Selected-response questions. Questions on a quiz or test that require a student to recognize the correct response. Examples of selected-response questions include true-false and multiple-choice questions.

Self-discipline. Students learn how to exert self-control and manage their own behaviors.

Self-reinforcement. A type of reinforcement administered by the student if the behavior meets a certain standard or expectation.

Self-regulation. The ability to monitor and adjust one's behavior or language in response to a situation; sometimes referred to as *self-control*.

Semantic cue. A cue that reflects an understanding of the meaning of language and aids the learner in predicting and reading unknown words by understanding the meaning of other words in a sentence or passage.

Separation anxiety. Excessive anxiety of a child concerning separation from home or from primary caregiver(s), beyond that expected of children of that age.

Sequence. Organization of ideas, steps, events, and stages in chronological or sequential order.

Sequencing. Breaking down a larger task, response, or behavior into its components so that a student can complete one component at a time.

Setting events. Events that affect the physical or emotional state of an individual at any given time.

Shaping. Successive approximations of a target behavior.

Shared reading. An activity in which a learner or group of learners follows along as a skilled reader, who can be a teacher or peer, reads the text fluently and with expression.

Short-term memory. Information that is held on a temporary basis in the brain.

Sight vocabulary. Printed words that occur with high frequency and are read automatically when encountered.

SNIPS. A five-step strategy that focuses on understanding and interpretation of visual aids such as pictures, graphs, charts, maps, time lines, and other visual representations. The SNIPS steps are: Start with questions, Note what can be learned from hints, Identify what is important, and Plug it into the chapter.

Social Action Approach. A social studies approach that involves students in making their own decisions about various issues that they study.

Specially designed instruction. "Adapting content, methodology, or delivery of instruction to meet the unique needs of a child with a disability and ensuring that the child has access to the general curriculum so that the child can meet the educational standards that apply to all children" [IDEA Sec. 300.26(b)(3)(ii)].

Speech. The spoken form of language.

SQ3R. Stands for survey, question, read, recite, and review. The study skills strategy involves reading a text several times and processing the information in many different ways.

Standardized test. A test in which the administration, scoring, and interpretation procedures are strictly followed.

Story grammar. A general outline of the structure of a story, such as the characters, time sequence, actions, settings, and resolution.

Standardized tests. Tests in which administration, scoring, and interpretation procedures are strictly followed.

Strategic instruction. A teaching method often used in middle and secondary schools that focuses on providing students with rules or guidelines so that they can approach learning activities or assignments more effectively and efficiently and with greater independence.

Strength-based assessment. An assessment approach that measures skills, achievements, and characteristics that create a sense of personal accomplishment, contribute to satisfying relationships, and help one to deal with adversity and stress.

Structured guide. A prepared, preplanned organizer such as an outline, semantic web, or concept map that organizes written pieces.

Structured interview. An assessment approach consisting of a set of questions that the interviewer considers and plans before meeting with an individual.

Student characteristics. A term that encompasses broad areas about the student, including the student's knowledge, motivation, skills, physical, social, and emotional attributes, and the student's home and community.

Student teams-achievement divisions (STAD). A type of cooperative learning in which the teacher focuses on team spirit in addition to academic and teamwork skills. STAD involves the teacher's introduction of content, team study, individual accountability on teacher-administered quizzes, team recognition, and opportunities for all students to succeed.

Summative assessment. Assessment that takes place at the end of the unit or marking period to show student growth and progress.

Supplemental aids and services. Provisions in the regular education classroom or in another educational setting that enable children with disabilities to be educated with children without disabilities to the greatest extent possible.

Supports. These include other people, such as one or more students who provide friendship activities or a teacher aide who provides behavioral support, or modifications to the environment that the IEP team identifies. The purpose of the support(s) is to reduce the discrepancy between a person and that person's environmental requirements.

Syntactic cue. A cue that assists learners in predicting the meaning of unknown words through knowledge of grammar and word order.

Syntax. The order or patterns of words in sentences and phrases.

Synthetic phonics. The process of changing letters into phonemes and blending the sounds to form words.

Task analysis. A process that identifies the individual steps or behaviors that comprise the skill.

Task assessment list. Identifies each of the components of the performance or product that must be present and indicates a rating of the quality of each component, rather than its presence or absence (as in a checklist).

Teaching method. A broad perspective based on theory, research, educational preparation and training, experiences, and/or philosophy. Sometimes referred to as an *instructional method,* a teaching method consists of a general plan that teachers will follow during instruction.

Teams, games, tournaments (TGT). A type of cooperative learning in which the teacher focuses on team spirit in addition to academic and teamwork skills. The teams-games-tournaments group is set up much the same as STAD, but there are no quizzes. After team members work and practice together, a tournament is held in which individual students compete as representatives of their teams. The teacher matches individuals from each team based on their prior performance.

Think-aloud. A comprehension monitoring strategy in which learners communicate thoughts while engaging in a task.

Timeout. A procedure in which a student is removed from the group or activity and placed in a neutral setting for a specified period of time.

Transformative Approach. An approach in social studies that infuses diverse perspectives into the curriculum.

Transition. A process that enables children and youth with disabilities to move easily, efficiently, and successfully from one school grade to another and from school to work and the community. Key points of transition include preschool to early elementary grades, elementary school to middle school or junior high school, middle school or junior high school to high school, and high school to work, postsecondary education, and the community.

Transition services. According to IDEA, transition services are a "coordinated set of activities for a student designed with an outcome-oriented process, that promotes movement from school to post-school activities, including postsecondary education, vocational training, integrated employment (including supported employment), continuing and adult education, adult services, independent living, and community participation" (Sec. 300.18).

Universal design. In education, the design of physical, social, and learning environments so that individuals with a wide range of abilities can have meaningful access and participation in general education. Universal design in education involves flexibility of materials, strategies, approaches, and technology. Universal design should guide developers, educators, users, and others in developing and implementing environments that support diverse users, regardless of their abilities.

Validity. Refers to the information that the assessment was designed to provide and the extent to which the assessment measures this information.

Venn diagram. A diagram usually made up of two or more overlapping circles. Venn diagrams can be used to show similarities and differences between events, people, situations, ideas, and concepts.

Vicarious reinforcement. Occurs when a model (person) that the student observes is reinforced for some appropriate behavior and the student's behavior increases accordingly even though the student is not directly reinforced.

Visual-Auditory-Kinesthetic-Tactile (VAKT). A multisensory approach. Fernald, the developer of this approach, believed that seeing, hearing, feeling, and touching individual words will help students to read and write them.

Visual cues. The shape or visual configuration features that allow readers to recognize a word or a group of words.

Wait time. The amount of time between a teacher- or student-initiated question and the response or the next question.

Word bank. A personal dictionary containing words that students can read.

Word wall. A large section of a classroom wall on which important words are posted for use in reading and writing.

Name Index

Subject Index